Contents

Irene C. Fountas & Gay Su Pinnell

Genre Study

Teaching with Fiction and Nonfiction Books

GRADES K–8 +

HEINEMANN
Portsmouth, NH

Heinemann
361 Hanover Street
Portsmouth, NH 03801–3912
www.heinemann.com

Offices and agents throughout the world

The authors and publisher wish to thank those who have generously given permission to reprint borrowed material:

Photos/Illustrations
[photos appear in *Frogs*] Figure 10.5: Top photo by Densey Clyne; bottom photos by Jim Fraser. Used by permission of Densey Clyne. [Puu Oo Crater Erupting] Figure 11.3: © Jim Sugar/CORBIS. [Saguaro cactus] Figure 11.8: © Jose Fuste Raga/CORBIS. [Crab Spider] Figure11.9: © George Grall/Getty Images. [Jumping spider] Figure 11.9: © George Grall/Getty Images. [Spider eating big black bug] Figure 11.9: Animals, Animal; © Wild & Natural. [Model shark] Figure 11.10: © Daniel Mirer/CORBIS. [Spirit Lake and Mount Saint Helens] Figure 11.11: © David Muench/CORBIS. [Woman Feels Cooled Lava] Figure11.11: © Jim Sugar. [Underwater background] Figure 11.14:
(credits continue on p. xi)

Library of Congress Cataloging-in-Publication Data
Fountas, Irene C.
Genre study : teaching with fiction and nonfiction books / Irene C. Fountas and Gay Su Pinnell.
p. cm.
Includes bibliographical references and index.
ISBN-13: 978-0-325-02874-3
ISBN-10: 0-325-02874-5
1. Literary form—Study and teaching. 2. Literature—Study and teaching. 3. Youth—Books and reading.
I. Pinnell, Gay Su. II. Title.
LB1575.F68 2012
372.64'044—dc23 2011048022

Editor: Betsy Sawyer-Melodia
Production: Michael Cirone
Cover and text designs: Lisa Anne Fowler
Cover photographs, top to bottom, left to right: Illustration by Will Sweeney, for LLI book *Little Bat*. Copyright © 2009 by Irene C. Fountas, Gay Su Pinnell, and Heinemann; Image ID E000548 © Photodisc/Getty Images/HIP; Image ID 5094266 © Jupiterimages/Getty Images/HIP; Image ID E007993 © Digital Vision/Getty Images/HIP; Image ID AA040372 © Photodisc/Getty Images/HIP; Image ID CHI0096D © Corbis/HIP; Montage (magnifying glass and fingerprint): © Brand X Pictures/Getty Images/HIP; Image ID BXP46997h and Image ID BAS_050, © Photodisc/Getty Images; Image ID CD087007 ©Pixtal/Age Fotostock/HIP; Image ID UNV-EF2-002-A © Houghton Mifflin Harcourt/HIP; Image ID Space 049 Heinemann disc "Art Explosion"; Image ID 42-24170722 © Mark Andersen/Rubberball/Corbis/HIP; Image ID SXECA07ASEAX_0586A © Houghton Mifflin Harcourt/Corbis/HIP.
Interior photographs: © Steve Jacob
Typesetter: Gina Poirier
Manufacturing: Deanna Richardson

Printed in the United States on acid-free paper
18 17 16 15 14 13 12 VP 1 2 3 4 5

Access to Additional Resources on the F&P Resources Site, including:

- Lists of series and sequels books
- Links to sites listing various award-winning books
- Printable Genre Thinkmarks

How to Access the *Genre Study* F&P Resources Site

STEP 1. Go to www.fountasandpinnell.com/resources

STEP 2. Follow the directions on the site to login and register for access to to your e-product

STEP 3. When prompted use fpgenreappendix12 as the "Product Code"

Acknowledgments

The making of a book takes a "whole village," and we have been privileged to work with a vital Heinemann team committed to excellence and truly dedicated to children and teachers.

We are ever grateful to Mary Lou Mackin whose intelligent, sensitive leadership and superb management skills guide all of our work, and to Michael Cirone whose skills as our long time, extraordinary production editor are unparalleled.

Lisa Fowler's brilliant artistry and design expertise, as well as her unending patience, have contributed enormously. We also thank Olive McRae for her continuous advice, and for always being available and brilliant in her thinking, and passionate about possibilities for teachers and students. She is able to take our work to new levels with her deep understanding, hard work, and unique talents. And special thanks to Samantha Garon, our superb Marketing Manager for her intelligent, thoughtful guidance of our work. As always, we are truly grateful for the vision, commitment, and leadership of Lesa Scott, Heinemann President.

To our devoted editor, Betsy Sawyer-Melodia, we express our special thanks, as without her, the many elements of the genre project would never have seen completion. She has been our patient, thoughtful, hard-working partner throughout this venture. Her thorough attention to detail, as well as her gifts in language, have been irreplaceable. We owe sincere appreciation to Kerry Crosby for her hard work and many contributions, her valuable feedback, and her ability to help us present material in a form that makes it accessible to teachers and children. We are also grateful to Alan Huisman for his detailed editing of our publications over many years. Jill Harden has been there for everything we have needed along the way with generous support and enthusiasm, from research to editing, and has played a key role in bringing this book to completion. And to Lynne Costa for her extraordinary attention to design and production in a very complex book, we are most appreciative. She has been a most valuable addition to the team.

We acknowledge the contributions of the many teachers and families who have produced the exciting examples of learning that appear in this book. Special thanks to Jo-Ann Quest Neubert, Katie Gribben, Patti Leary, Ellen Mantefel, Caitlin McArdle, Liz Ward and Maureen Wiklund for their generosity in sharing their teaching and wonderful examples of student work. We are grateful to Holly and Ryann Joseph for contributing a wonderful example how even young children notice the features of texts. We also acknowledge Dana and Jesse Ward for their continuous contributions to our work and their ever-spirited willingness to share their literacy.

As always, our work is supported by our generous professional colleagues at Lesley University, including: Cynthia Downend, Eva Konstantellou, Diane Powell, Kathy Ha, Toni Czekanski, and Margaret Crosby; and at The Ohio State University: Sherry Kinzel, Shelley Schaub, Jenny McFerin, and Wendy Sheets. Our special thanks to Jill Eurich for sharing her continuous feedback and insights into genres and how to help students engage in meaningful learning. We also wish to thank Pat Scharer for her vast knowledge of children's literature and her willingness to share it. And to Carol Woodworth, our masterful book expert, always quick to suggest, support, and expand our work wih her love and knowledge of children's books, we will always be grateful.

For their much-needed support with research, we thank Barbara Summers, Brenda Noe, and Forrest Bell. We thank Jan Rossi and Stacey Betts for their kind assistance in the production process. We'd also like to thank Sharon Freeman for the loving support she provides for every venture.

Ron Melhado and Ron Heath have been our deepest support over the years. Without their generous love and patience, this book would not be.

Finally, we are ever grateful to Charlotte Huck for what she taught us and for her passion for children's literature.

I. C. F and G. S. P.

Credits *(continue from p. ii)*

Kevin Tavares/istockphoto.com. [Great white shark inspects diver] Figure 11.14: Jeff Rotman/Photo Researchers, Inc. [Eugenie Clark carrying explorer flag under water] Figure 11.15 © Stephen Kogge. [Lemon Shark] Figure 11.15: Alexis Rosenfeld/ Photo Researchers, Inc. [Hammerhead Shark] Figure 11.15: Animals, Animal; © Osf/Howard Hall. [Great White Shark] Figure 11.15: Animals, Animal; © James Watt. [Mt. Saint Helens Ash] Figure 11.17: © Douglas Kirkland/CORBIS. [Worker adding cookie dough and strawberries and bananas] Figure 11.21: Courtesy of Blue Bell Creameries. [Cookie dough] Figure 11.21: Richard Nowitz/National Geographic Stock. [Nuts] Figure 11.21: Dmitry Rukhlenko/istockphoto.com. [Cookies] Figure 11.21: James Worrell/Photodisc/Getty Images. [View of the earth from the book] Figure 11.22: NASA photo. [Cotton King by Rick Spears from page 26 of *Mysteries of the Mummy Kids*] Figure 11.23: © Rick Spears. [Pilar Olivares from Reuters from page 26 of *Mysteries of the Mummy Kids*] Figure 11.23: © Pilar Olivares/Reuters/Landov. [Female mummy by Jeffery Newbury from page 52 of *Mysteries of the Mummy Kids*] Figure 11.24: © Jeffery Newbury.

Text

Figure 6.4: From *Ivy & Bean: Doomed to Dance* by Annie Burrows. © 2009 by Annie Burrows; Illustrated by Sophie Blackall. Published by Chronicle Books. Used with permission of Chronicle Books LLC, San Francisco. Visit ChronicleBooks.com.

Figure 6.5: From *Mieko and the Fifth Treasure* by Eleanor Coerr, calligraphy by Cecil Uyehara. Copyright © 1993 by Eleanor Coerr. Published by Puffin Books. Used by permission of G.P. Putnam's Sons, A Division of Penguin Young Readers Group, A Member of Penguin Group (USA) Inc., 345 Hudson Street, New York, NY 10014. All rights reserved.

Figure 10.5: From *Frogs* by Michael Tyler, from Mondo's *Bookshop* Reading Program. Text copyright © 1987 by Michael Tyler. Published by Mondo Publishing. Reprinted by permission of Mondo Publishing, 980 Avenue of the Americas, New York, NY 10018. All rights reserved.

Excerpt from *Whales Passing* by Eve Bunting. Published by The Blue Sky Press. Copyright © 2003 by Eve Bunting. Used by permission of Scholastic, Inc.

Figures 11.4, 11.6, 11.23, 11.24: From *Mysteries of the Mummy Kids* by Kelly Milner Halls. Text copyright © 2007 by Kelly Milner Halls. Reprinted with the permission of Milbrook Press, a division of Lerner Publishing Group, Inc. All rights reserved. No part of this excerpt may be used or reproduced in any manner whatsoever without the prior written permission of Lerner Publishing Group, Inc.

Figure 12.8: From *Jack and the Beanstalk,* retold by Blake A. Hoena. Copyright © 2008 by Stone Arch Books, and imprint by Capstone. All rights reserved.

Figure 12.10: "Manga" image by Jennifer Miller. Copyright © 2012 by Jennifer Miller. Used by permission of the artist.

Excerpt from *Far from Shore* by Sophie Webb. Copyright © 2011 by Sophie Webb. Published by Houghton Mifflin Books for Children. Reprinted by permission of Houghton Mifflin Harcourt.

Excerpt from *The Unsinkable Walker Bean* edited by Aaron Renier. Copyright © 2010 by Aaron Renier. Published by Roaring Books Press. Reprinted by permission of Henry Holt and Company, LLC.

"Thank You Note" from *If I Were in Charge of the World and Other Worries* by Judith Viorst. Copyright © 1981 by Judith Viorst. Published by Atheneum for Young Readers, an imprint of Simon & Schuster Children's Publishing Division. Reprinted by permission of Simon & Schuster and Lescher & Lescher, Ltd. All rights reserved.

Excerpt from *Harlem* by Walter Dean Myers. Copyright © 1997 by Walter Dean Myers. Published by Scholastic Press. Reprinted by permission of Scholastic Inc.

"Sleeping Bag" from *Toasting Marshmallows: Camping Poems* by Kristine O'Connell George. Text © 2001 by Kristine O'Connell George. Published by Clarion Books. Reprinted by permission of Houghton Mifflin Harcourt Publishing Company. All rights reserved.

"The Drum" from *Spin a Soft Black Song, Revised Edition* by Nikki Giovanni, illustrated by George Martins. Copyright © 1971, 1985 by Nikki Giovanni. Published by Farrar, Straus and Giroux. Reprinted by permission of Hill and Wang, a division of Farrar, Straus and Giroux, LLC.

"Chairs" from *All the Small Poems and Fourteen More* by Valerie Worth. Copyright © 1987, 1994 by Valerie Worth. Published by Farrar, Straus and Giroux. Reprinted by permission of Farrar, Straus and Giroux, LLC.

"Rope Rhyme" from *Honey, I Love and Other Poems* by Eloise Greenfield. Text copyright © 1978 by Eloise Greenfield. Published by HarperCollins Children's Books. Used by permission of HarperCollins Publishers and Eloise Greenfield.

"Paper Birch" from *Poetrees* by Douglas Florian. Copyright © 2010 by Douglas Florian. Published by Beach Lane Books. Reprinted with permission of Beach Lane Books, an imprint of Simon & Schuster Children's Publishing Division.

"Storm" from *Toasting Marshmallows: Camping Poems* by Kristine O'Connell George. Text © 2001 by Kristine O'Connell George. Published by Clarion Books. Reprinted by permission of Houghton Mifflin Harcourt Publishing Company. All rights reserved.

"Canada Geese" poem originally appeared in *The Great Frog Race and Other Poems* by Kristine O'Connell George. Text copyright © 1997 by Kristine O'Connell George. Published by Clarion Books. Reprinted by permission of Houghton Mifflin Harcourt Publishing Company. All rights reserved.

"The Anteater" from *Beast Feast: Poems and Paintings* by Douglas Florian. Copyright © 1994 by Douglas Florian. Published by Voyager Books. Reprinted by permission of Houghton Mifflin Harcourt Publishing Company. All rights reserved.

SECTION 1

An Inquiry Approach to Genre Study

Chapters in the first section present the central idea of this book—an inquiry approach to genre study within a readers' workshop. In Chapter 1, we define an inquiry approach and focus on the idea of learning from mentor texts. Chapter 2 focuses more closely on the description of genre study as a process. In Chapter 3, you will find the foundational understandings that students need to develop regarding genre. These understandings are critical in deeply comprehending texts. Chapter 4 describes the readers' workshop as well as how genre study may be integrated into language arts instruction. Finally, in Chapter 5 you will find a discussion of the systems of strategic actions that are involved in reading comprehension. Each is discussed through the lens of understanding genres of text.

CHAPTER 1

An Inquiry Approach to Genre Study

Learning from Mentor Texts

If there is certainty, or only one view, there is nothing to discuss and nothing to learn. Uncertainty is the foundation of inquiry and research.

—Peter Johnston

When we think of school, we think of wonderful books, and for good reason. What students read in school has profound lifelong effects. Books provide a foundation for all kinds of learning. We expect our students to become competent readers and writers who enjoy a variety of book types and know how to access the information in them. We also expect them to appreciate the writer's craft—the exquisite language and text features found in books. As our students read, they also learn how to write. But even more important, we envision our students living a rich reading and writing life in school—developing the habits, attitudes, and interests that will ultimately be the foundation for a lifetime of literacy. Good books will engage their intellect, wonder, and passion and become central to their lives.

For many of us, books are constant companions. We carry them everywhere, in a variety of forms—digital, audio, print—but no matter the form, they are still books. As we read, we meet new friends and revisit old friends, solve problems, enter different worlds, or wake up to new ideas and perspectives. And, as Anna Quindlen has said, "We read in bed because reading is halfway between life and dreams" (1998).

What Is Genre?

Genre refers to any type or kind of literary or artistic work or a class of artistic endeavor that has a characteristic form or technique, including music, drama, and studio arts. Written genres can include fantasy, biography, memoir, realistic fiction, forms, bills, brochures, maps, ads, magazine articles—hundreds of kinds of texts. Even televised sitcoms, plays, mysteries, and news items are written genres that people are reading aloud or reciting from memory.

Genre has changed over time. Genres like tragedy, epic, comedy, and satire used to be widely recognized and produced. They are still around today but are usually in different forms or are embedded within other genres. New genres have emerged, and the rules have changed. For example, in the eighteenth century, genres for writing were highly prescribed and writers were expected to follow those prescriptions if they wanted their writing to be appreciated (Gamble and Yates 2008). Today, we recognize that "genre boundaries are fluid, that new genres emerge and old ones fall out of common use" (Gamble and Yates 2008, 85).

As proficient readers with a lifetime of experience, we have built a large body of knowledge about text genres, and we use this knowledge every time we read, most of the time unconsciously. We enter texts with *expectations* that have everything to do with our enjoyment and appreciation (or dislike) and the meaning we take from them. As experienced processors of written texts, we automatically adjust reading (or listening) to suit the genre. When we receive a bill, we scan it for charges and the "bottom line." When we read a recipe, we look for the list of ingredients. When we read an ad, we are on guard for hidden costs or false advertising. When we read a mystery, we look for clues. When we watch a particular kind of television show, we know what to expect (although a fresh, new approach can still surprise us).

Purpose, Genre, and Audience

Genres have developed over centuries, and writers have always found ways to structure texts for their own purposes. A specific genre is a tool writers use to communicate with their audience and accomplish their purposes. Genre and purpose are interrelated in a complex way, and the audience must be considered in the process.

We might imagine a writer having a purpose and then selecting a genre appropriate for that purpose—one that will appeal to the desired audience. For example, if you want to tell a story, you use some kind of narrative, fiction or nonfiction, set in the past, present, or future. You shape the narrative to engage the audience. Sometimes writers have a favorite genre they gravitate to because of previous successes they've had communicating with an audience. They may use the genre for different purposes or multiple purposes and for speaking to many different audiences.

While "writers of fiction would all agree that they set out to tell a story, it is true that sometimes they have other purposes in mind" (Wilson 2002, 103) as well. They may wish to expose discriminatory treatment or help people understand aspects of the human condition. It is also true that readers may attribute purposes to a piece of fiction or nonfiction that were not intended by the writer. Sometimes writers target a particular audience and are surprised to find they have communicated with readers in ways they did not expect or have connected with untargeted audiences.

If you want to inform or persuade, you select some kind of nonfiction genre—usually categorical. You shape the text with the audience in mind, making it easier or more difficult depending on how much background knowledge you expect your audience to have.

Purpose in nonfiction genres may seem more straightforward, but it too can be complex. There are many nonfiction genres, and even factual texts may be organized in different ways. The way you select and organize facts may work to misinform and/or persuade.

As a reader, you choose texts in relation to your purpose. If you are seeking enjoyment or escape, you select a favorite genre that relaxes you. If you want to become immersed in a story, you choose realistic fiction, historical fiction, fantasy, or biography. If you want to gather information, you may choose nonfiction (although you may also get a great deal of information from some works of fiction).

In both reading and writing, there is a feeling that somehow purpose and audience come first and are related to choice. But as you become immersed in the acts of reading and writing, it is very likely that your purposes may change or you may develop multiple purposes.

Then, too, sometimes reading and writing are assigned. Choice does not play a role, and purpose and genre are inherent to the assignment. When students have undertaken the task of learning, there is some acceptance that with teacher support, they will accept the assignment for a purpose. In this case, any and all previously built knowledge will be very useful.

The Role of Genre in Understanding Reading and Writing

As we encounter book after book, we not only become absorbed in the story or interested in the information, we are also awed by the power of the writer's decisions about language. The genres that have existed through centuries of written language (and even before that in oral storytelling) have developed because writers needed ways to make their meaning and their message clear. Looking at aspects of genre, we see the writers' decisions—the essence of their craft. Everything—language, word choice, dialogue, structure or organization—rests on the choice of genre. As readers, we learn that knowing about the genre helps us make the predictions that support our thinking as we read the text and even help us remember it long afterward.

In this book we focus on the characteristics of literary genres in books—fiction, including realistic fiction, historical fiction, and fantasy; and nonfiction, including narrative nonfiction, expository nonfiction, and biography. Both fiction and nonfiction texts can take a variety of forms, each with its own defining characteristics—mysteries, survival stories, or graphic texts, for example.

When you want to write in a particular genre, you think about what you have read that is like what you want to write. If you were trying to write a mystery, for example, you might think about the crime or secret, the characters, what they are like, and what their motives might be. You'd think of the place(s) the characters inhabit, their relationships to one another, and the all-important series of steps they take to solve the mystery. You'd try to give the reader just enough information to stay engrossed in the story but not enough to solve the mystery before the characters do. Of course there are variations, but the process of construction is similar. You have learned the characteristics of mystery from your reading, listening, or viewing experiences.

If you are writing a biography, on the other hand, you might think about the importance of the subject and conduct research to uncover information about her life. You wouldn't want to write a dry collection of facts; instead, you would engage the reader by writing passionately about the person's impact or achievement, relating significant events, describing documented feelings or motivations, and exploring the hard or courageous decisions the person made throughout a particular span of life, in order to communicate the significance of the person's life and what it means for others.

The writing process varies by genre. Writing fantasy, we create an entirely imaginary world; writing historical fiction, we make the setting authentic; writing informational texts, we research, organize, and present facts in an accurate, logical way. As we write, we use deeply held concepts of the way texts are organized. But we also use this knowledge as we read. Imagine that you can see the internal structure of a skyscraper, including the hundreds of feet of foundation that lie underground, the skeleton of steel, the infrastructure of wiring that carries the electricity throughout the building, and much more. As proficient readers, we bring knowledge of the same kind of hidden organizational structure to a text, and we access it unconsciously because it is already in our brains. No one has to tell us the genre of a particular book—we recognize it soon after we begin to read (or perhaps even by looking at the cover), and we unconsciously access all the knowledge that we have about it. It helps us interpret and navigate our way through the text.

A Workshop Approach

We advocate a workshop approach in which students read extensively, make choices about what to read, and see reading as thinking. They take responsibility for their reading and understand its purpose in their lives. Teachers provide explicit instruction to the whole group, small groups, and individuals. The students view themselves as readers and writers and spend their school lives engaged in real reading, writing, and talking.

Elsewhere we have described a comprehensive framework for literacy education (Fountas and Pinnell 2001, 2006). In this book we concentrate on three major instructional contexts for reading and writing:

1. Interactive read-aloud.
2. Readers' workshop, which includes booktalks, a minilesson, conferences, independent reading, guided reading, literature discussion (book clubs), writing about reading, and group share.
3. Writers' workshop, which includes writers' talks, a minilesson, conferences, independent writing, guided writing, and group share.

Within these three contexts, we can have a deeper conversation about genre and its role in high-quality literacy programs.

An Inquiry Approach to Learning About Genre

In exploring genre study, we are not proposing an academic study of the labels and characteristics of each genre. Instead, we advocate teaching and learning in which students are engaged in exploration. By engaging deeply and constantly with a variety of high-quality texts, they build an internal foundation of information on which they can base further learning. They learn how to develop genre understandings and can apply their thinking to any genre.

People have always engaged in inquiry to make discoveries. Perhaps the strongest example of inquiry is the scientific method, but we also use the inquiry process in our daily lives. On the surface, it may seem that we learn things by taking in information or following directions (as with a recipe); in reality, learning is somewhere in between using what we are told and the discoveries we make ourselves. Using acquired information in the process of trying something out makes learning more memorable and more meaningful.

> Inquiry also requires a change in how we teach:
>
> If we now see children's learning differently, then we must now see ourselves, these children's teachers, differently as well. If the child is not the receiver of delivered curriculum, then we cannot be the deliverers of it. . . . Above all, the teacher is inquirer, inevitably providing—living—a demonstration of inquiry's way of turning toward puzzling phenomena and toward one another in exploring them. (Lindfors 1999, 117)

Through inquiry, students learn to think more critically about the decisions authors make as they plan and write texts. When they know how to look at a crafted work of fiction or nonfiction, the writer becomes real, and the search for the message is more exciting.

Taking an inquiry stance enables students to *learn how to learn*. They become empowered and develop a sense of agency. "A sense of agency empowers learners. It is the notion that gives children the mindset that if they 'act and act strategically, they can accomplish

GENRE STUDY	
Teacher-Directed Approach	**Student/Teacher Inquiry Approach**
Teacher provides a series of lessons related to the genre.	Students investigate the characteristics of each genre with teacher participation and guidance.
Teacher delivers the information to the students who make notes to help them remember it.	Students construct the understandings for themselves. Teacher facilitates and expands what they notice, making their understandings explicit and usually recording them.
Students remember the information.	Students learn "how to learn" about different text types so they can apply the process again.
Teacher assesses students' ability to share genre information.	Teacher assesses students' ability to use the noticing and naming process with a variety of text types.

Figure 1.1 Learning about genre: two different approaches

their goals'" (Johnston 2004, 29). They believe in themselves and their ability to *find out*, and the process itself is inherently pleasing to human beings. Ray describes the energy and satisfaction that results when students are able to influence the direction of their learning:

> Imagine what it would be like to go to school every day as a six-year-old or a sixteen-year-old, and to know how important your thinking is to what will happen in the classroom that day. To know that your teacher is waiting for you and your classmates and that her "Lesson Plans" for the day have huge spaces in them that she's waiting for you to fill with your thinking. (2006, 33)

We can assure meaningful, powerful learning by establishing readers' and writers' workshops in elementary and middle school classrooms and then using a large variety of high-quality texts to help students understand their inner workings. Genre study is much like exploration in science or social studies. Scientists gather data and organize information, looking for patterns. They make hypotheses and explore further to test them; they come to tentative conclusions that are always open to revision when more data are accumulated. Inquiring into genre with your students is an exciting exploration. "It is a line of inquiry—a road of curriculum, a trail of teaching, an excursion of knowing something about writing. It is some big thing that you and your class are digging into over time" (Nia, 1999).

Some educators have approached teaching about genre as direct instruction, and that is one choice for teachers. They explain the characteristics of various genres to students and then provide examples; students learn to name and identify these genres. But we have found that learning is deeper and more meaningful if students construct the understandings themselves.

Notice the difference between teacher-directed genre instruction and a student and teacher inquiry process (Figure 1.1). In student/teacher inquiry, you learn alongside your students. You are intentional in your teaching; you definitely have the goal of expanding students' specific knowledge of genres and their characteristics, and you are far more expert than your students. But when you inquire into texts together, there is always something more to notice and be surprised by. Your students are fully engaged, and most importantly, they learn a process they can apply for the rest of their lives.

The differences may seem subtle, but these two approaches play out very differently. In the inquiry approach students take more responsibility and ownership of learning. As they learn about genres, they simultaneously develop a process for finding things out, for comparing and contrasting texts, for detecting the characteristics that are truly indicative of a particular kind of text. They develop a scientific method for approaching and analyzing texts.

In the inquiry approach students explore texts so that they can *notice and name* the characteristics of each genre and *construct* a working definition that guides their thinking as readers and writers. The inquiry approach takes advantage of human beings' natural curiosity. We learn by searching for and identifying patterns in our environment, and these patterns help us make predictions. Inquiry empowers learners to construct new understandings. Inquiry also empowers us as teachers to teach both reading and writing in ways that make sense for our students and enable them to learn even more about reading and writing without us.

By genre study, we mean more than just learning the specific characteristics of each genre. We mean helping students learn how to learn about genre from other writers—how to study the way writers use craft and conventions in communicating meaning to their readers. Students think about the writer's purpose and audience and notice the features that help the writer achieve an effective communication. What is learned about genre in this way is *generative*—it can be applied to all the reading and writing students do for the rest of their lives.

Understanding Mentor Texts

Throughout our discussion of genre study in readers' and writers' workshops, we refer to *mentor texts* (Ray 2007 and Anderson 2005). You can probably think of someone who has been a mentor to you at some time in your life. A mentor is a trusted friend or peer with greater expertise than your own, someone who guides you and supports your learning and development. A text can have that same mentoring influence on an individual. After all, an author wrote (and probably researched or experienced) the text, so you are learning from that author's expertise and voice whether you are aware of it or not. Books and authors become models for what we may want to achieve in our own writing or the kinds of books we most admire. As the writer Cynthia Rylant says, "I learned how to write from writers. I didn't know any personally, but I read" (1995, p. 6).

Your own expertise in examining and analyzing a text plays a mediating role that helps your students learn how to look at mentor texts. The advantage of such texts is that you can revisit them again and again to seek answers to your questions and use them as models. Once you have read a book aloud to your students, it becomes a resource throughout the year. Ray says, "I study books with students so that they are able to stand on the shoulders of writers, to learn directly from them when I am not around. . . . The texts are just full of curriculum potential" (2007, 147).

Educators have written extensively about the powerful use of mentor texts as valuable resources for helping students as writers (Anderson 2005; Ray 2006; Calkins 2010). Student writers can borrow techniques from mentor texts and try them out when they draft pieces; they can consult mentor texts when they revise a text. If they have been introduced to a large number of high-quality texts, they have excellent models in many different genres. According to Fletcher, "If you want to improve your writing, you have to apprentice yourself to the best writers you can find" (2001). Mentor texts are also important for developing readers.

Through mentor texts, you simultaneously strengthen your reading comprehension and writing ability.

Throughout this book, we advocate for using high-quality picture books as mentor texts. These shorter texts are ideal for read aloud and allow you to share many clear examples of the genre. However, at the upper grade levels, and especially when exploring certain genres, like modern fantasy, it may prove challenging to find grade-level appropriate picture books or shorter texts. In these instances, you may choose to read aloud two or three chapters a day, over a period of a week or two, from a longer chapter book, as students read longer texts independently. We discuss this in more detail in Chapter 14. We have provided a list of mentor texts for each of the fiction and nonfiction genres in Section 2 in the appendix of this book (see Appendix A). These texts are meant to be used as exemplars of the genre, but they are only suggested texts—you may have others that you prefer to use.

Goals and Purposes of This Book

We have been working with a variety of genres for many years and have found that the more texts you encounter and study closely, the more you learn about the basic tools of the writer. Our primary interest in this book is to build your knowledge of genre and to help you apply genre knowledge to the effective teaching of reading comprehension, though we also make a link to writing. All of this teaching and learning takes place in a readers' and writers' workshop structure.

In writing this book we have three goals:

1. *To build your expertise in understanding specific genres and their characteristics.* Text genres are complex. Here we focus mainly on books and short stories rather than attempting to cover the entire world of texts (for example, newspapers, brochures, advertisements, and articles). We have written about the range of everyday reading elsewhere, but here we focus on the fiction and nonfiction books that students read in school and at home, including poetry, short stories, short informational texts, picture books, chapter books, and graphic texts.
2. *To help you understand an inquiry process you can use with your students to study the characteristics of any genre.* Learning is deepened and more likely to remain permanent and applicable if it is built from experience. The teaching we describe is intentional in the way it guides students' inquiry toward explicit understandings of a genre's characteristics. The students actively construct their own knowledge of each type of text.
3. *To show you how to help students apply their knowledge of genres in talking, reading, and writing.* It is through using genre understandings that your students think, talk, and read texts with deeper understanding and write effectively.

Others have written about using inquiry in learning, notably Lindfors (1999), who has studied language learning as a foundation for understanding other learning. Several renowned literacy experts have written extensively about the study of genre as inquiry—primarily as a way of teaching writing. Carl Anderson, Randy Bomer, Lucy Calkins, Ralph Fletcher, Heather Lattimer, Katie Wood Ray, Isoke Nia, and others have helped us understand that when students study text genres, they can apply their understandings to their own writing in those genres.

It is our hope to help students lay the groundwork for a lifetime of literary exploration, and understanding genre is a critical part of that foundation. As students explore different genres and their characteristics, they are more easily and confidently able to identify characteristics of texts that appeal to them as readers and as writers and can more fully engage with the texts they are reading. They are able to identify and understand the writer's craft and the writer's choices and confidently critique the accuracy and quality of a text. When they understand genre, they can engage more deeply with texts.

The following chapters help you take an inquiry stance in your teaching that will be exciting and interesting for you and your students as you guide them through a rich array of wonderful books.

Suggestions for Professional Development

Make a list of some of your favorite books. Review the list. What types of books are you reading? Are you reading a range of different types of books? If you are working with a group, share some of the characteristics of the types of books you read. Do not worry about assigning the appropriate genre to your description. You may want to revisit this list later with colleagues once you have read and studied more about genre and see how your thinking about your own reading has deepened or changed. Discuss what you like about these types of books and what you expect as a reader when you pick up these books. Use the following to guide your discussion or thinking:

- What types of books do you like to read? (Don't worry about correctly "labeling" the genre; just name some of the characteristics of the types of books you like to read.)
- Give some examples of these types of books.
- What appeals to you about this type of book?
- What do you expect as a reader when you pick up this type of book?

CHAPTER 2

What Is Genre Study?

In order to become competent, literate members of society, students must be able to navigate multiple genres.

—Heather Lattimer

Your students will encounter many genres and many texts during their lifetime and will need to be able to think about them analytically and critically. Genre study is a foundational inquiry that involves several steps and gives students the tools they need to navigate a variety of texts with deep understanding:

> They need to know how to confidently read, write, and discuss narrative, informational, persuasive, and analytical texts. Because these forms of text are unique and require unique strategies for reading and writing, it is not safe to assume that students who are competent with one genre will automatically master another. Students need to learn about particular genres through implicit experience and explicit instruction. (Lattimer 2003, 3–4)

"Implicit experience" is provided by immersion in excellent books; "explicit instruction" produces the conclusions students draw as they analyze and experience many examples in the inquiry process with the scaffolds you provide. There are six broad steps in a genre study (see Figure 2.1).

Your first step is to collect a set of high-quality mentor texts that are clear examples of the genre you are helping students understand. As described in Chapter 1, and in more detail in Chapter 14, using picture books or shorter texts as mentor texts allows you to share many clear examples of the genre. Have the

MAJOR STEPS IN GENRE STUDY

1. COLLECT
2. IMMERSE
3. STUDY
4. DEFINE
5. TEACH
6. READ AND REVISE

Figure 2.1 Major steps in genre study

students listen as you read the texts aloud (or have them read independently if they are reading longer texts at the upper grades), and discuss them. They can talk about what they noticed in each text, but when you have read and discussed about four or five, revisit them and study their common characteristics. Drawing out and listing what students have noticed *across* the texts will bring them closer to understanding the particular characteristics of a genre. Then, construct a working definition of the genre that can be revised as students study more examples. Make sure the definition includes the specific characteristics that differentiate this genre from others. Use the definition to guide discussions, all the while trying out your understandings with more examples. Over several days teach specific minilessons on these characteristics, grouping those that are related. Also help students notice the characteristics in small-group lessons or conferences related to their independent reading. Revise the lists and definition as needed and have students record them in the genre studies section of a reader's notebook (see Chapter 18) to use as a reference.

Genre Study and Comprehension

Much reading instruction helps students take words apart, develop strategies to acquire vocabulary, and process more complex sentences. These are important elements of instruction, but readers also need to learn that texts employ a predictable, consistent set of codes to organize and communicate information. Many children figure this concept out for themselves through avid reading or make the connection between formal instruction on genre and the texts they experience. Students may not grasp this understanding on their own. They make only superficial connections between texts and fail to notice the explicit patterns, structures, and features that can assist them both in processing texts more efficiently and in comprehending them better. Genre study through inquiry has the power to support deeper understanding of texts because your students can detect and use these codes and relate their thinking across texts. Genre study improves comprehension.

The Value of Genre Study for Readers

"Every piece of text comes to us as both a text—the piece it is—and a kind of text—an instance of genre" (Bomer, 1995, 117). When we encounter a text, we automatically (and usually unconsciously) assess the genre and proceed using the assumptions we have formed—the limits as well as the questions it raises. This is true even of very functional texts such as brochures or parking tickets. "Genre, an oft-overlooked cueing system in reading, constrains our predictions, lays down a track for our reading" (117). Genre study uses analytic thinking to connect texts, and it benefits readers in many ways (see Figure 2.2).

Through experience with texts, readers recognize common elements, as well as ways that texts in the same genre can vary. They use their knowledge of the predictable elements as a road map to anticipate the structures and elements of the text they are reading. For example, if you are reading a fantasy, you expect to read about a hero on a quest and a contest between good and evil. You are not surprised if magical things happen or if animals talk. If you are reading realistic fiction, on the other hand, you may still encounter a hero, but one who seems real and who must deal with real problems and situations in realistic ways. Both genres have a central story problem, sometimes more than one; you expect both to come to a satisfying or at least an edifying end.

Knowing these features helps you begin to comprehend a text even before starting to read. You have expectations and a kind of in-the-head graphic representation of what the text will be like—how information will be presented and organized. Anyone can memorize a list of characteristics for a genre; highly proficient readers hold these characteristics deeply in their consciousness and access them every time they read.

Through genre study, you help your students anchor their understandings in excellent examples of texts that matter to them because they have talked about them with others and built the understandings for themselves. They have also learned a process they will be able to apply to new types of texts. Genre study brings reading and writing together so that students can "read like writers" and in the process learn to think and talk analytically about texts. Finally, genre study through inquiry helps readers incorporate the academic language they need to talk about books with one another. In the process, they create a community of readers who have a shared language for thinking, talking, and writing about books.

THE VALUE OF GENRE STUDY FOR READERS

- Helps readers know what to expect when beginning to read a text.
- Heightens readers' ability to notice features and structures used by the writer as they process a text.
- Helps readers anticipate the structures and elements of the text.
- Develops the habit of "reading like a writer."
- Develops readers' ability to comprehend particular genres well.
- Helps readers understand what is common among texts in a genre and what can vary.
- Helps readers understand what particular genres have in common.
- Develops readers who can effectively process and comprehend a wide range of texts.
- Develops readers who have favorite genres and are articulate about them.
- Helps readers anchor understandings of genre in excellent examples of texts (mentor texts).
- Helps readers anchor understandings of genre in texts that are memorable and matter to them.
- Helps students use what they learn as readers to write and what they learn as writers to enhance their reading.
- Develops a shared language (academic language) that students can use to talk with one another about books.
- Supports the development of a community of readers and writers.

Figure 2.2 The value of genre study for readers

The Value of Genre Study for Writers

Genre study also helps students develop as writers (see Figure 2.3). They read to learn how to write. They learn about writing from writers who become their mentors. They can more easily apply this knowledge to their own writing, to include producing texts in particular genres. Genre study helps students learn not only a genre's

THE VALUE OF GENRE STUDY FOR WRITERS

- Helps writers notice what effective writers do to create texts in a genre.
- Helps writers learn how texts are created (the decisions writers make).
- Helps writers create the structures and elements of the genre they are writing.
- Develops the habit of "writing like a reader."
- Grounds teaching in real-world texts (rather than abstract lessons).
- Helps writers learn what illustrators do (the decisions they make).
- Helps writers develop a strong vision for the writing they will do.
- Develops a "habit of the mind" so that students actively notice the writer's decisions while they read.
- Grounds writing in excellent examples of well-written texts.
- Grounds writing in texts that matter or are memorable.
- Helps students use what they learn as writers to support reading and use what they learn as readers to help them write.
- Supports the development of a community of readers and writers who have a shared language to talk about the texts they read and write.

Figure 2.3 The value of genre study for writers

characteristics but also how to think deeply about *how* texts are created. They discuss the decisions authors and illustrators make to communicate what they want to say or show to readers.

When you have built up a large number of shared texts, you have created a rich resource for teaching writing. The texts are a bank of possibilities for writing and illustrating texts. Your teaching is grounded in excellent examples of real-world texts rather than abstract concepts—in texts that matter because students have shared them with their friends. Genre study helps writers develop a strong vision of the writing that they will do (Bomer 1995; Ray 2006). They get the "big picture" because they know so much about what their writing will be like.

Genre study helps students develop a "habit of the mind"—reading like a writer (Ray 2006). It brings writing and reading together. Students immersed in genre study can more easily choose the genre for their writing. They can take a piece in one genre and rework it into another. They understand the kinds of decisions writers make. They develop academic language for talking about texts—not only those they read but also those they write. This shared language supports a community of writers who can think and talk together about their thinking.

Genre and the Importance of Teacher Knowledge

The effectiveness of genre study in your classroom depends on your own growing knowledge of the characteristics of each genre (see Figure 2.4). When you have a strong knowledge of genre, you can scaffold and lead students to deeper understanding. But you don't need to know everything about a genre all at once. Using an inquiry approach means you learn alongside your students. You implicitly provide demonstrations of inquiry, and you participate in the process of constructing explicit understandings that guide reading and writing in a variety of genres.

Through genre study you deepen your appreciation of the complexity of texts. You also expand your knowledge of the features and structures that are characteristic of each genre. As you learn with your students, your own enjoyment of texts will grow and that enjoyment is contagious. Studying texts also helps you develop greater sensitivity to the deep understandings that you want your students to use as they talk and write. You also show your students how to use excellent texts as mentors for their writing. Through genre study, they learn to see authors as real people who write, revise, rewrite, and make decisions about their writing.

THE IMPORTANCE OF GENRE KNOWLEDGE FOR TEACHERS

- Deepens your appreciation for the complexity of texts.
- Allows you to use the features and structures of genres to guide the inquiry process.
- Increases your enjoyment of texts in various genres, which you communicate to students.
- Expands your awareness of the comprehension demands of texts.
- Promotes a deep understanding that will help you detect what students need to understand over time.
- Expands your ability to see features of mentor texts that will support students' writing.
- Expands your skill in helping students use texts as mentors.
- Increases your enjoyment of reading and talking about books.

Figure 2.4 The importance of genre knowledge for teachers

Studying genre through inquiry can only enhance the enjoyment of the texts you and your students study together. As students discover more in the texts they read and share these discoveries in their conversation, the process comes alive. Students begin to search actively for examples to support their findings; they even present good arguments. Texts become more meaningful for everyone.

Genre Study in Action

Let's look at an example of genre study in a third grade classroom, as Mrs. Lee, who is introducing her students to historical fiction, applies the six steps of the inquiry process.

1. **Collect.** Mrs. Lee begins by selecting a few high quality historical fiction picture books to read aloud over several weeks to immerse her students in the genre. She selects books that reflect a variety of time periods, historical events, and themes so that students can think beyond the topic to the characteristics common to all the texts. The texts Mrs. Lee selects are:

   True Heart (Moss)
   Gleam and Glow (Bunting)
   Pennies in a Jar (Chaconas)
   When Jessie Came Across the Sea (Hest)
   Freedom Summer (Wiles)
   Ma Dear's Aprons (McKissack)
   Ride Like the Wind: A Tale of the Pony Express (Fuchs)

Figure 2.5 Mrs. Lee immersing students in historical fiction texts

Figure 2.6 Mrs. Lee reviewing the noticings to create a working definition

2. **Immerse.** Mrs. Lee immerses the students in these mentor texts while they simultaneously choose their own books to read independently. Mrs. Lee doesn't have them look for characteristics of the genre right away. It's important for them to listen to (or read), think about, and discuss the content of the various texts with one another. Mrs. Lee reads a book and the students talk about the content and the themes or messages they encounter. Her students have a great deal of experience discussing what they notice about texts. She helps them notice that the setting often influences the actions of the characters in historical fiction.
3. **Study.** Next, Mrs. Lee has her students step back and closely study the characteristics the books have in common. What is evident in all of the books they have discussed? The students begin to think about the characteristics that define historical fiction. They talk about whether the things they notice occur *all* of the time or only *some* of the time. Students notice that the stories take place long ago, some of the characters use old-fashioned language, they tell what life was like, and that some tell about real people or events. "Tells about life in the past," and "imagined story set in the real world" are the only statements they agree meet the "all the time" criterion. The class creates a chart of noticings about historical fiction that they can add to as they read more examples (see Figure 2.7). This chart describes the

Historical Fiction

What we noticed:

- Imaginary story that could be real
- Has characters, plot and setting
- Shows life like it was in the past
- Tells about problems people had in the past

Figure 2.7 Historical fiction: what we noticed all of the time

characteristics that they notice *all* of the time. Another chart they create (Figure 2.8) describes the characteristics they notice *often*.

4. **Define.** The teacher and students then use the list of noticings to create a working definition of historical fiction (see Figure 2.9), a definition that may be revised over time as they continue to study the genre.
5. **Teach.** Mrs. Lee uses the list of noticings and the working definition to teach specific mini-lessons on the important features of the genre. For example:
   - Readers notice when a story tells about life as it might have been lived in the past so they can identify it as historical fiction.
   - Readers notice the setting in historical fiction to help them understand history.
   - Readers think about what life was like for the story characters and the challenges they faced in order to understand the problems and issues of the time.

Historical Fiction

Often:

- Is based on real people and events from the past
- Uses old-fashioned language

Figure 2.8 Historical fiction: what we noticed often

Historical Fiction

Historical fiction is a made-up story that takes place in the past and shows the way life may have been lived in the past.

Figure 2.9 Working definition of historical fiction

6. **Read and Revise.** Mrs. Lee places several baskets of historical fiction books in the classroom library for students' independent reading (see Figure 2.10). Included are books on a variety of historical periods and issues, harder-to-read books, shorter books, longer books, and more. There is also a basket of historical fiction books related to the civil rights movement, which the students are learning about in social studies. For the next few days, at the beginning of readers' workshop, Mrs. Lee provides quick book talks—short oral reviews—about the historical fiction texts she's added to the classroom library. She asks students to choose historical fiction when they are ready

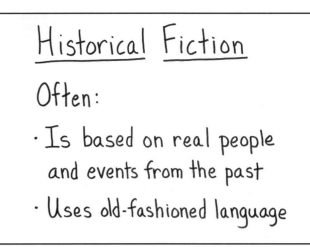

to read a new book independently and continues to read historical fiction aloud. During class discussions and sharing sessions students describe additional features they notice about the historical fiction they are reading, add more characteristics to their charts, and revise their working definition of historical fiction.

Understanding the Process

The different time periods, content, and other variations in the texts they read help Mrs. Lee's students think further about historical fiction as a genre. The idea is not to produce an extensive and uniform set of characteristics but to approach understanding the genre as a fluid process. Students build understandings over time and change and expand them as more examples are encountered. They explore themes and content through discussion, drawing out characteristics that make a text clearly identifiable as historical fiction. They refer to their charts of characteristics and their working definition to guide their thinking.

The charts are revised as the students read and discuss more texts. Mrs. Lee presents minilessons on the characteristics of historical fiction, and students look for these characteristics in their own independent reading. After a few weeks, students have developed:

- The ability to analyze a text and identify it as historical fiction.

Figure 2.10 Students making genre choices for independent reading

- A strong understanding of the characteristics of historical fiction.
- An understanding of the difference between historical fiction, realistic fiction, and nonfiction texts on historical topics.
- A shared language for talking about historical fiction.
- A higher level of appreciation for historical fiction.
- A greater understanding of the role of setting in relation to plot.
- A greater knowledge of history and its issues and challenges.

The students continue to refer to the genre throughout the year as they encounter more texts.

Figure 2.11 summarizes the steps in the inquiry process for genre study. Use it to guide your thinking as you discuss various genres.

STEPS IN THE INQUIRY PROCESS FOR GENRE STUDY	
1. **Collect** (Create Text Sets)	• Collect a set of mentor texts in the genre to read aloud. • Be selective; use high-quality, authentic picture books or shorter texts (when possible). • Collect books (at a range of difficulty levels) to place in a genre basket in the classroom library—books students can choose to read independently. • Collect multiple copies of books for genre book clubs (books of interest to the grade level) and guided reading groups (must be appropriate instructional level for the group).
2. **Immerse**	• Immerse students in several clear examples of the genre. As you read these mentor texts aloud, encourage students to think about, talk about, and identify common characteristics. • Give book talks on texts in the classroom library in the genre and invite students to select the genre for their independent reading. • Provide multiple copies of texts in the genre for book clubs and guided reading groups. Help students think about genre characteristics.
3. **Study**	• After the students have read several examples, have them analyze characteristics that are common to the group of texts. • List the genre features they notice on chart paper. Make sure that students are able to distinguish between characteristics that are *always* evident and those that are *often* evident.
4. **Define**	• Define the genre. Use the list of characteristics to create a short working definition.
5. **Teach**	• Teach specific minilessons on the important genre features on the list, using the mentor texts and adding new mentor texts to the initial text set.
6. **Read and Revise**	• Expand student understandings during individual conferences about their independent reading, and facilitate group share sessions. • Encourage students to talk about the genre in their book clubs, guided reading discussions, reading conferences, and any other appropriate instructional contexts. • Add more characteristics to the class charts and revise the working definition of the genre if needed.

Figure 2.11 Steps in the inquiry process for genre study

Suggestions for Professional Development

Explore some genres yourself (it will be more enjoyable if you work with colleagues). Gather four or five examples of picture books in two or three genres. You will be amazed at the quality of these shorter texts and their potential when used even at upper and middle grade levels.

1. Stack the books in piles according to genre.
2. Divide the texts and read them as partners or small groups.
3. Make a list of the things you notice across the texts.
4. Make charts like the ones in this chapter listing characteristics that always appear and those that often appear in texts in the genre. You will of course have much more background information than Mrs. Lee's students did, but don't try to make the lists exhaustive. The goal is to explore.
5. Create some genre text sets that will be exciting, engaging, and appropriate for your students. As you prepare these text sets, you may want to keep in mind which genres you will be asking your children to use as writers across the year since many of the sets will also become mentor texts for your writers' workshop.

CHAPTER 3

What Students Need to Know About the Genres of Texts

Genres are containers for thinking. They help us to orient ourselves to the kind of story we are hearing and its purpose.

—Pam Allyn

Students build their knowledge of genres over many years. Even as adults we often find ourselves learning the characteristics of new genres (or combinations of genres). This chapter outlines some of the basic understandings students need to develop about genres during the elementary and middle school (junior high) years. You may find many implications for high school as well. Having a deep understanding of the characteristics of genres is a strong foundation for all literacy-related learning. (Specific genres are discussed in more detail in Section 2.)

Many types of texts (mysteries for example) are sometimes called genres in casual conversation. Therefore, we need to distinguish between *genres* and the very identifiable types and specific *forms* they take. First, we cannot identify prose and poetry as genres: they are broad, overarching categories of the language of writing that can appear in *any genre*. For example, the book *Butterfly House* (Bunting, 1999) is a fictional text written in poetic form. If we establish prose and poetry as the two *ways* language is used in literature, we can move on to thinking about the genres of fiction and nonfiction and their various facets (see Figure 3.1).

Genres and Forms of Literature

The difference between prose and poetry is in the writer's purpose and the way the information is presented. Prose has sentences arranged in paragraphs that follow each other. Prose uses language that informs, shows, describes, and explains. Poetry is compact writing characterized by imagination and artistry and imbued with intense meaning. Both prose and poetry can evoke sensory images; both can tell a story; both can satirize or persuade. Sometimes the lines between prose and poetry are blurred: writers of prose may use figurative or poetic language to the degree that when it is read aloud, it sounds like poetry.

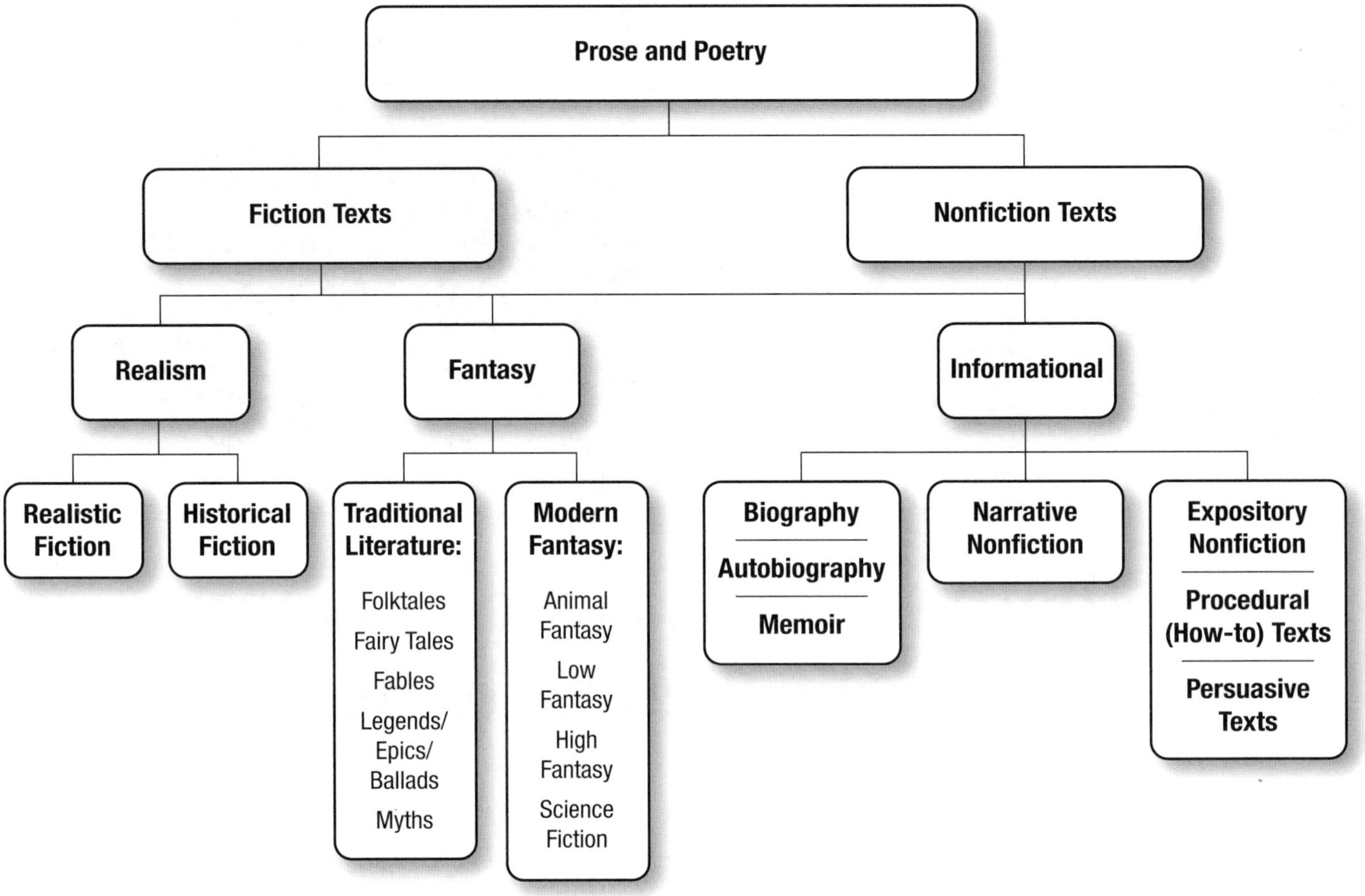

Figure 3.1 Genre categories

A genre is a type of text identified by definition and characteristics. The broader categories are fiction and nonfiction, and within these broad categories much depends on the setting and/or purpose of the text. There are a number of ways to categorize genres, but Figure 3.1 sorts the generally recognized genres in a way we find helpful. (The *Genre Quick Guide* (2012) defines and characterizes the fiction and nonfiction genres discussed in this book and can be used as a handy reference.)

Prose—the ordinary form of spoken or written language without the metrical structure of poetry—can be divided into fiction or nonfiction. Fiction is usually a narrative and is imagined rather than real. It includes elements such as setting, characters, a problem or conflict, a plot with events or episodes, and a problem resolution with some sort of conclusion. The left side of the chart in Figure 3.1 distinguishes between realistic fiction set in the present or the historical past and fiction set in fantasy worlds—this makes a difference in the way the text is written and the way it is read. The main purpose of fiction, whether realistic or fantasy, is to entertain.

Nonfiction, on the other hand, is intended to provide factual information. The information may be presented in narrative form using time (biography or narrative nonfiction, for example), or it may be presented using logic—in categories or some other logical organization (expository, procedural, or persuasive texts, for example). Nonfiction provides a great deal of factual information through text and visual images. The right side of the chart in Figure 3.1 distinguishes among nonfiction designed to explain, describe, inform, entertain, describe a process, or persuade, depending on the writer's purpose. Often nonfiction writing has more than one purpose and may not fall neatly into just one of these categories.

Special *forms*, which we discuss later in the chapter, are sometimes called *subgenres*; they cut across genres but have their own unique characteristics as well.

Fiction Texts

Fiction texts are narratives—they tell a story. These texts may be organized in many ways and may have unusual features, but the purpose is the same—to tell a compelling or entertaining story. Fiction texts may be realistic; that is, they are not true, but they are believable and stay within the parameters of the real world. Events in realistic fiction stories *could happen*, and characters and settings *could exist*, even if they are slightly preposterous or exaggerated. Fiction texts may also be fantasy, with characters, settings, events, or other elements that may be believable in the context of an alternative world but could not happen or exist in the real world.

Realism

Realism includes both contemporary realistic fiction, which is set in current times, and historical fiction, which takes place in the past.

Contemporary Realistic Fiction

Contemporary realistic fiction usually presents characters experiencing typical modern-day problems. It may also highlight social issues. Much contemporary realistic fiction for young readers is light-hearted and humorous, keying into issues that matter and are relevant to young readers. A good example of this is the much-loved *Tales of a Fourth Grade Nothing* (Blume 1972).

In the last twenty years, realistic fiction for children has also begun to focus on more serious topics. *A Taste of Blackberries* (Buchanan Smith 1973) and *Bridge to Terabithia* (Paterson 1977) both deal with the complex and moving theme of the loss of a close friend. Today, realistic fiction covers a range of issues and problems that young children or preadolescents and adolescents face, and is a way for young people to learn about others and recognize themselves in the stories they read.

Historical Fiction

Historical fiction depicts the way people lived in the past and focuses on the problems and issues of life in a particular historic time period. Setting (time and place) is very important in understanding historical fiction.

You might ask, "How far back in time does a book have to be set in order to be considered historical fiction?" There is no definitive answer to that question, because time, of course, is not stationary. Some books, such as the classic *Little Women* (Alcott 1868), which was first published in the 1800s, were written as contemporary fiction (the recent past of the writer), but have become historical fiction with the passage of time. Other classics, however, such as the Ramona books written by Beverly Cleary in the 1950s, remain contemporary because of their universal subject matter and because the setting is not significant to the story. Children still enjoy these books, although they may detect some elements that seem out of date.

Fantasy

Fantasy includes traditional literature and more modern types of fantasy, including simple animal fantasy, low fantasy, high fantasy, and science fiction.

Traditional Literature

Traditional literature comprises stories passed down in written or oral form throughout history. The stories are an integral part of world culture. Some stories appear in many cultures, adjusted to reflect specific cultural norms. For example, Cinderella stories are told throughout the world. In addition to the European and American versions many readers are familiar with, there are (among others) a Caribbean version (*Cendrillon: A Caribbean Cinderella Book*, San Souci, 2002), a Native American version (*The Rough-Face Girl*, Martin 1998), an African version (*Mufaro's Beautiful Daughters*, Steptoe 1987), and a Chinese version (*Yeh-Shen*, Louie 1996). Not only does traditional literature represent culture, it permeates culture. The stories are simple and the characters "flat" (simple and relatively unchanging), but we all know what the plot or theme will be when we hear "it's a Cinderella story." Moreover, these allusions appear over and over in the texts we read, and we process them automatically, accessing meaning. Authors constantly revisit the language, style, and themes of traditional literature as they craft fantasy and realistic fiction. Traditional fantasy "is the mother of all literature" (Tunnell and Jacobs 2000).

Works of traditional literature often have recurring motifs or patterns, such as "the quest" or "threes." They include some very clear structures; for example:

- Cumulative tales, such as "The House That Jack Built."
- Pourquoi tales, such as *Why Mosquitoes Buzz in People's Ears* (Aardema 2004), which tell or explain why something (usually a natural phenomenon) occurs.

The different kinds of traditional literature are well known, although we may not always need to distinguish them by type. There are beast tales featuring talking animals, trickster stories, "Noodlehead" tales about silly people, and tales of exaggeration (tall tales). Some folktales are realistic, but many have magical elements and are also called fairy tales. Sometimes tales are written by contemporary authors but *told* in the form of traditional literature because the writer has chosen to use characteristics of the genre. In these instances the genre lines are blurred, but true traditional literature began as oral stories.

Modern Fantasy

The fantasy genre also includes stories that began as written texts and are not traditional literature. These imaginative stories have a wide range of complexity, from simple animal fantasy to long, complex narratives that take place in other worlds to texts that use scientific concepts. This could be viewed as a continuum, but we think it is useful instead to consider four categories:

1. *Animal fantasy*, such as *The Tale of Peter Rabbit* by Beatrix Potter or *Charlotte's Web* by E. B. White, is very much like traditional literature. These texts have talking animals that get into many of the same dilemmas or situations that people would. Many have deeper meanings, and often the characters learn a lesson. The storylines are usually easy to follow and the characters do not change much.
2. *Low fantasy* has magical elements and is often quite complex but takes place in the real world. It can involve the struggle between good and evil, and may have heroes, powerful magic, magical objects, and other elements of fantasy. These "non-rational happenings occur in the rational world" (Gamble and Yates 2008), as in *The Borrowers* (Norton 1952) in which the tiny Clock family lives under the floor of an English country house and "borrows" all of their household objects from the humans who live above them.
3. In *high fantasy* the real world does not exist, because the writer has created an alternative world. Or, if the real world does exist, it does so in a parallel setting from which characters enter the alternative world. High fantasy is characterized by symbolism, rich and complex language, challenging vocabulary, and lots of action. Works of high fantasy are very complex and usually include a struggle between good and evil. All of these characteristics are true of the Earthsea trilogy (LeGuin), and the classic *The Lord of the Rings* (Tolkien 1937), which takes place completely in a fantastic world. Sometimes in high fantasy the alternative world exists alongside the real world as in the Harry Potter series. The lines between low and high fantasy are not always distinct, and that shouldn't be a problem for the reader.
4. *Science fiction* is fantasy based on scientific principles. Often, science fiction is set at some time in the future but it may have some of the same characteristics as low or high fantasy. In *Enchantress from the Stars* (Engdahl 1971) the characters, anthropologists, live in a future world in which they visit other planets and study the life there. Like much of science fiction, these texts help readers imagine what life in the future might be like. Science fiction also features technology or scientific advances, and often uses time travel or journeys through space.

Series and Sequels

Children tend to like series books and sequels. When students connect with a character or setting they relate to, they enjoy revisiting that place or character again and again. A list of excellent series books and books with sequels is included with the additional resources on the F&P Resources Site. Because you will want to use them in slightly different ways, Figure 3.2 differentiates between books that are only part of a *series* and books that have one or more *sequels*. Both, technically, are series books and can be called so, but let's look at some differences.

COMPARISON OF SERIES BOOKS AND BOOKS WITH SEQUELS		
	Series Books	**Books with Sequels**
Definition	A series is a set of books that are connected by the same character(s) and/or setting. Each book stands alone and they may be read in any order.	A sequel is a literary work that continues a story begun in a previous book. The central character usually remains the same and new secondary characters may be introduced. Books with sequels are generally meant to be read in order.
Setting	Settings tend to be constant.	Settings are more likely to change; characters may go on journeys or quests.
Themes	Themes are generally the same for all books in the series.	While the larger theme may be constant, there will be various layers within that theme as characters change.
Plot	Plot patterns are repetitive, although specific problems vary.	Plots are more complex and less predictable. Problems change as characters grow. One plot builds on another.
Characters	All characters tend to be "flat" and static. (In higher-quality series books, the main character is better developed.) They may learn a specific lesson but do not change over time.	Characters grow and develop over time. Main characters tend to be "round" and dynamic. The books build on previous learning. Relationships change as characters learn.
Primary Values for the Reader	Readers can read a large amount of text quickly with ease and enjoyment. Readers enjoy encountering familiar events, characters, and settings.	Readers get to know characters very well across several volumes. Readers explore more complex themes and plots. Readers enjoy higher-quality literary works.

Figure 3.2 Comparison of series books and books with sequels

Series Books

Series books focus on one character or a set of characters that appear over and over in successive volumes; generally they also have the same setting, although it may vary slightly (for example, from home to school to summer camp). Books in a series stand alone. A reader may select them in any order and enjoy the stories without having read prior volumes.

Often, series books are organized around the same theme or set of related themes. For example, the characters in the Berenstain Bears series are always dealing with the problems of everyday family life—sibling rivalry, sharing, caring for pets, and other issues. Both the Chet Gecko series (Hale) and the Geronimo Stilton series (various authors) feature animals who solve mysteries and have adventures, as do the characters in the 39 Clues series (various authors).

Plots in series books tend to be repetitive and formulaic, although the specific events and problems will vary within that structure. Plots are always resolved in an unambiguous way, and characters usually learn a lesson. These books generally contain stories with some humor and tell about daily life.

Although the literary quality of various series may be uneven, good series books offer many advantages to developing readers. For one thing, once a reader knows the characters and setting and understands the general nature of the plots, the reading becomes much easier. The text makes fewer demands on conceptualizing, and the reading is likely to be faster. In other words, the reader knows how the text "works." Once they find a series that they like, readers enjoy them. The repetitive plots may provide some security, and the characteristics of series books support the development of reading fluency. These books may be particularly helpful to struggling readers; they feel safe in their understanding and build up reading "mileage."

Books with Sequels

A sequel to a literary work continues the story that began with the first volume. Often, writers of sequels produce trilogies, but there can be more volumes as well. The characters are well drawn, and we see a great deal of change in them over time; that is, they tend to be "round" and dynamic. For example, in both the Little House series (Wilder) and the Betsy/Tacy series (Hart-Lovelace), the main characters grow to adulthood, taking on increasing responsibility and developing their roles within their families.

Sequels offer some of the same advantages to readers as series books do. Readers enjoy reencountering characters they know, particularly because these characters are usually well developed. Readers have the additional pleasure of seeing the character have new experiences and undergo further change.

Readers who enjoyed the plucky eight-year-old heroine Annabelle Doll in Ann Martin's *The Doll People* (2003) are treated to more Doll Family adventures in *The Meanest Doll in the World* (2005), and *The Runaway Dolls* (2010). Readers who journeyed with Dicey Tillerman and her three younger siblings in the novel *Homecoming* (Voigt 2003) are eager to read the sequels *Dicey's Song* (2003) and *A Solitary Blue* (2003), in which Dicey is also the main character.

Sequels usually have connected themes. The stories about the Doll family often feature the relationships between the more old-fashioned Doll Family and the more modern Funcraft family. The Tillerman books explore love in many dimensions. But as in all high-quality literary works, there are multiple themes across the books. The plots tend to be much more complex than those in series books, although complexity varies by the level of the book.

Sequels generally offer the advantage of familiar characters, with the settings changing as characters have further adventures. Thus, they encourage more reading, which is supported by the reader's previous experience. When they read sequels, readers bring with them their knowledge of the characters, so understanding is deepened. Sequels help readers carry meaning from one text to another; strategies such as making connections are more available. At the same time, readers are encountering the sophisticated language and vocabulary of good fiction.

Nonfiction Texts

All nonfiction is essentially informational, but the various types of nonfiction have different purposes and use different features to achieve those purposes. Nonfiction texts can be organized in logical ways, such as by categories of information (as with expository text), or they can aim to persuade or provide directions on how to do something. There are also narrative nonfiction texts that are organized very much like fiction in that they tell a story.

Narrative Texts

Many nonfiction texts are organized as narratives; they tell a story that is organized in time. Most accounts of history are organized as narratives, although they may also offer categorized information. We divide nonfiction narrative texts into two groups: biographical texts and narrative nonfiction texts.

Biographical Texts

Biographical texts tell the story of a person's life. The person the biography focuses on is called the *subject*. Biographical texts can be categorized further as biography, autobiography, or memoir. Writing a biographical text involves taking a point of view and making selective decisions about what to include in the text so that the reader agrees with the writer's perspective. Some biographical texts are more objective and well documented, and some are biased.

In a *biography*, the narrative is told in the third person—one person, or a team, writes the story of another persons's life (or part of it). We especially like picture book biographies that can be read aloud to upper elementary and middle school students. A biography of Marian Anderson, *When Marian Sang*, by Pam Munoz Ryan (2002), gives a chronological account of the singer's life. Within the beautifully crafted text, the writer has embedded words from the gospel songs that Marian sang in her church and that symbolize her life. The pencil illustrations in sepia tone, by Brian Selznick, open up the text like a stage set does an opera. The back of the book includes more information, written in expository style, as well as a timeline. These features—short narratives without extensive detail—are included in many biographies.

In an *autobiography,* a subject writes the story of his or her own life. In addition to his popular fiction novels for young people, Gary Paulsen has written two autobiographies: *My Life in Dog Years* (1999) and *Guts* (2002). In *Guts* he shares specific stories about experiences that led to the plots of his popular books.

Memoir is usually autobiographical and tells the story of a significant experience or aspect of one's life. The writer takes a reflective stance; memoirs are usually written in first person and convey intense emotion. Rather than relating every detail of an experience or producing an extended narrative, writers of memoir tell only *what counts*. They use many of the same techniques used by writers of fiction: memoirs have setting, characters, sometimes dialogue, exciting or scary events, problems, and visual imagery. The writer is relating a memory that makes a point. The goal is to make the reader understand and even share feelings, emotions, and conclusions. And because we have all had life experiences, memoir is a powerful genre for students. Through memoir, they can develop their craft and voice as writers, drawing on their own memories and making them more vivid. Author Tomie dePaola's *Nana Upstairs and Nana Downstairs* (2000) tells the story of treasured Sundays spent with his great grandmother during his boyhood. Memoirs often focus on memories of family members or of people, places, or events significant to the author.

Memoirs may be based on stories told and passed down in a family through generations. It is easy to identify a text written in the style of a memoir but not always easy to know whether the text is a true memory. Since memoir focuses on remembered feelings rather than on strict adherence to facts, many are formally classified on the copyright page as fiction. But you can look for a personal note from the author or some other indication that the memoir is a true memory.

Narrative Nonfiction

Narrative nonfiction texts use a narrative structure to provide information and literary language to make a topic interesting and appealing to readers. *Elephant's Story* (Blackford and Stojic 2008) begins with the birth of a young female elephant and describes elephant behavior as she grows to be a responsible member of her elephant family. Although this text uses narrative structure—it has a beginning, a series of episodes, and an ending—its purpose is different from that of most fictional stories. The writer wants not just to entertain readers but to help them understand animal habitats and behavior. This book also does what many narrative nonfiction texts do: it includes expository material in the back of the book to provide more information related to the topic.

LITERARY NONFICTION Much of narrative nonfiction that we encounter as readers can also be described as literary nonfiction, although this is not always the case. The term *literary nonfiction* describes nonfiction texts that employ literary techniques, such as figurative language, but these texts do not always take on a narrative form. Expository texts, for example, can present information in a non-narrative form while still using literary language.

Non-Narrative Texts

Some nonfiction texts do not tell a story but instead present information that is organized in some logical way. Narrative texts take place in time; non-narrative texts are organized in other ways. For example, *All About Frogs* (Arnosky 2008) presents facts about frogs in categories that are ordered logically, but readers can read them in any order.

We sort these types of nonfiction texts into three categories:

1. *Expository texts* are organized logically to offer the reader information about a topic. They often explain and describe, giving examples. They may use underlying structures like compare and contrast, problem and solution, cause and effect, or chronological and temporal sequence. Expository texts cover a broad range—factual texts, literary nonfiction, feature articles, reports, literary essays, and interviews.
2. *Procedural texts* include "how to" books that provide directions on how to do something or that teach or describe a process such as building a house. (This does not include processes in nature, such as caterpillar to butterfly or tadpole to frog.) They are almost always organized in temporal sequence, in which things must happen step by step. *Emeril's There's a Chef in my Soup! Recipes for the Kid in Everyone* (Lagasse 2005) is a good example of this organizational structure. *How a House Is Built* (Gibbons 1996), describes the complex and cooperative process of building a house.
3. *Persuasive texts* include everything from advertisements (which we don't examine here, since our focus is books) to persuasive essays. A persuasive text tries to convince the reader to do something, agree with an opinion, or join an opinion group. It offers statements of opinion and backs them up with reasons and evidence. *A River Ran Wild* (Cherry 2002) offers facts and descriptions in a way that persuades the reader to care for the environment. *All About Frogs* (Arnosky 2008) is an informational text that turns persuasive on the last two pages to convince readers to protect frogs' environment.

Hybrid Texts

The lines between genres are often blurred, and that's not a bad thing. Interest is often enhanced when the reader encounters features of one genre within another and/or one text structure within another. In fact, it is popular now for writers to mix genres and/or text structures. Although there are varying opinions on what characteristics make a text a hybrid, we define it at the broadest level as a text that blends more than one genre within a coherent whole. However, you will need to decide for yourself, as there is often no clear designation. We have developed criteria for identifying hybrid texts (see Chapter 12 for a detailed explanation and examples), but what is important is that you and your students examine different texts analytically and notice the writer's craft or the way the writer put the text together.

Text Structures

All non-narrative texts are organized, or *structured*, in a way that brings the message or information to the reader. The text structure influences the way readers take information from texts, so it is important to examine it here. In the discussion of fiction and nonfiction, we have already distinguished between narrative structure, which tells a story, and exposition, which presents information within some kind of categorization.

Fiction uses a narrative structure and nonfiction can be either narrative or non-narrative. The following underlying structures are prominent in nonfiction but can also appear in fiction:

- Argumentative—presents a series of persuasive statements or opinions with reasons attached.
- Descriptive—provides sensory details of a particular scene or event as well as emotional details.
- Chronological—describes events in the order they occur in time.
- Temporal—describes a process that always occurs in the same way and is repeated over and over.
- Compare and contrast—tells how entities are alike and how they are different.
- Cause and effect—focuses on why and how something occurs.
- Problem and solution—presents an issue or problem and describes a solution.
- Question and answer—presents a question and then an answer; the question and answer communicate a coherent overall meaning.

All text structures are valid; writers select the best structure for their purposes. Typically, nonfiction texts will combine many underlying structures even when the overarching structure is narrative or non-narrative.

Forms of Prose and Poetry

All genres may be presented in a variety of forms. They may take the form of longer books with chapters or sections or picture books or graphic texts. They may appear as articles in journals or newspapers or on the Internet. They may be written as diaries, log entries, or a series of letters or emails.

Forms of Poetry

Poetry may be fiction or nonfiction. It includes traditional poems, as well as songs and chants. It can be serious or humorous. Poetry comes in well-defined, specific forms, including free verse, lyric, narrative, limericks, cinquains, ballads, concrete poetry, Haiku, "found" poetry, list poems, and formula poems. We talk more about poetry and its various forms in Chapter 13.

Special Types of Fiction

There are some special types of fiction students need to recognize and understand because readers often gravitate to one or more of them. These types of fiction are complex and have their own special characteristics (we write in more detail about them in Chapter 7). They can be realistic or historical fiction, or they can be fantasy. Any of the forms may be combined. Some examples are mystery; crime; survival and adventure stories; horror; humor; animal stories; sports stories; stories about family, friends, and school; romance; and satire.

Plays

The structure of a dramatic text, unlike other forms of fiction, is directly influenced by its purpose—a play is written to be performed rather than just read. A play will include references to characters, scenery, and action, as well as stage directions, and usually consists of scripted (written) dialogue between characters. Plays can be realistic fiction, historical fiction, or fantasy, and they might also include elements of special types of fiction such as mystery, crime, or romance.

Literacy and New Media

In recent years, new *media* (formats for communicating information) have emerged that allow writers to deliver texts in forms that extend beyond printed words on a page. We often talk about the challenges of the *new literacies*. The term is related to the explosion of written or visual material that is available today and is constantly changing. Educators are advised to prepare readers and writers for today's world as well as for a world that does not yet exist. It seems inevitable that these formats will continue to grow and change in coming years, but two are especially significant.

Graphic Texts (Graphica)

In recent years graphic texts have burgeoned in popularity and have entered schools and classrooms. A graphic text integrates pictures and words to tell a story or to inform. Illustrations are equal to or more important than the printed text and tell much of the story, providing vital information. Graphic texts can be created in many genres, both fiction and nonfiction. The uniqueness of a graphic text lies in the way the illustrations and various types of text work together to communicate the author's meaning. This is done not just in pictures and text or special kinds of punctuation. The placement of the graphics and the lines around them mean something; there are special devices to indicate passing of time, change, or setting.

Thompson (2008) describes *graphica* as "an ever evolving medium with a wide range of possibilities" (6). Some have described graphica as a new genre, and certainly a graphic text has many unique features. But for now, we will talk about it as a medium of literature. Although the better-known graphic texts may be fiction, for example the popular Bone series by Jeff Smith, graphic texts can also be nonfiction, as is the case with the Graphic Science and Graphic History series and many others.

Formats of graphic texts include:

- *Comic strips*—panels of graphics and print that tell a story. They often appear in magazines or newspapers and have episodes about the same characters and/or a story line that continues over many issues.
- A *comic book*—an entire magazine presenting strips of comics that tell a longer story.
- A *graphic novel*—a book-length fiction text in which a majority of the story is told in pictures. A picture book would not be considered a graphic novel even though the illustrations are very important. A graphic novel specifically communicates setting, action, and events through pictures and special kinds of punctuation. A wide range of graphic novels are being published. The popular *Diary of a Wimpy Kid* (Kinney 2007) is described on the front cover as "a novel in comics." It has considerable text but comics appear on every page and add humor and artistry to the text. The dialogue is presented in speech bubbles. *The Invention of Hugo Cabret* (Selznick 2007) has long series of full-page pencil drawings that show action and feeling but not dialogue. The drawings alternate with full pages of print. Other graphic texts may be completely filled with comic strips.
- A *graphic nonfiction text*—similar to a graphic novel except that its purpose is to present factual information. Graphic nonfiction texts may use any of the text structures that all nonfiction texts use.
- *Manga*—graphic storytelling originating in Japan. Manga uses styled Japanese illustrations that are very distinctive and is often written specifically for boys (*shonen*) or for girls (*shojo*). Some texts are in the original Japanese format—written from right to left and from the back of the book to the front. Manga is popular with adults as well as children and therefore may have mature subject matter.

In this book, we focus on graphic novels and graphic nonfiction texts, the media most likely to be useful in elementary and middle school classrooms. Reading these texts may require more complex cognitive skills than the reading of text alone:

> To read a graphic novel students need to understand traditional literacy, including character, plot, theme, and writing craft, particularly dialogue, but they also have the opportunity to explore visual elements such as color, shading, panel layout, perspective, and even the lettering style. (Schwartz 2006, 59)

In other words, graphic texts make the same demands on the reader as any genre. But processing the *medium* requires some adjusting. We predict that this medium will continue to grow in popularity and deserves attention as legitimate literature. We talk more about graphic texts in Chapter 12.

Digital Texts

Books in electronic form are still books, and readers can easily learn to use bookmarks, add notes and comments, and save citations. Internet reading (and some computer program reading) is different. Every genre is available on the Internet today, but digital texts are distinguished by the way they are read:

> Digital texts are not linear. Hyperlinks embedded in websites allow the reader to go to completely different web pages or to a digital picture, video, or audio. The path of hyperlinks selected by the reader influences the direction and content of the text. In this way the reader's purpose and choices determine the reading sequence rather than the author. (Johnson 2009, 360)

Johnson goes on to caution that readers of digital texts must learn to stick to a purpose while reading. It is easy to become confused and frustrated while reading digital texts, or to simply become overwhelmed by too much information. Digital texts offer great opportunity and can be very engaging, but genre is still at the heart of reading and writing.

The Expanding World of Literature

The variety of literature available to both children and adults is amazing and is growing every day at an astonishing rate. The explosion of digital texts and the creativity of graphic texts are evidence that reading is more popular than ever. Books may take different forms, and we may explore them in many different ways, but whatever the medium or form, the genres all have their special ways of making meaning for us as readers. Teaching about genre can enrich students' experiences with and increase their appreciation for the texts they read and experience through interactive read-aloud. Awareness of genre increases students' ability to talk analytically with others about texts and to derive deeper meanings. In the language of curriculum goals and standards, knowledge of genre has everything to do with comprehension. Think of it as a "road map" (Bomer 1995) that helps readers explore texts based on their understanding of what to expect from the genre. It gives them increased power to see the craft behind the writing as well as the important meanings.

Suggestions for Professional Development

Creating your own mental road map for genre is very helpful. We all have an implicit knowledge of the variety of genres because of background reading and education, but it may be useful to consolidate understandings and share good examples.

1. Prepare a collection of read-aloud texts and guided reading texts that cover the range of genres. You'll need at least two examples for each genre; you may want to make one appropriate for younger students and one for older.
2. You may choose to meet in grade-level groups, but it will be even more productive to meet as a staff so you can discuss genre awareness across the grades.
3. Ask each participant to bring four or five favorite read-aloud books to the session.
4. Set up a long table (or use the floor) with the categories presented in Figure 3.1, "Genre Categories," laid out on sticky notes. (You can also use an enlarged version on chart paper, but the physical layout of texts makes a stronger impression.)
5. Ask participants to lay their books on the diagram (they can stack them). This will give your group a visual picture of where their favorite examples fit.
6. You may find that some genres are missing from the layout or chart. Talk about why.
7. Bring out the examples you collected earlier and ask participants to place them on the table or chart.
8. Discuss the implications of this chart for your literacy curriculum.
9. Divide into grade-level groups and generate some goals for broadening students' awareness of genre.
10. Make a list of genre categories that you want to expand in the school or classroom collections.

CHAPTER 4

A Workshop Approach to Genre Study

Children's ability to use language as a tool for thinking on their own has its origins in thinking together.

—Peter Johnston

Students experience authentic literacy by doing what readers and writers do in their daily lives: read, think, talk, and write. Students build a reading life and a writing life as they develop the attitudes, habits, and competencies of proficient readers and writers. A workshop is an ideal setting for engaging students in authentic literacy through inquiry. We describe three major instructional contexts for language and literacy across which students experience and learn important features of a variety of genres. We include several different talk structures within them.

Interactive Read-Aloud

In interactive read-aloud, you have the opportunity to explore a range of high-quality texts with your students. Freed from the need to decode words, students can give full attention to the meaning and the qualities of the text as you read it aloud. The word *interactive* is important. As you read aloud, pause briefly a few times and share your thinking; solicit students' comments, predictions, and questions; and invite them to discuss fiction and nonfiction texts with you and with each other.

We advocate using beautiful, content-rich, age- and grade-appropriate picture books—short stories or poetry or short informational pieces illustrated with beautiful art—as a foundation for thinking, talking, and writing (see the mentor texts in Appendix A and the list of children's books in Appendix D). At every grade level, picture books are ideal for reading aloud. They are a constantly expanding resource (you add to your collection over time) that can be used as examples or mentors in both readers' workshop and writers' workshop. You might also read some wonderful longer (chapter) books to your students, but be sure not to drag them out over several weeks. Remember that with shorter texts your students can gain important understandings that they will be able to apply to the many longer texts they read independently.

Readers' Workshop

You will need about sixty minutes for a readers' workshop. Some middle school teachers have very short periods (forty or forty-five minutes) that force them to alternate readers' and writers' workshop every few weeks, conduct a workshop over two days, or use a double period, but ideally you should have both workshops daily. The one-hour timeframe includes quick book talks, a short, explicit minilesson, and a short group share, with most of the time spent reading, thinking, talking, or writing. We suggest not including interactive read-aloud as part of readers' workshop in elementary school (there's usually no other choice in middle school), because doing so can use up a lot of time. Rather, the teaching and learning should flow smoothly from interactive read-aloud to readers' workshop (see Figure 4.1).

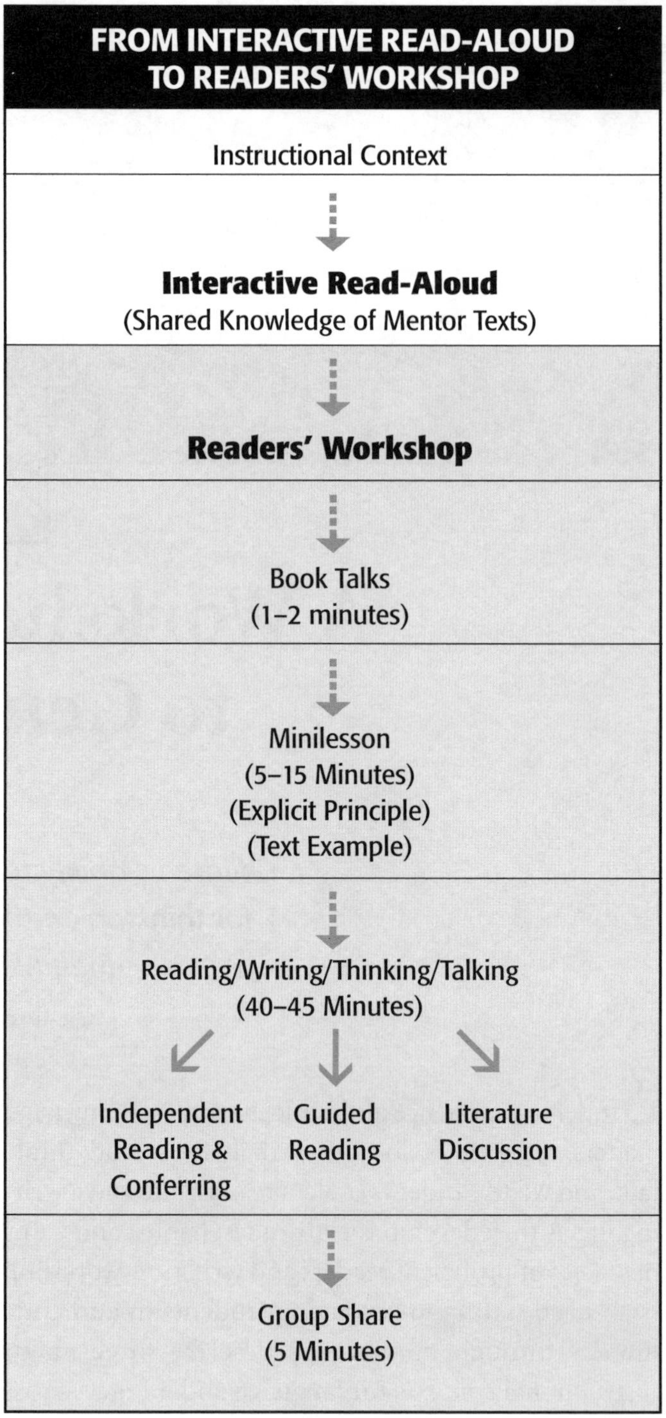

Figure 4.1 From interactive read-aloud to readers' workshop

Structure of Readers' Workshop

At the beginning of a readers' workshop give two or three thirty- to sixty-second book talks on titles, authors, or genres students may not know in order to entice them to read new books. Present a short, explicit whole-group minilesson on literary understandings (including genre), procedures for the workshop, or occasionally on reading strategies. Then students begin to work independently. They read a self-selected book at their independent reading level and may do some writing about reading in a reader's notebook—a general record of a student's reading that includes weekly letters to you as well as other forms of writing and your responses (Fountas and Pinnell 2011). We have developed two versions of our Reader's Notebook (see Chapter 18); one for grades 2–4 (*Reader's Notebook*), the other for grades 4–8 with a focus on genre (*Reader's Notebook: Advanced*). You can also explore other writing about reading options available through technology and the Internet: teachers have successfully created technological learning communities using blogs, list serves, and Twitter (see Hicks 2009).

While students are working independently:

1. *Independent Reading and Conferring* Hold short individual *conferences* with students to talk about their thinking related to their independent reading and their writing about reading in their reader's notebook.

2. *Guided Reading* Bring together a temporary group of children with similar reading ability for small-group reading instruction (*guided reading*). Select a text at the students' instructional level, introduce it, and have the students read the text silently. While they are doing so, you might sample the oral reading of students in the group, have a quick supportive interaction to support students' problem solving, or confer with other students in the class. When the group has finished reading, discuss and revisit the text with them as a group and make some specific teaching points based on their needs. You may then assign some hands-on word work or ask them to extend their understanding of what they have read by writing or drawing about their reading.
3. *Book Clubs* Bring together a small group of students who want to read, think about, and discuss the same book regardless of reading level. (Provide a group of texts from which students choose.) Have them read the book (or listen to an audio recording of it), prepare, and then talk about the book together. They may do this in one or several sessions. This activity is called *literature discussion* or *book club*.

At the close of the workshop, bring students together for a whole-group share in which you reinforce the minilesson principle by inviting students to share their application of the principle to their reading or extend their learning in other ways.

Three Types of Reading Instruction with Three Categories of Texts

The emphasis in reading instruction is on helping students develop the competencies and habits of proficient readers through a variety of experiences with text. A combination of whole-group, small-group, and individual instruction allows you to differentiate your instruction to meet your readers' varying needs.

Students develop their reading ability by encountering a variety of wonderful books with various levels of your support. As they develop the behaviors and understandings of proficient readers, they encounter three types of texts and have rich opportunities to build their understanding of various genres (see Figure 4.2):

1. *Grade, Age-Appropriate Texts* They experience age-appropriate, grade-appropriate texts during interactive read-aloud and literature discussion. These settings are wonderful for providing a base of text knowledge for genre study.
2. *Leveled Texts* With teacher-selected instructional-level texts and the support of your teaching in small-group guided reading, they expand what they know how to do as readers so they can apply their expanded reading power to other books and read increasingly challenging books over time. Leveled texts and their use are discussed in Chapter 19. We suggest that teachers use leveled texts for small-group reading instruction; however, we do not recommend that students choose books by level in the classroom, school,

DIFFERENT TEXTS FOR DIFFERENT PURPOSES	
Instructional Context	**Student/Teacher Inquiry**
Interactive Read-Aloud Literature Discussion (Book Clubs)	• Age- and grade-appropriate texts
Guided Reading	• Leveled books (A–Z+)
Independent Reading	• Classroom library—a variety of books organized by topic, author, illustrator, genre, awards, series

Figure 4.2 Different texts for different purposes

or public library. They need to learn the important strategies for choosing books they can understand and apply to any book collection.

3. *Choice Reading* With just-right books for independent reading, they develop mileage as readers, build their reading lives, learn to love reading, and develop their understanding of authors, illustrators, topics, and genres. They read many examples of the genres they are studying—books they can read without your support.

Planning and Managing Readers' Workshop

Begin the year by building a community of readers and carefully establishing the routines of independent reading. Teach students to choose texts that interest them and that are appropriate for their skill level. Help them learn how to choose books they can enjoy and understand without your help. During the readers' workshop, your students should read independently and silently or spend some time writing about their reading. The room should be quiet; some teachers play classical music very softly. When you confer with students individually, do it quietly, perhaps in a whisper. Insist on silent reading and a quiet classroom so that all students can concentrate for extended periods.

Once the routines of independent reading are well established, you can begin to call small groups together for guided reading and/or literature discussion. Again, this small-group instruction requires voices just loud enough to be heard within the small group.

Writers' Workshop

The goal of writers' workshop is to help students develop writing strategies and skills, learn about the writer's craft, and use writing as a tool for learning and communication. Like the readers' workshop, writers' workshop rests on the foundation developed through interactive read-aloud (see Figure 4.3).

Structure of Writers' Workshop

Writers' workshop, also scheduled for sixty minutes every day, begins with a writer's talk and a brief minilesson on any aspect of writing craft, conventions, process. Many

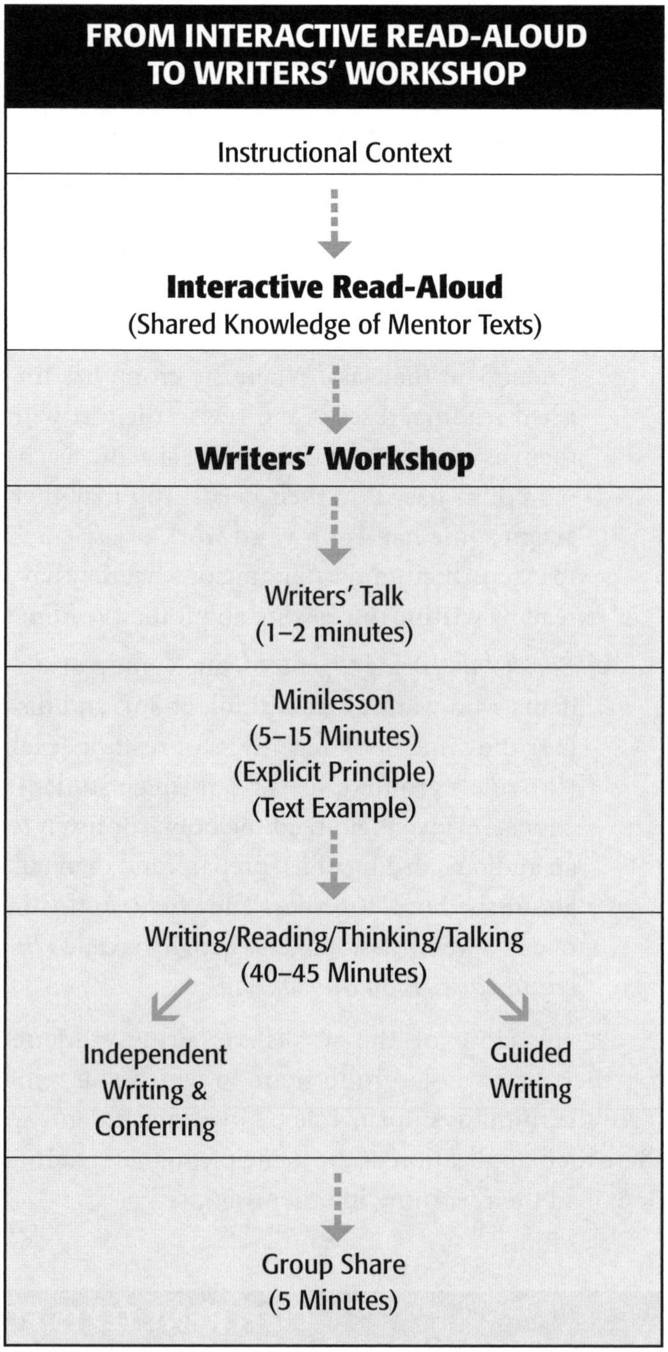

Figure 4.3 From interactive read-aloud to writers' workshop

of these lessons will incorporate mentor texts—the same texts students have listened to and discussed in interactive read-aloud. Students have already thought deeply about the texts and shared their understandings, so the texts truly do double or even triple duty. Identify a few wonderful examples that you can use over and over. Select them carefully; they increase learning and make your teaching efficient.

After the minilesson, students write their own pieces. Typically, all students are in some phase of writing, from using a writer's notebook to gathering thoughts and ideas to producing a "discovery" (first) draft to revising and editing. Some pieces are placed in their files as "final" drafts; a few are published.

Most of the time students choose their own topics; at other times you may assign topics. As students develop the ideas, they need to choose the genre that best suits the purpose. Sometimes you will ask them to write in a specific genre. Whatever the genre, they "get inside" it by experiencing it as a writer.

The time students spend writing independently is also quiet. Writers usually work individually, but sometimes they may work in small groups. While the students are working, you:

1. *Independent Writing and Conferring* Confer with individual writers to support their growth in any aspect of the writing process.
2. *Guided Writing* Bring a small, temporary group of students together for *guided writing*. Teach them about the craft, conventions, processes, and strategies of writing in a variety of genres, basing your instruction on the writers' needs, and help them create pieces of writing for different purposes and audiences.

Planning and Managing Writers' Workshop

Planning and managing a writers' workshop is similar to planning and managing a readers' workshop. First, focus on building a writing community and establishing the routines of independent writing. Have students work individually and silently in their writer's notebooks or on their writing pieces while you confer with them individually. While most students will work individually, you may call together small groups with similar writing needs for a guided writing lesson.

Books in Relation to Readers

Literacy teachers consider readers in relation to the texts they select. Throughout this book, we discuss the characteristics of fiction and nonfiction texts, but we need to understand that what makes a book "easy," "interesting," "hard," or "accessible" is always related to the person reading it. Finding books that are appropriate for readers and making them accessible is a complex process that calls for a detailed analysis of the demands of a text. Ten text factors may make a book easy, hard, or just right for your students (see Figure 4.4).

Genre refers to the type of text you are reading. There are easier and harder texts within every genre, but some genres pose particular challenges. For example, historical fiction requires that the reader have or acquire more background information about the setting (which is extremely important for comprehending the genre).

Form refers to particular ways fiction and nonfiction texts are presented. For example, a piece of fiction could be a novel with chapters, a short story, a picture book (illustrated short story), a mystery, or a graphic text. Books—both fiction and nonfiction—may make up a series.

Text structure refers to the way the text is organized. Fiction texts generally have a narrative structure that includes a problem and a sequence of events that lead to a resolution of the problem. As discussed previously, nonfiction texts may also be narrative, but most informational texts are organized categorically by subtopic and have underlying structures such as description, temporal sequence, comparison and contrast, cause and effect, and problem and solution. Often these structures are used in combination.

Content refers to the subject matter or topic. A nonfiction text, for example, usually focuses on a particular topic or subtopics related to an overall topic. The reading is easier if the reader already knows something about the topic, but it is more interesting if there is something new. Even a fiction text may include subject matter (historical events, geographic locations, cultures) that is either quite familiar or that requires background knowledge that readers do not have and cannot access quickly.

Themes and ideas are the big ideas and messages of the text. The more obvious and concrete they are, the easier they are to understand. Highly abstract and hard-to-grasp themes increase difficulty.

Language and literary features refers to the way the writer uses language, including dialogue and figurative

FACTORS RELATED TO TEXT DIFFICULTY	
Factor	**Definition**
Genre/form	The type or kind of fiction or nonfiction text (biography, expository, realistic fiction, fantasy); also, the particular form (mystery, picture book, short story)
Text structure	The way the text is organized
Content	The subject matter of the text—what it is about, the topic or information
Themes and ideas	The big ideas in the text, the overall purpose, the messages
Language and literary features	Plot, characters, figurative language, literary devices such as flashbacks
Sentence complexity	The length of sentences as well as the number of phrases and clauses
Vocabulary	The meaning of the words in the text
Word complexity	The length and sophistication of the words (syllables, tense, etc.)
Illustrations	The art in fiction and nonfiction texts; the photographs or graphic features of nonfiction texts
Book and print features	The number of pages, print font, length, punctuation, and the variety of readers' tools

Figure 4.4 Factors related to text difficulty

language, and literary elements such as a setting, plot, and characters. It also includes the use of literary devices such as flashbacks.

Sentence complexity refers not only to length but also to the number of embedded phrases and clauses the sentences have. The text may have long, complex sentences and/or unfamiliar language structures that make it hard for readers to derive meaning.

Vocabulary refers to the meaning of the words in the text. A person's oral vocabulary consists of all of the words he understands in speaking and listening. The closer a text matches the body of words in his oral vocabulary, the easier it is for the reader. The text may have too many words that the reader does not know (or does not understand the meaning of). In addition, words have multiple meanings and connotative meanings, and understanding them depends on the context in which the reader encounters them.

Word complexity refers to the ease with which words can be solved. For a text to be easy for a reader, most of the words (above 95 percent for readers who are not beginners [levels L and above], above 90 percent for early readers [levels A–K]) should be known or decodable with very little effort. A hard text may contain too many words that readers cannot solve using the visual information in print (for example, a lot of multisyllable words or unfamiliar letter combinations).

Illustrations are the graphic features of texts. In fiction books, the illustrations are usually drawings or paintings that extend or enhance meaning and support the mood. In graphic texts, the illustrations communicate a great deal of the meaning. In nonfiction texts, readers are required to take information from labeled pictures, maps, graphs, cutaways, diagrams, legends, and other features. They must integrate this information with the body of the text. The complexity of graphic features increases the difficulty of the text.

Book and print features are the physical characteristics of the text, including length, page size, layout, print size, and font. Even for older readers, dense print can make a text more difficult, and friendly layout makes it easier. Readers' tools like headings, chapter titles, an index, a table of contents, a glossary, and similar features give readers more information. But younger readers need to learn about these features, and too many of them pose a challenge.

Hard Texts

To understand what makes a text hard, think about what the text asks of the reader. Hard texts make too many demands. The challenge may lie in one or several interrelated factors, primarily those described in Figure 4.4.

A text can be too difficult even for a mature, competent reader. For example, without a great deal of prior study, you might find it difficult to read a text about the intricacies of the neurological system. Or, it might take you some time to read unusual forms of poetry or a novel with elusive literary references. Some genres may be harder to understand than others—for example, fiction written in blank verse or a very complex fantasy.

Your students' ability to access texts is related to their previous experiences in life *and* the texts they have previously read and understood. Therefore, they need to be immersed in a wide variety of genres from the time they enter the world of literacy. Hard texts require intensive concentration. When they are too hard, readers feel they are wasting their time and become frustrated, because they are just reading a string of words, not grasping ideas.

Easy Texts

When you read material that is very easy for you, the text doesn't demand much. Reading is smooth, and your focus is almost entirely on meaning. You don't have to figure out hard words or language patterns; you can concentrate on the ideas.

Easy reading is enjoyable if the material is interesting or uplifting. The content is within your understanding, even familiar. You know most of the vocabulary and recognize words instantly. The language patterns are familiar; you have seen them before and they take little effort. Organization is so clear that you don't recognize how you are getting the information. Reading goes along quickly, and you can easily adjust your reading speed to your purpose (scanning for information or "getting to the good part," for example). Easy reading provides escape, entertainment, and easy-to-grasp new content.

Just-Right Texts

While we all enjoy easy reading, texts that are a bit challenging are often more interesting and memorable and provide the most productive learning opportunities. Books that provide material for us to think about, that offer concepts to puzzle over, contribute to learning even for mature readers. When we read a book about history, science, or any challenging subject, we may encounter information that we have to read more than once to understand and add to our background knowledge.

For your students, just-right books are the best tool for learning not only about content but also about reading itself and are selected by teachers for guided reading instruction. The just-right book might help students use background knowledge to access content that offers some challenge but is within reach. Through reading books that are a little harder, students usually encounter some new words and have a chance to expand their word-solving skills. They expand their vocabularies greatly by encountering new words in books and building frames of meaning around them as they read. Also, as students read works of literature, they encounter language not normally used in conversation. They learn the structure of literary language and gradually expand the kinds of complex structures they can understand. As they read genres that are new to them, they discover different ways of organizing information in both fiction and nonfiction texts.

When you read a just-right book, you expect long stretches of fluent, easy reading, but you also expect places where you slow down to solve some aspect of text—content, language structure, words, and so on. Problem solving in the context of accurate reading while simultaneously maintaining comprehension and thinking about the ideas in the text develops the reading process. The just-right book makes demands on the reader, offering a chance to learn something new; but the demands are not so great that the reading process breaks down. Through reading just-right texts every day, students expand their ability to read.

In summary, students need to read texts that are *accessible*. For instructional reading, they need texts they can process easily enough that they can pay attention to and think deeply about the ideas being presented (see Figure 4.5), but also gain reading power through instruction.

Only easy and just-right texts offer the ease readers need to comprehend deeply. That's why it's important to increase students' access to texts by reading aloud and discussing books that they may need to listen to instead of read independently.

Assessment

Selecting the right book for the right purpose also depends on knowing your students—not only their reading skill but also the ways in which they process texts and how they understand them. We recommend systematic benchmark assessment conference, which involves:

- Using a programmed set of texts arranged in a gradient of difficulty (levels from A to Z) that are related to grade-level expectations (see Fountas & Pinnell *Benchmark Assessment System* 2011, Heinemann).
- Observing and recording reading behaviors while the student reads orally approximately 100 to 200 words aloud. With more proficient students they finish the text silently.
- Talking with the reader to determine the extent to which he has grasped and is able to talk about the key understandings required by the text.
- Scoring the reader's accuracy, fluency, and comprehension.
- Asking the reader to respond to a writing prompt that will further reveal his understanding of the text (optional but not necessary).

RELATIONSHIP BETWEEN TEXT COMPLEXITY AND LEARNING TO PROCESS TEXT		
Easy Texts	**Just-Right Texts**	**Hard Texts**
Support effective processing	Work to support and expand effective processing	Get in the way of processing
Provide enjoyment and learning	Provide enjoyment and learning	Create frustration and undermine motivation
Promote fluent reading	Promote fluent reading and quick problem solving	Hinder development of fluency
Provide easy comprehension	Provide opportunities to expand comprehension without experiencing frustration	Make comprehension too difficult so reading becomes meaningless
Texts That Build the Reading Process (arrow spanning Easy and Just-Right Texts)		

Figure 4.5 Relationship between text complexity and learning to process text

For levels A through K (approximately kindergarten through mid grade 2 level), an independent-level text is one a reader can read with 95 to 97 percent accuracy and satisfactory or excellent comprehension. For levels L through Z (approximately mid grade 2 through 8 or above), an independent-level text is one a reader can read with 98 to 100 percent accuracy and satisfactory or excellent comprehension. This means that the student can successfully process the text without teacher support. Students read independent-level texts individually during readers' workshop and at home, and they may later share their thinking about these texts in their writing and in end-of-workshop discussions. An instructional-level text is one students can read with 90 to 94 percent accuracy (levels A–K) or 95 to 97 percent accuracy (levels L–Z) and satisfactory or excellent comprehension. This kind of text is used for guided reading, so that you can stretch students' reading abilities.

In addition to a benchmark assessment conference, which is usually administered two or three times a year, you can systematically collect information as ongoing assessment using reading records, anecdotal information during your individual reading conferences, and in guided reading lessons. You can note observable reading behaviors as described above and you can also observe students' thinking as they talk or write about texts. If you are interested in what students know about genre, you can ask some specific questions during reading conferences (see *Prompting Guide, Part 2 for Comprehension*) and also ask them to include particular information in their writing about reading in their reader's notebook (see Chapters 17 and 18).

Curriculum for Teaching and Learning About Genre

The curriculum for teaching and learning about genre emerges from four components: systematic assessment, mentor texts, curriculum standards, and reading/writing behaviors and understandings. If you want students to think deeply about texts and use features and structures of genre, then consider these four factors. Two of the factors, reading/writing behaviors and understandings and mentor texts, are described in detail by grade and text level (guided reading) in *The Continuum of Literacy Learning* (Pinnell and Fountas 2008). In that document, which we use as a tool throughout this book, we provide a detailed description of the in-the-head actions readers and writers engage in. Reading involves twelve systems of strategic actions:

1. Solving words.
2. Monitoring and self-correcting reading.
3. Searching for and using information.
4. Summarizing information to remember it.
5. Adjusting reading to meet purpose and genre.
6. Maintaining fluency.
7. Making predictions.
8. Synthesizing new information.
9. Making connections with background information.
10. Inferring what the writer is implying but not telling directly.
11. Analyzing the text as a literary object.
12. Critiquing the text.

Writing involves specific behaviors related to craft, conventions, and process. We also provide a continuum for oral, visual, and technological communication that provides detailed descriptions of how oral language is used, as well as phonics and word study information.

Systematic Observation and Assessment

All good teaching begins with good assessment. Through systematic observation and assessment you gather the information you need to determine whether your students are meeting the expectations for proficient reading and writing and the thinking demands of the mentor texts (see Figure 4.6). You plan your curriculum based on:

- What students understand and are able to do as readers and writers.
- What they need to understand and be able to do.
- What texts and instruction will provide opportunities for new learning.

CURRICULUM FOR TEACHING AND LEARNING ABOUT GENRE	
• Mentor Texts (genre exemplars) • Curriculum Standards (related to genre) • *The Continuum of Literacy Learning* (description of the observable behaviors of proficient readers and writers)	• Systematic Observation of Individual Readers/Writers (from oral reading, talk about reading, writing about reading)

↓

Curriculum for Teaching and Learning About Genre

Figure 4.4 Curriculum for teaching and learning about genre

Mentor Texts

The mentor texts you read aloud interactively fuel the curriculum. Each of these texts makes specific demands on the reader in terms of the twelve systems of strategic actions listed earlier and provides the models for powerful writing in a variety of genres. We have described mentor texts extensively in *Teaching for Comprehending and Fluency: Thinking, Talking, and Writing About Reading, K–8* (Fountas and Pinnell 2006) and *Guiding Readers and Writers: Teaching Comprehension, Genre, and Content Literacy* (Fountas and Pinnell 2000), and we describe them further in this book.

Curriculum Standards (State, District, National)

Most countries have some kind of educational standards document. Standards define the expectations or goals for student learning. They may be issued at the district, province, state, or national level.

In the U. S., almost every state has issued standards that describe the competencies students are expected to achieve in reading and writing. Districts typically work toward these standards and may add to or adjust them for their own purposes. We have examined every state's standards and the U. S. Common Core State Standards and find they describe the same basic expectations we have included in *The Continuum of Literacy Learning* (see *fountasandpinnell.com* for a downloadable description of the alignment of our continuum with Common Core State Standards). The *Continuum of Literacy Learning* (Pinnell and Fountas 2011, 2008), however, is much more detailed with the specificity of behaviors and understandings because it is designed to be used for planning and using while teaching.

Reading/Writing Behaviors

As teachers we need a clear vision of what proficient readers and writers know and are able to do. Here, we are particularly interested in what they know about text genres, but we do not exclude other aspects of comprehending. We cannot separate genre knowledge from other thinking, such as inferring motivations of characters, noticing cause and effect or problem/solution, or using description. To understand genre, one must employ all the complex ways of thinking described in the Continuum.

Bringing It All Together

Obviously, a great deal of information feeds the curriculum. But it is "on the ground" teaching that makes the difference. In this book we focus on bringing these elements together to help students understand genre. In the process, they will learn a great deal that will help them expand all their abilities to comprehend texts and to write effectively in a range of genres.

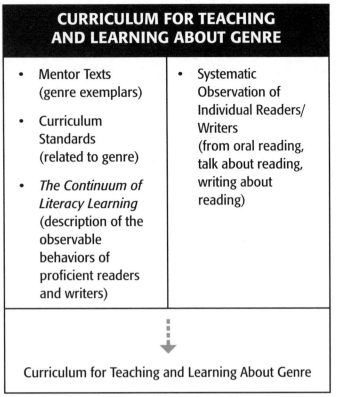

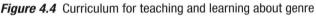

Suggestions for Professional Development

Finding the time for workshops can be challenging. If you have not implemented a readers' or writers' workshop in your classroom (or in your school):

1. Convene a group of grade-level colleagues who are interested in starting a readers' workshop or a writers' workshop.
2. Select one or the other workshop and work together on your schedules to find fifty-five or sixty minutes in the school day.
3. Plan how you will acquire the books you need to start your workshop (books for a classroom library and multiple copies for small-group guided reading and book clubs). Consult *Guiding Readers and Writers* for detailed information on getting started.
4. Collect books and begin the interactive read-aloud lessons to build the shared knowledge. You may want to use the text sets you developed following the professional development recommendations in Chapter 2.

If you already are implementing a readers' and writers' workshop, start planning to incorporate more genre study in the curriculum.

1. Get together with a group of colleagues, preferably your grade-level team, to discuss how you currently address genre in your readers' and writers' workshops.
   - What about your approach works? What are your concerns about the effectiveness of your approach in helping students learn the characteristics of different genres?
2. Talk about how you might begin to implement genre study and how that will shift the way you currently teach about different genres.
3. Select a genre to get started.
4. Have colleagues look at their classroom libraries or other libraries to select some excellent examples of a selected genre. Picture books will allow you to introduce several texts in a genre in a short amount of time as opposed to longer chapter books or novels. You may want to work from the text sets you developed if you followed the recommendations for professional development in Chapter 2.
5. Bring the texts to your next meeting and read and discuss them. Decide which texts will become part of your text sets for that genre. Everyone should have about three or four books to start. Make a plan to pass the books around the classrooms so that eventually everyone will get to use them.
6. Begin by immersing your students in these books during interactive read-aloud.
7. Meet back with colleagues and discuss the specifics of how you will continue the genre study during readers' workshop.
   - How will genre study change your readers' workshop?
   - How will it affect your reading minilessons and share?
   - How might it affect the way your students choose books during independent reading?
   - What implications will this have for writers' workshop?
8. Try it out in your classrooms and hold a follow-up meeting to discuss your results and questions.

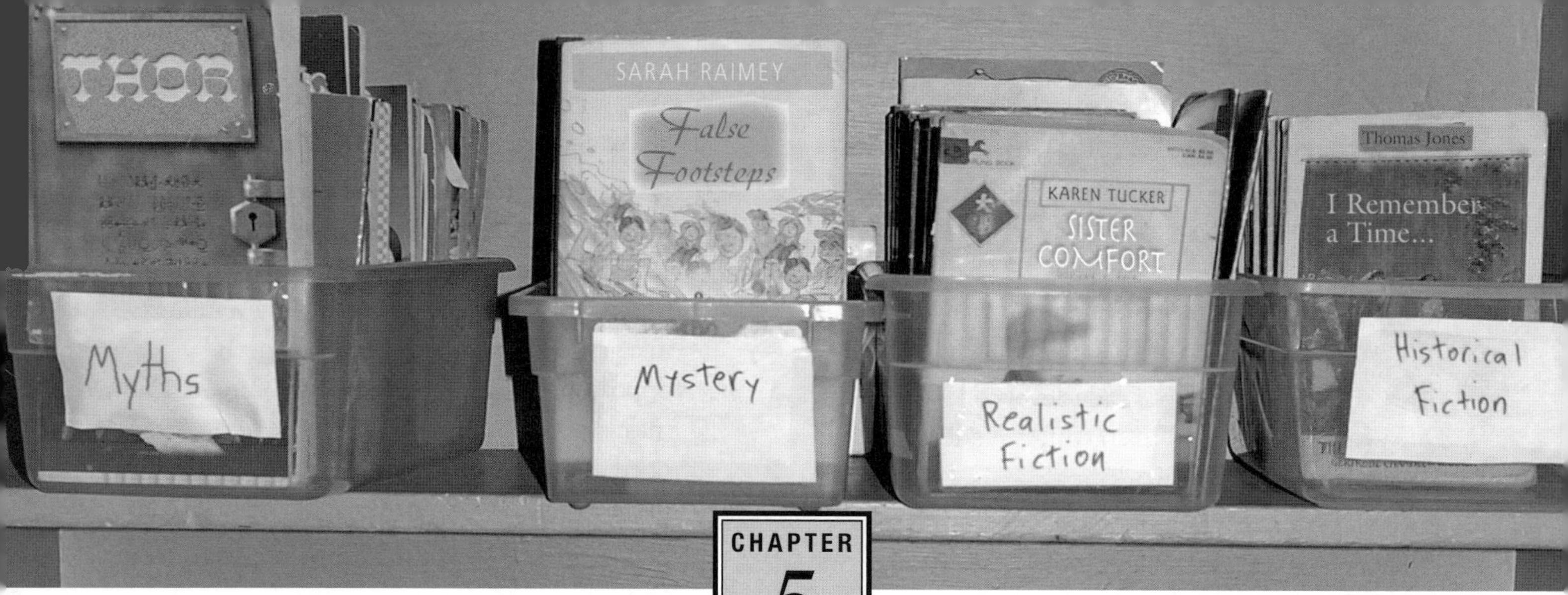

CHAPTER 5

Learning to Process Fiction and Nonfiction Texts

If a book is truly well written, the words between its covers are arranged in almost magical patterns that stir deep emotional responses in readers.

—James Jacobs and Michael Tunnell

Many things happen when you read a good book. Let's say you're reading one of the popular Harry Potter books, by J. K. Rowling. You might:

- Get carried along by the action.
- Appreciate the interesting and even bizarre characters, finding them humorous, inspiring, or repellent.
- Marvel at the imagination of the writer.
- Love learning the intricacies of the imagined game quidditch.
- Appreciate the use of satire (mocking bureaucracy and pompous individuals with authority).
- Notice the conflict of good and evil.
- Sympathize with Harry's problems and admire his character.
- Appreciate the humor; feel fear; feel empathy.
- Enjoy the magical world of Hogwarts.
- Notice how the author uses different language to show characters' speech.
- Notice the parallel between the "real" world and the wizard world.

These responses (only a few of those a reader might have) show why these books have been enjoyed (and understood at different levels) by both children and adults. Students can read them in fourth or fifth grade and again in eighth or ninth grade and have substantively different experiences. The levels of complexity in the texts trigger a complex thinking process in the reader, underscoring the idea that reading is thinking.

Most of us enter texts expecting to be engaged—to make meaning. We don't think about anything except wanting to read a good book, have an adventure, get some interesting information, or be inspired. Reading is a highly personal act: we participate with our own thoughts and emotions. When we are engrossed in a book and a stranger asks, "What are you reading?" we may feel our privacy is being invaded, although we usually respond courteously and sometimes have a conversation about the book. There is also a social aspect to reading. Many of us enjoy nothing more than talking about books with friends. We use words like *fascinating*, *intriguing*, or *disturbing*. We say things like "I couldn't put it down" or "I found it truly inspiring."

When we read biography, we want to gain new information or insights about the subject. When we read fiction, we expect to be privy to an adventure or a romance—to be taken away from our own everyday world. And when we read poetry, we want to savor beautiful language that stirs the senses and makes us think about the beauty of the world or of our own grief or joy. Very few people, if any, read a book solely to practice comprehension. And we do not expect or want our students to read for that purpose either. We want our students to engage in *deep reading*. Deep reading changes us.

> By *deep reading*, we mean the array of sophisticated processes that propel comprehension and that include inferential and deductive reasoning, analogical skills, critical analysis, reflection, and insight. The expert reader needs milliseconds to execute these processes; the young brain needs years to develop [them]. (Wolf and Barzillai 2009, 33)

According to Wolf and Barzillai, reading was invented in 5500 B.C., which makes it a relatively new cognitive function (compared with talking, eating, running, etc.) on the clock of human evolution. It is related to innate characteristics (like the development of language) but it is not, in itself, innate. According to these authors, the plasticity of the brain enables us to make new connections and "circuits" among genetically programmed structures such as talking, seeing, and thinking. "The very design of the human brain enables it to go beyond itself" (34). The process of reading substantively changes the neural networks over time.

> Readers actively construct meaning, questioning, analyzing, and probing:
>
> [T]hey learn to build knowledge and go beyond the wisdom of the author to think their own thoughts. By the time the expert reader has comprehended a text at a deep level, all four lobes and both hemispheres of the brain have contributed significantly to this extraordinary act—a neural reflection of the many processes involved. What we read and how deeply we read shapes both the brain and the thinker." (34–35)

Different kinds of texts place different demands on readers. Reading a book that is within our control but offers just a small challenge enables us to expand and enrich our in-the-head strategic actions. For example, the first time we read a book that flashes back in time or follows multiple generations across a long period of time, we learn how to use those structures to understand and enjoy the book. It is essential for students to experience a variety of rich texts—fiction and nonfiction—if they are to acquire the reading strategies they need.

Ways of Thinking About Texts

When we read, we *process* the text. A number of complex actions take place simultaneously in our brain. Our eyes pick up information from the print and match it with information in our head. Efficient readers not only recognize letters but also scan and recognize the patterns of letters that make words and the patterns of words that make meaningful language. All of this happens so rapidly and automatically that we are almost never aware of the process.

Most of the time our attention is on the meaning of the story or informational text. We may pause and "zoom in" if we meet a less familiar word or come across a word used in a new way—if a word is used ironically or metaphorically, for example. We may stop briefly to summarize mentally what we've read so far or to think about some new and puzzling information. We may pause to consider what the text reminds us of; we may even search back in the text to check our understandings or get missing information. Some part of our brain is constantly monitoring our grasp of the subject matter or our understanding of the story. But then we speed up again, giving our attention to the larger message. In fact, we must always hold the meaning in mind when we are problem solving; working out words is part of the search for meaning.

When we talk about *reading* in this book, we are always talking about *reading with understanding*. Comprehension is integral to processing any text successfully. Elsewhere we have defined and discussed twelve systems of strategic actions that proficient readers use to process, or work though, texts (see Fountas and Pinnell 1996, 2000), but here we examine these strategic actions through the lens of genre understandings and how they work for us.

The complexity of the brain makes it possible for readers to use hundreds of in-the-head strategies simultaneously. We may laugh when we recognize humor or feel empathy for characters; we may admire the writer's language and style of expression. Meanwhile, our eyes are traveling rapidly down the page; sometimes we scan or skip text, noticing only what's important to our understanding. Sometimes we search back in a text to find something we missed or confirm our thinking. Sometimes we move slowly to savor the language or think carefully about the story or the information. We are seeing letters and words and *at the same time* thinking about the meaning. And meaning is not found only in the particular book or article we are reading; reading brings meaning to life in our own head as we connect the text to our own experience, our background knowledge, and other texts we have read.

At any given time, readers employ systems of strategic actions that sustain reading across a text. Each system is a large and complex body of understandings and actions; all are taking place simultaneously in the brain as we look at print and pictures. We divide these systems into three broad categories of thinking:

1. *Thinking within the text* includes all the actions a reader uses to process the text and gain a satisfactory *literal* understanding. All the information is right there. The reader knows what happened in the story or has gathered the facts from a nonfiction text. When you observe your students' oral reading, you capture accuracy (word solving), monitoring, fluency, and other indications that the reader is processing the text efficiently. When you have students "retell" after reading a text, you are capturing memory or literal understanding. When students answer literal questions and often when they select the "right" answer from a list of multiple-choice questions, you are measuring thinking within the text. This ability to process the text is basic and important. The reader cannot comprehend without literal understanding, yet much more is expected for deep reading. If it is too difficult to think *within* the text, readers have little attention to give to the next two categories of thinking.
2. *Thinking beyond the text* includes what the reader *brings* to the reading. The information is in the reader's head. The thinking is cued by the print but goes far beyond it. It includes the text and the reader. Proficient readers make connections to their own prior knowledge of the world and of subject matter, and they constantly revise understandings as they encounter new information. They connect texts in a wide variety of ways—writing style, content, mood, or emotion. Readers make predictions, which they then confirm or discard; they infer what the writer is saying but not telling directly. Thinking beyond the text is essential for understanding and using genre knowledge.
3. *Thinking about the text* includes analytical and critical thinking. Here, readers hold up the text as an object for examination. On their own, they use their knowledge to reflect on the text. Thinking about the text is the essence of genre study, because readers are bringing to conscious attention *how* the writer has crafted the text. They also consider the quality or authenticity of the text and make judgments.

Think about these three ways of thinking. Much of reading instruction has been directed toward getting the words right and remembering important information. That's necessary but only a part of reading. To succeed, students need to think beyond and about texts. The assessment of reading is a complex process.

Our examination of the National Assessment of Educational Progress framework indicates that students are expected to work actively to build meaning across several texts—texts that may be in different genres. Additionally they need to comprehend hybrid texts, which blend more than one genre. The Common Core State Standards also set goals for higher level thinking with complex texts. Your instruction needs to ensure that all students have daily opportunities to articulate their thinking beyond and about texts in talk and writing. That kind of instruction is often limited to proficient readers; struggling readers often engage in tasks that require drill and recall.

Systems of Strategic Actions for Comprehending Texts

We define twelve systems of strategic actions for comprehending texts (see Figure 5.1). Thinking about these systems in categories helps make teaching more intentional, but in fact they are happening simultaneously in the reader's head and are interrelated. Each category reflects a complex system as part of a cognitive network.

Solving Words

Readers use a range of strategies to solve words. Good word solvers:

- Recognize many words automatically.
- Solve words by using analogy (how a word is like another word; for example, *and* and *hand*, *hand* and *handle*).
- Recognize and use letter clusters and parts of words (*-ble* in *double* and *trouble*).
- Connect words by how they sound and look and what they mean.
- Analyze words from left to right, using letters and word parts.
- Use *roots* or meaningful parts of words strategically to figure out the likely meaning of the word.
- Use language and text meaning to solve word meanings.

Efficient readers combine word-solving strategies like the ones above in a smoothly operating processing system. They take words apart "on the run" while continuing to pay attention to meaning.

When texts are highly literary, word meanings are not so simple. For example, in *Sky Boys: How They Built the Empire State Building* (Hopkinson and Ransome 2006) the words *canyons* and *forest* as used in the text require readers to understand the words differently than they ordinarily might:

> ". . . the concrete canyons of Manhattan." (7)
>
> "Before your eyes a steel forest appears." (9)

Some genres (expository texts and science fiction, for example) may include highly technical words, and these may be more difficult for readers to decode and understand. For example, nine- to twelve-year-olds might find the word *amplitude* in *Witness to Disaster: Tsunamis* (Fradin, 2008) especially challenging. These genres often provide a glossary of technical words and terms, but a simple definition is often only the beginning. Students need to construct networks of understanding around a word so that they understand it in many contexts. Meaning may be related to genre. The word *magnetic*, for example, can refer to magnetic fields in nonfiction texts or to a magnetic personality in fiction texts.

Monitoring and Correcting

An important aspect of comprehension is monitoring one's understanding of what is read. Proficient readers notice when they do not understand or when there is a mismatch between their reading and the print they see. They are always *monitoring* their reading to make sure it sounds right, looks right, and makes sense. When necessary, they correct their reading using the information from print as well as from their own sense of language and how it sounds.

Understanding genre characteristics is an important tool in helping readers learn to monitor accuracy and understanding. Readers know what to expect as they begin to read a text in a certain genre, and they automatically check their expectations against what they find. For example, in an expository text like *Vultures:*

SYSTEMS OF STRATEGIC ACTIONS FOR COMPREHENDING TEXTS		
Ways of Thinking	**Systems of Strategic Actions**	**Description and Challenges of Genre**
Thinking Within the Text	**Solving Words**	Using a range of strategies to take words apart and understand what words mean. • *Generally, decoding challenges are the same across genres, but as these challenges grow more sophisticated, readers develop more specific vocabulary related to content.*
	Monitoring and Correcting	Checking whether reading sounds right, looks right, and makes sense, and working to solve problems. • *Readers learn to monitor their understanding using genre characteristics as one of the tools.*
	Searching for and Using Information	Searching for and using all kinds of information in a text. • *When readers know the characteristics of a genre, it is easier to find information.*
	Summarizing	Putting together and remembering important information and disregarding irrelevant information while reading. • *The structure and patterns of genre help readers recognize and remember important information.*
	Maintaining Fluency	Integrating sources of information in a smoothly operating process that results in expressive, phrased reading. • *Knowing what to expect in the genre supports reading fluency. Dialogue is not exclusive to fiction texts but is more likely to occur in those genres, and it calls for more expressive reading. The phrasing and intonation will be different when reading different genres aloud.*
	Adjusting	Reading in different ways as appropriate to the purpose for reading and type of text. • *Readers take a stance toward a text that is related to the expectations they have of the genre. The stance requires them to behave in appropriate ways for reading in the genre.*

Figure 5.1 Systems of strategic actions for comprehending texts

SYSTEMS OF STRATEGIC ACTIONS FOR COMPREHENDING TEXTS		
Ways of Thinking	**Systems of Strategic Actions**	**Description and Challenges of Genre**
Thinking Beyond the Text	**Predicting**	Using what is known to think about what will follow while reading continuous text. • *Readers use genre characteristics to anticipate what will happen in a text.*
	Making Connections • **Personal** • **World** • **Text**	Searching for and using connections to knowledge gained from personal experiences, learning about the world, and reading other texts. • *Readers notice genre characteristics as they make connections between texts. They learn that they are able to make personal connections to texts in particular genres. They also learn that some genres seem to require more knowledge of the world than others, although all require some.*
	Inferring	Going beyond the literal meaning of a text to think about what is not stated but is implied by the writer. • *All texts require inference, but knowing the characteristics of a particular genre helps readers more quickly identify what the writer is showing but not telling.*
	Synthesizing	Putting together information from the text and from the reader's own background knowledge in order to create new understandings. • *Knowing genre characteristics helps readers identify information more rapidly because they understand the organization. They can give their attention to sorting what is already known, identifying what is new, and revising their own conceptual understandings.*
Thinking About the Text	**Analyzing**	Examining elements of a text to know more about how it is constructed and noticing aspects of the writer's craft. • *When readers have a frame for the structures and features of a genre, it is easier to notice them in a particular text; this also makes it easier to notice how the writer has used them.*
	Critiquing	Evaluating a text based on the reader's personal, world, and text knowledge and thinking critically about the ideas in it. • *Knowing about genres can help readers be much more specific in their criticism (for example, how the writer has created a literary text in the genre or whether the content is authentic and organized in a logical way).*

Figure 5.1 Systems of strategic actions for comprehending texts *(cont.)*

Animal Scavengers (Markle 2006), readers would expect to find general statements and definitions related to vultures at the beginning of the text, as well as some rationale for why vultures are important. Then they might expect information to be presented in categories. If the text suddenly presents seemingly unrelated information, they wonder why and look closer to determine whether they are misunderstanding or whether a section of the book has ended.

Searching For and Using Information

Readers know how to identify important information in a text—the ideas that will make a difference in their understanding. They have to search for and use visual features of print in order to decode words, and they also recognize and use print features such as punctuation, italics, and headings. They have to search for and use information about language structure to check on whether their reading sounds right in terms of grammar and the way sentences are formed. They also search for and use meaning—what makes sense. They use the meaning of individual sentences, paragraphs, sections, or chapters and the entire text. As they read, they unconsciously ask themselves whether the text meaning is clear. Sometimes they reread or search back in the text to check on their understanding.

Searching for and using information is very important when reading nonfiction. McKenna and Robinson define content literacy as "the ability to use reading and writing for the acquisition of new content in a given discipline" (1993/1997, 8). Readers are required to search for information in graphic features (diagrams, photographs, illustrations) and integrate it with what they read in the body of a text. They need to know where and how to look for information, and understand how information is presented in different genres.

Genre has everything to do with how a text is organized. When you read fiction, you expect to get information about the setting and characters at the beginning of the story. Then you expect one or more problems to be revealed as the story progresses. As you near the end, you look for the solution to the central story problem. Genre acts as a kind of road map to help you in your search (Bomer 1995).

Summarizing

Readers are always organizing the information they encounter so that they can remember and carry it forward to help them understand the rest of the text. In fiction and nonfiction texts some ideas are more significant than others, and those are the ones readers want to remember. After reading fiction, they have an organized memory of the plot, characters, and setting and the relationships among these elements. They know the significant events and the general order in which they happened. After reading nonfiction, readers have an organized memory of the information—usually in meaningful categories. They do not remember every detail, of course, but a *summary* helps them re-access the text as needed. The organizational patterns of the genre are frameworks within which they can reorganize information and hold it in their brains.

Maintaining Fluency

Proficient readers use several kinds of information (from the words in print, from language, and from background knowledge) in a smooth, integrated way. Although they may slow down for various reasons, they generally maintain a good momentum (see *Teaching for Comprehending and Fluency*, Fountas and Pinnell 2006). Fluency is often measured using reading rate alone, a misleading practice. Students come to think that reading faster is better. Reading too fast in order to achieve a higher fluency score can undermine thinking and comprehension. The optimum rate is not too fast and not too slow.

Oral language involves rhythm, pauses, facial expression, and gestures. In written language, readers have only the print, although the punctuation cues them to the kind of expression they should use. They have to use that punctuation along with their understanding of the meaning to produce expressive oral reading. We define fluency in terms of six dimensions:

1. Pausing: the way the reader's voice reflects the punctuation.
2. Phrasing: the way the reader groups words into meaningful phrases.
3. Intonation: the way the reader's voice goes to higher and lower pitches to reflect meaning.

4. Word stress: the way the reader selectively says one or more words in a sentence with slightly more emphasis than the rest.
5. Rate: the speed at which the reader reads.
6. Integration: the way the reader uses the first five dimensions in a smooth and orchestrated way.

When reading orally, proficient readers pause and change the tone of voice to create phrase units that make the text meaningful. For example, "Still . . . I wish we could see it again, and again, and again," requires a longer pause after *still* and brief pauses after each *again*. Noticing the punctuation means, to an extent, reproducing the writer's intended meaning or even giving a text some of our own interpretation. Good readers notice and use punctuation to aid in this process.

Readers also *sound* different when reading texts in different genres. For example, although dialogue is not exclusive to fiction, it is more likely to occur there, and the voice changes to reflect that someone is speaking. Intonation when reading factual material with bullets might be quite different from the intonation used when reading a fictional mystery.

Adjusting

Proficient readers adjust to the purpose for reading, the style of the text, the genre, and even the audience. They take a stance toward a text and read differently based on that stance (Rosenblatt 1994). They automatically adjust the speed and style of their reading. For example, they:

- Scan for information and then slow down to read carefully.
- Read aloud with expression.
- Search back in a text to help them remember something.
- Slow down to figure something out and then move along rapidly.
- Integrate information in graphics or illustrations with the information in the print.

If you know the genre of a text, you automatically adjust the way you read. Your expectations are different. You read a mystery in a different way than you do a fantasy that requires you to enter and believe in another world. The more you understand about the structures and patterns of genre, the easier it is to adjust your stance toward the reading.

America's White Table (Raven 2005) uses poetic language to tell the fictional story of the little known custom of setting a small table in remembrance of soldiers missing during the Vietnam War. The mood is somber; the objects on the table are symbols for sorrow, peace, and hope. When you begin reading, you know that you are reading a fictional text but also that you need to call up background knowledge. The way the print is placed encourages you to read it (or hear it in our head) as poetry. You probably don't read or scan the text quickly but go slowly to understand and enjoy the language. When you reach the story within the story, in which a mother tells her daughters about her uncle's experience in Vietnam, the illustrations are rendered in sepia tones and draw on more background information. You respond to the story in light of your own personal experiences but also consider other perspectives. There are layers of meaning in this simple story, changing slightly the way you think and process the print and the pictures. You might go back and read this story again in order to notice more. How different your reading might be if this were strictly an informational book about the Vietnam War!

Predicting

Anticipation propels readers through the text. Language has a redundancy that helps you read. For example, in the sentence "Three women walked slowly toward the town, clutching their bundles of food," plurality is signaled by the word *three*, the form of *women*, the word *their*, and the *s* on *bundles.* you make predictions at every level of reading—within sentences, paragraphs, chapters, and longer texts. You use your knowledge of the patterns of language to narrow possibilities and solve words more easily. You also anticipate what might happen next in a story, or you generate expectations regarding the kind of information that will be available given the topic or the way the text is organized. Prediction helps you comprehend. Of course, readers who are actively monitoring also know when a prediction isn't right; that's where surprise comes in and often makes reading more enjoyable. That's also where learning comes in, as misconceptions are untangled while reading about a topic.

Understanding genre and its characteristics helps readers make predictions at the *text level*, which can mean deeper engagement and better comprehension: readers actively seek confirmation of their predictions. Engagement is the *cognitive involvement* a person invests in something and it is an important factor in comprehension. (Campbell, Voelkl, and Donahue 1997; Pinnell and Fountas 2009).

Making Connections

Readers are always making connections between what they are reading and what they already know. Every time they read, they bring their own personal experiences. These connections enrich the reading. Three kinds of connections expand the meaning readers take from texts.

- *Personal connections.* Readers make connections between the text and their own lives. For example, *Me llamo María Isabel* (Ada 1996) is the story of a little girl, Maria Isabel, whose new teacher renames her "Mary" on her first day in her new school because there are already two Marias in the class. This story can be enjoyed and understood by anyone, but readers who have experienced being new in a place where their language and customs are not the majority bring a different meaning to it. They connect knowledge of the topic, plot, characters, or setting to their personal experiences. The character of María Isabel experiences such connections herself when she reads *Charlotte's Web* (White 2001): "Now as she turned the pages, she thought that maybe the secret was that *everyone* has problems. She felt close to poor little Wilbur, being fattened up for Christmas dinner without even knowing it. He was a little like her parents, who were so eager to go to the pageant, not knowing what was waiting for them." These kinds of personal connections promote engagement with the text.
- *World connections.* A key factor in understanding a text is the extent to which readers can connect it with what they already know. Using background knowledge is especially important when reading informational text, but it is also helpful when reading fiction, especially books that incorporate scientific information or current or historical world events. Background knowledge helps readers interpret what they are reading as well as evaluate it. *A Nest for Celeste* (Cole 2010) is a work of fantasy that is set in a New Orleans plantation in the 1800s and features a mouse called Celeste. Celeste becomes a friend of the famous naturalist John James Audubon's young assistant, Joseph Mason. On almost every page, there are beautiful pencil drawings that enhance the mood and message, but the text is not easy. To understand it readers need to connect with what they know about animal fantasy—they need to think from the point of view of Celeste—as well as history and the work of Audubon. Knowing about bird characteristics and basket weaving (Celeste's specialty) might not be necessary but would extend comprehension. And some of the nuances of the text would be evident only to experienced readers: the birds speak in different dialects, for example, and the story is reminiscent of the fable "The Lion and the Mouse." To understand this seemingly simple book, readers must call on their knowledge of content, history, and fantasy, and those with stronger connections will comprehend it more deeply and gain a different view of Audubon.
- *Text connections.* Reading can bring to mind other texts readers have experienced. For example, a character in one book might remind them of another, or they might suddenly realize that two novels have a similar plot. While reading historical fiction, they might remember a biography they have read of someone living in a similar time. They have available all of their knowledge from previous

reading when they encounter a new text. Such connections create a network of understandings that enrich their reading. These connections help them not only recognize literary references (such as quotations from Shakespeare or the Bible) but also sense subtler relationships among texts. Young readers who have heard or read the Curious George books (Rey) or *Five Little Monkeys* (Christelow 2007) will make connections with *Me . . . Jane* (McDonnell 2011), a biography of Jane Goodall, when they hear it read aloud. The first books are playful and entertaining, the last is informational. It doesn't matter which is read first; one helps readers understand and appreciate the other. Through genre study, you deliberately teach your students to compare and contrast texts and to make connections among them.

Inferring

To truly understand a text readers have to go beyond the literal meaning so that they derive what is not *said* directly but is *implied*. For example, when María Isabel opens her beautiful new book in *Me llamo María Isabel*, the reader knows how she feels without a literal description: "She loved the sea and had always dreamed of seeing a real dolphin, so she opened the book eagerly. On the inside cover the teacher had written the name Mary Lopez. María Isabel stared at the words." Empathy for fictional or historical characters is derived from inference. Readers also make inferences when they form tentative theories about the significance of or reasons for events. All texts require inference. Readers have to search for and interpret different kinds of information when reading different genres. Knowing a genre's characteristics helps them know how and where to look for the information on which to base an inference.

Synthesizing

When readers synthesize new information from a fiction or nonfiction text, they integrate it with what they already know or feel. Making connections with personal experience, background knowledge, or other texts leads them to revise their understandings. When you read a book about the Underground Railroad, you add to or change your understanding of the way it worked. For example, reading a novel like *The House of Dies Drear* (Hamilton 1968/2006) might increase your appreciation of the danger the conductors on the Underground Railroad encountered. Reading an expository text like *The Underground Railroad* (Bial 1995) would help you better understand the logistics of the operation. Reading a biography like *Moses: When Harriet Tubman Led Her People to Freedom* (Weatherford 2006) would tell you more about Harriet Tubman and help you better appreciate her sacrifices and contributions.

In a sense, every worthwhile book you read probably changes your thinking or knowing a little bit, and some books may have an even greater influence on your life. *Anne Frank: The Diary of a Young Girl* (Frank 1952, 1989) has profoundly affected millions of readers.

Synthesis can also mean taking new perspectives. Reading a variety of texts on the same topic but in different genres can expand thinking. You may have read about Jackie Robinson in books about the history of baseball, for example, or you may have read a biography about him. But reading *Testing the Ice: A True Story About Jackie Robinson* (Robinson 2009), a memoir written by Jackie's daughter, expands your perspective and gives you new insight into the man. Memoir is often very personal and highlights particular emotions and concepts in a subject's life. In this book, Sharon Robinson describes a childhood memory of her father (who couldn't swim) testing the ice on a deep lake before allowing his children to ice skate. She compares this "testing the ice" to the way he paved the way for other African Americans in baseball. The theme of the story is courage—two different kinds of courage that are metaphorically linked.

Analyzing

Comprehending a text may mean bringing to it your knowledge of textual elements and features. Readers can gain greater understanding by closely examining elements of a text and thinking about how it is constructed. For example, successful readers recognize plot development and can make judgments about the motives and actions of characters. They derive the underlying organization of a text—how time is used, for example, or whether the setting is significant. They also know how to use graphic features to find information and let the illustrations set the mood or tone of the piece.

Readers uncover the major theme—what the writer is trying to convey—and analyze the way the writer conveys that idea. In *Annie and the Old One* (Miles 1985), for example, a Navajo girl, Annie, secretly undoes each night the weaving that her grandmother has completed during the day because she believes her grandmother will die when the weaving is finished. Finally, she helps her grandmother weave the rug. The reader understands how the writer uses the symbol of weaving to convey that time cannot be held back. Also implied in the story is the acceptance of death. You may read *Annie and the Old One* at a superficial, literal level, but the deeper meanings of this book can be understood only by analyzing it closely, perhaps by discussing it with others.

Genre study requires students to analyze texts closely. They notice aspects of text such as structure, symbolism, speeded up and slowed down action, and figurative language. In *Sky Boys* (Hopkinson and Ransome 2006), for example, the authors artfully bring together a factual account of the construction of the Empire State Building and a fictional narrative that takes place during a specific period in history—the Great Depression—and all the complex feelings experienced by the workers:

> In this new, ingenious,
> assembly-line construction
> each man works as fast as he can
> knowing that down below
> a hundred jobless men are ready
> to take over his spot in a flash.
> Yet knowing, too,
> That the quicker he finishes
> The sooner he'll be back in line himself,
> waiting and desperate for work.
> (19–20)

In *Bats at the Library* (Lies 2008) a close analysis highlights the writer's use of *rocket* instead of *fly*: "Then squeezed together, wing to wing, we rocket through the opening" (6). In addition, the illustrator has made

connections to familiar stories, depicting the little bats like the ducklings in *Make Way for Ducklings* (McCloskey 1941, 2010) and turning the title of *Goodnight Moon* (Wise Brown 1947, 2005) into *Goodnight Sun*. Readers who understand the structures and features of genre have a framework to bring to their analysis, which makes it easier to notice how the writer has exercised craft.

Critiquing

Proficient readers bring a critical eye to everything they read. They evaluate the quality and authenticity of fiction and nonfiction texts. They assess whether a fictional text is consistent with what they know to be true from their own experiences. They also evaluate the writer's craft—whether language is used skillfully and appropriately, and whether characters seem real. They discover bias in writing, detect inaccuracies (using background information), and analyze the text for accurate portrayals of individuals and groups of people. They are able to analyze a text for racial, cultural, or gender-related stereotypes. In nonfiction texts, they need to be able to assess the accuracy or completeness of the information.

Detecting misinformation in any kind of text is essential if readers are to add to their knowledge; moreover, critical reading is essential to responding intelligently to current events and making responsible decisions as a member of society. "Critical readers recognize that a text represents one particular view of the world and that however authoritative it may appear, is written by an author who has a particular ideology or set of assumptions" (Gibbons 2009, 87). Knowing the genre of a text helps them be alert to the writer's perspective. Through close study of texts during genre study, student readers learn to be more specific in their criticism. They learn to detect how language works to make a particular argument or state a point of view.

Strategic Actions as an Integrated System

It is important to emphasize again that the complex actions readers take while reading are going on all at once and with great speed. Readers are certainly not aware of everything going on in their brains while reading, and most of the time they would not even be able to talk about the process. But they know it is happening because they are constructing meaning.

Strategies are not discrete; they don't happen one at a time and you cannot teach them one at a time. You employ these interrelated and complex strategies in a fluid way, your attention most of the time focused on your search for meaning.

Learning to Read by Reading

The network of strategies we have described helps you understand the challenges of developing good readers across the grades. The wide range of learning activities that make up the language and literacy framework contribute to the learning process in different ways; a wide variety of texts is basic to the process.

When you read aloud to students, they are freed from some of the basic processes of word solving, searching for and using information, and so on. While listening to and discussing the text, they are free to expand strategies such as inferring, summarizing, and synthesizing.

Literature study makes it possible for students to go deeper into texts they have read or that have been read to them. They can analyze the elements of fiction and nonfiction texts as well as critique them. They learn to talk with one another about texts in a way that deepens comprehension and helps them notice characteristics they might not have on their own. As teachers, you demonstrate and guide students to make inferences or notice the language used by the writer.

In guided and independent reading, students read a wide range of texts for themselves. This rich variety, plus skilled teaching, helps them apply processing strategies to an increasingly challenging array of texts. To be able to write letters in their reader's notebooks, they have to reflect on their reading, again deepening their awareness. Small groups of students in guided reading are introduced to texts that have been intentionally selected because they are within students' control but offer different kinds of challenges. Text selection is all about helping students read texts that will expand their network of reading strategies.

Some direct teaching of word-solving strategies and other skills is necessary. You need to remember, however, that strategic actions are not developed only by doing isolated exercises; they are employed while reading continuous text. Also, strategies are not developed through "practice" with one book. The reality that you become a reader by applying all your knowledge and skills to reading continuous texts has strong implications for the kind of reading students do as well as the time they are given to do it.

Suggestions for Professional Development

1. Explore the relationship between comprehending strategies and genre understandings and how they support one another.
2. Choose a reader in your classroom who is reading on grade level. Observe and analyze his reading behaviors while reading a text. Pick two texts you know are at the student's instructional level (a text that is within his reach but will still offer a few areas for problem-solving). Try to pick one text in a genre with which you know he is familiar and one in a genre with which he has more limited experience.
3. Before reading the first text, ask the student what he knows about the genre and what he expects from the reading.
4. Introduce the first text and listen to him read about 150 to 200 words aloud into a tape recorder. Have a brief conversation with the student after the oral reading. Discuss the whole selection, not just the part the student read orally. Make it a real conversation, but give the student opportunity to talk about his predictions and inferences. Ask for a brief summary as well as what the student thinks about what was read.
5. Using the chart in Figure 5.1, note evidence of the student's use of strategies. For expanding strategies (those that help readers think beyond and about text such as inferring), you will need to make hypotheses from your conversation after reading. Think about how knowledge of this genre affected the way the reader applied the different strategies while reading.
6. Repeat the process with the text from a new genre. Analyze the student's reading again and think about how not knowing the genre might have affected his processing of this text. Do you see the same level of engagement in terms of strategies for thinking within, beyond, and about text?
7. Have a conversation with colleagues about what you noticed using Figure 5.1 as a guide.

SECTION 2

Understanding Genres

The chapters in Section 2 are devoted to a detailed description of the characteristics of fiction and nonfiction genres. The information in these chapters is foundational. It is a body of understandings that your students will develop over a long period of time with many rich experiences with texts of different genres.

Chapter 6 focuses broadly on fiction texts—the elements of all fiction and the demands they make on readers. Then, we divide fiction into realism and fantasy. In Chapter 7, you will find a discussion of contemporary realism as well as historical fiction. Both genres present stories that could take place in the real world, either in the present or the past. In Chapter 8 the focus on fiction continues, this time with a description of fantasy. This chapter includes information about traditional literature and modern fantasy, including simple animal fantasy, low fantasy, high fantasy, and science fiction.

Chapter 9 focuses on understanding biography, a form of nonfiction that is usually told in narrative form. Biography, autobiography, and memoir are discussed, with genre characteristics and examples. The next two chapters present information about nonfiction texts. Chapter 10 focuses on the purpose, organization, and audience of nonfiction texts, and Chapter 11 presents an analysis of the unique aspects of their design.

While this entire book is devoted to the study of genre, it is important to acknowledge that genres are not always clearly categorized. There are "hybrid" genres that incorporate fiction and nonfiction genres within the same text, and that is good because we want students to learn to read, think, and talk across genres. In Chapter 12, we define hybrid texts and include examples. We also discuss the use of multigenre text sets to help students learn to address themes and content across genres. In this chapter we also address the increasingly popular medium of graphic texts. Graphic texts can be produced in any genre, and they make special demands on readers.

Finally, in Chapter 13, we describe the forms of poetry. Poetry may occur in any genre, fiction or nonfiction, but the reader's challenge is to learn to understand and enjoy the many forms of poetry. All of the chapters in this section have implications for instruction, both in reading and in writing.

CHAPTER 6

Understanding Fiction Texts

Exploring Realism and Fantasy

Students can discover the many pleasures of reading when they are treated to books with authentic, rich language and convincing stories about life.

—Kathy Short

Fiction has the power to take you into other lives, times, landscapes, and situations—some so real that you easily believe in and recognize them, others fantastic and strange. Many of you see reading fiction as a way to escape everyday life and have vicarious experiences. At the same time, you realize that when you read fiction you can gain real insight into yourself and into the human spirit. You may even feel that you understand human problems better through reading fiction than through reading nonfiction reports or articles on the same topics. Fiction is about the emotions you *experience* rather than being just about acquiring and processing information. The characters in books often feel like friends whom you gradually come to know; sometimes you remember these "friends" throughout your life.

Lovers of fiction usually enjoy sharing their interest and talking about it with others. You may notice and share your admiration of a writer's skillful use of language or point out strong imagery, but you seldom spend a great deal of time thinking about how fiction "works." You just enjoy it. As teachers, however, it is helpful to call up your implicitly held knowledge consciously so that you can help students put themselves in the position of fiction writers.

Think of the challenging task of the fiction writer. She has to create characters and place them in a setting that is described well enough that readers can easily imagine it. She constructs a believable problem or problems and describes a series of events through which the characters move with increasing tension to the "high point" or resolution of the story. After that, she wraps it up with "falling action" leading to a satisfying end. And this is an oversimplified description of how fiction works. Plots twist and turn, characters do surprising things, endings vary widely. Many scholarly volumes have been written to describe just one of the elements of fiction. Not wishing to become so analytic that we no longer experience the joy of reading fiction, here we'll explore aspects of how fiction works that apply to *all* fiction. (Subsequent chapters discuss the unique features of realism and fantasy.) We also discuss texts that cross genre lines and texts that have become classics.

You need to consider the elements of fiction as you read aloud to students, select and introduce texts in guided reading, support literature study, and guide students' choices for independent reading. No matter what the setting, you need to consider the age appropriateness of the text and whether it will be engaging. In guided reading lessons, you also need to consider the text's level of difficulty.

A Comparison of Fiction and Nonfiction Texts

Fiction was not always as popular and respected as it is today. Nonfiction commanded the respect of the majority of serious readers. As recently as two centuries ago, fiction was considered frivolous by much of society.

Today, we consider a large number of fiction texts to be great literature—serious works of intellect.

Although there is some overlap in fiction and nonfiction genres, and the lines that separate them are not always sharply defined, fiction and nonfiction texts have some important differences (see Figure 6.1).

In general, when describing fiction, we can say that the content is imaginary rather than real (although it may be based on real events or portray realistic problems and situations). The characters may seem real, but they are creations of the writer, as are the story problems and the events. The settings may be real places or imagined worlds. Often fiction texts have illustrations that extend the meaning or create a mood. Usually, you read a fiction text from beginning to end. Nonfiction texts contain factual (real) content and the events or people they describe exist or existed in the past. Nonfiction texts are designed to inform, and they often have illustrations that extend or support the information being presented.

An important difference between fiction and nonfiction is the *structure*—the way the text is organized. The events in fiction texts are usually presented chronologically, although there may be some variation (flashbacks, flash-forwards, or stories within stories, for example). With the exception of biography and some narrative texts, nonfiction texts are usually organized by topics and subtopics. They have distinct sections and often have organizational aids such as headings to help clarify information. Nonfiction texts (excluding biographies) often do not have to be read from beginning to end; instead, you can search the text for interesting or needed information and read only a part of it or read it in any order.

The lines between fiction and nonfiction are sometimes blurred. For example, real events can be accurately portrayed within a fiction text. Jean Fritz wrote biographies that engage students while presenting factual details. In books like *Will You Sign Here, John Hancock?* (Fritz 1997) and *And Then What Happened, Paul Revere?* (Fritz 1996) she set a standard of authenticity by not drawing inferences, making up events, or having the characters say words that are not recorded in history.

Fictionalized biography may also include the unspoken thoughts of a subject and some imagined events. Books like *The Secret Soldier: The Story of Deborah Sampson* (McGovern 1990) read like novels but are based on facts. In historical fiction you are also likely to find a great many real historic details that provide accurate information. In *Elijah of Buxton* (Curtis 2009), the author uses real characters and events from history but weaves them into a historical novel. In many contemporary realistic fiction books, characters live in real, recognizable cities or towns, and may grapple with real events and issues. Sorting out what is fact and what is fiction requires careful and thoughtful consideration.

An important aspect of literacy instruction is convincing students that they need to distinguish between fiction and nonfiction, and equipping them with the skills and genre knowledge necessary to do it.

Fiction Genres

Fiction texts are usually organized as stories, or narratives, and they have imaginary characters and events. Figure 6.2 describes the structure and elements of a

COMPARISON OF FICTION AND NONFICTION TEXTS		
Fiction Texts	**Nonfiction Texts**	
	Biographical and Narrative Nonfiction Texts	**Expository, Procedural, and Persuasive Texts**
Content is imagined.	Content is real (may be fictionalized to a degree).	Content is real.
Purpose is to entertain, to show life's problems, and to communicate a message.	Purpose is to engage interest in or create appreciation for a subject.	Purpose is to inform and engage interest in facts, often to persuade or show how to do something.
Texts have elements such as characters, setting, story problem, events, and problem resolution.	Texts have details about a subject, often presented chronologically.	Texts present information, often in categories, and use structures such as compare/contrast, problem/solution, description, temporal sequence, and cause/effect.
Texts are usually read from beginning to end.	Texts are usually read from beginning to end, although readers often know the end.	Texts can be read in parts, not necessarily in order, according to interest.
Illustrations and graphics extend the meaning and the mood and help the reader visualize characters and events.	Illustrations and graphics extend the meaning and the mood and help the reader visualize the setting and the subject's world.	Illustrations, drawings, graphics, and organizational tools extend information and/or make it easy to find.

Figure 6.1 Comparison of fiction and nonfiction texts

wide range of fiction genres. Some are based on realistic events—either contemporary or historical—and some are based on worlds, events, or characters that do not or could not exist.

Fiction texts can be categorized as realism (contemporary realistic fiction and historical fiction); or fantasy, including traditional literature (folktales, fairy tales, fables, legends, epics, ballads, and myths) and modern fantasy (animal fantasy, low fantasy, high fantasy, and science fiction). By the end of elementary school, students should be familiar with all of these genres and should have read, discussed, and studied many examples of each—most of them at every grade level, with some challenging genres read more frequently at the higher grades. In middle school and high school, students should be able to think deeply about all of them.

Realism

Both contemporary realistic fiction and historical fiction focus on universal human themes, including friendship, love, family, loss, adventure, loneliness, survival, and discrimination. These stories are imagined but they are true to life because they include characters and events that could exist—either today or at some time in the past. Both realistic and historical fiction can take many special forms, including mysteries or adventure stories that take place in the past or in modern times.

FICTION GENRES	
Genre	**Sub-Genres**
Realism	• Contemporary Realistic Fiction • Historical Fiction
Fantasy	Traditional Literature: • Folktales • Fairy Tales • Fables • Legends, Epics, Ballads • Myths Modern Fantasy: • Animal Fantasy • Low Fantasy • High Fantasy • Science Fiction

Figure 6.2 Fiction genres

Both historical fiction and realistic fiction help students better understand themselves and others, but historical fiction demands that the reader understand past times. Through reading historical fiction, readers can visit distant lands or times past and learn about people from other cultures, all the while making connections to familiar issues and problems. Historical works also have the added value of helping students understand the unique challenges and realities of the past. We discuss the characteristics of contemporary realistic fiction and historical fiction in more detail in Chapter 7.

Fantasy Genres

Fantasy, including traditional literature, modern fantasy, and science fiction, also employs all of the elements of fiction—characters, setting, and plot—but the reader must suspend reality in order to enter the fantasy world.

Traditional Literature

Traditional literature, including folktales and fairy tales, fables, epics, ballads, legends, and myths, consists of the written versions of oral tales that have been passed down from generation to generation in every part of the world. At a time when very few people could read or write, these tales (sometimes sung as ballads) served as entertainment and, more importantly, as an oral record of history and of customs. Traditional literature includes a wide variety of texts, from simple to highly complex. Since traditional literature comes from the oral traditions of cultures around the world, it is no wonder anthropologists learn about cultures by studying folklore. Studying traditional literature is a wonderful way to learn about cultures other than our own. We discuss the characteristics of the specific genres of traditional literature in more detail in Chapter 8.

Modern Fantasy

Modern fantasy has some similarities to traditional literature, but all works of modern fantasy have more contemporary content and began as written stories. Here, too, the lines are blurred. A modern fantasy may be based on a traditional story but contain so many unique elements that the authorship is clear. For example, *Ella Enchanted* (Levine 2004) is based on the Cinderella story but has a decidedly original and modern narrative and characters. In contrast, a text that sticks very close to a known version of a traditional tale is identified as being "retold" by the author.

When we read modern fantasy, we accept the elements of the imagined world; within those parameters, the text is believable. The writer describes the setting and characters in a way that helps us suspend reality and believe in the world we have entered. Once we accept the world of wizards and the setting and rules of Hogwarts, for example, the Harry Potter series is believable. Within any work of fantasy, the writer must be consistent; in other words, characters cannot suddenly fly, perform magic, or change shapes unless the potential is there and the groundwork has been laid. The writer of fantasy must create a text that is coherent in that the actions of characters are possible in the world the writer has created.

In fantasy, as in realistic and historical fiction, characters usually deal with human problems—love, loss, challenging situations. Even though the settings and events are not realistic, readers have the opportunity to learn some universal truths. Many readers identify strongly with Harry Potter's struggles at Hogwarts—universal struggles that have to do with friendship, loyalty, and self-discovery. Sometimes the fantastic world is even more effective than realistic settings at helping readers reflect on real life. We discuss the characteristics of the specific genres of modern fantasy in more detail in Chapter 8.

Elements of Fiction

Fiction texts incorporate literary elements students need to know about if they are to fully appreciate the meaning and craft of a text.

Narrative Text Structure

Fiction texts are stories and use narrative structure. A simple narrative structure (see Figure 6.3) follows a traditional sequence that includes a beginning, a series of events or episodes, and a resolution and ending. There may be some variations in this structure (and it may vary from culture to culture), but the general pattern is this:

1. There is a beginning in which important elements such as the setting, characters, and central problem are introduced.
2. There is a series of events or episodes in which the plot unfolds as the main character takes action to solve the problem.
3. The problem reaches a high point during a culminating event, sometimes called a *climax.*

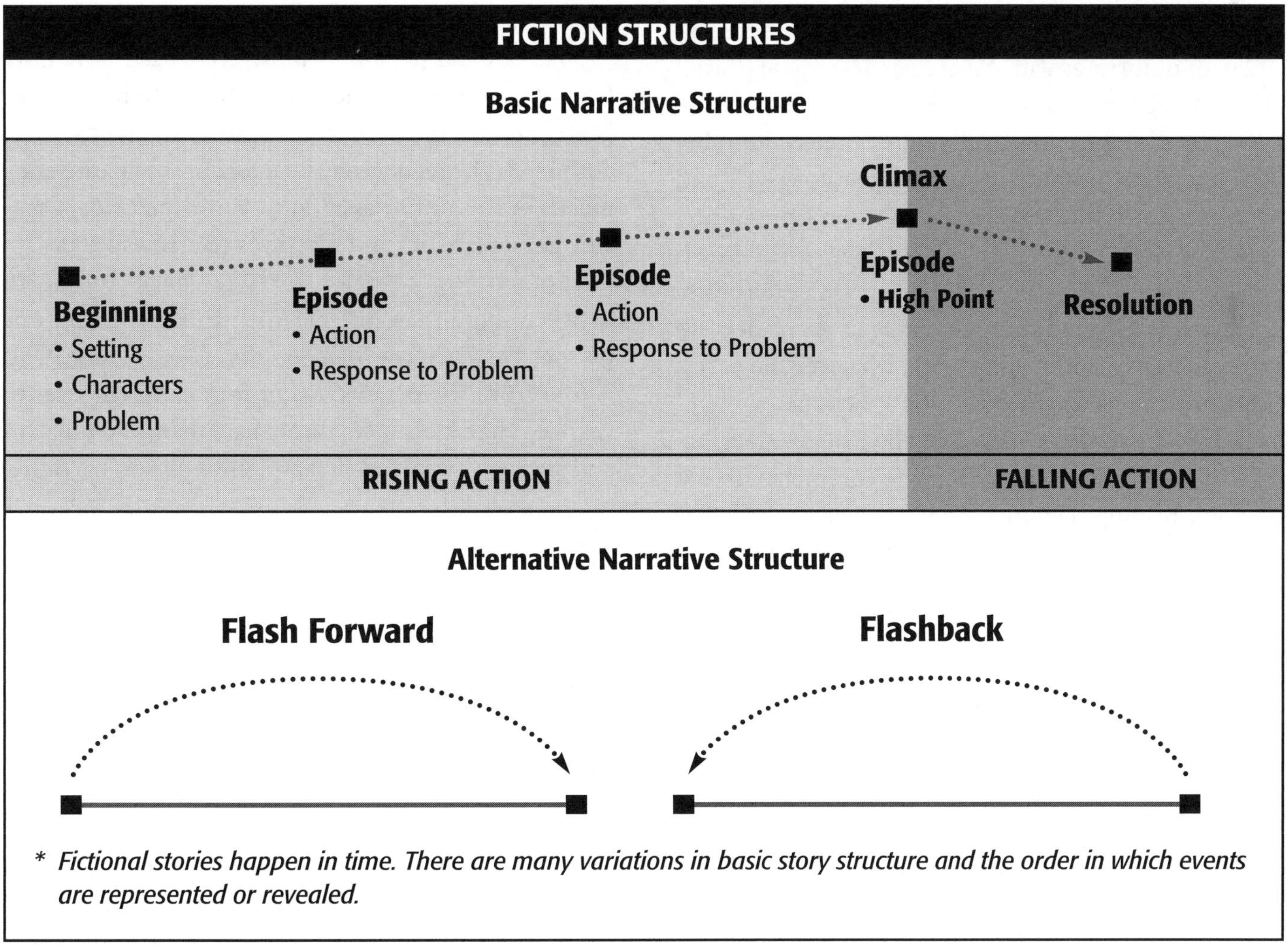

Figure 6.3 Fiction structures

4. There is a conclusion or resolution, often followed by a *denouement*, in which the final outcome of the problem is described, perhaps including subsequent events.

In the Harry Potter series, J. K. Rowling develops a single overarching problem or theme—the struggle between good and evil—over seven volumes. Within each volume are subthemes related to the main theme; most are resolved, but at the end of each book, the author communicates that there is still more work to be done. The final book in the series has a denouement that gives the reader a long view of Harry's adult life.

There are many ways in which the simple narrative structure of fictional stories can vary. Many stories begin at the end; they describe the current state of a character and then move back to the beginning to tell about events that have already occurred. Some mysteries start with the solution, then the reader observes a detective solving the mystery step by step. There are stories within stories as with *Night Boat to Freedom* (Raven 2008). Some narrative structures are highly complex—telling several stories the reader must connect, jumping back and forth in time, telling the same story over and over but from different perspectives, and presenting many subplots. Most fiction writers signal when time is passing and problems are solved; sometimes the entire narrative is delivered through dialogue. As readers we can recognize a compelling story, whatever the variations, and that is what we love about fiction.

The more students know about how stories are structured, the easier it will be for them to comprehend what they are reading. Dymock (2007) has suggested that teaching students about narrative structure—eventually helping them understand even very complex structures—will give them a significant advantage in thinking analytically about texts. This makes sense. The more students understand about how a text is crafted, the easier it will be for them to access the meaning.

Narrator or Perspective

In every fictional text someone has to tell, or *narrate*, the story. An author may choose to tell a story using a first-, second-, or third-person perspective, although the first and third person are the most common. Third- and second-person stories are told by an author; first-person stories are told by a character in the story.

With a third-person perspective, the author decides how much she knows about what is happening in the story. The narrator may be able to see and know everything that happens within the world of the story (third person omniscient), or she may have limited knowledge (third person limited or limited omniscient), for example, knowing only what is in the mind of one character but not another. The omniscient narrator, such as the narrator in the classic three-book fantasy epic *Lord of the Rings* has total knowledge.

In books written in the first person, the narrator speaks as one of the characters, telling the story as "I." A good example is *Missing May* (Rylant 1993), in which the young narrator, Summer, struggles to come to terms with her Aunt May's death. The first person narrator may be the protagonist, telling his own story, or he may be telling someone else's story.

The second person, *you*, is rarely used in fiction; from this perspective the "you" referred to in the story is a character in the narrative, so designated by the author. Or the reader may be made into a character by means of the author assigning "you" (the reader) specific characteristics and reactions (Burroway 2000).

Sometimes, complex texts go back and forth between more than one narrator and more than one perspective. *The View from Saturday* (Konigsburg 1998) is told from the perspective of four different twelve-year-old characters—Noah, Nadia, Ethan, and Julian—and alternates between first and third person narrative.

Characters

The characters are the individuals in the story. They may be people or animals or, as in some fantasy texts, something other than human or animal. One character is considered the *main* character or *protagonist* (a story may have more than one). There are also usually a number of supporting characters. There is sometimes an *antagonist*, a negative force, who creates conflict or tension. In the classic tale "Little Red Riding Hood," Little Red Riding Hood is the protagonist and the wolf is the antagonist.

Stories are usually told from the protagonist's point of view, and readers are usually most deeply concerned with the protagonist's feelings and experiences. Authors reveal characters to the reader through what they say or think, how they look, how they behave, and what others think or say about them. With a well-written, believable story, the characters change and grow as they experience the events of the plot.

When you read fiction, you "see things through the character's eyes and language but also through the author's eyes and language" (Wood 2008, 172). At the same time, you often see *more* than the character sees. In *Bridge to Terabithia*, told in the third person, you experience the story through the main character Jess's eyes, but you also see his family's struggles with money, the pressures on Jess being the middle child and the only boy, his artistic spirit and his dreams of distinguishing himself as a runner, and his relationship with his father. You see how Jess sometimes pushes himself beyond his endurance. You understand all of this against the background of changing times after the Vietnam War, times that are changing very slowly in Jess's backwater town. As a reader, you are perfectly positioned to understand the impact that all of these forces have on Jess's life, because you bring your own understanding to the characters and story.

Round and Flat Characters

In high-quality texts, the characters seem real to the reader. Major characters are round, as opposed to flat. A round character is a fully-developed one—you know how the character thinks and feels or what she does and is likely to do in many settings. A flat character is one-dimensional. The writer has not revealed much about the character, and she usually either does not change or changes very little. The character plays a role in the story but the reader doesn't come to "know" her. In *A Nest for Celeste* (Cole 2010) the author reveals much about the main character Celeste's thoughts and dreams. A secondary character, Joseph, is less well developed. Another character, a cat, exists mainly to move the plot in a specific direction, adding elements of drama and danger. The writer's decisions about characterization help the reader focus attention on the important characters and let others slip into the background. Of course, complex texts like those in the Harry Potter series have many interesting characters that hold the reader's attention. If you stop to consider these minor characters, however, you realize that most of them remain essentially the same. After you get to know them, you expect them to change very little. Harry, on the other hand, grows and changes in every volume.

Illustrations play an important role in helping you understand characters, although usually they only support the written text. The dark and somber tones of the beautifully illustrated *Night Boat to Freedom*, with occasional splashes of the brilliant color red (symbolizing both slavery and freedom), help you understand Christmas John's emotions and bravery. Many fiction texts for older readers have few if any illustrations, so the writer must do all the work of helping the reader envision characters. Yet the images that grow from words alone can be very strong. In graphic novels, on the other hand, illustrations play a major role in revealing characters. Much of the action is carried through dialogue and short descriptions, but frame after frame show how characters look and feel. In *Foiled* (Yolen 2010), the character Aliera is revealed as a mousy, unpopular girl who changes when she puts on a fencing mask. When she becomes a fencer, her inner spirit is clear. Aliera's facial expression and posture show the many facets of her personality.

Static and Dynamic Characters

Characters may also be static or dynamic. Static characters remain the same; they do not change over the course of the story. They may be flat or round but are unchanging. For example, Cinderella does not change (she is just as good at the beginning of the story as at the end) and neither do her stepsisters. As discussed previously in Chapter 3, characters in many series books tend to be flat; they may learn some lessons during the story but do not change much. The characters Ivy and Bean, in the eponymous series by Annie Barrows, are well developed, likable, and funny. They have problems, get into trouble, and learn a few things, but essentially, they remain the same.

A fiction writer has the challenge of showing not only *how* characters change but *why* they change. Good writers of fiction show character development not by making statements about characters but by showing what characters think and do and what others say about them. In *One Green Apple* (Bunting 2006), the change in the main character, Farah, who gradually assimilates into the new culture, is made more explicit by the metaphor of many apples blending to make cider.

The main character or protagonist in a well-written story must be round and is almost always dynamic. For example, in the classic *Abel's Island* (Steig 1976), the main character Abel, a mouse, changes from snobbish and fussy into someone who appreciates the natural world and all that he used to take for granted. In *Danitra Brown Leaves Town* (Grimes 2005), the third book in a series, two friends, Danitra and Zuri, exchange letters while spending a summer apart. Through Grimes' poetry, the characters' unique voices come through clearly, and they develop throughout the series as they grow slightly older and encounter new problems.

We often feel we know memorable characters from fiction as real people, and that's a good thing. We want students to encounter strong characters that will inspire them and draw them deeper into their reading. In *Sarny: A Life Remembered* (Paulsen 1999), a young slave girl is freed following the last days of the Civil War and faces much adversity as she attempts to rebuild her life. The author paints such a rich and detailed picture of the courageous Sarny that the reader is fully engaged and left wanting to know what will happen next for her. While students may not be able to relate to the specific challenges that Sarny faces, they feel that they know her because the author has created such a fully realized character.

Plot

The plot of a story is the action—the problem and the events that stem from it. All fiction texts use some form of narrative structure, which can be simple or complex. A strong plot holds the story together and keeps the reader interested, making it the most important element in determining appeal. Younger children tend to prefer simple plots they can easily follow. As they grow more experienced, they are drawn to more complex plots.

Time is an important element of plot, and writers make various uses of time. The plot may move in chronological order—that is, the story is told in the order the events happen. Tension and conflict increase until the overall problem is resolved. By contrast, a plot may have episodes that do not necessarily occur in chronological order but that are linked to one another by common characters or a unified theme.

The writer may also use devices like *flashback* or *flash-forward* in which the action moves suddenly into the past or into the future to relate events that have relevance for understanding the present. Flashbacks and flash-forwards expand time, so that the story can encompass a wider span. Epilogues perform the same function by providing additional information in a compressed form.

Writers also use stories within stories to explain events. In *Maniac Magee* (Spinelli 1999) the author provides a series of stories about the main character prior to the beginning of the action of the main plot.

Conflict

A successful narrative plot must involve conflict, tension, and action—these are the characteristics that engage us as readers.

> We know the plot of a story only after the fact, for only when the reading is completed can we decide what the plot was. The notion of tension, on the other hand, is always present in our reading, pulling us along, challenging us to stretch our imaginations. In emotional terms, tension might be referred to as the suspense, anxiety, nervousness, strain, urgency, excitement, or fear that grips us as we read. (Peterson and Eeds 1990, 28)

Most plots are built around some sort of conflict, which may take any one of these forms:

- *People in conflict with nature.* Individuals strive to overcome or survive forces such as weather, climate, natural disasters, or geography. In *Hatchet* (Paulsen 1987, 2007), a young boy must learn to survive alone in the Canadian wilderness after a plane crash. He faces challenges such as making a shelter, finding food, staying warm, and fending off wild animals.
- *People in conflict with other people.* A protagonist and an antagonist collide. In *Cousins* (Hamilton 1992) the main character, Cammy, dislikes her cousin Patty Ann, who is pretty, smart, and in

Cammy's opinion, spoiled. Just when Cammy wishes that Patty Ann would "disappear off the face of the earth," a tragic turn of events occurs.

- *People in conflict with society.* The main character struggles to overcome societal ills such as poverty, war, or racism. In *Roll of Thunder, Hear My Cry* (Taylor 1976, 2004), an African American family struggles against poverty, racism, and illness in the deep South of the 1930s.
- *People in conflict with themselves.* The protagonist struggles with conflicting personal goals, actions, or identity. In the classic *The Hundred Dresses* (Estes 1944, 2004) Maddie struggles with her own guilt over knowing that she did little to defend the friendless Wanda against the cruel teasing of their classmate Peggy.

Setting

Setting is the place and time in which a story takes place. It may be set in the past, present, or future, but whatever the setting it almost always affects the action, characters, and theme of the book. Sometimes the setting is very important to the story, as in *Night in the Country* (Rylant 1991), a picture book that explores the sights and sounds of nighttime in the country. In other fiction texts, the setting is almost incidental, merely a backdrop to the characters and plot—these stories could take place in other places or times and be relatively unchanged. In historical fiction, time plays an essential, defining role in the story, and the place is often significant as well.

If the setting is very important to the story, the fiction writer must find a way to slow down the action, as if to say *now I'm going to tell you what this place is like*. Often we are told about the setting through the eyes of a character. In *The Hunger Games* (Collins 2008) the young heroine, Katniss, says:

> Our part of District 12, nicknamed the Seam, is usually crawling with coal miners heading out to the morning shift at this hour. Men and women with hunched shoulders, swollen knuckles, many who have long since stopped trying to scrub the coal dust out of their broken nails, the lines of their sunken faces. But today the black cinder streets are empty. Shutters on the squat gray houses are closed. The reaping isn't until two. May as well sleep in. If you can. (4)

Collins has created a mental picture that alerts us to the miserable conditions in Katniss' home and simultaneously alerts us that something even more terrible than the daily drudgery is about to happen.

Theme

The theme (also called the big idea) of a story is the underlying message or messages in the text or the bigger meaning below the story's surface. The theme reveals the author's purpose. The big idea is often stated at the end of a story and is sometimes voiced by one of the characters. In *Ella Enchanted* (Levine 2004), the main character, Ella, articulates one of the themes of the book—that the power to change lies within us—when she says:

> I had been able to break the curse myself. I'd had to have reason enough, love enough to do it, to find the will and the strength. (228)

Most of the time, themes are not explicitly stated and must be uncovered by the reader. In fact, we would not want explicit moralizing, which might make a story flat and uninteresting. In *Elena* (Stanley 1996) a young Mexican girl overcomes obstacles in order to get an education and make a better life for herself. A similar theme can be found in *Lyddie* (Paterson 1991, 2004), which is about a young girl who labors in a mill and struggles to achieve more education. As with many high-quality stories, several themes can be derived from *Elena* and *Lyddie*. They both deal with the value of independence, persistence, and hard work, as well as the importance of higher learning. We need to help our students become sophisticated enough to identify the main theme of a story or to discern and discuss multiple themes.

Style and Language

Another element of fiction is the writer's style—the way she chooses words and arranges them to create a meaningful text. Some prolific writers have recognizable styles, but they also vary their style according to the audience and purpose for which they are writing. For example, Cynthia Rylant tells simple stories with homespun details that communicate feelings related to home and family. In her Henry and Mudge books, Rylant speaks in a simple, childlike voice that seems very natural and focuses on those details of life that would be important to a young boy like Henry.

William Steig uses long, complex sentences full of sophisticated vocabulary and images. He also uses language that imbues his animal characters with whimsical and vivid personalities. *Amos and Boris* (1971, 2009) tells about an unlikely friendship between a whale and a mouse:

> During that time, they developed a deep admiration for one another. Boris admired the delicacy, the quivering daintiness, the light touch, the small voice, the gemlike radiance of the mouse. Amos admired the bulk, the grandeur, the power, the purpose, the rich voice, and the abounding friendliness of the whale. (16)

Steig's writing, rich with figurative and descriptive language, brings these two characters vividly to life and also clearly shows the contrast between Amos the mouse and Boris the whale.

Jean Craighead George uses details and action to weave eventful, adventurous stories. A hallmark of her work is the well-researched detail that establishes authenticity. In *My Side of the Mountain* (1959, 2004) young Sam runs away and learns to live off the land in the mountains of upstate New York. George's descriptions of place allow you to explore the landscape along with Sam:

> Thinking that I ought to have a bucket of water in case things got out of hand, I looked desperately around me. The water was far across the meadow and down the ravine. This would never do. I began to think the whole inspiration of a home in the tree was no good. I really did have to live near water for cooking and drinking and comfort. I looked sadly at the magnificent hemlock and was about to put the fire out and desert it when I said something to myself. It must have come out of some book: "Hemlocks usually grow around mountain streams and springs." (33)

Upper elementary and middle-level students need to read books with a wide variety of writing styles. They will not only develop greater appreciation as readers but also come to know their own tastes and preferences. Exposure to a range of high-quality texts will influence them as writers as well.

Figurative Language

Many writers use figurative language to bring their words to life. Figurative language compares things in order to allow the reader to see something more clearly or better understand the feelings or thoughts of a particular character. In *Lester's Dog* (Hess 1993), a young boy is frightened of a dog, and says, "All of me is trembling, and my legs feel like loose jello." Later in the story, he finds a kitten and says, "I hear it mewing, mewing like a stuck record." Each of these quotes contains a *simile*, which makes a comparison using *like* or *as*.

A *metaphor* is a direct comparison. In *Tuck Everlasting* (Babbitt 1975, 2007) one of the characters compares the cycle of life to a wheel:

> It's a wheel, Winnie. Everything is a wheel, turning and turning, never stopping. The frog is part of it, and the bugs, and the fish and the wood thrush, too. And people. But never the same ones. Always coming in new, always growing and changing, and always moving on. That's the way it's supposed to be. That's the way it is. (62)

Symbolism

Writers often use symbolism to communicate the theme or message of a story. By understanding symbolism, readers delve into layers of meaning, going deeper than the literal level. *Circle of Gold* (Boyd 1996) is the story of a family struggling after the father's death. A gold pin comes to symbolize the main character's hopes that her family's situation will get better and that her mother will be happy again.

The color red plays a powerful symbolic role in *Night Boat to Freedom*. The cloth that lured Granny Judith into slavery was red, but toward the end of the story Granny presents her grandson with a red shirt, explaining, "It's your freedom color . . . 'cause tonight you've got to row yourself to safety, Christmas John" (23). The color red has come to symbolize freedom rather than enslavement.

Voice

Sometimes fiction writers tell you something about themselves through their writing. Their feelings, experiences, principles, and attitudes are revealed through a story's characters, problems, and resolutions. Every decision or choice writers make about plot, language, setting, and so on, is part of their voice as a writer. When you study an author like Gary Paulsen with your students, reading several of his books, you become familiar with his voice. He writes about male characters who grow stronger, more capable and confident, because of their struggles to survive. His style is action-packed and suspenseful as he describes the struggle between people and nature. At the same time, his descriptions communicate his obvious reverence and respect for nature. As students consider the voice of their favorite authors, they can also begin to develop a writer's voice of their own.

Mood

Using language, sometimes in combination with illustrations, writers evoke an emotional atmosphere in a literary work. In *The Fighting Ground* (Avi 1994) the author provides an almost moment-by-moment account of a twenty-four-hour period during the Revolutionary War. The resulting mood is intense. By contrast, in the beginning of *Autumn Street* (Lowry 1986), a work of fiction that is autobiographical, the beginning language and layout evoke a mood of reflection and sadness, signaling that a poignant story will follow:

> It was a long time ago.
>
> Though it seems, sometimes, that most things that matter happened a long time ago, that is not really true. What is true is this: by the time you realize how much something mattered, time has passed; by the time it stops hurting enough that you can tell about it, first to yourself, and finally to someone else, more time has passed; then, when you sit down to begin the telling, you have to begin this way:
>
> It was a long time ago. (1)

Mood is important because it captures readers' interest and involves them *emotionally* in the story. Sensing the mood, you read with that emotional backdrop, thus enhancing your comprehension of and appreciation for the writing. You want your students to talk about the mood of the stories they read—how they built expectations from the beginning as well as how the story made them feel.

Illustrations

A picture storybook is a cohesive literary work in which illustrations and text work together to convey meaning. In *Dandelions* (Bunting 2001) the gouache paintings convey the sweeping landscapes and open, empty land of the western frontier. In *Wilfrid Gordon McDonald Partridge* (Fox 1989) pastel watercolors of round-shaped characters dressed in soft colors convey the reflective, warm mood of older people in a nursing home.

Most easy chapter books for younger readers have illustrations that greatly enhance the meaning. For example, the Ivy and Bean books by Annie Barrows have illustrations on every two-page spread (see Figure 6.4). The illustrations are very helpful to younger readers in conveying the significance of the very close friendship between the two girls as they encounter problems in their everyday lives. Other easy chapter books, such as the Arthur series by Marc Brown, have black-and-white illustrations every four or five pages.

Most chapter books for older readers do not have illustrations but may have one or two drawings or photographs or some design features at the beginning or end of chapters. In works of high quality, text and illustrations work together to convey the author's message. *A Taste of Blackberries* is illustrated with soft charcoal drawings that convey the mood of sadness a young boy feels when his friend dies tragically and he must deal with the loss.

The typography of a book should be appropriate for the age group for whom it is intended. Easy chapter books have slightly larger print and more space between lines. The books shouldn't look "babyish," but a little easier font helps these readers. Longer chapter books have fonts similar to adult fiction.

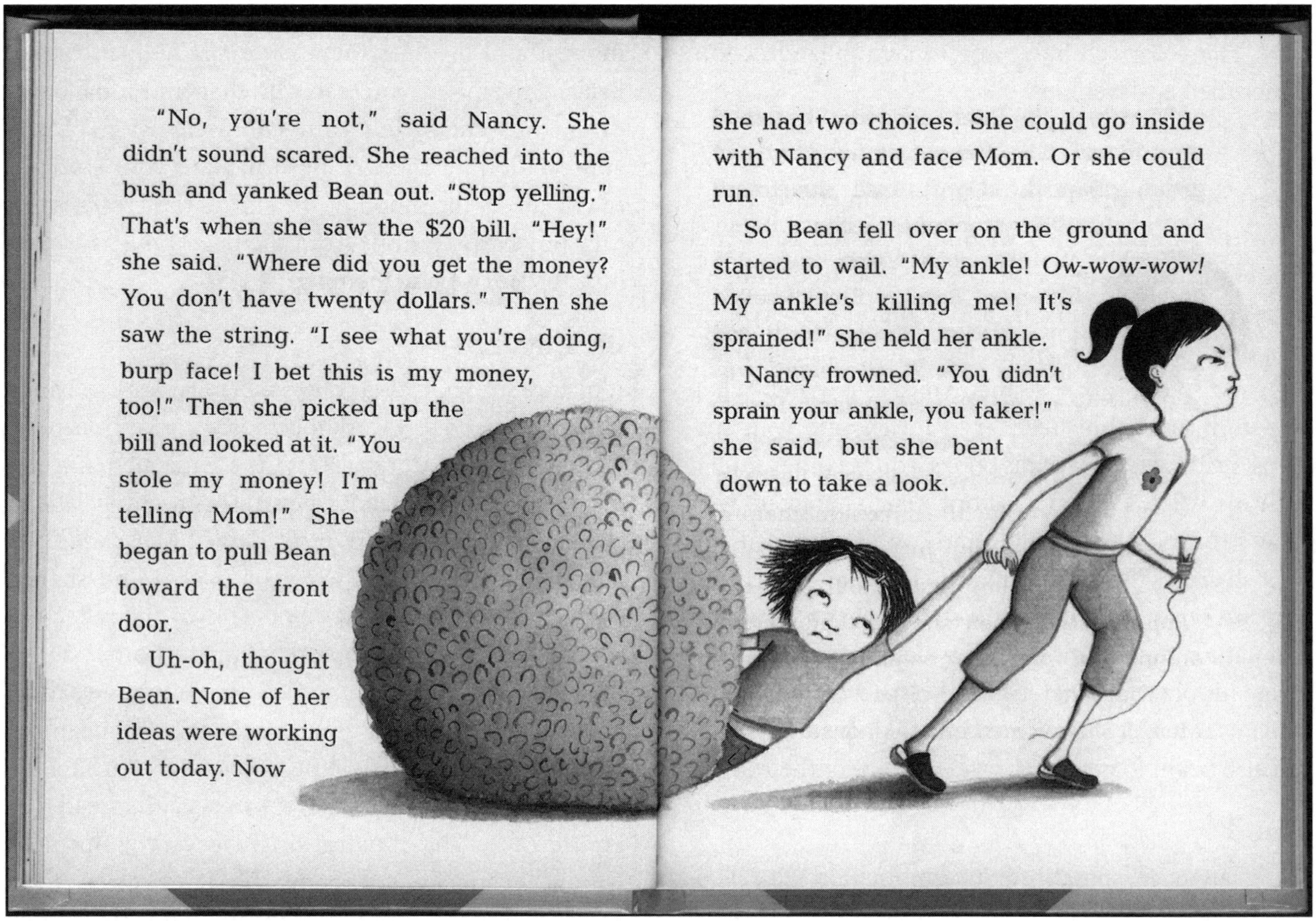

"No, you're not," said Nancy. She didn't sound scared. She reached into the bush and yanked Bean out. "Stop yelling." That's when she saw the $20 bill. "Hey!" she said. "Where did you get the money? You don't have twenty dollars." Then she saw the string. "I see what you're doing, burp face! I bet this is my money, too!" Then she picked up the bill and looked at it. "You stole my money! I'm telling Mom!" She began to pull Bean toward the front door.

Uh-oh, thought Bean. None of her ideas were working out today. Now she had two choices. She could go inside with Nancy and face Mom. Or she could run.

So Bean fell over on the ground and started to wail. "My ankle! *Ow-wow-wow!* My ankle's killing me! It's sprained!" She held her ankle.

Nancy frowned. "You didn't sprain your ankle, you faker!" she said, but she bent down to take a look.

Figure 6.4 Pages from *Ivy & Bean*, Book 1

In *Mieko and the Fifth Treasure* (Coerr 2004), each chapter is introduced with a Japanese character written in calligraphy (see Figure 6.5); the characters are explained in the back of the volume. This artistic enhancement adds to the book's interest for readers and adds considerably to readers' understanding of the significance of the characters and the art of producing them.

Design

Design refers to the format of the text. The elements of design include the way print is placed on the page, the size and shape of the book, the illustrations, the binding, and the cover. In a work of high quality, all of these elements work together harmoniously. In *Mieko and the Fifth Treasure*, the cover shows Mieko painting calligraphy, a tree full of apple blossoms visible through the window; the soft pink, brown, and lilac tones help convey the grace of the art form. The back cover shows the Japanese character for friendship in the middle of a parchment-colored page. The only graphics in the book are the Japanese characters, placed within plenty of white space at the beginning of chapters with one-word titles, which underscore the theme of simplicity and beauty.

There is often a difference in the artistic quality of hardbound and paperback versions of a book. The cover image often changes on the paperback, and of course there is no book jacket. Nevertheless, paperback books are a reality in the classroom, and you want students to notice what publishers do to make a book attractive. Students can talk about the illustrations on the cover and the copy and illustrations on the back of the book, as well as any other design features. You need to teach students to be critical of the design of a book.

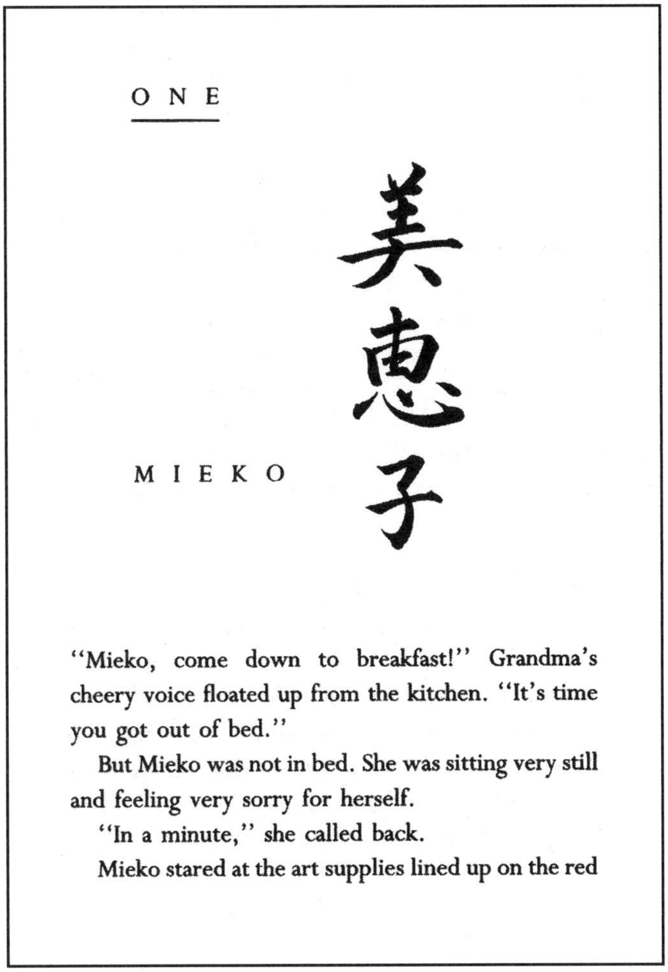

ONE

美恵子

MIEKO

"Mieko, come down to breakfast!" Grandma's cheery voice floated up from the kitchen. "It's time you got out of bed."

But Mieko was not in bed. She was sitting very still and feeling very sorry for herself.

"In a minute," she called back.

Mieko stared at the art supplies lined up on the red

Figure 6.5 Page from *Mieko and the Fifth Treasure*

For example, a cover that is intended to attract buyers should also represent the meaning, theme, and mood of the book. There are some books with covers that don't fit the story, and you want students to notice.

Classic Fiction

Given all these ways to look at the quality of literature, you will always want to look for new books that will engage students and present them with opportunities to learn. At the same time, there are books that over the years have come to epitomize the characteristics of high-quality literature. These books have also remained popular with elementary school children. *Little Women* (Alcott 1868/2011), for example, was originally written as realistic fiction; Alcott was writing about her own adolescence and early adult years. Now, over a hundred years later, young people read this classic novel as historical fiction. Laura Ingalls Wilder began writing her famous Little House series in the 1930s, but she too was writing about her childhood. Born in 1867, she was helping children understand what life was like on frontier farms at a much earlier time in history.

Classic books like these bring adventure and historically relevant experience to children in a timeless way. They engage readers from one generation to the next. Classics exist in all genres, and they include themes and issues that are important throughout the ages. The characters are believable, the style appealing, and the stories relevant and captivating.

Classics may change, of course, finally waning in popularity as new classics arise to meet the special interests of a generation. The Chronicles of Narnia series, for example, is still read and enjoyed, but *The Adventures of Tom Sawyer* (Twain 1876, 2011) is not as popular with today's youth as it has been with generations past.

Teachers can count on the quality of these classics, and they are also widely available in libraries and schools. And you can probably count on enjoying these books yourself.

Award-Winning Books

Many high-quality books win awards; most of these books become classics, although some do not. You want to be aware of these award-winning books because, again, you can count on their quality.

The Caldecott Medal was established to honor Randolph Caldecott, a great English illustrator of the nineteenth century. The award is presented annually by the Association for Library Service to Children (a division of the American Library Association) to the most distinguished American picture book for children. The award is largely presented for the artwork, but the text must be worthy of the illustrations. Many of these beautiful picture books are excellent resources to read aloud. *Once a Mouse* (Brown 1989) is a good example of a Caldecott Medal winner that has stood the test of time. The book can be enjoyed at several levels, including a sophisticated analysis of the fable and how the illustrations symbolize power. Another example is Jerry Pinkney's 2009 retelling of the classic tale *The Lion and the Mouse*.

The Newbery Medal, also awarded by ALA's Association for Library Service to Children, annually recognizes an author of the most distinguished book in children's literature. The award, established in honor of John Newbery, the first English publisher of children's books, called the "father of children's literature," has been awarded since 1922. The recipient must be a citizen of or reside in the United States and is chosen every year by two committees.

Other popular children's book awards include the Coretta Scott King Book Awards that promote understanding and appreciation of the culture of all peoples and honor African American authors and illustrators; the Theodor Seuss Geisel Medal that honors the authors and illustrators of beginning reader books; and the Sibert Medal and NCTE Orbis Pictus Award, both of which recognize outstanding nonfiction books for children.

These and other book award lists are excellent sources of high-quality texts for young people. A complete list of links to guide you to the various book award websites and lists, as well as brief descriptions of the different book awards, is included with the additional resources on the F&P Resources Site.

Evaluating Fiction Texts

In addition to keeping an eye out for award winners, you need to evaluate works of fiction on your own. Throughout their comprehensive textbook, Kiefer and her colleagues (2010) have identified some key questions to ask as you evaluate children's literature. The list in Figure 6.6 is drawn from that work. Many questions apply to all fiction texts, but some are specific to contemporary realism, historical fiction, and fantasy.

We hope that this chapter has helped you to think about the characteristics of a variety of fiction texts. This information will be helpful to you as you think about selecting books for different purposes across the language and literacy framework. Some of this information will be appropriate (related to their level of sophistication) to teach your students, but the larger purpose is to expand your own thinking about the quality and variety you provide for students. We will expand our discussion of fiction texts in subsequent chapters when we talk about the demands they place on readers.

QUESTIONS TO ASK WHEN EVALUATING FICTION TEXTS	
All Fiction Texts	• Does the plot tell a good story that readers will enjoy? • Is there action that will engage readers? • Does the plot build toward a credible resolution? • Does the story communicate big ideas over and above the particular setting and plot? • Does the theme emerge naturally from the story? • Does the writer avoid obvious themes and moralizing? • Are the characters appealing, well developed, and believable? • Does the writer show how and why characters change? • Does the writer avoid cultural, racial, and geographic stereotypes? • Is the style of writing appropriate for the plot, purpose, and age group intended? • Is the point of view appropriate to the story? • Are the illustrations of high quality? • Do the illustrations extend meaning, communicate mood, or enhance the reading experience? • How well designed is the format of the book? • What is the quality of the book (paper, binding, cover)?
Realistic Fiction (Contemporary)	• Is the plot believable and authentic in today's world? • Does the story reflect problems typical of the age range intended? • Do the themes have authenticity today? • Is the description of the setting currently authentic? • Does the writer describe characters that readers can relate to and empathize with?
Historical Fiction	• Are the description of the setting and the events of the plot accurate and authentic for the period of history? • Are enough details provided to enable the reader to understand the setting? • Is the story interesting and relevant for today's children although set in the past? • Is there a good balance between fact and interesting narrative? • Does the writer do a good job explaining the perspectives of characters who live in the time period? • Does the writer use language and expressions appropriate to the time period? • Does the text help children understand the problems of the past in a way that helps them think about their own lives? • Does the story illuminate today's problems? In what ways?
Fantasy	• Has the writer described the setting in a way that readers can understand? • Is the story logical and consistent within the world the writer has described? • Does the story communicate universal truths that readers can understand? • Is the story original and engaging? • Does the writer describe characters that are believable? • How has the writer made the fantasy elements believable within the story?

Figure 6.6 Questions to ask when evaluating fiction texts

Suggestions for Professional Development

1. Schedule a meeting with grade-level or cross-grade-level colleagues to discuss fiction texts and get to know a greater range of books.
2 Bring four novels and four picture storybooks appropriate for your grade level, two that are very popular with your students and two that you especially like. Sharing the titles and contents among yourselves.
3. Place all the books into genre groups. Ask:
   - What genres are best represented?
   - What genres are missing?
   - Are there some popular authors?
   - What implications does this information have for independent reading (book talks), guided reading, and literature study?
4. Discuss the books you and your colleagues have selected as high quality using the questions in Figure 6.6. Discuss the characteristics of the books.
5. Now discuss the books your students find most interesting. Add to your list using a different color or prepare a separate chart. Discuss:
   - What makes these books so appealing to students?
   - Are there differences between the books teachers think are good and the books students think are appealing?
   - What implications does this discussion have for your teaching—read aloud, independent reading, guided reading, and literature study?

CHAPTER 7

Realism in Fiction Texts

Contemporary Realistic and Historical Fiction

Realistic fiction serves children in the process of understanding and coming to terms with themselves as they acquire "human-ness."

—Charlotte Huck

Realism as a genre is a relatively recent addition to our literary history. According to Buss and Karnowski (2000), Defoe's *Robinson Crusoe,* written in 1719, marked the beginning of realism as a genre. Today realism is popular among all audiences. We like realism because, although the writer draws from his reality or life experience, it often intersects with our own and/or becomes ours (O'Conner 2010). In this chapter we take a closer look at both contemporary realistic fiction and historical fiction, and the demands these texts make on readers (see Figure 7.1). At the end of this chapter you will find a list of mentor texts for both contemporary realistic fiction and historical fiction. These are suggested titles to be used as exemplars of the genre, but you may have excellent examples of your own that you prefer to use. These mentor texts may be used to build text sets for interactive read-aloud or book clubs. We do not advocate engaging in a focused genre study of historical fiction for grades K–1 or 2–3, though you may find high-quality historical fiction picture books appropriate to these grade levels for reading aloud.

Both contemporary realistic fiction and historical fiction can take a variety of forms—mysteries, adventure or survival stories, family stories, or a combination of forms. They both use literary elements, including characters, plot, and setting. They can be written in straight narrative style or in poetic style; they can take the form of letters or diaries.

The main difference between contemporary realistic fiction and historical fiction is that the latter is set in the past—a simple but significant difference! When readers process contemporary realistic fiction, settings

REALISM		
Imagined stories that take place in the real world, either past or present, and recount events that could really happen.		
Genre	**Definition**	**Characteristics**
Realistic Fiction (Contemporary)	An imagined story set in the real world that portrays life as it could be lived today, and focuses on the problems and issues of today.	• Imagined story but set in the real world • Has narrative structure with characters, plot, and setting • Portrays life as it could be lived today • Focuses on the problems and issues of living today Often: • Has convincing and believable characters, plot, and setting • Based on real events • Tells about relationships between people and sometimes animals • Has bigger themes (universal implications) • Represents diverse perspectives and cultures • Helps us to understand people and our world
Historical Fiction	An imagined story set in the real world that portrays life as it might have been lived in the past, and focuses on the problems and issues of life in the past.	• Imagined story but set in the real world • Has narrative structure with characters, plot, and setting • Portrays life as it might have been lived in the past • Focuses on problems and issues of life in the past Often: • Has convincing and believable characters, plot, and setting • Based on real people or events from the past • Connected to the author's own personal experiences • Begins as contemporary fiction but has been around long enough to acquire historical significance • Uses old-fashioned language in dialogue • Communicates important understandings of history

Figure 7.1 Characteristics of realism

may be familiar and easily integrated into their experiences. At other times, although the setting is still contemporary, it may be unfamiliar and the writer may have to help readers understand them. For example, as you read *Muktar and the Camels* (Graber 2009), you may absorb a great deal that is new to you about the nomadic life of some Somali people.

In historical fiction, the setting is almost always different from the reader's experience (unless it takes place in a time the reader remembers, which is not likely for our students). The writer of historical fiction has to paint a picture of times past, and there are often challenges associated with doing so. The writer must present the authentic perspectives and language of the people who lived during a specific time; however, he must also take care not to endorse all the beliefs and prejudices of the time. For example, the setting for *Foster's War* (Reeder 2000) is World War II. An author's note warns the reader that although the derogatory term *Jap* is used in some of the book's dialogue, it is done to authentically re-create a specific place and time period.

The Value of Realistic Fiction

Realism allows authors to present a vast and colorful array of human lives and experiences to their readers. By experiencing this variety, students can develop their preferences and tastes as readers. They can begin with books that are close to their own lives, but they can also broaden their horizons. Realism enables readers to learn from the struggles of others. The vicarious experiences readers have help them develop empathy for others in modern times and to understand the hardships that people endured in the past.

Contemporary Realistic Fiction

Students tend to like contemporary realistic fiction because it closely mirrors real life. They can identify with characters that are about their own age (or a little older) and who experience problems similar to their own.

Common Themes

An exciting or interesting plot and memorable characters are the elements that attract students to realistic fiction, but you also want these texts to have a larger message. Readers learn from books as the theme is identified and absorbed. Most realistic stories have a primary theme and may also have several secondary themes that are linked to the primary theme in some way. Some of the larger themes that appeal to students, along with examples, are:

- *Living in a family.* These books emphasize family relationships and the day-to-day challenges, rewards, and humor of families living together. In *The Relatives Came* (Rylant 1993), a raucous and loving crowd of relatives arrives for an extended stay at a rural home. In Beverly Cleary's Beezus and Ramona series, the focus is on the relationship between the precocious Ramona and her older sister Beezus.
- *Finding peer acceptance.* In *Rules* (Lord 2008), twelve-year-old Catherine struggles to balance the love she has for her younger, autistic brother, with her desire to fit in and be "normal." With great humor and insight, the book chronicles Catherine's attempts to form new friendships while coming to accept her family's unique challenges.
- *Becoming one's own person.* Many of today's contemporary realistic fiction books deal with the difficulties of forging one's own identity, especially for immigrants or children from other cultures. In *My Name is Yoon* (Recorvits 2003), a Korean girl struggles to hold onto her Korean identity while embracing her new "American" self.
- *Making and keeping friends.* In *Enemy Pie* (Munson 2000), the perfect summer for a young boy is ruined when a new boy moves into the neighborhood and becomes his "number one enemy." Fortunately, with a father's help, the two boys become friends.

- *Growing up.* In *Becoming Naomi Leon* (Ryan 2004), the eleven-year-old Mexican-American protagonist, Naomi, must contend with changes and challenges both at home and at school.
- *Learning about sexuality.* Judy Blume has written several timeless classics about young people and sexuality, including *Are You There God? It's Me, Margaret* (1970) and *Then Again, Maybe I Won't* (1971). A more contemporary book is *The Secret Blog of Raisin Rodriguez* (Goldschmidt 2006), which deals with those same issues.
- *Coping with human problems.* Books in this category can run the gamut from moving to a new home to coping with divorce, illness, and death. In *Fred Stays with Me!* (Coffelt 2007), a small girl's bond with her pet dog, Fred, helps her navigate the new territory of her parents' divorce.

The themes above, among many others, support students as they encounter the challenges of growing up. They make connections with their own lives and experiences, and as they read more, they make meaningful connections across texts.

Demands on the Reader

For all realistic fiction, you need to ask, *what are readers asked to do in order to understand what they are reading?* Students who experience a variety of texts stretch their processing powers by meeting the demands for comprehension.

You might assume that contemporary realistic fiction exists mainly to provide entertainment, but this genre is quite demanding. If books in this genre are read at a superficial level—as a series of events with characters that you take at face value—then your understanding and even your enjoyment is not as deep. Inherently, human beings find pleasure in thinking and learning something new, and realistic fiction, even though it is not "true," provides this opportunity. The demands that realistic fiction makes on readers are summarized in Figure 7.2.

Deeper thinking about texts requires that you derive the author's message(s), but there are many variations in interpretation. What a text means to one reader might be different from what it means to another; nevertheless, a well-crafted text guides you to seek the writer's meaning.

An example of a realistic fiction text with an explicit message is *Bag in the Wind* (Kooser 2010), a picture book that could be read aloud to older students.

CONTEMPORARY REALISTIC FICTION: DEMANDS ON THE READER

- Consider point of view or perspective of the author.
- Understand literary elements such as figurative language.
- Identify the important characters and secondary characters.
- Identify the conflict or problem of the story.
- Understand the prominent theme or author's message.
- Understand characters from how they look; what they do, think, or say; and what others say or think about them.
- Follow the events of the plot and make predictions about its resolution.
- Understand the meaning and significance of the climax or plot resolution.
- Relate the primary message or theme to our own life–make the story our own.
- Remember important parts of the story to relate it to other texts.

Figure 7.2 Contemporary realistic fiction: demands on the reader

In this book, the writer traces the journey of a yellow plastic grocery bag as a way to promote reuse and recycling. Another realistic text, *Orange Peel's Pocket* (Lewis and Zong 2010), has a meaning that requires deeper understanding. An adopted Chinese American child realizes that she knows little about her birthplace. She travels around her neighborhood collecting not just mementos but valuable information about her heritage from each of the shop proprietors she meets along the way. On one level, the story is simple; on a deeper level, readers can understand that:

- Each adult tells Orange Peel something very important about her birth country and gives her an object that symbolizes it.
- Her adopted mother (not Chinese—a detail learned only from the illustrations) supports Orange Peel in learning about her birth country.
- The writer places the red silk knot (for luck) last in the story (to be discovered by Orange Peel right before her talk) to make the story more interesting.
- The writer wants to show respect for elders.
- The illustrations show Orange Peel's thinking as she imagines the different aspects of China.

Other understandings would no doubt emerge from an in-depth discussion of the book.

Characters

Realistic fiction is all about characters. In previous times, fiction for children was often didactic, with "perfect" characters. An extreme example is *Elsie Dinsmore* (Finley 1867/1999). The main character always behaves perfectly and is therefore not believable to modern-day readers. Believable characters have flaws, just like real human beings, and we like to read books that involve imperfect families and a variety of relationships, some dysfunctional (O'Conner 2010). You recognize both the naughtiness of the young boy David in *No, David!* (Shannon 1998), and the exasperation and love of his mother. You admire the engaging quirkiness of Marshal in *Marshal Armstrong is New to Our School* (Mackintosh 2011) as he goes against the crowd. Characters who appear in longer books with more complex plots are often more complex as well. Understanding these more complex characters can create greater challenges for the reader. The reader must gather information about the character not just from what the author describes directly, but also by inferring information from the way the character behaves, the character's dialogue with others, and the thoughts of the character or thoughts of others about the character. Readers will come to know more complex characters slowly over the course of the story rather than all at once and in a superficial way. The reader must pick up on more subtle clues about character, and this is both challenging and rewarding.

Plot

Readers of realistic fiction must follow the plot—what happens in the story after the exposition of the problem, which sets the plot in motion. Most fiction follows a pattern called *progressive plot*, in which a series of events takes place, all of them tied to the same story line (Buss and Karnowski 2000). Readers need to realize how the events in the story are related to the whole story line and the problem. Some realistic fiction involves a series of separate episodes that don't necessarily follow one another but are related through the setting or the characters. *Seedfolks* (Fleischman 2004) has an episodic plot, a series of stories that take place in an inner-city neighborhood. The narrator changes every chapter so that each of several characters is telling a story, yet all the stories are related to the main story line and message. The more complex the plot, the greater the challenges to the reader, especially when techniques like flashbacks and foreshadowing are introduced.

One element, not always in keeping with reality, that readers of realism still desire and expect is a satisfying ending. Writers of fiction must always work hard to find a balance between creating a believable story and satisfying the reader. The reader of realistic fiction is always implicitly asking, *Is this real? Do I believe it?* and finally, *Do I like it?*

Writer's Message

A major demand of realistic fiction is to grasp the writer's message and even to go beyond it with your own interpretations, although you may not consciously set out to identify the message. You may sit down to read fiction for a variety of reasons, but your goal isn't usually to find out the writer's message. You just want to enjoy a good book. But true comprehension—and in the process, true enjoyment—comes from reading about a series of events and resulting actions of characters and finding greater meaning in them.

A critical part of deep understanding is using the structure of the story to help you derive the messages. Readers of realistic fiction need to understand the structure of the story in order to follow the plot. In the previous chapter, we described narrative structure, which is characteristic of works of contemporary realism. On one level, story structure can be very simple: introduction of the characters, setting, and problem and a series of episodes building to problem resolution. But narrative structure can be very complex.

Fiction texts sometimes have challenging structures, such as stories within stories or flashbacks that challenge the reader to understand how the story is unfolding. Additionally, readers are required to enter fully into the story, and it helps if the writer has given the reader a coherent plot in which details fit together.

Readers must attend to important details that are related to the resolution of the problem or to understanding characters. You also must infer from the writing the motivations of characters and what they are like as people. Certainly, the farther the story is from the reader's own experience, the more background knowledge (or knowledge of other texts) is needed to understand the events and characters. Readers have to follow the events of the plot and make predictions as to future events and plot resolution.

Understanding of messages and enjoyment are increased if you understand the literary devices (such as figurative language) the writer uses. In addition, you must not only grasp the larger message, or theme, of the story but also connect it to your own life. Finally, every text read can be connected to the future reading we will do as literate persons. Simply finishing a book without reflecting on it in a way that leads you to remember something important about it will not contribute to your life as a reader. Readers make connections between characters, themes, and settings. These connections increase comprehension and lead to more reading.

Historical Fiction

There are certain universal human problems and issues that seem to remain constant through the ages. As students read historical fiction, they see that people from times past experienced the same hopes and fears that we do today. However, these hopes and fears are played out in different ways according to the customs and events of the times in which the story is based.

The Value of Historical Fiction

An essential genre in the classroom library, historical fiction makes several important contributions. According to Rycik and Rosler (2009), contemporary realism has tended to dominate the awards for children's books (Newbery Medal and Honor winners). But in recent years, the popularity of historical fiction has been on the rise. For example *Elijah of Buxton* (Curtis 2009), the story of the first freeborn citizen in a Canadian settlement of escaped slaves, won both the Coretta Scott King Award and was a Newbery Honor book (see the additional resources on the F&P Resources Site). Reading historical fiction:

- Breathes life into the events of the past.
- Helps readers value the events and accomplishments of the past.
- Helps readers vicariously experience life in the past.
- Encourages readers to integrate fact and fiction and to distinguish between the two.
- Helps readers see the challenges of the past more clearly.
- Helps readers view the present from a larger perspective.

Historical fiction can be read purely for entertainment, but high-quality historical fiction can also be used to teach history (Rycik and Rosler 2009). In addition to delivering the values listed above, historical fiction should provide good stories that students like to read. As with all fiction, characters should be well developed and plots should be interesting and believable. Well-written historical fiction will help readers understand more about the writer's craft.

Influence of Setting on Theme and Plot

The setting in historical fiction is usually quite important to the plot. For example, *A Time of Angels* (Hesse 2000), set in 1918, depicts the main character, Hannah, living in a crowded tenement in Boston while separated from her parents during World War I. They battle a flu epidemic and Hannah nearly dies. The reader needs to understand that during that time period, influenza was much more dangerous than it is today; and it would also be helpful for the reader to know something about what life was like for poor immigrants. The historical novel *Catherine, Called Birdy* (Cushman 1995) tells the story of a spirited girl living in medieval times. Although at that time women were considered chattel, Catherine successfully outwits the suitors her father tries to force on her. Understanding the times is essential to appreciating the way the writer has drawn the character.

In *Jump Ship to Freedom* (Collier 1987), Daniel and his mother are slaves. Their owner has stolen the money Daniel's father earned to free them. Caught stealing it back, Daniel is forced aboard a ship that is sailing to the West Indies—and certain slavery. The time period and setting are important to understanding the dangers Daniel faces, and the writer makes Daniel's actions reasonable and believable in the circumstances.

Each story above depends on the setting for the development of plot and characters. The people's actions and their character are related to particular circumstances they face—circumstances that are often radically different from those faced by people today. Nevertheless, as characters, they must face and overcome fear, sadness, and loneliness, just like people today.

Common Themes

In addition to the themes that occur frequently in all realism, historical fiction has some particular themes, including:

- *The devastation of war. The Fighting Ground* (Avi 1994) is the story of a thirteen-year-old boy who runs away to fight in the Revolutionary War and comes to understand himself and his father better.
- *The search for freedom. Jump Ship to Freedom* (Collier 1987) depicts the hardships and risks faced by enslaved people and the courageous lengths they went to in search of freedom.
- *Changes over time in culture and attitudes.* Set in 1945, *Year of Impossible Goodbyes* (Choi 1991), is the story of ten-year-old Sookan and her family, who endure the cruelties of the Japanese occupation of Korea and find their culture virtually destroyed.
- *The helplessness individuals feel when caught up in larger changes and events.* In *The Watsons Go to Birmingham—1963* (Curtis 2000), a family gets caught up in events surrounding the civil rights movement of the 1960s during a visit to relatives in the South. The novel *Annexed* (Dogar 2010) tells the story of Anne Frank from another perspective—that of her friend Peter, whose family shared the secret room the Frank family hid in during the war.

In the examples above, imagined human feelings take place against a background of significant historical events. Perhaps the major advantage readers of historical fiction have is the realization that during those times, real people lived—people like us.

Demands on the Reader

Historical fiction challenges readers in ways similar to and in addition to contemporary realistic fiction (see Figure 7.3). As with contemporary realistic fiction, readers are required to follow the plot, understand characters, and discern the major theme or message, but historical fiction makes some additional demands. As you read historical fiction, you are integrating factual knowledge of the past with an imagined plot and set of characters. Historical fiction may require more background knowledge to understand. Readers of all types of fiction need to be able to follow and understand the dialogue that brings a character to life (O'Conner 2010). But in the case of historical fiction, the reader may have to understand dialogue that is far different from his own speech. The writer may use archaic language—both words and language structures—to make characters more authentic.

HISTORICAL FICTION: DEMANDS ON THE READER
■ Consider point of view or perspective.
■ Make hypotheses about why the author has selected the time in history and setting to tell the story.
■ Understand literary elements such as figurative language.
■ Understand archaic language authentic to time and place.
■ Identify the important characters and secondary characters.
■ Sort out imaginary characters from authentic historical characters.
■ Identify the conflict or problem of the story.
■ Understand the problem in the light of historical events and problems.
■ Understand the prominent theme or author's message.
■ Understand characters from how they look; what they do, think, or say; and what others say or think about them.
■ Understand characters in the light of the culture, time in history, and physical setting.
■ Follow the events of the plot and make predictions as to resolution.
■ Distinguish imaginary events from authentic historical events.
■ Understand the meaning and significance of the climax or plot resolution.
■ Relate the primary message or theme to your own life–make the story your own.
■ Relate present events and circumstances to those of the past.
■ Remember important parts of the story to relate it to other texts and/or check the authenticity of the story.
■ Sort out fact from fiction before, during, and after reading a text.

Figure 7.3 Historical fiction: demands on the reader

The reader is required to sort out fiction from authentic events and characters from the past. You may speculate on why the author chose the particular time, setting, or culture within which to play out the major theme of the story, and you will want to understand the problem or characters' actions and motivations in light of the setting. As part of reading critically, you should evaluate the text's accuracy when reporting real events.

Types of Realistic Fiction

It is important to have a wide variety of realistic fiction texts to use when reading aloud, when asking students to choose books to read independently, and during small-group discussions (either guided reading or book clubs). It is by experiencing variety that you begin to know your own taste as a reader.

The content, organization, and characteristics of fiction texts are highly interrelated and influence one another. Some text types (mystery, for example) have been called subgenres, but a mystery simply presents the reader with a puzzle to solve; it is organized so that the reader continuously looks for information. A mystery can be historical or contemporary fiction, it can be fantasy or science fiction, and that overlap is true of most of these types of texts—many fit into more than one category.

A special type of text is a popular and well-read kind of text distinguished by its content. The special

SPECIAL TYPES OF FICTION TEXTS		
Type	**Definition**	**Characteristics**
Mystery	Stories dealing with the solution of a crime or the unraveling of secrets.	• Characters seem real • Can be realistic or fantasy • Setting can be today, the past, or the future • Main character can be detective or spy • Problem or crime needs to be solved • Need to think of motives of characters to solve the mystery • Main character looks for clues • Usually one or more suspects • Need to put together clues to try to solve the problem or crime while reading • Some clues hidden and not obvious • Mystery solved at the end, sometimes there's a surprise • May have misleading clues (red herrings) • Suspenseful • Gaps the reader needs to fill to solve the mystery • Foreshadowing helps the reader notice clues
Crime	Stories of how a criminal committed a crime and was (usually) brought to justice	• Someone breaks the law • Often is about murder • Includes violence • Tells why the crime was committed • Tells about the victim • Has characters in law enforcement • Usually has science or technology • Criminals usually caught and punished and sometimes killed • Good characters and bad characters • Strong characters who have flaws
Survival	Stories in which a character or characters must struggle against nature or other people in order to stay alive	• Main character struggles to stay alive • Main character has or learns skills to stay alive • Can involve struggle against nature or people • Can involve science and technology • Setting can be the past, present, or future • Can be realistic or fantasy • Characters become stronger • Characters may change during ordeal

Figure 7.4 Special types of fiction texts

continues

SPECIAL TYPES OF FICTION TEXTS		
Type	**Definition**	**Characteristics**
Adventure	Stories that presents a series of exciting events; often involves journeys or dangerous and suspenseful events	• Exciting story • Usually a journey to an exciting place • Setting is a place with danger • Danger from natural causes • Has a hero who is brave • Has a lot of action and not too much description • Characters keep moving; fast paced • Has human or natural enemies • Sometimes hero has a mission or quest • Sometimes has mystery • Can be realistic or fantasy • Can be told in first person or third person
Horror	Stories in which events evoke a feeling of dread in both the characters and the reader	• Good and evil characters that may be human or animal • Monsters and beastlike characters • Usually includes violence • Struggle of good and evil • Includes victims
Humorous Stories	Stories that are full of fun and that are meant to entertain	• Can occur in all genres • Compares things in funny ways • Characters say and do funny things • Makes fun of people and/or animal characters • Has language that is funny (like what characters say or the narrative)
Animal Stories	Stories that provide the experience of relating to, loving, and caring for animals; often focuses on the relationships between humans and animals	• Real stories about pets, domestic animals, and wild animals • Stories that could really happen • Characters learn and change (human and animals) • Tells about the feelings humans and animals have for each other • Helps the reader learn more about animals • Sometimes has a sad ending
Sports Stories	Stories that revolve around specific individual and team sports	• Tells about the sport–the rules and the action • A lot of action, some of it games in which the sport is played • Suspenseful • Winning and losing • Shows characters' motivations and love of the sport • Often tells about teamwork

Figure 7.4 Special types of fiction texts *(cont.)*

SPECIAL TYPES OF FICTION TEXTS		
Type	**Definition**	**Characteristics**
		• Tells about working hard to be good at the sport • Tells about overcoming challenges
Stories About Family, Friends, and School	Stories that focus on the everyday experiences of children of a variety of ages, including relationships with family and friends and experiences at school	• Tells about the setting • Characters can be of all ages • Characters struggle with family relationships • Characters want to make friends and encounter the ups and downs of friendship • Characters relate to one another as friends and enemies at school • Problems related to school—studies, sports, friendship • Relationships with teachers
Romance	Stories that focus on the development of romantic and sexual love between characters; may be contemporary or historical	• Believable characters • Tells about love between people • Tells about competition • Settings realistic in today's world—usually school or neighborhood • Disappointments and happiness • A believable outcome • Ending may be happy or sad • Characters change and learn
Westerns	Stories that use a setting in the Western United States or in cattle herding areas of other countries; often historical	• Believable characters • Setting is important—either past or present but involving horses • Rural or ranch settings • Conflict between good and evil • Some violence • Elements of survival
Satire	Texts that prominently use satire—type of writing that uses ridicule or scorn in a humorous way to expose vices and follies; often embedded in a text	• Uses sarcasm • Uses irony • Ridicules or makes fun of some human weaknesses or foolishness • Comments on society • Offers alternatives • Tone of mockery • Has a point of view that the reader agrees with or not • Requires figuring out what is being made fun of and why • Requires looking beyond the text to the deeper meanings the writer is expressing

Figure 7.4 Special types of fiction texts *(cont.)*

types of texts in Figure 7.4 are those most common in realistic fiction. (In Chapter 8 we discuss fantasy and refer back to Figure 7.4, because each of these types can also occur in fantasy and science fiction.)

Mystery

Mystery stories follow a formula; the problem is to solve a puzzle or crime. Mysteries may consume readers! Nina Sankovitch (2011) writes of her sister, an art historian: "Mysteries were her candy, her vodka tonic, her bubble bath. She loved mysteries rich in detail, deep with atmosphere, and dark in motive." (p. 6) The protagonist moves through a series of events in search of clues. Elements of surprise and suspense are often present. Main characters tend to be round, but supporting characters are often flat. However, the main character is not always required to be dynamic (for example, Sherlock Holmes remains essentially unchanged throughout the entire series of Sherlock Holmes mysteries). At the end of the story, the puzzle or mystery is solved; usually there is conflict between the main character (the sleuth) and the villain.

In some mysteries, characters solve intricate puzzles, as in *The Westing Game* (Raskin 1997). Others involve a detective at work, following clues, as in *Coffin on a Case* (Bunting 1993). Readers in the elementary grades may be introduced to mysteries through series like Nate the Great or Encyclopedia Brown. Although these are formula fiction, they do reveal the structure of mysteries. In the Nate the Great series, the main character, Nate, uses some of the "hard-boiled" language that foreshadows more mature mystery or detective stories:

> I, Nate the Great, sat down
> next to a noisy cat.
> This case was going
> slower than the tortoise.
> This case had come to
> a dead end. (26)

Many young readers get hooked on series mysteries that have been popular for generations and are still read today, such as Nancy Drew and the Hardy Boys. These series are formulaic but do give readers "mileage" because they can be read quickly. Predictability has value. Sankovitch says that "mysteries tell me there is order in the universe" (p. 192). At the same time, there are many new mystery series, such as the danger.com series by Jordan Cray; the popular *The 39 Clues* series (various authors); and the Cabin Creek mysteries by Kristiana Gregory. Although parents and teachers often discourage reading mystery series as well as other series books, it does readers no harm to devour hundreds of these books! Students tend to read to a satiation point and then move on, but in the process they have increased their vocabulary and reading efficiency. You wouldn't want students to read *only* series books, but that will not happen if you have plenty of high-quality texts on hand and are always talking about them. A natural next step is to provide some more substantive mysteries.

Although some mysteries are formulaic, many others have well developed characters and strong themes. In *The Way to Sattin Shore* (Pearce 1994), a young girl pieces together evidence surrounding the mystery of her missing father. *Hoot* (Hiaasen 2005) and *Flush* (Hiaasen 2010) are humorous and suspenseful mysteries set in the contemporary world. In contrast, *The Other Side of Dark* (Nixon 2011) is a darker story with a young heroine who wakes from a four-year coma to discover her mother was murdered and the killer is probably looking for her. These mysteries give readers all the enjoyment of solving a puzzle, as well as suspense, but also deal with human issues and problems.

Mysteries can also be historical fiction or even fantasy. In *The House of Dies Drear* a family moves into a Civil War–era house that was once a critical stop on the Underground Railroad, and the main character must piece together clues to learn the dangerous truth about the past.

Mysteries demand active, attentive reading. You have to notice and interpret details that might not be so important in other kinds of texts. The reader is actively searching for information throughout the book in order to solve the central puzzle.

Crime

Mysteries often involve crime, but there are also stories that focus on crime or violence and don't necessarily involve a mystery. A character breaks the law, and violence is often involved. The reader learns how and why the crime was committed, and the perpetrator is brought to justice. Crime novels usually have strong characters (who are good but often flawed), and there is usually a strong contrast between good and bad characters. At the elementary and middle school level, crime stories likely also involve mystery; straight crime stories tend to be more popular with adults, as evidenced by bestselling authors like James Patterson. Many of the stories involving crime for younger readers also focus on social issues and mature content. Walter Dean Myers' *Monster* (2001) follows a sixteen-year-old on trial for murder. *When Dad Killed Mom* (Lester 2003) follows two children coming to terms with their father's crime. *The Afterlife* (Soto 2005) tells the story of a murder from the perspective of the teenage victim.

Survival

Survival stories offer tense excitement. Intermediate readers can imagine testing themselves in dangerous situations, often pitted against the forces of nature. The main character must overcome adversity in order to stay alive, and often must act alone in doing so. In *A Girl Named Disaster* (Farmer 1997), set in Africa, an eleven-year-old girl flees her village and a horrible marriage and embarks on a year-long journey of survival.

Another kind of survival story involves enduring the inhumanity of fellow human beings. In *After the War* (Matas 1997), fifteen-year-old Ruth, a victim of the Holocaust, risks her life to lead a group of children to Palestine. Stories of the Holocaust illustrate the resilience of the human spirit. Both *Good Night, Maman* (Mazer 2010) and *The Day of the Pelican* (Paterson 2010) are stories in which the main characters must survive extreme hardship and violence related to historical events.

Adventure

Survival stories are certainly adventure stories as well, but you may also encounter stories that don't necessarily involve survival but do involve exciting or suspenseful events. Usually there is a journey to an exciting place, with a setting that involves some danger or at least major challenges. The hero has to be brave, and there is a lot of action. One of the classic science fiction adventure stories is Jules Verne's *Journey to the Center of the Earth* (1864/2007). Another classic, *Paddle-to-the-Sea* (Holling 1941/1980), tells the story of a young Native American boy who sets a carved wooden figure and canoe afloat in Canada; the story follows the adventures of the figure on its journey across lakes and rivers on its way to the Atlantic Ocean. More contemporary popular adventure series are the Magic Tree House series, by Mary Pope Osborne, and the Percy Jackson series, by Rick Riordan; both fall into the fantasy genre.

Horror

Horror stories are related to the vicarious enjoyment of fear. No wonder horror movies are so popular: you can sit safely in a theater but have your senses stimulated by fear. Horror stories appeal to readers for the same reasons, and many students eat them up. These texts often involve elements of fantasy, but they may also fit into the category of realism, in which case they usually involve crime and violence. Mary Downing Hahn has written several ghost stories, including *Wait Till Helen Comes* (2008), that have well-paced plots and fully realized characters who must deal not only with scary occurrences but also with recognizable issues related to family and self-identity.

Humorous Stories

As with all fiction, humorous stories center on a problem, but the writer's interpretation of events has a lighter tone. The characters' actions and dialogue may be funny, or characters may find themselves in hilarious situations.

Humorous fiction engages student readers and is often the impetus for their reading more books by a specific author or additional books in a series. Humorous writing also often employs an element of surprise; it makes readers more aware of the way the author uses language to give characters voice or to describe situations. Judy Blume's *Tales of a Fourth Grade Nothing* and Thomas Rockwell's *How to Eat Fried Worms* are humorous classics. Mo Willems' *Knuffle Bunny* books and Elephant and Piggie series are very funny and well-suited to younger readers.

Animal Stories

Realistic animal stories are believable; the animals do not talk or have human characteristics. You do not know what they think or how they feel, although you may infer fear or pain from the description of events and behavior. These stories may be serious or humorous. *The Incredible Journey* (Burnford 1963, 1997) is the story of three loyal pets who make a challenging and at times harrowing cross-country trek in an attempt to be reunited with their family. Although the animals in the story are the main characters, they do not speak; instead, their actions convey their thoughts and feelings. A stray dog figures strongly in the plot of *Because of Winn-Dixie* (DiCamillo 2000), which also recounts the many serious problems faced by its human characters, including loneliness, abandonment, and alcoholism. *Sable* (Hesse 2010) tells the story of ten-year-old Tate and the challenges she faces with her family and others when she rescues a stray dog. Animal stories like these often allow readers to connect emotionally with the text, since these animal characters often respond to challenges with a simple loyalty and bravery that can seem an antidote to more complex human struggles.

Sports Stories

Like mysteries, sports stories tend to be formulaic. For example, author Matt Christopher's novels in the Peach Street Mudders series are very popular with elementary students who enjoy his exciting descriptions of games and events. It's important to point out, though, that Christopher's characters experience internal conflict as well as the challenge of sportsmanship, and they grow from the experience.

Many sports stories have complex themes that go beyond the simple lessons of teamwork and competition. *Thank You, Jackie Robinson* (Cohen 1997) is a sensitive story in the form of a memoir by a young Jewish boy. His father dead, Sam forms a friendship with an African American cook, Davy, who takes him to see Jackie Robinson. An autographed ball by Robinson becomes a symbol of Sam's devotion to Davy.

Stories About Families, Friends, and School

Much realistic fiction has to do with our relationships with others and our everyday lives. Modern realistic fiction is very popular with elementary and middle school students. They enjoy reading about individuals who share their fears, anxieties, and hopes. They like stories about growing up, like *Dear Mr. Henshaw* (Cleary 1983), and stories about families, like *Fig Pudding* (Fletcher 1996). Andrew Clements is a popular author who has produced many texts that focus on the everyday problems of children: *The Report Card*, (2008), *Frindle* (1998), and *Lost and Found* (2010) among others.

Of course, stories about family, friends, and school are enduringly appealing to young and old readers alike. These themes cut across genre lines, and many good examples can be found in historical fiction as well. The structure of family units, the dialogue and gestures between friends and family members, and the customs and norms of relationships may change over the years, but the underlying challenges and issues often remain the same. It is appealing to young readers to recognize and explore these differences while still relating to characters and emotions.

Romance

As students grow into preadolescence and adolescence, romance becomes increasingly popular, especially for girls. The Sweet Valley High series continues to be popular with many readers, as do other books with themes of romance. Romances focus on the development of romantic and sometimes sexual attraction between characters. Usually, the texts used in school imply sexual attraction rather than describe it explicitly; you have to judge what is appropriate in your own setting. Not all romances are flimsy or formulaic. Eve Bunting's novel *Jumping the Nail* (1993) is the story of two teenagers who must struggle to preserve their growing romance and make difficult decisions in the face of opposition from their friends.

Westerns

Western stories have been popular for a long time, but their popularity peaked in the 1960s and has declined steadily since then. A western is a fictional story set in the rural parts of the American West, primarily in the latter half of the 19th century, though some are set in more contemporary times. This kind of text often describes a time when cattle ranching was a booming industry and people's imaginations were taken with the idea and romance of the vast, empty landscapes of the west. Westerns often involve strong, tough characters who must pit themselves against the harsh elements and customs of the rugged west. Sometimes these characters are flat and unchanging, but there are more complex characters and plots in some westerns, and many feature a central male character on a journey to adulthood. *My Friend Flicka* (O'Hara 1941/2008) is a classic Western tale. Set on a ranch in Wyoming in the 1940s, it's the story of young Ken, the son of a strict and demanding rancher father. Ken struggles to find his own identity as he tries to please his father and ultimately gains confidence and strength by raising and training his loyal horse, Flicka. Another classic western, *The Red Pony* (Steinbeck 1937/1994), chronicles the boyhood of young Jody Tiflin and his relationship with his rancher father. The natural elements and the rugged landscape play a major part in both of these stories and in the characters' lives.

Satire

We place satire here because it applies to very sophisticated works of fiction that are related in intentional ways to the real world. Satire is also a writing technique, one that mocks or makes fun of some aspect of society. But we call works that are dominated by this technique *satires*. In satire, the writer uses sarcasm and irony to ridicule human weaknesses or foolishness. The satire is a comment on society, and the reader is required to consider this view and agree or disagree with it. Satire requires a high level of thinking; it cannot be truly understood at a superficial level. The classic example is Jonathan Swift's essay "A Modest Proposal" (1729), in which the author proposes that poor people eat their young as a solution to poverty. Swift's *Gulliver's Travels* (1726) mocks society's bureaucratic aspects. In *The Pushcart War* (Merrill 1964), war breaks out between truck drivers and pushcart peddlers in New York City. *The Butter Battle Book* (Seuss 1984) is a commentary on the foolishness and futility of war.

Exploring Mature Themes

In the past several decades, both contemporary realistic fiction and historical realistic fiction have broadened students' worlds by helping them understand a wide range of human problems, including death, divorce and remarriage, poverty, mental illness, physical disability, child abuse, aging, war, and prejudice. In *Lyddie* readers come to understand the courage it takes for a young girl to endure the hard work of a nineteenth-century textile mill. The narrative in the Tillerman series, by Cynthia Voigt, follows the day-to-day struggle for survival of the four Tillerman children, while *Missing May* (Rylant 1993) and *The Higher Power of Lucky* (Patron 2008) deal with complex contemporary issues of loss, loneliness, and self-identity.

Realism: Learning About Ourselves and Others

Realism enables student readers to learn from the struggles of others. The vicarious experiences they encounter helps them develop empathy for their contemporaries and understand the hardships people just like themselves endured in the past. Many avid readers experience finishing a compelling text as "waking up." They have been immersed in another world—experiencing a range of emotions—and they think and talk about the characters long after reading. Their lives have been changed, if even in a small way, through the experience of fiction.

Suggestions for Professional Development

OPTION 1: Meet with grade-level colleagues to examine realism in fiction texts.

- Prepare for the meeting by selecting four books: two contemporary realistic fiction books and two historical fiction books. You may want to consult the lists of mentor texts that we have provided at the end of this chapter.
- These books should be appropriate for average students at your grade level. They may be required by the school curriculum but in any case should be easily available.
- Use the values listed in this chapter (as well as Figure 4.4 in Chapter 4) to help you make your selection.
- Ask every member of the group to read all four books and to come to the meeting prepared to talk about them. (Work in small groups if you have more than six or seven people.) You may also decide to jigsaw these books to save time, assigning a few people to each text.
- For each book:
    - Talk about the demands this text makes on readers. What will readers need to understand to comprehend this book?
    - List the demands made by each book on chart paper. Then compare your lists across the texts. How is contemporary realistic fiction different from historical fiction?

OPTION 2: Work with grade-level colleagues (and across grade levels) to explore your students' preferences in realistic and historicalal fiction books.

- Before meeting, make a list of the most popular realistic and historical fiction being read in your class. Are there particularly popular series that fall within these genres?
    - If you have reader's notebooks, go through the list of books they have read.
    - If not, interview them. You might also convene the entire class and ask them to help you make a list on chart paper of their favorite books. If they are aware of the different genres, ask them to specifically list their favorite realistic or historical fiction books. If not, keep the list general and you can sort the list yourself after the discussion. Ask them if there is a particular series they really enjoy.
- Bring your list to the meeting.
    - First, talk with grade-level colleagues about the books your students are reading.
    - Make a combined list of the most popular titles and series in the realism category (remember this includes realistic and historical fiction).
    - Compare your lists across grade levels.
    - Discuss what this list tells you about your students as readers. How do preferences change across grade levels?
    - If you notice that many of your students' choices are series books, draw some conclusions about the role of series books.
    - You may want to evaluate whether you have adequate variety and breadth of realistic and historical fiction (series and otherwise) in your classroom.
    - If one or two series or texts emerge as very popular, analyze the text, asking: What is engaging to the readers?
    - If you had difficulty compiling this list because your students are not reading in these two genres, talk about why that might be and how you might increase interest in realistic and/or historical fiction.
    - If you have time, make a list of other non-series realistic fiction and historical texts you know that might have the same qualities of the most popular books/series you have listed to broaden the range of choices you can offer your students.

CHAPTER 8

Fantasy in Fiction Texts

Traditional Literature and Modern Fantasy

A good fantasy is deeply rooted in human experience.

—Nikki Gamble and Sally Yates

Traditional literature and modern fantasy, including science fiction, allow you to soar above the confines of the real world while keeping you grounded in the familiar world of human experience. Often, it is the fantastic flight from reality that allows these stories to reveal universal truths. In high-quality fantasy you learn a great deal about yourself, and the characters in these stories are some of the most unforgettable you will meet: Goldilocks, Peter Rabbit, the Mad Hatter, Willy Wonka, Harry Potter, Bilbo Baggins, and hundreds of others. Many fantasy and traditional literature stories have become classics, and readers are likely to return to them again and again.

Good fantasy must be rooted in reality to be believable—even while introducing you to something that never was and never could be. You accept that Snow White would fall asleep for a very long time, only to be awakened years later by a prince's kiss. To be believable, fantasy must have internal consistency. The writer of fantasy creates new laws—different from the real world—but then must live within them. The plot and setting must have an inner logic that readers can understand. Characters should be believable within the setting. At the end of this chapter you will find a list of mentor texts for traditional literature and modern fantasy. These suggested titles can be used as exemplars of the genre, but you may have excellent examples of your own that you prefer to use. These mentor texts may be used to build text sets, and for interactive read-aloud or book clubs.

For the most part, traditional literature and fantasy stand the test of time. Contemporary realistic fiction can become dated, but the fantasy world has a long life simply because it is a product of the imagination. Many good works of fantasy appear as sequels; once a compelling character has been created, readers want to visit the imaginary world of that character again.

The genres of fantasy include traditional literature, modern fantasy, and science fiction (see Figure 8.1). Traditional literature includes folktales, fairy tales, fables, legends, epics, ballads, and myths. These tales have been handed down through centuries; they originated in oral

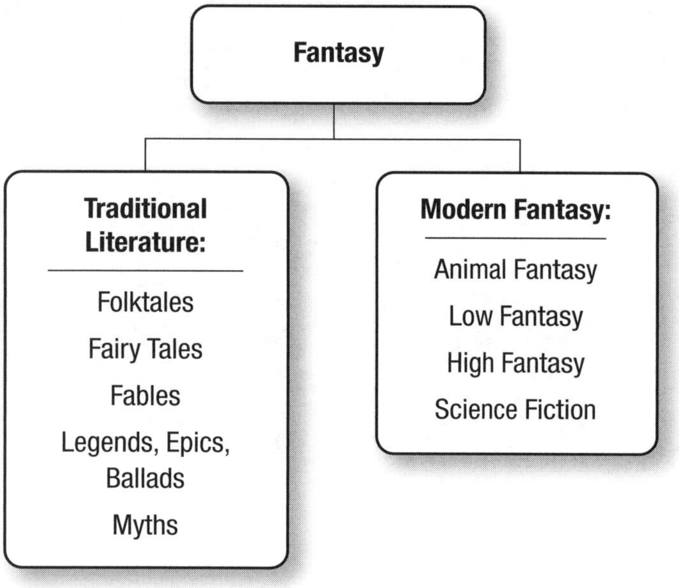

Figure 8.1 The genres of fantasy

story telling and were intended for the entertainment and enlightenment of adults. These oral stories gave people a way to remember the past and teach cultural values. Today, they seem to be the purview of children; they are retold in writing, and there are many variations reflecting various cultures around the world.

Unlike traditional literature, modern fantasy stories originated as written texts. What distinguishes this genre is that "the reader is presented with story elements that run counter to the natural and physical laws of our known world" (Darigan, Tunnell, and Jacobs 2002, 194). Within this genre we distinguish between simple animal fantasy, low fantasy, high fantasy, and science fiction. The four categories are not discrete; there is overlap, but in general, the demands they make on readers increase with complexity.

Motifs in Traditional Literature and Modern Fantasy

Reading traditional tales can give students a good foundation for studying and understanding modern fantasy. Since the roots of modern fantasy lie in traditional literature from the whole of human history, it is not surprising to find a number of recurring themes, ideas, or subjects, called *motifs*. Most of us have these motifs deeply embedded in our minds as metaphors. All cultures seem to have folktales, and similar motifs are found in many geographic areas and societies, but there will be variations. In the multicultural classrooms of today, it is good to remember that children who are not familiar with traditional European motifs may be familiar with others.

Darigan, Tunnell, and Jacobs (2002) have identified six basic fantasy motifs: the struggle between good and evil, magic, secondary or alternative worlds, the hero's quest, special character types, and fantastic or magical objects (see Figure 8.2). Any one of these motifs appearing in a story makes it a fantasy; and they occur across all types of fantasy. Some works of fantasy may include only one of these motifs; others may include all. A classic fairy tale from traditional literature includes all these motifs. A work of modern fantasy that includes all these motifs would be considered high fantasy.

The Struggle Between Good and Evil

A characteristic of most traditional literature and modern fantasy is that the main characters tend to be either good or bad, while secondary characters are simply background players or are relegated to either the good group or the evil group. The struggle between good and evil is most evident in high fantasy like *The Lord of the Rings* (Tolkien 1954/2005), in which forces of good and evil engage in an epic battle. But you can also recognize the struggle between good and evil in many folktales and fairy tales. Some, like "The Three Little Pigs," act more as cautionary tales. Others, like "Little Red Riding Hood," were originally quite violent in their depiction of true evil (the wolf devours the innocent grandmother and attempts to do the same to a little girl). Ursula Le Guin's Earthsea trilogy lifts the motif to new complexity as the hero, Ged, struggles to bring about peace within himself as he flees and then finally faces his own shadow.

Magic

In fantasy worlds, objects may be magical, and people and animals may have magical powers. Magical transformations happen. There are many examples of magical objects in folktales and fairy tales: Cinderella rides to the ball in a magic coach transformed from a

BASIC MOTIFS IN TRADITIONAL LITERATURE AND MODERN FANTASY		
Motif	**Definition**	**Application to Stories**
Struggle between good and evil	Distinguishable good and evil sides in the basic conflict around which the story is built	• Characters fit into either good or evil categories • May involve internal conflict between good and evil • Usually most evident in high fantasy • Usually no neutral characters
Magic	Characters or objects that possess supernatural powers	• People transformed into animals or vice versa • Objects that can be used for magical purposes • Inanimate objects that talk • Wishes that come true with either good or evil consequences
Secondary or alternative worlds	An established and unusual setting where magical events are believable	• Carefully designed and described setting that operates with a different set of governing rules • Inner consistency (conforming to the "rules" of that setting) • Certain aspects help readers recognize the setting as a real world
Hero's quest	A heroic character who is called to complete a mission	• Endurance of danger and hardship—life's trials • Entry to an imaginary world • Magical creatures and powers • Secondary characters who help and protect the hero • Successful completion of the quest
Special character types	Characters that have unusual traits and powers	• Characters reminiscent of traditional tales, like mermaids, fairies, giants, witches and wizards, and elves • Characters from the author's imagination that become well known, such as hobbits or munchkins • Characters who change or transform themselves in various ways • Animal characters who talk
Fantastic or magical objects	Props that are imbued with magic and help characters achieve their missions	• Objects that are given or come to characters in unusual ways • Props that propel the hero forward in the quest • Objects that are used as tools for magic • Objects that are important in the struggle between good and evil

Figure 8.2 Basic motifs in traditional literature and modern fantasy

pumpkin and pulled by horses that were once mice; Jack's beans grow overnight into a massive beanstalk that he climbs in order to enter another world. In *The Wainscott Weasel* (Seidler 2009) and *Olivia* (Falconer 2000) animals talk and act like humans. Susan Cooper has written a series of books including *The Dark Is Rising* (1965) and *The Grey King* (1976) that feature magical objects that assist the main character, Will, who himself possesses magical powers.

Through magic, people may be transformed into animals and vice versa. In the Animorph series (Applegate 1996) a group of teens have the ability to transform into any animal they touch. Human-to-animal transformation also takes place in *The Frog Princess: A Tlingit Legend from Alaska* (Kimmel 2006) when a princess refuses to marry her suitor and instead goes to live with the frog people.

People in a very ordinary world may have only one magical object or hint of magic, as in *The Devil's Arithmetic* (Yolen 1988), where the time warp is the only extraordinary event and the rest of the story is set in reality. Or magic may permeate the entire fantasy world, as in Lloyd Alexander's Prydain series.

Works of fantasy also have magical characters, who may or may not be human. As in traditional tales, works of fantasy may include fairies, ogres, giants, and wizards. Human characters with magical powers may come from the past or from the future.

Secondary or Alternative Worlds

In many traditional stories, magic takes place primarily in the real world, with characters occasionally traveling from the real world into a fantasy world, as in "Jack and the Beanstalk." But in modern fantasy, the reader may encounter a variety of alternative worlds.

Sometimes modern fantasies start out in the real world and the characters then enter a fantasy world, as in classics like *Where the Wild Things Are* (Sendak 1963), *Alice in Wonderland* (Carroll 1865), and *The Wizard of Oz* (Baum 1900). Sometimes the real world and the alternative world exist side by side, as in the Harry Potter series and in *Weslandia* (Fleishman 2002). In *The Water Mirror* (Meyer and Crawford 2001), part of the Dark Reflections trilogy, the authors create a magical version of the Italian city of Venice, complete with a flying stone lion and a journey into hell.

In other fantasy texts, such as *The Wonderful Flight to the Mushroom Planet* (Cameron 1988), the real world does not exist, although these new worlds do have recognizable features. The reader is directly introduced to the secondary world and is expected to suspend disbelief, derive the rules of that world, and understand how the characters must behave within it.

Hero's Quest

Heroes have special qualities and special origins, and they are called to battle evil. The hero embarks on a quest that often involves entering a strange and hostile world and enduring trials or tests. The hero frequently is guided by an older and wiser being (for example, Merlin in the Arthurian legends). The hero succeeds in his quest and in the process grows and matures, returning home triumphantly. In the popular Redwall Abbey series (Jacques 1987), Matthias Mouse sets out to recover the lost sword of the legendary Martin the Warrior. With the aid of his friends, Matthias defends Redwall Abbey and in the process fulfills his destiny.

Special Character Types

Nowhere are the vivid imaginations of authors more evident than in the wonderful and unusual characters they create in fantasy stories. In traditional literature, you might encounter fairy godmothers, witches, ogres, giants, and animals with unusual abilities, such as the well-known "tricksters" Anansi and Hare. In modern fantasy, colorful characters include the Oompa-Loompas from *Charlie and the Chocolate Factory* (Dahl 1964), the Munchkins from *The Wizard of Oz* (Baum 1900), the fantastic mythical creatures from Rick Riordan's Percy Jackson series, and characters such as Mr. Tumnus and Aslan from *The Lion, the Witch, and the Wardrobe* (Lewis 1950).

Fantastic or Magical Objects

The characters in traditional tales often possess inanimate objects that have high significance—the magical and transformative wand of Cinderella's fairy godmother, for example. Snow White eats an apple on which a spell has been cast and falls asleep for years. There are magic cooking pots and magic coins.

Writers of modern fantasy use fantastic objects in a variety of ways. Often, the very appearance of the object signals the genre of the text. Opening a magic box, finding a crown, or discovering a magic stone begins the adventure, as in William Steig's *Sylvester and the Magic Pebble* (1970) and *The Amazing Bone* (1976). In the Harry Potter series, somewhat archaic artifacts (brooms, cauldrons, and quills) are transformed into magical objects. In the Earthsea series, the author uses a unique object, the hero's shadow, in a highly symbolic way. Throughout his quest, Ged is chased by the shadow. Finally, he turns and faces it—that is, faces himself, resolving the inner conflict. In a way, the shadow is magical because Ged thinks it is.

Building a Foundation for Understanding Fantasy

These motifs appear in many of the traditional folktales and fairy tales we know. As teachers, it is important for us to make the connections between these simple tales and the challenging literature that our students will be expected to understand. Early experiences with traditional literature and simple fantasy (animal tales, for example) provide a strong foundation for what is one of the most complex genres.

Traditional Literature

Within every culture a rich array of stories have been created to serve various purposes: to entertain, to preserve and recount important events or people from history, to teach values, to caution against dangers, and to inspire the young. These stories have no authors; rather, they are part of general cultural knowledge. Studying traditional literature is a wonderful way to learn about cultures other than our own.

Traditional stories were originally oral rather than written. Later, some written fairy tales were produced (such as those written by Hans Christian Anderson). These modern fairy tales, with the elements of traditional stories, led the way to modern fantasy.

One characteristic of traditional literature is that characters are relatively flat and static. You don't get to know much about their personalities or their thoughts and feelings, and they change very little (even though a happy ending may result in a change of circumstance). Characters are either bad or good. They are symbolic of desirable and undesirable human traits; their one-dimensional quality is appropriate to the lessons the stories deliver. Characters in traditional literature are also somewhat stereotypical. Good characters are usually beautiful or handsome, while bad characters are often ugly or frightening. In some tales, however, a bad character may be beautiful outside but evil internally, such as the witch in "Snow White and the Seven Dwarfs." Or a character may be ugly or flawed externally but good inside, such as the Beast in "Beauty and the Beast." These characters are usually transformed back into physically ugly or physically beautiful characters when the heroine sees their inner evil or their inner goodness.

In traditional literature you often encounter language such as "once upon a time," "there once was," and "in a land far away." This language is appropriate because most folktales are set in the distant past or another world. Traditional literature tales also tend to have simplistic plots that are easy to remember. Often, goodness, faithfulness, and kindness are rewarded; there is a strong moral tone in many tales. The underdog—the weakest or smallest character—frequently triumphs through cleverness or persistence, as in "The Tortoise and the Hare" and the Anansi the Spider tales.

Traditional tales often have recurring patterns such as the numbers three (three tasks, three guesses, three brothers) and seven (seven swans, seven brothers), and repeated refrains as in "The Gingerbread Man" ("You can't catch me. I'm the gingerbread man!"). Endings are usually satisfying but simplistic: Cinderella ends with the familiar language "and they lived happily ever after."

Types of Traditional Literature

We provide a list and definitions of several kinds of traditional literature (see Figure 8.3).

TYPES OF TRADITIONAL LITERATURE		
Traditional Literature: Literature that has been passed down over time in the oral tradition, with some additional literature written and published in later times.		
Type	**Definition**	**Characteristics**
Folktales (including modern rewritings)	An imagined story that features characters and events that could not exist in the real world. Narrative structure, written or oral, handed down over many years. • Beast tales • Cumulative tales • Pourquoi tales • Trickster tales • Noodlehead tales (fool tales) • Realistic tales • Tall tales	• Animals that talk • Imagined story that features characters and events that could not exist in the real world • Narrative structure, written or oral, handed down over many years • Simple, easy-to-follow plot • Triumph of good over evil • Goodness rewarded and evil punished • Characters who are flat and do not develop • Time, place, and characters and conflict established quickly • Brief conclusion • Repetition (of words, numbers, verses, responses, chants, and poems) • Recurring motifs (magical powers, transformations, magical objects, wishes, trickery) • Culture and values of the place of origin reflected Often: • Original source of the tale referenced • Proverbs from the place of origin • Recognizable literary patterns (cumulative tales, pourquoi tales, beast tales, realistic tales) • Figurative language and imagery • Simplistic characters who are completely evil or completely good • Small and powerless characters who triumph • Happy ending
Fairy Tales	A type of folktale that emphasizes magic and the supernatural.	• Imagined story that features characters and events that could not exist in the real world • Narrative structure, written or oral, handed down over many years • Simple, easy-to-follow plot • Triumph of good over evil • Goodness rewarded and evil punished

Figure 8.3 Types of traditional literature

TYPES OF TRADITIONAL LITERATURE		
Traditional Literature: Literature that has been passed down over time in the oral tradition, with some additional literature written and published in later times.		
Type	**Definition**	**Characteristics**
Fairy Tales *(cont.)*		• Characters who are flat and do not develop • Time, place, and characters and conflict established quickly • Brief conclusion • Repetition (of words, numbers, verses, responses, chants, and poems) • Recurring motifs (magical powers, transformations, magical objects, wishes, trickery) • Magic and the supernatural (wicked witches, demons, monsters, dragons) • Culture and values of the place of origin reflected Often: • Original source of the tale referenced • Figurative language and imagery • Simplistic characters who are completely evil or completely good • Small and powerless characters who triumph • Romance and adventure • Happy ending
Fables	An imagined story that features characters and events that could not exist in the real world. Brief and moralistic and primarily meant to instruct.	• Imagined story that features characters and events that could not exist in the real world • Narrative structure, written or oral, handed down over many years • Brief and moralistic (implicit or explicit moral) • Primarily meant to instruct • Animals who speak as humans • Flat, impersonal characters who represent aspects of human nature Often: • No more than three characters • Plot based on a single incident • Associated with Aesop

Figure 8.3 Types of traditional literature *(cont.)*

continues

TYPES OF TRADITIONAL LITERATURE		
Traditional Literature: Literature that has been passed down over time in the oral tradition, with some additional literature written and published in later times.		
Type	**Definition**	**Characteristics**
Legends, Epics, Ballads	An imagined story that features characters and events that could not exist in the real world. Long narrative or cycle of stories that revolves around the actions of a single hero.	• Imagined story that features characters and events that could not exist in the real world • Narrative structure, written or oral, handed down over many years • Connected with myths • A long narrative or cycle of stories that revolves around the actions of a single hero • Gods and human heroes • Heroes who embody the ideal characteristics of greatness of the time • Moral values of society expressed Often: • A quest • Otherworldly creatures • Written as poetry or in a poetic way
Myths	An imagined story that features characters and events that could not exist in the real world. Seeks to explain the beginnings of the world, nature, natural phenomena, or human behavior.	• Imagined story that features characters and events that could not exist in the real world • Narrative structure, written or oral, handed down over many years • Explanation of the beginnings of the world, nature, natural phenomena, or human behavior • Characterized by type of explanation offered (creation myths, nature myths, hero myths) • Gods and goddesses that take the form of men and women • Gods and goddesses that are immortal and possess supernatural powers • Gods and goddesses that represent virtues Often: • Relationships among the gods, and between humans and gods • Difficult tasks or obstacles for hero or heroine to overcome • Otherworldly creatures

Figure 8.3 Types of traditional literature *(cont.)*

Folktales

Folktales are about everyday people, or "folk," although often kings and queens, and princes and princesses figure in these stories too. Folktales exist all over the world in every culture, and have themes, motifs, and settings related to elements of a particular culture. There are several types of folktales, but a folktale might fall into more than one category.

BEAST TALES *Beast tales* feature animals that talk. Classic examples are "Little Red Riding Hood," "Goldilocks and the Three Bears," and "The Three Little Pigs." Animal fantasy is always popular with children of all ages, and there are many different retellings of classic beast tales. *Martina the Beautiful Cockroach: A Cuban Folktale* (Deedy 2008) features a pretty cockroach who knows nothing of marriage. Her grandmother advises her to ask suitors to pass the "coffee test." All fail until she meets a mouse who turns the tables.

CUMULATIVE TALES In *cumulative tales* like "The Pancake" or "The Gingerbread Boy," all story events are repeated in each new episode; this gives them a rhythmic quality. In *The Gingerbread Cowboy* (Squires 2006), the well-known tale is given a Wild West twist, and a new line is added to the classic refrain.

POURQUOI TALES *Pourquoi* means *why* in French, and *pourquoi tales* try to explain why things (usually natural phenomena) are the way they are: how the earth was created or why animals look or act the way they do, for example. In the West African tale *Why Mosquitoes Buzz in People's Ears* (Aardema 1976), a mosquito's actions trigger a long chain of events that ultimately explains why mosquitoes buzz in people's ears.

TRICKSTER TALES *Trickster tales* feature a clever, usually physically weaker or smaller animal who outsmarts larger and more powerful animals. The trickster is mischievous but lovable. Gerald McDermott has written trickster tales from several different cultures, including the American Southwest (*Coyote: A Trickster Tale*, 1999) and Pacific Northwest (*Raven: A Trickster Tale*, 2001), the Amazon (*Jabuti the Tortoise*, 2005), India (*Monkey: A Trickster Tale*, 2011), and West Africa (*Zomo the Rabbit*, 1996). Each of these tales features a lovable and clever main character and reflects the traditional folklore of that particular culture.

NOODLEHEAD TALES *Noodlehead* or "fool" tales, like "The Three Sillies" or "The Fools of Chelm," are humorous stories featuring a foolish character or characters who often behave in ways contrary to what is expected, making mistake after mistake but often coming out on top in the end. Some current retellings include *The Three Sillies* (Kellogg 1999) and *Noodlehead Stories* (Hamilton and Weiss 2006).

REALISTIC TALES *Realistic tales* that do not involve talking animals can still be called folktales if they have been passed down orally over time. An example is the popular folktale "Stone Soup," in which a hungry traveler or group of soldiers tricks a whole town into contributing to a pot of soup. Often, these stories are humorous, portraying the foibles and customs of rural people. An interesting retelling, *Stone Soup* (Muth 2003), transports the action from its traditional European setting to China, and the hungry traveler is replaced by three wise monks who attempt to teach the villagers to focus on the happiness that comes from sharing rather than just filling their stomachs.

TALL TALES *Tall tales* are legends that have grown over time and are characterized by a great deal of exaggeration. Tall tales revolve around a central, legendary character who acquires extraordinary physical features or abilities. Tall tales such as "Pecos Bill," who was raised by coyotes and could ride and tame a tornado, and "Paul Bunyan," who was so large and powerful that he created the Great Lakes by digging, reflect both the myth and reality of westward expansion in North America during the 1800s. *Doña Flor* (Mora 2005), set in the American Southwest, is a tall tale about a giant woman who can, among other things, make tortillas big enough to use as rafts on the river. *John Henry* (Lester 1994) is the legendary story of the boy whose ultimate feat was beating a steam drill in a race to cut through a mountain. In *Thunder Rose* (Nolen 2007), a young African American girl has remarkable abilities, including the ability to form a ball out of lightning and hold a cow over her head.

Fairy Tales

A fairy tale (also called a *wonder tale*) is a folktale characterized by magical elements, including people with magic powers, supernatural beings, and magic objects. *The King with Horse's Ears and Other Irish Folktales* (Burns 2009) is a collection of many favorites that have been told in Ireland for centuries. Some feature fairies dancing to fairy pipes; the title story is about a king who kills his barbers so no one will find out he has horse's ears.

Some fairy tales—Cinderella, Sleeping Beauty, and Beauty and the Beast, for example—are common to cultures all over the world. *Glass Slipper, Gold Sandal: A Worldwide Cinderella* (Fleischman 2007) is a blending of many versions of Cinderella into a single tale. The many variants of each of these stories make them well suited for classroom study. These tales are usually set in medieval times, and there may be both human and animal characters. Almost always, there are magical transformations and symbolic objects, such as the glass slipper in "Cinderella" or the pea under the mattress in "The Princess and the Pea."

Fables

Fables are tales that feature animals or other natural objects that have human qualities. Examples are "The Tortoise and the Hare," in which the slow, steady tortoise ultimately wins the race, and "The Wind and the Sun," in which the sun wins a contest with the wind. The most famous fables are those attributed to a Greek slave, Aesop, who supposedly wrote in the fifth century, B.C. There is, however, disagreement about whether Aesop actually wrote these fables—he may have been transcribing oral tales from that time. There is even some question as to whether Aesop existed or is himself a legend.

Originally, the Greeks intended fables to be instructive essays for adults, but over centuries these tales have been embraced by children as well. The objective of a fable is to communicate a moral lesson, which is often explicitly stated and summed up in the last part of the tale. For example, "slow and steady wins the race" is the lesson from "The Tortoise and the Hare." "Don't judge someone's potential by his appearance," could be the moral of "The Lion and the Mouse."

Many fables have been used as the basis for modern stories. *Amos and Boris* (Steig 2009) is a version of "The Lion and the Mouse" that features a whale and the mouse who saves him. Students reading this book can connect it to the fable, enriching their analysis.

Stories with moral lessons appear in many different cultures. For example, in *The Night Visitors* (Young 1993), Ho Kuan follows the ants that have eaten all of his grain. In this Chinese folktale from the Tang Dynasty, we learn that "you can learn from all—no matter how small."

Legends, Epics, Ballads

Legends, epics, and ballads may tell the struggle of a person who has triumphed over evil (or even been defeated after a heroic struggle). The hero usually undertakes a journey or quest. These works were originally memorized and performed by storytellers who traveled from village to village sharing these tales. Often, they took the form of long poems and were sometimes sung as ballads (for easier memorization). These extended tales were a way for people to become knowledgeable about their history; they created solidarity and community in a time when there was no written communication. Often, over many years, these stories grew more exaggerated.

Some legends have grown up around modern phenomena. For example, no one really knows how the secret of silk was smuggled out of China, but there are many stories. In *Red Butterfly: How a Princess Smuggled the Secret of Silk Out of China* (Noyes 2007) a Chinese princess who grew up in the luxury of her father's kingdom is given in marriage to a king of a desert country; she carries the mulberry seeds and silkworms with her in her elaborate hair.

Legends and epics focus on heroes and their accomplishments. The subject of a legend may be an imaginary character or a real person whose reputation grows to an exaggerated degree over the years. Legends originated in and grew through oral tradition, but some were eventually written down, including those featuring Robin Hood, King Arthur, and Prince Rama.

An epic is a long story or series of stories about a legendary hero who may or may not have supernatural powers. Usually, an epic involves a quest or journey and a series of tasks or tests, in which the hero triumphs. Homer's epic poems *The Iliad* and *The Odyssey* are well known; probably some parts of them began as songs or as traditional literature. The legend of King Arthur is recounted in many different epics, the first we know of being Sir Thomas Malory's *Le Morte d'Arthur* (1485). Many modern fantasies take their inspiration from Malory's work, including *The Sword and the Circle* (Sutcliff 1994) and *The Once and Future King* (White 1958). For younger students, Mary Pope Osborne's Magic Tree House series includes several stories that involve King Arthur. Also for younger students, *Rama and the Demon King* (Souhami 2005), tells the tale of Prince Rama from the Indian epic the Ramayana, and *Gilgamesh the King* (Zeman 1998) is based on an ancient Mesopotamian epic about a tyrannical king.

Myths

Myths offer explanations for natural phenomena and usually have to do with the creation of the world and its people and animals. Every culture in the world had myths that explained the phenomena people did not understand, such as the sun's journey across the sky each day. Virginia Hamilton's *In the Beginning: Creation Stories from Around the World* (1991) retells twenty-five creation myths from such diverse cultures as China, Tahiti, Micronesia, and Australia.

Myths are more abstract than folktales and fairy tales and require a more sophisticated reader. For example, Roman, Greek, or Norse myths include stories of gods and goddesses who have supernatural powers and take different forms. Picture books such as *Jason and the Golden Fleece* (Riordan 2005) and *King Midas and the Golden Touch* (Craft 2003), along with classic collections such as *D'Aulaires' Book of Greek Myths* (D'Aulaire 1961) and *D'Aulaire's Book of Norse Myths* (D'Aulaire 1967) are useful in introducing students to the study of myths. For younger children, Rosemary Wells' *Max and Ruby's First Greek Myth: Pandora's Box* (1993) and *Max and Ruby's Midas: Another Greek Myth* (1995) adapts these two popular myths to a more contemporary setting and situation, starring Wells' beloved Max and Ruby characters.

The Benefits of Traditional Literature

Although folktales provide entertaining reading, they may also have significant themes for students to think and talk about. Often, they teach lessons about honesty, loyalty, and courage. Since the issues are black and white and the plots are simple, it is usually easy for even young students to derive the big ideas or messages. Children who in the early elementary grades participate in interactive read-aloud that includes traditional literature enter the upper elementary grades with an advantage. They will be familiar with particular vocabulary words, characters, common sayings, figurative language, symbolism, and traditional writing styles. These stories and characters will appear or be referenced again and again in literature, film, and conversation. (See Figure 8.10, page 109.)

Modern Fantasy

Modern fantasy is fiction in which the writer takes events, places, and people that could not exist in the real world and makes their existence believable. The reader of fantasy is entering another world—one that has been carefully structured by the writer according to tenets he has established.

Fantasy shares the six basic motifs mentioned earlier (see Figure 8.2). Some texts may use only one of the motifs; others may have all six. The degree to which these motifs are included in the story or longer text increases the complexity for readers.

Four main types of modern fantasy—animal fantasy, low fantasy, high fantasy (see Figure 8.4), and science fiction (see Figure 8.7, page 108)—help us understand the demands of these texts on readers. We discuss science fiction separately further along in the chapter.

1. *Animal fantasy* features animals that talk and often behave like humans. Sometimes people interact with these animals; in other texts all of the characters are animals.
2. *Low fantasy* takes place in the real world but involves unreal elements such as magic. Low fantasy does not usually include all of the basic motifs found in traditional literature.

TYPES OF MODERN FANTASY		
Modern Fantasy: Imagined stories that feature characters and events that could not exist in the real world.		
Type	**Definition**	**Characteristics**
Animal Fantasy	An imagined story with animal characters who behave like people, and a setting that could not exist in the real world but seems real.	• Narrative structure with characters, plot, and setting • Imagined setting that seems real • Animals who behave like people • Characters who do not change or develop • Magical elements • Modeled on traditional literature Often: • Grounded in reality • Simple plot • Moral or lesson at the end • Themes that express folk wisdom or proverbs of a culture
Low Fantasy	An imagined story that features characters and events that could not exist in the real world. Features talking animals, toys, and dolls, characters who have magical powers or use magical objects.	• Narrative structure with characters, plot, and setting • Imagined setting that seems real • Talking animals, toys, and dolls • Recurring motifs found in traditional literature (magical powers, transformations, magical objects, wishes, trickery) • Characters with magical powers or who use magical objects • Conflict between good and evil Often: • Set in medieval times • Characters with unusual traits (tiny, large, very strong) • Language similar to that in folktales • Reveals universal truths or lessons

Figure 8.4 Types of modern fantasy

TYPES OF MODERN FANTASY		
Modern Fantasy: Imagined stories that feature characters and events that could not exist in the real world.		
Type	**Definition**	**Characteristics**
High Fantasy	An imagined story that features characters and events that could not exist in the real world. Characters have magical powers or use magical objects. Setting is a complete imaginary world or alternate imaginary world that exists alongside the real world.	• Narrative structure with characters, plot, and setting • Complete imaginary world or an alternate imaginary world that exists alongside the real world • Recurring motifs from traditional literature (magical powers, transformations, magical objects, wishes, trickery) • Characters with magical powers or who use magical objects • Heroic characters who grow and change • Conflict between good and evil Often: • Hero on a quest or mission • Hero who is starts out as an ordinary character • Wise character who advises the hero • Reveals universal truths about life • Symbolism • Elevated (complex, poetic) or medieval-sounding language • Has sequels
Science Fiction	An imagined story that features characters and events that could not exist in the real world. Involves technology or scientific advances and takes place in a future that may or may not seem possible.	• Narrative structure with characters, plot, and setting • Complete imaginary world or an alternate imaginary world that exists alongside the real world • Characters with magical powers or who use magical objects • Heroic characters who grow and change • Conflict between good and evil • Technology or scientific advances • Takes place in a future that may or may not seem possible Often: • Time travel • Recurring motifs from traditional literature (magical powers, transformations, magical objects, wishes, trickery) • Aliens or outer space • Combines elements such as magic with scientific information

Figure 8.4 Types of modern fantasy *(cont.)*

3. *High fantasy* takes place in a wholly imagined world. The real world does not exist. High fantasy usually includes most or all of the basic motifs found in traditional literature.
4. *Science fiction* is fantasy that involves technology or scientific advances and takes place in a future that may or may not seem possible.

Values of Modern Fantasy

Modern fantasy has great appeal for children in today's hurried world, where there is little time to pause and feed the imagination. In most modern fantasy, characters have human problems; readers have the opportunity to learn some universal truths even though the setting is not realistic. For example, hundreds of thousands of children relate to Harry Potter's school experiences even though he attends a school for wizards. We list several values of modern fantasy (see Figure 8.5).

Fantasy has another advantage: while realistic fiction can sometimes become dated and lose its appeal with readers, fantasy (especially works that create a completely new and different world) remains viable. Books that deal with contemporary issues head on may be appealing to students of that time but may sound ridiculous or old-fashioned to the next generation. Because fantasy takes the reader outside the realm of what is real, it often remains fresh and engaging for many years. That is certainly the case for modern fantasy classics such as *Watership Down* (Adams 1972, 2005), *The Lion, the Witch, and the Wardrobe* (Lewis 1950, 2005), as well as countless others.

VALUES OF MODERN FANTASY

- Allows readers to escape to another time and place—beyond the real world.
- Fuels the imagination by opening the reader to the impossible.
- Offers complex plots and language related to traditional literature with which the reader is familiar.
- Permits the reader to glimpse new worlds and heroic deeds.

Figure 8.5 Values of modern fantasy

Story Elements in Modern Fantasy

Scholars have identified a number of story elements that commonly occur in fantasy; those most frequently cited are shown in Figure 8.6. These story elements overlap with the previous discussion of motifs shared by traditional literature and modern fantasy.

Animals That Behave Like Humans

In many works of fantasy, animals take on human qualities. They may talk, wear clothing, walk upright, engage in battles, cook and eat food—do anything human characters would do. Animals are given personalities; you not only hear their conversation, you are aware of their thoughts. The anthropomorphism of animals can be placed on a continuum. Sometimes animals talk, think, and have adventures but are in every other way true to their species. In *Watership Down* for example, the rabbit characters have dreams, fears, and aspirations. They talk and even have extrasensory perception, but they still exist in a realistic rabbit world, not wearing clothing, living in burrows, and displaying typical rabbit traits. In the Skippyjon Jones series (Schachner 2005) the exuberant main character, a Siamese kitten, dresses, talks, and behaves just as a young boy might.

Toys That Come to Life

In some works of fantasy, toys come to life and have adventures. The classic example is the story of *Pinocchio* (Collodi 1883), the puppet who was given the chance to become a real boy and whose nose grew every time he lied. A Newbery Medal–winning book, *Hitty: Her First Hundred Years* (Field 1929), is the story of a wooden doll passed from owner to owner over a century. The story is told in Hitty's own words, so we know what she thinks and feels, but she displays no other human traits. Other good examples are *The Castle in the Attic* (Winthrop 1985), in which a magical toy castle transports a boy into another world, and the classic *The Velveteen Rabbit*

COMMON STORY ELEMENTS OF MODERN FANTASY		
Element	**Definition**	**Characteristics**
Animals that behave like humans	Animals have human characteristics, such as the ability to talk	• Animals act like people • Combination of human and animal characters or all animal characters • Usually set in the real world but with unreal characters
Toys and objects that come to life	Inanimate objects come to life	• Inanimate objects talk and have personalities
Eccentric and extraordinary characters	Characters are very unusual in some way: have magical powers, are humorous, or are very eccentric	• Exaggerated character traits • Humor • Magical happenings
Time travel	Characters travel through time or settings that shift from one time period to another	• Often have special settings conducive to time travel • Sometimes connect time travel to objects • Characters enter other worlds • Characters from different generations meet
Ghosts and the supernatural	Ghosts appear to living people	• May be benevolent or dangerous • Often but not always frightening • Usually resolved when the ghost's problem is solved
Imaginary worlds	A completely imaginary world	• May begin in the real world but characters are transported to an imaginary world • Settings with very unusual features that seem believable within that world
Tiny people	Human characters are much smaller than humans in the real world	• May exist within the real world alongside humans • May encounter danger from ordinary household pets such as cats • May exist in imaginary tiny worlds

Figure 8.6 Common story elements in modern fantasy

(Williams 1922), in which a boy's beloved stuffed rabbit becomes real.

Eccentric and Extraordinary Characters

Roald Dahl is known for the eccentric and memorable characters he has created in books like *Charlie and the Chocolate Factory* (1964) and *James and the Giant Peach* (1961). Characters from older classics like Mary Poppins, Dr. Doolittle, and Pippi Longstocking endure over the years to delight both children and adults. Although these characters are described in vivid detail and are full of life, they are static in that they do not change and develop much over the course of the story or stories. Readers can count on Mary Poppins' prim, take-charge attitude and her unwavering magical powers in story after story, just as they can count on Pippi Longstocking's cheerfulness, strong-mindedness, and sense of fun.

Time Travel

One way of altering a setting quickly and removing characters from the real world is to have them travel in time. In *The Root Cellar* (Lunn 1996), a twelve-year-old orphan girl sent to live with relatives on a farm in Canada discovers that entering an old root cellar allows her to travel back in time to more than a century earlier.

In many stories about time travel characters experience settings and challenges that change their present lives. They meet memorable people who help them gain new perspectives. In *Tom's Midnight Garden* (Pearce 1958), when an old grandfather clock chimes thirteen, Tom enters the past and plays in a garden with a little girl dressed in old-fashioned clothing. They become friends, and eventually he realizes that the old woman living upstairs in the present is that same girl. For younger readers, Mary Pope Osborne's Magic Tree House series and Jon Scieszka's Time Warp Trio series feature time travel to the sites of well-known events or time periods in history and prehistory.

Ghosts and the Supernatural

Children like scary stories that may incorporate evil characters with magical powers. Certainly when children are younger they are exposed to a great many stories, many of them traditional literature, that feature witches and other slightly scary creatures. As they grow and their ability and desire to discern reality from fantasy becomes more pronounced, young readers may become more skeptical of these characters.

Stories about ghosts and other supernatural characters may be mysterious and suspenseful, or they may have elements of humor or folklore. *A Stranger Came Ashore* (Hunter 1994) tells the legend of a Selkie (a seal-person in Scottish folklore) who emerges from the sea and pretends to be a man. Ghosts that appear in works of fantasy are sometimes benevolent and sometimes frightening. In *Breathe* (McNish 2006), Jack and his widowed mother move into an old farmhouse, and Jack must battle a sinister ghost mother who has enslaved several ghost children. *Wait Till Helen Comes* (Hahn 1994) features a malevolent and seductive ghost who waits in a pool to drown children who come too near. A ghost story often gives the main character an opportunity to battle his or her own inner demons or unresolved issues, and the vanquishing of the ghost is often symbolic of the character's conquering fear or loss.

Imaginary Worlds

One of the creative ways writers of fantasy convince readers to suspend disbelief is to create complete imaginary worlds totally separate from reality. Writers create these imaginary worlds in part by rendering them in great detail and creating lasting images. Sometimes the reader enters into these imaginary worlds immediately, and there is no acknowledgment that any other world exists. In *The Gammage Cup* (Kendall 1959) the author has created an imaginary world inhabited by a race of people called the Minnipins—tiny people who become epic heroes. In other stories, the main characters recognize that they have entered another world very different from the real world. A classic example is *Alice in Wonderland* (Carroll 1865), first published over a hundred years ago, in which Alice is transported from the real world, via rabbit hole, to an extraordinary world with extraordinary characters. *The Wizard of Oz* (Baum 1900) begins in the rather colorless reality of Midwest America and moves quickly to the magical Land of Oz, with Dorothy trying throughout the story to get back home. In some stories like this the characters enter and leave the imaginary world in a dreamlike way; readers of *The Wizard of Oz* are left wondering if Oz was just a place that unfolded in Dorothy's brain while she was unconscious from the bump on her head or if it really existed. In *Where the Wild Things Are* (Sendak 1963), Max is sent to his room for mischievous behavior, and his own imagination transports him to the land of the Wild Things and back home again.

Another kind of imaginary world is a kingdom presented in great detail. Often these kingdoms are reminiscent of medieval times, with kings, queens, knights, and castles and battles between good and evil forces. The Redwall Abbey series describes such a kingdom, Redwall Abbey, inhabited by peaceful animal citizens and rat warlords bent on destroying that peace. *The Search for Delicious* (Babbitt 1969) describes a young boy's quest to prevent civil war from erupting in his kingdom. Lloyd Alexander's Westmark trilogy features a kingdom in which a printer's apprentice helps a princess gain her rightful place against the wishes of the chief minister. (The kingdom itself is not magical.)

Tiny People

Frequently, imaginary worlds are peopled by characters who are very small. The variance in dimension is often the impetus for creating the world. In Mary Norton's classic *The Borrowers* (1952) the tiny Clock family lives beneath the floorboards of a country house in England. Their adventures stem from the challenges of being small in a big world and of trying to remain unnoticed by the humans living in the house. Their ingenuity in "borrowing" and adapting objects to suit their size is part of the fun of reading about their world.

Elements of Fantasy

Fantasy has the same elements as all works of fiction—setting, characters, and plot. The fantasy aspect of the story is created by manipulating or changing one or all of these elements in a way that takes the reader away from reality.

Setting

Setting is very important in works of fantasy; in many fantasies the action takes place in a setting entirely separate and different from the real world. The writer creates a secondary world that has its own features and rules. Once created, the writer must stay within those rules in developing the plot.

In modern fantasy, settings are described in greater detail than they are in traditional tales, because they are so important to characters and action. Compare "once upon a time in a faraway land" with the detailed descriptions of Redwall Abbey in a medieval-like kingdom where monks must defend their abbey against marauders. The characters must act within this setting, using both the attributes of their own species and weapons of the time. For example, the invading rat king uses a battering ram but also forces moles to dig tunnels for him. Some authors include maps of imaginary worlds along with their descriptions in the text, making the fantasy world seem more concrete and real.

Time is often manipulated as part of the setting in fantasies. Characters travel backward or forward in time (forward time travel is most often a characteristic of science fiction). Traveling back in time, characters may have to face real problems that existed in history. In *The Devil's Arithmetic* (Yolen 2004), a spoiled Jewish girl, Hannah, is transported to a Polish village in the 1940s, where she is captured by the Nazis and taken to a death camp. Popular series books that feature travel back to historic periods or events or specific cultures include Mary Pope Osbourne's The Magic Treehouse series, and John Scieszka's Time Warp Trio series.

Characters

Characters in fantasy may be "real" human beings living in a fantastic world. Alternatively, they may be normal in all ways except for some fantastic power or ability. An example is the character Will in Susan Cooper's The Dark is Rising series, who discovers that he is "the last of the immortal Old Ones" and must battle the powers of darkness. Characters in fantasy may also be supernatural beings, either good or evil.

Works of fantasy often include animal characters that have been humanized. The world of *Mrs. Frisby and the Rats of Nimh* (O'Brien 1986) is inhabited by mice, rats, crows, and cats, all of who have their own distinct personalities. These characters are animals with both human and species-correct characteristics.

As in all fiction, characters in fantasy must be believable and well developed, even though they depart from reality. In contrast to traditional literature, where characters are generally flat, the main characters in fantasy are round; especially in the series books, they tend to grow and change.

Plot

The action of the story must be related to the setting and the qualities of characters. In realistic fiction, the story must be possible within our modern world. Characters must be believable as individuals, and their actions must be in keeping with their capabilities and motivations. In fantasy, the story must be possible *within the parameters of the created secondary world*, and characters must be believable within their capabilities and motivations as described by the writer. For example, Harry Potter can fly on a broomstick, but if he falls off it, he plummets to earth (but is always miraculously saved by others with special abilities). When he flies on his broom to play quidditch, the rules are carefully described, and the players can't depart from them. Harry needs his wand to defend himself against evil wizards, who also use their wands.

Science Fiction

Science fiction is a type of fantasy in that one, two, or all three of the elements (setting, events, and characters) are altered so that they are not consistent with the real world. However, true science fiction includes technology and/or is based on scientific advances. The writer of fantasy is asking the reader to enter a world that never was or could be. The writer of science fiction is hypothesizing about what might be possible at some time in the future or in another version of the past or present.

Types of Science Fiction

It is sometimes hard to distinguish between science fiction and other types of modern fantasy, because texts have features of both and inevitably there will be some overlap. It is not important to strictly delineate between fantasy and science fiction, since science fiction remains part of the fantasy genre. We describe some common types of science fiction (see Figure 8.7).

BLEND OF FANTASY AND SCIENCE Works of science fiction often combine elements such as magic with scientific information. Here, there is not so much emphasis on using scientific information accurately. In the Hunger Games trilogy (Collins 2010) the characters do have some advanced scientific equipment but the text also has some classic story elements of fantasy (struggle between good and evil, the trial of the hero).

TECHNOLOGY AND SCIENCE Some science fiction is very carefully grounded in scientific possibilities and raises important ethical questions about the use of technology. In the novel *Eva* (Dickinson 1990), a girl's consciousness and spiritual essence are scientifically transplanted into the body of a chimpanzee after a terrible accident. She learns to deal with the mixture of beings that coexist within her body.

OUTER SPACE AND ALIEN WORLDS For decades, people have been fascinated with outer space. Some science fiction involves aliens coming to earth or human beings traveling through space to other planets and solar systems. *The Green Book* (Walsh 1986) is the story of a family trying to survive in a new settlement on a faraway planet after the devastation of earth. Interestingly, the value of reading figures strongly in the plot; allowed to take only a limited amount of supplies, books become valuable as the only way to cope with the loneliness.

FUTURISTIC STORIES Science fiction is frequently futuristic. *The Ear, the Eye and the Arm* (Farmer 2002) takes place in Zimbabwe in the year 2194. The three

TYPES OF SCIENCE FICTION	
Element	**Definition**
Blend of fantasy and science	Stories mix elements of fantasy, such as magic, with scientific information.
Technology and science	Stories are based on technological or scientific advances.
Outer space and alien worlds	Stories feature aliens coming to earth or people traveling in outer space.
Futuristic stories	Stories feature a world of the future that may or may not come to be.

Figure 8.7 Types of science fiction

books in the Hunger Games series reveal a future world brought about by mass destruction; the novels are a warning of what could happen if people do not protect their world. Their "reality TV" setting using advanced technology makes them very modern.

In *The Giver* (1993), and *Gathering Blue* (2000), Lois Lowry creates two different but equally complex futuristic worlds that revolve around oppressive civilizations and the central characters' quests to find their own voices and freedom. The first is set in a highly technical society, while the second features a society with only rudimentary technology. In both cases, it is the futuristic aspect of the stories that characterizes them as science fiction.

Values of Science Fiction

The values of science fiction are much the same as those for modern fantasy in general. Readers have the opportunity to stretch our imagination and escape from the here and now. In addition, reading science fiction can:

- Raise questions about the future, demanding new thinking on the part of the reader.
- Engage the reader in thinking about ethical issues related to science and technology.

The Demands of Modern Fantasy on the Reader

Modern fantasy stretches readers' comprehending strategies in ways that realistic fiction cannot. The list in Figure 8.8 suggests some demands on comprehension that are unique to this genre.

Sequels and Series

Like realistic fiction, works of fantasy may be written as a series or sequel. Some series center on the same characters and themes but each can stand alone, making it possible to produce an unlimited number of volumes. A series can also be an ongoing story in which the characters grow and change across a limited number

MODERN FANTASY: DEMANDS ON THE READER

- Suspend disbelief and enter worlds far different from our own.
- Recognize and understand the significance of symbolism.
- Deal with abstract ideas.
- Understand complex story structures with many layers and movement across time and space and between reality and fantasy.
- Manipulate the concept of time to understand the action of the plot.
- Understand characters' motivations and qualities even if they are different from people in our world.
- Follow complex plots with many characters and events.
- Attend to details and descriptions of imaginary worlds and characters.
- Identify and understand multiple themes.
- Cope with language that may be very different from everyday speech in the real world.
- Read, solve, and understand invented words that require us to make connections to archaic or difficult known words (for example, the evil rat in the Redwall Abbey series refers to his "henchrats").
- Make connections to traditional literature to understand the meaning of motifs and symbols.

Figure 8.8 Modern fantasy: demands on the reader

of volumes, as in the Harry Potter books, the Hunger Games trilogy, and the Earthsea trilogy.

Fantasy sequels make possible many heroic quests as the saga continues over time. Readers eagerly wait for the next book because they want to continue the experience. Always, there is the continuing struggle between the forces of good and evil until the last volume of the series when the story ends and the hero has triumphed.

Fantasy Series Books

Previously in this book we have made a distinction between a set or series of books and books with several sequels. We may informally call both categories a "series," but there is a difference worth noting. In the former, books include the same characters and usually the same setting, and they may be read in any order. Characters do not develop much. Their appeal is in their unchanging nature. In a series of sequels, action takes place over time. Characters change and develop; the setting may also change. Most readers like to read the books in order. Again, the contrast between these two types of series books is not sharp; rather, it is a continuum.

Fantasy series books are very popular with readers and provide an opportunity for children to begin reading fantasy in an easy way. The series books we highlight on the F&P Resources Site include both low and high fantasy books, as well as animal fantasy.

Fantasy Books with Sequels

Once readers have entered a fantasy world, they have the prior knowledge (and often the motivation) to keep reading about that world. They are eager for the next volume. The volumes in a series or sequels offer a powerful experience for the reader. Some are humorous or fun, and some provide the complex stories that make up a saga. The list on the F&P Resources Site includes fantasy books with sequels. These high-quality works feature characters that stay with readers forever.

Evaluating Fantasy

Good fantasy must meet the same criteria as those for all fiction—a compelling story and engaging characters. The setting, characters, and action of the fantasy story must be believable to the reader, even those elements that could not really exist. The writer must describe the setting and characters in a way that helps readers suspend reality and believe in the world we have entered. Once you accept the premise the writer has introduced, the rest of the story becomes believable.

Within any work of fantasy, the writer must be consistent; in other words, characters cannot suddenly fly or perform magic unless the groundwork for that potential has been laid. The writer of fantasy must create a text that is coherent in that the actions of characters are

possible within the parameters the writer has laid out. Nor should the fantasy suddenly be made unbelievable at the end (having the person realize the events were a dream, for example). Readers of fantasy also expect a high degree of originality and creativity in characters, setting, and plot.

Figure 8.9 lists some questions to ask in identifying and analyzing modern fantasy. Answering these questions will help you think about how the writer of fantasy manipulates setting, time, characters, and actions to create believability.

Traditional Literature and Modern Fantasy in the Classroom

Even though your students are living in the real world, reading fantasy and science fiction can greatly contribute to their reading capabilities. Traditional literature, which includes the oral history of the cultures of our diverse world, is the foundation for the more complex works of modern fantasy that transport readers to other worlds and endless imaginative possibilities.

ANALYZING MODERN FANTASY

- How is the world of the story different from our world today?
- How has the author altered the setting so that the secondary world is different from the real one? (The writer may alter a few characteristics or many.)
- What is the evidence that the characters are different from real people? How are they different from people in the real world?
- Is there evidence that time has been altered? How was it altered and how does this change contribute to the story?
- How has the writer made the story believable, encouraging readers to suspend disbelief?
- What motifs or recurring patterns from traditional literature are used in the story?
- What is the underlying message or theme of the story?

Figure 8.9 Analyzing modern fantasy

TRADITIONAL LITERATURE: DEMANDS ON THE READER

- Suspend disbelief and enter worlds different from our own.
- Identify the important characters and what human traits they represent.
- Recognize and understand the significance of symbolism.
- Identify the struggle between good and evil in the story.
- Recognize the message or moral of the story.
- Recognize language commonly used in traditional literature.
- Identify the values the story is teaching.
- Identify common motifs found in traditional literature.
- Recognize recurring patterns.

Figure 8.10 Traditional literature: demands on the reader

Suggestions for Professional Development

OPTION 1: Work with colleagues to examine traditional literature.

- Ask each person to bring a picture book folktale appropriate for students in grades 1–8. (See the mentor texts in Appendix A and the list of children's books in Appendix D.) In addition, find several different versions of the same folktale—for example, Little Red Riding Hood—from different parts of the world if possible.
    - In small groups, participants read as many of the books as they can.
    - Use Figure 8.2 to identify recurring motifs in the examples of traditional literature you have read. Compare how the motifs are used in the different tales.
- Now look at the versions of the same folktale.
    - How are the versions similar (characters, motifs, plot)?
    - How are the versions different?
    - How do the differences reflect the origin [country, region, culture] of the story?
- Discuss how traditional literature study could be integrated with the social studies curriculum in your school.
- Discuss how traditional literature can be used as a springboard to help students read the genre of fantasy.

OPTION 2: Work with colleagues to examine modern fantasy texts.

- Prepare for the meeting by selecting four books of modern fantasy. (Try to include science fiction.) You may want to consult the lists of mentor texts that we have provided at the end of this chapter. These books should be appropriate for average students at your grade level. They may be required by your school curriculum but in any case should be easily available.
- Ask every member of the group to read all four books and to come to the meeting prepared to talk about all of them. (Work in small groups if you have more than six or seven people.)
- Using Figures 8.3 and 8.4, analyze and discuss the books. For each book:
    - Talk about the demands this text makes on readers. What will readers need to understand to comprehend this book?
    - List the demands made by each book on the chart.
    - Compare your lists across the texts.

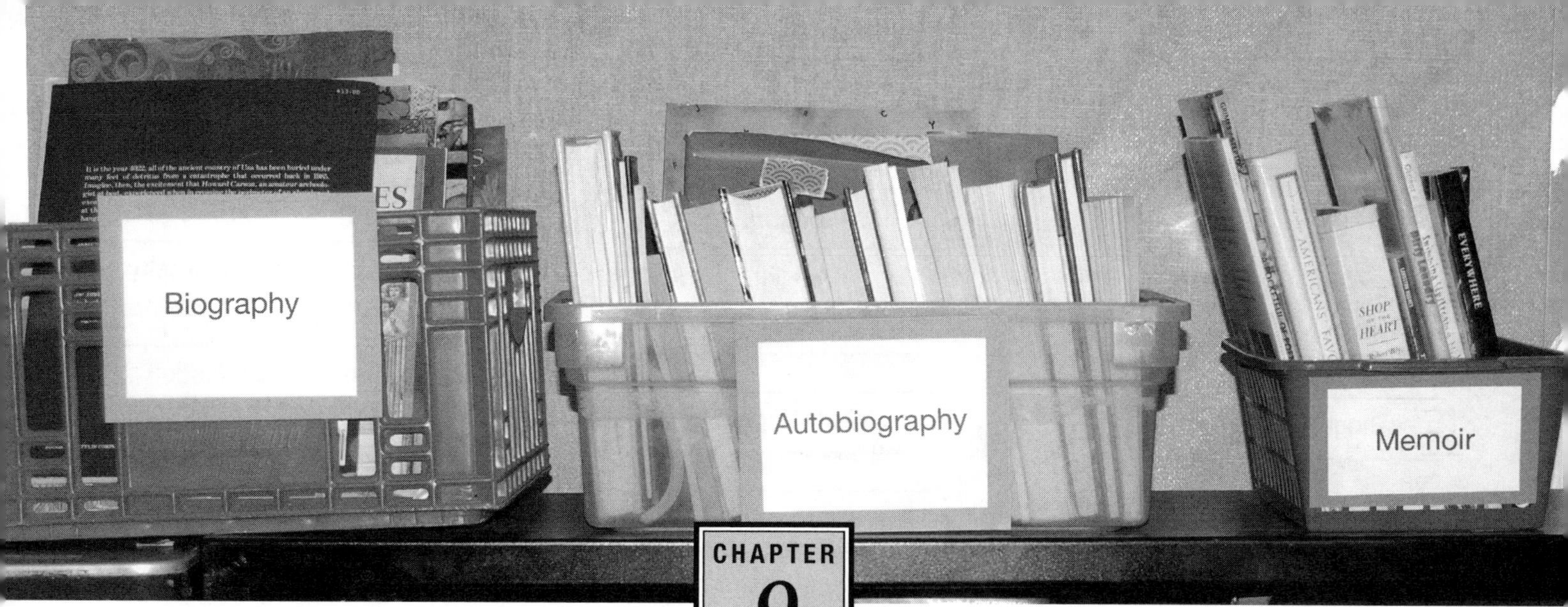

CHAPTER 9

Understanding Biography

Learning from the Lives of Others

As a life story, a biography tells readers how a person navigates the extremes of success or failure, riches or poverty, happiness or sadness, innovative change or stagnant sameness, determination or aimlessness.

—Myra Zarnowski

We love reading stories about real people—people who lived long ago and people we know in our world today. The subjects of these stories are often even more compelling than the vivid characters we encounter in fiction! Biographical texts tell about the extraordinary lives of people well known to us, like political figures, artists, musicians, and celebrities, and ordinary people whom we have never encountered before. They trace entire lives from birth to death or focus on a brief but significant period of time. They may be shaped by the time period or the setting in which they take place, or they may chronicle the achievements of people who shaped their times.

One thing all biographical stories have in common is that they are based on actual facts and events that can be documented; this places them in the category of nonfiction, despite being told in a narrative style like fiction. It is important for students to be able to recognize the purpose and organization of the nonfiction texts they read as well as to distinguish them from fiction. We consider all nonfiction texts to be "informational," as their ultimate purpose is to share true information with the reader, as opposed to fiction, which departs from the actual but nevertheless communicates truths.

In this book, we organize the genres of nonfiction into three main categories:

- *Biography, autobiography, and memoir.* Biographical texts are usually narratives as well. They too tell a story—one that focuses on a real person or events in a person's life or on a particular time in a person's life.
- *Narrative nonfiction.* Narrative nonfiction texts tell a story—just like fiction. We find nonfiction narratives in highly literary texts

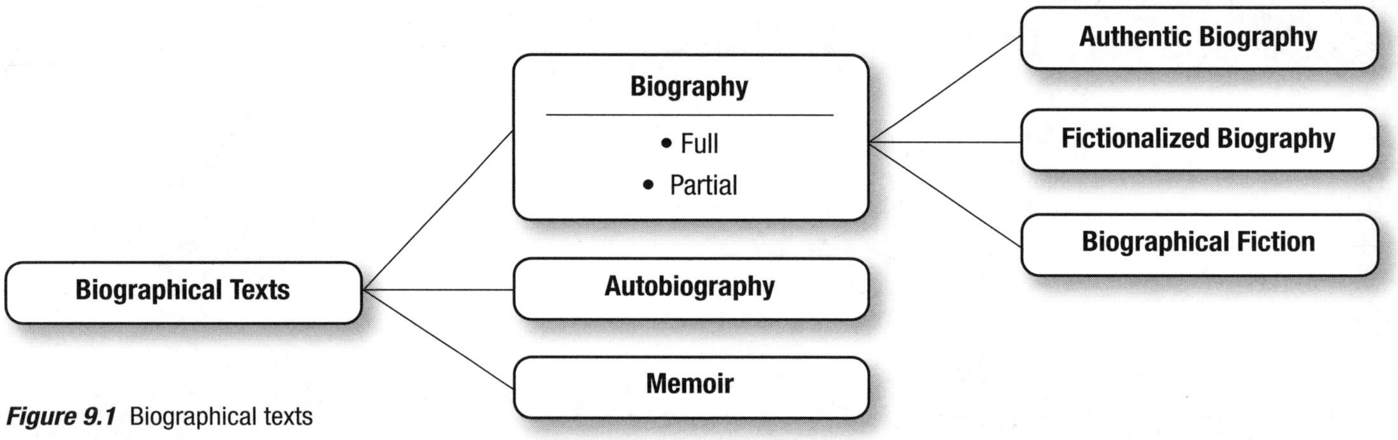

Figure 9.1 Biographical texts

that present true information in story form, and in historical narratives that recount history in chronological order. The story format makes the narrative text easy to follow.

- *Expository, procedural, and persuasive texts* present information in many different ways but most frequently in categories. These categories help the reader relate information.

This chapter focuses on biographical texts, or stories about real people and events (see Figure 9.1). We'll talk more about the other genres of nonfiction in Chapters 10 and 11. At the end of this chapter you will find a list of mentor texts for biography, autobiography, and memoir. These are suggested titles to be used as exemplars of the genre, but you may have excellent examples of your own that you prefer to use. These mentor texts may be used to build text sets, and for read-aloud and book clubs. We do not advocate engaging in a genre study of biography for grades K–1, though you may find some high-quality age-appropriate biographies such as simple biographies of authors for these grade levels that you might want to use for reading aloud and exposing them to a variety of texts.

Full Biographies

Biographical texts may be biographies, autobiographies, or memoirs. Biographies may be "full' biographies in that they tell the story of all or most of a person's life (or if the person is still alive, the story up to the point of publication). Even in full biographies, the writer must be selective in telling the story. Only the important details can be included. *Albert Einstein: A Biography* (Meltzer 2008) is the life story of Albert Einstein, Nobel Prize–winner for his theory of relativity. The volume has many quotes from Einstein and a letter he wrote in 1939 to Franklin Roosevelt. It also includes many photographs. Einstein's theory led to the development of the atomic bomb and the end of World War II, but he was an advocate for peace and campaigned for nuclear disarmament. He was also a civil rights advocate. This multifaceted portrait of the famous scientist allows readers to witness the internal, human conflicts with which Einstein grappled.

Partial Biographies

Biographies can also be "partial" in that they focus on one important part of the subject's life. In this case the writer may describe one incident or one period of time in greater depth. Often additional background information is provided in an introduction or author's note. *The Librarian of Basra: A True Story from Iraq* (Winter 2003) describes a courageous librarian's success in saving over 30,000 volumes from being burned. This true story offers insight into the lives of ordinary Iraqi people during the American invasion and highlights their love of books and learning.

Almost all biographical texts have a narrative structure. Figure 9.2 defines genres of biographical texts and also lists characteristics you and your colleagues or students are likely to notice.

GENRES AND CHARACTERISTICS OF BIOGRAPHICAL TEXTS		
***Biographical Text:* Provides factual information in narrative style about all or part of a person's life.**		
Genre	**Definition**	**Characteristics**
Biography	Told by another person, provides factual information in narrative style about all or part of a person's life.	• Tells the story of a person's life or part of it • Uses a narrative structure • Provides factual information about a subject's life • Tells why the subject's life is important enough to be written about • Written in third person (not told by the subject) • Tells the setting and the culture the person lived in and what influenced the subject Often: • Uses made up dialogue (fictionalized) • Includes direct quotes • Has photographs • Tells the story at any point in subject's life • Uses some imagined scenes or dialogue but based on fact • Has a point of view toward the subject (likes or doesn't like) • Adds factual statements as additional information • Conveys a larger message
Auto-biography	Told by the subject, provides factual information in narrative style about all or part of the author's life.	• Tells the story of a person's life or part of it • Told by the subject • Written in first person • Uses a narrative structure • Provides factual information about the subject's life • Tells why the subject's life is important enough to be written about • Has a limited perspective (subjective) Often: • Includes direct quotes • Has photographs • Tells the story at any point in subject's life • Tells the setting and the culture the person lived in and what influenced the subject • Adds factual statements as additional information • Conveys a larger message

Figure 9.2 Genres and characteristics of biographical texts

continues

GENRES AND CHARACTERISTICS OF BIOGRAPHICAL TEXTS		
Biographical Text: **Provides factual information in narrative style about all or part of a person's life.**		
Genre	**Definition**	**Characteristics**
Memoir	Provides factual information in narrative style about a significant time, place, person, or event in the author's life, and explains the significance.	• Tells the story (memory) of a significant time, place, person, or event in a subject's life • Told by the subject • Uses a narrative structure • Provides factual information about the subject's life • Tells why the time or event is important enough to be written about • Written in first person • Has a limited perspective (subjective) Often: • Includes direct quotes • Has photographs • Tells the story at a significant point in subject's life • Tells the setting and the culture the person lived in and what influenced the subject • Adds factual statements as additional information • Conveys a larger message

Figure 9.2 Genres and characteristics of biographical texts *(cont.)*

Distinguishing Between Biography, Autobiography, and Memoir

The three related genres of biographical texts have different purposes and characteristics. A *biography* is a factual account of a person's (the subject's) life written by another person, who is called a biographer. An *autobiography* is an account of a life written by the subject himself or herself. A *memoir* is a briefer, more intense account that presents a single memory or set of related memories. Memoirs are always autobiographical because the writer is remembering a significant time, place, or person; but some memoirs focus more on another person who was influential and memorable (for example, the writer's account of his experience *with* a famous person).

Biographies (at least those that are published) usually have subjects who are known to a larger group for some kind of achievement. But often a biography reveals a relatively unknown person who has made a significant contribution to society in some way. Memoir is different. We all have memorable experiences that touch the senses or raise deep emotions. All of us can describe people who have been important to us or moments that have influenced our lives. Writing short memoir allows writers to describe, create dialogue, and share experiences with readers. As we write memoir with them, our students can develop most of the techniques that writers use for fiction and nonfiction.

Biography

Biography is the most common genre for conveying the stories of real people. Dozens of biographies may be written about well-known people. Readers select biography for a variety of reasons: they admire (or dislike) the subject; they want the subject's perspective on a period of time and on other people; they want to be inspired. Curiosity drives the process.

Readers of biography need to be analytic and critical. The writer of a biography generally takes a position, and although genuine scholars try very hard to be objective, it is usually easy to tell whether the writer admires the subject or not. Biographies of living people can be *authorized*, in which case the subject collaborates with the writer or provides information. They can also be *unauthorized*, in that the subject has not approved the material (it may still be true). Many biographies are of deceased people. Here, the writer has to rely on historical sources. Usually, the more research a writer has done and the better documented the biography is, the surer you can be that the information is reliable.

Biographies and autobiographies usually use chronological sequence in telling the story; however, they do not always have to begin at birth and end at death. A biography can start at any time in a person's life and then move back to the person's early life from there or proceed forward. A biography that chronicles the entire life of an individual is a *complete* biography; however, many biographies could be considered *partial* biographies because they focus only on a part of the individual's life. Memoirs are usually partial autobiographies, covering a single event or a shorter time period than the entire life. You want to help your students notice whether a biography or autobiography is partial or complete, be aware of where in the person's life the story begins, and speculate why the writer chose the particular structure.

It takes years and exposure to many texts to build a deep understanding of the nuances of biography (as well as autobiography and memoir), but you can build a strong foundation through interactive read-aloud and literature discussion.

Understanding Biography

People who are the subject of biographies usually have accomplished something important or performed some admirable acts of courage or service. They may be very well known public figures or unknown persons whose accomplishments only become widely known with the publication of their stories. Often, the lives of seemingly ordinary people can teach us something about the world or about ourselves, but the subject must have some qualities or achievements that make her worth writing about, and biography must make clear what are those qualities or achievements. As you pursue a discussion of turning points, students can consider "what if" a different decision had been made.

Literature includes an array of stories about real people who lived in the past or who are still alive today. Students are likely to become confused about distinguishing between true (authentic) biography and biography with a substantial amount of detail that is imagined by the writer (fictionalized biography). You want students to read and enjoy the whole range of stories, but they need to learn how to tell the difference between what is true and what is imagined. It is useful to examine the relationship of authentic biography to biographical fiction and historical fiction (see Figure 9.3). The overlapping circles indicate that you should be thinking of a continuum rather than discrete categories.

All the categories have much to offer students. In every category there are high-quality texts that students like to read. All these texts can engage their interest in history and people who lived in other times. The lines are not always clearly drawn. The classification really depends on how much inventing the writer has done. Some of the characteristics of authentic biography and fictionalized biography are described below.

Authentic Biography

Almost all biographies are fictionalized to some degree. We believe that a biography can be slightly fictionalized and still be authentic. Our definition of *authentic biography* is biography that:

- Is thoroughly grounded in research.
- Recounts events that are documented.

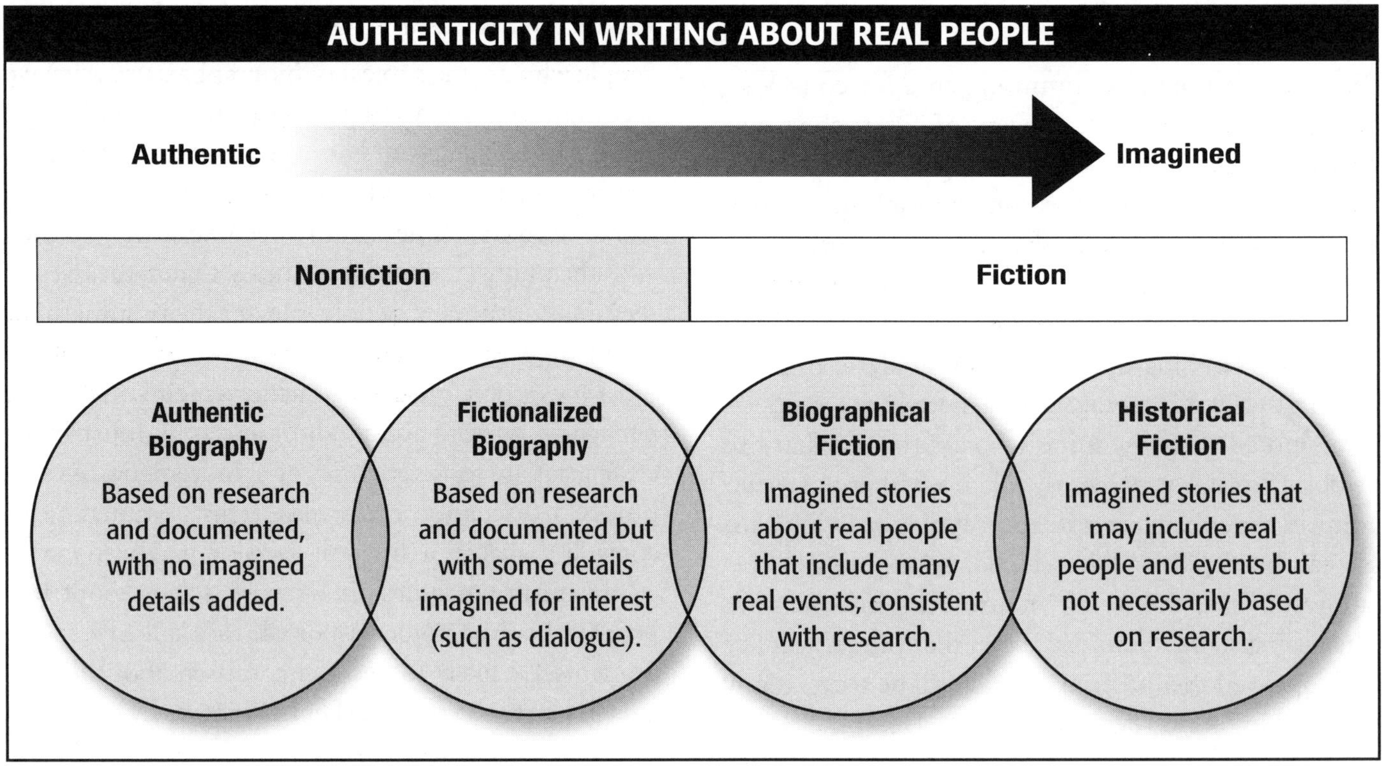
AUTHENTICITY IN WRITING ABOUT REAL PEOPLE
Authentic
Imagined
Nonfiction
Fiction
Authentic Biography
Based on research and documented, with no imagined details added.
Fictionalized Biography
Based on research and documented but with some details imagined for interest (such as dialogue).
Biographical Fiction
Imagined stories about real people that include many real events; consistent with research.
Historical Fiction
Imagined stories that may include real people and events but not necessarily based on research.

Figure 9.3 Authenticity in writing about real people

- Includes no imagined details and no dialogue that is created by the writer.
- Does not attribute imagined feelings to the character. (This does not mean that the text does not have dialogue or feelings; but these are based on materials such as original letters, diaries, or recorded interviews.)
- Is written by someone who has searched for actual comments by the subject or comments from those who have written or talked about the subject. (Often, biographers rely on many sources—respected historians who have written about the subject and documented their efforts).

The author of the biography *Eleanor: Quiet No More* (Rappaport 2009), about former first lady Eleanor Roosevelt, cites letters and other sources that give us confidence that the feelings the author attributes to her subject are authentic. She uses Eleanor's own words on every page spread. You cannot be absolutely sure of the authenticity of the material unless you go to those sources yourself to check, and sometimes readers do just that.

While many biographies tell the reader more about the lives of well-known figures from history and the arts, biography can also introduce the reader to the amazing accomplishments of lesser-known people. The award-winning biography *Snowflake Bentley* (Martin 1998) tells the story of photographer Wilson Bentley, whose career focused on the magic of snowflakes, using gentle prose and highly detailed woodcuts. The story also includes information in sidebars about snowflake science. The *Queen of the Falls* (Van Allsburg 2011) features an unlikely real-life daredevil—the sixty-two year old charm-school teacher who was the first person to ever go over Niagara Falls in a barrel.

Fictionalized Biography

Fictionalized biography engages the reader by providing a few imagined details and, sometimes, invented dialogue. The biographer usually bases these details on reliable sources. Fictionalized biography tends to follow a person's life closely and is based on research. The main events of the story and characters are authentic. The writer uses many documented details but imagines some of the dialogue and guesses at the subject's thoughts and motivations. In children's literature, in particular, very easy biographies are often fictionalized so that they will deliver more of a "story" to younger readers. Biographies for older readers tend to be more factual.

Fictionalized biographies interest students in the lives of real people and provide a bridge to authentic biographies. *Mama Miti: Wangari Mathaai and the Trees of Kenya* (Napoli 2010) tells about the Kenyan environmental activist who received the 2004 Nobel Peace Prize. In the interest of literary quality, the author may have slightly fictionalized scenes in which Mama Miti talks with women. But the writer may have listened to or watched the Nobel Prize winner being interviewed and either replicated her style of talking and/or took personal stories from the interviews.

There is a big difference between a small amount of imagined detail and a heavily fictionalized work. In the past, many biographies geared toward young readers were highly fictionalized, because it was thought that authentic biography would not engage children. But today, writers have learned how to write in a more literary and engaging way and to base details solidly on sources. Students need to learn to look at a text analytically and check the documentation; the ultimate focus should be on authenticity.

The engaging biography *You Never Heard of Sandy Koufax?!* (Winter 2009), appears to be slightly fictionalized because the writer talks directly to the reader and narrates the book from the invented perspective of an anonymous former teammate of Koufax. The writer offers some documented sources and includes charts of baseball statistics. The entire book is highly engaging and offers great information and perspective. *Gregor Mendel: The Friar Who Grew Peas* (Bardoe 2006) is a well-researched biography of Gregor Mendel, the first person to apply the scientific method to biology. At times in the text, the writer includes details about her subject's feelings that may be imagined, but she also quotes the subject's own writing, and there is no imagined dialogue.

Unusual Biographies

Sometimes biographies are presented in unusual ways or feature unexpected subjects. *Animals Marco Polo Saw* (Markle 2009) is the story of the explorer's travels on the Silk Road in 1271. It begins with Marco Polo's birth and ends in 1298 with the handwritten publication of

his stories. A subtext, told in sidebars, focuses on the interesting animals Marco Polo saw on his journey over the Silk Road. This book is both a biography and an expository text.

Biography can be presented in poetic form as well as in prose. *Django: World's Greatest Jazz Guitarist* (Christensen 2009) is a biography of Django Reinhardt written in free verse. It is slightly fictionalized but based on historical events. *When Marian Sang: The True Recital of Marian Anderson* (Ryan and Selznick 2004) is the life story of the great singer Marian Anderson. The main text is presented as a "libretto," in lyrical language, by Pam Munoz Ryan. The text includes stanzas of words from the songs Marian sang at each point in her life. At the end of the story an author's note provides more specific facts and a timeline of notable dates. The writer does attribute specific feelings to the subject—saying, for example that "her heart beat wildly. Would she be able to utter one note?" But it is easy to imagine Marian feeling this way as she sang at the Lincoln Memorial for 75,000 people, an event that is well documented.

The biography *When Harriet Met Sojourner* (Clinton 2007) links two great women who fought against slavery. Page spreads alternate between Isabella (later Sojourner) and Araminta (later Harriet). The writer carefully reveals the parallels in their lives; both are presented as strong women.

Biographical Fiction

In *biographical fiction*, a great deal of the story is invented. A real person may be identified and used as a starting point, but the writer imagines the events, actions, characters, and dialogue. An example of biographical fiction is *Amelia and Eleanor Go for a Ride* (Ryan 1999). In this entertaining story, Amelia Earhart takes Eleanor Roosevelt for a ride in her airplane. The event really happened and these two famous women really existed, but the writer has changed some of the true details of the event to create a good story (for example, she never mentions that two other pilots were present and did most of the flying). At the end of the text, the author's note provides a factual account of Eleanor's interest in aviation and the event in question. She also explains why she deviated from the facts.

In *Ella Fitzgerald: The Tale of a Vocal Virtuosa* (Pinkney 2002), a talking cat tells the story using a rap music style that changes to narrative but is still quite colorful. The scratchboard illustrations introduce lively action. Obviously the cat narrator is fictionalized, as are many of the scenes depicted (such as Ella and Dizzy Gillespie being launched into space on a trumpet), but the people and events in the story are based on fact.

Moses: When Harriet Tubman Led Her People to Freedom (Weatherford 2006) tells of Harriet's own spiritual journey that led her to become the "Moses of her people." The entire text is a work of poetry and art based on a true story but drawn from the writer's imagination.

Students enjoy biographical fiction, and it often sparks their interest in reading more about the person. However, you need to help upper elementary and middle level students distinguish fiction from nonfiction wherever possible.

Historical Fiction and Biography

Unlike biography, the main purpose of historical fiction is not to provide information about a real person's life. Instead, historical fiction aims to tell a good story. In doing so it also often features real people from history. In *Pink and Say* (Polacco 1994) set during the Civil War, Abraham Lincoln features prominently and appears briefly to shake the main character's hand. Contrast this book with *Abraham Lincoln* (D'Aulaire 2008) a simple, colorfully illustrated biography that describes Abraham Lincoln's life from boyhood to presidency. Both books will appeal to young children in the vividness of their narratives and illustrations, but one aims to entertain and provoke thought, while the other aims to inform the reader about the life of a man.

Judging the Quality of Biographies

As you select authentic and fictionalized biographies for students, you will need to apply overlapping but slightly different criteria to judge their quality. We list some questions to ask about both categories of texts (see Figure 9.4). For fictionalized biographies, while we accept the inclusion of invented details and dialogue, we expect the text to be based on truth. Also, the language and details must be authentic in terms of the time and setting in which the subject lived. You also need to think about how the writer supports readers by explaining difficult concepts or providing some background. Fictionalized biographies sometimes have glossaries, pronunciation guides, or timelines that help readers understand the subject's life and circumstances.

In authentic biographies, every detail is documented—places the subject lived, time, actions, dialogue, and so on. It's not that the book is heavily footnoted; that would ruin the experience for the younger reader. But somewhere in the text the sources are provided, and there should be consistency with other nonfiction texts about the same subject or the times. It is also important to notice what the writer includes and what is left out, because important missing information can bias readers' view of the subject. For example, biographies of the founding fathers of the United States often omit the fact that many of them owned slaves.

In both kinds of biographies, information needs to be interesting, clear, and available. The information in the text must have value for students, not just in learning to read biography but in finding out more about life and the world in which they live.

The Demands of Biography on the Reader

Biography makes unique demands as it often asks the reader, as described previously, to make subtle distinctions between factual and fictional details within the same text. Sometimes these details are subtle and therefore more difficult to distinguish, and sometimes they are more apparent. We describe some of the demands of biography on the reader (see Figure 9.5).

EVALUATING AUTHENTIC AND FICTIONALIZED BIOGRAPHY	
Authentic Biography	**Fictionalized Biography**
• Is the book based on sound research, with details documented? • Is it true in every detail? • Is the subject's life worth reading about, and will it be interesting and informative to students? • Is the subject worthy of the biography? • Will information about this subject further students' understanding of historical or current events? • Has the writer used documented dialogue and details to make the story more interesting to readers? • Is the style clear and readable? • Are illustrations authentic and reflect research? • Is the subject presented in a multidimensional way, with both strengths and weaknesses evident? • Has the writer left out any important details about the subject that would influence the reader's view? • Is the information consistent with other biographies of the individual or of people who lived at the same time? • Does the writer avoid bias in presentation–in what is included as well as what is omitted? • Is the organization of the text clear–is it easy for readers to find and understand information? • Are tricky concepts that require background knowledge explained? • Are there any features to help readers understand the text (maps, timelines, glossary, etc.)?	• Is the book based on sound research even though some details that cannot be absolutely substantiated are added? • Are added details supported by other information (such as historical information)? • Does the writer tell the story in an interesting way that will engage readers? • Is the subject's life worth reading about, and will it be interesting to students? • Is the subject presented in a believable way? • Are invented dialogue and detail authentic for the times? • Did the writer make the subject "come to life" and seem real? • Are illustrations true to the times, and do they make the book more interesting? • Can students relate to the subject as a real person with strengths and weaknesses? • Is the author's interpretation of the subject fair and objective? • Is the book readable and interesting? • Is the writer objective in the presentation of the subject? • Is the biography consistent with other information about the individual or the times? • Is the organization of the text clear–is it easy for readers to find and understand information? • Are tricky concepts that require background knowledge explained? • Are there any features to help readers understand the text (maps, timelines, glossary, etc.)?

Figure 9.4 Evaluating authentic and fictionalized biography

BIOGRAPHY: DEMANDS ON THE READER

- Readers must distinguish between true (authentic) biography and fictionalized biography.
- Readers must analyze texts and check documentation.
- Readers must judge the authenticity of language and details—whether they are authentic to the time and setting.
- Readers must evaluate text for bias.
- Readers must use tools such as pronunciation guides and timelines.
- Readers must notice turning points, or when important decisions were made

Figure 9.5 Biography: demands on the reader

Autobiography

An autobiography is a life story written by the person who lived that life. Autobiographies are interesting because the subject can provide many more authentic details than anyone else can, but by their nature, autobiographies are also biased. No one is capable of taking an entirely objective view when writing about one's own life. A good autobiography, however, will not leave out important information or distort events that are historically documented.

Although an autobiography can never be truly objective, it has another advantage:

> . . . autobiography provides the unique viewpoint of self-revelation. What writing about oneself loses in objectivity it gains in wholeness. No one has as complete a view of a life as the one who has lived it." (Darigan, Tunnell, and Jacobs 2002, 374)

We are driven by curiosity to read autobiographies of people we admire and perhaps also those of people we have less regard for because we want to see the world and events from their perspective. Writing an autobiography, the writer is in a place of tension. In recent decades (as public scrutiny has become more tolerant) autobiographies have probably become more honest. Autobiographies for children and adolescents are not as complicated, but they still have challenges. The subject of an autobiography must be someone who is worth reading about but must also be someone who people *are interested* in reading about.

The Wall: Growing Up Behind the Iron Curtain (Sis 2007) in an autobiographical story in which the popular children's author Peter Sis reveals what it was like to grow up in Cold War–era Prague. After an introduction that establishes the history and setting, Sis tells the story in third person using a spare and graphic text. In sidebars, he provides specific information such as definitions of terms and a timeline of historical events. Sidebars also complement and explain the graphics. Sis also includes excerpts from the journals he kept over the years. This autobiography is full of information and requires close study.

Many popular autobiographies feature writers whom children have come to know and love from reading their books. These autobiographies are especially useful in classroom teaching. *Author: A True Story* (Lester 2002) is a picture book autobiography that chronicles author Helen Lester's life from childhood through the publication of her first book. Cynthia Rylant's *But I'll Be Back Again* (1993) describes the author's life and helps readers understand the source of some of her writing. In *Guts: The True Stories Behind* Hatchet *and the Brian Books* (Paulsen 2001) Gary Paulsen describes the true adventures that led him to write his popular books.

Many autobiographies deal with cultural subjects. In *Dancing to Freedom: The True Story of Mao's Last Dancer* (2007) Li Cunxin tells the story of his journey from a rural village in China to a career as a professional ballet dancer. A related text is *Mao and Me: The Little Red Guard* (Hong, 2008): Chen Jiang Hong was born in 1966 and his father was sent away for "re-education" during the Cultural Revolution. Hong became a Little Red Guard and later a children's author.

Autobiographies may be written by ordinary people trying to affect social change. *I Am Rosa Parks* (Parks and Haskins 1997) is a brief autobiography that introduces readers to Rosa Parks and the Montgomery, Alabama bus boycott. Told in Rosa Parks' own voice, the simple story is well suited to young readers. In *Escape From Slavery: The Boyhood of Frederick Douglass in His Own Words* (Douglass 1993) Douglass's own words tell the story of his childhood in slavery.

Evaluating Autobiography

The first tenet in evaluating autobiography is: Is the writer being honest? In a sense, you can never know the answer to that question, because the author is telling his or her own story. But you can apply your own background knowledge (or information from research) to the text you are reading. You know that the writer must write from her or his own perspective, but you can still search for an honest voice. Many of the criteria for evaluating autobiography (see Figure 9.6) are the same as those for biography.

As with biography, you need to consider *authenticity*, which is essential. You assume that the writer is telling the truth but understand that it is shaded by his or her own thoughts and views. But accuracy can be checked. Some parts of a subject's story might be left out because they are not appropriate for children to read about, but in general, the important details should be there. The style of an autobiography should be clear, readable, and interesting. The text should also be "reader friendly"—that is, organized in a way that helps readers find and understand the information. Finally, an autobiography should reveal the writer as a real person; readers should realize that the individuals telling their stories struggled with adversity and had to make decisions about their lives. Readers should be able to connect with writers as people.

EVALUATING AUTOBIOGRAPHY

- Is there evidence that the writer is telling the story honestly?
- Is the text authentic? Can it be substantiated by information from other sources?
- Is the writing style engaging and interesting?
- Is the text organized in a way that supports the reader's understanding?
- Has the writer tried to be as objective as possible and/or explained his/her own biases?
- Has the writer considered the intended audience (younger children; adolescents)?
- Does the writer seem like a real person?

Figure 9.6 Evaluating autobiography

Memoir

Much of the writing that students do in writers' workshop is *memoir*. Memoir is a personal account of events as recalled by the writer. Ray provides this definition:

> Memoir is a type of autobiographical nonfiction where a writer takes a reflective stand in looking back on a particular time in his or her life. The time may be connected to a particular event that happened during that time, or to a person, a place, or an object from that time that is particularly vivid. Memoir is most often written in first person, in the past tense, and generally has some quality of reflection attached to it. In other words, readers don't just get the memory, they also get a sense of the person who is remembering. Sometimes personal essays fulfill the intentions of memoir. (2006, 192)

Ray goes on to say that while autobiographers are obligated to recount faithfully the events of their life and give the reader some kind of order, writers of memoir can take more liberties. We agree that the important thing about memoir is sharing a feeling, an insight, a perception, or an experience. Memoir is a unique type of biographical text, and lots of ordinary people write memoir—sometimes for an audience and often just so they can understand an experience, person, place, or object and remember it. A writer may take on the *style* of memoir to communicate truths for various purposes. Or the writer may draw on past experiences by changing elements such as setting or characters, yet the text has the quality of memoir. We have included a few fictional texts below because they communicate important ideas and offer excellent models.

A memoir usually focuses on a few events or a shorter period in a person's life rather than the entire story from birth to death. The details are vivid, and the reader gets a real sense of the writer's feelings or what the experience was like. In *Winterdance: The Fine Madness of Running the Iditarod* (Paulsen 1994), the author recalls his own experience running the 8,810-mile dog sled race across Alaska. He provides an intense, action-packed description of the experience and also recounts his own feelings. He describes surviving a storm, depending on a hook to save himself and his dogs. Later, he writes:

> I knew what scared me wasn't the canyon and wasn't the hook hanging by one prong but the knowledge, the absolute fundamental knowledge that I could not stop, would not stop, would never be able to stop running dogs of my own free will. (19)

In *When I Was Young in the* Mountains (1993), the well-known children's book author Cynthia Rylant evocatively describes the simple pleasures of growing up in the country. In *Bigmama's* (1998) Donald Crews describes boyhood summers at his grandmother's house in rural Florida. Both books focus on the value of close families and the intense pleasures of childhood freedom. *Saturdays and Teacakes* (2004) is a luminous memoir of the Saturdays author Lester Laminack spent visiting his grandmother as a young boy. The author's poetic language keeps the momentum going and helps the reader hear sounds, like the creak of an old metal glider, and feel motions, like pedaling a bike.

In what might be described as "fictionalized memoir," writers will sometimes take on the style of memoir because they want to show a true event from the perspective of a real person who lived through that event. *Nasreen's Secret School* (2009) is the true story of a little girl in Afghanistan who loses both of her parents in the war. Told from the point of view of her grandmother, the story shows how education helped Nasreen recover. In *Erika's Story* (Zee 2003) the author narrates a true story in the voice of Erika, an infant thrown from a cattle car on its way to a concentration camp in Germany during World War II. This book is an example of the way illustrations and narrative work together to perfectly create mood. The only color in the stark black-and-white drawings is the pink of the infant's blanket, until the final spread, when the drawings burst into full color—still a soft pastel palette—to show that Erika—and hope—has survived and blossomed again.

Some memoirs do not tell a specific story but instead provide descriptions and sensory images that show what life was like at a certain time or in a certain place. *No Star Nights* (Smucker 1989) tells what it was like to live in a mill town in West Virginia about thirty years ago. The illustrations show the dark, smoky air, but the text reveals happy memories.

A memoir can also be a story told to the writer, who chooses the style of memoir for a specific purpose. *Hamzat's Journey: A Refugee Diary* (Robinson 2009) is the story of Hamzat, a young Chechnyan refugee who lost his leg to a land mine and was taken to the United States for surgery. Although the narrator speaks in Hamzat's voice, Hamzat is not the author.

Often famous people who have made remarkable accomplishments use memoir to tell of significant events (turning points) in their life. *I Dreamed I Was a Ballerina* (2001) describes one performance that led the author, Anna Pavlova, to become one of the greatest ballerinas of all time.

Evaluating Memoir

Memoir may be evaluated using the same criteria you apply to biography and autobiography (see Figures 9.4 and 9.6) except that here you may not be so concerned about accuracy and authenticity. What matters is the

message, the images, and the purpose. Of course, if you are using memoir as part of a serious study of a subject, you will need to check the facts. (See Figure 9.7.)

Easy Series Biographies

The first biographies students read might be some of the very simple texts on the market today. These simplified biographies are written in clear language and usually have quite a few illustrations (drawings or photographs). Some biography series are especially designed for younger readers. They include drawings or photographs and simple text for early readers to understand.

Picture Book Biographies

Some simple biographies are beautifully illustrated picture books that are of high artistic quality. These texts are valuable resources in the upper elementary and middle school classroom because:

- They engage students in learning about people's lives.
- When read aloud, they provide opportunity for students to develop background knowledge about historical events or people who live today.
- They introduce readers to the genre.
- They can provide role models for students.
- More so than in the past, many are about leaders or outstanding people from various cultures and minority groups.
- They are high-quality literature for students to enjoy and discuss.

In a picture book biography, the illustrations greatly enhance the meaning of the text. Well-written text that meets the criteria for high-quality biography is accompanied by illustrations worthy of the text. *Bill Pickett: Rodeo-Ridin' Cowboy* (Pinkney 1996) is the story of a famous black rodeo performer. The illustrations by Brian Pinkney are scratchboard renderings hand-painted with oil, and they vividly portray rodeo in action. Floyd Cooper's *Mandela: From the Life of the South African Statesman* (1996) is an account of the life of the great leader of the African National Congress. The soft, pastel paintings (oil wash on board) create a reflective mood and impart warmth that offsets the seriousness of the story.

In *Wilma Unlimited: How Wilma Rudolph Became the World's Fastest Woman* (Krull 1996), the illustrator, David Diaz, uses striking, colorful drawings set against photographs that are symbolic of periods in Wilma's life. The combination of background photographs, drawings, and text provides texture and makes the story more dramatic.

Collected Biographies

Collections of short biographies often appear in a single volume. Usually, the subjects are united by some kind of theme or similarity. *Five Brave Explorers* (Hudson 1995) includes stories about African Americans who explored new worlds. In *Seven Brave Women* (Hearne 1997), the author tells the story of seven generations of women in her family, from her great-great-great grandmother to her mother. Hearne uses short portraits of these women to tell not only what they did as individuals but what the times were like in which they lived.

Elements of Biography

The literary elements of biography and autobiography are in some ways the same as those of fiction, with some important differences.

Setting

Setting is often significant in biography—the time and usually the place where the subject lives affect his or her life. For example, in *Alvin Ailey* (Pinkney and Pinkney 1995) the reader learns that Alvin Ailey's early experiences with music and dance in Los Angeles in the 1940s had a major impact on his achievements later in life.

Characters

The characters in biographies and autobiographies are not invented by the writer. The main "character," of course, is the subject of the biography. Other characters are also real people, but the writer selects whom to include; she makes judgments about which supporting characters are important in the life of the subject. Subjects are not always famous; they are not always heroes. Ordinary people who perform heroic acts are excellent role models for students. Some biographies focus on infamous characters from history, and these also provide important information. As with fictional characters, the subject of a biography must be believable and interesting, and a successful biographer will make readers feel they know the subject well.

Theme

Above and beyond telling the story of a person's life, a biography often has a theme or larger message. The subject may be selected because she has an inspiring story to tell. Biographies have themes like courage, the conflict of good and evil, persistence and hard work, kindness to others, community service, using one's true talents, self sacrifice, and love. They include some of the same conflicts that occur in fiction—for example, people struggling against natural forces, against other people, or even against themselves. In excellent biographies, the writer focuses on those aspects of a person's life that contributed most strongly to their achievements. Those aspects, then, often carry the meaning or message of the entire text—that is, the theme.

Sequence of Events

The sequence of events in biography, including problems and resolutions, are real events that are there for the writer to chronicle, so we do not talk about these events as a "plot" as we do in fiction. The writer, however, should tell about events in an interesting way and must make many decisions about which parts of the individual's life to share in detail and the order in which to tell the story. The reader must consider turning points, or when important decisions are made.

Perspective

The writer of a biography does take a perspective. An authentic biography is told from an objective perspective; the author's point of view should not create bias or overwhelm the reader's understanding of the subject and his or her life. On the other hand, the text should be more than a dry recital of facts. Good biographies often include letters, drawings, notes, or other authentic documents that give the subject life and voice.

MEMOIR: DEMANDS ON THE READER

- Recognize why the author is telling the story.
- Recognize the significance of the events or period of time the author is telling about.
- Understand the author's feelings about the people and events in the story.
- Notice turning points, or when important decisions were made.
- Use tools such as pronunciation guides and timelines.
- Analyze the text and check that information is factual.

Figure 9.7 Memoir: demands on the reader

Art

Biographies, autobiographies, and memoirs may also include art that extends the meaning of the text. They may have authentic photographs of people or artifacts that help readers understand the time, the setting, or the events in the subject's life. They may have drawings or paintings that create mood and expand meaning. As in fiction, the art and text should be harmoniously intertwined so that the entire text is coherent. They should also be accurate.

Graphic and Textual Features

Biographies may also have graphs, maps, charts, and other features that provide information to readers. As in all nonfiction texts, these graphic features should be accurate in every way. Biographies are enhanced by captions under pictures as well as by labels for photographs or drawings.

Biographies also frequently have textual features that support the reader by providing more information or making it easier to find information in the text. Longer biographies may be organized by chapters or sections. They may have a table of contents, an index, a glossary, or a pronunciation guide.

Structural Patterns in Biographies

A biographer typically uses description to help the subject seem real and important to readers and also to describe events in a temporal sequence. Like a fiction writer, a biographer may start with an important event and then reflect on the subject's earlier times. The organizational structure of a biography is quite similar to narrative; after all, the biographer is telling a story.

Biography has many of the features of fiction that appeal to students, among them:

- A narrative structure.
- A strong central character (or subject).
- An important setting—time, place, and circumstances.
- A series of events during which problems arise and are resolved.
- A major culminating point that represents the individual's greatest achievement. (There may be several of these points.)

High-quality biographies also have the advantage of authenticity and believability. Biography has features of nonfiction in that it:

- Is based on research.
- Is accurate in details and events.
- Provides selected and organized information.
- Is designed to inform the reader.

Value of Biography

Because of the combined features above, biography can be a bridge between fiction and nonfiction. Students may be captivated by the fact that the stories are true. The narrative structure makes the material more available to them because it is familiar from their reading of fiction.

The important questions for students to ponder are related to the turning points in biography, or when important decisions were made. Have students consider: What if a different decision were made by the subject? This gives students new understanding of the impact of history on peoples of the world. By reading biography, students can learn about other cultures and times. They can explore the conflicts between people, internal conflicts, and struggles against nature and society. People of achievement typically have shown courage in overcoming obstacles and have made contributions to society. Biographies help students understand both past times and current times more clearly.

Biographies can be inspiring as students read about how ordinary people stretch to meet the challenges that arise in their lives and achieve greatness. For many readers, the impact of biography is even more powerful than fiction because the subject and the story are real. In addition, biography makes it possible to integrate literature study and social studies within the curriculum. Students are reading and learning more about genre; at the same time, they are exploring history or current events and people.

The wide variety of biographical texts gives students the opportunity to learn about and through the lives of real individuals who have made important contributions. Some are famous and documented in history; some are unknown. But the subjects of biographies can inspire students. The literacy curriculum is enriched when a variety of biographies, autobiographies, and memoirs are available to students.

Suggestions for Professional Development

Set up four meetings to discuss biography and autobiography with colleagues at your particular grade level. You might enjoy doing this as a lunch discussion group, during a planning period, or as part of a study group or in-service course. If you do not have the time to do all four suggested activities, pick one or two that will impact your teaching at your grade level. You'll be looking at four kinds of texts:

- Fictionalized and authentic biographies
- Picture book biographies, both fictionalized and authentic
- Autobiographies
- Memoirs

Ask your school librarian for help or go to a public library if you don't have a good collection of these books in your classroom. You will find many high-quality biographies, autobiographies, and memoirs for a variety of grade levels listed as mentor texts at the end of this chapter. *Guiding Readers and Writers: Teaching Comprehension, Genre, and Content Literacy* (Fountas and Pinnell 2001) includes a complete list of autobiographies by writers of children's books. For each meeting, each participant should bring at least four examples for discussion.

MEETING 1: FICTIONALIZED AND AUTHENTIC BIOGRAPHIES

1. Share the titles and authors of the books each member of the group has brought.
2. Decide whether each title is fictionalized or authentic. Provide a rationale for your classification.
3. Working in pairs or small groups, use the chart in Figure 9.4 to evaluate and discuss the books. Find evidence in the text to support your judgments. For example, if you determine that the writer provides details to make the character seem real, read a short example aloud to the group.
4. After examining the texts, select a few for more in-depth discussion. Ask:
   - What are the features of this text that will make it appealing to students at the grade level or reading level?
   - What will be challenging to students?
   - What has this writer done to make information accessible to students?
5. One of the outcomes of this meeting will be to increase your knowledge of biographies. Make a list of those you want to read and those you would like to order for your classroom when resources are available. Include all necessary information, including ISBN number, so that ordering will not be a chore.
6. Reflect as a group on how your new understandings of biography will impact study of biography in your classroom.

MEETING 2: PICTURE BOOK BIOGRAPHIES—BOTH FICTIONALIZED AND AUTHENTIC

1. In your first meeting, you might have looked at some picture books along with chapter books, but in meeting 2 you will be focusing on picture book biographies.
2. Share the titles and authors of the books everyone brings to the meeting and spend some time reading them and looking at the art. Because these biographies are usually short, members of the group can read them at the meeting. You might even have time to read some aloud to the group.
3. Determine whether each biography is fictionalized or authentic. This should be a very quick process.
4. Look at each book and discuss the following questions:
   - How do the illustrations and text complement each other?
   - What do the illustrations add to the story that would be missing with text only?

- What mood/emotion do the illustrations evoke and how does this mood add to your understanding of the subject or events?
- Are the illustrations of high quality? Are they appropriate for the subject and the meaning the writer wants to convey?

5. Leave the meeting with a list of books you want to order for your own classrooms. You can also exchange books and read some of them aloud to your students. Discuss their responses at a follow-up meeting.

MEETING 3: AUTOBIOGRAPHY

1. Follow the same procedures for sharing that you used in meeting 1 and 2.
2. Using the chart in Figure 9.6, apply the criteria for evaluating autobiography. Discuss and provide evidence for your decisions.
3. Discuss the collection of autobiographies using the following questions:
   - How has the writer been selective in choosing the details and events to describe?
   - What message does the writer want to convey in telling his or her life story?
   - What would be appealing to students about this autobiography?
   - What would students learn from reading this autobiography?
4. Leave the meeting with a list of autobiographies that you want to read and/or acquire for your classroom library.
5. Reflect on how your new understandings of autobiography will impact your study of this genre with your students.

MEETING 4: MEMOIR

1. Follow the same procedures for sharing that you used in previous meetings.
2. Use the charts in Figures 9.4 and 9.6 to examine and discuss the memoirs everyone has brought to the meeting (with memoir you may not be as concerned with evaluating accuracy and authenticity). Provide evidence from the text for your statements.
3. Discuss the collection of memoirs using the following questions:
   - Why did the writer select the particular time period or event to focus on in the memoir?
   - What message does the writer want to convey in telling about this memory?
   - What would be appealing to students about this memoir?
   - How could you use this memoir to help students in their own writing (in a series of writing minilessons, for example)?
4. Leave the meeting with a list of memoirs you want to read and/or acquire for use with your students.
5. Reflect on how your new understanding of memoir will impact your teaching in reading and writing.

CHAPTER 10

Nonfiction Texts

Purpose, Organization, and Audience

Good nonfiction rejects the voice from nowhere that characterizes encyclopedias and text books, a stance that acts as if reality were undisputed and God-given, in favor of a particular person's situated understanding of the topic.

—Randy Bomer

We sometimes think of nonfiction texts as simple—presenting facts in a straightforward way—as opposed to fiction, which has imaginary characters, plots, complex language, and a number of literary techniques. Content knowledge is seen as the major factor in comprehending nonfiction, and background information is indeed very important. But it is just as important to recognize *how* the writer of nonfiction presents information. Nonfiction texts are crafted by a writer for a wide variety of purposes, and their structure ranges from simple to highly complex.

We consider all nonfiction genres to be informational, in the sense that each imparts facts. We can further separate nonfiction into two categories: narrative and nonnarrative. Biography, autobiography, and memoir are all narrative, as is narrative nonfiction. Expository, procedural, and persuasive texts are all nonnarrative. (See Figure 10.1.)

You use nonfiction texts every day for many purposes. You might start the day by reading the directions on medication, the label on your cereal, or the operating directions on your treadmill. You may read a newspaper, and probably you'll take a look at your calendar. As the day goes on you might go online via your tablet or laptop to search for a phone number, order something from a catalog, read advertisements, and peruse menus and timetables. If you're cooking, you might read a recipe or the directions for microwaving something. You will read your mail—letters, an investment statement, a newsletter from your college, or the latest issue of a magazine. You might listen to the news (which means someone is reading a report aloud to you) or read it on the Internet. You might visit your networking site of choice to read messages from friends. Finally, relaxing in the evening, you might read the guide on your TV screen or a program at a concert. You could

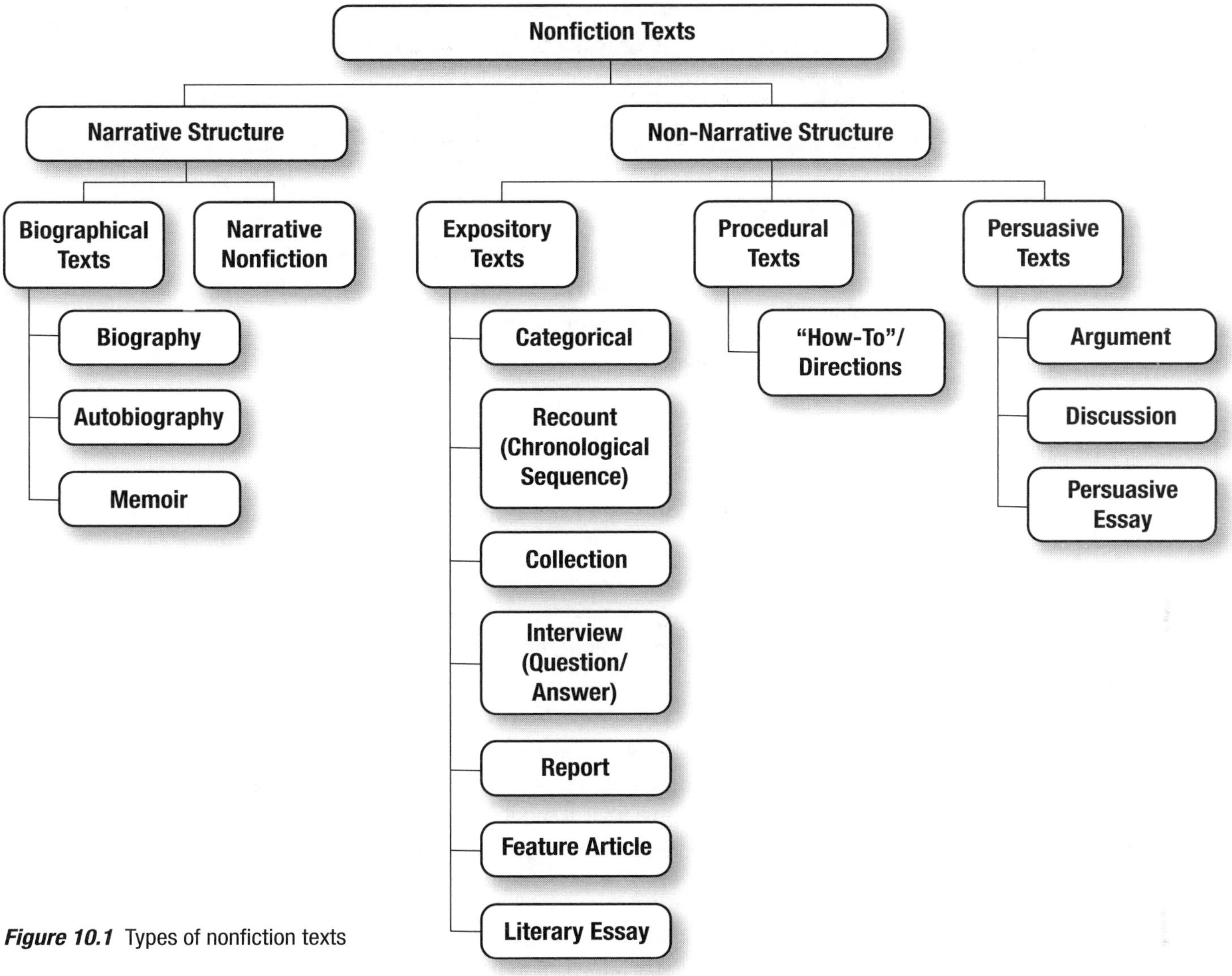

Figure 10.1 Types of nonfiction texts

pick up a new book about the Silk Road, a book about health, or guides to next summer's gardening.

Nonfiction reading permeates our lives in essential ways. It guides our actions, helping us know what to do and how and when to do it. Through nonfiction, we expand our knowledge of the world; it shapes our opinions. We gain knowledge that helps us make better personal decisions about health, finances, property, and relationships. We gain knowledge that helps us become better at our jobs and better citizens.

As students engage with nonfiction across the elementary and middle school grades, they build a foundation for their lifelong appreciation of these texts. They need exposure to a far greater variety than textbooks offer. It is important that they read many different kinds of texts for a range of real purposes (see Figure 10.2). As they process texts, they learn to adjust their reading according to the purpose, style, and type of text. This flexibility expands their reading ability. Complex nonfiction texts present a challenge to students, partly because of their great variety and also because of the many ways writers can craft texts to provide information. It takes many years for readers to become skilled in reading the various genres and types of nonfiction texts.

In Appendix A you will find a list of mentor texts for narrative nonfiction, expository nonfiction, procedural texts, and persuasive texts. These are suggested titles to be used as exemplars of the genre, but you may have excellent examples of your own that you prefer to use. These mentor texts may be used to build text sets, and

GENRES AND CHARACTERISTICS OF NONFICTION TEXTS		
Nonfiction: **Provides factual information about a subject; often uses exposition but may include narration, description, or persuasion; employs underlying text structures such as compare and contrast.**		
Genre	**Definition**	**Characteristics**
Narrative Nonfiction	Provides factual information in narrative style and chronological structure about a particular topic.	• Provides factual information about a topic • Information is presented in the form of a story • Uses chronological text structure Often: • Has characters and setting • Uses literary language • Conveys a larger message • Includes organizational tools (table of contents, headings, index, glossary, pronunciation guide, appendices) • Includes graphic features that support or enhance the text (photographs, illustrations, captions, charts, diagrams, tables and graphs, timelines)
Expository Nonfiction	Provides factual information about a topic using a clear (non-narrative) organizational structure with a major topic and supporting information.	• Provides factual information about a topic • Information is presented with a clear (non-narrative) organizational structure, for example, categories of information in a logical sequence • Has a major topic and supporting information Often: • Conveys a larger message • Has information organized by categories or subcategories • Includes organizational tools (table of contents, headings, index, glossary, pronunciation guide, appendices) • Includes graphic features that support or enhance the text (photographs, illustrations, captions, charts, diagrams, tables and graphs, timelines)
Procedural Text	Provides factual information in order to give directions or teach or describe a process.	• Provides factual information • Gives directions or teaches or describes a process Often: • Organized as step-by-step directions • Describes steps in a simple or complex process • Describes human invented processes • Uses temporal sequence • Uses cause and effect • Has diagrams or drawings with labels

Figure 10.2 Genres and characteristics of nonfiction texts

GENRES AND CHARACTERISTICS OF NONFICTION TEXTS		
Nonfiction: **Provides factual information about a subject; often uses exposition but may include narration, description, or persuasion; employs underlying text structures such as compare and contrast.**		
Genre	**Definition**	**Characteristics**
Persuasive Text	Presents a series of factual, logically organized reasons to support ideas in order to convince the reader to think or do something.	• Provides factual information • Convinces the reader to think something or do something • Presents a series of logically organized reasons to support ideas • Takes a stance or specific side of an argument Often: • Includes both facts and opinions • Is biased • Presents pros and cons of a given situation • Presents two (or more) alternate points of view • Related to social or scientific issues

Figure 10.2 Genres and characteristics of nonfiction texts *(cont.)*

for read-aloud and book clubs. At grades K-1, we recommend a study of the characteristics of nonfiction texts as a general category, as opposed to studying the more detailed and nuanced characteristics of specific nonfiction genres appropriate to older students.

Value of Nonfiction Texts

Nonfiction texts provide information to students in the content areas, but they have value above and beyond learning facts. Reading high-quality nonfiction texts, suitable in level of difficulty, provides a way for students to expand the reading process. With your support and teaching, they learn to adjust their reading for different kinds of texts and different purposes. We list some of the values of nonfiction texts (see Figure 10.3), which we briefly discuss below.

Nonfiction texts introduce readers to a variety of ways of thinking. They learn how ideas build on one another and how facts are used to support generalizations. They can recognize a logical sequence of ideas or follow events and descriptions over time. In factual texts, however, information does not need to be presented in a linear way (as in narrative). Writers organize their ideas into categories and use a variety of tools, such as graphic illustrations, headings and subheadings, indexes, and tables of contents, to direct our attention in several directions.

Nonfiction texts also help readers learn to integrate information from a variety of sources. For example, writers use non-textual devices such as graphs and maps. Readers learn to move back and forth between the text and information presented graphically. You need to gather information from both and integrate it as you read. Or you can read the text first and then go back to pick up information from the graphic features.

Nonfiction texts are excellent models for writing. Reading them, students learn how to organize and express their own ideas. They learn how to present the logical sequence of an argument or write objectively, presenting both sides of an argument. As they read high-quality expository texts, they are exposed to examples of clear language, word choice, sentence style, and how writers use detail and example to explain concepts clearly.

VALUE OF NONFICTION TEXTS

High-quality nonfiction texts:

- Provide accurate information to expand students' knowledge.
- Introduce readers to a variety of ways of organizing and presenting ideas and information.
- Provide examples of different structures for presenting ideas.
- Help readers learn to integrate information from text and other sources.
- Engage the reader with the topic.
- Provide examples that help students in their own nonfiction writing.
- Present content in an interesting way.
- Provide information that will help students make connections to fiction texts.
- Provide information that will help students critique fiction texts.
- Have great variety, which will stretch readers' powers.
- Leave readers interested in pursuing even more information on the topic.

Figure 10.3 Value of nonfiction texts

High-quality factual texts with engaging illustrations are inherently interesting to students because they provide information about the world in which they live. Today, we have superb examples of texts that engage readers in every way and effortlessly build knowledge foundations. Information on any topic can be accessed in seconds through online and print sources.

Factual texts can be integrated with fiction texts in classroom instruction. Students who read historical fiction will be interested in factual texts about the same time period. Realistic fiction texts may be set in different parts of the world; informational texts about these same places will enhance students' understanding of the plot. Some fiction texts may feature scientific or technological concepts; reading expository texts provides information that students can use to read critically.

Deep reading requires making connections. Through connecting texts, students enrich the experience of reading both fact and fiction. Each has value for the other. Reading fiction can spark interest in nonfiction texts; reading nonfiction texts can give readers the information and tools they need to better understand fiction texts as well as think critically about them.

Nonfiction texts require the reader to become flexible, adjusting to a wide range of texts. The variety of informational texts we encounter every day is astounding. Some are simple, others are complex, but all have their particular organizational structure and even vocabulary. Reading this wide variety of texts and recognizing the differences helps students learn more about themselves as readers. (See Figure 10.8, page 147.)

Narrative vs. Non-Narrative Structure

Writers of nonfiction texts have a number of decisions to make as they think about text structure. Depending on purpose, they can use either narrative or non-narrative structure, or a combination of both. Narrative texts tell a story; in the case of nonfiction, the text presents true information but it "reads" a little like fiction because it is organized in chronological order. That is certainly true of biographical texts, which tell the story or stories of a person's life.

That is also true of narrative nonfiction that is not biographical but does use chronological structure to engage readers and carry them along. *Salmon Summer* (McMillan 1998) uses a narrative structure to describe a day in the life of a real Alaskan Aleut boy who is finally old enough to fish with his father. By following the activities of this family, we gain a great deal of information about their relationships with one another, their culture, and this particular fishing industry.

Narrative nonfiction and biography differ from fictional stories in that they may not use the typical story structure of plot, climax, and resolution. But readers will recognize the chronological text structure because it is so close to narrative structure. Narrative nonfiction is also usually distinguished by literary quality—not just the fact that a chronological sequence is used. A high-quality nonfiction history narrative, for example, usually has a central message that goes beyond simply presenting historical facts in an organized way. Writers of nonfiction books for children often use a narrative structure because it is familiar to young readers. But students must learn the flexibility it takes to recognize and adjust their reading to gain information from the many different ways texts are organized.

Literary nonfiction refers to nonfiction that uses literary styles and techniques (such as figurative language). We do not consider these two terms—literary nonfiction and narrative nonfiction—to be interchangeable. Literary nonfiction does not always take a narrative form (for example, an expository text might be considered literary nonfiction when literary elements are present).

Non-Narrative Text Structures

Most non-narrative texts use one of three kinds of structures—expository, procedural, or persuasive (see Figure 10.2). These three categories can be distinguished by *purpose*:

- Expository texts are designed to inform, explain, or describe. Within this category, we will see that writers have many choices for organizing texts.
- Procedural texts give directions or teach or describe a process. They may be simple how-to books, longer instructional manuals, or much longer, complex texts.
- Persuasive texts are intended to convince the reader to think something or do something. Persuasive texts can be obvious or they may be quite subtle.

These categories are helpful in recognizing the types of texts, but we also need to realize that many texts do not fit neatly into one category. A text can be all three—expository, procedural, and persuasive.

Categories of Nonfiction Texts

The way nonfiction texts are organized includes strong underlying patterns that readers are required to recognize and understand for deeper comprehension. You need to recognize the wide range of nonfiction texts that exist and that you use in various ways to organize your life. You may not think of something like a lesson plan or schedule as being a nonfiction text, but it is. Some guides and schedules can be quite tricky to read and interpret. And there are highly abstract and complex texts, such as government reports, that are easy to label as inaccessible. You can group nonfiction texts (excluding biographical texts which we discuss in Chapter 9) into several large categories (see Figure 10.4) based on the primary or overarching text organization as well as the purpose of the written text.

The categories in Figure 10.4 are not mutually exclusive but may overlap. Generally, more complex texts include combinations of the simpler forms. The Internet is a good example. "Reading" the Internet requires knowing how to read labels and search for information. When you reach a website, you find information in categories that you must access, and you also find links to other websites. You need to use key words, interpret labels and buttons, and keep the general pattern of categorization in mind. Once you access the information, however, you'll be reading reports, articles, lists, explanations, stories, emails, discussions, and so on. The website, a text in itself, is a gateway to all the other kinds of informational texts.

Expository Texts

Categorical Texts

A great many expository nonfiction texts present information by category and provide details about the topics. The categories are usually presented in some logical order, but readers can often skip around, seeking information of most interest. There is no need to read from beginning to end. This feature allows skillful readers to seek out new information or facts that support their own area of investigation. You skim and scan for information, zooming in on the answers to questions. Naïve readers often plod along, reading every word, unable to sort out the details to gain the essential information. Using categories, noticing the organization of the information by topic and subtopic, and using features such as headings helps students read with understanding.

Killer Creatures (Llewellyn 2008) is an example of a text organized by categories. The table of contents

CATEGORIES OF NONFICTION TEXTS			
EXPOSITORY TEXTS			
Type	**Description**	**Requires readers to:**	**You might find this type of informational text in:**
Categorical Text	Information presented in logical categories (and subcategories) of related information; all categories clearly related to a major topic; there may be diagrams to show categories of information and how they are related	• Understand the major categories of information and why facts are grouped together • Identify and understand subcategories • Understand the relationship between categories • Understand comparison/contrast, problem/solution, description, cause/effect	Informational books and articles Textbooks
Recount (chronological sequence)	Past events ordered in chronological sequence; may start in the present and move back in time, but time periods are clearly signaled; often uses timelines and diagrams to show time periods	• Gather information • Follow a sequence in time • Understand events in relation to time periods • Think about why past events are important • Remember the most significant events	Historical accounts Reports of natural phenomena set within time periods Newspaper articles Letters/email Diaries Journals Logs Textbooks
Collection	A body of material organized as a reference or list; items organized, sometimes with descriptors, into a database that may be printed, accessed via Internet, or on a computer flash drive; may be included as reference tools in a factual text	• Recognize the way the document is organized • Use alphabetical order to locate information • Scan to pick up information. • Use tools like a table of contents and an index. • Relate items of information to the bigger picture • Conduct searches–hard copy or online.	Catalogs Directories Encyclopedias (brief entries) Dictionaries Atlases Almanacs List books Joke and riddle books Glossaries Database

Figure 10.4 Categories of nonfiction texts

CATEGORIES OF NONFICTION TEXTS			
EXPOSITORY TEXTS *(cont.)*			
Type	**Description**	**Requires readers to:**	**You might find this type of informational text in:**
Interview (question and answer)	Information organized as a series of questions with responses; based on a verbal interview or on frequently arising or logical questions about a topic; often may be read in any order	• Construct meaning by putting together information from sometimes fragmented responses • See the relationship between answers to questions • Follow the logical order of questions • Search for questions of interest and read selectively	Transcribed interviews Blogs or electronic surveys Books based on frequently arising questions, or questions people might ask about the topic
Report	Brings together information from several sources and synthesizes them into a single text that informs the reader about some general principles; may include a wide range of graphics.	• Gather information • Notice important details and summarize information • See how content is divided and organized • Draw out generalizations • Think about relationships between facts and ideas • Synthesize information • Evaluate accuracy • Recognize bias • Distinguish fact and opinion • Notice and get information from graphics	Articles Books on content topics Financial reports Research reports Speeches on social or political topics
Feature Article	Presents information organized around a central theme or idea; uses many different kinds of text structures to weave a cohesive sequence of ideas	• Derive central ideas or themes of the article • Gather information supporting the central idea or theme • Think critically about the ideas and how they are related	Newspaper or magazine articles Articles in literary magazines or books

Figure 10.4 Categories of nonfiction texts *(cont.)*

continues

CATEGORIES OF NONFICTION TEXTS			
EXPOSITORY TEXTS *(cont.)*			
Type	**Description**	**Requires readers to:**	**You might find this type of informational text in:**
Literary Essay	Presents information in an analytic way to draw conclusions about works of literature	• Understand how ideas are presented to support conclusions • Follow analyses and understand how they build on one another toward conclusions	Articles in literary magazines or books
PROCEDURAL TEXTS			
How-To, Directions	A set of instructions about how to perform a task; usually organized as a step-by-step set of directions; there may be diagrams or drawings with labels	• Gather information • Follow the description of a sequence of actions • Consider the significance of each step in a complex process • Understand the conventions in which instructions are written • Recognize the logic of the instructions or the temporal sequence • Problem solve by searching in the document for missed steps or errors	Guides of all kinds Pamphlets Manuals Recipes Class lectures on how to do something
PERSUASIVE TEXTS			
Argument	A persuasive text that presents a series of logically organized reasons for a belief, attitude, or proposed action	• Gather information • Follow a line of thought • Identify the sequence of ideas • Understand points made on one side of an argument • Judge or evaluate the accuracy or validity of the argument • Recognize bias • Distinguish fact from opinion • Notice persuasive language • Recognize the unexpressed (or explicit) values behind the writing	Essays Speeches/debates Position papers Advertising Propaganda Editorials and op-ed pieces Reviews Letters to the editor

Figure 10.4 Categories of nonfiction texts *(cont.)*

CATEGORIES OF NONFICTION TEXTS			
PERSUASIVE TEXTS *(cont.)*			
Type	**Description**	**Requires readers to:**	**You might find this type of informational text in:**
Discussion	Presents the pros and cons of a situation, event, or phenomenon; generally seeks full disclosure of information in an objective way; presents specific information	• Gather information • Follow a line of thought • Understand points made on both sides of an argument • Contrast two points of view • Evaluate the objectivity and accuracy of the text	Articles in newspapers or magazines Textbooks Books on natural phenomena or social/political science
Persuasive Essay	A persuasive text that provides a body of information related to social or scientific issues; tries to help the reader develop generalizations and principles on which to make decisions; may include any or all of the other types of factual texts	• Gather information • Decide which information is important • Discover relationships among ideas • Follow a line of argument • Develop generalizations and principles from the information • Evaluate the accuracy, completeness, and logic of the piece • Evaluate the proposed solution	Government reports Position papers Scientific reports Long essays Treatises Literary essays presenting opinions

Figure 10.4 Categories of nonfiction texts *(cont.)*

clearly presents the categories of "killers," from big cats to crocodilians to extinct killers. The well-organized text presents photographs with grisly details of the killings as well as clear relationships between the animals' characteristics and the ways they kill. Readers can easily find areas of interest using the glossary.

Recount (Chronological Sequence)

A recount is a description that tells of past events and is usually ordered sequentially in time. The recounting may be about a brief time (minutes of a meeting) or a longer period (a history of a town). It may be informal (a letter or email about a vacation) or formal (a history text).

Telling events in order is usually the only way the recounting resembles a narrative. True narrative structure would have characters, a story problem, a plot, and an end to the story. Sometimes works of nonfiction will have all those elements; the difference is that the characters are real (or real but anonymous) and sometimes there are many critical points in the story. But some writers create chronological descriptions in a way that mimics the narrative structure.

Lewis and Clark (Kroll 1994) is a sequential account of the historic journey to explore the American West. There are no digressions and only the essential background information is provided. *The Way West:*

Journal of a Pioneer Woman (Knight 1993) provides excerpts from the journal of a family traveling by wagon from Iowa to the Oregon territory in the 1800s.

A recount requires readers to follow a sequence, identify and think about important points on the sequence, and remember what is significant. As we will discuss later, chronological sequence can also be an *underlying structure* included in any kind of nonfiction text.

Collection

A collection is an organized list or catalog of items that have something in common. At the very simplest, a telephone directory is a collection of names, addresses, and phone numbers. Joke and riddle books would also be in this category. More complex collections might include concise encyclopedia entries and almanacs. *Lies (People Believe) About Animals* (Sussman and James 1987) is an example of a more complex collection. Each page has a photograph and text that succinctly specifies the lie and the truth, along with an explanation. *Name That Style: All About Isms in Art* (Raczka 2009) explains the basics of fourteen different art styles spanning the 1430s to the 1970s. *Independent Dames: What You Never Knew About the Women and Girls of the American Revolution* (Anderson 2008) is an interesting example of a collection. It follows a timeline, so the writer uses chronological sequence as well, but the important organizational spine is women's accomplishments related to the American Revolution.

Sometimes writers use a well-known and established system as an organizing tool. Examples are alphabet and counting books, which are usually geared to younger children. Many alphabet books, however, have little to do with learning the alphabet! *A Is for Africa* (Onyefulu 1997) presents Africa in images and facts organized by the alphabet. The writer/photographer's goal is to present favorite images reflecting the diversity of the continent as a whole. The alphabet serves only as a way to organize and present the information.

Readers of collections need to use organizational conventions—alphabetical order and the hierarchical nature of categories, for example—to access information. You may need special skills to search for information. Collections seldom require readers to read from beginning to end; instead, you use searching techniques. You may scan rapidly for information, picking up just the detail you need in order to find what you want. Or you may move around randomly in the text, looking for what is interesting or new.

Interview (Question/Answer)

Interviews organize information as a series of questions with responses. These may be based on actual verbal exchange between a subject and an interviewer (who has ideally conducted research on the subject beforehand and brings some expertise to the interview); or they may be based on frequently arising or logical questions about a topic. Many interviews include explanatory text in paragraph form that provides background or summary information that pertains to the interview or the subject, or may summarize parts of the interview. Some books for young readers consist almost entirely of question and answer format interviews, or may include discrete sections that use an interview format. A highly imaginative book for younger readers that uses an interview format is Bob Raczka's *The Vermeer Interviews* (Raczka 2010). The author clearly states that the answers given to the questions he poses are imagined (questions are about the subjects in the paintings and their surroundings), but using the interview format allows him to give details about the art techniques, historical context, and cultural elements related to the paintings, and the text provides straightforward analysis and information.

Report

Reports are comprehensive documents that usually bring several kinds of nonfiction texts together in a logical way. The writer of a report has done wide reading on a topic—using several sources—and has then synthesized it into a single report. The central core of a report is the communication of one or more main ideas or principles, with supporting details. Information is organized categorically; most textbooks are some kind of report. Reports may take the form of articles or books on topics in the physical or social sciences. Reports may deal with any form of human endeavor; a financial report, for example, would bring together profit and loss statements and would usually include tables or graphs. Research reports survey a body of information, summarize it, and draw out main principles.

Your own school experiences may lead you to think of reports as boring or dry, but like any other kind of nonfiction text, the degree to which it is interesting depends on factors like writing style, voice, layout and graphics, and topic presentation. Of course, your own interests are also a factor, but good books can always grab you if they have the right features.

Many interesting nonfiction books can also be called reports. Look at the page from *Frogs* (Tyler 1997) in Figure 10.5. Each page of this book presents a different kind of information about frogs. The information is logically organized, full of descriptive information, and accompanied by detailed illustrations.

All frogs are similar in important ways.

They have smooth skin which must be kept moist. For this reason they always live in or near damp places.

Desert habitat where frogs keep moist by living underground until it rains (right)

Habitat with natural springs where tree, land, and water frogs live (bottom left)

Dam near Snowy Mountains where tree and land frogs live (bottom right)

11

Figure 10.5 Page from *Frogs*

To comprehend a report readers need to notice important details and summarize them as they go, creating a network of understandings. They need to be able to discern how the content is organized, relating information from one section to another. They constantly match the information in the text with their own background knowledge, either revising their concepts or questioning the accuracy of the text. They not only acquire the information provided but also think about what might have been left out; they judge the completeness of the report, try to detect bias, and distinguish fact from opinion. If appropriate, they integrate information from text and graphics.

Feature Article

A feature article presents information organized around a central theme or idea. In past years, feature articles were mainly found in newspapers or magazines and other printed texts, although now many feature articles appear in online publications. Feature articles deal with a wide variety of subjects and may use many different kinds of text structures to weave a cohesive sequence of ideas. They usually have an interesting angle on a topic that engages readers.

Literary Essays

A literary essay is a very formal written presentation of analytic thinking. The writer reads and thinks analytically about a text or a connected body of texts (for example, several works by the same author or with the same theme, setting, etc.) and then presents the thinking in the form of an essay. The essay brings different kinds of information together and juxtaposes ideas that lead to the main points. This type of text reaches its height in literary criticism, but middle school and high school students can begin to appreciate literary essays. (Few literary essays appear in children's literature.)

Expository Texts and Literary Quality

The distinguishing feature of narrative nonfiction is not so much type as literary quality, and expository texts can also have a literary quality. To create higher engagement and greater enjoyment, the writer may employ many of the techniques of the writer's craft: figurative language, lyrical description, unique or surprising comparisons, interesting ways of organizing and presenting information. *All About Turkeys* (Arnosky 1998) has labeled diagrams, sidebars, and other nonfiction text features, and the language is clear, straightforward, and interesting:

> Two gobblers claiming the same territory almost always results in vicious fighting. The combatants lash out at each other with their feet and sharp spurs. Fights among gobblers often end in a death. (11)

Here, little figurative language is used, but the exquisite drawings, use of print and pictures together, and the presentation of information in interesting ways work together to create literary quality.

Whether a nonfiction text has literary quality or not is a matter of personal judgment. As you closely examine nonfiction texts, look for those that will appeal to your students and engage their interest. Chances are, those are the texts that fit into the category of literary nonfiction.

Procedural Texts

Procedural texts may be highly practical (such as recipe books or instruction manuals), or a guide to help you understand how to do something like plant a garden. The line between these nonfiction texts is not always clear. A cookbook may involve rich descriptions of a geographical region, for example. *Cook's Illustrated Cookbook* (America's Test Kitchen 2011) provides a great deal of description about the trial and error process used to derive each excellent recipe. Even a procedural text may have a larger message.

How-To Texts or Directions

Many procedural texts are meant to help the reader perform tasks. The text usually provides identifiable, step-by-step instructions. Readers are required to identify and follow a sequence of actions. It helps to visualize these actions, picturing how one leads to another. Often, the reader must interpret diagrams as part of understanding the text. Readers need to check the significance of each step: are all essential or can they be skipped? The reader also needs to match the steps with time required. *Growing Vegetable Soup* (Ehlert 1991) describes all of the steps involved in planting, growing, and preparing the vegetables for vegetable soup—and even eating the finished product! *The New Way Things Work* (Macaulay 1998) is an updated guide to the workings of hundreds of different machines. This book uses both descriptive text and step-by-step directions. Sometimes writers use a "how-to" format to write humorous texts.

Persuasive Texts

Persuasive texts are designed to convince the reader of the validity of a set of ideas—usually of a particular point of view. You process persuasive texts every day as you encounter advertisements, newspaper editorials, and commentators on the news or talk shows. As readers, it is important to bring your critical thinking skills to bear—to recognize persuasion and evaluate the points made. While the categories are not mutually exclusive, we describe three major kinds of persuasive texts.

Arguments

The purpose of an argument is to persuade. The writer presents a series of connected points, all of which lead to a one-sided conclusion. The text may contain facts as well as opinions of the writer and others. In children's literature, you will not find many texts that are written purely for the sake of argument; however, the texts students read in special programs (such as antidrug or antismoking campaigns) would present strong, logical arguments, supported by facts. Seldom would you find both sides of the argument presented in such texts.

In most works of quality literature, a text will have more than one purpose. Texts featuring natural phenomena, for example, may simultaneously report information, using description and detail, but also have the underlying purpose of persuading readers to value the environment. Most of the time, this message is implicit, but when it is explicitly stated, we could call the text *a supported argument*. An example is *Once a Wolf* (Swinburne 2001), which provides accurate information about and wonderful photographs of wolves. The writer dispels myths about wolves and tells of their origin, arguing for a new view of wolves:

> Doug Smith and other wolf biologists believe that their work with the wolves is about fixing what humans have destroyed in the past, righting a long-standing wrong. "Wolf reintroduction is not a science. It's an art," Smith points out. "You go on gut feelings, on hunches, learn as you go. We have so much to learn, but the wolves are teaching us. They are teaching us that if we are tolerant, we can live side by side with them. (44)

Readers of argument must select important information and evaluate the accuracy, completeness, and logic of the piece. They need to follow the line of argument and assess how well each point builds on the other and whether ideas the writer claims are related really are logically connected. Argument requires that readers follow the line of thought the writer is exposing. That might mean understanding the information and how it is related to the claims the writer is making. It would also mean evaluating the writer's claims. Is the information accurate? Are the writer's claims warranted? In a sense, readers of argument must constantly create the *other side* in a critical way.

Discussion

A discussion is similar to an argument in that points of view are expressed; however, a discussion is more objective. Most writers do come to a conclusion, but the discussion involves full disclosure of different points of view. Specific information, such as description and explanation, are often included in a discussion. A newspaper article is the classic example of a discussion, although you are confronted with imperfect examples just about every day. A discussion is supposed to include all relevant information and provide both sides on an issue. When a newspaper article displays bias and opinion, it becomes an editorial. Of course, in the real world, you know that reporting is biased because individuals can never be totally objective, but sometimes the writer has no intention of being objective.

When you read a discussion, you need to gather information and notice what is important, as well as follow a logical argument. Here, though, your task is to evaluate the extent to which the pros and cons have been expressed. A true discussion presents different aspects of the event under discussion. You find discussion in many newspaper and magazine articles, as well as in books on controversial topics such as global warming.

Persuasive Essay

A persuasive text provides a body of information related to a major social or scientific issue. It is related to both argument and discussion in that ideas are organized logically and build toward a conclusion. But a persuasive essay is usually much more formal; the writer claims to have gathered all the information needed to make significant decisions. The writer may have performed research and also has surveyed the field. Most texts read by elementary students would not approach the formality of a persuasive essay, but some books, like *Once a Wolf* and *Fire in the Forest: A Cycle of Growth and Renewal* (Pringle 1995) come close, because they present a great deal of information that has social significance. They work to persuade and they prompt students to think deeply. By reading (or hearing) books like this, students are laying the foundation for much more sophisticated reading and writing.

The demands on readers of persuasive essays are similar to those for arguments and discussions. Since the document is related to significant decisions, the reader must evaluate whether the information is accurate and *complete* and whether the piece is organized logically and honestly.

Underlying Structural Patterns in Nonfiction Texts

In the previous descriptions of types of nonfiction, we referred to the *overarching* or *primary* design used by the writer. The writer has decided to present information in a certain way, and as readers we form expectations based on this presentation. Do we look for categories of information? Do we follow a sequence? Answers to these questions help us predict the kind of information we will be reading: we know where to find answers because we know how the text "works" in general. But as readers of nonfiction, we are also challenged to detect and interpret *underlying* structural patterns that also help us derive information. These patterns appear within the primary text organization and represent the complexity involved in reading nonfiction. Almost every nonfiction text contains *multiple* examples of these structures.

Nonfiction texts are not put together randomly. The coherence of the text depends on the way information is presented, and there are some typical patterns that writers of nonfiction use. These patterns are not formulas but rather descriptions of how information can be presented so that readers can more easily comprehend the writer's message. As writers consider their content, they don't simply choose one of these structures or patterns; they work with the ideas, and the patterns for communicating emerge. There is a match between the content and the way it is organized.

Eight structures often appear in nonfiction texts (see Figure 10.6). Almost all the types of texts listed earlier employ several or even all of these structural patterns.

UNDERLYING STRUCTURAL PATTERNS IN NONFICTION TEXTS

Pattern	Definition	
Categorical	• Presenting information in categories, often with subcategories, signaled by headings and subheadings	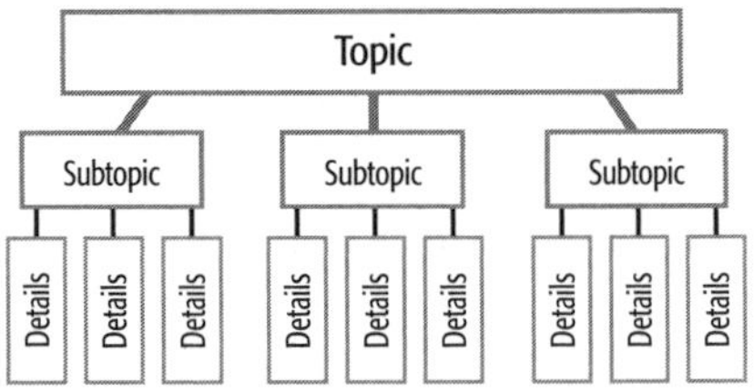
Description	• Using language to provide details and form images so that readers can determine how something looks, moves, taste, smells, or feels	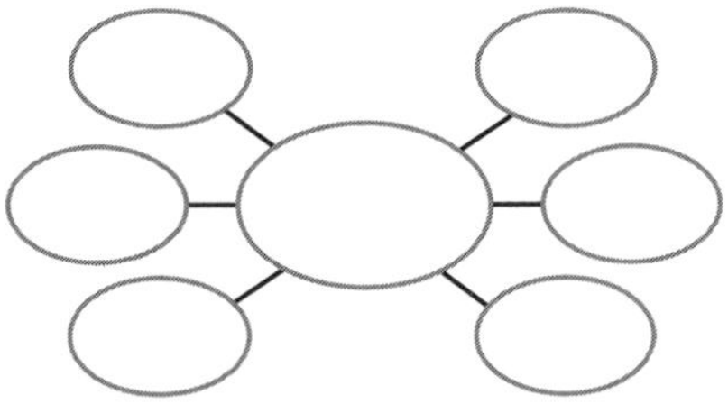
Sequence (Chronological)	• Describing a series of events in the order they happened in time (as in an historical account)	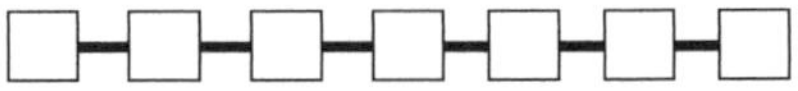
Sequence (Temporal)	• Presenting a sequence of actions for doing something (a process that always happens in the same way)	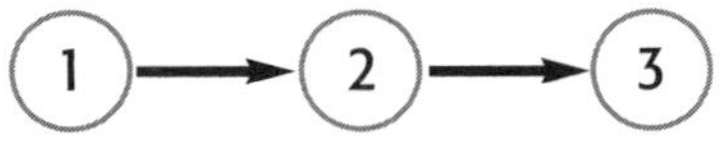
Compare/ Contrast	• Comparing two ideas, events, or phenomena by showing how they are alike and different	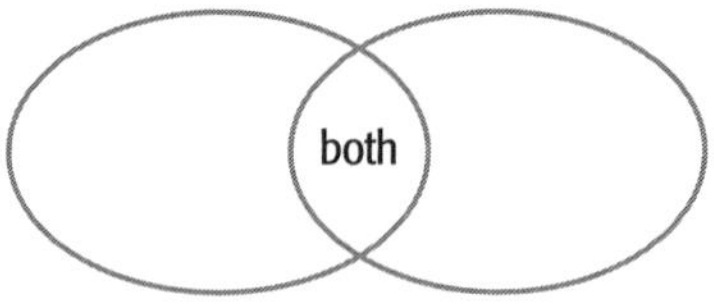
Cause and Effect	• Proposing the reasons or explanations for various phenomena	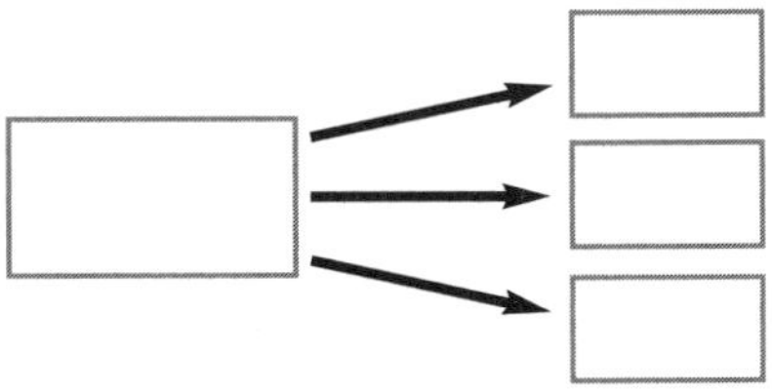
Problem and Solution	• Identifying problems and hypothesizing solutions	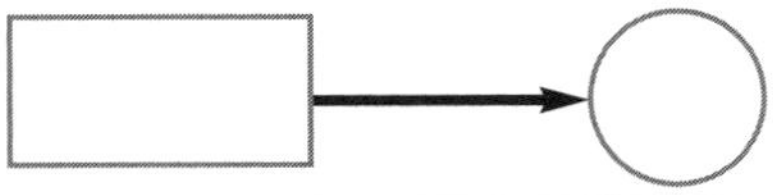
Question and Answer	• Posing a question or a series of questions that are then answered; often used in sidebars or as headings	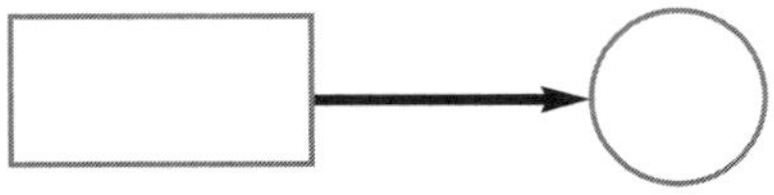
Combination	• Combining or embedding the above structural patterns within a text (almost all nonfiction texts use a combination of patterns)	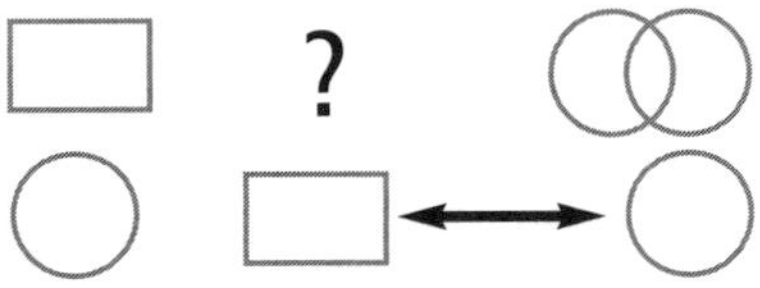

Figure 10.6 Underlying structures in nonfiction texts

Categorical

A categorical pattern appears frequently in nonfiction texts. There are different ways to present categorical information. Sometimes a writer will start with a single aspect of a topic and build ideas through successive sections of the book, finally summing up. On the other hand, a writer may begin with a larger topic and break it down into sections.

Typically, a beginning chapter or section communicates the main idea or thesis. The following sections or chapters present one set of information after another related to the main topic. *Amazing Journeys* (Bacon 1991) begins with an introduction that presents the idea of the book. Chapters titled "Journeys of Discovery," "The Age of Exploration," "Sailing the Sea and Sky," "Journeys for Science," "Some Amazing Animal Journeys," and "More Amazing Journeys" follow, providing specific information about different kinds of journeys.

Description

Description is used in almost every expository nonfiction text. The entire text may be devoted to describing something, but usually description is integrated with other structures. The writer of expository texts describes characteristics of the subject or topic. The writer may emphasize key concepts and use details to support those ideas. The writer of *Safari* (Bateman 1998) uses description (accompanied by outstanding photographs) to help readers understand the life of wild animals. A text inset for each animal provides specific facts:

> The leader of an elephant herd is always the oldest female, known as the matriarch. She remembers where the deepest water holes are and knows the best places to find food.
>
> The face of one of these wise old female elephants makes me think of a map. The creases and wrinkles are like the mountains and rivers. The flat places are the wide plains. (5)

Description is basic to providing information. The writer has to decide *how much* description to provide and then must use language that rouses sensory images and helps the reader visualize how something looked, felt to the touch, smelled, sounded, tasted, or felt while moving. Here is some language from *Outside and Inside Bats* (Markle 1997):

> Squeeze your arm and pat your knees to feel the bones inside. Like you, a bat has a hard, bony inside framework, or skeleton, that gives its body shape. Now bend your fingers, arms, and legs. The body can only bend where bones meet. The bat's body, like yours, is made up of different kinds of bones. (10)

To understand description readers must notice important details and bring them together in a larger vision. They make inferences in that they call up sensory images in response to the words; they also make connections between their own experiences or knowledge and the descriptions in the text. Description relies on the ability to make connections; for example, if they have never seen the color red, it might be hard to understand a description that focuses on that color. In the pieces above, the readers are asked to make connections between their own knowledge and what the writer is describing.

Sequence (Chronological and Temporal)

Sequence, both chronological and temporal, refers to time. The writer organizes the ideas or information in a text in the order in which they happened (or the order in which they are *recommended* to happen).

Temporal sequence is used to describe procedures for accomplishing a task. *The Story of Snow: The Science of Winter's Wonder* (Cassino 2009) includes a two-page layout showing how to catch snow crystals. Temporal sequence is also used to describe processes that occur over and over in the same order. *Sugaring Time* (Lasky 1986) follows the production of maple syrup, beginning with the snow melting and sap running. Directions are usually organized, step by step, in temporal order.

Chronological sequence tells a story in the order things happened. *The Children We Remember* (Abells 1983) is a factual photo essay organized like a story, beginning before World War II and continuing through the war.

Compare/Contrast

To compare one or more ideas, events, or phenomena means to show how they are similar; to contrast them means to show how they are different. Writers often explain ideas using comparison or contrast or both. This structure is especially helpful in preparing an argument or in discussing issues, but it is also useful in description. In *The Grizzly Bear* (Potts 2006), the writer helps readers understand grizzlies by comparing them to other animals: "Many animals travel in groups, herds, or packs. The grizzly does not. Grizzly bears like to be left alone" (23). The contrast is brief, almost an aside, and calls for prior knowledge on the part of the reader.

Cause and Effect

Cause-and-effect patterns provide readers with explanations. The writer may be explaining why a natural phenomenon occurs or explaining the events of history. Cause and effect is a useful structure in writing explanations, arguments, discussions, or reports.

In *The Sun* (Bacon 1991), the writer makes the case that pollution causes the greenhouse effect and that gases are destroying the ozone layer. In this easier text, the cause/effect relationship is only briefly explained, without much detail. Going further would mean explaining *how* the gases destroy ozone. Just how much to explain when using the cause-and-effect structure is a decision that writers and publishers make.

An explanation provides details and descriptions in a way that helps readers understand underlying causes or reasons for natural phenomena, events, or actions. An explanation can be a supported hypothesis about how or why something works (or failed). Explanations appear in scientific articles or books. Textbooks contain many explanations, which is not surprising because they are designed to teach. In *Stones, Bones, and Petroglyphs: Digging into Southwest Archaeology* (Goodman 1998), a hypothesis is offered for why the ancestral Pueblo people left their cliff dwellings.

> In the 1200s, many groups built their pueblos, or towns, around springs. Some even put towers near their water supply to guard it. Could a water shortage be the answer?
>
> Trees create new rings of growth each year—wider rings during years with wet weather, narrower ones during dry years. Scientists, looking at thirteenth-century tree rings from this region, discovered a long drought from A.D. 1274 to 1299. Less rain meant less food from crops, less water for drinking, and perhaps less reason to stick around. (15)

Comprehending explanation requires understanding the way ideas and events are related. We understand the effect and the probable cause the writer is arguing. We evaluate the explanation for feasibility and accuracy. Often graphics add information that is helpful.

Problem and Solution

The Sun (Bacon 1991) proposes a solution to the problem of pollution, instructing readers in some simple ways to stop pollution. Problem and solution is a structure often used in arguments and persuasive essays. A writer clearly defines a problem and then proposes a solution. Cause and effect is often used in combination with problem and solution. In high-quality nonfiction texts, the problem is made clear, as are the reasons it is important to address the problem. The solution is logically related to the problem; it is feasible and there is good evidence that it will solve the problem.

Sometimes an entire text can be organized around a central problem or question. In *Daily Life in a Covered Wagon* (Erickson 1997), the writer describes many problems encountered by a family moving west. The subtitle of *Black Holes: A Journey to the Heart of a Black Hole—and into One of the Greatest Mysteries of the Universe* (Couper and Henbest 1996) lays out the central question or problem around which the entire text is organized—finding out about the mysteries of space.

Question and Answer

Questions and answers are often inserted into a nonfiction text to raise questions in the reader's mind and/or to convey answers with some precision. Sometimes these are presented as headings and/or sidebars. *Do Animals Have Feelings Too?* (Rice 1999) asks a question in the title; the entire text then addresses this guiding question. *Mysteries of the Mummy Kids* (Halls 2007) has an embedded interview with Johan Reinhard, mummy finder. In *Moon Bear* (Guiberson 2010) the author poses questions about Asian bears and how they thrive in their natural habitat. *Lifetimes* (Rice 1997) tells about the expected lifetimes of animals and plants, including the mayfly, which lives one day, and the giant sequoia, which lives about two thousand years. Overall, *Lifetimes* is a persuasive text designed to help readers appreciate the environment. In a sidebar running along the bottom, the writer poses questions for readers; these are not answered in the text but are intended to spark thinking and/or discussion.

Combining Structural Patterns

Structural patterns rarely appear in isolation, although a text may be primarily organized around one of them. Usually, structures are embedded within each other and within the larger organizational structure. In addition to describing problems and solutions, *Daily Life in a Covered Wagon* also uses categories; the information is presented by topics, which include mishaps, food for the journey, children's activities, and sickness and death. Interesting descriptive details let readers know what pioneer life was like, and the voices of pioneers appear from their personal diaries. A range of photographs, drawings, paintings, and reproduced documents support and extend the text, which also has a fully developed timeline (1800 to 1890), a glossary, and an index.

You want your students to learn to recognize these structural patterns and use them in comprehending informational texts. You also want to help them use these patterns in their writing. Students are often directed to "write two paragraphs comparing and contrasting" something. This formulaic writing prompt appears frequently on tests but is quite unlike the process used by writers of high-quality nonfiction texts. Writers think about their subject and purpose, and the structural patterns emerge from that. Teaching students to recognize patterns in the texts they read is the foundation for making these patterns available to them as writers.

Use of Graphics

Comparisons and contrasts may be shown in charts or graphs reporting numerical data. Description may be enhanced by cross-sectional drawings. A timeline can show chronological order or sequence. A flowchart can show temporal sequence. A map can provide supporting details that make information clear.

Language Signals for Structural Patterns

Structural patterns are not always easy for readers to detect if they have not had a lot of experience reading nonfiction. Some ways in which writers use language to signal they are employing a structural pattern are listed in Figure 10.7. Sometimes the signal is a particular word or phrase. For example, the word *therefore* or an *if . . . then* structure would signal the reader that the writer is coming to a conclusion involving cause and effect. The words *while* or *like* and *unlike* signal a comparison. These signals help us show our students what the author is trying to achieve.

The Importance of Text Structure

Text structure refers to the overall way the writer has organized the content. It is strongly related to genre (Fountas and Pinnell 2006). You expect both fiction and nonfiction texts to be organized in recognizable patterns. For example, fiction has one or more story problems (usually with a major, overarching problem), and you expect to identify these problems and read about their resolution. This knowledge of texts guides reading and supports understanding. It is usually easy to recognize patterns in fiction because you have had so much life experience hearing and reading stories.

Nonfiction texts, too, have recognizable organizational types that occur over and over. Readers who have had limited experience in reading nonfiction sometimes find it difficult to recognize the types or patterns. As proficient readers of nonfiction, we pick up a book, immediately notice how it "works," and adjust our behavior accordingly. This adjustment is automatic and unconscious. For example, if you notice that information is presented in categories, you scan them looking for interesting information. You may end up reading the entire text, but you know that is not absolutely necessary. If you notice chronological sequence, you usually start reading at the beginning but know it's possible to

LANGUAGE SIGNALING STRUCTURAL PATTERNS IN NONFICTION TEXTS	
Pattern	**Language Signals**
Categorical	Reference to main idea particular to text: *related to, like, a kind of, another kind of*
Description	Descriptive details—words like *on, over, beyond, within, like, as, among* Descriptive adjectives Metaphor and simile
Sequence (Chronological)	*First, second, third, fourth, etc.; before, after, then, next, earlier, later, last, in addition to, at the same time, meanwhile, at last, in the end, at the beginning, long ago, to begin with, secondly, lastly, finally, most important, not long after, to begin with, when, now, until, on (date), at (time)*
Sequence (Temporal)	*First, second, third, fourth, etc.; before, after, then, next, finally*
Compare/Contrast	*While, yet, but, rather, most, either, like and unlike, same, as opposed to, as well as, likewise, on the other hand, although, the same, similarly, opposites, whereas, besides, equally important, even more important, however, moreover, also, however, alike, different from, unless, compared to, similar to, resembles*
Cause and Effect	*Because, since, thus, so that, if . . . then, therefore, nevertheless, due to, this led to, as a result, then . . . so, for this reason, on account of, consequently, in order to, cause, effect*
Problem and Solution	*Propose, conclude, a solution, the problem or the question, research shows, the evidence is, among, a reason for, therefore, hence, indeed, nevertheless, furthermore*
Question and Answer	*Who, what, where, when, why, how, how many*

Figure 10.7 Language signaling structural patterns in nonfiction text

skip time periods with which you're already very familiar. If you notice that the text presents a set of directions, you immediately decide whether you are interested in the process; if you're not, you may not read it at all. This recognition of the type and organization of a text supports understanding from the beginning.

Text structure also refers to the underlying patterns that writers select to present information. These repeating patterns raise expectations in the reader's mind. Readers detect patterns such as problem and solution or cause and effect and this influences they way they store, understand, and use the information from the text. These underlying structures make reading informational texts a very complex process. Reading nonfiction is far more than just taking in a string of facts. Recognizing structural patterns helps readers to identify a problem and its cause as well as a solution or several possible solutions. The reading process is really a thinking process, supported by the text; the reader has gained new ideas and even new questions.

As students become familiar with the many different purposes, styles, and typeset formats of nonfiction texts, they will become skilled in reading these often complex texts, and will learn to adjust their reading accordingly, which will, in turn, expand their reading ability. Most importantly, they will learn to enjoy and seek out the amazing array and variety of high-quality nonfiction texts.

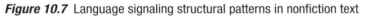

Suggestions for Professional Development

There are so many complexities to informational texts that analyzing them can sometimes be overwhelming. We tend to focus on the graphic features, and those are important. But for this session, focus only on the meaning of texts and how they are organized.

1. Gather a group of nonfiction texts that are considered appropriate for your grade level and meet with a group of colleagues to discuss them. You may want to limit the collection to expository texts, but include a couple of textbooks for comparison. Refer to the last column in Figure 10.3 under the "Expository" category to help guide your selection. You can also refer to the list of mentor texts at the end of this chapter.

EXPOSITORY AND NARRATIVE NONFICTION: DEMANDS ON THE READER

- Analyze texts and check documentation.
- Evaluate texts for bias.
- Distinguish between fact and opinion.
- Identify the main idea and supporting details.
- Understand how facts are used to support generalizations.
- Recognize the author's purpose or message.
- Identify and use the organizational structure of the text.
- Follow sequence of events and descriptions.
- Integrate information from a variety of sources.
- Use tools such as headings, illustrations, maps, captions, diagrams, labels, and timelines.

Figure 10.8 Expository and narrative nonfiction: demands on the reader

2. For each text, decide:
   - What are the big ideas and the major theme or themes? In other words, what does the writer really want to convey to the reader over and above facts? (the "so what?")
   - What is the primary or overarching organizational structure of the text? How does the text work? (Different sections may have different patterns.) Use Figure 10.3 to help you determine the organizational structure.
   - What underlying text structures or patterns can you identify? List them for each text. Use Figure 10.6 to help you identify text structures and patterns.
   - What are the author's explicit and implicit messages?
3. End with a general discussion of the challenges and opportunities to learn associated with each text. If you have easier and harder texts, compare them in terms of complexity and/or quality.
4. Select one text to read aloud to students, have a conference about it with an individual student, or use it for small-group reading. Keep theme, overall structure, and underlying structures in mind when planning your discussion or introduction.
5. Reflect on how this lesson went with colleagues.
   - How did your close study of the text improve/help your instruction?

CHAPTER 11

Nonfiction Texts

Analysis of Design

New worlds and new interests lie waiting for children between the covers of informational books.

—Charlotte Huck

Nonfiction texts are strikingly different from fiction texts in their use of *design features* that support readers. After the text is written, authors and illustrators (and professional designers) decide how to lay out the information and select graphics that present information in interesting ways. Graphics help readers understand the information in the body of the text, and they also add important information. Of course, as in all writing, drafting and designing are recursive processes. The raw text may suggest the way the text is designed; adding a design feature may require revision or more writing or rewriting.

Proficient readers notice and derive information from design features and also learn how to use them in our own writing. Five design features in particular have implications for helping students understand nonfiction genres. Today many fiction texts also incorporate some of these features, and students encounter hybrid texts as well (see Chapter 12), so recognizing and using them is increasingly important in all reading.

Readers often use design features without being aware of it. Over the years you noticed them and gradually learned to use them. Early exposure to nonfiction texts goes a long way in building this unconscious knowledge. Figure 11.1 shows an enterprising first grader's use of design features as she casually writes a book at home. Ryann has obviously noticed many details as she's read simple texts. She's created a cover with a title, illustrated with the sole figure of her mom. Turning the page we see the title again, along with the table of contents. And notice how Ryann has organized information. She has carefully selected the information for the pages, each of which is identified as a section. She has clear categories for the information she presents and has written meaningful headings and printed them in a larger font. We can tell that she has read some "about" books. Print is placed consistently at the bottom of each page. Illustrations show details that precisely match the text. Each section has a concluding sentence, and there is even a little humor as

Figure 11.1 Ryann's book about her mom

continues

she calls paying bills a "balancing act." There are page numbers and a section called Meet the Illustrator. In Meet the Illustrator, she expresses gratitude to her readers and hopes that they will "connect" with her words. On the back cover (she offers two versions), she entices readers with a summary of the book.

Ryann is well on her way to understanding the wide range of design features that characterize nonfiction texts, and she did not develop this knowledge in one or two lessons. She has books in her home and has probably noticed a lot from hearing books read aloud and from her own browsing (even before she could read). Casually, an adult might have pointed out things like a dedication, a title, headings, or page numbers. The adult might have used the table of contents to locate information. These encounters were not "direct instruction," but what adults attend to, children will notice. At school, her

Figure 11.1 Ryann's book about her mom *(cont.)*

teacher may have been more intentional in drawing features to her attention. Whatever has happened—probably something to do with her own need to publish—Ryann is motivated to study texts closely. In the next few years, her knowledge of text features will grow. As teachers, the more we are aware of text design, the better job we can do to help our students use features to their advantage in gaining and comprehending information.

Design Features of Nonfiction Texts

Designers make hundreds of decisions as they place information and illustrations on the pages of nonfiction texts. We will discuss these decisions in five categories: (1) text divisions; (2) organizational tools; (3) graphic features; (4) print features; and (5) layout features. (See Figure 11.2.) Learning to recognize and use

DESIGN FEATURES OF NONFICTION TEXTS		
Text Divisions	• Chapters/Sections/Subsections • Body copy (paragraphs) • Headings, subheadings	• Titles • Introduction/Preface • Foreword/Afterword
Organizational Tools and Sources of Information	• Table of Contents • Bibliography • Index • Glossary • Lists	• Pronunciation Guide • Appendices • Author Information • References • Dedication
Graphic Features	• Photographs (color or black and white, enlarged, zoom) • Paintings (oil, acrylic, watercolor, pastel) • Drawings (scale, labeled, colored or black and white) • Captions • Labels • Insets	• Charts (rows and columns) • Diagrams (cutaways, cross-sections, flow diagrams, webs, trees) • Tables and graphs (bar, line, pie) • Maps • Timelines (horizontal or vertical) • Sidebars
Print Features	• Type size • Type style (regular, bold, italic, underlined)	• Typeface (font) • Color
Layout	• Format • Columns • White space • Shading	• Placement (sidebars, insets, illustrations, and graphics) • Bullets and numbers

Figure 11.2 Design features of nonfiction texts

design features is critical, because design reveals the text structure to readers and gives our students an incredible advantage in comprehending a text.

Text Divisions

Let's focus first on the body of the text. Many longer texts are organized into chapters or sections, sometimes into subsections, and then into paragraphs. The paragraphs present ideas and supporting details. Paragraphs follow each other in a logical order. They are clustered into the chapters or sections; sometimes sections represent categories of information, sometimes time periods, and sometimes some other organizational structures. Subsections further divide larger categories (e.g., time periods) into subcategories that, again, provide related information. Text divisions signal to readers the way the text "works"—the way the writer has structured or organized it.

Additional information may be provided in special ways. For example, a writer may want to provide a short passage giving extra information to inform or engage readers. Sometimes this material is not appropriate for the body of the text because it disrupts the flow or creates an overload of information. Of course, we read everything on the page, but the body can be understood without the additional information even though it is interesting. That material can be included in a box, often called a *sidebar*. Additional information can be provided in many different and creative ways—splashes, blasts, bubbles, starbursts, lines of print running along the bottom of each page or in the corners.

Sometimes photographs or drawings are included to illustrate the topic, and they must be labeled and explained. Again, this material does not belong in the body of the text. The writing appears as labels and legends next to the illustrations. An *inset* might show a magnified or more detailed area of a map or photograph. The writer may also want to provide introductory material or comments and extra information after the text formally concludes. For example, a picture book written in a poetic way to engage readers will often have a substantive, denser page or two at the beginning or end with specific information about the topic. This kind of information is contained in the *introduction, preface, foreword, afterword,* and *author's* or *illustrator's notes*, which are separate from the main body of the text. An introduction or preface is usually what the writer or another person wants to say to the reader about the book they are about to read. It provides information useful in understanding the text. The afterword is an epilogue (further comment, interpretation, or information); it can be a critical or interpretive commentary by someone other than the author. Additionally, information may be provided about the writer to interest readers and to establish qualifications related to accuracy of information.

Texts may be divided in many ways, and there are texts that have unusual sections and divisions not mentioned here. Writers and designers study the structure of the text carefully and break it up in a way that reflects what they want to communicate.

Organizational Tools and Sources of Information

A great design feature of nonfiction texts is the inclusion of tools that help the reader process and understand the text. These organizational tools and sources of information are increasingly included in nonfiction texts for younger as well as older children.

Table of Contents

One of the first organizational tools readers encounter in many nonfiction books is the table of contents. A table of contents gives readers an initial view of how the parts of the text will be organized (see Figure 11.3). A more complex table of contents shows not only major sections but also lists the subsections (see Figure 11.4).

The table of contents can help readers:

- Understand the organization or structure of the whole text.
- Go right to the section of interest.
- Remember information after reading by helping them recall the categories of information.
- Go to particular sections for discussion with others or for responding in writing.

Headings

One of the most important organizational tools in a nonfiction text is the headings. Headings and subheadings show readers how the text is divided. Printed in fonts that are large and noticeable, they are highly visible signals that inform readers about the kind of information—and its function—they are going to encounter. This quick preview serves readers very well. The page layout from *All About Dinosaurs* in Figure 11.5 shows the main heading "What Dinosaurs Ate."

Index

The index is a wonderful research tool. We use indexes (indices) regularly in our everyday lives—the index in a cookbook, for example, lets you search for recipes by ingredient or by name. An index enables readers to search for precisely the information they want. Located at the back of a text, it provides one or more page numbers that mention the particular item of interest.

The index for *Mysteries of the Mummy Kids* (Halls 2007), shown in Figure 11.6, lists a variety of words, including names of explorers and mummies, technical words, and places where mummies have been found or are displayed. Readers can choose a topic or an idea and find related information in the text.

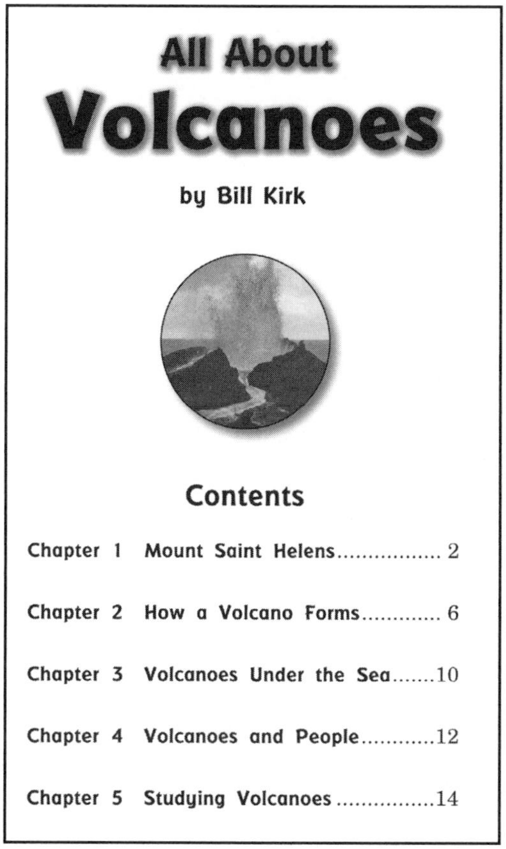

All About
Volcanoes
by Bill Kirk

Contents

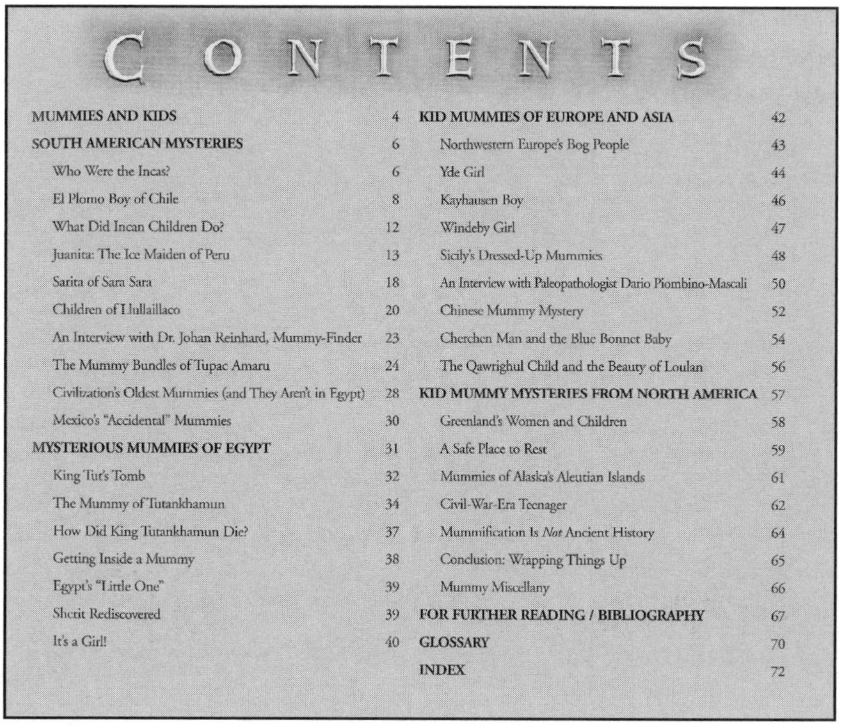

CONTENTS

Figure 11.3 Table of Contents from *All About Volcanoes (left)*

Figure 11.4 Table of Contents from *Mysteries of the Mummy Kids (top)*

What Dinosaurs Ate
Some dinosaurs ate only plants.
Their teeth were flat.
This dinosaur had flat teeth.
12
Some dinosaurs ate meat.
Their teeth were long and sharp.
This dinosaur had lots of
long, sharp teeth.
13

Figure 11.5 Main heading from pages 12–13 of *All About Dinosaurs*

Figure 11.6
Index for *Mysteries of the Mummy Kids*

INDEX

72

Today we can search the Internet in much the same way; the "old-fashioned" index was the precursor of the powerful computer search engines we now use. Digital books have searching power that allows you to find key words in seconds (if you know them). When we want to find something, the key word, whether located in the index or entered into a computer search engine, is the best way to find information.

Glossary

The glossary provides definitions of words in the text that may be unfamiliar. For glossaries in books meant for children and adolescents, the words are chosen with several questions in mind:

1. What words may be unfamiliar to readers (in general or as used in this text)?
2. What words are key to comprehending this text (and cannot be fully defined in context)?
3. What words will be helpful to students' development of vocabulary?

The words are often of a technical nature, as in the glossary shown in Figure 11.7. Here, the writer has hypothesized that readers might not be familiar with the precise definitions of *college* and *gravity.* These words are defined in context, but it helps readers to be able to get back to definitions that are all in one place. Also, the writer has guessed that the word *mission* as used in this particular context might need a definition. The words *space suit* and *spacecraft*, which are more technical, are defined in context as well.

Pronunciation Guide

A pronunciation guide provides phonetic spellings and diacritical markings to help readers pronounce words correctly. The pronunciation guide is often embedded within the text, as in Figure 11.8, or it may appear in a separate section at the back of the text, along with the glossary and index. Frequently, the words may be place names or the names of people, both of which may be hard for most readers to pronounce. The pronunciation guide may also help readers say technical words (or just difficult key words).

Glossary

college	a school where students can study after high school
gravity	a force that pulls people toward Earth
mission	a special job for an astronaut
spacecraft	a machine that flies into space
space suit	special clothing that an astronaut wears for space flights

Figure 11.7 Glossary from *All About Astronauts*

Of course, when you read silently, you tend to move past the words without stopping to say them aloud or even wondering how to say them. Comprehension is not damaged, because conceptually you know what the word represents. But the pronunciation guide helps if you need to say the word aloud. Also, knowing how to pronounce a word sometimes helps you feel more comfortable with the text and more easily remember information.

Appendices

Appendices contain extra material that informs readers but does not necessarily fit into the body of the text. A variety of information can be included in an appendix, including:

- Suggestions for further reading and study.
- Follow-up articles.
- Lists of examples or locations.
- Additional information written in a style different from the text.
- Facts and/or research that supports the text.

Figure 11.8 Pronunciation guide on a page from *All About the Sonoran Desert*

Plants of the Desert

This tall plant is a cactus. The cactus can live here because it **stores** water in a special way.

When it rains, the cactus roots soak up water. The plant **swells** up and gets bigger. The cactus uses the water until it rains again.

saguaro
(sah WHAR oh) cactus

The saguaro cactus can grow taller than a house.

About the Author/Illustrator

Readers are often interested in knowing more about the person who wrote or illustrated the book. For nonfiction texts, author or illustrator information also helps readers judge the quality of information in the text. The information can be a personal note from the author or illustrator or a short biography showing background experience. The author/illustrator information is usually in the front or back of the text or on the back cover.

References

References, presented in a standardized format (usually alphabetical), list the sources of information cited in the text. Often the list includes important Internet articles or sites. Readers can use this list to examine original sources in order to gain more information or check the accuracy of the text.

Graphic Features

Perhaps the most engaging design features for nonfiction texts are the graphics. Designers use a wide range of visual tools in order to present information to readers. Examples are discussed below, but there are many variations, and we are always discovering new ones.

Photographs

Photographs make a text come alive! So many wonderful photographs are available today. You can see animals in their natural habitats; the camera zooms in and shows you things you would never be able to see with the naked eye (see Figure 11.9). A photograph can be historical or modern, black and white or in color. Historical photographs like the one in Figure 11.10 establish the reality of historical events or places. Concepts can also often be illustrated more clearly when the text is accompanied by photographs; the photographs in Figure 11.11, for example, depict dormant and active volcanoes.

Figure 11.9 Close-up photograph from *All About Spiders*

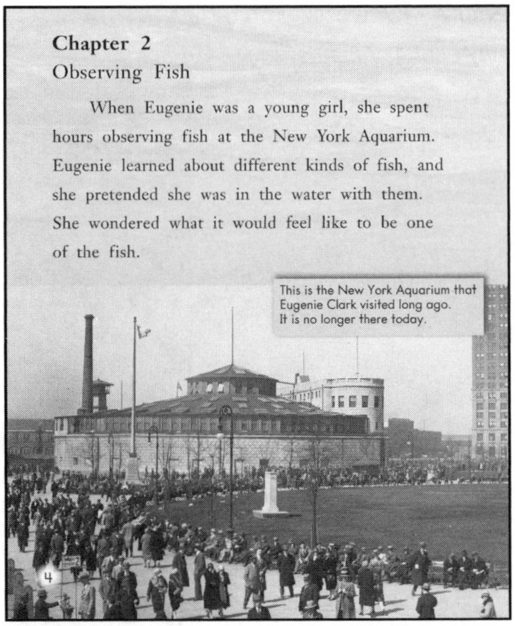

Figure 11.10 Historical photograph from *Eugenie Clark*

Paintings and Drawings

Paintings and drawings add greatly to the attractiveness of a text. They can also add to its tone or mood and show processes or events that are not easy to photograph. The drawing in Figure 11.12 illustrates how bats find food. Beautiful color paintings like the one in Figure 11.13, which shows a mother sea turtle laying her eggs and then filling the hole with sand, help us imagine moments or events, often from nature, that would be difficult to capture on film.

Paintings may be in acrylic, watercolor, pastel, or oil; they may involve techniques like collage. Drawings may be black and white or colored; they may depict people or events. When they illustrate a process, we usually call them *diagrams* (there is more information on diagrams below). They may be labeled or include a "scale" that gives readers perspective on size.

Captions

Captions explain illustrations. They orient readers and enable us to make the connection between information in the picture and the body of the text. Underneath the photograph in Figure 11.14 a caption explains that the diver is studying a great white shark from the safety of a shark cage.

Some volcanoes are active. They burst, or erupt, often. Some volcanoes are dormant. This means they have not erupted for a very long time. Dormant volcanoes seem to be sleeping. Before 1980, Mount Saint Helens was dormant for more than 100 years.
active volcano
This rock is lava that has cooled.
dormant volcano
Not all volcanoes look like Mount Saint Helens when they erupt. When this big volcano erupts, red-hot lava flows from openings in the mountain.
Some kinds of lava move slowly, and some kinds move very quickly. When lava cools, it becomes hard rock. The rock becomes part of the mountain.
8
9

Figure 11.11 Photographs illustrating concepts from *All About Volcanoes*

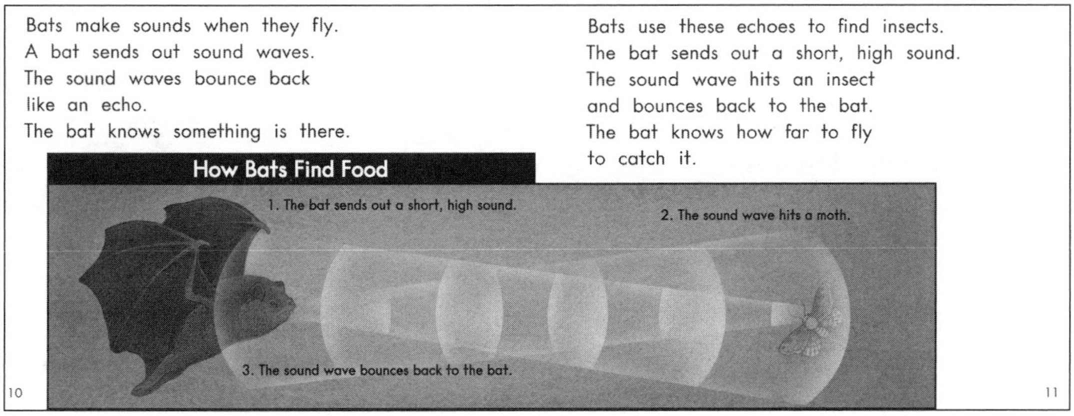
Bats make sounds when they fly.
A bat sends out sound waves.
The sound waves bounce back
like an echo.
The bat knows something is there.
Bats use these echoes to find insects.
The bat sends out a short, high sound.
The sound wave hits an insect
and bounces back to the bat.
The bat knows how far to fly
to catch it.
How Bats Find Food
1. The bat sends out a short, high sound.
2. The sound wave hits a moth.
3. The sound wave bounces back to the bat.
10
11

Figure 11.12 Drawing from *All About Bats*

Mother Sea Turtle
digs a deep hole.
The hole is for her eggs.
She lays many eggs
in the hole.
8
Then she fills the hole
with sand.
Her eggs are safe
under the sand.
9

Figure 11.13 Color paintings from *Mother Sea Turtle*

Figure 11.14 Caption from *Eugenie Clark*

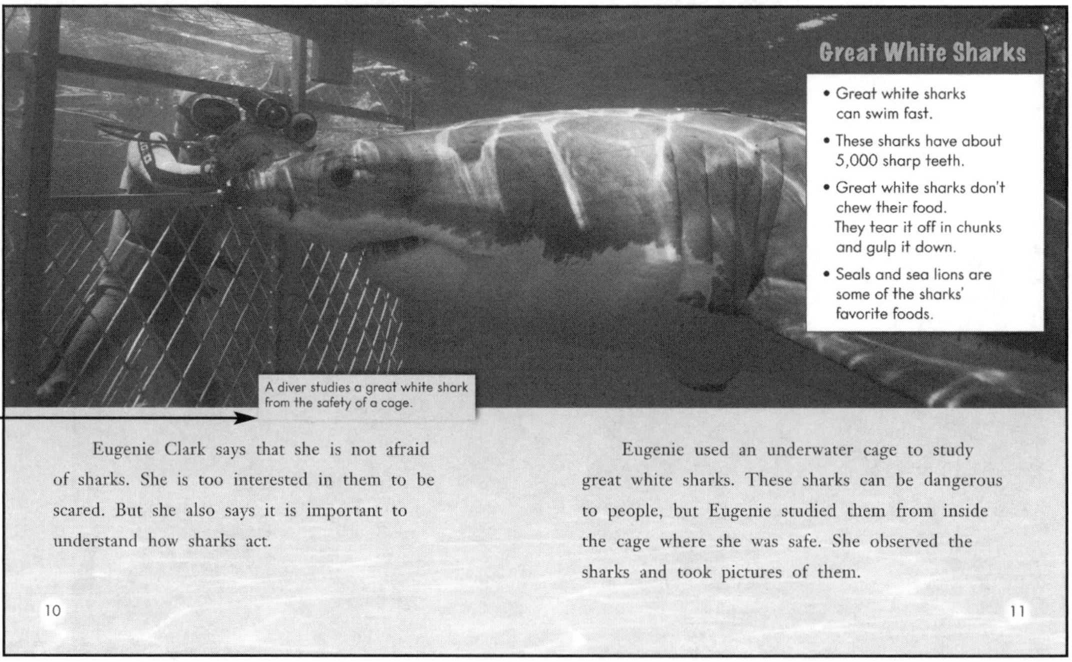

Great White Sharks
• Great white sharks can swim fast.
• These sharks have about 5,000 sharp teeth.
• Great white sharks don't chew their food. They tear it off in chunks and gulp it down.
• Seals and sea lions are some of the sharks' favorite foods.
A diver studies a great white shark from the safety of a cage.
Eugenie Clark says that she is not afraid of sharks. She is too interested in them to be scared. But she also says it is important to understand how sharks act.
Eugenie used an underwater cage to study great white sharks. These sharks can be dangerous to people, but Eugenie studied them from inside the cage where she was safe. She observed the sharks and took pictures of them.
10
11

Charts

Charts take a variety of forms and pull out information from the text. They are an excellent way to show categories of information and problem/solution or cause/effect relationships, or to compare and contrast items. In charts, information is ordered so that readers can see important relationships. The chart in Figure 11.15 not only lists three different kinds of sharks but also provides photographs of each.

Diagrams

A diagram is a drawing that explains something by outlining its parts and their relationships—the way they "work." A diagram can also explain a sequential process; the one in Figure 11.16 depicts the steps taken to turn milk into ice cream.

Diagrams are excellent for showing temporal sequence—the life cycles of animals or the formation of precipitation, for example. Diagrams can also be

Figure 11.15 Chart from *Eugenie Clark*

Figure 11.16 Diagram from *From Milk to Ice Cream*

cutaways and cross sections that show the inner workings of something. A cross section of a tree, for example, might show the rings that represent its entire life. A cutaway of a volcano might show what happens inside the mountain when a volcano erupts (see Figure 11.17). Cutaways and cross sections help us understand how natural and human-made phenomena work; they extend description and sometimes capture temporal sequence. Diagrams can also be flowcharts, webs, or trees, all of which show how ideas are related to one another.

Tables and Graphs

Tables and graphs are very useful in showing and comparing numbers. Readers can quickly see comparisons, growth curves, and proportions. Numbers can be represented in many ways—bar graphs, line graphs, and pie graphs are examples. In the book *Far From Shore* (Webb 2011) the author uses line graphs to show declines in the dolphin population (see Figure 11.18). Tables and graphs are clarified by *keys*—explanations that tell what each symbol represents. They also usually have substantive titles that help readers know what the table means, and they are explained in the body of the text.

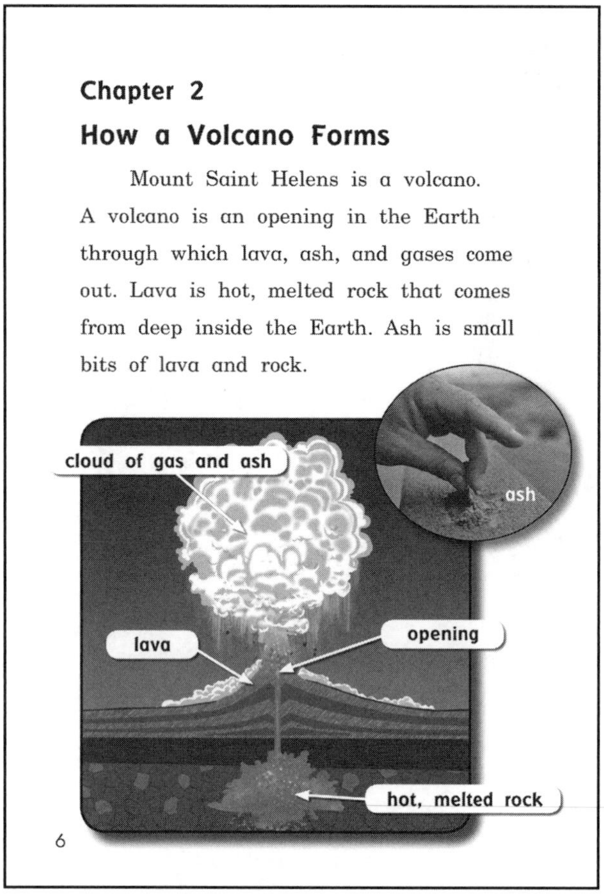
Chapter 2
How a Volcano Forms
Mount Saint Helens is a volcano. A volcano is an opening in the Earth through which lava, ash, and gases come out. Lava is hot, melted rock that comes from deep inside the Earth. Ash is small bits of lava and rock.
cloud of gas and ash
ash
lava
opening
hot, melted rock
6

Figure 11.17 Cutaway diagram from *All About Volcanoes*

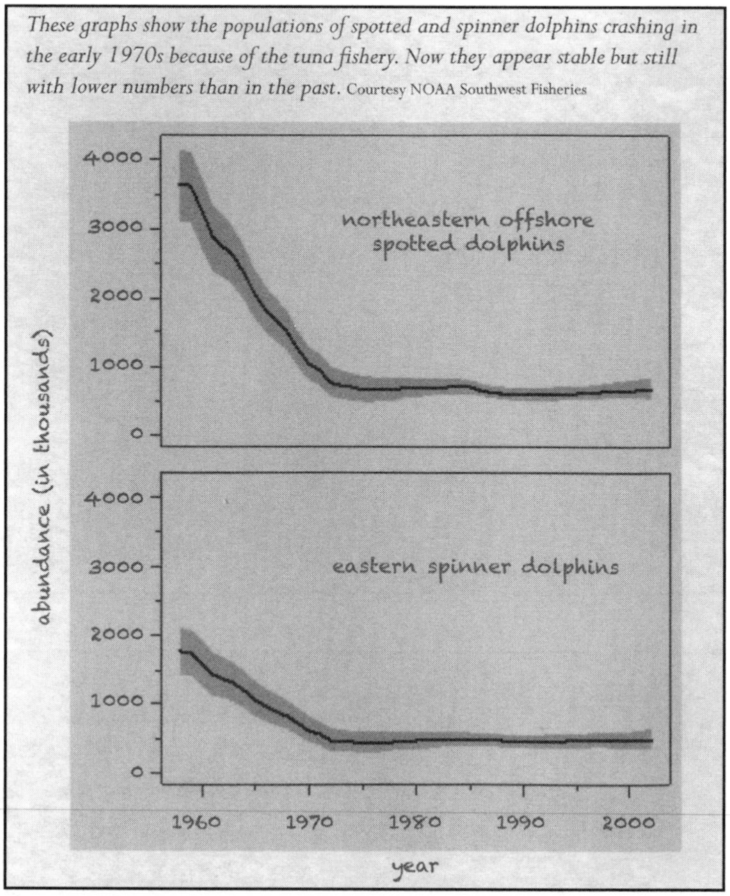
These graphs show the populations of spotted and spinner dolphins crashing in the early 1970s because of the tuna fishery. Now they appear stable but still with lower numbers than in the past. Courtesy NOAA Southwest Fisheries
abundance (in thousands)
4000
3000
2000
1000
0
northeastern offshore spotted dolphins
eastern spinner dolphins
1960
1970
1980
1990
2000
year

Figure 11.18 Line graphs from *Far from Shore*

Maps

Maps are common in nonfiction texts, because the geographic setting is often highly relevant to the topic. Maps help readers understand the relationship between their own world and what they are reading. They place the subject of the text in geographic perspective. In Figure 11.19, the map showing where redwood trees grow includes a smaller inset pinpointing the location of the region of the United States (Oregon and California) depicted in the larger map.

Timelines

Timelines place events along a line that shows the passage of time (see Figure 11.20). A timeline helps readers keep track of events in chronological order. This is especially helpful when dealing with a series of complex events. Readers are not required to remember everything from the body of the text; they can glance at the timeline and keep it all in perspective.

The Value of Graphics

In recent years, technology has made it much easier to produce high-quality graphics, and designers can make texts more engaging and accessible. Today, readers are sophisticated about graphic features and expect good ones; We can also easily produce features such as charts, diagrams, and graphs on our own computers. However, design features can be confusing if they are simply inserted into the text without a clear purpose beyond decoration, or if they are cluttered and hard to understand. You want to help your students understand the strong link between the information and how it is organized in a text and the way the graphic features extend meaning and make it clearer.

Print Features

The print in a text also communicates meaning. In the example in Figure 11.21, the labels on the small photos are in a playful red font, while the body of the text is in

Where Redwood Trees Grow
Redwood trees grow by the sea. The weather there is just right for them. It is not too cold or too hot. There is a lot of rain and fog by the sea. Redwood trees grow well in rain and fog.
Oregon
Redwood Trees
USA
California
6
7

Figure 11.19 Map and inset map from *All About Redwood Trees* (top)

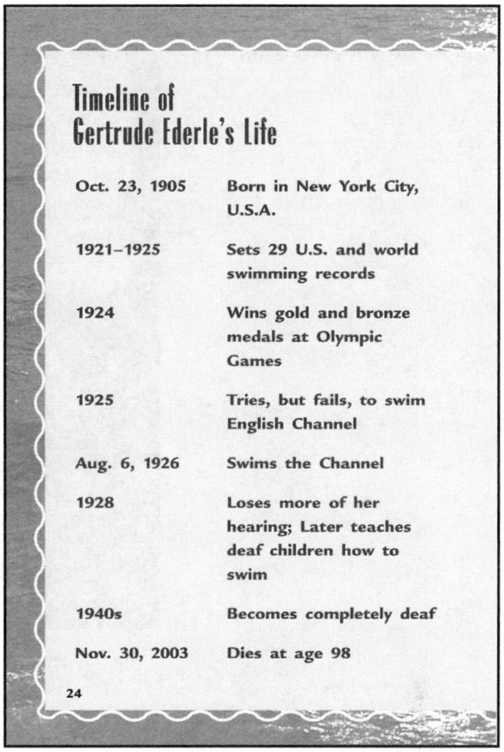
Timeline of Gertrude Ederle's Life
Oct. 23, 1905 Born in New York City, U.S.A.
1921–1925 Sets 29 U.S. and world swimming records
1924 Wins gold and bronze medals at Olympic Games
1925 Tries, but fails, to swim English Channel
Aug. 6, 1926 Swims the Channel
1928 Loses more of her hearing; Later teaches deaf children how to swim
1940s Becomes completely deaf
Nov. 30, 2003 Dies at age 98
24

Figure 11.20 Timeline from *You Can't Stop Trudy* (right)

a different, black font. The caption accompanying the photo on the left page is in the same font as the smaller photo labels but is black on a white background to make it more visible against the backdrop of the color photograph. In good design, color, size, style, and font are carefully selected to communicate meaning and help readers access the way the text is organized and the underlying structures.

Layout

Layout refers to the manner in which the print and illustrations are arranged on a page. Layout, too, communicates meaning. It draws the eye to important information. Layout is related to the purpose of the text. For example, the purpose of the page layout in Figure 11.22 is to help readers better understand what it is like to be an astronaut. It features a photograph, caption, and labels on the left page that show what the earth looks like to astronauts on the moon. More information about the meaning of the word *astronaut* is provided in a "fun fact" on the right page. The design of the pages reinforces the subject matter, and the simple black font on a light background allows readers to focus on the most important ideas by setting the text clearly apart from the illustrations.

Another machine whips the mix. This makes the ice cream taste rich and creamy. Then it is time to add flavorings, such as chocolate or vanilla. Treats such as fruit, nuts, and cookies can go in, too.
A worker adds cookie dough.
Strawberries and bananas
Cookie dough
Nuts
Cookies
10
11

Figure 11.21 Print features in *From Milk to Ice Cream*

Every aspect of layout is carefully considered by the book designer, including the amount and placement of white space, whether the print will be arranged in columns or across the whole page, the placement of sidebars and insets in relation to the body of the text, the shading of material, and the use of bullets and numbers to emphasize lists.

Figure 11.22 A page layout from *All About Astronauts*

Chapter 2
Becoming an Astronaut
It takes a lot of study and hard work to become an astronaut. The men and women who become astronauts must be excellent students. In college, they study math and science. They need to learn all about Earth, other planets, and outer space.
Fun Fact
The word *astronaut* means "sailor among the stars."
Earth
moon
4
This is what Earth looks like to astronauts on the moon.
5

Analysis of a Text

The more you help your students notice and occasionally critique design features in nonfiction texts, the greater awareness they will have regarding their use. In their own writing, students function as both writer and designer. There is no better way for them to learn about design features than to have them try out the techniques in their own nonfiction writing. Noticing is the key.

To summarize our discussion of the design elements of nonfiction texts, let's take a look at one example, *Mysteries of the Mummy Kids* (Halls 2007). Figures 11.23 and 11.24 show two double-page spreads from the book. Figure 11.25 shows an analysis.

Meaning

Mysteries of the Mummy Kids is a nonfiction text illustrated with photographs and some maps. Our analysis first mentions some big ideas and an overarching theme, because in high-quality nonfiction, readers gain more than a collection of facts to remember. The writer puts information together in powerful ways to help readers infer larger meanings and thus develop a sense of the important or big ideas as well as the theme the writer wants to convey. The theme may or may not be explicitly stated, but readers come away with something worth thinking about. In the case of *Mysteries*, a great deal of detailed factual information is presented, which makes the text interesting. Readers should not expect to remember all the various mummies and their settings, but should grasp the big ideas listed in column two. They may also derive the theme intended by the writer (which is stated) as well as others that they construct for themselves (for example, the briefness of human life contrasted to the length of time a mummy survives).

Organizational Structure

Mysteries of the Mummy Kids has an overall organizational structure—categories of mummies by region—and many underlying text structures, notably description and chronological sequence, but also including temporal sequence, problem/solution, and question and answer.

Design

The design involves the way the body of the text and additional material are laid out and signaled to readers. This text has sections and subsections with headings and subheadings. The body of the text is presented in paragraphs. Organizational features include a table of contents, glossary, index, bibliography, and suggestions for further reading. Graphic features such as black-and-white and color photographs and maps add to the interest and provide more information. Overall, these graphic features help readers remain oriented to the

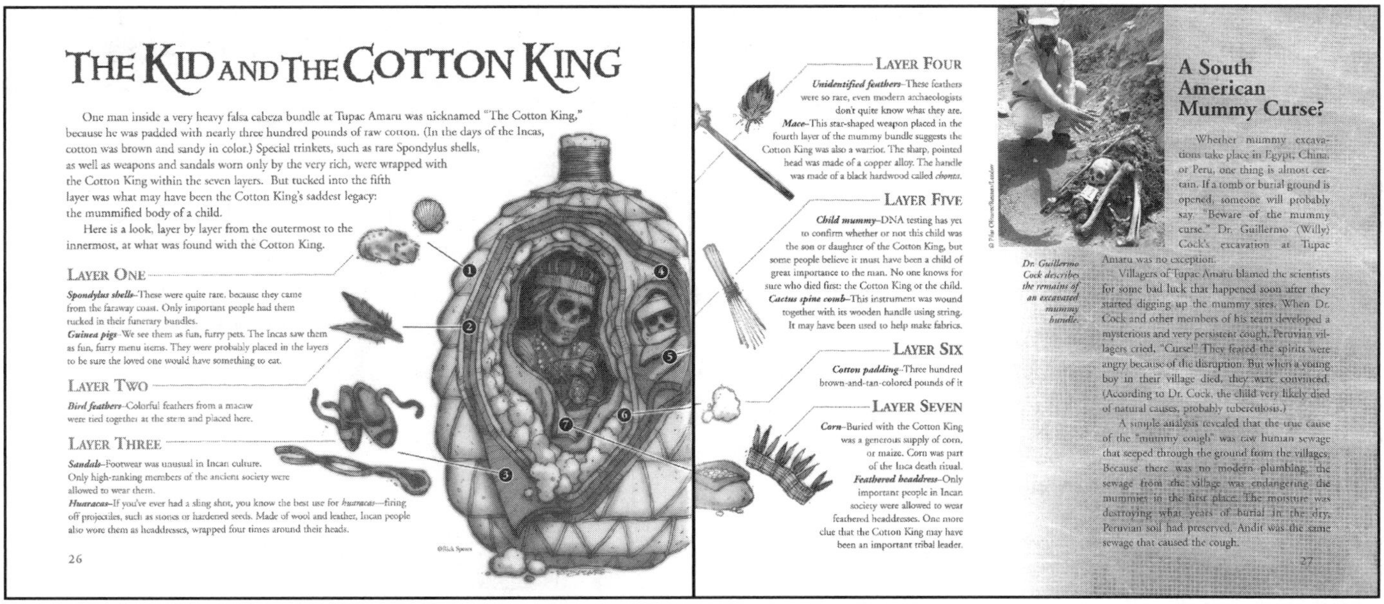

THE KID AND THE COTTON KING

One man inside a very heavy falsa cabeza bundle at Tupac Amaru was nicknamed "The Cotton King," because he was padded with nearly three hundred pounds of raw cotton. (In the days of the Incas, cotton was brown and sandy in color.) Special trinkets, such as rare Spondylus shells, as well as weapons and sandals worn only by the very rich, were wrapped with the Cotton King within the seven layers. But tucked into the fifth layer was what may have been the Cotton King's saddest legacy: the mummified body of a child.

Here is a look, layer by layer from the outermost to the innermost, at what was found with the Cotton King.

LAYER ONE

Spondylus shells–These were quite rare, because they came from the faraway coast. Only important people had them tucked in their funerary bundles.
Guinea pigs–We see them as fun, furry pets. The Incas saw them as fun, furry menu items. They were probably placed in the layers to be sure the loved one would have something to eat.

LAYER TWO

Bird feathers–Colorful feathers from a macaw were tied together at the stem and placed here.

LAYER THREE

Sandals–Footwear was unusual in Incan culture. Only high-ranking members of the ancient society were allowed to wear them.
Huaracas–If you've ever had a sling shot, you know the best use for *huaracas*—firing off projectiles, such as stones or hardened seeds. Made of wool and leather, Incan people also wore them as headdresses, wrapped four times around their heads.

©Rick Spears

26

LAYER FOUR

Unidentified feathers–These feathers were so rare, even modern archaeologists don't quite know what they are.
Mace–This star-shaped weapon placed in the fourth layer of the mummy bundle suggests the Cotton King was also a warrior. The sharp, pointed head was made of a copper alloy. The handle was made of a black hardwood called *chonta*.

LAYER FIVE

Child mummy–DNA testing has yet to confirm whether or not this child was the son or daughter of the Cotton King, but some people believe it must have been a child of great importance to the man. No one knows for sure who died first: the Cotton King or the child.
Cactus spine comb–This instrument was wound together with its wooden handle using string. It may have been used to help make fabrics.

LAYER SIX

Cotton padding–Three hundred brown-and-tan-colored pounds of it

LAYER SEVEN

Corn–Buried with the Cotton King was a generous supply of corn, or maize. Corn was part of the Inca death ritual.
Feathered headdress–Only important people in Incan society were allowed to wear feathered headdresses. One more clue that the Cotton King may have been an important tribal leader.

Dr. Guillermo Cock describes the remains of an excavated mummy bundle.

A South American Mummy Curse?

Whether mummy excavations take place in Egypt, China, or Peru, one thing is almost certain. If a tomb or burial ground is opened, someone will probably say, "Beware of the mummy curse." Dr. Guillermo (Willy) Cock's excavation at Tupac Amaru was no exception.

Villagers of Tupac Amaru blamed the scientists for some bad luck that happened soon after they started digging up the mummy sites. When Dr. Cock and other members of his team developed a mysterious and very persistent cough, Peruvian villagers cried, "Curse!" They feared the spirits were angry because of the disruption. But when a young boy in their village died, they were convinced. (According to Dr. Cock, the child very likely died of natural causes, probably tuberculosis.)

A simple analysis revealed that the true cause of the "mummy cough" was raw human sewage that seeped through the ground from the villages. Because there was no modern plumbing, the sewage from the village was endangering the mummies in the first place. The moisture was destroying what years of burial in the dry, Peruvian soil had preserved. And it was the same sewage that caused the cough.

27

Figure 11.23 Page spread from *Mysteries of the Mummy Kids* showing a main section, labeled diagram, photograph, captions, and sidebar

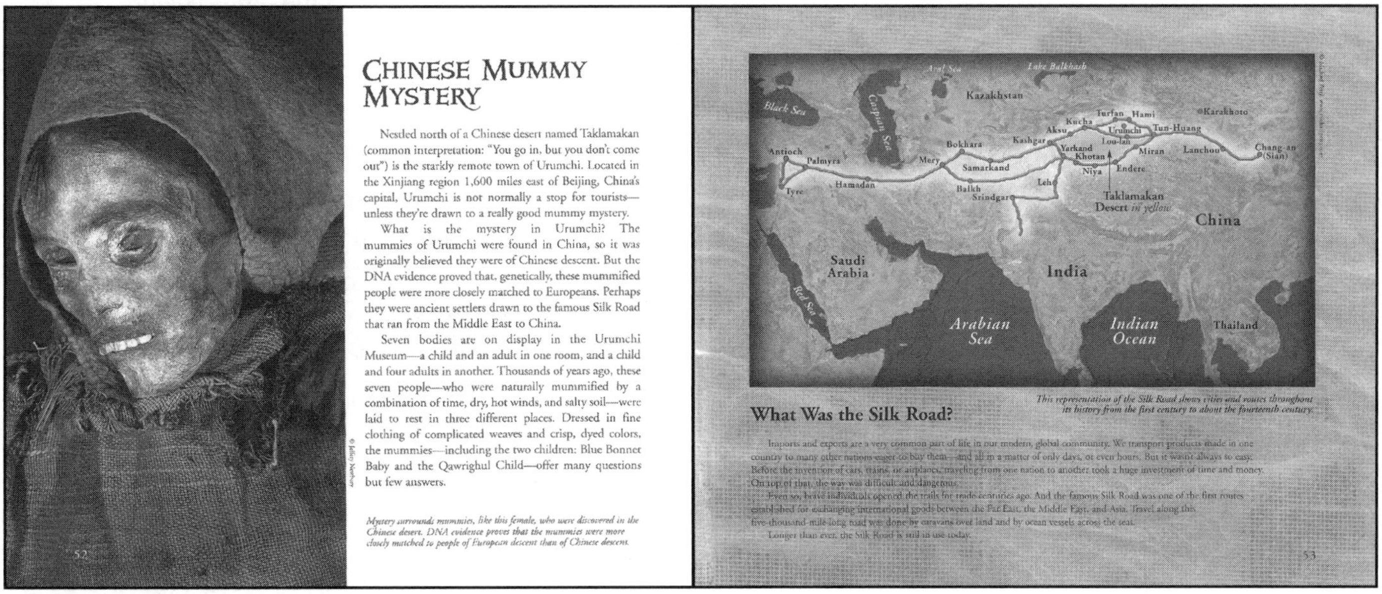

CHINESE MUMMY MYSTERY

Nestled north of a Chinese desert named Taklamakan (common interpretation: "You go in, but you don't come out") is the starkly remote town of Urumchi. Located in the Xinjiang region 1,600 miles east of Beijing, China's capital, Urumchi is not normally a stop for tourists—unless they're drawn to a really good mummy mystery.

What is the mystery in Urumchi? The mummies of Urumchi were found in China, so it was originally believed they were of Chinese descent. But the DNA evidence proved that, genetically, these mummified people were more closely matched to Europeans. Perhaps they were ancient settlers drawn to the famous Silk Road that ran from the Middle East to China.

Seven bodies are on display in the Urumchi Museum—a child and an adult in one room, and a child and four adults in another. Thousands of years ago, these seven people—who were naturally mummified by a combination of time, dry, hot winds, and salty soil—were laid to rest in three different places. Dressed in fine clothing of complicated weaves and crisp, dyed colors, the mummies—including the two children: Blue Bonnet Baby and the Qawrighul Child—offer many questions but few answers.

© Jeffery Newbury

Mystery surrounds mummies, like this female, who were discovered in the Chinese desert. DNA evidence proves that the mummies were more closely matched to people of European descent than of Chinese descent.

52

This representation of the Silk Road shows cities and routes throughout its history from the first century to about the fourteenth century.

What Was the Silk Road?

Imports and exports are a very common part of life in our modern, global community. We transport products made in one country to many other nations eager to buy them—and all in a matter of only days, or even hours. But it wasn't always so easy. Before the invention of cars, trains, or airplanes, traveling from one nation to another took a huge investment of time and money. On top of that, the way was difficult and dangerous.

Even so, brave individuals opened the trails for trade centuries ago. And the famous Silk Road was one of the first routes established for exchanging international goods between the Far East, the Middle East, and Asia. Travel along this five-thousand-mile-long road was done by caravans over land and by ocean vessels across the seas.

Longer than ever, the Silk Road is still in use today.

53

Figure 11.24 Page spread from *Mysteries of the Mummy Kids* showing sections, photograph, and a map

central ideas of the text as those ideas are explored across geographic regions and cultures.

The print features and layout reveal that *Mysteries of the Mummy Kids* is a challenging text with fairly dense print. Headings and subheadings are in a bold, enlarged, noticeable font. Different fonts are used for the body of the text, picture captions and legends, and maps. Sidebars are shaded but substantial, so they could be confused with the body of the text. There is not much white space; every square inch is loaded with information. Nevertheless, the layout is fairly clear for the sophisticated reader.

Special Sets of Nonfiction Texts

Build your classroom collection of nonfiction books strategically. Although you don't want students to choose books by level, you want to be sure the range of nonfiction books for independent reading includes

ANALYSIS OF *MYSTERIES OF THE MUMMY KIDS*		
MEANING		
Ideas and Themes	Important ideas: • Mummies preserve human characteristics. • Mummies appear all over the world; many were people who were special to someone or to many people. • People are very curious about solving the mysteries of mummies; there are many secrets left to discover.	Emerging theme: • Mummification reminds us of the human connection across cultures and across time; all people love, experience loss, and want to preserve those people who were special to them.
ORGANIZATION/STRUCTURE		
Overall Organizational Structure	Present in the text: • Categorical • Subcategories within each larger category	Description: • First section provides definitions and overview; each section provides the same type of information relative to a region: South America, Egypt, Europe and Asia, North America
Underlying Structural Patterns	Present in the text: • Description • Chronological Sequence • Temporal Sequence • Problem/Solution • Question/Answer	Description: • Many mummies are described with details of their entombment and the larger setting. • Many stories are told about how mummies were discovered; also, change over time in some settings is described. • The process of mummification is described in some sections. • The text tells about solving the mysteries of the mummies. • Several embedded interviews are included. Questions often appear in the subheadings.
DESIGN		
Structural Features	Present in the text: • Sections with titles and subtitles • Body and paragraphs • Sidebars	Description: • Each section has a meaningful title in bold: *South American Mysteries*, for example

Figure 11.25 Analysis of *Mysteries of the Mummy Kids*

ANALYSIS OF *MYSTERIES OF THE MUMMY KIDS*		
DESIGN *(cont.)*		
Organizational Features	Present in the text: • Table of Contents • Glossary • Index • Bibliography and Suggestions for Further Reading	Description: • Table of Contents has section titles and subheadings • Questions often appear in subheadings
Graphic Features	Present in the text: • Photographs with captions • Maps • Diagram	Description: • Text includes a great many photographs of mummies, artifacts, and the people who discovered them • Maps help the reader understand the region of the world and the universality of mummies • Diagram of layers that formed the padding of one mummy
Print Features	Present in the text: • Variety of fonts	Description: • Print font differs for headings, body, captions, and sidebars • Sidebars are shaded and usually have photographs • Some substantial sidebars
Layout Features	Present in the text: • Dense print layout • Single-spaced throughout	Description: • There is very little white space and the print is dense, although broken up by many photographs • Single spacing with double spacing in some places; for example, interviews

Figure 11.25 Analysis of *Mysteries of the Mummy Kids (cont.)*

the variety of texts necessary for every student to do a good job choosing books. You can supplement their experience with excellent nonfiction texts that you read aloud. You may want to refer to the list of nonfiction mentor texts in Appendix A.

Presenting books in sets helps you guide student choice and/or make sure they explore content areas you want to cover. Many teachers build baskets of books by topic, author, and even theme. Exploring books in sets, especially when they are supplemented by book talks and read-alouds, helps students build meaning across informational texts.

Many publishers produce sets of nonfiction texts. There is usually a unifying theme, such as animals, people, parts of the world, or technology, but the theme can be just about anything. These sets of books also have consistent design features and organizational structures. Once students read one or two volumes in a set, they find the others more accessible. Unlike some fiction series, nonfiction sets may be read in any order. Here are some recommendations:

1. There are over a hundred volumes and a wide variety of topics to choose from in the DK Eyewitness (DK Children) and Eyewitness Juniors (Knopf) sets. These books have high visual appeal and contain accurate information. They have close-ups and labeled line drawings. Processes are explained in boxed text and arrow arrangements or timelines. Pictures have detailed captions that offer additional information.

2. David Macaulay has produced an excellent set of nonfiction books, including *Cathedral* (1981), *Castle* (1982), and *Pyramid* (1982), in which he provides detailed drawings that show the long and complex process of building various ancient, large-scale structures. He has also written several more recent nonfiction books that deal with the intricacies of how things are built, including *Building Big* (2000), *The Way We Work* (2008), and *Built to Last* (2010).
3. The If You . . . series (Scholastic) takes an up-close look at a period of time (such as Colonial times or westward expansion) or a historical event (such as the signing of the Constitution) by providing descriptive details about what life would be like.
4. Seymour Simon has produced a rich and extensive collection of books (Smithsonian) characterized by vivid color photographs. The books cover a wide range of scientific topics, including the solar system, the stars, the sun, hurricanes, earthquakes, lightning, whales, sharks, the brain, and other parts of the body.
5. For younger readers, Gail Gibbons has also produced a colorful and engaging collection of nonfiction titles that deal with a range of topics, including weather, nature, animals, how-to books, and planets. Each is characterized by colorful illustrations and accessible text.
6 Ruth Heller's World of Language series (Puffin) engages the reader with vibrant color illustrations and simple, poetic text. Each book addresses a different part of the English language, including nouns, verbs, and adjectives.
7. The Magic Tree House series by Mary Pope Osborne has corresponding nonfiction research books that act as companions to the titles in the fiction series. These entertaining books are full of facts, maps, illustrations, and resources related to the subject matter of the fiction books.

Publishers have also created sets of nonfiction texts designed specifically to be used in reading instruction. Apply the same evaluative criteria to sets of reading books as you do to any nonfiction texts. You should especially be sure that the writing is not distorted or formulaic. The text must meet criteria for high-quality nonfiction *and* be interesting and accessible to your students.

Demands of Nonfiction Texts on Readers

Students are often highly motivated to read nonfiction; for many, it is more engaging than fiction (Bennett-Armistead and Duke 2007). Duke has argued that nonfiction is limited, at least in early elementary grades. This has been steadily improving. In many schools students may be exposed mostly to textbooks for their nonfiction reading. We advocate using a rich variety of nonfiction texts both for interest and motivation and to help students learn *how to read* nonfiction, with all its complexity.

It is obvious from the descriptions in this chapter that nonfiction texts demand much of readers. The variety and structural patterns place unique demands and offer unique learning opportunities (see Figure 11.26).

As this figure indicates, the process of reading nonfiction texts is complex—these operations are going on rapidly and simultaneously in the head of the competent reader. Select texts carefully to provide many opportunities for students to comprehend a variety of types of nonfiction. Choose texts that are accessible to your students. If they are too hard, the reading process breaks down and students don't have the opportunity to use effective reading strategies.

Evaluating Nonfiction Texts

It is necessary for readers to think critically about all texts, but it is even more important to do so about texts that they rely on to provide accurate information. You want your readers to think about whether a text offers authentic information and also to notice aspects of the writer's craft that they can use in their own writing. The more you think critically about the texts, the better you can help them.

Because time for reading is limited, it is also important to select excellent examples of informational texts

NONFICTION TEXTS: DEMANDS ON THE READER

Nonfiction texts require readers to:

- Gather information.
- Follow a sequence of events or procedures.
- Follow a logical line of thought.
- Summarize and remember important details and other information.
- Recognize and use underlying patterns of the text—established sequence, temporal sequence, comparison/contrast, cause/effect, problem/solution, description/categories.
- Scan to pick up information.
- Use organizing tools to find information.
- Relate ideas and facts to each other.
- Use prior knowledge to interpret and understand information.
- Synthesize information by integrating it with prior knowledge.
- Evaluate the text for accuracy and completeness.
- Distinguish fact from fiction.
- Search texts for missing information.
- Recognize perspective and bias.
- Notice and get information from graphics.
- Recognize implicit or explicit underlying values expressed by the writer.
- Judge or evaluate the logic of an argument.
- Evaluate the logic and feasibility of a proposed solution.

Figure 11.26 Nonfiction texts: demands on the reader

for the classroom library (independent reading), guided reading (small-group instruction), and read-aloud and literature discussion. Encountering good examples will not only engage your students but also help them notice the craft. Figure 11.27 lists several categories for evaluating nonfiction texts and suggests some questions to ask yourself and perhaps discuss with your colleagues. All seven areas in the table are related to the quality of the text:

1. The most important questions are related to the *authenticity or accuracy* of the text. Is it up to date? Is it fact or fiction? Is it accurate? If it isn't, the other features don't matter so much, because you won't use it with students. Of course, times change and scientists discover more, so what is a high-quality text today might not be appropriate ten years from now. If you do discover out of date information in a good text, you can use it but explain the more up to date information.
2. Be sure that the *organizational structure* is clearly signaled to readers and that it is helpful rather than confusing.
3. Take a look at the *language*. Is it appropriate for the topic? Does it capture attention? Is it interesting? Select texts that are engaging rather than didactic, with as little bias as possible.
4. Are the *concepts* well developed and clearly explained? How much background information is required? Are the concepts just mentioned or "thrown in," or are they elaborated? Is there sufficient evidence for the writer's points?
5. Does the writer's *voice* communicate with and engage readers? Sometimes the voice is the same throughout the text; but there may be another style for a particular purpose. If so, how easy is the text for the reader to follow?
6. Has the writer considered the *audience*? How appropriate is the language and will it engage the readers?
7. Finally, consider the *design features*. Do they contribute to meaning in a coherent way? Are they useful? Are they of high quality and do they make the text more readable?

As you work with nonfiction texts, asking these questions will become more familiar and unconscious, and the more you discuss and critique texts with your students, the more they will become able to think critically about nonfiction texts.

EVALUATING NONFICTION TEXTS	
Element	**Questions to Ask**
Authenticity	• Are the writer's credentials revealed and do they support the authenticity of the text? • Are details accurate and consistent with other sources? • Is the text up to date? • Does the writer avoid inappropriate anthropomorphism (humanizing animals and objects)? • If fiction is mingled with fact, does the writer clearly signal which parts of the text are made up?
Organizational Structure	• Is the organizational structure of the text clear? • Is it easy for readers to gather information? • Does the layout clearly reveal the structure (headings, subheadings, etc.)? • Do sections of the text provide coherent information sufficient for the reader to understand the text (rather than fragmentation)? • Is the organizational structure of the text clearly revealed in the text design? • Is the text logically ordered? • Is the organizational structure consistent throughout the text? Are any changes adequately signaled? • Is the text sequenced in a way appropriate to the type and subject matter? • Are there cross-references in the text to direct the readers to needed information?
Language	• Is the language accessible to students? • Does the language capture attention and spark curiosity? Is it interesting? • Are there features to help readers understand the language (glossary, quick definitions within the text)? • Is the language appropriate to the type of text (report, expositions, etc.)? • Is the language appropriate to the subject area? • Does the text have illustrations or other graphic features that support the language? Are different concepts or words illustrated? • Is the language inclusive (avoiding stereotypes)? • Does the writer avoid didacticism and propaganda?
Concepts	• Are concepts well developed with examples that help readers understand them? • How much background knowledge is required of readers? • Are concepts elaborated rather than just mentioned? • Are concepts well supported by facts? • Do understandable descriptions support concepts? • Are relationships among concepts made clear? • Does the writer provide sufficient evidence for generalizations? • Does the writer answer the significant questions at issue?

Figure 11.27 Evaluating nonfiction texts

EVALUATING NONFICTION TEXTS	
Element	**Questions to Ask**
Voice	• Does the writer communicate a scientific attitude? • Is there a consistent voice in the text? If the voice changes, is the variation clearly significant and does it fulfill a real purpose? • Is the writer's voice likely to engage readers? • Has the writer communicated the information in an interesting way?
Audience	• Is the purpose of the text clear? • Do the information and language fit the purpose? • Does the writer appear to keep the audience in mind? • Is the text interesting?
Design Features	• Do the format and layout contribute to the meaning and are they easy for readers to use? • Are organizational features useful and clear? Do they signal the contents? • Are the design features consistent throughout the text? • Are the graphic aids of high quality? • Do graphic aids add meaning to the text? • Is there a good balance between illustrations and text? • Are the graphic aids accurate? Do legends and keys help readers interpret graphics? • Do illustrations capture attention and add interest to the text? • Do the print size, font, and style make the text readable?

Figure 11.27 Evaluating nonfiction texts *(cont.)*

Suggestions for Professional Development

Examine informational texts with your grade-level colleagues. You may want to use the same books you collected for the professional development activity in Chapter 10.

1. Select three texts—one on a science topic, one on a social studies topic, and one on a topic of your choice.
2. Look at the analysis of *Mysteries of the Mummy Kids* in Figure 11.25. Then, using the blank form for analyzing nonfiction text factors in Appendix C, analyze each of the three texts. Work in pairs or small groups.
3. Compare your analyses. Then discuss what you learned.
   - How effective is the text in using a combination of characteristics to provide information about the topic?
   - What variety did you find across the three texts?
   - What are the opportunities for your students to learn from reading this text?
   - What text features would you draw students' attention to in introducing this text?

CHAPTER 12

Reading Across Genres

A Close Study of Hybrid Texts, Graphica, and Multigenre Text Sets

Modes mix, genres blend.
I'm for teaching an expansive
and flexible view of genre.

—Tom Romano

The ability to read across texts is a critical competency for a literate person. You want your students to learn to think analytically about a topic, idea, or theme by synthesizing information from several texts—not just one. Thinking across texts makes understanding richer and helps readers take multiple perspectives; it also helps you become more critical in your reading. Many teachers foster deeper thinking by using a series of texts in different genres that focus on one topic or theme.

This book categorizes written works according to characteristics and special forms. Yet in each chapter we have had to emphasize that often the lines between these categories are blurred. In order to engage readers and get their messages across, writers very often blend categories in ways that make the material more exciting. In literature written for children and young people, this blending of genres has become even more common in recent years. Hybrid texts offer a much wider scope for the writer and provide the variety that engages readers.

In addition to the explosion of beautiful, high-quality picture books, other formats have become increasingly popular as well. As technology makes it easier to produce color images, illustrations have become more frequent and more dominant in both paper and electronic texts. *Graphica*, for example, a form rapidly expanding in popularity across the world, is a medium of literature that integrates pictures and words to tell a story or inform; illustrations are equal to or more important than text and tell much of the story or provide much of the information.

The Benefits of Reading and Thinking Across Genres

Combining genres does not mean that understanding individual genres is less important. Readers can more fully appreciate unusual text construction when they recognize embedded genres. Also, when they encounter a new and unusual medium, such as graphica, they need to be able to apply all the genre knowledge they already have to understand the text.

Today, students have access to more variety in texts than at any time in the history of written language. While this richness is wonderful, thinking across genres also makes greater demands. Some of the important benefits for students are:

- They gain multiple perspectives on a topic or idea when they read a variety of genres and forms.
- They learn to read more critically, especially when they find conflicting views or facts.
- Different genres engage their interest and attention in different ways, leading to more active involvement.
- Comparing texts on the same topic or idea but in different genres helps them understand genre characteristics and purposes.
- Reading one genre helps them better comprehend similar ideas or themes in another. For example, reading historical fiction and then authentic diaries or histories may make the nonfiction material more interesting. Conversely, reading nonfiction first may make historical fiction more interesting because they have background information.
- They may accomplish different purposes within the same arena. For example, they may collect facts but then be inspired by biography or poetry.

Keep in mind also that on standardized tests today students are expected to draw information from more than one kind of text (see the NAEP framework). This expectation is also a clear expectation of the Common Core State Standards.

These are all good reasons for your students to read and think across genres. But there is one more reason—it's fun! By carefully guiding your students' independent reading and making intentional choices for texts you read aloud, discuss in book club, and choose for guided reading, you can raise the level of enjoyment in your classrooms. Variety is the spice of life, and that is true of the reading menu as well. Three approaches to creating this menu are laid out in Figure 12.1. All the materials have great potential not only for enlivening the learning in your classroom but for increasing students' understanding of genre.

Hybrid Texts

In her definition of hybrid texts Calkins (2010) calls them "a mixture of non-narrative and narrative structure." These texts may present an idea supported by facts, and then tell a story that relates to or illustrates the idea. Or, they may tell an imagined but realistic story, interspersed with related factual information. Some texts like this begin with a story, a letter, a diary entry, or a mini-biography and then move into expository structures that are clearly set off from the narrative text in some way. Because texts structured this way often can't be broken down into boxes and bullets, teach children to instead treat them like photographs and quotes, asking, *What does this letter or story teach me?*

It's easy to define a hybrid text as one made up of a blend of genres, but it becomes much harder when you examine hundreds of texts. As you read the literature on and examples of hybrid texts, many questions surface. For example, for a text to be called a hybrid:

- How much of the text must be in a second genre? Is just an embedded paragraph or sidebar enough?
- What genres are mixed? Should it be always be fiction and nonfiction?
- When text structures are mixed (narrative and exposition, for example), can we call the text a hybrid? When two structures are used in fiction (such as a letter within a piece of realistic fiction), can we call it a hybrid text?

READING AND THINKING ACROSS GENRES		
Materials	**Definition**	**Thinking Across Genres**
Hybrid Texts	A nonfiction and a fiction genre are included within one text. Genres may be blended or in different sections.	• Enhance engagement by presenting ideas and content in interesting ways. • Require readers to sort out genres. • Require readers to notice aspects of the writer's craft.
Graphica	A kind of text that integrates pictures and words and arranges them cumulatively to tell a story or convey information. Most but not all have the look of comic strips. The illustrations carry a great deal of the information.	• Are highly appealing to readers. • Are available in a great variety of genres. • Help readers think across genres within a new and unique media. • Help readers notice new aspects of the writer/illustrator's craft.
Multigenre Text Sets	A group of texts that have a common theme or topic is selected for reading aloud to students. The set is characterized by a variety of genres.	• Explore big ideas through different genres. • Lead to comparing genres.

Figure 12.1 Reading and thinking across genres

- Does the writer's purpose play a role in identifying a hybrid text? For example, is it a hybrid when a writer suddenly switches from description and explanation to argument and persuasion?
- When two forms are mixed (print narrative with some pages of graphic texts, for example), can we call the text a hybrid?

In answer to these questions, we have developed these criteria for identifying hybrid texts (see Figure 12.2):

1. A hybrid text is one that blends more than one genre in a coherent whole. In order for a text to be considered a hybrid, it must be a blend of a fiction genre and a nonfiction genre. A blend of two different fiction genres (e.g., fantasy embedded within an historical fiction text), or of two different nonfiction genres (e.g., real newspaper articles [expository nonfiction] embedded within a biography) does not constitute a hybrid text. The text may combine one or more of the following fictional genres with one or more of the following nonfiction genres:
   a. Fiction: realistic fiction, historical fiction, modern fantasy, including science fiction, and traditional tales or stories written like them.
   b. Nonfiction: narrative nonfiction; biography, autobiography, and memoir; and expository, persuasive, and procedural texts.
2. Texts may have other genres embedded within them or have whole sections that are set apart

CHARACTERISTICS OF HYBRID TEXTS		
Genre	**Definition**	**Characteristics**
Hybrid Texts	A text that blends fiction and nonfiction genres in a coherent whole; may have genres or structures embedded within a text or have sections set apart that are written using different structure.	• Combines fiction and nonfiction in one text • Second genre(s) accounts for a significant amount of the text • Clearly differentiates between the two different genres Often: • Uses different text structures for the different genres

Figure 12.2 Characteristics of hybrid texts

and clearly a different genre. For example, *Dinner at Aunt Connie's House* (Ringgold 1993) is a blend of fiction and biography. It tells the fictional story of a family's annual dinner, combined with the factual biographical information about several famous African American women. More smoothly blended genres may be problematic for readers as it becomes more difficult to clearly identify the book as fiction or nonfiction.

3. A substantial and/or very significant part of the text is in a genre other than the main genre. One paragraph or a sidebar of narration within an expository text does not make it a hybrid. Readers need to make a judgment about the degree to which the text is hybrid, and there will always be disagreement.
4. In fiction, the embedded text would need to be factual information rather than another form of fiction. In other words, a fictionalized letter embedded in a historical fiction text would not make it a hybrid. But if a substantial amount of real historical documents are embedded, then the text is a hybrid. In the science fiction series beginning with *Ender's Game* (Orson Scott Card 1991), characters frequently communicate via emails embedded in the regular text; however, these books are not hybrids. The email strings introduce another kind of form/structure, but they are fictional.

When it comes to hybrids and to the understanding of fiction and nonfiction genres, in general, an exact designation isn't necessary. The important goal is to think analytically about a text and notice the writer's craft. There will always be texts that you find difficult to categorize, and wrestling with this dilemma often raises interest. Just thinking about the genres and their characteristics has instructional value. We suggest that you work with clear genre examples when you introduce each genre in a study. Then your students will be able to think analytically about hybrids.

The Value of Hybrid Texts

According to Romano (commenting on *The Collected Works of Billy the Kid,* by Michael Ondaatje), "Each genre is a color slide complete in itself, possessing its own satisfying composition, but also working in concert with the others to create a single literary experience" (2000, 3–4). Romano suggests that the multigenre approach reflects the world of writing, which is large and contains multitudes:

> We have fiction and restaurant menus, sonnets and graffiti, recipes and dissertations, love letters and legal documents. In fact, modes of writing are often blended. Narrative needs description. Vivid anecdotes clarify exposition. Fiction can build tension when characters engage in back-and-forth exposition through dialogue. Modes mix, genres blend. I'm for teaching an expansive and flexible view of genre. (43)

Hybrid texts have great potential benefit for students (see Figure 12.3). Using multiple genres gives writers a broader scope, allowing them to layer meanings in a way that helps readers see a topic from many different points of view. Mixing genres can enliven expository texts with narrative and anecdotes. It can ignite readers' interest in information because it is situated within an engaging story.

In many ways, hybrid texts more closely resemble the kind of reading experiences you may have when surfing the Internet to explore a topic. You may find yourself reading fiction or informational articles, personal stories or memoirs, and editorials and opinion pieces, as well as viewing video.

Ray (2006) makes the point that classifying writing is a gray area (189). She also makes the case for studying genre as a way of teaching writing. Instead of teaching students to use different modes (short story, feature article, personal essay), the point of departure should be genre: "If the move toward a draft begins with an answer to the question, 'What have you read that is like what you're trying to write?' the complexity of mode will be intact. It can't *not* be intact, because this is how things get written in the world outside school. . . . It's as simple as knowing exactly the kind of thing you'd like your students to write, and showing it to them" (59). Ray doesn't use the term *hybrid* and says little about multiple genres; however, she does suggest this:

> Sometimes writers combine several different kinds of writing in the creation of a single text, creating a sort of writing collage on a given topic. Based on the topic, these multigenre texts can do the combined work of memoir, poetry, feature article, essay, recipe—basically any kind of writing—in a single text. (254)

Romano (2000) also advocates having students write multigenre reports, one "composed of many genres, each piece self-contained, making a point of its own, yet connected by theme or topic and sometimes by language, images, and content" (p. x), because it will help them connect more deeply with their topics.

THE VALUE OF HYBRID TEXTS

- Consider point of view or perspective of the author.
- Understand literary elements such as figurative language.
- Identify important characters and secondary characters.
- Identify the conflict or problem of the story.
- Understand the prominent theme or author's message.
- Understand characters from how they look; what they do, think, or say; and what others say or think about them.
- Follow the events of the plot and make predictions about its resolution.
- Understand the meaning and significance of the climax or plot resolution.
- Relate the primary message or theme to our own life—make the story our own.
- Remember important parts of the story to relate it to other texts.

Figure 12.3 The value of hybrid texts

The Demands Hybrid Texts Make on Readers

While hybrid texts can be highly engaging, they also make unique demands on readers (see Figure 12.4). Readers must be able to recognize shifts in genre and adjust their thinking accordingly. They have to draw out real information to separate it from the imagined text and think deeply about the author's real purpose. In addition to the demands of the genres embedded in the text, readers must deal with the complexities of layered or blended genres.

For example, when reading The Magic School Bus series, even adults are sometimes momentarily unsure whether the books are nonfiction or fantasy. In *The Magic School Bus on the Ocean Floor* (Cole 1994), readers learn that "the deepest valleys and the tallest mountains on earth are found under the ocean." You read the definition of *submersible*. At the same time you see a

HYBRID TEXTS: DEMANDS ON THE READER

Readers need to:

- Recognize when a writer is blending or layering genres.
- Determine by analyzing text structure the particular way the writer has mixed genres.
- Meet the demands of all genres included in the text.
- Make subtle shifts in the use of strategic actions to process the text effectively.
- Sort out the real information from the material in the text that is imagined.
- Notice the way the text is organized in order to present different kinds of information.
- Make hypotheses about the writer's purpose.
- Notice aspects of the writer's craft and hypothesize why the writer made those choices (for example, to make a text more interesting or to arouse readers' feelings).

Figure 12.4 Hybrid texts: demands on the reader

school bus that has been magically transformed into a submersible vehicle for exploring the ocean floor. At the beginning of the book, that same bus, driven by Ms. Frizzle, has charged right into the ocean with students on board. The book is a fantasy, yet the information is factual. The illustrator has done much to help readers. Interesting facts and descriptions are placed on what looks like yellow notebook paper. Dialogue is in speech bubbles. The narrator of the fictional text is one of the students, and everything Ms. Frizzle says imparts real information about the ocean. The result is a highly entertaining text but not necessarily an easy one. You get caught up in the humor of the imaginative adventure story and at the same time must notice the signals and get a sense of where to find the various kinds of information.

Hybrid texts are complex, but meeting their demands can stretch readers' thinking. Tolan and Calkins (2010) comment on how both narrative nonfiction and hybrid texts can support students' thinking:

> We read differently when a text is structured as an expository text—organized to advance ideas, with information divided into compartments—and when a text is organized as a story. Nonfiction texts can be either—or both, combining both expository and narrative structures.... Often, when kids read nonfiction, they read as if they're wearing blinders, taking in one specific page of a text at a time, not seeing how one page links with the broader text. By helping children think of these nonfiction (narrative) texts as stories and helping them use their knowledge of story structure to determine importance (and unimportance), you help them synthesize as they read. (3)

Genre Study with Hybrid Texts

Students can read (or hear read aloud), enjoy, and understand hybrid texts long before they study or analyze them. Even younger readers can understand simple examples as "partly true and partly not true." But once students are grounded in a basic understanding of a number of genres, studying hybrid texts will be interesting and have great benefit. After all, students today are expected to draw meaning across texts that may be of different genres. Looking at hybrids is good practice. Some hybrid texts are excellent and engaging but provide a large amount of detail with very busy illustrations that the individual reader needs to examine. At the end of this chapter you will find a list of hybrid mentor texts. These books are suggested titles to be used as exemplars of the genre, but you may have excellent examples of your own that you prefer to use. These mentor texts may be used to build text sets, and for read-aloud and book clubs.

One teacher began her students' investigation of hybrids by framing combined genres in general. She called their attention to the distinguishing features that *make* a text hybrid rather than to one specific text. The students had participated in other genre study activities, so they were familiar with the process. An excerpt from the beginning of their study is provided in Figure 12.5.

BEGINNING A STUDY OF HYBRID TEXTS	
TEACHER:	You know how we studied biography and expository nonfiction books? Those are two kinds or genres of texts. And at the beginning of the year we studied realistic fiction. We shared some texts that were all the same kind, and you read some individually and shared your thinking. We made a chart of what we noticed. Take a look at our chart for expository nonfiction books. What kinds of things did we put on the chart?
DARIUS:	We said what expository nonfiction texts are like.
KARL:	It's also what makes them different from other kinds of books. Like for biography, it was about a real person and his life.
CLAUDIA:	We didn't put in what would be in all books—like it had paragraphs or something, just the important things.
TEACHER:	We were studying one kind of text when we made those charts. But sometimes writers like to use two or even more kinds, or genres, of text in one book. So you might have a book that is one part fiction and one part nonfiction. Do you all know The Magic School Bus series?
STUDENTS:	Yes.
TEACHER:	Do you think it's fiction?
STUDENTS:	Yes.
MARIAH:	Because a school bus couldn't really fly or go under the ocean.
DENTON:	So it's a fantasy.
TEACHER:	But does it give you a lot of factual information also?
CLAUDIA:	Yes, it gives true information, like Ms. Frizzle couldn't be real but she gives them lessons about things that are real.
TEACHER:	When a writer uses both fiction and nonfiction genres in one book, it is called a hybrid. That word means mixed. The writer has mixed nonfiction and fiction genres in one book. There are different ways of doing it, and we will be looking at some of them. Why do you think a writer would mix genres to make a hybrid text?
DARIUS:	It's more entertaining, like the Magic School Bus is funny but you still learn things.
TEACHER:	It may be to make the factual information more interesting. It can also be to make a fictional story seem more real.

Figure 12.5 Beginning a study of hybrid texts

Over several days the class discussed the books as they were read aloud. They examined them further during independent reading. Then the group began to generate characteristics they noticed. They added to the list over the next few days, sometimes striking out a characteristic that, while important, was not important in distinguishing hybrid texts. Their finished list and resulting definition are shown in Figures 12.6 and 12.7.

Students wrote the definition and list of characteristics in their reader's notebooks, and over the next few weeks during readers' workshop they shared hybrid texts they had read. Sometimes texts were hard to categorize, and there was no emphasis on "right" or "wrong." The entire experience sharpened students' attention to text structure, organization, and author's purpose.

Including Hybrid Texts in Classroom Instruction

Hybrid texts are valuable instructional materials. Here are five ways you can integrate them into your literacy instruction:

1. *Use hybrid texts for genre study.* Undertake a study of hybrid texts or introduce hybrid texts in studies of other genres, distinguishing them as representing the genre (fantasy, for example) but also including another genre. In the latter case, use clear, memorable examples to establish a clear understanding of the genre before introducing blended or hybrid examples.
2. *Provide hybrid texts for independent reading.* Place a collection of hybrid texts in a labeled basket so that students can explore them. Also, place good examples of hybrid texts in collections that focus on content area topics. Students can share their experiences with these texts in readers' and writers' workshop.
3. *Use hybrids as mentor texts to discuss the writer's craft in readers' and writers' workshop.* The texts you have read aloud or that students have shared can be reexamined during minilessons in readers' and writers' workshop.
4. *Encourage students to create their own hybrid fiction and nonfiction texts.* Students will enjoy using a variety of genres to get their messages across. They can even incorporate multimedia to make report writing more exciting.

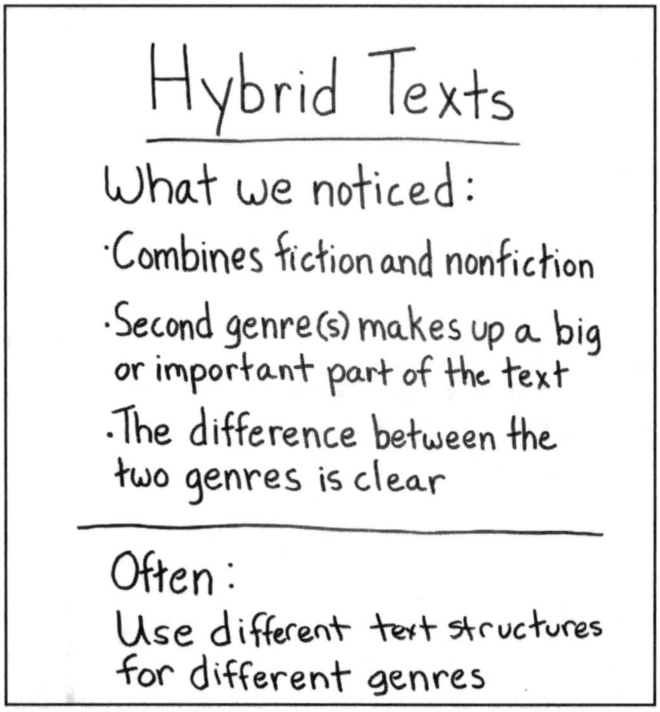
Hybrid Texts
What we noticed:
·Combines fiction and nonfiction
·Second genre(s) makes up a big or important part of the text
·The difference between the two genres is clear
Often:
Use different text structures for different genres

Figure 12.6 Noticings about hybrid texts

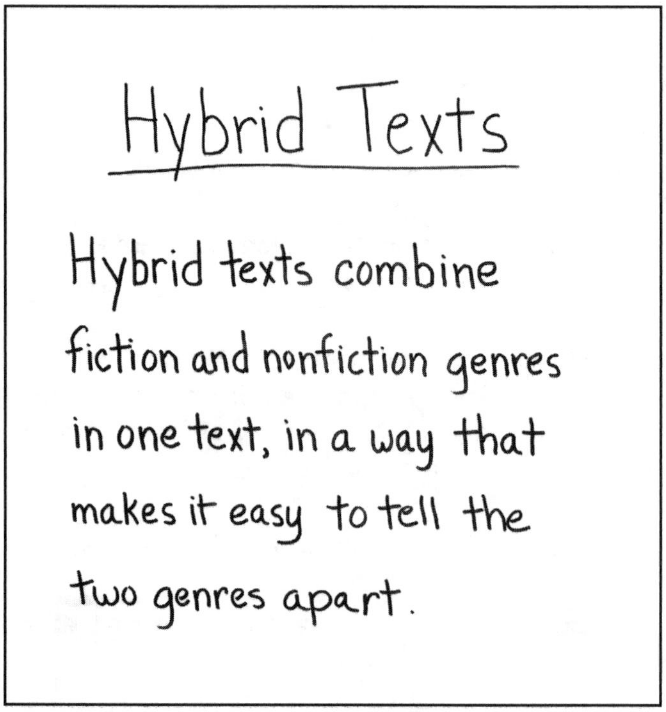
Hybrid Texts
Hybrid texts combine fiction and nonfiction genres in one text, in a way that makes it easy to tell the two genres apart.

Figure 12.7 Working definition of hybrid texts

5. *Use hybrid texts to enrich content area study.* Exciting and informative hybrid texts can make content area study come alive as students move beyond expository textbooks to sample texts that evoke feelings and show different perspectives.

Graphica

Reading graphic novels is an exciting experience. The reader encounters page after page of action and must derive the characters' emotions from the expression on faces and body posture. You infer causes and transitions by looking from frame to frame and thinking about what happened between frames. There is some third-person narrative, but you infer the setting, plot, and action mostly from the dialogue and pictures. Yet graphica has all the characteristics of the genre in which it is written. It is no wonder that graphic texts are becoming more and more popular with children, young people, and adults (see Figure 12.8).

Defining Graphica

In *Adventures in Graphica: Using Comics and Graphic Novels to Teach Comprehension, 2–6*, Thompson (2008) defines graphica as "a medium of literature that integrates pictures and words and arranges them cumulatively to tell a story or convey information; often presented in comic strip, periodical, or book form; also known as comics" (6).

Rollins (2006) defines graphica as "a form of sequential, visual storytelling" (8). He claims that "anything shorter than seventy or so pages is seldom graced with the title 'graphic novel'—it is usually called an 'extra-long one shot'" (8). He goes on to say that graphic novelists tend to use mature themes and are more inward looking, even darker than other writers; that many graphic novels are autobiographical; and that they are not appropriate for young children. We take a slightly broader view.

Graphica is not a genre but rather a special kind of text—as Thompson says, a medium, available in many genres, that uses many formats. A graphic text can be:

- A historical account, such as *The Sinking of the Titanic* (Doeden, il. Barnett and Miller, 2005).
- A fantasy with a character who develops super powers, as in *Foiled* (Yolen, il. Cavallaro, 2010).
- A biography, like *Satchel Paige: Striking Out Jim Crow* (Sturm and Tommaso 2007) or *Maus I: A Survivor's Tale: My Father Bleeds History* (Spiegelman 1973).
- A traditional tale, like *Jack and the Beanstalk: The Graphic Novel* (Hoena, il. Tercio, 2009).

Figure 12.8 Pages from the graphic novel *Jack and the Beanstalk*

Figure 12.9 describes some general characteristics that apply to all graphica, as well as five formats.

The most significant characteristic of graphica is the art, which in certain graphic texts is called *anime*, stylized Japanese illustrations that are quite distinct (see the example in Figure 12.10 on page 207). *Anime* is the art form that appears in *manga*, comic texts that originated in Japan and have now spread around the world. Not all graphic texts use the *anime* style. There is increasing variety in the medium. Artists have different ways of integrating text with pictures.

Comic Strips

The form of graphica we are probably most familiar with is the comic strip, which is a feature in many newspapers and magazines. Comic strips have every characteristic of graphica. Usually they are short and humorous, but they can be continuing stories with episode after episode. Comic strip authors/artists like Charles Schultz have been popular for decades, and some of the classic newspaper strips such as *Dick Tracy* (Chester Gould), *Pogo* (Walt Kelly), and *Prince Valiant* (Harold Foster) are being reissued.

Comic Books

Comic books, too, have been around for many years. Many of the superheroes popular in movies today were originally comic book characters. Comic books are longer than comic strips, are published as inexpensive paper booklets, and can have a variety of content. Some are clearly entertaining and meant for children; some have political and social messages. Often, they come in a series, carrying a story over from one issue to the next.

Criticized as not being "real" reading in the 1950s, comics occupy a new place in our reading culture today. The world of comic books is changing rapidly and expanding and becoming more and more popular. According to Cornog and Perper (2009), comics

CHARACTERISTICS AND FORMATS OF GRAPHIC TEXTS (GRAPHICA)		
General	**Definition**	**Characteristics**
Graphica	A medium of literature that integrates pictures and words to tell a story or inform (often presented as panels with art)	• Pictures carry a lot of the meaning and are equal to or more important than the print • Dialogue is very important • Sometimes full of action and adventure
Graphic Text Formats	**Definition**	**Characteristics**
Comic Strip	Panels of graphics and print that tell a story; often in a magazine or newspaper; the story continues or is about the same characters	• Short story • Three to eight panels • May be humorous, romantic, or adventurous • May mock something in today's society
Comic Book	An entire volume presenting strips of comics that tell a longer story	• Multiple-page volume that looks like a magazine • Story line may carry over from one issue to the next • Often about superheroes • Wide range of story lines

Figure 12.9 Characteristics and formats of graphic texts

CHARACTERISTICS AND FORMATS OF GRAPHIC TEXTS (GRAPHICA)		
Graphic Text Formats	**Definition**	**Characteristics**
Graphic Novel	A book-length fiction text with comic strips on every page and a story line that continues across the text (may also be an anthology of shorter texts)	• Similar to comic book but longer • Panels are like paragraphs • Dialogue in speech bubbles uses first person • Text boxes tell part of the story and are in first or third person • Print features (like boldface type) create mood and tell reader how to read it aloud • Usually read left to right and top to bottom but may vary • Often uses all uppercase text • Artwork as important as text • Text and art inseparable • Gutters (white space) between panels have meaning • Gutters often leave reader to infer what happened • Has a full story from beginning to end • Like fiction, with characters, story problem, and problem resolution • Wide range of story lines
Graphic Nonfiction Text	A book-length nonfiction text with comic strips on every page and information presented in categories or sequence	• Similar to comic book but longer and for a different purpose (to inform) • Engages the reader with art • Wide range of topics
Manga	A form of graphic storytelling that uses stylized Japanese illustrations to represent characters; often separated into shojo for girls and shonen for males; usually for middle school and young adults	• Graphic storytelling from Japan • Written specifically for girls or for boys • Special way of illustrating characters • Some mature story lines • May read from back of the book to the front or from right to left

Figure 12.9 Characteristics and formats of graphic texts *(cont.)*

Figure 12.10 Example of Manga

can enhance reading. They cite Krashen, who has reported research suggesting that children who read comics read more for pleasure. Dowdy, Dunko, and Hartz (2011) describe the potential of both comic strips and comic books for engaging students in “reading and writing: “The brain is helped to process information when it is presented in a variety of ways” (18). They describe a workshop approach to involve students in studying and creating their own comic strips and comic books.

Graphic Novel

A graphic novel is a work of fiction created using comics or other kinds of illustrations. Usually, a graphic novel has comic strips or other dominant illustrations on every page and some written narration that carries part of the story line. It may be any fiction genre, such as realistic or historical fiction. There are also many short graphic stories, such as fantasies, folktales, or fairy tales, as well as graphic anthologies of shorter stories.

Even young children can read graphic stories. A simple example of a graphic story for younger students is *Little Mouse Gets Ready* (2009) by Jeff Smith, the author of the popular Bone graphic novel series. The Benny and Penny series of graphic stories by Geoffrey Hayes features two adorable mouse siblings who will appeal to the primary grade reader.

But graphic novels can also be quite complex and sophisticated. *The Arrival* (Tan 2006) uses symbolism and some of the techniques of film to communicate what a new immigrant feels on entering a place like America. The book’s endpapers show black-and-white drawings (like passport photos) of immigrants from all over the world. Within the text, large and imaginative black-and-white drawings communicate the mood.

Fantasy is a popular genre for graphic novels, and a frequent motif is the superhero. *Foiled* (Yolen 2010) features a female heroine who becomes an excellent fencer. On a date with her lab partner, Aliera discovers she can conjure up magical things with her foil. The colors used for the text are black, blue, and white, giving it a somewhat dark look; however, when Aliera uses her foil, objects and creatures appear in very bright colors. Color signals the change from the everyday world to the imaginary one. On one page, the author signals the change of time by three vertical panels, each a picture of Aliera at a different age. The chapter titles are fencing moves, from “Engagement” to Disengagement,” that have a double meaning.

Another example of fantasy is the mysterious *Brain Camp* (Kim and Klavan 2010). Two teenagers, Lucas and Jenna, who have both been turned down many times by camps and educational programs, suddenly receive invitations to attend a camp that promises to be unlike any other. Danger is foreshadowed in the first four pages, which show two campers appearing to choke. Readers predict that Lucas and Jenna were invited to the camp to take their place. This dark and scary text borders on horror.

American Born Chinese (Luen Yang 2008) follows three separate storylines involving three different characters: Jin Wang, who is the only Chinese boy in his new school; Danny, troubled by his pesky cousin; and a character from Chinese folklore, the Monkey King. The three characters all have problems to solve and must find a way to help one another. The work is a fantasy but the problems of the two boys will be familiar to most readers.

The Invention of Hugo Cabret (Selznick 2007) is a graphic novel over five hundred pages long. This historical fiction book is about Hugo, who lives in a Paris train station where he takes care of the clocks. The story is told with a series of alternating pictures and whole pages of print.

Graphic stories are often new versions of classic stories. *Jack and the Beanstalk* (Hoena 2009) retells this folktale in an engaging graphic format. *Rapunzel's Revenge* (Hale and Hale 2008) is a graphic fantasy that offers a comic twist on the classic story of Rapunzel. In this version, Rapunzel leaves the castle and goes on adventures with an outlaw named Jack. *The Odyssey* (Hinds 2010) is a highly sophisticated piece of traditional literature based on Homer's epic poem. The myth is told through beautiful pencil and watercolor paintings. The story is narrated by Odysseus, but dialogue is also included. The same author has also created the graphic novels *Beowulf, The Merchant of Venice,* and *King Lear.*

Sometimes graphic novels come in a series, such as the Babymouse books (Holm and Holm 2005). These humorous books feature a dynamic, irrepressible little mouse. The design and content seem appropriate for younger students, but the text is surprisingly sophisticated. We see many of Babymouse's thoughts and daydreams, and there are literary allusions such as "the Midas touch."

One of the most popular graphic novel series begins with *Diary of a Wimpy Kid: Greg Heffley's Journal* (Kinney 2007). The books are a series of journals kept by the main character, Greg Heffley, who has to deal with typical middle school social situations and family relationships. The stories also have quite a bit of narrative text, but are illustrated throughout with comics, most with dialogue. Many upper elementary age students love to read books in the Wimpy Kid series, though the content is clearly aimed at middle school students.

Graphic texts are rapidly growing in number and popularity. Writing about graphic fiction in the United States, Cornog and Perper (2009) say:

> To one degree or another, virtually every popular literary genre shows up in graphic novel form. Some genres are abundantly represented, such as horror-supernatural, action-adventure, and fantasy of all types. Other categories, though seemingly tailor-made for comics-style storytelling, are not yet as prevalent in this country as one might think: science fiction, Westerns, and war stories. A few genres, like romance fiction and children's humor, are only now becoming more widely available as American publishers are reaching out to new audiences. (67)

Graphic Nonfiction Texts

Graphic nonfiction texts can be any type—biography, narrative nonfiction, or exposition. Graphic nonfiction texts are appealing to many readers because they make a topic come alive. Graphic biographies can make a subject's life seem more accessible to a reader, and more immediate. There are several graphic nonfiction series titles that utilize a graphic format to present information about significant people and events from history. The Graphic Biography titles from The Graphic Library series (Capstone Press) focus on subjects from U.S. history, such as Thomas Jefferson, George Washington, and Molly Pitcher, as well as more current subjects that represent different aspects of American culture, such as science (Marie Curie, Jane Goodall, Jonas Salk), sports (Jackie Robinson, Jim Thorpe), activism (Rosa Parks, Cesar Chavez, Martin Luther King, Jr.) and technology (Steve Jobs). The graphic texts in the Inventions and Discovery series of Graphic Library include details about both inventors' lives, and their inventions. These books show the inventions in various stages and prompt the reader to imagine what it might have been like to make such influential and life-changing discoveries. Other graphic biographies such as *Anne Frank: The Anne Frank House Authorized Graphic Biography* (Jacobson

2010) take a more serious tone and the graphics reflect that with detailed, sophisticated graphics that use a more muted color palette.

Expository texts also work well as graphica. The Graphic Library series mentioned earlier also includes a series of graphic nonfiction texts that encompass a wide range of events from U.S. history, including the signing of the U.S. Constitution, the Lewis and Clark expedition, and the Apollo 13 mission; as well as a science series with titles that focus on scientific concepts such as electricity and cell life. For younger readers the "You Wouldn't Want to Be" series (Scholastic) uses a humorous tone and illustrations to emphasize the challenges and hardships related to significant events in U.S. history (American colonists, the Mayflower voyage) and world history (the construction of the pyramids and of the Great Wall of China). As with graphic biographies, graphic expository nonfiction can run the gamut from very simple, to highly sophisticated texts with graphics that mirror the complexity of the themes or content. *The United States Constitution: A Graphic Adaptation* (Hennessey 2008) provides detailed background information on events that led to the creation of the U.S. Constitution. In the nonfiction text *How to Clean a Hippopotamus: A Look at Unusual Animal Partnerships* (Jenkins and Page 2010) the authors present the idea of symbiotic relationships in nature using a graphic text design. Although the book utilizes Jenkins' usual cut paper illustrations, it also employs the style of the graphic novel to show a series of illustrative frames from different points of view.

Manga

Manga is the Japanese word for comics; it literally means "whimsical pictures." In Japan, both children and adults read manga, and this body of literature includes a broad range of genres. The roots of manga are in the traditional style of Japanese art dating back to the twelfth century. The art, called *anime,* is stylized in particular ways. During the 1950s, the popularity of manga started to increase rapidly and its scope broadened. Manga is available as comics but also as hardbound and paperback books that are read from right to left. Today manga is popular all over the world and it has influenced comics in many countries, particularly Taiwan, South Korea, and China.

Manga started to become popular in the U.S. in the 1970s, partly through film. (Many graphic texts, especially those with comic strips, have a film-like quality.) In the U.S., the term *manga* is generally used to refer to comics published in Japan or comics done in that style, and they are published as books and magazines to be read right to left (some are reversed as left to right). Not all graphic texts use anime. Looking through many graphic texts, we find a wide variety of styles.

The Conventions of Graphic Texts

Even though graphic texts vary widely and there are no "rules," most graphic illustrator/writers recognize some conventions and stick to them, especially if they are producing comic-type texts. To read graphic texts successfully, students need to recognize and use these conventions. You can study these conventions in the same way you study the features of a genre, by having students read and study a number of examples of graphic texts and articulate what they notice. The conventions of graphic texts include the following (students studying graphic texts will probably point out others as well):

1. Speech bubbles are in circles and have an arrow pointing to the speaker. They tell what the characters are saying.
2. Thought bubbles are in circles and have dots pointing to the speaker. They tell what the characters are thinking but not saying out loud.
3. Narrative boxes are usually rectangles or squares and tell what is happening or provide other information.
4. The lettering conveys how something is said. Often the words are in all caps. They can be in bold or italics, large or small. They can also be wiggly or jagged.
5. The panels hold the pictures and tell the story. They show how characters feel, what they do; they show the action—how the story moves in sequence. We read them from left to right and top to bottom. Sometimes the panels become larger when something important happens.

6. The gutters are the white space between the panels. Gutters have significance, too, because readers have to infer what went on between the panels. Sometimes the space between panels indicates time has passed.
7. The pictures in the panels show the characters and what happens in the story. The pictures are often drawn as comics but can take other forms as well. They may be rendered in color or black and white.
8. Sound words often enhance the action, a visual representation of what we would be hearing.

Another way to help students learn how to read graphic texts is to bring some good examples into your guided reading lessons. There are examples of graphic texts at every level of difficulty and in a variety of genres (go to www.fountasandpinnellleveledbooks.com for specific titles). After several lessons, students develop a heightened awareness.

Specific Demands Made by Graphic Texts

Authors such as Thompson (2008) and Cornog and Perper (2009) have discussed the appeal of graphic texts and their accessibility. But you also have to think about the additional demands these texts place on readers (see Figure 12.11). Readers of graphica must meet the demands of the specific genre and in addition develop a way of "reading" the large number of illustrations. Their eyes have to move across the panels left to right and down the page, and this process can be complex if the writer/illustrator has used panels of varied sizes and shapes.

Compared to regular texts, there is usually less print to provide the information or tell the story. Some graphic texts have a lot of print, but in general the ratio of print to pictures will be about equal or smaller. Readers, therefore, must infer the story from images and dialogue; some graphic texts have no narration boxes. You have to use the pictures to distinguish characters and infer their traits and feelings. You also have to infer what happens between the panels, as each is a step in time. You have to construct the action mentally!

You have to know how to recognize and use the conventions of graphica automatically so that your attention is free to concentrate on the story. For example, you should automatically infer what happens between panels, note the passing of time, and—assisted by size of font, punctuation, and style of print—"hear" the dialogue. You need to recognize and use sound words to make the action more exciting.

Finally, just as in other forms, you need to notice aspects of the writer/illustrator's craft. Readers should notice how the pictures and the text work together to communicate meaning, how the illustrations and color contribute to the mood, and how the style and size of panels are related to the information or the action that is taking place. A good graphic text is a coherent work of art.

The Art

The salient characteristic of a graphic text is the art. Sometimes print does not even appear and when it does, it is secondary and sparse. Prentis Rollins (2006), a comic book artist who has worked on characters such as Superman and Batman, has produced a very interesting doubled-sided flip book. One side is *The Resonator*, an action-packed work of science fiction with black-and-white drawings. Flipped over it becomes *The Making of a Graphic Novel,* which details the complex and time-consuming process of producing a graphic novel. According to Rollins, comics have come into their own. There has never been a more exciting time for this medium.

While most art in graphica has intensity and action, strong characters, and either black-and-white or bright-colored drawings, other examples feature wispy pastels, and still others are just down to earth and funny. Aaron Renier, author/illustrator of *The Unsinkable Walker Bean* (2010) (see Figure 12.12), provides a great summary of the process of making this adventure story book.

1. The story was conceptualized and planned.
2. The art was drawn in pencil.
3. It was then inked with several pens.
4. Words were lettered with a felt-tip pen.
5 Pencil lines were erased.

GRAPHIC TEXTS: DEMANDS ON THE READER

In addition to the demands of the particular genre, a graphic text requires readers to:

- Interpret a large number of visual images.
- Move through the text top to bottom and left to right.
- Follow a sequence of actions shown in art.
- Recognize and use onomatopoetic words to follow the action.
- Infer what happens between the panels.
- Infer action and information from dialogue.
- Use the imagination to bring the text to life.
- Infer the story from images within minimal text or dialogue only.
- Infer character traits from facial expressions and dialogue.
- Infer feelings from characters' expressions and plot.
- Notice how the writer has communicated through the combination of visual images and text.
- Distinguish characters and learn about them through dialogue even when they are not named.
- Understand and use the conventions of graphica (speech and thought bubbles, narrative boxes, lettering, gutters and panels, pictures) and be able to process them automatically.
- Derive meaning of words from graphics.
- Notice how pictures and text work together to communicate meaning.
- Notice the style and size of panels, and relate to the importance of the information or the action taking place.
- Notice the style and mood of the illustrations.
- Notice aspects of the writer's or illustrator's style.
- Notice the use of color and line.

Figure 12.11 Graphic texts: demands on the reader

6. Some pages were scratched and ripped with razor blades (to create rain and splashes).
7. White-out with a foam applicator was used to make white shapes.
8. Black colored pencils were used to draw the illustrations.
9. Each page was scanned into a computer.
10. Then colors were added by computer, laying them under the drawings.

The creators, inspired by old, faded children's books, worked from a palette of seventy-five colors (the only ones used in the book). According to Renier, it is easier to write a long graphic novel when there are a limited number of colors to choose from, and their limited

Figure 12.12 Pages from *The Unsinkable Walker Bean*

number makes the colors feel more unified. Seventy-five may seem like a lot, but the colors are about the same intensity, so the book has a coherent "look" to it. Renier's description makes clear that a team of people with varied skills create a graphic text. That's true when any text is published: author(s), editor(s), copy editor(s), and illustrator(s) all contribute.

Creating Graphic Texts

Once your students have begun to study graphic texts, they will want to make their own. Good mentor texts will be very useful, especially if the students have studied them carefully. You can encourage them to go beyond cartoons and support their writing and craftsmanship. Two helpful resources are:

- *Adventures in Cartooning* (Sturm and Frederick-Frost 2009).
- *The Making of a Graphic Novel* (Rollins 2006).

These texts tell about the steps that professional writer/illustrators use. Of course, your students will be doing all the steps themselves and may need to modify the process. The basic steps in creating a graphic text by hand are:

1. Think of the story you want to tell.
2. Make a story plan or board that has the narration and the dialogue you want to use.
3. Using a pencil, draw the pictures for a series of panels that tell the story. Be sure they are in order. (You can change the order if needed.) Make big panels for something that is exciting or important, and little panels or differently shaped panels to show action.
4. Do the lettering in pencil for the narrative boxes and the speech bubbles. Decide how to make the speech bubbles (round, dotted, star shaped, wavy). Decide what the print should look like (size, font, lines).
5. Add the color (optional) using markers, colored pencils, or watercolors. Decide whether you want light or heavy color as well as how many colors to use.
6. Ink the lines. Using an extra-fine marker, outline the pencil markings. (Then you can erase any pencil marks that show.)
7. Put in sound words as needed.

8. Scan the comic into the computer and use a program to make adjustments (optional).

There are quite a few computer programs students can use to make their own cartoons. They can try out different styles for graphic texts and use them for many genres. They may want to extend a fiction book they've read or liven up a report by including a graphica section. They might even create an entire work in this interesting new way.

Using Multigenre Text Sets

Throughout this book, we have suggested the value of compiling text sets that have similar content or that have similar themes. Text sets can revolve around any organizing principle: author, topic, setting, historical event, scientific idea, social issue, or genre. Students think in deeper ways as a result of immersion in a text set.

Text sets comprising *multiple genres* encourage students to think more deeply about a particular topic, theme, or big idea. The purpose is to explore a theme through different literary lenses. Instead of noticing elements related to the specific genres, students generate a list of important perspectives that communicate a big idea. With some topics you want readers to gain information, but you also want them to grapple with the broader issues as communicated by various authors in various genres and formats. A multigenre text set is a great way to accomplish all these purposes. A study of nature conservation for intermediate students might include biographies of environmental activists, expository nonfiction books that impart information about the natural world and the environment, persuasive texts that address issues of conservation, and fictional texts that tell a good story even while imparting a message about conservation (see an example in Figure 12.13). There are hundreds of age-appropriate fiction and nonfiction books to choose from—we recommend beginning with books that are both the clearest examples of the genre, and also the highest quality texts available. You may want to explore award winning books, both contemporary and classics (see our list of links to websites featuring award-winning books) and the mentor texts listed in Appendix A. There are other resources available for finding excellent books, including Internet resources and recommendations from colleagues.

You can immerse your students in multigenre text sets using the same general process described in Chapters 1 and 2; ask students what they learned about the central theme or topic; and have them list what they noticed about each text. After several books have been read, you can also ask them what the particular genre contributed. Questions like these may be appropriate:

- How did the genre influence your thinking?
- Why do you think the writer chose this genre?
- What was important about the genre the writer selected?
- How was [text/genre] different from [text/genre]?
- What specific contributions did this text/genre make to your thinking and why?
- Which did you enjoy more and why?
- How would this text be different if written in another genre?
- What genres do we need to look for to understand more about this topic/theme?

Using these multigenre text sets communicates to students that genre is significant and helps them think and talk about genre characteristics and how various genres contribute to our learning.

Exploring New Genres and Forms

The popular forms of text we have explored in this chapter have enormous potential. As teachers, we need to recognize that the world of literacy is changing around us every day. New forms are created; the line between video and print is blurred. Electronic books now come alive with illustrations that move and include sound. This new world resonates with students. Given the opportunity they will find ways of expressing themselves and communicating that were unheard of even a generation earlier. And new possibilities are just around the corner. The important thing is to keep exploring!

A TEXT SET ON NATURE CONSERVATION			
Title and Author	**Description**	**Approximate Grade Level**	**Genre**
The Great Kapok Tree: A Tale of the Amazon Rain Forest by Lynne Cherry	• A fable about a man who enters the rainforest in order to chop down a Kapok tree. • The many animals of the rainforest come to the man while he sleeps and ask him not to cut down the tree. • A convincing plea for rainforest conservation.	4	traditional literature: modern fable
The Wolves Are Back by Jean Craighead George	• Narrative nonfiction text that uses chronological order to tell the story of how wolves were brought back from near extinction. • Facts about wolves are woven into the narrative. • Factual sources are cited.	4	narrative nonfiction/ persuasive text
Nature's Green Umbrella: Tropical Rainforests by Gail Gibbons	• Nonfiction text describing tropical rainforests. • Includes facts about tropical rainforests including many of the plant and animal species that live there, and the importance of the rainforest. • Detailed, labeled color paintings.	4	expository nonfiction
Manfish: A Story of Jacques Cousteau by Jennifer Berne	• Biography about one of the world's best-known oceanographers • Written in literary language that captures the magnificence of the ocean. • Author's Note at the end provides facts about the subject. • Full-color paintings complement the text.	4	biography
Wangari's Trees of Peace by Jeanette Winter	• A biography of environmentalist Wangari Maathai, a 2004 Nobel Prize winner. • Describes Maathai's efforts to restore trees to her barren homeland and encourage other women to take action.	4	biography
Footprints on the Roof: Poems About the Earth by Marilyn Singer	• Poetry collection focuses on an appreciation of nature and our earth. • Different perspectives range from the point of view of an astronaut in space to a worm in its underground home. • India ink drawings on rice paper contribute a spare, beautiful effect.	4	poetry

Figure 12.13 A text set on nature conservation

Suggestions for Professional Development

Professional development relative to reading across genres can take many forms. Here are three options:

1. With grade-level or cross-grade-level colleagues, put together a multigenre text set.
   a. Select an area of the science or social studies curriculum and collect books appropriate to the grade level, or select a topic or theme appropriate across several grades and incorporate more variety.
   b. Have everyone read all the books (assemble multiple copies or introduce an efficient system for passing them around).
   c. Meet again to discuss each one in turn, limiting the time.
   d. Discuss how the different genres contribute to your thinking.
   e. Generate a list of themes and topics conducive to being studied through multiple genres.
   f. Talk about what your students might gain from this type of study. What would you need to do to prepare them for this type of study?
2. Collect a group of hybrid texts (or those you think might be hybrids) and bring them to a meeting.
   a. Discuss whether the texts are hybrid; if so, what makes them so? What genres are included? How are the genres blended or placed together in one text?
   b. Don't worry if you argue and can't agree! Argument will make the session more lively and informative. We are always refining our thinking about genre.
   c. Reflect with colleagues on how this experience will impact your teaching.
3. Select a good example of graphic text. (*Maus* is appropriate for adults.)
   a. Get copies for participants to read.
   b. Talk about the text and how it made you think.
   c. Discuss how reading the graphic text was different from reading other genres.
   d. Take a look at some graphic texts for children and discuss their appeal. Would they be appropriate for struggling readers?
   e. Discuss the possible uses of graphica in the classroom.

CHAPTER 13

Poetry

For me poetry has always been a way of paying attention to the world.

—Naomi Shihab Nye

This chapter is about poetry—the different types, the qualities, and the benefits to your students. The important thing about poetry is how it makes us feel—about ourselves, the world, and others. Poetry, like prose, is a form of writing, but it is a form that focuses primarily on emotions, language, and sensory imagery. Poetry can pack great feeling and intensity into few words. The unique form of poetry and its power to move you is what you must convey to your students if you want to help them build a lifelong love of and appreciation for poetry.

Why is poetry important? Those who are familiar with poetry know its benefits. They can read poetry to relax the mind and become reflective. They can enjoy language that is used in unusual and beautiful ways. Perhaps most importantly, poetry allows you to look at the world through the eyes of a poet, seeing the ordinary in new ways.

In the poem "Birches" (Fletcher 1997) the poet describes white birch trees against a blue sky this way: "lines drawn bold and white/down the sky's blue canvas." By noticing these ordinary trees and writing about them in a poetic way, using figurative language and making surprising comparisons—the sky is a canvas on which nature has drawn the white birch trees—the poet sharpens your awareness of the world around you. You see it differently, and therefore more closely and vividly.

Poetry enriches life by capturing the essence of meaning in the sparest of language. Poetry brings together sounds and words in ways that may evoke intense imagery and profound meaning. The best poetry frequently contains an element of surprise. You encounter language that you want to read over and over, and when you do, you experience the poem anew each time. Your thoughts and emotions may be aroused by a single word. Poetry slows down thinking and opens new avenues of thought.

Poetry has strong oral roots; at one time, all poetry was memorized and performed aloud because people could not read. Poetry is found throughout history and around the world; for example, ballads were a popular way of telling stories during the Middle Ages. Today, poetry is still wonderful to hear read aloud as it tells stories or evokes images and feelings. Any topic—

nature, everyday life, human relationships, war, history—can be the subject of poetry.

Being rooted in an oral tradition means that poems have rhythm, tonal quality, and sometimes rhyme. We love the way they *sound*. As Robert Frost has said, "All poetry is a reproduction of the tones of actual speech." Poetry, like music, is meant to be heard more than one time; it can and should be listened to again and again, each time evoking the same or often new responses and opening up new discoveries.

Perhaps the most important thing about a poem is how it makes us feel—the images it conjures; the memories it stirs; the humor, sadness, or happiness it evokes. People write and read poetry for those feelings and emotions. Frost writes, "A poem begins with a lump in the throat; a home-sickness or a love-sickness. It is a reaching-out toward expression; an effort to find fulfillment. A complete poem is one where an emotion has found its thought and the thought has found the words."

Poetry covers the whole range of emotions. Whatever we are feeling, we can find poems to read and we may even express our own thoughts in poetic form. The emotion depicted in poetry is not always sad. Poetry can also bring wonderful humor into our lives. Poems can make us laugh or see the absurdity of life, as with this excerpt from a popular poem by Judith Viorst:

Thank You Note

I wanted small pierced earrings (gold).
You gave me slippers (gray).
My mother said that she would scold
Unless I wrote to say
How much I liked them.
    Not much.

The Elements of Poetry

Some of the elements of poetry—the elements you notice when you read or hear poetry—are listed in Figure 13.1. These elements give poetry its unique quality. Not every element is included in every poem. They are "tools for crafting meaning" (Heard 1998). Although it is often difficult to identify the elements that make a poem because poets continue to explore new forms and ways of writing, you need to help your students recognize these elements so they can choose to use them in their own poems. The characteristics of poetry are shown in Figure 13.2. These are the characteristics that will help students recognize a piece of writing as poetry.

Figurative Language

Poets often make comparisons to infuse their language with meaning. Two types of comparisons (figures of speech) are commonly used in poetry: (1) *metaphor*, which is a direct comparison, and (2) *simile*, which is a comparison that uses *like* or *as*.

In "Sleeping Bag" (see Figure 13.7 on page 203), the poet writes, "I'm a caterpillar in a cozy cloth cocoon that zips." The poet is directly comparing herself to a caterpillar and her sleeping bag to a cocoon. The word *cocoon* adds meaning to the ordinary word *sleeping bag*. In Alfred, Lord Tennyson's "The Eagle" (see Figure 13.16 on page 208) the writer describes an eagle, creating an image of powerful, almost violent action by comparing his speed to a thunderbolt: "He watches from his mountain walls,/And like a thunderbolt he falls."

Figurative language may consist of only one or a few words for effect, or the poet may use an extended metaphor throughout the poem. Figurative language gives poetry the element of surprise and helps the reader to see familiar things in new ways.

Imagery

Poets use language to create sensory impressions. As you read, you form mental images that are pleasurable. The words and their arrangement evoke a sense of sight, sound, touch, smell, taste, or movement. "Storm" (see Figure 13.13 on page 208) creates the image of an arriving storm by helping you imagine the "whistle-sharp, wet, and cold" wind as well as the birds as they dart from tree to tree. The poem builds to the final word—*rain*—and you feel that you have watched the rain come. In "Canada Geese" (see Figure 13.14 on page 208) you can imagine the birds' lonely cry, calling "goodbye."

THE ELEMENTS OF POETRY		
Element	**Definition**	**Characteristics**
Figurative Language	The comparison of two objects or ideas either directly (metaphor) or using *like* or *as* (simile); the connotation of one word changes or elaborates the meaning of the other.	• Can be only a word or two, or be sustained throughout the poem • Compares two things that we might not think are like each other at first • Makes us see things in new ways
Imagery	The use of language to create sensory impressions (mental images).	• Evokes a sense of sight, sound, touch, smell, taste, or movement
Personification	A way of speaking about animals as if they were people or inanimate objects as if they were living.	• Is a kind of metaphor • Uses contrast to evoke images
Rhythm	A pattern of recurring strong and weak syllabic stress in the flow of poetry.	• Is the beat or cadence of the poem • Related to the structure or metrical form

Rhyme and Sound	Either identical or very similar recurring final sounds in the words at the ends of lines of verse.	• Organized in different ways to form the structure or patterns of the poem:
		  • *Couplet:* two rhyming lines (usually of the same length or number of syllables) in succession
		  • *Triplet*: three rhyming lines in sequence

Repetition	Repeated words or phrases that help to create the rhythm and momentum of a poem.	• Can repeat any word in any place in the poem • Can repeat a word every line or the same word within a line
Alliteration	The repetition of an initial sound in neighboring words or in stressed syllables.	• Adds to the sound quality of a poem • Works with rhythm to create tonal quality
Assonance	The repetition of identical or similar vowel sounds in words.	• Repeated vowel sounds followed by different consonant sounds • Creates a partial rhyme
Consonance	The repetition of the final consonant sound in words with difference vowels.	• Does not rhyme. • Creates tonal harmony within a poem.

Figure 13.1 The elements of poetry

continues

THE ELEMENTS OF POETRY		
Element	**Definition**	**Characteristics**
Onomatopoeia	The use of words to suggest an actual sound.	• Uses many words that exist in language (buzz, pop, moan) • Sometimes changes the spelling of words to emphasize sound (zoooooom) • Sometimes includes made-up words to represent sounds
Layout/ Line Breaks (Shape)	The way a poet lays out the lines of a poem to support the central meaning or add meaning.	• Groups words/ideas together to convey meaning • Reveals the form or structure • Supports rhyme and rhythm • May take a shape that creates imagery, movement, or suspense • May take concrete shape that adds to the meaning

Figure 13.1 The elements of poetry *(cont.)*

THE CHARACTERISTICS OF POETRY FOR CHILDREN		
Definition	**Characteristics**	
A form of writing that uses compact language, pattern (verse), and rhythm to express feelings and ideas.	• Can be fiction or nonfiction • Uses fewer words to convey meaning • Appeals to the thoughts and feelings of the reader • Uses rhythm • Placement of words helps you know how to read • Looks different from prose	Often: • Makes you see, smell, hear, and feel things • Uses rhyme • Uses repetition • Uses figurative language • Uses patterns (verse) • Has a shape that can tell you about the meaning • Offers a new way of seeing things • Tells about nature

Figure 13.2 The characteristics of poetry for children

Personification

Poets often use personification, which attributes human characteristics to nonliving things, to help you see or feel things in new ways. The poem "Undecided" (Fletcher 1997) is full of personified images. When the poet tells you that "the wind speaks with winter's tongue," you feel the cold. When he describes the "sky using the pond as a mirror" or the "pond wearing bracelets of sky," you see the images of matching blue.

Rhythm

Meter is the rhythmical pattern in verse. Rhythm is measured in small groups of syllables, called *feet*. In English, a foot is an unstressed syllable followed by a stressed syllable. Therefore, meter, or rhythm, is made up of stressed and unstressed syllables. Most poetry has rhythm; the origins of poetry are rooted in chants and songs. Rhythm helped people memorize songs. Sometimes poets create their own rhythm, which may have complex or subtle patterns, but most poems, when performed aloud, have this kind of tonal pattern.

Rhythm can be slow or fast and can change within the poem. Read "Rope Rhyme" (see Figure 13.11 on page 207) aloud and you will feel the rhythm of jumping rope.

Rhyme and Sound

Rhymes are identical (or very similar) recurring final sounds in words at the ends of lines of verse or within a line. There are many different rhyme schemes, and we will not try to define them all here. The big idea is to examine the poem to see how the poet has arranged rhyme. Here are two examples:

- A *couplet* is two rhyming lines (often of the same length or number of syllables) in succession. The two rhyming lines may form a stanza of a poem.
- A *triplet* is three rhyming lines in sequence, often forming a stanza of a poem.

Repetition

Repetition adds to the rhythmic quality of a poem, emphasizes the sound of words, and makes poetry exciting. Repetition may involve the same word said several times, or a repeating refrain may tie the stanzas together. Notice the powerful impact of the repetition of the word *darkness* in this excerpt from Walter Dean Myers' long illustrated poem (1997):

Harlem

There is lilt,
Tempo, cadence
A language of darkness
Darkness known
Darkness sharpened at Mintons
Darkness lightened at the Cotton Club
Sent flying from Abyssinian Baptist
To the Apollo. (14)

Alliteration

Alliteration is the repetition of an initial sound in neighboring words or in stressed syllables. Alliteration adds to the tonal quality of a poem and works with rhythm to create poetic artistry. We see an example of alliteration in the fourth line of "Canada Geese" (see Figure 13.14 on page 208): "sketching, stretching skyward."

Assonance

Assonance also involves repetition. The poet repeats identical or similar vowel sounds to create a partial rhyme. The final consonant sound is usually different. In the poem "Storm" (see Figure 13.13 on page 208), paired words such as *lace* and *lake*, *blow* and *cold*, *uneasy* and *tree*, provide a harmonious inner sound.

Consonance

Consonance also refers to the repetition of sounds—the repetition of *final* consonant sounds in words with different vowels. The words do not rhyme, but they help to create harmony within the poem. This is a subtle technique you might not always notice. You see a trace of it in "The Drum" (see Figure 13.8 on page 203). The author uses the words *drum, him*, and *rhythm*, three words that carry a great deal of meaning and end with the same sound.

Onomatopoeia

Onomatopoeia is the representation of sound with words. Many onomatopoetic (usually called *sound words* with younger students) exist in every language. English examples are *pop, bang, thump, swish, swoosh,* among countless others. Poets select and use words like these to make sound come alive in their poems. Sometimes they change or exaggerate the spelling. In "Rope Rhyme" (see Figure 13.11 on page 207), the *clappedy-slappedy* helps you recall just how a jump rope sounds when it hits the ground.

Layout/Line Breaks (Shape)

One of the first things we notice about poetry is that it *looks* different from prose. The lines of poetry—the way they appear on a page—often reflect the meaning or some other aspect of the poem. The way in which the poem should be read is indicated with lines and white spaces. Line breaks are carefully designed to signal to the reader the meaningful phrase units that represent deeper meanings. And increasingly, poets are using the shape of their poems to reinforce the content or ideas.

The line breaks in "Storm" (see Figure 13.13 on page 208) help you "scoop up" these meaningful phrases. Each line has a powerful image. The author has also used the shape of the poem to increase the tension. The poem starts slowly with "late in the afternoon" but on the very next line, the wind picks up and increases in volume, followed by the heavy black clouds. The reader has a feeling of backing away from the "thunderous load of storm."

Crafting Tools

Over time, and as appropriate to their grade level, you help your students understand the terms defined above as elements of poetry. They can notice them in the poetry they read and discuss, but eventually they will want to use them as tools in their own work. In *Awakening the Heart* (1998) Georgia Heard names the following as "tools for crafting meaning": image, metaphor, simile, personification, words, line-breaks, beginnings and endings, titles, and observation. All of these elements represent decisions writers make as they convey meaning to their audience. The tools for crafting sound are rhyme, repetition, rhythm, alliteration, line-breaks, assonance, and consonance.

Poets think about layout and shape, and they also think about white space—places on the page where there are no words. They signal places to take a breath or pause. A characteristic of poetry and something that readers love about it is that the page is not crowded. White space has meaning in poetry; it leaves time to reflect, to fill in thinking around the spare language. A volume of poetry may have illustrations but still leave lots of room on the pages.

When you consider the craft of poetry, it is also important to think about the *tone*—the poet's attitude as revealed in the poem. Notice the determined, even angry, tone of "The Drum" (see Figure 13.8 on page 203). The tone is highly related to the mood—how the poem makes the reader feel. Mood depends not only on the poet's tone and choice of words but also on the connection the poem makes for the reader. Poems remind us of our own life experiences. "Storm" (see Figure 13.13) has a suspenseful, exciting, even menacing mood, depending on your own experience with storms. "Rope Rhyme" (see Figure 13.11 on page 207) might take you back to your own childhood, creating a sentimental or reflective mood.

It's amazing how many tools poets have at their disposal, although not all of these tools are employed at once. Many poems have no rhyme or rhythm but may use imagery or shape to communicate meaning. Also, poets bend the rules and merge tools all the time, so you shouldn't look for pure examples.

At the end of this chapter you will find a list of mentor texts for poetry. These are suggested titles to be used as exemplars of poetry, but you may have excellent examples of your own that you prefer to use. These mentor texts may be used to build text sets, and for aloud-aloud and independent reading. We have included collections of poetry by a single author, as well as collections that include poems by several different authors. As we describe below, just as with prose writing there is great variety in poetry—in subject matter, tone, form, and language. We have included a variety of titles, but you will want to add your own mentor texts as well, depending on the focus of your poetry study.

Variety in Poetry

Students learn best by inquiry, and you can learn a great deal by working alongside them. Embarking on the study of poetry does not mean you have to know as much as your college literature teacher, but the more you do know about the types and forms of poetry, as well as the crafting tools, the better you will be able to notice and guide student learning.

In the past, each type, or form, of poetry was "taught" as a label with rules or examples. Students then wrote a poem in the particular form. Of course, enthusiastic teaching can make just about anything work, but the result was often superficial learning, and students sometimes learned to hate particular forms of poetry. You won't want to study every form of poetry in one year, but select a few important types and investigate them through inquiry. The learning your students do will be much more likely to stay with them and be available as they read poetry throughout their lives.

Qualities of Poetry

Poetry is best defined by its qualities. It is laid out in patterns of stressed and unstressed syllables that create rhythm and thus imply a speaker. A poet selects word images and puts them together to create powerful feelings in the reader or listener. Compressing meaning into few words, often in conjunction with figurative language, creates a multilayered work open to a variety of interpretations. A poem's word patterns may include rhythm, rhyme, assonance, alliteration, and word repetition. A poet uses line breaks, white space, and capitalization to create a visual image and to tell the reader how the poem is to be read. All poems are written in verse, although they do not all rhyme; trivial or comic rhyming verse such as doggerel is not considered poetry.

Often, writing suggestive of the qualities of a poem can be called poetry. When the line between prose and poetry is blurred, a given text may accurately be categorized in either of the larger categories.

Poetry and Genre

As we stated earlier in Chapter 3, poetry is *not* a genre; it is a form of writing within which poems can be written in any genre. You can study poetry that is biography, history, contemporary or historical fiction, informational, and so on. Although we categorize prose in these well-defined genres, it would be cumbersome and possibly boring to divide poetry into these same categories. Therefore, we tend to study poetry by emphasizing the different forms (or types) into which it can be sorted. If your students know the characteristics of prose genres, however, they can identify the same categories for poetry.

Types of Poetry

The type, or form, of poetry is the way its parts are organized—the organization that unifies the work and determines its total effect. Poets choose the form to fit meaning and purpose. (They often find a form they like and use for most of their poems.) The forms of poetry students are most likely to study in elementary and middle school are listed, defined, and described in Figure 13.3.

As teachers you can approach each type using an inquiry approach similar to that described in Chapter 2. First, you immerse students in several examples of the form or type by reading them aloud several times and letting students discuss and enjoy them and (if appropriate) add a copy to their personal poetry anthologies. Once they have experienced several poems, work together on a noticings chart and a working definition (see Figures 13.17 and 13.18 on page 209).

Some important types of poetry may be explored every year: free verse, lyric poetry, and narrative poems, for example. There are many examples of poems in these categories, from simple to more sophisticated. Other types, such as epics, may have a place in the curriculum at certain grade levels. Still others, such as haiku, are fun for students to learn and have in their repertoire, but there is not enough time to include all of them each year. We recommend that teachers plan the types of poetry that will be explored at each grade level. (See Suggestions for Professional Development at the end of this chapter.)

Poetry Workshop

How do you open the world of poetry to your students? The key to poetry appreciation is to experience it before studying it. Teachers have had extraordinary success helping students learn to love reading and writing poetry by first immersing them in poems that they themselves love and can relate to. Today, there are many high-quality volumes of poetry written especially for children and adolescents that you can enjoy as much as your students do. Readers can find humor, poems about friendship and everyday life, poems about nature, even stories and novels written entirely in poetry (verse).

TYPES OF POETRY		
Type	**Definition**	**Characteristics**
Free Verse (sometimes called blank verse)	Poetry that does not rhyme but does have rhythm; may use some rhyme, alliteration, or other language pattern.	• Does not have to rhyme • Usually has rhythm determined by the poet, but seldom with a regular beat • Written without rules (writer makes his own rules) • Uses figurative language • Can be short or long
Lyrical Poetry	Songlike poetry that has rhythm and sometimes rhyme, and is memorable for sensory images and description.	• Sounds like a song • Lots of descriptive, figurative language • Helps you form a picture in your head • Usually short • Has rhythm and sometimes rhyme
Narrative/ Ballad	A story poem that relates an event or episode; gives the effect of a song; may be a lyric, a sonnet, or free verse, but it must tell a story.	• Tells a story, sometimes a long tale • Has rhyme and rhythm • Uses repetition • Tells about an important event or heroic deeds • Can be a fantasy • Can be funny or serious
Epic/Saga	A long narrative poem, usually about the great deeds of a folk hero (epic), or a similar and more sophisticated narrative poem with less emphasis on the hero (saga).	• Uses sophisticated language • Usually describes lofty or high goals and ideals • Usually involves a hero and a long quest
Haiku	An ancient Japanese form of non-rhyming poetry that creates a mental picture and makes an emotional statement.	• Has seventeen syllables • Does not rhyme • Lines 1 and 3 have five syllables • Line 2 has seven syllables • Usually has two parts: (1) a description; (2) a statement of mood or feeling • Usually expresses a truth about the natural world • Meaning not evident immediately • Appears simple but abstract; meaning makes it more complex

Figure 13.3 Types of Poetry

TYPES OF POETRY		
Type	**Definition**	**Characteristics**
Limerick	A nonsense form of rhyming verse, usually surprising and humorous.	• A five-line irreverent rhyming poem • Lines 1, 2, and 5 rhyme • Lines 3 and 4 rhyme • Silly subjects • Humorous • Sometimes has a surprise
Concrete Poetry	Poems with words (and sometimes punctuation) arranged to present a concrete picture of the idea the poem is conveying.	• Arrangement of text looks like or is related to the meaning • May look like an object or show movement • Shows meaning through both the words and the shape of the poem
Sonnet	A fourteen-line verse consisting of three four-line stanzas (quatrains), each with its own rhyme pattern, and ending with a couplet	• Has rhythm that makes it pleasurable to listen to • Often conveys strong emotions • Often tells about historical events

Figure 13.3 Types of poetry *(cont.)*

Elsewhere we have written about using a poetry workshop to help students learn about poetry in a meaningful and enjoyable way (see Fountas and Pinnell 2001, Chapter 24). Here we discuss using the workshop structure to help students learn about the genres of poetry.

Many teachers have implemented readers' workshop (see Chapter 15) and writers' workshop (see Chapter 18) in their classrooms. Usually the workshops take about sixty minutes each, every day. Once a week, several times a month or a week per month, a combined two-hour workshop can focus on reading and writing poetry. The poetry workshop has a particular structure (see Figure 13.4).

Poet talk. The workshop begins with a short "poet talk" in which the teacher tells students something interesting about a poet or their poetry they have come to know through reading his poems. This element is optional and quite short, but it helps students realize that poets are people! Websites of various poets who are popular with young people provide plenty of information.

Read-aloud and minilesson. A time for reading, enjoying, and talking about poems. By reading aloud the same poem a few times, the teacher helps students experience and enjoy it. Students share their noticings and talk about what the poem says to them. They internalize examples as a foundation for learning poetry genres. As students become more experienced, these known examples help them notice the characteristics of poetry and the subdivisions within it. A short minilesson refers to the examples and helps students develop a specific understanding.

STRUCTURE OF THE POETRY WORKSHOP (60 MINUTES)		
Element	**Approximate time**	**Description**
Poet Talk	2 minutes	Teacher provides a brief talk communicating something interesting about a poet or his poetry—usually one whose poetry has been read to the class.
Poetry Read-Aloud and Poetry Minilesson	18 minutes	Teacher helps students experience and enjoy poetry by reading one or two new poems and inviting students to respond to them. These familiar poems are then used as models during minilessons on analyzing writing craft and mentoring students as they try their hand at writing poetry. The students glue the poems in their anthologies.
Poetry Projects: Reading, Writing, Illustrating, Conferring	30 minutes	Students respond to and illustrate poems they have glued in their notebooks. They read and select new poems for their own personal poetry anthologies; collect language or ideas in a writer's notebook; draft, revise, and edit their own poems; and create illustrations for poems they have collected or written. Teacher confers with individuals about their poems.
Poetry Sharing	10 minutes	Students perform or share poetry.

Figure 13.4 Structure of the poetry workshop

Projects: reading, writing, illustrating, conferring. Following the reading and minilesson, students do their own work with poetry, which may include reading poems and selecting one to copy and/or illustrate in their personal poetry anthologies. This work naturally evolves into writing *about* poems (what they say to students, how they make students feel) and then to making comments or writing their own poems, sometimes "borrowing" ideas, style, and language from the poets they are reading. Students participate in a wide range of exploration and production. The teacher also confers individually with students, listening to them read their poems aloud and helping them reflect on their work.

Sharing. During the workshop, students share their poems by reading them aloud or performing them. Here, too, the discussion of characteristics may be an integral part of the conversation. The teacher may also give small groups of students specific help with the craft of poetry.

Learning About Poetry from Poetry

Let's follow along as a fourth-grade teacher, Marian, uses a poetry workshop to immerse her students in poetry and help them define the form and generate some broad characteristics by experiencing it. She follows the steps of the inquiry process:

- Collect.
- Immerse.
- Notice.
- Define.
- Teach.
- Read and Revise.

The powerful inquiry process gets students to think actively; they construct their understandings as they come to their own conclusions.

Collect

Marian begins by collecting poems that will be touchstones for her students' beginning inquiry into poetry. She wants them to understand some very basic characteristics:

- Poetry expresses ideas and feelings in fewer words than prose.
- Poetry has rhythm when you read it out loud.
- Poetry appeals to the thoughts and feelings of the reader.
- The way the lines are arranged on the page helps us know how to read a poem.

Marian's students have had limited experience with poetry. Many are familiar only with rhyming poetry or doggerel (verses that amuse but are not real poems). Without making a value judgment about any type of poem, Marian wants to expand her students' experience so they will have broad understandings to build on as they explore different types of poetry.

Marian has been collecting poetry and poetry anthologies—some general and some by a single poet—for several years. She has also created several of her own personal anthologies of poems she has collected. She has illustrated these anthologies or found appropriate photographs or drawings and written responsive comments for some of the poems (a page from one of her personal anthologies is shown in Figure 13.5).

A teacher-created anthology is a wonderful model for students; it demonstrates your appreciation for and thinking about poetry and is a quick source of poems to use during minilessons. It is also a great addition to the collection of poetry books assembled in poetry baskets. Some ideas for teacher anthologies are:

- Poems about nature
- Poems about animals
- Funny poems about school
- Family poems
- Poems that tell a story
- City poems
- Historical poetry
- Traditional rhymes and jingles
- Poems about many cultures
- Poems with different moods (happy, sad, reflective, silly, playful)

Marian selects a series of specific poems (see Figure 13.6) that provide a range of examples, prompt good discussions, and reflect a variety of topics and themes.

Marian plans to read two or three poems a day (depending on the time needed to discuss them) during the first week. Looking at these poems, she sees that:

- They are mostly unrhymed.
- Metaphor and visual imagery are easy to identify in almost every poem.
- The poems have rhythm, often indicated by the layout.
- Some poems seem intended to be read slowly, others fast, depending on the content.
- Content is varied: ordinary activities, family relationships and conversations, animals, plants, and ordinary objects.
- The poems are short enough to read and talk about during the time allotted.
- The feelings in the poems vary: humor, awe, appreciation of beauty, anger.

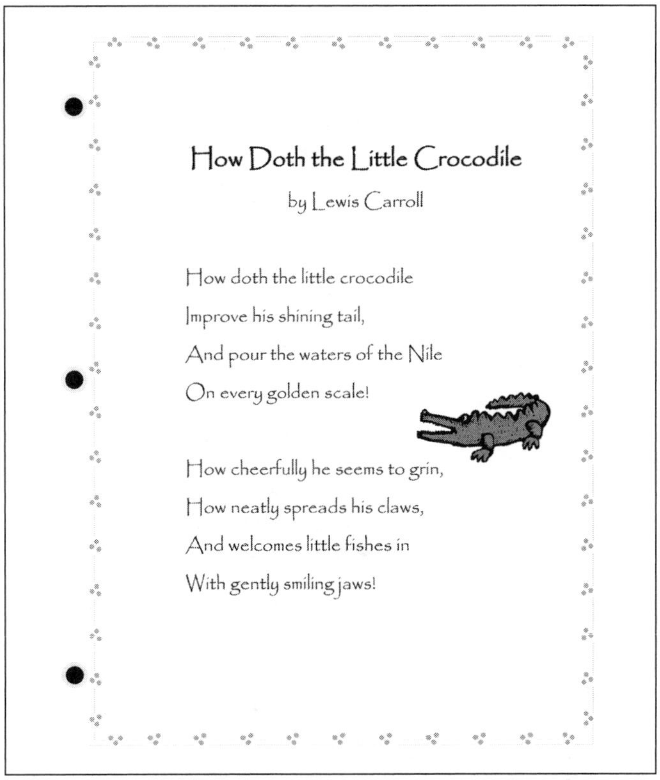

How Doth the Little Crocodile

by Lewis Carroll

How doth the little crocodile
Improve his shining tail,
And pour the waters of the Nile
On every golden scale!

How cheerfully he seems to grin,
How neatly spreads his claws,
And welcomes little fishes in
With gently smiling jaws!

Figure 13.5 Page from Marian's personal poetry anthology

MARIAN'S POETRY SELECTIONS			
Poem	**Important Characteristics**	**Poem**	**Important Characteristics**
"Sleeping Bag"	• Content that is familiar to most students • Action words • Sound words *(scoootch)* • Metaphor • Humor	"Storm"	• Layout and shape indicate movement • Sight, sound, and touch imagery • Metaphor • Sounds words *(rumble, thunderous, whistle-sharp)* • Exciting–scary • Builds to climax.
"The Drum"	• Extended metaphor • Dialogue • Strong feeling–anger, determination	"Canada Geese"	• Metaphor • Visual and sound imagery • Layout to guide pace and pause of reading • Lonely
"Chairs"	• Description • Metaphor • Layout to show pace and pause of reading • Whimsical • Seeing ordinary objects in new ways	"The Anteater"	• Shape of poem represents animal • Action words for visual imagery *(snaking)* • One rhyme–lines 11 and 13 • Humor
"Paper Birch"	• Visual imagery • Metaphor • Layout throughout to show pace and pause of reading • Sound word *(birrrrrrrrrrrrrch)* • Pattern at beginning–two 2-word lines followed by a 3-word line. • One rhyme (lines 8 and 10) • Visual imagery • Peaceful–beauty of nature	The Eagle"	• Visual imagery • Familiar animal • Descriptive words *(wrinkled sea)* • Simile • Power of nature
		"Rope Rhyme"	• Rhythm • Rhyming couplets • Layout at end to show pauses in reading • Happy, active

Figure 13.6 Marian's poetry selections

Immerse

Marian has allotted plenty of time for her students to experience and respond personally to the poems. She starts with "Sleeping Bag" (see Figure 13.7), a humorous poem, knowing that most of her students have used a sleeping bag even if they had not been camping. She also plans to read "The Drum" (see Figure 13.8), and, if time allows, "Chairs" (Figure 13.9).

The goal is simply to have the students listen carefully to and enjoy the poems, talk about their thinking, and say what they notice about the written poem. Marian has prepared printed copies of each poem so that each student can glue them into their personal poetry anthologies.

Day one. At the beginning of the poetry workshop, Marian invites students to the meeting circle. (A transcript of a portion of the lesson is shown in Figure 13.10.) Marian reads each poem aloud, asking students to listen and comment. Since they do not have a print version, they are not distracted by the layout but can concentrate on the way the poem sounds. By reading the poem two or three times, Marian helps them think about the meaning of the poem, what the poet said to them, and what they noticed about the way the poet said it. They talk about words or phrases they love and images they want to remember. They came up with some good discussion points. Marian guides the discussion lightly, listening to students and occasionally extending what they say. After oral reading, Marian gives them the duplicated poem so that they can notice the layout while hearing the poem once again. At the end of the lesson, Marian asks her students to think across the three poems in order to briefly summarize the discussion.

Sleeping Bag

It's so cold outside,
I'm getting dressed inside
my sleeping bag.
I wriggle, scoootch,
scrunch, and jiggle. Flop.
Front flips, back flips—
I'm a caterpillar in a cozy cloth cocoon
that zips.

—Kristine O'Connell George
From *Toasting Marshmallows: Camping Poems*

Figure 13.7 "Sleeping Bag"

The Drum

Daddy says the world
Is a drum
Tight and hard
And I told him
I'm gonna beat out my own rhythm.

—Nikki Giovanni
From *Spin a Soft Black Song: Poems for Children*

Figure 13.8 "The Drum"

Chairs

Seem
To
Sit
Down
On
Themselves, almost as if
They were people,
Some fat,
Some thin;
Settled comfortably,
On their own seats,
Some even stretch out their arms
To
Rest.

—Valerie Worth
From *All the Small Poems and Fourteen More*

Figure 13.9 "Chairs"

EXCERPTS FROM A POETRY WORKSHOP CONVERSATION	
TEACHER:	I am going to share three poems with you today. The first poem is called "Sleeping Bag." What do you think of that?
JORGE:	Why would somebody write a poem about a sleeping bag?
MARIAH:	Don't they usually write poems about nature and stars and stuff? That's weird!
TEACHER:	Listen while I read the poem and then maybe you can talk about why you think the poet, Kristine O'Connell George, wrote it. [Reads "Sleeping Bag" aloud.]
KENT:	It's a funny poem.
HAYLEAH:	I tried to get dressed inside a sleeping bag and it isn't very easy. You do have to wiggle around like that.
SARI:	You have to wiggle just to get out of it.
FAWN:	I liked when it said *skoootched*.
TEACHER:	Yes, it is pretty funny. Listen while I read it again and then talk about what the poet is saying to you. [Reads "Sleeping Bag" aloud for a second time.]
REGI:	She is saying it's warm and cozy inside so it's better to get dressed in a bag.
PABLO:	She's telling us what it feels like.
LAURA:	She uses words that are funny, like *jiggle* and *scrunch*, so it's like you can feel him or hear him moving.
MARIAH:	She said it's like a caterpillar being happy in a cocoon.
TEACHER:	Do you think that is a good comparison?
MARIAH:	Yes because when it's zipped up, you're kind of rolled up in it.
HAYLEAH:	I like a sleeping bag because it's warm.
TEACHER:	Yes, the poet uses the word *cozy.* That's warm and also kind of snug and safe feeling, isn't it? Marcos, what were you thinking about the poem?
MARCOS:	I don't know if you could do flips in a sleeping bag, but it's pretty funny.
TEACHER:	I'm going to give you a copy of the poem to look at while I read it again. [Passes out the printed copies and reads the poem again. She pauses at periods and at the ends of lines.] What did you notice this time when you looked at the poem while I read it?
JORGE :	Some lines are longer and some are shorter.
SARI:	*Scooootch* has too many *o*s.
FAWN:	*Wriggle, scoootch, scrunch, and jiggle* come right after each other kind of just like she is moving.
MARCOS:	Then it says *flop* with just a period after it like you're supposed to stop.
DANTE:	It says the cocoon has a zipper.

Figure 13.10 Excerpt from poetry workshop conversation

EXCERPTS FROM A POETRY WORKSHOP CONVERSATION

TEACHER:	You are noticing a lot about the way the poet wrote this poem. What are you thinking now about why someone would write a poem about a sleeping bag?
MARIAH:	I think it was just to be funny so that people would laugh.
GABE:	I think so we know what it feels like–so good you want to stay in it.
JOHN:	I'd never think about a sleeping bag that way, but it was right.
TEACHER:	So sometimes poems can be about ordinary things. The poet can use language to help us see something in a new way. Would you agree?
HAYLEAH:	Yes.
JOHN:	Why doesn't it rhyme?
TEACHER:	I'm glad you asked that, John. Poems sometimes rhyme, but they don't *have* to rhyme. This poem does have rhythm, though. Listen one more time while I read it and then tell me what you notice about my voice. [Reads the poem aloud again.]
DANTE:	Your voice stopped at the ends of lines.
JOHN:	You had a rhythm in the way it sounded.
TEACHER:	I looked at the lines, the white spaces the poet left, and the punctuation and thought about the meaning. I tried to read it the way I think the poet wanted it to sound. You can try that with a partner during work time. Our next poem is really short. It's by Nikki Giovanni from a collection called *Spin a Soft Black Web*. Nikki Giovanni likes to write poems about her family and about African Americans and their lives. This one is called "The Drum." [Reads "The Drum" aloud.] What is the poet saying to us?
DANTE:	She says the world is like a drum?
HAYLEAH:	Is it round or something?
MARA:	The world is tight and hard.
JORGE:	Kind of hard . . . like hard to get a job or something?
TEACHER:	A drum has a skin that is stretched really tight so that it's hard and makes a great sound when you hit it. But it is full of tension. Does that make you think of anything? Listen to me read it again. [Reads "The Drum" aloud for a second time.]
DANTE:	Maybe it's kind of tense or tight, nervous. Not really a good world all the time.
TEACHER:	You could be right. And what about the girl's answer? I'll read it again and think about her answer and how it might be different from her dad's description. [Reads the poem a third time.]
HAYLEAH:	The girl doesn't agree with her dad. She's going to take the drum and beat on it the way she wants to.
MARIAH:	She's not afraid of the world and thinks she can make it better.

Figure 13.10 Excerpt from poetry workshop conversation *(cont.)*

continues

EXCERPTS FROM A POETRY WORKSHOP CONVERSATION

TEACHER:	Wow! Does everyone agree with that? [Gives them a duplicated copy of the poem.] Read this short poem to a partner and then buzz about what you noticed about the way the writer wrote the poem. [Students take turns reading the poem aloud and talking for about a minute.] I think we have time for our third poem. It's by Valerie Worth. This poet is known for "small poems" and there are several collections of them in our library. This one is called "Chairs." I guess you are probably wondering why someone would write a poem about chairs. Listen while I read this one. [Reads "Chairs" aloud two times.] What is the poet saying to you?
DANTE:	There are different kinds of chairs and they could be like people. Some are big and some are skinny. They do have arms.
MARYA:	It says "to rest" at the end and you rest in a chair.
KENT:	It's like the chairs are really people.
STEVEN:	You think about chairs and now when you look at them they're funny.
SARI:	At first it sounded like you stopped after every word.
TEACHER:	You are right, Sari. The first six lines had just one word each. In fact, most of the lines of this poem are short. [Gives students a copy of the poem.] Take a look at it. You can see the first six lines. That's what Sari noticed in my voice. I'm glad you noticed that the poet was comparing chairs to people, Kent. I'll read it once more so that you can look at the way it is laid out. [Reads the poem again.] You've heard three poems today and you have noticed some very important things about poetry. What did you notice after thinking about all three?
SARI:	Poems can be about a lot of different things, even things that you wouldn't usually think about.
MARYA:	The lines are important because sometimes they are really short and you have to read kind of choppy.
GABE:	They had a lot of comparisons in them and words used different ways.
FAWN:	Sometimes you get a kind of surprise in the poem.
DANTE:	They sound like they have rhythm when you read them.
JOHN:	They don't all rhyme.
TEACHER:	Those are great things to notice. Glue these poems in your anthologies. Glue the poem on the left side of a page layout. On the right side, draw with colored pencil, paint with watercolors, or use paper scraps to illustrate the poem.
KARIN:	Could we cut out some chairs and glue them in?
TEACHER:	Sure, that would be interesting! Bring your anthology to group share at the end of our workshop.

Figure 13.10 Excerpt from poetry workshop conversation *(cont.)*

During work time, students read poems to a partner, glue the poems in their blank personal poetry anthologies, and illustrate them on the opposite page by drawing or finding an appropriate picture (on the Internet or in magazines), occasionally taking a digital picture and printing it. They also write a brief comment below each poem to show their response—what they think about it. As the students grow in their ability to think analytically about poems, their comments move from a simple "I thought the poem was funny because" to deeper insights in which they respond to the writer's craft or elements.

During poetry share, students briefly revisit one of the poems with a partner and make a few more comments about what they learned about poetry that day.

Day two. Continuing to immerse the students in poetry, Marian reads "Rope Rhyme," by Eloise Greenfield (see Figure 13.11). The students enjoy this vigorous rhyme. Marian varies the process and invites the students to read the poem in unison after they have heard it several times and discussed the layout; they even shout the words at the end.

After reading and discussing "Rope Rhyme," the class does the same with "Paper Birch" (see Figure 13.12) and then "Storm" (Figure 13.13). Student comments that emerge from the discussion are:

- Poems can be read fast or slowly.
- Poems can be read loudly or softly; some parts should be read loudly and some read softly.
- There are patterns in poems (like the number of words in lines).
- The shape of a poem can show the meaning or make us feel what the poet means.
- Poets say a lot in just a few words.
- Poets choose words very carefully.

Day three. On the third day Marian introduces "Canada Geese" (see Figure 13.14) and "The Anteater" (see Figure 13.15). These two poems are a nice contrast. Students talk about the feeling of loneliness communicated by "Canada Geese": the steel gray sky, the lonely cry, the windswept autumn, and the call goodbye all fit a somber mood. In contrast,

Rope Rhyme

Get set, ready now, jump right in
Bounce and kick and giggle and spin
Listen to the rope when it hits the ground
Listen to that clappedy-slappedy sound
Jump right up when it tells you to
Come back down, whatever you do
Count to a hundred, count by ten
Start to count all over again
That's what jumping is all about
Get set, ready now,
  jump
    right
      out!

—*Eloise Greenfield*
From *Honey, I Love*

Figure 13.11 "Rope Rhyme"

Paper Birch

Paper birch.
White birch.
Canoe birch too.
Beautiful
Native
Tree to view.
Smooth white birch bark
Grows where it's cold.
Paper birrrrrrrrrrrrrch:
A sight to behold.

—*Douglas Florian*
From *POETREES*

Figure 13.12 "Paper Birch"

"The Anteater" has a lively and amusing quality. Students also notice the repetition of vowel and consonant sounds in *sketching, stretching* and the alliteration in *tacky tongue* and *snaking . . . snout*. The first poem does not rhyme and the second has only two rhymes. Students are beginning to see that many poems have no rhyme and that when poets use rhyme, they do so selectively and carefully.

Day four. Marian reads aloud Tennyson's classic poem "The Eagle" (see Figure 13.16) which gives students a good chance to notice alliteration and to experience a poem with a different pattern—three lines

Storm

Late in the afternoon
the wind begins to blow
whistle-sharp, wet and cold.
Whitecaps lace the lake.
Uneasy, the birds
dart from tree to tree
as heavy black clouds
rumble towards us,
an oncoming train
hauling a thunderous
load of storm.
Rain!

—*Kristine O'Connell George*
From *Toasting Marshmallows: Camping Poems*

Figure 13.13 "Storm"

The Anteater

The
anteater's
long
and
tacky
tongue
is
snaking
from
its
snout.
A thousand termites riding in,
But no one riding out.

—*Douglas Florian*
From Beast Feast: Poems and Paintings by Douglas Florian

Figure 13.15 "The Anteater"

Canada Geese

Padded drum
Of beating wings
Fills the steel gray sky.
See them stretching, stretching skyward.
Hear their lonely cry. See them in the windswept
Autumn. Hear them call
goodbye.

—*Kristine O'Connell George*
From The Great Frog Race and Other Poems

Figure 13.14 "Canada Geese"

The Eagle

He clasps the crag with crooked hands;
Close to the sun in lonely lands,
Ringed with the azure world, he stands.

The wrinkled sea beneath him crawls;
He watches from his mountain walls,
And like a thunderbolt he falls.

—*Alfred, Lord Tennyson*
From *Piping Down the Valleys Wild,* collected by Ellen Raskin

Figure 13.16 "The Eagle"

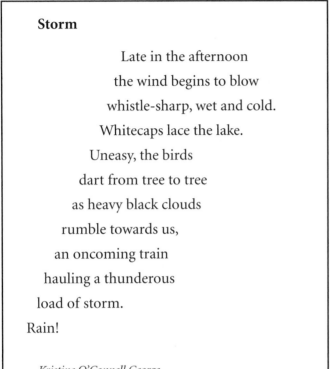

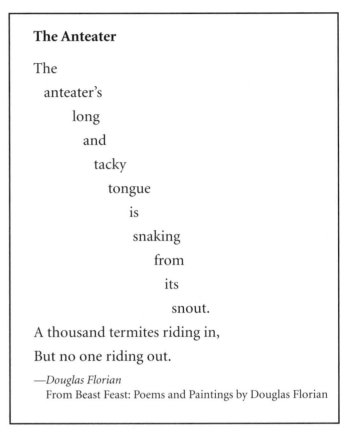

rhyming per stanza. This poem lends itself to a choral reading by the group, which everyone enjoys; they emphasize the powerful simile "like a thunderbolt."

Notice

After nearly a week of poetry reading and discussion, Marian feels that the students are ready to begin noticing things about the poems. Using their personal anthologies, they spend some time rereading the ten poems in small groups. As they work, Marian asks them to think about what they notice is always true about poetry based on these poems. During their whole-class discussion, Marian writes what they notice about poetry on a class chart (see Figure 13.17). These noticings, which they modify and add to over time, become a reference for their continued study of poetry during the rest of the year. Marian encourages students to continue finding poems they like. She introduces them to the collections of poems in the classroom library (see the list of mentor texts for poetry in Appendix A) and helps them find the topics and types of poems that interest them.

Define

Using their list of noticings, Marian and her students create their own working definition of poetry. It's challenging to create a definition that captures the "big idea" of poetry without getting into each of the details they noticed, but they do (see Figure 13.18). Students copy the list of noticings and the definition into their reader's notebooks.

Teach

Marian teaches several more poetry minilessons in which she zeroes in on the things the students have noticed about poetry. She explores each bulleted statement with her students in greater depth, always beginning with reading and discussing interesting poems. They search for examples of different elements of poetry in the poems they have collected and share these examples with the class. Over time, students experience a variety of poems and begin to compare them, identifying poems with similar characteristics.

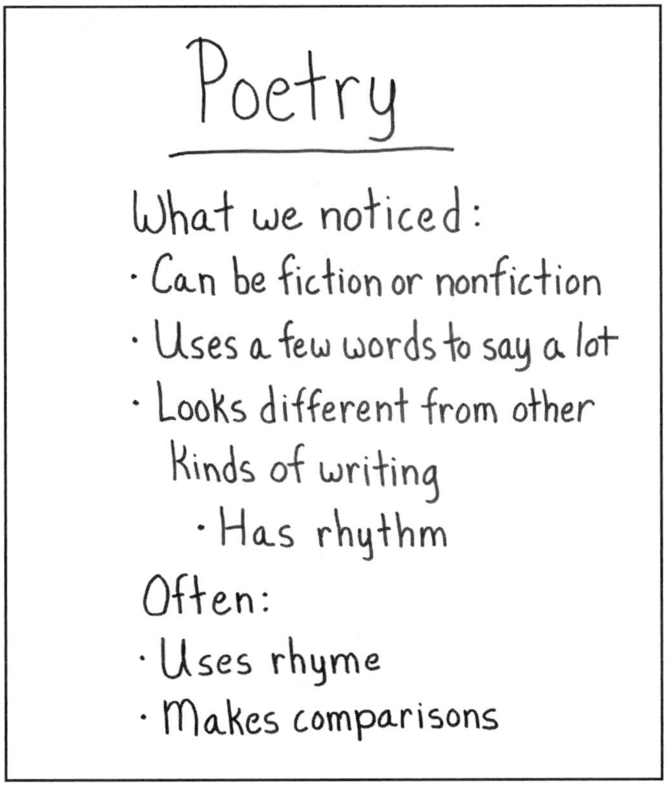
Poetry

What we noticed:
· Can be fiction or nonfiction
· Uses a few words to say a lot
· Looks different from other kinds of writing
· Has rhythm
Often:
· Uses rhyme
· Makes comparisons

Figure 13.17 Poetry: What we noticed

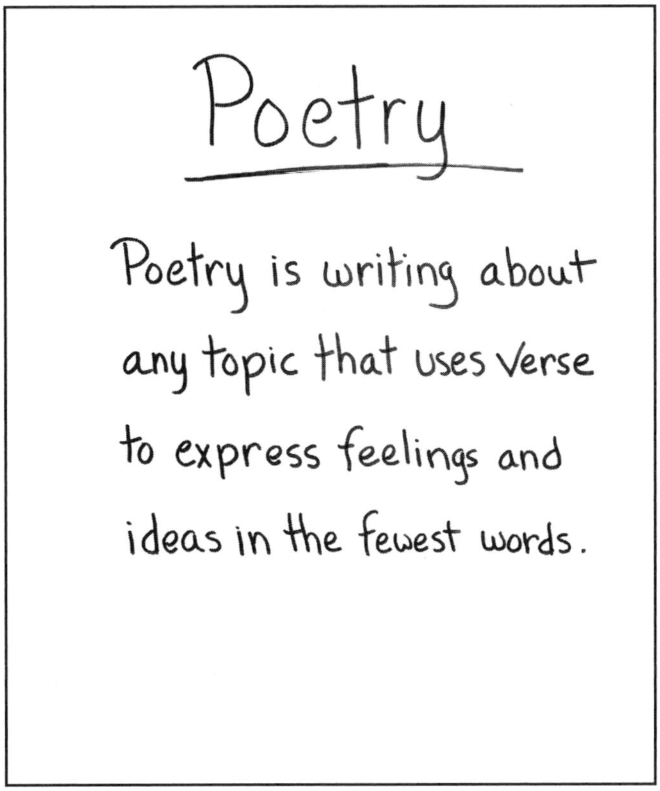
Poetry

Poetry is writing about any topic that uses verse to express feelings and ideas in the fewest words.

Figure 13.18 Working definition of poetry

Read and Revise

As they read and explore poetry in greater depth, Marian and her students revise their noticings chart and their definition. They refine statements, add words like *imagery* (once they fully understand the concept), and add characteristics they notice as they read a greater variety of poems. They identify the characteristics of poetry that they notice all of the time, and those that they notice often (see Figure 13.2). For example, they add "uses comparisons," an important characteristic of poetry, to the "often" list, after Marian reads several poems that use simile and metaphor.

Repeat the Process

Marian's students have a good grounding in the essential elements of poetry, but they do not yet have a sophisticated understanding of the different types. To extend their learning during the year, Marian repeats the inquiry process, focusing on a particular type or form of poetry (see Figure 13.3). Students begin to talk in very specific ways about the characteristics of each.

An Environment to Foster Poetry

Creating an environment in which to foster poetry requires giving it a place of importance in the classroom conversation. It's not an add-on or even a unit presented once a year. Poetry, like prose, needs to be part of students' daily reading and writing lives. The classroom should be a place where students:

- Listen to poetry read aloud.
- Read poetry and choose poems they find relevant.
- Read poetry aloud.
- Trust that others will appreciate their ideas about poems.
- Trust that others will encourage their efforts to write poetry.
- Collect poetry in a personal anthology (paper or electronic).
- Connect personally with poetry
- Analyze poetry and gradually learn the terms to describe the elements, types, and craft.
- Illustrate poetry.
- Respond to poetry in oral and written language.
- Perform poetry.

Goals for the Poetry Curriculum

Some suggested goals for creating a poetry-rich classroom and implementing an effective learning program include:

1. Making poetry accessible to readers for their enjoyment. Be sure your collection has all types of poems: content-area poems, poems with different moods (happy, sad, reflective, silly, and playful), poems that tell stories, poems that evoke images, poems from many cultures, traditional rhymes and jingles, and rich examples from the past.
2. Create poetry centers. One center can house the poetry collection—placed face-out in bins. Poetry books can be categorized by poet, topic, type, or any other designation that means something to students. Also place your personal anthologies in this center. Give students a separate place to display their personal poetry anthologies rather than hide them in a desk. Create a space where copies of poems are available and students can illustrate their work through photographs, drawings, or computer images.
3. Help students learn about individual poets and choose some favorite poems that they reread and collect. Provide anthologies of the poems of particular poets and place them in the classroom poetry collection.
4. Help students develop a personal poetry collection. Model the process (and add poems to your collection) by developing your own anthology.
5. Place particular emphasis on your collection of free verse. Freed from rhyme (or from too much rhyme), students can more easily see the

essence of poetry. Free verse has every element of poetry except rhyme. Mary Oliver has said, "Free verse is not, of course, free. It is free from formal metrical design, but it certainly isn't free from some kind of design. Is poetry language that is spontaneous, impulsive? Yes, it is. It is also language that is composed, considered, appropriate and effective." (1994, 67).

6. Help students appreciate the meaning and sound of poems by reading them aloud and encouraging students to read them to one another.
7. Help students read poetry to learn how to write it. Encourage inquiry and close study of poetry. Encourage students to try out elements of the craft and to share their efforts with others. Guide their writing through minilessons and individual conferences.
8. Develop a love for poetry and poetic language by sharing high-quality poetry and other texts written in poetic ways during interactive read-aloud. Point out language you find especially beautiful and encourage students to do the same.

9. Help students learn and memorize some favorite poems. In this way, they can step into the shoes of the poet, try on the language, and make it their own.

Collecting Poems

Meeting the goals above requires creating a good poetry collection. Here are some ways to begin the collection:

- Over a vacation period spend some time creating a few personal poetry anthologies of your own favorites. Place poems in categories you like—animal poems, school poems, funny poems, poems about nature, etc. These anthologies will be very popular and will give students great access to poems.
- Use the school and/or public library to check out as many poetry books as you can. Look for a good variety. Select poems from these books as you teach minilessons, and place the poems in the appropriate class anthologies.
- The Internet is another good source for poems, but be sure to check for copyright information before printing and using poems.

- Encourage students to copy poems and bring them from home and/or share poetry books with the group.
- Look for children's poetry anthologies on remainder tables or at garage sales.
- With your colleagues, create some poetry sets (for example, poetic biographies, funny poems, epics, shape poems). Have these spend a month or so in one classroom and then travel to the next. You'll get greater variety for less money.

Always look for what students love most, where gaps exist, unique and engaging examples, and the best quality.

Finding Joy in the Teaching of Poetry

Fortunately, we have begun moving away from dissecting poems in an isolated way in a poetry unit or poetry month, and instead have begun creating a culture of enjoyment in the power and depth of poetry and its rich layers of meaning. Studying poetry by emphasizing the sounds of the language, student choice, more contemporary poems, multiple interpretations, personal poetry anthologies, and poetry performances is active and rich for both teachers and students.

The important thing about poetry is how it makes you feel. If the enjoyment and meaning of poetry is lost, then all the study in the world will not accomplish your learning goals. The inquiry process is key to helping students invest in poetry and make it their own.

Suggestions for Professional Development

OPTION 1: With colleagues across grade levels, create a curriculum map for teaching poetry through inquiry. Use your district curriculum, state standards or curriculum maps, and *The Continuum of Literacy Learning* (Pinnell and Fountas 2011) as resources.

1. Gather examples of the types of poetry you want students to learn across the grades.
2. Examine the examples and talk about the appropriate grade level(s) for each.
3. Select the types of poetry you think should be explored every year (growing in complexity). (You might want to consult your district or state curriculum goals as well as *The Continuum of Literacy Learning*).
4. Look at the additional types of poetry you want students to learn.
5. Tentatively place the various types of poems within a grade level or several levels.
6. Create some poetry baskets with poetry collections, anthologies, novels in verse, and picture book poems to put in a central location.
7. In grade-level groups, create a poetry curriculum map for the year.
8. Meet again midyear to share inquiry experiences and again at the end of the year to evaluate the process and make revisions.

OPTION 2: With colleagues, create your own personal poetry anthologies. Working with colleagues on this project will make it more fun and will multiply your exposure to different types of poems and poets; however, you can also start and add to your anthology on your own. Your own personal poetry anthology will be a wonderful resource to share with your students as part of your poetry genre study and a place to collect poems that are meaningful to you.

1. Gather a collection of published poetry anthologies or poems that you have used in the past with your students. Ask each of your colleagues to bring at least two poetry anthologies and/or a small packet of poems they enjoy or have used with students in the past.
2. Bring blank papers for drawing or bound spiral notebooks with blank pages (e.g., a sketchbook) for everyone to use as their own personal anthologies. Have everyone bring markers, crayons, or any other art supplies you think would be fun to use as you respond to poems in your own anthologies.
3. Pass around the collections of poems and poetry books you have brought. Have everyone select three poems that speak to them in some way. The poems might be related to each other in their form, theme, or emotional content; or they might be just three isolated poems that connect to them in some way. Whether you are currently studying farms with your students and choose poems about animals or whether you have a deep emotional connection to a poem, select anything that is meaningful to you for whatever reason.
4. Spend time sharing the poems you have found with your colleagues. You can discuss the following:
   - Why did you select the poem?
   - What does it say to you?
   - Are the poems you selected related to each other? In what ways?
5. Spend time copying either by hand or by gluing a photocopy of the poems you collected into your blank anthology. Write or draw a response to accompany the poem.
6. If there is time, share what you have created.
7. Reflect on what you learned about the genre of poetry from this process of reading, selecting, sharing, and responding to poetry. How will this experience impact your instruction in the classroom?

SECTION 3

Expanding Reading Power Through Understanding Genres

All of the chapters in this book have implications for classroom teaching, but the chapters in this section directly address instruction for genre understanding. In these chapters you will find many examples drawn from years of working with teachers of kindergarten through middle school. The heart of the curriculum for genre study is interactive read-aloud and the literature discussion that is embedded within it. In Chapter 14, we describe how teachers support students' thinking and talking about genre through interactive read-aloud and book clubs. Awareness of genre emerges through intentional conversation in these settings.

The next two chapters discuss the use of minilessons and group share. The structure of readers' workshop is particularly designed to provide the instruction students need to gain greater depth of understanding about genres. Chapter 15 focuses on fiction texts and Chapter 16 on nonfiction.

The readers' workshop structure also includes time for students' independent reading of books of their own choice and for individual reading conferences with the teacher. In these settings, too, genre understandings can be effectively built. Chapter 17 focuses on developing genre understandings through conferences and independent reading.

Chapter 18 describes the role of writing about reading in helping students to develop deeper understanding of texts and their genres. An advanced reader's notebook is presented.

In Chapter 19, you will find many suggestions for using the structure of guided reading to teach genre understandings. In this small group setting, you can differentiate instruction to give students support in using genre understandings as they read texts on the appropriate level for effective processing.

This book takes reading as a major focus, but genre study also contributes greatly to students' writing. In Chapter 20, we address the connection between reading and writing with a variety of examples. The more students know about the structure and characteristics of a genre, the more resources they have to draw on when writing in the genre. This chapter, too, suggests the use of mentor texts in writers' workshop.

CHAPTER 14

Thinking and Talking About Genre

Interactive Read-Aloud and Literature Discussion

What is the use of a book, thought Alice, without pictures and conversations?

—Lewis Caroll, *Alice in Wonderland*

This chapter examines the potential for genre study within two powerful talk structures: (1) interactive read-aloud, a whole-group instructional context that is valuable in itself and also provides important resources for readers' and writers' workshop, and (2) the small-group instructional context of literature discussion, also called book clubs. Through interactive read-aloud and literature discussion, teachers engage students in thinking and talking about excellent, age-appropriate texts. In both situations, students' reading levels are not an issue.

In interactive read-aloud, decoding isn't an issue either. The texts selected are age and grade appropriate so that your students have the interest and ability to understand them. Read aloud the text to students so they do not need to worry about the words. Use your voice to convey the meaningful phrase units within long, complex sentences. Students can understand the text because they can give their full attention to the meaning, the writer's craft, and, in many cases, the illustrator's craft.

Interactive read-aloud is an ideal instructional context for studying genre. Through reading aloud, you immerse your students in many high-quality examples of a genre. They can concentrate on what they are noticing about the type of text, generate their own list of characteristics, and genre definitions emerge from their discussion.

As students become more acquainted with a genre, participating in small literature discussion groups helps them deepen their knowledge by considering a text and how it fits the characteristics and definition. Reading level doesn't matter, because teachers offer texts that are age and grade appropriate in terms of content and theme. But student selection is very important. Students choose a text they want to read from a limited set of choices and talk about it with their peers. If the book is too hard, students may listen to a recording of the text or to someone reading it aloud. There's no stigma attached to this approach: many proficient adult readers listen to audio books while driving or at home, or use a variety of listening devices.

Every text that matters to you stays in your memory to be accessed in connection with later learning. The more texts your students read, the more knowledge they have to bring to reading and to other life experiences. Take every opportunity to build a "treasure chest" of texts that your students will remember and use to learn more all of their lives.

When students think and talk about literature, they develop the ability to notice the way writers craft a text. They develop a shared language that helps them communicate articulately about these texts. Communication is important because they learn ways of talking with one another as literate people.

The more you help students explicitly understand the features of each genre, the better they can apply them when they read and use them when they write. The learning is *generative.* Students learn *a way of looking at and thinking about texts.* They *become more observant;* they become *analytical,* because they notice more. In genre study, help them look at texts in a particular way in order to determine characteristics common to a genre. They also learn that genres are not absolute. They are fluid, often combined, and sometimes new. Genre study requires close analysis that reveals a great many literary aspects of texts.

Interactive read-aloud and literature discussion focus on a literary product. The text is complete, the writer's decisions are made, and all its attributes are there for discussion. Students can "hold the text still," examine it, and think about the writer's decisions. The texts they access, the thinking and talking they do, and the close analysis in which they engage develop a repertoire of possibilities that students can use to boost their reading and writing abilities.

The Continuum of Literacy Learning (Pinnell and Fountas 2010) describes the text characteristics and specific curriculum goals for both these instructional contexts, Grades K–8. Here, we offer a closer description of the structures and examples.

Selecting Texts

Students need to experience age-appropriate, grade-appropriate texts whatever their reading level. Some students cannot read on grade level, but they can all think in a way appropriate to their age group. They want to meet memorable characters, experience engaging plots, learn interesting information, and discuss the problems of their peers. It is important to use engaging, age- and grade-appropriate texts as the first experiences in genre study. Notice the short list of criteria for selecting texts to use for genre study (see Figure 14.1). Of course, the texts must be high-quality, but they must also engage students' interests and be appropriate for their age and experience. Text characteristics need to be considered in relation to students' maturity and cognitive development.

CRITERIA FOR SELECTING TEXTS FOR GENRE STUDY

- Texts that will engage readers/listeners by stirring the emotions, providing interesting information, offering vicarious experiences, or are relevant to their lives.
- High-quality examples that have well-crafted text and illustrations.
- Texts that are clear examples of the genre.
- Mostly short rather than long texts so that students can experience a greater variety of examples.
- Texts that are appropriate for students' age and experience.
- Content that is accessible to readers given their background and experience.

Figure 14.1 Criteria for selecting texts for genre study

It is harder to select texts for read-aloud and literature discussion than for guided reading (small-group reading instruction). With guided reading, you can use systematic assessment to determine students' appropriate reading level (always remembering that accuracy is not the only criterion). But with interactive read-aloud and literature discussion, you need to consider students' abilities to understand themes of varying abstractness, bring content knowledge to texts, and analyze aspects of texts.

If you want relatively inexperienced students to understand genre, you need to start with simple, clear examples of the genre. Students need to understand simple narrative structure before you introduce complexity. We suggest questions to ask as you search for texts to use in interactive read-aloud and literature discussion (see Figure 14.2). This is not a rigid step-by-step process but rather a guide to your thinking as you browse through books.

As you consider books, think about characteristics that will engage your students' interests. Think about the content, themes, and ideas, and choose texts that will expand students' thinking, help them take new perspectives, and enhance their understanding. You also want them to be able to grasp the deeper meanings of the text.

Each text you select needs to stretch your students' understandings and their ability to comprehend texts. But it is not wise to use a book to exemplify genre features if your students cannot understand it. Just because a book is short and has illustrations does not mean it is easy to understand. Many of these texts are sophisticated in their craft and require experience and maturity to understand. You would not usually expect third graders, for example, to understand the highly symbolic and beautifully written *An Angel for Solomon Singer* (Rylant 1996), but the book would spark an excellent discussion as part of genre study in grades 5 or 6. Another very sophisticated text is *The Harmonica* (Johnson 2004), a story of the Holocaust. Students need a great deal of background information to understand how and why the boy in this book survived. On the other hand, *Grandma's Purple Flowers* (Burrowes 2008) and *Aunt Flossie's Hats* (Howard 2001) are both accessible enough that younger students can understand them and appreciate their artistry.

Studying Genre Through Connected Texts

Previous chapters on specific genres have included mention of *text sets* (a group of texts connected in some way) created to help students learn to look closely at writing (Harste, Burke, and Short 1998). For example, the books in a text set might:

- Have the same or similar themes.
- Have similar elements (same setting, characters).
- Share the same topic or have similar content.
- Be organized in the same way (have the same structure).
- Be written by the same author.

QUESTIONS TO ASK WHEN SELECTING TEXTS FOR INTERACTIVE READ-ALOUD AND LITERATURE DISCUSSION IN A GENRE STUDY

- Is the text well written and illustrated?
- How will the texts engage the students' interests?
- Will the students make connections between the text and their own lives?
- Will the students understand and connect to the characters, the subjects, or the storyteller?
- Are the concepts interesting but not so heavy that the students cannot understand them?
- Are the themes within the students' ability to understand?

Figure 14.2 Questions to ask when selecting texts for interactive read-aloud and literature discussion in a genre study

- Be illustrated by the same artist.
- Exemplify particular aspects of writers' craft (interesting lead, dialogue, description, first-person narrative, ways to show time is passing, perspective, ways to show what characters are like, use of figurative language, ways to end a text).
- Exemplify a particular genre.

Teaching for Comprehending and Fluency: Thinking, Talking, and Writing About Reading, K–8 (Fountas and Pinnell 2006) includes an extensive discussion of text sets and their use. The DVD that accompanies the book contains a list of suggested text sets for each week of each month of the year for each grade, kindergarten through grade 8.

For genre study, you can develop text sets in specific genres for interactive read-aloud, book club choices, and baskets for the classroom library (independent reading choices). Of course, the texts may be connected in other ways as well, and you want to be sure that students think and talk about the meaning of each text *before* looking for genre characteristics. Once students have had the opportunity to learn about the genre in whole-group discussions (interactive read-aloud), they can use their genre knowledge in small-group book discussions, guided reading discussions, and independent reading. This process provides rich learning across texts.

Developing a Shared Language for Talking About Texts

We have written extensively about the development of a shared vocabulary for talking about books and how it is developed over time in *Teaching for Comprehending and Fluency*. We suggest specific terms that might be learned at each grade and text level in *The Continuum of Literacy Learning*.

If students talk about texts every day, they build a shared language that gradually grows more complex. This kind of vocabulary is referred to as *academic language*. Students need to learn these academic terms by encountering age-appropriate concepts in a number of texts and fully understanding the concepts. The purpose of terms like *genre* and *setting* is not simply to identify and define them; a shared language facilitates conversation about important elements of texts. A general process for teaching new terms is described in Figure 14.3, using *setting* as an example. (Terms like *setting* are not too technical, but consider the age group and grade level.) The last three actions listed enter the conversation at appropriate stages in the process.

Acquiring language to talk about books is a cumulative process. Don't throw so many terms at students that they do not understand what you're talking about. When to use academic terms depends on your students' experiences with talking about texts. Here are some steps to keep in mind:

1. Talk about a concept in everyday language.
2. Use examples until students understand the basic concept.
3. Provide the label for what students already understand (name it) and invite them to use the new vocabulary (as appropriate for the age/grade).

Terms that are particularly important to use in genre study are listed in Figure 14.4 on page 223. The arrow indicates the point at which you introduce the term explicitly and help students understand it. The continued shading means you are using the term as shared language following teaching. A complete glossary of terms related to genre and literary elements is included in Appendix B at the end of this book.

This chart is only a guide. (See Chapter 15, Figure 15.3 for potential genre studies in each grade.) If your students have very little experience talking about texts, you may need to raise their awareness of concepts they are assumed to know. Also, students frequently pick up a term without internalizing a good definition for it. They may talk about *plot* and *setting* but cannot apply the terms correctly when they talk about books and can't give examples. That is not what you want; superficial knowledge is quickly forgotten.

The use of labels needs to change over time. For example, teachers in kindergarten or first grade might have rich conversations with students in which they talk about the people or animals in a story and how they felt; discuss the problems, the surprises, the beginnings and endings; and use terms like *author, illustrator, character,*

DEVELOPING A SHARED LANGUAGE FOR TALKING ABOUT SETTING	
Process	**Examples**
1. Talk about the concept of *setting* in everyday language. Consider different types of texts in which setting plays an important role (biography, historical fiction, fantasy, some realistic fiction).	• "Let's talk about the place the subject lived and what it was like in those times." (Biography) • "Where did the story take place? What was it like there?" • "What was important about where and when the story took place?" • "What was it like for people to live in [the time period and the place]? How is that important to the story?" • "Why is it important for you to think about how people lived in those times?"
2. Introduce the term when you are sure students have some good examples in their heads.	• "We have been talking about when a story takes place and where the writer of the story lived. Let's look at some of the books we have read together and think about the setting in each of them."
3. Create a chart with students that will remind them of the specific term and refer to it often.	The setting is the time and place of a story. • The setting for Nasreen's Secret School is Afghanistan in the 1990s, after the Taliban took over. • The setting for Mailing May is Idaho in 1914. • The setting for Neville is a modern-day suburban neighborhood. • The setting for A Nest for Celeste is a plantation near New Orleans. The writer describes the setting to help readers understand how it influences the experience.
4. Use the term in conversation when discussing books with students, sometimes writing an example when appropriate.	• "The setting for this historical fiction book is . . ." • "What was important to know about the setting?" **Hannah Is My Name** Author: Belle Yang Setting: Taiwan and the United States in the 1960s What we noticed: • The story mostly takes place in the city of San Francisco. • There are crowds of people and lots of activity. • Some of the story takes place at Hannah's school.

Figure 14.3 Developing a shared language for talking about setting

continues

DEVELOPING A SHARED LANGUAGE FOR TALKING ABOUT SETTING	
Process	**Examples**
5. Help students understand when the setting is important and when it is not.	• "What do you need to understand about the setting in order to have a good understanding of the story? Why?" • "Could this story have happened anywhere or any time? Or is the setting important here?"
6. Help students understand that for some genres, the setting will almost always be important.	• "Let's talk about the role of the setting in genres like historical fiction, realistic fiction, or biography. Is it important? Why? What about some of the other genres we have read?" • "Let's look at some different kinds of books and talk about how important the setting is."
7. Help students understand that stories and nonfiction books can have meaning for their lives even though they may not have lived in the same time or place.	• "What can you learn from this story (book) even though the people lived in a different time than we do?" • "What can you learn from this story (book) even though the people lived in a different place than we do?"

Figure 14.3 Developing a shared language for talking about setting *(cont.)*

problem, and *solution.* By third or fourth grade, you will begin to use more sophisticated terms, differentiate among genres in more detail than *fiction* and *nonfiction,* and use more specific terms like *biography* or *setting.*

Using Interactive Read-Aloud to Study Literary Genres

The time invested in interactive read-aloud saves time later. If you set aside fifteen or twenty minutes every day for interactive read-aloud, your teaching is more productive and efficient in all other areas of literacy instruction. Reading aloud and talking about a shared text builds community and engages the thinking of all students. Both teachers and students look forward to an enjoyable activity. A structured and well-planned approach to interactive read-aloud allows you to use *intentional conversation* to achieve the specific goals of instruction.

Intentional conversation is real conversation directed toward an instructional goal. Students and teacher interact with one another by talking naturally. They look at the person who is speaking and respond. The students and the teacher take turns and ask questions. Teachers aren't doing all the talking, repeating all the students' remarks, or talking after every student's comments. However, teachers *are*:

- Demonstrating ways to think about texts by sharing their own thinking.
- Inviting students to talk about particular aspects of a text.
- Asking questions that spark thinking rather than call for a "right" answer.
- Asking questions that call for thinking beyond and about the text.
- Helping students become listeners who notice things
- You may want to refer to *Prompting Guide, Part 2 for Comprehension* where you will find specific language to use in interactive read-aloud and book discussions.

Structure of Interactive Read-Aloud

Establishing a simple structure for daily interactive read-aloud tells students that this is a serious and important activity and they are expected to join in the

ACQUIRING A SHARED VOCABULARY FOR TALKING ABOUT TEXTS										
Term	**Quick Definition**	**GRADES**								
		K	1	2	3	4	5	6	7	8
General										
Author	Person who wrote the text	→								
Illustrator	Person who provided the illustrations, graphics	→								
Author's Note	A note by the author that provides personal information or extra factual information				→					
Illustrator's Note	A note by the illustrator that provides personal information or extra factual information				→					
Foreword	An introductory section that helps the reader understand a text						→			
Dedication	A printed inscription in a book dedicating it to a person or cause from the author	→								
Cover	The protective covering that binds together the pages of a book	→								
Book Jacket	The removable outer cover of a book	→								
Endpapers	The leaves of paper in a book that appear before the title page and after the text				→					
Prologue	The introductory part of a text						→			
Epilogue	The concluding part of a text						→			
Graphic Texts	Texts that integrate pictures and words to tell a story or convey information				→					
Poetry	Condensed language arranged to create an emotional response through meaning, sound, rhythm, imagery	→								
Hybrid Text	A text that blends fiction and nonfiction genres in a coherent whole							→		

Use the term as shared language following teaching

Figure 14.4 Acquiring a shared vocabulary for talking about texts

continues

ACQUIRING A SHARED VOCABULARY FOR TALKING ABOUT TEXTS										
Term	**Quick Definition**	**GRADES**								
		K	**1**	**2**	**3**	**4**	**5**	**6**	**7**	**8**
Talking About Fiction Texts										
Setting	The time and place of the story			→						
Character	People, animals in a story	→								
Main character	The character the story is mainly about		→							
Problem	The central issue or conflict that characters in the story face	→								
Events	What takes place in the story			→						
Solution (Resolution)	The point in the story when the problem is solved (and how)	→								
Mood	The emotional atmosphere the writer evokes using language and sometimes illustrations						→			
Tone	The attitude of the writer or illustrator toward the story or toward the reader							→		
Figurative Language	Language that compares things in order to allow the reader to see something more clearly						→			
Simile	Figurative language that makes a comparison of two different thinks using *like* or *as*					→				
Metaphor	Figurative language in which something is described by comparing it to something else							→		
Symbol	Person, object, or situation that has a meaning beyond its literal sense							→		
Round Characters	Characters that are well developed, in that they change over time								→	
Flat Characters	Characters that do not change (usually supporting characters)								→	

Use the term as shared language following teaching

Figure 14.4 Acquiring a shared vocabulary for talking about texts *(cont.)*

ACQUIRING A SHARED VOCABULARY FOR TALKING ABOUT TEXTS

Term	Quick Definition	GRADES K	1	2	3	4	5	6	7	8
Talking About Fiction Texts *(cont.)*										
Plot Type	Various kinds of plots–romance, tragedy, satire, irony, comedy, mystery, adventure								→	
Plot Structure	Various points in the plot–initiating event, rising action, climax, falling action								→	
Fiction and Nonfiction	The two basic types of texts	→								
Realistic Fiction	A narrative that is set in contemporary times and is imagined but could be real				→					
Historical Fiction	A narrative that is set in the past and is imagined but could be real; often based on real events				→					
Folktale	An imagined story, written or oral, handed down over many years, featuring the triumph of good over evil, repetition, and recurring motifs	→								
Fairy Tale	A kind of folktale that emphasizes magic and the supernatural		→							
Fable	A brief, moralistic tale primarily meant to instruct			→						
Legend	A narrative that usually revolves around the actions of a single hero						→			
Epic	A long narrative, usually centered on a hero and describing the hero's achievements						→			
Ballad	A kind of folktale adapted for singing						→			
Myth	A narrative that seeks to explain the natural world or human behavior				→					
Fantasy	Simple imagined stories that include talking animals, magic, or lessons. Might include heroes, quests, symbolism, and a clash between good and evil			→						

[shaded box] Use the term as shared language following teaching

Figure 14.4 Acquiring a shared vocabulary for talking about texts *(cont.)*

continues

ACQUIRING A SHARED VOCABULARY FOR TALKING ABOUT TEXTS										
Term	**Quick Definition**	**GRADES**								
		K	1	2	3	4	5	6	7	8
Talking About Fiction Texts *(cont.)*										
Science Fiction	A form of fantasy that includes technology or science							→		
Special Types: Mystery	Characters collect clues to solve crimes or other unknown problems				→					
Special Types: Adventure	Character(s) go on an exciting quest or experience conflict with nature, humans, or technology				→					
Special Types: Satire/Parody	Writing technique that mocks some aspect of society							→		
Talking About Biography Texts										
Timeline	A representation of the sequence of events in the subject's life—arranged in a list or diagram				→					
Caption or Legend	An explanatory title or similar information under maps, graphs, or illustrations				→					
Accuracy and Authenticity	The extent to which the text reflects facts and truth				→					
Biographical Genres	Categories of biographical writing: biography, autobiography, memoir				→					
Events	The important events of a person's life, arranged in time				→					
Subject	The person the biographical text is about					→				
Life Decisions	The critical decisions in a person's life					→				
Setting	The characteristics of the time and place the subject lived in and their influence				→					

[shaded box] Use the term as shared language following teaching

Figure 14.4 Acquiring a shared vocabulary for talking about texts *(cont.)*

ACQUIRING A SHARED VOCABULARY FOR TALKING ABOUT TEXTS										
Term	**Quick Definition**	**GRADES**								
		K	**1**	**2**	**3**	**4**	**5**	**6**	**7**	**8**
Talking About Nonfiction Texts										
Information	Facts and ideas that are in the text and can be learned	→								
Chapters or Sections	The divisions of a text; may be chapters		→							
Accuracy	The extent to which the text reports correct information				→					
Table of Contents	A list of the major sections or informational of a of a text (may be the same as the headings)		→							
Heading	A phrase in a large font or boldface, usually set off by white space, that provides information about the topic of the section			→						
Subheading	A phrase in a larger font than the text (but smaller than the heading) that provides information about the topic of a division of a section				→					
Topic	The subject of a text or of one of its parts	→								
Caption	A title or explanation for a picture or illustration		→							
Category	A defined division of a classification system					→				
Sidebar	Information on a topic that is separate from the rest of the main text				→					
Diagram	A simplified drawing showing the workings or structure of something			→						
Chart	Information in the form of a table, graph, or diagram				→					
Index	A list of topics and names in the text				→					
Glossary	A list of key words and their definitions usually placed at the back of a text				→					

Use the term as shared language following teaching

Figure 14.4 Acquiring a shared vocabulary for talking about texts *(cont.)*

discussion. All students need to be able to hear the text being read and see the art. Some approaches include:

- Students sit on the floor (perhaps in a circle) with enough room so that they are not touching each other; the teacher sits on a chair or slightly raised surface.
- Students bring chairs to a meeting area and sit in a circle or clustered group.
- Students sit comfortably at their desks in whatever arrangement the teacher prefers (a horseshoe or three-sided rectangle works well.) The teacher walks around the room while reading, making sure every student sees the illustrations.
- We provide a list and description of simple techniques to develop students' oral discussion skills in Figure 14.5.

Before Reading

The process really begins with deciding to implement genre study and creating a text set such as that described earlier in this chapter. The greater the potential for engaging students, the stronger the foundation you will lay. If your goal is to help students learn about genre, select clear examples of a particular genre to begin.

As you go over your selections, think about what you will say to introduce the text to your students. These "opening moves" should be taken very seriously. Your first words engage student interest and provide a frame for their thinking. Examples of how to start a read-aloud session for genre study are shown in Figures 14.6 and 14.7.

Notice that the teacher does not mention the genre or tell the students a great deal about the characteristics of genre. She does tell them the book is based on a true story. She alerts them that one character will be telling the story and encourages them to think about what the storyteller is saying. The students are not listening, thinking, and talking in order to detect genre characteristics. If you turn the interactive read-aloud into an exercise, students will look for a characteristic or two and may miss the key understandings of the text. The first goal is always to become engaged with the text and understand it as fully as possible. All discussion related to understanding the text will be useful when it is revisited as an example of genre.

Before reading aloud, place sticky notes in a few places (no more than three or four) where you plan to stop to invite brief student comments. On the note, jot a comment or question that will invite thinking. Think about how this sequence can develop a line or chain of thinking. These quick stops keep students active; they can share their ongoing thinking immediately rather than waiting for the end of the story. For example, they can make predictions about what a character is going to do based on the evidence they have heard so far. A chain of thinking might focus on character with attention to how characters are revealed in different ways by a writer and how readers can infer their traits and motivations.

Reading the Text (with Conversational Routines)

Read to the students, stopping only briefly and only a few times, so as not to lose the momentum and engagement with the text. Read to demonstrate how to communicate the meaning of the text. Students need to talk as well; their talk is their thinking. That's why the word *interactive* is used before *read-aloud*. The entire session is a highly organized and orchestrated process within which people in a social community interact to develop a richer understanding than any one reader could gain himself.

Invite students to make comments, and help them respond and listen to the comments of their classmates. Not all comments need to be directed to you or to the whole class. Here are some ways to implement "turn and talk," a routine that encourages quick discussions by partners or small groups:

1. Students have an identified partner or partners. At the signal "turn and talk" or "turn and talk about ___," they turn to each other (on floor or in chairs) and have time for one or two quick interchanges about the issue at hand. (If there is an uneven number of students, you can partner with a student.)
2. Partners talk and then turn to another pair and quickly share a summary of what they have been saying.

FOSTERING DISCUSSION DURING INTERACTIVE READ-ALOUD		
Step	**Teaching Points**	**Attention to Genre**
Selection and Preparation	• Select a sequence of texts to read over a few days or weeks. • Select texts that are engaging and age-appropriate.	• Select good examples of the genre.
Opening	• Make brief opening remarks that set the tone for the lesson.	• Draw attention to an aspect of genre that you plan to discuss after the reading. • Invite children to think about the type of book rather than naming the genre before reading.
Reading Aloud	• Read the text aloud, letting your voice reflect the meaning. • Move along with good momentum, not losing the meaning of the text. • Make brief stops to make comments, ask a question, or invite children to share their thinking. • Use routines like "turn and talk" occasionally so that all students can talk with a partner or a small group about some aspects of the text.	• Select places to stop and call students' attention to aspects of the text that will help them notice characteristics of genre. • Ask them to remember some aspects of the text and talk about them again later.
Discussion	• Invite students to reflect on the meaning they took from the text and what they noticed about the writing. • Sometimes, make a short chart or statement to record some of their thinking.	• Draw attention to aspects of the text that are important when thinking about the genre. • Sometimes write text characteristics on a chart. • Name the genre.
Self-Evaluation	• Invite students to evaluate the interactive read-aloud session.	• Give feedback to the students about what they noticed.
Record of Reading	• Add the book to the record of books the class has read together.	• Note the genre after the title and author on the list.
Written or Artistic Response (Optional)	• Occasionally, extend students' understanding of the text with readers' theater, drawing, or writing.	• Extend the meaning of the text by connecting it to other books in the same genre.

Figure 14.5 Fostering discussion during interactive read-aloud

Figure 14.8 captures the thinking Brian and Juan did when they turned and talked about the book *The Harmonica*.

When you teach this routine, you can demonstrate it with a student as your partner so the others can have a vision of what they are being asked to do. Afterward you can ask them to self-evaluate their exchanges using these questions:

- Did we express our own ideas?
- Did we share quickly?
- Did we listen carefully to each other?

After the Reading

After you finish reading, invite the students to share their thinking about the text. You can participate, sharing your thinking as a reader, but don't overwhelm them. Rather, gather evidence of their understanding. An example of an after-reading discussion is shown in Figure 14.9.

This is a significant interchange. The students have already discussed what happened in the story and shared their theories about it. The teacher asks them to dig down deeper to answer the question that she posed in the beginning—why did the boy tell his story? As the discussion continues (see Figure 14.10), a definition emerges.

As these students hear several examples of historical fiction over a week or so, they expand their knowledge of the genre, drawing out more generalizations. The teacher lists their observations on the genre characteristics chart for historical fiction (see Figure 14.11), and they are ready to construct a working definition (see Figure 14.12). They have not arrived at the highly sophisticated literary definition given in Chapter 7, but they are getting there.

Illustrations add considerably to students' understanding of texts you read aloud, so it is important to bring them into the discussion. Illustrations like those in *The Harmonica* are somber, while the illustrations in *Hannah Is My Name* are brighter and more whimsical—both reflect the tone of the stories.

Through daily interactive read-aloud, you can provide examples of beautifully crafted texts with illustrations that communicate meaning and mood and make genre come alive in your classroom. The texts become resources for extended discussions in

OPENING REMARKS FOR *THE HARMONICA*

TEACHER: Today we are going to think and talk about a book that takes place during the Holocaust. It is inspired by a true story. You remember that during World War II, Jewish people and many other people were imprisoned in concentration camps. The writer has written it in the voice of a boy. As you listen to the boy's story, think about why the writer wanted to tell the story.

Figure 14.6 Opening remarks for *The Harmonica*

OPENING REMARKS FOR *HANNAH IS MY NAME*

TEACHER: We've been talking about immigration. Today, we are going to read a story about a family from Taiwan, which is near China. The author is Belle Yang [show picture]. Belle and her family came to the United States from Taiwan when she was a young girl. She based this book on her own experiences. She tells the story from the point of view of the main character, Hannah. The title is *Hannah is My Name.* As you listen to this little girl–her parents call her Tadpole–think about why her name is so important to her.

Figure 14.7 Opening remarks for *Hannah Is My Name*

book clubs and examples for minilessons in readers' and writers' workshop.

Using Book Clubs (Literature Discussion) to Study Literary Genres

A book club (or literature discussion) involves bringing together a small group of students—all of who have read the same text. They meet to discuss the book in depth and thus create a richer meaning than any one reader could gain alone. Book club selections may be in any genre; they may be picture books (in essence, illustrated short stories) or longer texts such as novels. All texts should be engaging and of high quality. They should be chosen by the students (usually from three or four texts you have preselected). Give a brief book talk on each book and have students write their first, second, and third choices. Try to be sure each student gets his first or second choice. (There may be a second round of book clubs using the same initially grouped

TURN AND TALK ABOUT *THE HARMONICA*

The teacher reads pages 14–15: "Like a length of kindling, in one stroke, they split our family."

TEACHER: Turn and talk to your partner about what you are thinking.

BRIAN: Probably, he'll never see his parents again.

JUAN: I wonder if they could have run away. But they kind of just pretended the war wasn't happening.

BRIAN: That's right. They were just dancing and listening to music.

JUAN: I think music was really important to them.

The teacher continues to read and stops on pages 18–19: "Often to keep from losing hope, I touched the harmonica, cold inside my pocket. Sometimes I played it to keep from losing hope."

TEACHER: Turn and talk about what you think the boy meant.

BRIAN: He still has the harmonica. That's all he's got left of his family.

JUAN: I said music was important. He's remembering his parents.

BRIAN: As long as he has the harmonica, he won't give up.

The teacher reads through pages 24–25: "He worked us, beat us for no reason, without mercy. Yet he recognized beauty. I could not imagine how that could be. I felt sick, black inside, playing music for the commandant, who wore ugliness and death upon his shoulders like epaulets."

TEACHER: Turn and talk about what he was really saying about the commandant.

JUAN: He really hates playing for the commandant. He maybe feels guilty about it.

BRIAN: But he has to do it because he gets bread. Also, the commandant is really mean and would kill him if he didn't do it.

JUAN: He thinks it isn't fair that he does this and all the other prisoners don't get anything.

Figure 14.8 Turn and talk about *The Harmonica*

texts, so students get to talk about two of the books in the collection.) You can use book clubs for genre study in two ways:

- Offer students a set of books in one genre, such as historical fiction. They enter the discussion knowing the genre and can focus some of their discussion on how the author and illustrator evoked strong feelings and details from the time period.
- At the end of any book club discussion, have students identify the genre and compare the selection to texts of the same genre that have been read aloud by referring to the characteristics chart they have constructed together. They may add new characteristics to the chart.

Book Club Structure

Figure 14.13 suggests a simple structure for book clubs. Students need to be responsible and independent. For that to happen, teach them the routines they need and participate in the discussion to reinforce and expand their social conventions as well as their talk.

Before the Discussion

Select texts that are good examples of the genre and then give students time to read them during readers' workshop. Use picture books, which will be quick to read and offer a good foundation for discussion. But you may also want to select some longer chapter books as choices. Remember that you may have to make accommodations, such as reading the book aloud or having some students

EXCERPT 1 FROM *THE HARMONICA* DISCUSSION	
TEACHER:	You've talked a lot about how the boy must have felt. Why do you think the author wanted to tell this story?
VERA:	The boy turned something that was really bad into something that was good. He knew he wasn't just playing for the commandant. He was playing for all the prisoners.
JOHN:	It said he was really playing for everyone—like his parents and his father who gave him the harmonica.
SAM:	Remember how they really loved music and his father used to tell him about the music guy [Schubert] who never gave up. The music was the main thing about the story.
JUAN:	It seems like he wanted to say to never give up hope, even though he was living in a concentration camp.
TEACHER:	Maybe so, and the music was really important, wasn't it?
SAM:	The music was what kept him going.
TEACHER:	So, I asked you to think about why the author wanted to tell this story. Is that why?
JOHN:	To share a story about someone who survived the Holocaust. And also to say that even when things are really bad you shouldn't give up.
TEACHER:	That's what it said in the information the writer provided in the back. Let me read it to you. [The note is about Henryk Rosmaryn and his experience during the Holocaust.]

Figure 14.9 Excerpt 1 from *The Harmonica* discussion

A CONTINUATION OF *THE HARMONICA* AFTER-READING

TEACHER: You know we have read and talked about several books that take place during a specific time period, like *The Harmonica*, which takes place during World War II. Can you think of some other books like *The Harmonica* that show what life was like during a particular time in history?

HALEEMA: It was like *Willy and Max*. That was about the Holocaust too.

TEACHER: Yes, *The Harmonica* and *Willy and Max* are alike in that they are from the same time period, and they both tell something about what life was like for some people during that time. I'm also thinking of *Just As Good* by Chris Crowe. Take a look at our record of reading. Are any of these other stories set in the past?

MARTY: What about *Ruth and the Green Book*? It says in the beginning that their car was a 1952 Buick.

TEACHER: That's right. Let me read a bit from a couple of these books, and then I want you to tell me what you noticed.

[Reading p. 10 of *Ruth and the Green Book*] "We had picnics at roadside stops for lunch and dinner because all the restaurants had signs in the windows that said we couldn't eat there. It seemed like there were 'White Only' signs everywhere outside our Chicago neighborhood."

[Reading p. 5 of *Just As Good*] "I'd been aching for a miracle ever since Coach O'Brien banned me from his Little League baseball team. 'Look around, Homer,' he said. 'You see any Negroes playing in the major leagues?' 'Jackie Robinson. He's already a star for Brooklyn.'"

What are you noticing about these two books? Turn and talk for a minute. Then I'll write some of your comments.

Students talk briefly with a partner. Then they talk again as a whole group.

JESSICA: They're both set in the past. [Teacher writes on chart.]

PAUL: They're both talking about the way things were a long time ago, like when African American people weren't allowed to eat in restaurants or play on baseball teams with white people. [Teacher writes on chart.]

MAUD: They're fiction but they're talking about things that really happened. [Teacher writes on chart.]

They go on to generate a few more characteristics that the texts have in common, adding a few comments about *Willy and Max*.

TEACHER: All of these books we have been talking about are historical fiction. We'll read another historical fiction book tomorrow. I really like historical fiction because of what you said—they tell something about the way things were a long time ago, and some of the challenges people faced.

Figure 14.10 A continuation of *The Harmonica* discussion

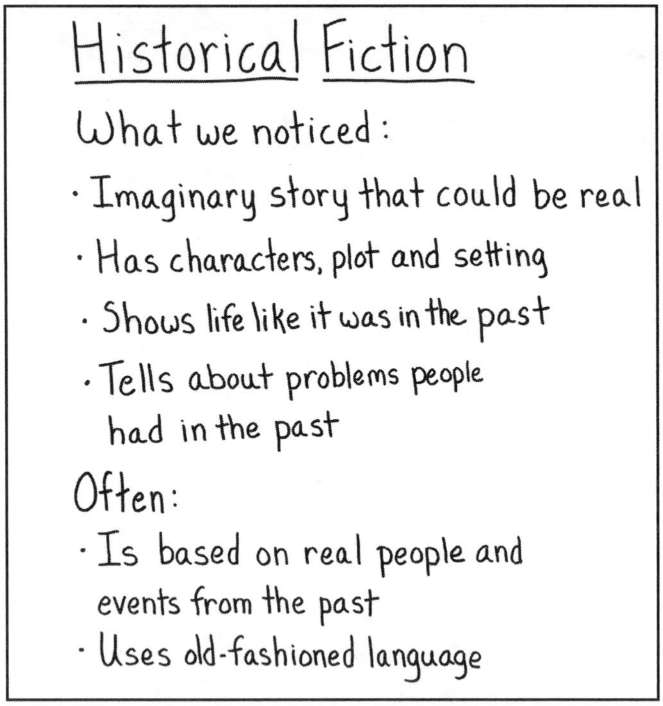
Historical Fiction
What we noticed:
· Imaginary story that could be real
· Has characters, plot and setting
· Shows life like it was in the past
· Tells about problems people had in the past
Often:
· Is based on real people and events from the past
· Uses old-fashioned language

Figure 14.11 **Noticings chart for historical fiction**

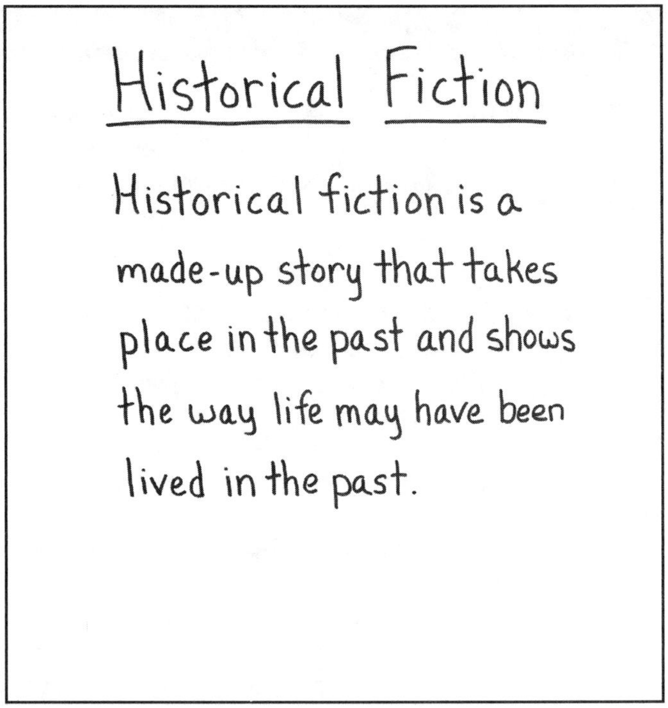
Historical Fiction
Historical fiction is a made-up story that takes place in the past and shows the way life may have been lived in the past.

Figure 14.12 **Working definition of historical fiction**

listen to an audio version to make the text accessible to everyone. Book clubs need to be scheduled far enough in advance that students can read the book and prepare (see the mentor texts listed at the end of Chapter 7 for historical fiction texts at different grade levels).

Students then read or revisit the text and prepare for the discussion. They can use their reader's notebooks or Genre Thinkmarks (see Appendix) to note page numbers they want to visit and why. Or they can place sticky notes in the book at appropriate pages with notes or questions on them. It is important for each participant to bring their own thinking to the discussion.

During the Discussion

When first implementing book clubs make it an important occasion—show students how to prepare and be a member of the group, sharing your thinking and language that facilitates authentic talk. Don't monopolize the discussion but intervene to keep it on track. *Teaching for Comprehending and Fluency* contains specific descriptions for implementing book clubs and getting started. There are also minilessons for the first thirty days, so your students will learn the social conventions and techniques for authentic talk.

Students do not always come to book club knowing how to hold a discussion, which involves such techniques as:

- Getting a turn.
- Being sure everyone in the group has a turn.
- Listening and looking at the person who is speaking.
- Staying on topic.
- Building on the ideas of others.

Some teachers find it helpful to teach students some temporary hand signals to support these techniques. However, having students assume roles, such as the person who talks about the illustrations or describes the characters, stifles the discussion and makes it artificial and ritualistic. With these artificial roles, students never truly learn to engage in discussion. The temporary routines below will help younger children stay with an idea long enough to develop it:

1. One student starts talking.
2. Others who want a turn hold out two fingers, which means, "I want to add something on the same topic."

3. Others who want a turn put up a thumb, which means, "I want to change the topic."
4. The speaker calls first on the members with two fingers out.

It is also helpful to model language such as the following:

- "I agree with ___ because..."
- "I disagree with ____ because..."
- "I'd like to add to that."
- "I don't understand. Can you say more about that?"
- "Can you give us an example?"

This language will be useful to students throughout school and in later life. An extensive list of language to use in book discussions is included in *Prompting Guide, Part 2: Teaching for Comprehension* (Fountas and Pinnell 2012).

Figure 14.14 is an excerpt from a discussion of *Uncle Jed's Barbershop*. The students are having a real conversation about the central message of the story. At the end of the discussion, the teacher can ask: "How is *Uncle Jed's Barbershop* like the other historical fiction books we have read?" This doesn't need to be heavy handed; a short reference or discussion is enough.

After the Discussion

After the discussion, students are encouraged to summarize and evaluate what they talked about. They can consider questions like these:

- Did we come prepared for the discussion?
- Did we share our thinking?
- Did we make sure everyone in the group had a turn to speak?

STRUCTURE FOR BOOK CLUBS

Step	Action	Focus on Genre
Prepare (read, think, mark)	Students read during readers' workshop and at home during the days preceding the book club meeting. They prepare for the club by marking or noting what they want to discuss.	In addition to the parts they want to think about, students note the genre and mark particular places in the text that are characteristic of the genre.
Discuss (talk and listen)	For 20 to 30 minutes students share their thinking as they talk and listen to others. They add to the thinking of others and support their thinking by referring to specific evidence from the text.	In addition to the points they want to make, students take a few moments to look at parts of the text that are characteristic of the genre.
Summarize and Evaluate (reflect)	Students make summary comments and briefly evaluate what went well in the group. If they need to read more, they plan how much to read before the next book club discussion. (Usually, only one book club meeting is needed for a picture book discussion.)	In addition to the summary, students think about anything they want to add to the genre chart or that they want to tell the whole class.
Extend (optional) (represent and respond to meaning)	Students reflect by writing or drawing (or a combination). They may share some of their book club discussion with the whole class.	Students report to the class what they found out from this example of genre.

Figure 14.13 Structure for book clubs

- Did we listen to and look at each person who was speaking?
- Did we give reasons for agreeing or disagreeing?
- Did we ask questions when we didn't understand what someone meant?
- Did we call each other by name?
- Did we use examples from the book when we made our points?
- Did we encourage everyone to participate?

The group might decide to share their noticings with the whole class, or you might ask them to report what they learned about the genre from this example so that they can check it against the characteristics chart.

After the discussion, you also have the option of asking students to extend their understanding of the text by writing or drawing or other means. Some ways to extend the text are:

- Write a letter about your personal response to the text in your reader's notebook (see Chapter 18).
- Draw or sketch something from the text that shows a significant event.

EXCERPT FROM A BOOK CLUB DISCUSSION OF *UNCLE JED'S BARBERSHOP*	
DAMIEN:	He was really old but he did get his barbershop. It was nice that he got it before he died.
KARIN:	That was because he was really patient and also because he always put other people first.
AMY:	I agree with Karin because when he almost had the money, he had to give $300 for her operation. He didn't stop or anything. He just loved her so much he just gave it to them.
TEACHER:	Karin and Amy, is there a page or part of the text you can take us to that really shows that?
AMY:	It's on page 14. It says that money didn't matter. [Reads.] He couldn't let anything happen to his Sarah Jane.
DAVID:	I want to bring up that I think Uncle Jed just never gave up. On page 17 it shows where they lost all their money. Why did they lose their money?
SHAWN:	I think it's kind of like the bank went broke. They maybe put their money in the stock market or something or they loaned it to people who couldn't pay it back.
XANDRA:	That happened to some people my parents know.
SHAWN:	So then all the money they saved was gone.
DAVID:	But he didn't give up. He just started over. And he even cut people's hair free when they didn't have the money. But that didn't help him much.
AMY:	I disagree with David because it did really help him in the long run. When people got money again they would stick with him. Look on page 21. All those people are really happy for him and it says, "That day they all came to him."
TEACHER:	What do you think Margaree Mitchell, the writer, wanted to say with this story? What is the big idea?
DAMIEN:	That the girl's uncle was important to her and she loved him.
SHAWN:	Also, that it's important not to give up on your dreams.
XANDRA:	Maybe too that people had to work harder back then to get the things they wanted.

Figure 14.14 Excerpt from a book club discussion of *Uncle Jed's Barbershop*

- Select a quote that is significant and write what it makes you think about.
- Make a T-chart in your reader's notebook (2 columns). On one side write "What I think" and on the other side write "Why." Provide evidence from the text.
- Write a book review or recommendation.
- Write the title, genre, and the reasons you think the text fits the genre (or does not).

Learning Over Time

This chapter describes how you can use interactive read-aloud and literature discussion to help students learn about genre. The Interactive Read-Aloud and Literature Discussion Continuum in *The Continuum of Literacy Learning* details specific behaviors and understandings to notice, teach, and support in students' literacy learning at grade levels K through 8. Behaviors and understandings that are particularly important to notice, teach for, and support in genre study include the students' ability to:

- Hypothesize the significance of the setting in influencing characters' decisions and attitudes.
- Discuss the characteristics of the work of some authors and illustrators (connecting texts).
- Recognize how the writer or illustrator has placed ideas in the text and in the graphics.
- Make connections to other texts by genre.
- Notice how the writer has organized a nonfiction text (categories and subcategories, sequence, and others).
- Notice and understand when the writer uses temporal sequence, comparison and contrast, and description. (Move toward recognizing a full range of underlying text structures, including those three along with problem/solution and cause and effect.)
- Recognize the genre of the text and use it to form expectations of the text.
- Understand biography as the story of a person's life.
- Identify and discuss cultural and historical perspectives that are in conflict in the text or that are different from their own perspective.
- Critically examine the writer's word choice.
- Recognize, understand, and discuss some obvious symbolism.
- Recognize and discuss the differences between narrative and other structures.
- Recognize the narrator of the text and discuss how the choice of first- or third-person point of view contributes to the effectiveness of the writing.
- Recognize and discuss aspects of narrative structure (beginning, series of events, high point of the story, ending).
- Think critically about informational texts in terms of quality of writing, accuracy, and the logic of conclusions.
- Think critically about realistic fiction texts in terms of authenticity of characters, accurate portrayal of current issues, and appropriate voice and tone.
- Think critically about historical fiction in terms of authentic portrayal of characters within the setting and accurate reflection of historical events.
- Think deeply about social issues as revealed in realistic and historical fiction and discuss ideas with others.
- Identify the sources of conflict in fiction texts and draw implications for the issues of today.

Students will develop these behavioral understandings across the grades. The understandings are related to thinking *beyond* and *about* the text. Some are appropriate for primary students; others you would not expect until readers are older and more experienced. Many are the same from grade to grade, but reading power is still expanding because students are performing the operations on harder texts. Higher-level thinking is supported because in interactive read-aloud students are freed from reading the words and the books for book club are either at students' independent level or available in audio form.

Suggestions for Professional Development

With grade-level colleagues, create a genre text set.

1. Gather a set of read-aloud texts that are appropriate for the grade level and that are good examples of one genre. (You may want to consult district or state standards to determine required genres.)
2. Read the texts and decide which ones to use for interactive read-aloud and which to use for book clubs.
3. Prepare "opening remarks" for the read-aloud books and book talks for literature discussion choices.
4. Have one member of the group take about two weeks to use the books and the genre study process with students. Remember, you will need multiple copies of the texts you select for book clubs.
5. Schedule a meeting so that your colleague can report results. Pass the text set to the next person in the group to try.
6. Continue to pass along the text set until everyone has had a chance to use it in their classrooms. (If you have enough copies of all the books, all members of your group can implement the plan simultaneously.)
7. Schedule a final meeting to compare all the results. Change, add, or drop texts so that you refine the set to include those that work best. Save the texts (or a record of where to find them) for next year! You may want to leave one copy of each book in classroom libraries so students can choose them for independent reading.

be real
· Has characters, plot, and
setting
· Shows life like it was
· Tells about problems people
the past

CHAPTER 15

Learning About Fiction Genres Through Minilessons and Group Share

We want our students to make a lifelong commitment to reading and writing. And so we begin by painstakingly caring about the literacy landscape, and then we proceed to do the best literacy teaching imaginable."

—Shelley Harwayne

The previous chapter describes how students' deep understanding of the characteristics of each genre can grow out of interactive read-aloud. This chapter (which focuses on fiction genres) and the next (which focuses on nonfiction genres) describe how you can work toward very specific genre understandings through short, explicit whole-group lessons at the beginning of readers' workshop, followed by a group share at the end of the workshop.

The talk, noticings, and comparisons of carefully selected texts that take place during interactive read-aloud are the foundation for the enhanced knowledge of specific elements of genre that students develop in a structured readers' workshop. (See Figure 15.1.) The texts you and your students have shared during interactive read-aloud become mentor texts for the explicit minilessons presented in readers' and writers' workshop. These minilessons follow your inquiry-based study, so that students can achieve even deeper levels of understanding.

If students do not know much about the characteristics of a genre, it's best to begin by establishing some broad understandings—for example, the difference between fiction and nonfiction. Most younger students can already categorize texts as fiction or nonfiction, but many have only vague understandings.

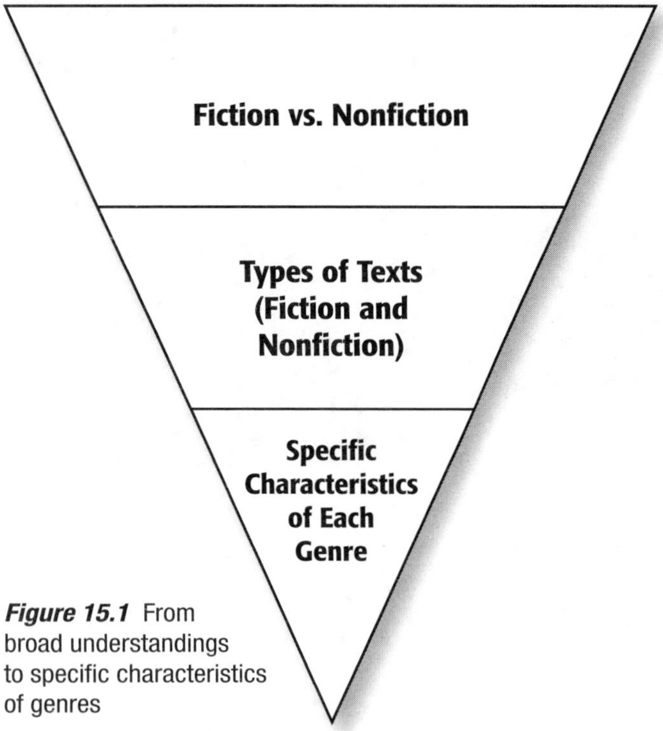

Figure 15.1 From broad understandings to specific characteristics of genres

Some common misconceptions that persist even in older age groups are:

- Any text that *could* be true (for example, realistic fiction) is nonfiction. Some students may believe that just about anything printed is true.
- Any text that contains facts is nonfiction even if it includes fictional characters (the Magic School Bus series, for example, which is a hybrid text).
- Books about real people are always nonfiction.

It's important to check on the specific understandings your students have about genre. Can they differentiate between fiction and nonfiction even when the lines are blurred? This time is not wasted. It only takes a few minutes for students to generate a simple chart like the one in Figure 15.2 after reading, discussing, and labeling five or six good examples of fiction and nonfiction.

Once students have built some important global understandings, they can begin to build a network of understandings about more specific types of fiction and nonfiction. While still sorting texts into fiction or nonfiction for example, they can begin to distinguish characteristics of biographical and other nonfiction texts. Further, within biographical texts, they can begin to distinguish between biography, autobiography, and memoir. Within fiction, they can distinguish between realistic texts and fantasy, itself divided into traditional literature and modern fantasy, including science fiction. All of this learning requires many experiences

CHARACTERISTICS OF FICTION AND NONFICTION	
Fiction	**Nonfiction**
▪ Not real ▪ Tells a story ▪ Has a beginning and an ending ▪ Has characters and a problem ▪ Sometimes describes people and places that could really exist (realistic fiction) ▪ Sometimes describes people and places that could have existed in the past (historical fiction) ▪ Sometimes describes people and places that could not really exist (fantasy)	▪ Tells about something real or true ▪ Gives factual information ▪ Can tell a story with facts ▪ Can tell a story of someone's life (biography) ▪ Can describe how to do something or how something works ▪ Can be written to persuade the reader ▪ Can be written by people telling about their own lives ▪ Can include a variety of text features to communicate information

Figure 15.2 Characteristics of fiction and nonfiction

with texts over a long period of time, so it is a good idea to articulate the curriculum for learning about genre over several years. As students grow more knowledgeable, they can appreciate the fine differences that exist in the literature—for example, how to distinguish authentic biographies, fictionalized biographies, and biographical fiction. Also, they learn to analyze and write hybrid texts that contain more than one genre.

The Structure of Genre Study

In Chapter 2 we outlined steps in a genre study: (1) collecting a text set for a particular genre or subgenre; (2) immersing students in the texts through interactive read-aloud (and providing more texts in book clubs, guided reading, and independent reading); (3) creating a list of characteristics of the group of texts; (4) co-constructing a working definition of the genre; and (5) reading and revising the lists and definition.

Learning about genre takes a long time, so you repeat this process over and over across the grades as you share more complex understandings. Generally, teachers in kindergarten and first grade select realistic fiction, animal fantasy, different forms of traditional literature, and simple nonfiction texts on topics that children have the background knowledge to understand for specific studies. This doesn't mean they would not also be exposed to a greater variety of texts. Young students may respond to stories about children in times past but do not usually understand the complexities of historical settings. As children move beyond the first two years of school, their ability to understand a wide range of genres and attend to more complex themes and concepts expands rapidly. Be sure to evaluate the age group's ability to comprehend complex genres such as high fantasy and science fiction. Historical fiction and biography also make particular demands in that some understanding of the social conditions and perspectives of the period of history are necessary for deep understanding.

Most students will not automatically categorize texts and internalize the features of genre; they require instruction. Once the characteristics of genre are deeply known, however, they are an important advantage to the reader. Keep your students in mind while collecting interesting and engaging text sets—their ages and experience and also their interests (but you can create new interests with high-quality, interesting texts). If a genre is relatively new or the students have not previously studied this genre, they need clear, easy-to-understand examples.

As you immerse students in the genre through the talk structures of interactive read-aloud and literature discussion, engage in intentional teaching. After your students hear and discuss some clear examples (there's no set number, but four or five is about right) and list features they notice, keep a clear understanding of the elements of the genre in your own mind so you can help them create a simple working definition of the genre.

You may return to the genre during the year, using further examples. The teachers in your school may decide to study a given genre every year or every other year so that students have the opportunity to think analytically about increasingly complex texts appropriate to their age level. In Figure 15.3 you will see an example of how you might begin to think about genre study across the grades, Kindergarten through Grade 8. As you develop a plan across grades, consult your district and state standards and think about the particular needs and strengths of your students and school. Remember the plan is not rigid like stone, but more like clay that guides your broad thinking.

The Structure of Readers' Workshop

After you are confident students have a working definition of the genre, teach specific minilessons in readers' workshop. You can address the noticings individually or cluster them to study the various elements. There's no need to reread the mentor texts during the minilesson, because they will be very familiar, but they're on hand for students to remember and revisit as needed.

The simple organizational outline of readers' workshop in Figure 15.4 works for writers' workshop as well. Since we have written extensive descriptions of readers' and writers' workshop elsewhere (see Fountas and Pinnell 2001, 2006), we will only summarize here.

Connection

Begin the workshop by making a connection to previous minilessons. In this way you help students link previous principles to the new one that you teach. For example, you might say (statements of the principle are in italics):

- "We have been thinking about, talking about, and reading realistic fiction. Michael, can you read the definition for us?" [Michael reads.] "Last week we learned that [reading from chart] *realistic fiction is a story that is not true though it could really happen. It has characters, a problem, and a solution.*"
- "One thing you noticed was that in realistic fiction the writer usually tells about the setting. What is setting?" [Students respond] *"Readers think about the setting, or when and where the story takes place, to help them understand the story."*

  "Let's look back at a few books we read together to think about how the setting helps readers understand the story."

Often you construct the minilesson principle with your students, after looking at several examples. Sometimes you might begin with the principle on the chart and talk about how it applies to your shared examples. In either case, be sure to help your students understand how the new principle they are learning relates to the big ideas that define the genre.

POTENTIAL GENRE STUDIES ALONG THE K–8 CONTINUUM

Grades	Kindergarten	First Grade	Second Grade
Potential Genre Studies in Each Grade *Note: Within these genres, students might be reading many different forms of text (e.g., plays, series, chapter books, graphic texts, picture books, etc.) as well as different types of fiction (e.g., mysteries, adventure stories, horror, humor, etc.) and nonfiction (e.g., reports, literary essays, feature articles, interviews, etc.)*	• Fiction vs. Nonfiction • Folktales • Poetry	• Fiction v. Nonfiction • Realistic Fiction • Folktales • Simple Expository Texts (e.g. informational books) • Procedural Texts • Poetry	• Fiction vs. Nonfiction • Realistic fiction • Animal Fantasy • Folktales • Fairy Tales • Fables • Expository Texts (e.g. informational texts) • Procedural Texts • Poetry (add in specific types of poetry)
Other genres that students might be exposed to through read-aloud or independent reading, but not studied through inquiry	• Realistic Fiction • Animal Fantasy • Fairy Tales • Narrative Nonfiction • Simple Expository Texts (e.g. informational books) • Procedural Texts	• Animal Fantasy • Fairy Tales • Narrative Nonfiction	• Myths • Persuasive Texts • Narrative Nonfiction • Simple Biographies • Memoirs

Figure 15.3 Potential genre studies along the K–8 continuum

POTENTIAL GENRE STUDIES ALONG THE K–8 CONTINUUM			
Grades	**Third Grade**	**Fourth Grade**	**Fifth Grade**
Potential Genre Studies in Each Grade *Note: Within these genres, students might be reading many different forms of text (e.g., plays, series, chapter books, graphic texts, picture books, etc.) as well as different types of fiction (e.g., mysteries, adventure stories, horror, humor, etc.) and nonfiction (e.g., reports, literary essays, feature articles, interviews, etc.)*	• Realistic Fiction • Folktales • Fairy Tales • Fables • Myths • Expository Texts (e.g. informational texts, interviews) • Biographies • Memoirs • Poetry (add in specific types of poetry) • Tests Special types of fiction read across genres: • Mysteries • Adventure Stories • Animal Stories • Family, Friends, and School Stories • Graphic Texts	• Realistic Fiction • Historical Fiction • Folktales • Fairy Tales • Fables • Myths • Fantasy • Expository Texts (e.g., informational texts, feature articles, interviews, research reports) • Biographies • Autobiographies • Memoirs • Narrative Nonfiction • Poetry (add in specific types of poetry) • Tests Special types of fiction read across genres: • Mysteries • Adventure Stories • Animal Stories • Family, Friends and School Stories • Graphic Texts	• Realistic Fiction • Historical Fiction • Folktales • Legends, Epics, Ballads • Myths • Fantasy • Expository Texts (e.g., informational texts, feature articles, interviews, research reports, literary essays) • Persuasive Texts • Biographies • Autobiographies • Memoirs • Narrative Nonfiction • Poetry (add in specific types of poetry) • Tests Special types and forms of fiction read across genres: • Mysteries • Adventure Stories • Animal Stories • Family, Friends and School Stories • Graphic Texts
Other genres that students might be exposed to through read-aloud or independent reading, but not studied	• Narrative Nonfiction • Autobiographies • Fantasy • Historical Fiction • Persuasive Texts	• Legends, Epics, Ballads • Fantasy • Science Fiction • Persuasive Texts	• Science Fiction • Hybrid Texts

Figure 15.3 Potential genre studies along the K–8 continuum *(cont.)*

continues

POTENTIAL GENRE STUDIES ALONG THE K–8 CONTINUUM			
Grades	**Sixth Grade**	**Seventh Grade**	**Eighth Grade**
Potential Genre Studies in Each Grade *Note: Within these genres, students might be reading many different forms of text (e.g., plays, series, chapter books, graphic texts, picture books, etc.) as well as different types of fiction (e.g., mysteries, adventure stories, horror, humor, etc.) and nonfiction (e.g., reports, literary essays, feature articles, interviews, etc.)*	• Realistic Fiction • Historical Fiction • Legends, Epics, Ballads • Myths • Fantasy • Science Fiction • Expository Texts (e.g. informational texts, feature articles, interviews, research reports, literary essays, speeches) • Biographies • Autobiographies • Memoirs • Narrative Nonfiction • Persuasive Texts • Hybrid Texts • Poetry (add in specific types of poetry) • Tests Special types and forms of fiction read across genres: • Adventure Stories • Mysteries • Satire/Parodies • Graphic Texts	• Realistic Fiction • Historical Fiction • Legends, Epics, Ballads • Myths • Fantasy • Science Fiction • Expository Texts (e.g. informational texts, feature articles, interviews, research reports, literary essays, speeches) • Biographies • Autobiographies • Memoirs • Narrative Nonfiction • Persuasive Texts • Hybrid Texts • Poetry (add in specific types of poetry) • Tests Special types and forms of fiction read across genres: • Adventure Stories • Mysteries • Satire/Parodies • Graphic Texts	• Realistic Fiction • Historical Fiction • Legends, Epics, Ballads • Myths • Fantasy • Science Fiction • Expository Texts (e.g. informational texts, feature articles, interviews,research reports, literary essays, speeches) • Biographies • Autobiographies • Memoirs • Narrative Nonfiction • Persuasive Texts • Hybrid Texts • Poetry (add in specific types of poetry) • Tests Special types and forms of fiction read across genres: • Adventure Stories • Mysteries • Satire/Parodies • Graphic Texts
Other genres that students might be exposed to through read-aloud or independent reading, but not studied	• Students should be reading independently across all genres.	• Students should be reading independently across all genres.	• Students should be reading independently across all genres.

Figure 15.3 Potential genre studies along the K–8 continuum *(cont.)*

STRUCTURE OF READERS' OR WRITERS' WORKSHOP		
Connection	**Establish Context**	• Teacher helps students link previous minilesson principles to the new one that will be taught. • Students understand how the learning relates to the big ideas.
Minilesson	**State the Principle**	• As an inquiry approach, students think and talk about the examples and co-construct the principle. • Principle stated in clear, explicit, and concise language. • Principle tells what readers or writers do and why.
	Refer to Examples (Mentor Texts, Charts, Student or Teacher Writing)	• Teacher demonstrates and models with high-quality text examples to help students understand the principle. • Discussion fosters a shared language. • Students suggest examples and share noticings. • Students know how the examples are helping them as readers/writers.
	Have a Try (When Applicable)	• Students quickly try out the principle in the whole-group setting, often with a partner or in threes. • Students actively process the new information with support. • Directly related to what readers and writers need to be able to think about independently during the workshop.
Application	**Apply New Learning on Own** **Confer with Teacher**	• Students apply what they have learned in the minilesson to their own reading or writing if applicable. • Teacher holds brief individual conferences to support the students' reading and writing and make a teaching point. • Teacher may reinforce minilesson principle with individuals. • Teacher may assess the reading or writing of individuals. • Teacher may link principle to guided reading or book club discussions (or guided writing lessons).
Group Share	**Extend Learning**	• Students share new learning with the whole group. • Students extend learning through sharing more examples and insights. • Teacher expands learning through building on student examples. • Teacher gains feedback on student learning. • The group evaluates how today's workshop went.

Figure 15.4 Structure of readers' or writers' workshop

Minilesson

The minilesson includes the statement of a principle, some examples, and sometimes "having a try." Involve students in the inquiry process so they construct their knowledge, or you may sometimes include teacher-led demonstrations and modeling. Your approach may depend on the particular principle.

Take an inquiry stance in your language and how you approach the principle. According to Ray, an inquiry stance "repositions the curriculum as an outcome of instruction rather than the starting point" (2006). Together, you and your students derive the principle based on the previous study of clear examples of genre or craft. The inquiry stance is active and exciting. You learn as much as your students as you think alongside them, and the students get inside the understandings because they construct them for themselves.

As an alternative, you might tell the students the principle in clear terms and then invite them to offer examples to help them understand it. This approach is most effective if you have previously immersed the students in the genre and they have clear examples as a reference. The goals of the minilesson are listed in Figure 15.5.

When you teach minilessons, think about what you want your students to learn how to do as readers—the systems of strategic actions you want them to be able to use. Think about how they will use what they learn on their own. To select and plan minilessons, draw on your assessment and observation of student behaviors, and consult district and/or state standards and guidelines. What do students already know? What do they need to know? What examples will they need to access? How much demonstration will be needed? The characteristics of effective minilessons are listed in Figure 15.6.

Stating the Principle

State the principle in explicit language. A minilesson in readers' workshop may focus on an important principle related to processing texts or thinking beyond and about texts. The twelve systems of strategic actions described in Chapter 5 are the foundation for minilessons throughout grades K–8. *The Continuum of Literacy Learning* includes specific descriptions of curriculum goals for minilessons based on your assessment of student needs.

Minilessons in a genre study generally require students to think beyond and about the texts they are hearing read or are reading independently. Specifically, they prompt students to think and talk about examples in a way that helps them notice and analyze the characteristics related to the genre.

Begin with an introductory lesson that builds on the definition the students have helped create. You might prepare for the lesson by asking all your students to select a book in the genre for their independent reading. Although students should not choose books by level, a good variety of texts at a range of difficulty levels needs to be available in the classroom library. Display the books face front in labeled tubs or baskets to help students quickly find books they like in a variety of genres.

Referring to Known Examples

In a genre study, the same mentor texts can be used for both reading minilessons and writing minilessons. Mentor texts not only make your teaching efficient but also provide the coherence that makes instruction more meaningful for students. You can return to mentor texts that students know well many times to help them understand the characteristics of texts in a particular genre. The texts need not be reread. Students will remember a text because they have had the opportunity to discuss it and list features they noticed. Revisit parts of the text as needed.

MINILESSON GOALS

- Teach readers how to think in a new way about texts.
- Help students use mentor texts they know well so that they can learn from and refer to the examples.
- Make new understandings explicit and accessible so readers can retrieve them when needed.

Figure 15.5 Minilesson goals

EFFECTIVE MINILESSONS

- Have a clear purpose.
- Use clear language that gets young readers (K–2) to think about an important idea as they start reading (e.g., *Think about the problem in the story* or *Think about why the author is telling about this topic*).
- Use clear language that refers to what readers do and why (grades 3–8). *(e.g., Readers ____ so that ______.* or *Readers ______ in order to ______.)*
- Include a statement of the principle and examples from shared texts.
- Help students understand what they are learning how to do and how it helps them as readers (and writers).
- Use high-quality mentor texts, teacher or student writing, graphic organizers, and charts everyone can see.
- Are grouped and sequenced according to concepts so that students build one understanding on the next.
- Develop related understandings over several days so that students make connections and develop deep understandings and gain the bigger ideas.
- Are relevant to the needs of readers. (What will be helpful to most readers and also meet the demands of the curriculum?)
- Are brief, concise, and to the point (about five to ten minutes).
- Are well-paced to engage and hold students' interest.
- Engage readers' thinking from beginning to end.
- Stay focused on a single idea (no digressions that waste time, divert attention, or confuse).
- Foster community through the development of a shared language.
- Help students become better readers and writers.

Figure 15.6 The characteristics of effective minilessons

Carry genre study over into writers' workshop using the same examples. If students are writing memoir, for example, the authors of the examples they revisit will become professional mentors. The same is true of biography, autobiography, expository texts, and short fiction.

Having a Try

Learning is helped along if students have a chance to apply the principle during the minilesson or immediately after it, whether as a whole group, in a small group, or with a partner. This activity is directly related to what readers and writers need to be able to do independently in the workshop. Having a try might involve:

- *Reading.* Students and teacher talk about the characteristics in one or two mentor texts. Then the students turn and discuss with a partner the characteristics in another example or in their independent reading.
- *Writing.* After noticing a genre characteristic with the teacher, students select a writer's notebook entry, give it a try, and explain to a partner what they did.

The time spent having a try is brief. The teacher observes in order to gather information on how well students understand the minilesson principle and reinforces it.

Application

Immediately following the minilesson, students apply what they have learned to their own reading or writing, if that is appropriate. They are accountable for trying out new thinking because they know they will be expected to discuss the principle again during the sharing session. The charge can be anything: "Think about the setting and why it is important." "Choose a character and be prepared to share how the writer helped you know what that character was like." "Think about an important decision the subject of your biography made and be prepared to talk about it." At the end of the minilesson, for example, you might say:

- *Reading.* "While you are reading today, notice what the writing is like so you can identify the genre [nonfiction book, biography, fantasy, realistic fiction, other]. Be prepared to share what you noticed during group share."
- *Writing.* "While you are writing today, you may want to use the examples of [biography, memoir, short fiction] to help you think about what to write or how to write it. Share your thinking with us in group share."

The examples above are just suggestions. There are many ways to foster student thinking based on the particular genre being studied.

Students then begin reading or writing independently. Typically, the room is completely silent except for the low-voiced conferences you have with individual students or the small-group work you do in guided reading or writing or literature discussion. Independent work includes:

- *Reading.* Students silently read a book of their own choosing. Students do not choose books by level but according to their interests. They may be asked to choose a book in a particular genre following the study and are expected to read a specific number of books in a variety of genres during the year. They might also write about their reading once a week in a reader's notebook. (The routines of readers' workshop, as well as how to get started in the first twenty days of the school year, are described in Fountas and Pinnell 2001.)
- *Writing.* Students work on their own pieces. The writing may involve any aspect of the writing process, including writing in the writer's notebook (planting seeds), getting thoughts down on paper (writing a discovery draft), revising, editing, and producing a final draft that may be published in some way. (The routines of writers' workshop are described in Fountas and Pinnell 2001, 2006.)

While students are working independently in readers' workshop, you might:

1. Confer with individual students regarding their reading or their writing about reading.
2. Bring small groups of students together for guided reading. (Guided reading as it contributes to genre study is described in Chapter 19.)
3. Bring small groups of students together for literature discussion, often called *book clubs.* (The role of book clubs in genre study is described in Chapter 14.)

In the earliest grades (K–1) you might have students rotate to literacy centers for work with words, listening to a book, responding to books with art, or other engaging, meaningful independent activities.

Group Share

For a brief period at the end of the workshop, students have the opportunity to share their learning with the entire group. During this time they expand and deepen their understanding of the minilesson principle. This sharing period is more than students' coming prepared to say something; you actively teach, connecting their examples to the minilesson principle. Sharing approaches vary. For example, you can:

- Have students sit in a circle and some students share their thinking with the entire group.
- Have each student share one brief thought ("popcorn") around the circle.
- Have students talk first in pairs or threes and then gather a few comments for the larger group.

Sharing at the end of readers' workshop takes only a few minutes and is very valuable. Students' observational powers are sharpened because they know they are expected to share with the group. They benefit from the thoughts of their peers. Reinforce the minilesson principle with students' own examples and at the same time quickly assess student understanding. Sharing provides you with immediate feedback on the effectiveness of the minilesson.

By sharing during a genre study, students learn from one another. For example:

- *Reading.* Students can share with a partner what they noticed about the features of the genre in the books they are reading. After this brief "buzz," some students can share comments with the entire group. Or students can go around the circle and quickly share features they have noticed in the books they are reading.
- *Writing.* Students can share how they used a mentor text to help them craft their writing. Or they can share how they used what they know about a genre to help them write in a genre.

There are many other ways students can share their understandings. Readers'/writers' workshop provides a predictable and productive series of opportunities that support students in learning the specifics of reading and writing.

Genre Study in Readers' Workshop

When introducing genre study in readers' workshop, keep in mind the close relationship between your intentional teaching in interactive read-aloud and the minilessons and group shares that take place in the workshop. Together, they provide the powerful teaching that helps your students not only comprehend texts deeply but also talk and write about them analytically. These goals will not be accomplished by dipping randomly into a genre or literary element. Genre study needs to be systematic, well planned, and connected. Ideally, with colleagues in your school, construct a tentative genre study curriculum map across a grade level and if possible across several grades (see examples in Figures 15.7, 15.8, and 15.9). Students need to learn that texts employ a predictable, consistent set of codes that make up the genres and their elements and characteristics. They need to become familiar with a wide range of genres. They also need to study genres with texts that become more complex across the grades. Plan conceptual units that help students build strong understandings, one upon the other, in each genre.

Moving from interactive read-aloud to a readers' workshop enables you to establish a foundation through inquiry and also to ensure that students have clear examples as anchors. As you teach, bring these specific examples back to mind (along with previous discussions, characteristics, and definitions) to ground your points. (See Figure 15.10.)

Using Minilessons and Group Share to Support Genre Study

Let's walk through the process of moving from interactive read-aloud to a readers' workshop during genre study and look specifically at how minilessons and group share supports the process. Figure 15.9 provides a snapshot of a three week genre study in the month of October in a fifth-grade classroom. You will also want to glance back at Figure 15.8, an example of a fifth grade curriculum map, to see how this realistic fiction genre study relates to other genre studies across the school year. This genre study and the ones that follow in this chapter help students to see a relationship among genres. This example is not a rigid path requiring that one thing be done before another. Rather, think through the relationships yourself and help students build the map of genres in their own heads. The three-week example of a genre study is only one example of a way a teacher might approach the study of realistic fiction. Genre studies usually last about two to four weeks. Decide what your students need and think about what literary elements you will revisit or focus on in subsequent genre studies. Thinking through these points will help you determine how long to spend on a given genre.

In the three-week example (Figure 15.9), Matt begins the genre study of realistic fiction by immersing his fifth grade students in realistic fiction picture books (using picture books quickly builds a repertoire of shared texts) during interactive read-aloud. Notice that Matt does not incorporate genre study into his reading minilessons and group share in the first week. However, he has made sure realistic fiction books are available at a range of levels in his classroom library. As students discuss the genre in interactive read-aloud, becoming more familiar with the elements of realistic fiction, Matt introduces book club

SAMPLE CURRICULUM MAP FOR GENRE STUDY, GRADE 2			
Month	**September**		**October**
Time spent	**2 weeks**	**4 weeks**	**2 weeks**
Genre Study	**Mini Study:** **Fiction vs. Nonfiction**	**Realistic Fiction**	**Author, Illustrator, or Craft Study**
Process	Collect a variety of fiction and nonfiction texts.	Collect a text set of realistic fiction texts (including picture books, plays, short stories and short chapter books).	*Author, Illustrator, or Craft Study:* Collect a text set of books that represents the category you plan to study.
	Immerse students in both nonfiction and fiction texts during interactive read-aloud. Give book talks on a variety of fiction and nonfiction texts.	Immerse students in realistic fiction during interactive read-aloud. Give book talks on realistic fiction at a range of reading levels for independent reading.	Immerse students in this text set during interactive read-aloud. Give book talks on realistic fiction at a range of reading levels for independent reading.
	Create list of characteristics defining difference between fiction and nonfiction.	Create a list of characteristics defining realistic fiction.	
	Co-construct a definition for fiction and nonfiction to distinguish between the two.	Co-construct a definition of realistic fiction. Read and revise definition.	Teach minilessons on principles related to the study. For example: • Literary elements • Analyzing the author's or illustrator's craft • Themes and messages across texts • Making connections across texts by the same author or illustrator
	Teach a series of minilessons focusing on how readers can tell they are reading fiction or nonfiction and have students try classifying their own reading.	Teach a series of minilessons on one or two of the defining elements of realistic fiction. For example: • Characters • Setting • Problem resolution • Themes and messages • Perspective • Illustrations	Help students notice the genres of the texts.
	Students choose from a variety of genres available in the classroom library for independent reading to apply their learning.	Students choose from a variety of genres available in the classroom library for independent reading to apply their learning.	Students choose from a variety of genres available in the classroom library for independent reading to apply their learning.

Figure 15.7 Sample curriculum map for genre study, grade 2

SAMPLE CURRICULUM MAP FOR GENRE STUDY, GRADE 2		
Month	**November**	
Time spent	**3 weeks**	**1 week**
Genre Study	**Expository Texts**	**Author, Illustrator, or Craft Study**
Process	Collect four or five nonfiction read-aloud titles that are clearly expository texts, not biography, how-to, or narrative nonfiction. Immerse students in this genre through interactive read-aloud. Give book talks on expository texts at a range of reading levels for independent reading. Create a list of characteristics defining expository nonfiction. Co-construct a definition of expository nonfiction. Read and revise definition. Teach a series of minilessons on one or two of the defining elements of expository nonfiction. For example: • Information in text • Text structure • Big ideas • Tone, voice, and perspective • Text features Students choose from a variety of genres available in the classroom library for independent reading to apply their learning.	*Author, Illustrator, or Craft Study:* Collect a text set of books that represents the category you plan to study. Immerse students in the text set during interactive read-aloud. Give book talks at a range of reading levels for independent reading. Teach minilessons on subjects related to the study. For example: • Literary elements • Analyzing the author's or illustrator's craft • Themes and messages across texts • Making connections across texts by the same author or illustrator Help students notice the genres of the texts. Students choose from a variety of genres available in the classroom library for independent reading to apply their learning.

Figure 15.7 Sample curriculum map for genre study, grade 2 *(cont.)*

continues

SAMPLE CURRICULUM MAP FOR GENRE STUDY, GRADE 2		
Month	**December**	
Time spent	**3 weeks**	**1–2 weeks**
Genre Study	**Animal Fantasy**	**Author, Illustrator, or Craft Study**
Process	Collect a text set of animal fantasy texts. Immerse students in animal fantasy using this text set during interactive read-aloud. Give book talks on animal fantasy texts at a range of reading levels for independent reading. Create a list of characteristics defining animal fantasy. Co-construct a definition of fantasy. (You can choose if you want to specify animal fantasy). Read and revise definition. Teach a series of minilessons on one or two of the defining elements of animal fantasy. For example: • Characters • Setting • Problem resolution • Lesson/Message • Perspective • Illustrations • Common motifs/elements of fantasy Students choose from a variety of genres available in the classroom library for independent reading to apply their learning.	*Author, Illustrator, or Craft Study:* Collect a text set of books that represents the category you plan to study. Immerse students in the text set during interactive read-aloud. Give book talks at a range of reading levels for independent reading. Teach minilessons on subjects related to the study. For example: • Literary elements • Analyzing the author's or illustrator's craft • Themes and messages across texts • Making connections across texts by the same author or illustrator Help students notice the genres of the texts. Students choose from a variety of genres available in the classroom library for independent reading to apply their learning.

Figure 15.7 Sample curriculum map for genre study, grade 2 *(cont.)*

SAMPLE CURRICULUM MAP FOR GENRE STUDY, GRADE 2			
Month	**January**		
Time spent	**1–2 weeks**	**2–3 weeks**	**1–2 weeks**
Genre Study	**Author, Illustrator, or Craft Study**	**Procedural Texts (How-to-Books)**	**Author, Illustrator, or Craft Study**
Process	*Author. Illustrator, or Craft Study:* Collect a text set of books that represents the category you plan to study. Immerse students in the text set during interactive read-aloud. Give book talks at a range of levels for independent reading. Teach minilessons on subjects related to the study. For example: • Literary elements • Analyzing the author's craft • Themes and messages across texts • Making connections across texts by the same author Help students notice the genres of the texts. Students choose from a variety of genres available in the classroom library for independent reading to apply their learning.	Collect a text set of procedural or "how-to" texts. Immerse students in procedural texts during interactive read-aloud. Give book talks at a range of levels for independent reading. Create a list of characteristics defining procedural texts. Co-construct a definition of procedural (how-to) texts. Read and revise definition. Teach a series of minilessons on some of the elements or demands of procedural texts. For example: • Gathering information • Considering the significance of each step in a complex process • Understanding the conventions in which instructions are written • Analyzing the logic of text or critiquing it for errors Students choose from a variety of genres available in the classroom library for independent reading to apply their learning.	*Author, Illustrator, or Craft Study:* Collect a text set of books that represents the category you plan to study. Immerse students in the text set during interactive read-aloud. Give book talks at a range of levels for independent reading. Teach minilessons on subjects related to the study. For example: • Literary elements • Analyzing the author's or illustrator's craft • Themes and messages across texts • Making connections across texts by the same author or illustrator Help students notice the genres of the texts. Students choose from a variety of genres available in the classroom library for independent reading to apply their learning.

Figure 15.7 Sample curriculum map for genre study, grade 2 *(cont.)*

continues

SAMPLE CURRICULUM MAP FOR GENRE STUDY, GRADE 2		
Month	**February**	
Time spent	**1–2 weeks**	**3–4 weeks**
Genre Study	**Author, Illustrator, or Craft Study**	**Folktales and Fairy Tales** (You may want to focus on a couple of types of folktales only and follow with fables.)
Process	*Author, Illustrator, or Craft Study:* Collect a text set of books that represent the category you plan to study.	• Beast Tales • Cumulative Tales • Pourquoi Tales • Trickster Tales • Noodlehead Tales • Realistic Tales • Tall Tales Collect a text set of folktales. (At this grade level, it is not necessary to make a distinction between folktales and fairy tales as they are both forms of folktales, and the main goal is for students to begin to understand how traditional literature is different from the other genres they have read.)
	Immerse students in the text set during interactive read-aloud. Give book talks at a range of reading levels for independent reading.	Immerse students in folktales during interactive read-aloud. Give book talks on different folktales and fairy tales at a range of reading levels for independent reading.
	Teach minilessons on subjects related to the study. For example: • Literary elements • Analyzing the author's or illustrator's craft • Themes and messages across texts • Making connections across texts by the same author or illustrator	Create a list of characteristics defining folktales. Co-construct a definition of folktales. Read and revise definition.
	Help students notice the genres of the texts. Students choose from a variety of genres available in the classroom library for independent reading to apply their learning.	Teach a series of minilessons on one or two of the defining elements of folktales. For example: • Characters • Setting • Problem resolution • Themes and messages: Reflections of the culture • Perspective • Illustrations

Figure 15.7 Sample curriculum map for genre study, grade 2 *(cont.)*

SAMPLE CURRICULUM MAP FOR GENRE STUDY, GRADE 2		
Month	**March**	
Time spent	**1–2 weeks**	**1–2 weeks**
Genre Study	**Reviewing Fiction vs. Nonfiction** (or further types of folktales) Note: If your students have a good grasp of the differences between fiction and nonfiction, you may also want to revisit realistic fiction and fantasy and discuss the differences between these two types of fiction.	**Author, Illustrator, or Craft Study**
Process	Spend time reviewing what you and your students have learned about fiction and nonfiction and/or realistic fiction and fantasy by revisiting texts and charts you created during the inquiry process. Have students spend time reading their choice of genre during independent reading and identifying the texts as fiction or nonfiction or categorizing them by genre.	*Author, Illustrator, or Craft Study:* Collect a text set of books that represent the category you plan to study. Immerse students in the text set during interactive read-aloud. Give book talks at a range of reading levels for independent reading. Teach minilessons on subjects related to the study. For example: • Literary elements • Analyzing the author's or illustrator's craft • Themes and messages across texts • Making connections across texts by the same author or illustrator Help students notice the genres of the texts. Students choose from a variety of genres available in the classroom library for independent reading to apply their learning.

Figure 15.7 Sample curriculum map for genre study, grade 2 *(cont.)*

continues

SAMPLE CURRICULUM MAP FOR GENRE STUDY, GRADE 2		
Month	**April**	
Time Spent	**3–4 weeks**	**1–2 weeks**
Genre Study	**Realistic Fiction**	**Author, Illustrator, or Craft Study**
Process	Revisit realistic fiction with another text set of realistic fiction texts (including picture books, plays, short stories, and short chapter books). Immerse students in realistic fiction during interactive read-aloud. Give book talks on realistic fiction at a range of reading levels for independent reading. Revisit the list of characteristics defining realistic fiction. Revise or add any new noticings to your chart. Revise/co-construct a definition of realistic fiction. Read and revise definition. Teach a series of minilessons on one or two of the defining elements of realistic fiction that you may not have addressed previously. For example: • Characters • Setting • Problem resolution • Themes and messages • Perspective • Illustrations Students choose from a variety of genres available in the classroom library for independent reading to apply their learning.	*Author, Illustrator, or Craft Study:* Collect a text set of books that represents the category you plan to study. Immerse students in the text set during interactive read-aloud. Give book talks at a range of reading levels for independent reading. Teach minilessons on subjects related to the study. For example: • Literary elements • Analyzing the author's or illustrator's craft • Themes and messages across texts • Making connections across texts by the same author or illustrator Help students notice the genres of the texts. Students choose from a variety of genres available in the classroom library for independent reading to apply their learning.

Figure 15.7 Sample curriculum map for genre study, grade 2 *(cont.)*

SAMPLE CURRICULUM MAP FOR GENRE STUDY, GRADE 2		
Month	**May**	**June**
Time spent	**4 weeks**	**3 weeks**
Genre Study	**Expository Nonfiction**	**Author, Illustrator, or Craft Study or Review of Fiction and Nonfiction**
Process	Revisit expository nonfiction with another text set of four or five nonfiction read-aloud titles that are clearly expository texts, not biography, how-to, or narrative nonfiction. Immerse students in this genre through interactive read-aloud. Give book talks on expository nonfiction at a range of reading levels for independent reading. Revisit the list of characteristics defining expository nonfiction you made at the beginning of the year. Revise or add any new noticings to your chart. Revise/co-construct a definition of expository nonfiction. Read and revise definition. Teach a series of minilessons on one or two of the defining elements of expository nonfiction. You will probably want to choose an element you did not address previously. For example: • Information in text • Text structure • Big ideas • Tone, voice, and perspective • Text features Students choose from a variety of genres available in the classroom library for independent reading to apply their learning.	Depending on student need, review differences between fiction and nonfiction. Conclude the year with another author, illustrator, or craft study.

Figure 15.7 Sample curriculum map for genre study, grade 2 *(cont.)*

CURRICULUM MAP FOR GENRE STUDY, GRADE 5		
Month	**September**	
Time spent	**3 weeks**	**1–2 weeks**
Genre Study	**Memoir**	**Author, Illustrator, or Craft Study**
Process	Collect a text set of memoirs. Immerse students in the text set during interactive read aloud. Give book talks on memoirs at a range of reading levels for independent reading. Create a list of characteristics defining memoir. Co-construct a definition of memoir. Read and revise definition. Teach a series of minilessons on one or two of the defining elements of memoir. For example: • Perspective • Setting • Message/ Theme • Imagery • Communication of emotion • Tone, attitude, mood • Style/Language Students choose from a variety of genres available in the classroom library for independent reading to apply their learning.	*Author, Illustrator, or Craft Study:* Collect a text set of books by an author you plan to study. Immerse students in this text set during interactive read-aloud. Give book talks at a range of reading levels for independent reading. Teach minilessons on subjects related to the study. For example: • Literary elements • Analyzing the author's or illustrator's craft • Themes and messages across texts • Making connections across texts by the same author or illustrator Help students notice the genres of the texts. Students choose from a variety of genres available in the classroom library for independent reading to apply their learning.

Figure 15.8 Curriculum map for genre study, grade 5

CURRICULUM MAP FOR GENRE STUDY, GRADE 5		
Month	**October**	
Time spent	**3–4 weeks**	**1 week**
Genre Study	**Realistic Fiction**	**Author, Illustrator, or Craft Study**
Process	Collect a text set of realistic fiction texts (including picture books, plays, short stories, and short chapter books). Immerse students in realistic fiction during interactive read-aloud. Give book talks on realistic fiction at a range of reading levels for independent reading. Create a list of characteristics defining realistic fiction. Co-Construct a definition of realistic fiction. Read and revise definition. Teach a series of minilessons on one or two of the defining elements of realistic fiction. For example: • Characters • Setting • Plot and problem resolution • Themes and messages • Tone • Mood • Perspective • Illustrations • Style/Language Students choose from a variety of genres available in the classroom library for independent reading to apply their learning.	*Author, Illustrator, or Craft Study:* Collect a text set of books that represents the category you plan to study. Immerse students in the text set during interactive read-aloud. Give book talks at a range of reading levels for independent reading. Teach minilessons on subjects related to the study. For example: • Literary elements • Analyzing the author's or illustrator's craft • Themes and messages across texts • Making connections across texts by the same author or illustrator Help students notice the genres of the texts. Students choose from a variety of genres available in the classroom library for independent reading to apply their learning.

Figure 15.8 Curriculum map for genre study, grade 5 *(cont.)*

continues

<table>
<tr><th colspan="3">CURRICULUM MAP FOR GENRE STUDY, GRADE 5</th></tr>
<tr><th>Month</th><th colspan="2">November</th></tr>
<tr><td>Time spent</td><td>3–4 weeks</td><td>1 week</td></tr>
<tr><td>Genre Study</td><td>Biography</td><td>Author, Illustrator, or Craft</td></tr>
<tr><td>Process</td><td>Collect a text set of biographies (including picture books, plays, short chapter books)

Immerse students in the text set during interactive read-aloud. Give book talks on biographies at a range of reading levels for independent reading.

Create a list of characteristics defining biography.

Co-construct a definition of biography.

Read and revise definition.

Teach a series of minilessons on one or two of the defining elements of biography.
For example:
• Subject
• Attitude, tone
• Illustrations
• Influence of setting
• Decision points
• Larger messages

Students choose from a variety of genres available in the classroom library for independent reading to apply their learning.</td><td>Author, Illustrator, or Craft Study: Collect a text set of books that represents the category you plan to study.

Immerse students in the text set during interactive read-aloud. Give book talks at a range of reading levels for independent reading.

Teach minilessons on subjects related to the study. For example:
• Literary elements
• Analyzing the author's or illustrator's craft
• Themes and messages across texts
• Making connections across texts by the same author or illustrator

Help students notice the genres of the texts.

Students choose from a variety of genres available in the classroom library for independent reading to apply their learning.</td></tr>
</table>

Figure 15.8 Curriculum map for genre study, grade 5 *(cont.)*

CURRICULUM MAP FOR GENRE STUDY, GRADE 5			
Month	**December**	**January**	
Time spent	**3 weeks**	**1–2 weeks**	**3 weeks**
Genre Study	**Historical Fiction**	**Author, Illustrator, or Craft Study**	**Expository Texts: Feature Articles** (or other forms of expository texts)
Process	Collect a text set of historical fiction texts (including picture books, plays, short stories, and short chapter books). Immerse students in the text set during interactive read-aloud. Give book talks on historical fiction at a range of reading levels for independent reading. Create a list of characteristics defining historical fiction. Co-construct a definition of historical fiction. Read and revise definition. Teach a series of minilessons on one or two of the defining elements of historical fiction. For example: • Characters • Setting • Plot and problem resolution • Themes and messages • Tone • Mood • Perspective • Illustrations • Style/Language Students choose from a variety of genres available in the classroom library for independent reading to apply their learning.	*Author, Illustrator, or Craft Study:* Collect a text set of books that represents the category you plan to study. Immerse students in the text set during interactive read-aloud. Give book talks at a range of reading levels for independent reading. Teach minilessons on subjects related to the study. For example: • Literary elements • Analyzing the author's craft • Themes and messages across texts • Making connections across texts by the same author Help students notice the genres of the texts. Students choose from a variety of genres available in the classroom library for independent reading to apply their learning.	Collect four or five examples of feature articles from newspapers, magazines, etc. (or collect examples of other expository texts). Immerse students in this genre through interactive read-aloud. Provide access to feature articles in print and online at a range of reading levels for independent reading. Create a list of characteristics defining feature articles (or other forms of expository texts). Co-construct a definition of feature articles as one type of nonfiction. Read and revise definition. Teach a series of minilessons on one or two of the defining elements of feature articles. For example: • Information in text • Text structure • Big ideas • Tone, voice, and attitude • Text features Students choose from a variety of genres available in the classroom library for independent reading to apply their learning.

Figure 15.8 Curriculum map for genre study, grade 5 *(cont.)*

continues

CURRICULUM MAP FOR GENRE STUDY, GRADE 5		
Month	**February**	
Time spent	**1–2 weeks**	**2-3 weeks**
Genre Study	**Author, Illustrator, or Craft Study**	**Tests**
Process	*Author, Illustrator, or Craft Study:* Collect a text set of books that represents the category you plan to study. Immerse students in the text set during interactive read-aloud. Teach minilessons on subjects related to the study. For example: • Literary elements • Analyzing the author's or illustrator's craft • Themes and messages across texts • Making connections across texts by the same author or illustrator Help students notice the genres of the texts. Students choose from a variety of genres available in the classroom library for independent reading to apply their learning.	Collect several examples of test questions. Give students the opportunity to look at the tests and try them. Create a list of characteristics defining the "testing genre." Co-construct a definition for tests as a genre. Teach minilessons around analyzing the language of testing, testing strategies, and the defining characteristics of the testing genre. Students choose from a variety of genres available in the classroom library for independent reading to apply their learning.

Figure 15.8 Curriculum map for genre study, grade 5 *(cont.)*

CURRICULUM MAP FOR GENRE STUDY, GRADE 5			
Month	**March**		**April**
Time spent	**3–4 weeks**	**1–2 weeks**	**3–4 weeks**
Genre Study	**Legends, Epics, Ballads, Myths**	**Author, Illustrator, or Craft Study**	**Persuasive Texts**
Process	Collect a text set of legends, epics, ballads, or myths (including picture books, plays, short stories, and short chapter books). Immerse students in the text set during interactive read-aloud. Give book talks on books in this genre at a range of reading levels for independent reading. Create a list of characteristics defining legends, epics, ballads, or myths. Co-construct a definition of legends, epics, ballads, or myths. Read and revise definition. Teach a series of minilessons on one or two of the defining elements of legends, epics, ballads, or myths. For example: • Characters/Heroes/Gods • Setting • Plot and Problem resolution (good v. evil) • Themes and messages (reflections of culture/society) • Symbolism • Style/Language • Common motifs	*Author, Illustrator, or Craft Study:* Collect a text set of books that represents the category you plan to study. Immerse students in the text set during interactive read-aloud. Help students notice the genres of the texts. Teach minilessons on subjects related to the study. For example: • Literary elements • Analyzing the author's or illustrator's craft • Themes and messages across texts • Making connections across texts by the same author or illustrator Students choose from a variety of genres available in the classroom library for independent reading to apply their learning.	Collect examples of persuasive texts from picture books, newspapers, magazines, online, etc. Immerse students in this genre through interactive read-aloud. Provide access to persuasive texts in print and online for students' independent reading. Create a list of characteristics defining persuasive texts. Co-construct a definition of persuasive texts. Read and revise definition. Teach a series of minilessons on one or two of the defining elements of persuasive texts. For example: • Information in text • Text structure • Message • Perspective • Tone, voice, and attitude • Evaluating logic, accuracy, completeness • Language/Style Students choose from a variety of genres available in the classroom library for independent reading to apply their learning.

Figure 15.8 Curriculum map for genre study, grade 5 *(cont.)*

continues

CURRICULUM MAP FOR GENRE STUDY, GRADE 5		
Month	**May**	**June**
Time spent	**3–4 weeks**	**4 weeks**
Genre Study	**Fantasy**	**Narrative Nonfiction or Author Study, Illustrator, or Craft Study**
Process	Note: You will want to decide whether you want to simply label this genre "fantasy" or distinguish between modern fantasy and traditional literature for your students. Collect a set of fantasy texts. Immerse students in the text set during interactive read-aloud. Give book talks on texts in this genre at a range of reading levels for independent reading. Create a list of characteristics defining fantasy. Co-construct a definition of fantasy. Read and revise definition. Teach a series of minilessons on one or two of the defining elements of fantasy. For example: • Characters • Setting • Plot and problem resolution • Themes, lessons, messages • Common motifs • Style/Language Students choose from a variety of genres available in the classroom library for independent reading to apply their learning.	Follow the process for author, illustrator, or craft study noted previously. Or Collect a text set of narrative nonfiction texts. Immerse students in this genre through interactive read-aloud. Provide book talks on narrative nonfiction for a range of reading for students' independent reading. Create a list of characteristics defining narrative nonfiction. Co-construct a definition of narrative nonfiction. Read and revise definition. Teach a series of minilessons on one or two of the defining elements of narrative nonfiction. For example: • Text structure • Information in text • Message • Tone, voice, and attitude • Evaluating accuracy • Language/Style Students choose from a variety of genres available in the classroom library for independent reading to apply their learning.

Figure 15.8 Curriculum map for genre study, grade 5 *(cont.)*

EXAMPLE OF A GENRE STUDY OF REALISTIC FICTION			
	Interactive Read-Aloud	**Reader's Workshop**	**Writer's Workshop**
Week 1	*Genre Study:* Immerse students in realistic fiction texts (Matt spent the weeks leading up to this study collecting a text set of realistic fiction books.)	*Book Talks:* Realistic fiction texts at a range of reading levels for independent reading. *Minilessons:* Matt has been teaching a series of minilessons on how writers use punctuation to show meaning (craft) that he will continue until he is ready to bring the learning from genre study into readers' workshop (after students have an understanding of the characteristics and a definition for the genre.) *Independent Reading:* Students begin to explore realistic fiction texts during independent reading. Matt makes sure his classroom library contains many baskets of realistic fiction on a variety of topics at a range of reading levels. *Book Clubs:* Matt decides to begin book clubs in his class around realistic fiction to further explore the genre. *Share:* Students share examples of writers' use of punctuation in relation to the minilessons at the beginning of the week. As the students become more familiar with realistic fiction in their book clubs and independent reading, they begin to share examples of realistic fiction during group share.	Students work on finishing a writing project that they might already be writing and begin planting seeds in their writer's notebook in preparation for writing their own fiction stories.
Weeks 2–3	*Genre Study:* At the beginning of the week, Matt helps his students create a list of the characteristics of realistic fiction based on the clear examples they have heard the week before. They work together to construct a definition of realistic fiction.	*Book Talks:* Realistic fiction texts at a range of reading levels for independent reading. *Minilessons:* While Matt works on listing the characteristics and defining realistic fiction with his students during interactive read-aloud. He spends the first two days of this week finishing his minilesson series on the craft of punctuation during readers' workshop. After he is confident his students have a working definition of realistic fiction, he further integrates the learning into readers' workshop by incorporating it into his reading minilessons. He decides to focus on	Students work on finishing a writing project they might already be writing and begin planting seeds in their writer's notebook in preparation for writing their own fiction stories.

Figure 15.9 Example of a genre study of realistic fiction

continues

EXAMPLE OF A GENRE STUDY OF REALISTIC FICTION			
	Interactive Read-Aloud	**Reader's Workshop**	**Writer's Workshop**
Weeks 2–3	During his planning time, Matt begins collecting a text set for his upcoming author study. He plans to study Judith Viorst, since she writes many realistic fiction books, to continue immersing students in realistic fiction during the author study.	two elements of realistic fiction over the remainder of this week and next week based on his students' noticings: character and plot/problem/resolution. Each day's minilessons for the remainder of this week and next week address a different aspect (what characters do, what they say or think, how they look, what others say about them, how they change) of the following umbrella minilesson principle. *Readers notice how the writer shows what the characters are like to help them understand realistic fiction.* (See Figure 15.13 for a detailed look at this minilesson.) *Independent Reading:* Students continue reading realistic fiction during independent reading and begin applying what they learn about characters to their own reading. *Book Clubs:* Matt supports students in thinking about characters during their realistic fiction book clubs. *Share:* At the beginning of the week, students continue to share examples of characters and how writers show what they are like in realistic fiction from their independent reading. As the minilessons begin focusing on character in realistic fiction, the students share about the characters in their books with examples related to the minilesson principle.	

Figure 15.9 Example of a genre study of realistic fiction *(cont.)*

EXAMPLE OF A GENRE STUDY OF REALISTIC FICTION

	Interactive Read-Aloud	Reader's Workshop	Writer's Workshop
Week 4	*Genre Study:* Matt continues to immerse students in realistic fiction texts and the class works to revise the definition according to new discoveries and understandings. Toward the end of the week, Matt begins to read books from the Judith Viorst text set for his upcoming author study.	*Book Talks:* Realistic fiction texts at a range of reading levels for independent reading. *Minilessons:* Matt uses the first two days of the week to finish looking at character in realistic fiction and then, begins focusing on plot/problem and resolution in relation to their definition of realistic fiction. He and his students and he co-construct the umbrella minilesson principle: *Readers think about the plot of a story, particularly the problem(s) and resolution(s), to help them understand a realistic fiction story.* Over the remainder of the week and possibly into part of the next week, Matt's related minilessons address: • How to identify the main problem(s) of a story • Noticing the most exciting place in the story—often the resolution • Noticing how characters respond to the problem/resolution (bringing together last week's work around characters and this week's work around plot) *Independent Reading:* Students continue reading Realistic Fiction during independent reading and try applying new understandings from the minilessons to their own reading. *Guided Reading:* Matt tries to select leveled realistic fiction texts when possible to share with his guided reading groups. *Share:* Students begin the week by sharing about the characters in their books in application of the day's minilesson. As the minilessons shift to addressing plot/problem/resolution in Realistic Fiction, they begin sharing about the problem and resolution in their independent reading.	Students begin a discovery draft of a fiction piece.

Figure 15.9 Example of a genre study of realistic fiction *(cont.)*

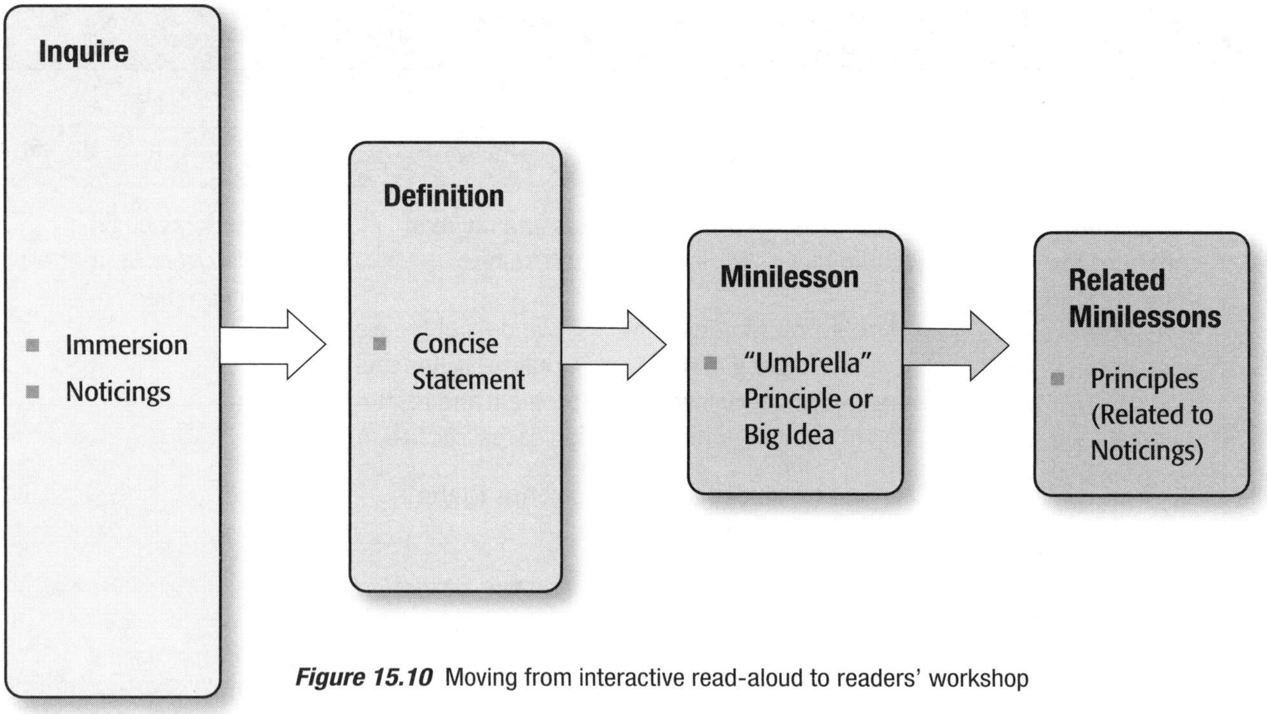

Figure 15.10 Moving from interactive read-aloud to readers' workshop

discussions of more picture books or longer texts during reading workshop, and they share examples of these elements from their own independent reading.

Toward the end of the inquiry period, Matt asks students to summarize what they notice about all of the realistic fiction books they experienced, and they construct a list of noticings (see Figure 15.11).

Having been grounded in several shared texts and having made an explicit list of characteristics together, Matt and the students next come up with a working definition of realistic fiction, which takes some time. The definition includes the important ideas and the essential elements and is concise (see Figure 15.12).

The grounding texts, the list of characteristics, and the definition set the scene for two or three weeks of powerful teaching

Building on the list of characteristics and the definition, Matt decides to focus on two important elements of realistic fiction for his reading minilessons and group share over the next two weeks: character and plot/problem and resolution. He decides character will be a good place to start exploring realistic fiction since he feels it is an accessible subject for his students based on their previous experiences and will help them analyze and critique the author's craft in creating a realistic fiction story. He has also noticed many of his students struggling with inference. He hopes discussing character in relation to realistic fiction will not only strengthen their understanding of the genre but will give them specific opportunities to support their ability to infer understandings of character and character change from text. To launch his formal study of realistic fiction during readers' workshop, he presents an umbrella minilesson on character (see Figure 15.13). In this lesson, he links the umbrella lesson and its principle to previous inquiry work, asking students to read their definition of realistic fiction and discuss what they already know about characters in realistic fiction texts.

These students clearly understand quite a bit about characters in realistic fiction (although their knowledge may be somewhat superficial). Most do not yet know how this information will be useful to them as readers (and ultimately as writers). Matt spends several days developing the students' understanding of character using the mentor texts from the inquiry study as examples to demonstrate the minilesson principles related to this umbrella lesson (See Figure 15.14 for a more detailed look at this week-long focus on character). Matt's goal is to keep the information developed during minilessons accessible during the

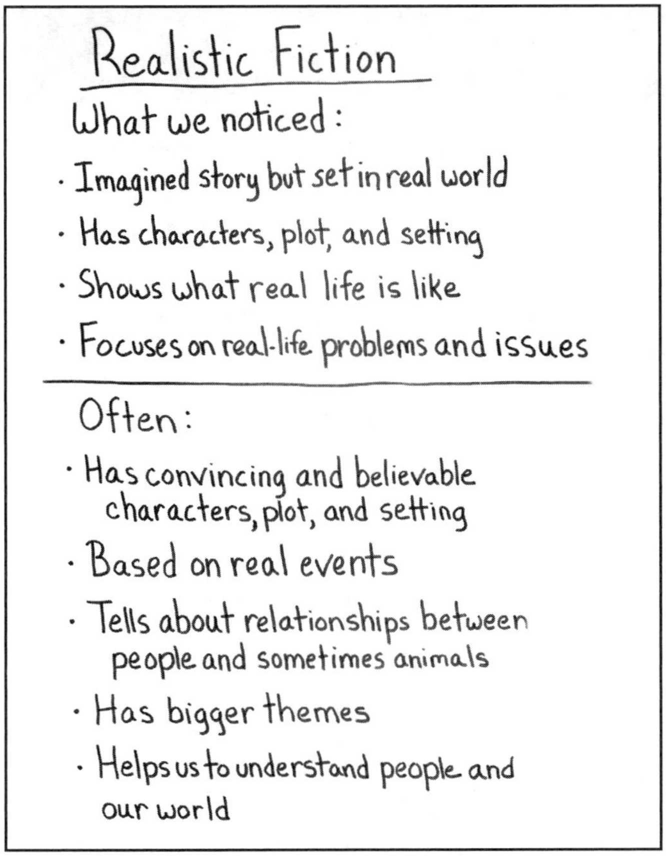
Realistic Fiction
What we noticed:
· Imagined story but set in real world
· Has characters, plot, and setting
· Shows what real life is like
· Focuses on real-life problems and issues
Often:
· Has convincing and believable characters, plot, and setting
· Based on real events
· Tells about relationships between people and sometimes animals
· Has bigger themes
· Helps us to understand people and our world

Figure 15.11 Noticings about realistic fiction

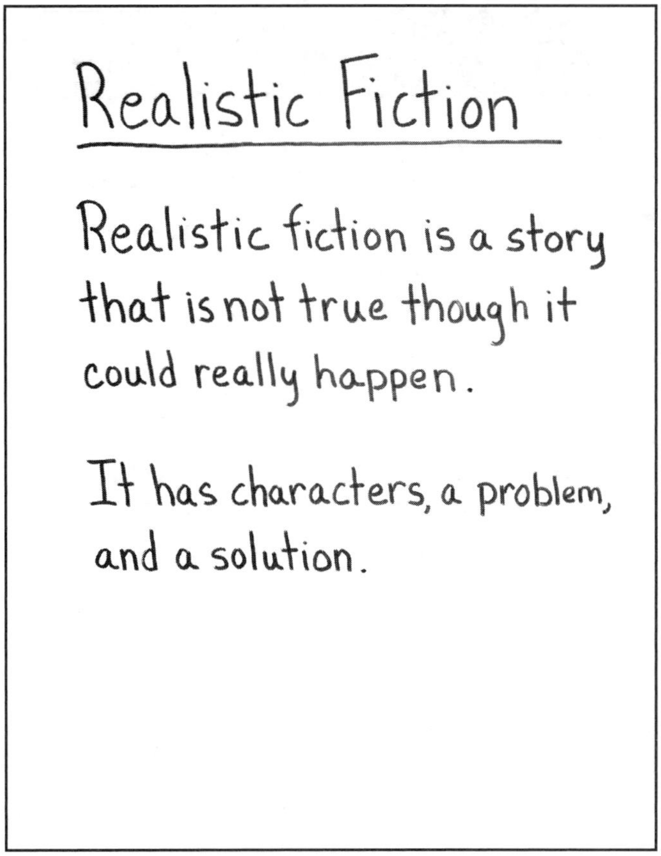
Realistic Fiction
Realistic fiction is a story that is not true though it could really happen.
It has characters, a problem, and a solution.

Figure 15.12 Working definition of realistic fiction

work periods. Application time really means reading and/or writing about reading in connection with the minilesson principles. The minilessons put an intentional framework around the reading.

While students are reading independently, Matt has as many individual conferences as possible to support individuals and ensure students will be able to share their thinking clearly when he calls them back together. He makes sure he talks with students who he thinks may have difficulty applying the minilesson principle to their own reading. At the end of the workshop, students meet for a brief sharing period. Matt allows plenty of time to share because he thinks it's important for students to apply and hear one another's thinking about the principle. Alternatively, he could have students share their thinking in twos or threes so that everyone gets a chance to talk. When students have read books that are not realistic fiction, Matt resists the temptation to talk at length about these other texts. The goal is to focus on characters in realistic fiction. When students are confused about the genre they are reading or can't decide about the genre, Matt quickly notes that he will need to confer with these students individually or address some of their confusion during guided reading. A couple of Matt's students are reading hybrid texts—a blend of fiction and nonfiction genres with the same text. Matt helps them to think about character within the context of these texts by clarifying which parts of the book are fiction and which are nonfiction. He tells students they will talk more later about texts that combine genres.

Through this series of minilessons (first on character, and then on plot/problem/resolution), Matt knows that in addition to learning more about realistic fiction, his students are learning about important aspects of character and plot that will also carry into other genres (for example, biography or historical fiction). Though he doesn't mention this to his students now, he will undoubtedly refer back to the learning from this series of minilessons as his students explore other genres throughout the year.

EXCERPT FROM AN UMBRELLA MINILESSON ON CHARACTER DURING REALISTIC FICTION GENRE STUDY

TEACHER:	We have read many realistic fiction books and you have noticed a lot about what they are like. Rachel, would you read the definition we wrote for realistic fiction based on what we know now?
RACHEL:	[Reads] "Realistic fiction is a story that is not true though it could really happen. It has characters, a problem, and a solution."
TEACHER:	So, if you know that a text is realistic fiction, you know to expect some things. One of the things we wrote in our definition is that realistic fiction texts have characters. Over the next few days, we are going to spend time thinking about characters in the books we are reading. What are some things you already know about most of the characters in realistic fiction from the books we have shared?
CATHY:	They will have a problem to solve, or they might have more than one problem but the big problem will be solved before the book ends.
LEAH:	There will be important characters and less important characters.
RENE:	The characters will like each other or they might not be nice to each other. They seem real.
OSCAR:	The main character usually changes or learns something by the end.
FRANKIE:	They usually talk with other characters.
TEACHER:	You already know a lot about what we will be talking about this week. Have you ever thought about how the writer helps you to get to know the characters in the books we have read? This week, we will be looking closely at realistic fiction, finding evidence for our thinking, and analyzing how writers reveal characters to us. Would someone like to read the minilesson principle for this week? Stan?
STAN:	Readers think about the ways authors provide information about characters to help them understand realistic fiction.
TEACHER:	What words or phrases stand out for you from this statement? [Reads the minilesson principle again.]
FRANKIE:	Authors provide information about characters.
TEACHER:	I am going to highlight that part of the principle. Writers don't just tell you about the characters, they show you. Let's look at the character Meg in *Courage to Fly*. What is Meg like at the beginning of the story?
MARIAH:	She's scared all the time.
TRAVIS:	She doesn't want to play with any of the other kids—she's shy.
TEACHER:	That's right. How do you know that?
RACHEL:	It says she's like a frightened bird. And you can tell she's shy because she always said no when the girl down the hall asked her to play.
OSCAR:	Some kids from her class call her "Nutty Meg."
TEACHER:	All of these things help you get a sense of what Meg is like at the beginning of the story. Today when you're reading your realistic fiction book, I'd like you to first identify who the main character is and then think about how the writer shows you what the character is like. Be prepared to talk with a partner and share with the group at the end of writers' workshop.

Minilesson Principle

Readers think about the ways authors provide information about characters to help them understand realistic fiction.

Figure 15.13 Excerpt from an umbrella minilesson on character during realistic fiction genre study

WEEK-LONG FOCUS ON CHARACTER IN REALISTIC FICTION			
Week-long Focus on Character within Realistic Fiction Genre Study	**Minilesson Statements**	**Teacher Decision-Making and Thought Process**	**Strategic Actions Engaged/Supported Through Minilesson** *Note: Though students will have to engage all of the strategic actions simultaneously and flexibly in order to fully understand their reading, specific minilessons will help support some areas of strategic actions in particular.*
Day 1	**Umbrella Minilesson:** Readers notice how the writer provides information about the characters to help them understand realistic fiction. (see Figure 15.13 for a look at this lesson in more detail)	Matt introduces this umbrella minilesson based on the students' noticings about character. He hopes looking more closely at characters in relation to realistic fiction will not only strengthen his students' understanding of the genre but will also give them opportunities to strengthen their ability to infer from text, an area with which his students need support.	• Inferring • Synthesizing • Analyzing • Critiquing
Day 2	**Related Minilesson:** Readers notice what characters do and what they say to understand what they are like.	Matt decides to start by looking at how authors give readers clues about the characters from their actions and dialogue. He is hoping this lesson will support his readers in inferring from the text. Matt has also noticed his students struggle with finding evidence from the text to support their thinking. By looking closely at the character's dialogue and actions, he will help students stay grounded in the text and find evidence to support their thinking. Matt uses the mentor texts they have already read during the immersion process to illustrate the minilesson principles. Though Matt decided to spend one day on this minilesson principle, he could have easily broken this down further over two or three days if he felt his students needed that level of support.	• Searching for and Using Information • Inferring • Synthesizing

Figure 15.14 Week-long focus on character in realistic fiction

continues

WEEK-LONG FOCUS ON CHARACTER IN REALISTIC FICTION			
Day 3	**Related Minilesson:** Readers notice what other characters think about or do to the main character to learn more about the main character.	Matt feels his students will benefit from looking at other ways characters are revealed in the text not only to support their ability to infer, but to help them think in more depth about the craft of realistic fiction. He plans to revisit the concepts raised in Day 2 and Day 3 of readers' workshop during writers' workshop so that students will begin thinking about how to reveal their own main characters through action, dialogue, and interaction with other characters. Again, he will use the same set of realistic fiction mentor texts for both readers' and writers' workshop.	• Searching for and Using Information • Inferring • Synthesizing
Day 4	**Related Minilesson:** Readers notice how the writer makes the characters seem real to think about the quality of the story.	After Matt spent time developing his students' ability to infer what characters are like and how they change in realistic fiction, he felt they were ready to think more critically about author's craft. In this minilesson, he demonstrates how to analyze whether a character seems real using some of the understandings that developed around characters' actions and dialogue during the previous three days. He wants his readers to think critically about how writers craft realistic characters not only to develop their critical eye as readers, but so they can also revisit this in crafting their own characters during writers workshop.	• Searching for and Using Information • Analyzing • Critiquing
Day 5	**Related Minilesson:** Readers think about how characters change to understand the meaning of the story.	Matt has also noticed his students need support in synthesizing information to form new understandings about text. As students look at character development, they will need to gather information from several parts of the story, synthesize it and come to new understandings about characters. He also thinks looking at character development will further support their understanding of plot and help them think deeper about the craft of realistic fiction.	• Searching for and Using Information • Inferring • Synthesizing

Figure 15.14 Week-long focus on character in realistic fiction *(cont.)*

Mapping a Sequence of Minilessons

As teachers, you can see the big picture if you plan a sequence of genre studies in advance and then identify some possible lessons. You need to see the relationships among principles if you are going to help students. Therefore, collect text sets and jot down observations you think are important to help students generate. Of course, they will come up with more or word them differently, and it's important when you make the chart to use their words unless the words are confusing. Creating the chart is a negotiation between you and your students. The same is true of minilesson principles, which can be expressed in several ways.

Let's now look at Matt's preplanning and overall structure for studies of realistic fiction, historical fiction, and folktales as examples (Figures 15.15, 15.17, and 15.19). These plans provide Matt with some guidelines as he goes through the inquiry process with his students. As we saw from his four-week study of realistic fiction, he could not possibly teach every element of realistic fiction or he would be spending a year studying one genre. The planning laid out in Figures 15.15, 15.17, and 15.19 allows him to think about his students' understandings about the genre in more depth and also helps him to support his students' developing systems of strategic actions. He will select the minilesson principles he thinks will best support his readers where they are in their learning. Having these in-depth plans across genres helps him to see where he might be able to revisit a literary element in more depth or address one he wasn't able to get to in an earlier study.

Studying Realistic Fiction

The diagram in Figure 15.15 illustrates Matt's planning of a realistic fiction genre study. Notice the coherence of his plan. The reading workshop minilessons provide explicit, direct teaching, but they rest on solid knowledge of examples and the students' experience during the genre study inquiry. The characteristics and definition are theirs, and Matt easily turns them into clear, explicit principles, each of which will be a follow-up minilesson.

Of course, the study of the literary elements of realistic fiction and the fiction writer's craft continues over several years. You could spend the entire year studying realistic fiction, but that is impossible: students need broader genre knowledge. Fortunately, as you move on to other genres, there are always ties back to the learning about realistic fiction. For example:

- Historical fiction has many of the same characteristics. The primary difference is the setting (time period).
- Fantasy also has many of the same characteristics, but the setting and/or characters could not exist in the real world.
- Biography requires understanding the setting to appreciate the decisions the subject had to make.

You can create continuous connections between genres while at the same time helping students contrast them to see what makes a genre unique.

You might focus on a genre like realistic fiction for a few weeks, but it depends on the grade level and the experience of the students. Within the time you allot, spend only a few days on some elements (see Figure 15.16) and much more time on others. Come back to the concepts related to revealing and understanding characters and their development many times; students benefit from the study of characters several times a year every year in greater complexity and with more sophisticated texts.

It's important to remember that you can start with any genre of fiction. Matt chose realistic fiction because he thought it would be most accessible to his group. But when he goes on to study historical fiction or fantasy, he'll find that everything they learned about the elements—characters, setting, etc.—also apply to those genres. In fact, the contrast helps students understand the unique and distinctive features that define genres.

<table>
<tr><th colspan="4">FROM INTERACTIVE READ-ALOUD TO READERS' WORKSHOP: REALISTIC FICTION</th></tr>
<tr><th>Inquiry</th><th colspan="3">Definition</th></tr>
<tr><td rowspan="5">What we noticed about realistic fiction:
• Tells a story that could be true
• Takes place in the real world
• Shows what real life is like
• Focuses on real-life problems and issues
• Has narrative structure with characters, plot, and setting
• Has important characters and less important characters
• Has characters that have feelings about each other
• Shows and tells what characters are like
• Sometimes shows how characters change and tells why
• Takes place somewhere that is described
• Sometimes where the story takes place is very important in the story and sometimes it isn't</td><td colspan="3">Realistic fiction is a story that is not true but has characters, a problem, and a solution that could be real.</td></tr>
<tr><th colspan="2">Minilessons to Extend Learning About Realistic Fiction</th><th>Strategic Actions Supported</th></tr>
<tr><td>Characters</td><td>• Readers decide who the important characters are and think about why they are important to help them understand the story.
• Readers think about what the characters are like to help them understand the story.
• Readers notice whether characters seem real to think about the quality of the fiction story.
• Readers notice what characters say, think, and do to understand them.
• Readers think about what others say about or do to a character to learn more about them.
• Readers think about how characters change and why to help them understand the plot in fiction.</td><td>• Searching for and Using Information
• Inferring
• Critiquing

• Searching for and Using Information
• Summarizing
• Analyzing

• Searching for and Using Information
• Inferring

• Searching for and Using Information
• Inferring
• Synthesizing</td></tr>
<tr><td>Setting</td><td>• Readers think about when and where the story takes place to help them understand the story. This is called the setting.
• Readers think about whether the setting is important to help them understand the story.</td><td>• Searching for and Using Information
• Making Connections
• Analyzing</td></tr>
<tr><td>Plot and Problem Resolution</td><td>• Readers notice the problem to help them understand the meaning of a story.</td><td>• Searching for and Using Information
• Summarizing</td></tr>
</table>

Figure 15.15 From interactive read-aloud to readers' workshop: realistic fiction

FROM INTERACTIVE READ-ALOUD TO READERS' WORKSHOP: REALISTIC FICTION			
Inquiry	**Minilessons to Extend Learning About Realistic Fiction**		**Strategic Actions Supported**
• Has a problem that is resolved at the end; sometimes has one important problem and more related problems • Has a point in the story where things change and the problem is solved • Communicates one or more messages or big ideas • Sometimes the big ideas are not said but the writer shows the meaning • Shows how the writer feels about the story, the place it happened, or the characters • Can make you have feelings: happy, sad, afraid • Sometimes the story is told by one of the characters ("I") and sometimes it's just told by the writer ("they," "he," "she") • You can picture it happening • Sometimes gives more information in the pictures	**Plot and Problem Resolution,** *(cont.)*	• Readers think about the main or most important problems to help them understand the meaning of the story. • Readers notice the exciting point in a story where the problem is solved to help them understand the story.	• Searching for and Using Information • Summarizing • Searching for and Using Information • Summarizing • Analyzing
	Themes and Messages	• Readers think about the author's message to help them understand the story. • Readers think about what the author really meant but did not say to help them understand the important messages in the story.	• Inferring • Synthesizing • Inferring
	Tone	• Readers notice how the story makes them feel to help them think about the story.	• Inferring • Analyzing
	Mood	• Readers notice what the writer feels about the story and the characters to help them think about its meaning.	• Inferring • Synthesizing • Analyzing
	Point of View	• Readers notice who is telling the story to help them understand it. • Readers notice when an outside person (writer) is telling about the people in the story so they can understand the point of view. • Readers notice when the writer tells about the feelings and actions of one character so that they can understand the point of view. • Readers notice when a character is telling the story so that they can understand the point of view.	• Searching for and Using Information • Analyzing
	Illustrations	• Readers think about the information in the pictures and how they make them feel, to help them understand the story.	• Inferring • Analyzing

Figure 15.15 From interactive read-aloud to readers' workshop: realistic fiction *(cont.)*

ELEMENTS OF REALISTIC FICTION	
Characters	• Readers notice the characters in the story—the people or animals—so they can understand the problem. • Readers think about whether the characters seem real to help them understand the story. • Readers decide who the important characters are (main characters) so they can think about the story problem. • Readers think about why the main characters are important to help them understand the problem in the story. • Readers think about how writers reveal what characters are like—through telling how they look, what they say, do or think and what others say about them. • Readers think about the less important characters in a story to help understand their role in the plot. These are minor characters. • Readers think about how the characters feel about each other to help them understand the story problem and solution. • Readers think about how characters change to help them understand the plot and resolution. • Readers think about why characters change to help them understand the plot. • Readers notice how the writer tells or shows readers what the characters are like to help them understand the craft of realistic fiction.
Setting	• Readers think about the setting—when and where the story takes place to help them understand the story. • Readers think about whether the setting is important in the story to help them understand it. • Readers identify the characteristics of the setting that are important to the plot or that affect the characters so that they can understand the story. • Readers think about whether a setting is familiar or unfamiliar to them and adjust their reading in order to get a full picture of what the setting is like. • Readers notice details about the setting of a story in order to picture it in their minds. • Readers think about how the conflict in a story is resolved to help them understand the messages of a text.
Plot	• Readers think about the problem or plot in a story to help them understand it. • Readers notice the problem to help them understand a realistic fiction story. • Readers think about the main or most important problems to help them understand the plot of the story. • Readers notice the exciting place in a book where the problem is solved to help them understand the story. This is called the climax. • Readers identify the conflict in a story in order to understand what drives the plot (character against character; character against nature; character against society; character against himself—inner conflict). • Readers think about the conflict in the story to help them understand it. • Readers think about the different kinds of conflict to help them understand the story. • Readers identify the subplots in a story to help them understand it.

Figure 15.16 Elements of realistic fiction

ELEMENTS OF REALISTIC FICTION	
Plot *(cont.)*	• Readers identify how the events are presented in a story to help them understand the plot. • Readers identify different kinds of problems and plots to understand special types of realistic fiction (mystery, survival). • Readers notice when the same actions begin and end the story in order to understand that the story will repeat itself (circular plot). • Readers notice when a writer repeats lines and builds on them until the story ends in order to understand how it is organized (cumulative plot).
Theme	• Readers think about the theme or the author's message to understand what the story really means. • Readers notice more than one message or theme in a text to help them understand its full meaning. • Readers notice when an author states the theme or themes in the writing of a text to help them understand the writer's goal. • Readers think carefully about the specific language an author uses in order to understand exactly what the author is trying to say.
Point of View	• Readers notice the way an author tells the story in order to understand the writer's perspective or attitude. • Readers notice the person who tells the story in order to understand how the writer wanted readers to understand it. • Readers notice when a text is written in third person narrative in order to understand the action and all the characters ("he," "she," "they"). This is called third person. • Readers notice when the writer speaks directly to the reader in order to understand the writer's perspective ("you"). This is called second person. • Readers notice when a character in the story is a narrator in order to understand the character's perspective ("I," "me," "we," "us"). This is called first person. • Readers think about how the narrator shapes the information they get as readers in order to understand the point of view. • Readers consider the narrator's bias in order to understand the narrator's perspective. • Readers think about how the story might be different if the point of view changed in order to understand how the perspective shapes the story. • Readers critique the point of view of a story to think about its meaning.
Tone/Mood	• Readers think about how the story makes them feel to understand how the writer created the tone. • Readers think about the mood of a piece of writing in order to understand the author's writing style.
Style/ Language	• Readers notice the way the writer uses words and language in order to understand the author's writing style. • Readers notice the writing patterns in books in order to understand the author's style. • Readers think about how writers make things seem believable or real in order to make the story come alive.

Figure 15.16 Elements of realistic fiction *(cont.)*

Using Inquiry and Readers' Workshop to Study Historical Fiction

Historical fiction has the same elements as realistic fiction, but you have to adjust your understanding of them because of the historical setting. Historical fiction demands that you stretch your thinking to understand the perspectives of people who lived in the near or distant past. There are many high-quality historical fiction picture books available, from simple and easy to understand examples to very complex treatments of mature topics. A genre study of historical fiction can also be coordinated with curriculum goals for social studies or history.

As shown in the curricular plan in Figure 15.17, the same elements are important for all fiction. The only real difference is the setting, and the minilessons make it clear that the time and place have a big influence on readers' thinking.

With this in-depth approach, the learning in one area strengthens learning in another. If you've already presented an umbrella minilesson followed by a series of related minilessons on the elements of realistic fiction, students will bring a basic knowledge of elements like character and setting to their study of historical fiction. As students acquire more understanding, the process goes more quickly.

You might also conduct a broad inquiry into fiction using a text set that includes a variety of types of fiction; however, if students are novices with regard to genre study, it is probably better to start with texts that can be connected without "noise." Too many variables make it harder for students to see the common elements.

Begin by collecting a high quality text set with clear examples of the genre. Then immerse students in reading, discussing, and enjoying the books. The list of noticed characteristics in Figure 15.17 is an example that helps push students a little harder to think in different ways, but the list should be generated *with* students, not presented to them. Then move on to the definition, again using Figure 15.17 as a guide but allowing students to work through the process of creating their own.

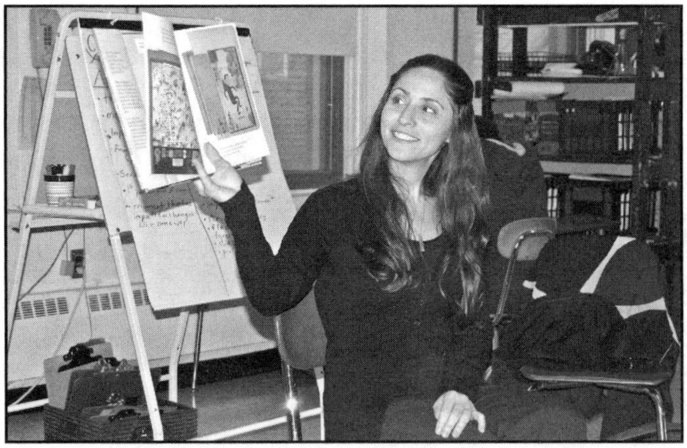

Provide a fairly large sample of historical fiction texts in the classroom library baskets for students' independent reading.

You can increase the intensity of the inquiry by:

- Reading aloud historical fiction books each day (even after minilessons begin).
- Teaching a daily minilesson on a specific characteristic of historical fiction.
- Having students read historical fiction in book clubs (either picture books they've heard read aloud or listened to on CD, or chapter books selected from a limited set).
- Selecting historical fiction for some guided reading lessons (if the level is appropriate).
- Having students read a book of historical fiction independently so they can apply the minilesson principle and present their thinking during group share.

Using Inquiry and Readers' Workshop to Study Traditional Literature

Traditional literature is one of the categories of fantasy. It describes stories passed down orally over time. (Modern fantasy includes animal fantasy, low or high fantasy, and science fiction). In early elementary school, most students have learned to tell the difference between stories that could or could not be real or true (fiction and nonfiction, or realism and fantasy). This

FROM INTERACTIVE READ-ALOUD TO READERS' WORKSHOP: HISTORICAL FICTION

Inquiry

- Tells a story that could be true
- Shows what life was like in the past
- Has narrative structure with characters, plot, and setting
- Focuses on problems and issues of life in the past

Often:

- Has convincing and believable characters, plot, and setting
- Based on real people or events from the past
- Connected to the author's own personal experiences
- Begins as contemporary fiction but has been around long enough to acquire historical significance
- Uses language of the times in dialogue

Definition

Historical fiction is an imagined story that shows life like it used to be, and focuses on the problems and issues of life in the past.

Minilessons to Extend Learning About Historical Fiction		Strategic Actions
Characters	• Readers think about what the characters are like so that they can tell whether the story seems real.	• Searching for and using information • Inferring • Critiquing
	• Readers think about whether the characters seem like real people who lived in the past so that they can understand history.	• Searching for and using information • Summarizing • Analyzing
	• Readers decide who the important characters are and think about why they are important to help them understand the story.	
	• Readers think about how the characters feel about each other to help them understand the story.	• Searching for and using information • Inferring
	• Readers think about how characters change and why; so they can understand the plot in historical fiction.	• Searching for and using information • Inferring • Synthesizing
	• Readers notice how the writer shows that characters lived in the past so that they can identify historical fiction.	
Setting	• Readers think about when and where the story takes place and if it has happened in the past to help them understand the story. This is called the setting and it is very important in historical fiction.	• Searching for and using information • Making connections • Analyzing
	• Readers recognize the setting for the story and think of what they know about it so they can understand the story.	• Synthesizing
	• Readers think about the important role of the setting to help them understand history.	• Analyzing
	• Readers think about how the writer shows that characters are people who lived in the past (how they talk, how they look and behave) to help them understand what life was like in the past.	• Searching for and using information

Figure 15.17 From interactive read-aloud to readers' workshop: historical fiction

continues

FROM INTERACTIVE READ-ALOUD TO READERS' WORKSHOP: HISTORICAL FICTION		
Minilessons to Extend Learning About Realistic Fiction		**Strategic Actions**
Plot and Problem Resolution	• Readers think about the problem of the story and how it fits into the past to help them understand historical fiction. • Readers think about the events that took place in the past to help them understand the plot of historical fiction.	• Searching for and using information • Summarizing
	• Readers notice the point in the where the problem is solved to help them understand the story. • Readers think about whether the problem is solved in a way it would have in the past so that they can understand historical fiction.	• Searching for and using information • Analyzing
	• Readers think about how the author shows time in a story so that they can understand the plot. • Readers think about the choices characters have within their setting so that they can understand the plot.	• Analyzing
Themes and Messages	• Readers think about the importance of the author's messages for today's world so they can learn from historical fiction. • Readers think about what the author really means but does not say to help them understand the important messages in the story.	• Inferring • Synthesizing
	• Readers recognize recurring lessons from the past so that they can understand history and its implications for today.	• Inferring • Synthesizing
Mood	• Readers think about how the story makes them feel to help them understand the story. • Readers think about how and why their feelings toward characters or events change as they read so that they can understand the overall feeling developed by the writer.	• Inferring • Synthesizing • Analyzing
Point of View	• Readers notice who is telling the story to help them understand the problem or plot. • Readers notice when an outside person (writer) is telling about the people in the story so they can understand the point of view. • Readers notice when the writer tells about the feelings and actions of one character so that they can understand the point of view. • Readers notice when a character is telling the story so that they can understand the point of view.	• Searching for and using information • Analyzing
Illustrations	• Readers think about the information in the pictures and how they make them feel to help them understand the story and the setting.	• Inferring • Analyzing

Figure 15.17 From interactive read-aloud to readers' workshop: historical fiction *(cont.)*

distinction may seem simple, but it requires students to compare stories with their own experience and what they know about the world. When you consider that many children begin school believing that beings like fairies and Santa Claus could be real, helping them sorting fantasy from realism is no easy task. If students are not clear on what makes a text a fantasy, you can quickly make a visible comparison like the one in Figure 15.18. This kind of chart can be revisited as new fantasy elements are discovered and students learn more labels related to genre.

You can approach the study of fantasy the same way you study realistic and historical fiction. Children hear folktales from the time they are born—stories with simple plots and flat characters who don't really change. Even young children can understand these simple texts. Many kindergarten, first-grade, and second-grade teachers read several versions of stories like "The Three Little Pigs" and children compare them. In the process, students internalize many of the elements of folktales, such as talking animals, simple conflicts, happy endings, victory for the weaker or smaller characters, and repetitive language.

When you study fantasy, however, the variety and complexity becomes evident. In many ways, fantasy is the most complex and demanding fiction genre. Readers must suspend disbelief and temporarily treat as true plots, characters, and settings that are unreal. You enter unreal worlds and need to understand and remember their parameters. (In high-quality fantasy, nothing can violate the "rules" of the fantasy world.) Fantasy often involves the struggle between good and evil, literary devices such as symbolism, and lofty language.

Characters in fantasy are often larger than life and undertake impossible quests; most of them fall neatly into the category of good or bad, but that doesn't mean they are simple. They may have weaknesses and flaws to overcome; they make big mistakes, for which they pay. Fantasy can follow a very structured form that involves adventure, but you must recognize underlying universal themes, such as the struggle between good and evil. Often, novels of fantasy are quite long (many are part of series totaling thousands of pages) and involve multiple quests and battles as the plot moves toward final resolution.

Traditional literature is a great place to start an inquiry into fantasy because it forms a strong foundation for understanding the entire genre. The roots of fantasy lie in traditional literature, which encompasses folktales, fairy tales, fables, legends, epics, ballads, and myths. A common characteristic of all these forms is that they originated as oral stories and were shared and passed down orally over many generations. Now, of course, there are written versions, and there are

COMPARING FANTASY AND REALISM

Could Be Real or True	Could Not Be Real or True
▪ Real people ▪ Real animals ▪ Places that are like the real world today or in the past • Realistic Fiction • Historical Fiction	▪ Fairies, giants, elves ▪ People that can fly or do magic ▪ Animals who talk or act like people ▪ People that become animals or animals that become people ▪ Impossible tasks ▪ Magic • Folktales • Fairy Tales • Fables • Legends, Epics, Ballads • Myths • Modern Fantasy • Science Fiction

Figure 15.18 Comparing fantasy and realism

Historic Fiction
What we noticed
Imaginary story that could be real
Has characters, plot, and setting
Shows life like it was
Tells about problems people had in the past

modern tales that are written in the *style* of the original oral tales. Modern fantasy and science fiction (as well as many works of poetry and realistic and historical fiction) allude to traditional literature, and the time you spend on traditional literature pays off when students study modern fantasy and other genres. As students learn more, they can sort traditional literature into subcategories that will help them analyze characteristics in greater detail, always realizing that some texts are difficult to place into just one category.

A plan for studying folktales, beginning with inquiry, is laid out in Figure 15.19. Because of the wide variety of folktales it is important to remember that every characteristic is not in every tale and those that are not always present are listed under "often" (see Chapter 8).

As with realism, you can examine many of the story elements, but your minilessons should help students see these elements in the light of an unreal world in which impossible things exist and can happen. Folktales also reveal the values of a group of people. They teach what is good and right. They use patterned language and often use repetition, possibly to help people remember and tell them without the help of written language.

Once you have presented broad minilessons related to the literary elements, your students can study more detailed aspects of folktales—motifs or particular forms, for example. (See Chapter 8). The minilessons you use for this and other genres that build upon your genre study will ultimately deepen your students' knowledge and understanding of a variety of literary genres and elements.

<table>
<tr><th colspan="4">FROM INTERACTIVE READ-ALOUD TO READERS' WORKSHOP:
LEARNING ABOUT FOLKTALES</th></tr>
<tr><th>Inquiry</th><th colspan="3">Definition</th></tr>
<tr><td rowspan="6">What we noticed about folktales:
• Imagined story that features characters and events that could not exist in the real world
• Has narrative structure, written or oral, handed down over many years
• Has simple, easy-to-follow plot
• Shows triumph of good over evil
• Shows goodness rewarded and evil punished
• Has characters who are flat and do not develop
• Quickly establishes time and place, and characters and conflict
• Has brief conclusion
• Uses repetition (of words, numbers, verses, responses, chants, and poems)
• Uses recurring motifs (magical powers, transformations, magical objects, wishes, trickery)</td><td colspan="3">A folktale is an imagined story handed down over many years that shows good winning over evil, some kind of repetition, and recurring elements or motifs.</td></tr>
<tr><th colspan="2">Minilessons to Extend Learning About Folktales</th><th>Strategic Actions</th></tr>
<tr><td>Types</td><td>• Beast tales
• Cumulative tales
• Pourquoi tales
• Trickster tales
• Noodlehead tales
• Tall tales
• Realistic tales</td><td></td></tr>
<tr><td>Characters</td><td>• Readers notice the people, animals, and objects so that they can understand the tale.
• Readers think about what the characters in a tale are like so that they understand whether they are good or bad.
• Readers decide who the good and important characters are so that they can make predictions.
• Readers think about the bad characters in a tale so that they can predict how the story will end.</td><td>• Searching for and using information
• Inferring
• Analyzing
• Inferring
• Predicting
• Analyzing
• Predicting</td></tr>
<tr><td>Setting</td><td>• Readers notice how the writer describes the setting (the time and place where the story takes place) so that they can understand the tale.
• Readers notice what the setting is like so that they can understand the plot and the way characters behave.</td><td>• Searching for and using information</td></tr>
<tr><td>Plot and Problem Resolution</td><td>• Readers identify the problem in the story so that they can understand the folktale.
• Readers notice how the problem in the tale is solved so they can understand the folktale.</td><td>• Searching for and using information
• Inferring</td></tr>
</table>

Figure 15.19 From interactive read-aloud to readers' workshop: Learning about folktales

continues

FROM INTERACTIVE READ-ALOUD TO READERS' WORKSHOP: LEARNING ABOUT FOLKTALES			
Inquiry	**Minilessons to Extend Learning About Folktales**		**Strategic Actions**
• Reflects culture and values of the place of origin Often: • Mentions the original source of the tale • Includes proverbs from the place of origin • Have recognizable literary patterns (cumulative tales, pourquoi tales, beast tales, realistic tales) • Uses figurative language and imagery • Has simplistic characters who are completely evil or completely good • Has small and powerless characters who triumph • Has happy ending		• Readers identify the main problem of the story so they can understand the folktale. • Readers notice the exciting place in the story (the climax) so that they can understand how the problem is resolved. • Readers notice the way the story ends so that they can understand the resolution of the problem.	• Searching for and using information
	Themes and Messages	• Readers think about the messages or lessons the story teaches so they can learn from the folktale. • Readers think about the lesson of the story so they can understand how the tale gives information about human values. • Readers identify the part of the story that reveals the lesson so they can understand the purpose of the tale.	• Searching for and using information • Inferring • Analyzing • Searching for and using information
	Mood	• Readers think about the way a tale makes them feel so they can understand the meaning of the story. • Readers think about how the story makes them feel so that they can understand the purpose of the story (make readers afraid, promote doing the right thing, entertain).	• Inferring • Synthesizing • Inferring
	Perspective	• Readers notice who is telling the tale to help them understand the story. • Readers notice that stories are almost always told in third person so that they understand this characteristic in folktales.	• Searching for and using information
	Illustrations	• Readers notice how the illustrations show the characters and the actions so that they can understand the setting for folktales.	• Searching for and using information • Analyzing

Figure 15.19 From interactive read-aloud to readers' workshop: Learning about folktales *(cont.)*

Suggestions for Professional Development

OPTION I: Explicit minilessons are key to developing in-depth understanding of genres. To help you build specific minilessons:

1. Form grade-level groups.
2. Collect one type of fiction, such as realistic fiction, historical fiction, traditional literature, or modern fantasy. Read four or five and discuss their characteristics. List the characteristics you notice and create your definition.
3. Discuss the characteristics and make a list of large, umbrella categories for your minilessons.
4. Select one umbrella category and list the specific elements within it.
5. For each element, write a minilesson statement of principle. State what readers need to think about and why.
6. Teach your minilessons for a couple of weeks and then reconvene to talk about what worked well and to problem solve.

OPTION 2: Toward the end of the year, create a master plan for the coming year with grade-level colleagues. You can vary the plan as you make decisions during the year, but having this overall approach will allow you to make the most efficient use of materials and time.

1. Make a list of the areas you want to address in readers' workshop for the year. Consider genres, authors, and literary elements.
2. Lay out the year in months and identify studies for each month.
3. Create text sets to support each study.
4. Meet with cross-grade-level colleagues to create a spiraling curriculum that develops essential understandings over the years (see *The Continuum of Literacy Learning*).

CHAPTER 16

Learning About Nonfiction Texts Through Minilessons and Group Share

Schools, if they are to become scholarly communities, need to create structures so that children have access to the experts and the information they need.

—Shelley Harwayne

Genre study is as important for nonfiction as it is for fiction. Nonfiction texts vary widely and have a large number of complex features that readers need to notice and use to guide text processing and comprehension. Even more important, reading nonfiction requires more than just gleaning facts and information. High-quality nonfiction has big ideas and overarching themes. When you read nonfiction, ask these implicit questions and more:

- What's the point?
- Why did the writer select (or omit) certain facts?
- What is the writer's purpose?
- What is the writer's attitude toward the topic?
- Is the writer trying to persuade me of something?
- Is the writer showing me how to do something?
- What does the writer want me to think (believe, do)?
- What is the message or messages—the big idea or ideas that I should be getting?
- What is the relevance/significance of the topic to me and/or others in the world?

A nonfiction text has a message beyond the facts given. *Wild Dogs: Past and Present* (Halls 2005) provides a great deal of information about different species of wild dogs in all parts of the world. The book, beautifully illustrated with photographs, tells in great detail about the origin and history of wild dogs and their current status. The author describes the link between domestic and wild dogs and the strong relationships between the various kinds of wild dogs in each region of the world (coyotes, wolves, and foxes in North America, for example). Readers interested in the topic will find an abundance of fascinating information but will also be thinking about important bigger ideas and questions:

- Creatures evolve and change through thousands of years and are affected by climate change and other factors in the physical world.
- Animals in the wild are interdependent; the extinction of one species affects many others.
- Dogs and people have had a long and mutually dependent relationship; dogs were sometimes worshipped and sometimes demonized.
- Dogs (wild and domesticated) work in packs and help one another survive.
- You need to protect wild dogs and other animals so that species do not die out.
- Even the most pampered dog today is related to wild dogs.
- DNA evidence gives you wonderful information that helps you learn about species and their history so you can appreciate and protect them.
- Should people learn more about wild dogs in order to understand their own pets?
- How long would it take a domesticated dog to learn how to survive in the wild?
- The writer has put together ideas in a clear way, making connections that matter.
- The more you learn about wild animals, the more you can do to protect and appreciate the special roles they play in nature (a hypothesis about the overarching theme).

These are not specific facts but rather thoughts generated by a synthesis of information and conclusions. Anyone reading the book might list many more.

If you come away from the book merely being able to retell ten or fifteen facts, you have gained something from the reading but have not deeply understood what you have read. Your goal as a teacher is to help your student readers put information together, raise questions, draw conclusions, form hypotheses, infer the writer's purposes, detect persuasion and evaluate it, and think critically about the topic.

This chapter explores how you can use minilessons and group share in readers' workshop to help your students learn about nonfiction texts. Even after students have learned to distinguish broadly between fiction and nonfiction, which in itself represents complex learning when you consider the great variation in texts, they need to learn about the genres within nonfiction that make different demands on readers.

Types of Nonfiction Texts

We describe five categories of nonfiction: (1) biographical texts; (2) narrative nonfiction; (3) expository nonfiction; (4) procedural texts; and (5) persuasive texts (see Figure 16.1).

These categories are related to:

1. *Purpose.* Writers select a genre that will meet their objective. If they want to tell the story of a person's life or their own, they select biography, autobiography, or memoir. If they want to provide some comprehensive and clear information about a topic, they expose or set forth the facts in a logical, organized, and detailed way that readers can follow. If they want to tell a story that gives accurate information, they may choose narrative nonfiction. If they want to tell readers how to do something, they describe the *procedure.* If they want to convince readers of something, they set up an argument with evidence that is *persuasive.*
2. *Audience.* Writers need to know who will be reading their text as it will influence the language and text structure they use. Audience relates to the age group you are writing for, as well as the assumed level of understanding of the topic. The writer should signal that they know who they are writing for as early as possible in order to maintain the interest and trust of the reader—they do this by using the right vocabulary, words, and expressions throughout—language that will appeal to and hold the interest of their target audience.

CATEGORIES OF NONFICTION TEXTS	
Category	**Examples**
■ **Biographical Texts:** Present factual information about real people in the form of a story	■ Biographies, autobiographies, memoirs
■ **Narrative Nonfiction:** Presents factual information in the form of a story	■ Informational texts, feature articles, literary essays
■ **Expository Nonfiction:** Uses a logical organization to present factual information; non-narrative	■ Informational science or social studies texts, feature articles, reports, literary essays, interviews
■ **Procedural Texts:** Teach or demonstrate a procedure; usually use temporal sequence	■ How-to guides, descriptions of how something is done
■ **Persuasive Texts:** Present reasons and evidence to convince the reader to agree with a point of view	■ Persuasive essays, editorial and op-ed pieces, reviews, letters to the editor

Figure 16.1 Categories of nonfiction texts

3. *Text structure.* Writers select a structure or organizational pattern that fits the purpose. Biography and autobiography rest on narrative structure because they tell a story. Memoir, too, may be a story. (Sometimes memoir is simply a descriptive piece that is not a narrative). Writers of expository texts, feature articles and reports, typically do not use narrative structure but select from a range of possible organizational patterns that fit the topic (they sometimes adopt narrative structure for a particular purpose). Writers of procedural texts usually demonstrate a process step by step. Writers of persuasive texts must present arguments, reasons, and evidence.

Let's look at an example of a nonfiction text. *Wild Dogs: Past and Present* is an expository text. Its purpose is mainly to inform and engage the reader. But it also has an element of persuasion, not explicitly stated but embedded in the text. It also has a few short narratives, mainly located in insets or sidebars. But again, the main purpose of the book is *to inform*. The writer decided that a nonfiction text with an expository organization was best suited to this purpose.

As experienced writers, you may not even be aware you are making such choices about the genres you write in, but you have a large body of understanding about texts that you automatically draw on as you begin to write. Writing a memoir about a beloved grandmother, you unconsciously draw on your knowledge of narrative structure. Presenting a report for school or for work, you may choose an expository organizational structure. Writing a letter to the editor of your local newspaper, you may draw upon your understanding of persuasive texts and arguments. You often take these choices for granted, but they are choices, perhaps the most important ones that writers make.

As writers, your students need to understand that genre and structure are not just "assigned." Writers make decisions according to purpose and audience. In writers' workshop, you sometimes need to assign writing in particular genres. But through genre study and the use of mentor texts, you can explore the way writers make decisions and create a context within which your students understand they are building a repertoire of possibilities from which they can choose.

Interactive Read-Aloud and Readers' Workshop

Begin genre inquiry (see Figure 16.2) during interactive read-aloud, which if possible should take place outside the readers' workshop. During daily interactive read-aloud lessons, students can discuss the texts they've heard and begin to notice their characteristics. The texts used in interactive read-aloud become excellent mentor texts for subsequent readers' workshop minilessons.

Students listen to four or five mentor texts, list their characteristics, and create a working definition before you teach an umbrella minilesson followed by minilessons on specific characteristics. Then, as you provide the sequence of minilessons you have designed, you can continue to enrich students' immersion in nonfiction texts and build your collection of mentor texts. The sequence is described below.

1. Interactive read-aloud of mentor texts.
2. Daily book talks that help students choose their own independent reading in the genre.
3. Individual conferences during independent reading, quick moments in which you help students notice features of the books they have chosen.
4. Guided reading lessons in which you help students link nonfiction texts with the mentor texts you have read aloud.
5. Book clubs in which small groups of students discuss nonfiction texts.
6. Group share in which students think together and learn more about the genre.

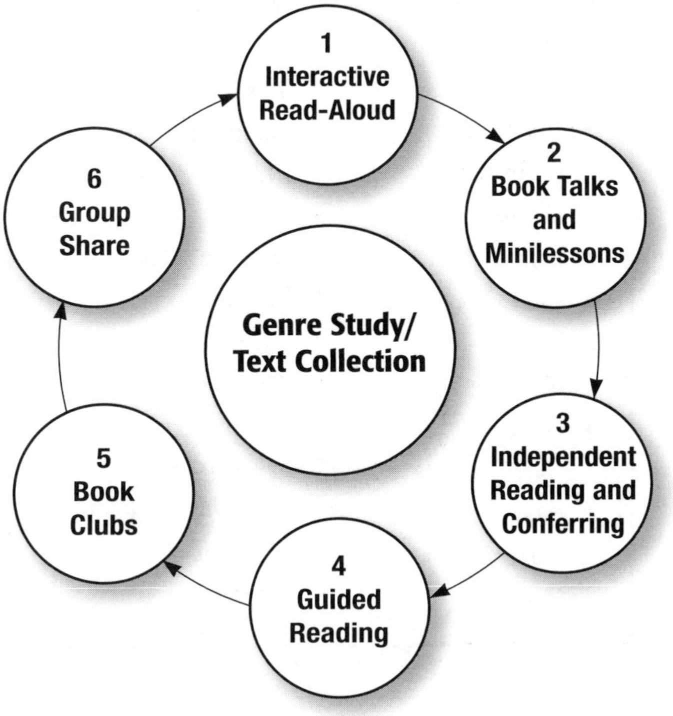

Figure 16.2 Genre study inquiry

Genre Study for Nonfiction Texts

The process of genre study for nonfiction texts is the same as it is for any kind of text; the difference is the features you help students notice. We have outlined this inquiry process in a number of earlier chapters. You might start genre study with the broad categories of nonfiction. Depending on your grade level, you may want to follow up with a specific type of nonfiction (e.g., procedural texts). Figure 16.3 applies the process to expository nonfiction texts.

Collect

Students will need at least four or five very clear examples of the genre (see the mentor texts listed at the end of Chapter 10). Genre study is a process engaged in over time; you can build knowledge of each category, always relating it to the larger category of nonfiction.

Immerse

Read the mentor texts aloud over a week or so, enjoying them and discussing the topic. Ask students what they notice about the way the text was written. "Why did the writer make the decision to ______?" can be asked about any feature students notice—facts, headings, sidebars, comparisons, pictures with legends, problem and solution, labels, glossary, and so on. After reading four or five excellent examples, you and your students are ready to make a list of characteristics.

Make additional expository nonfiction texts available to students, assembled in bins or baskets, that reflect a variety of reading levels (although students do not choose books by levels and the books are not labeled with levels). Genre study is not a single lesson or even a series of lessons. Immerse students in the

PROCESS OF GENRE STUDY—EXPOSITORY NONFICTION TEXTS	
Collect	Collect four or five nonfiction read-aloud titles that are clearly expository texts, not biography, narrative nonfiction, or procedural texts. (Persuasion, if included, should be a minor characteristic.) Make sure there are baskets of expository nonfiction texts (organized by topic) that represent a range of reading challenges. Decide whether to introduce the word *expository* or whether to simply refer to nonfiction or informational texts. The decision depends on students' level of experience.
Immerse	• Immerse students in the genre by reading the mentor texts aloud over a week or two. • Give book talks on expository nonfiction texts at a variety of levels to interest students in selecting books for independent reading. Later, confer individually with students during independent reading. • Organize book clubs using expository texts (multiple copies) and meet with clubs over time. • Select some expository texts (multiple copies) for guided reading (small-group reading instruction). Teach lessons over several weeks, being sure to refer to the genre and point out features or ask students what they notice. • Once inquiry is underway, place students at tables with a small pile of expository nonfiction books. Some can be books you have read to them and some can be new. Ask them to list what they notice to report to the whole group.
Notice	Help students notice and list characteristics of expository nonfiction. For example: • Provides factual information about a topic • Information is presented with a clear (non-narrative) organizational structure • Has a major topic and supporting information • Often conveys a larger message • Often has information organized by categories or subcategories • Often includes organizational tools (table of contents, headings, index, glossary, pronunciation guide, appendices) • Often includes graphic features that support or enhance the text (photographs, illustrations, charts, diagrams, tables and graphs, timelines) • Table of contents • Glossary • Index • Headings and subheadings • Drawings • Illustrations • Photographs • Captions • Labels • Insets • Charts • Diagrams • Cutaways/ cross-sections • Maps • Pronunciation guide • Borders • Websites • Bibliography • Introduction • Fun facts • Sidebars • Author's note • Illustrator's note • Bullets, asterisks, stars • Bold print • Italics • Changing type colors • Appendix • Foreword/Afterword • Timelines • Chapter titles

Figure 16.3 Process of genre study—expository nonfiction texts

PROCESS OF GENRE STUDY—EXPOSITORY NONFICTION TEXTS	
Define	With students, construct a definition of expository nonfiction. For example: An expository nonfiction text gives factual information in an organized way with a major topic and supporting information.
Teach	Using mentor texts that students know as clear examples, present a series of minilessons that reflect the list of characteristics. For example: Readers notice and read all of the design features on the page to help them learn about a topic. One broad characteristic may require several specific minilessons. The umbrella lesson in this example can lead to several minilessons on the variety of organizational and graphic features and their purposes.
Read and Revise	Read many more expository nonfiction texts, checking and adding to the list of characteristics.
Plan later genre studies on biography, narrative nonfiction, procedural texts, and persuasive texts.	

Figure 16.3 Process of genre study—expository nonfiction texts *(cont.)*

genre being studied throughout readers' workshop and in their independent reading. The most important characteristic is the topic. Is it interesting and relevant? The goal is that over a few weeks students will read several expository texts that will fuel their own learning about the genre and about which you can converse with them during individual conferences. Provide books in the genre for book clubs so your students have more opportunities to discuss expository texts. The goal of literature discussion is to think and talk about meaningful topics, ideas students can take away with them above and beyond a collection of facts. They help each other learn more than any one of them could learn alone. Figure 16.4 is an example of collections of texts for primary and intermediate grade levels that might be used in different contexts (text levels for guided reading are in parentheses).

Notice

During immersion, help students pay special attention to, and create a class chart with the features that are particularly important in identifying an expository text (see Figure 16.3). Also have your students write the list in their reader's notebooks (see Chapter 18). It's easy for them to notice graphic features such as maps, diagrams, and charts, but you also need to be explicit about the features that distinguish expository texts from fiction (they are factual, for example).

Students new to genre study may suggest features that are appropriate but do not distinguish the genre—has illustrations or has descriptive language, for example. Focus their thinking as you read a series of texts aloud by constantly comparing texts with ones previously read: "What did you notice about this book and all the others we read?" By the time the class begins

IMMERSING STUDENTS IN EXPOSITORY TEXTS

Interactive Read-Aloud	Independent Reading (Book Talks)	Guided Reading	Book Clubs
PRIMARY			
Slow Down for Manatees by Jim Arnosky (Grades K–3) *Lots and Lots of Zebra Stripes Patterns in Nature* by Stephen Swinburne (Grades K–2) *Trains* by Gail Gibbons Grades K–1) *I Face the Wind* by Vicki Cobb (Grades K–3) *What Living Things Need: Water* by Vic Parker (Grades K–2) *How Big Were the Dinosaurs?* by Bernard Most (Grades K–1)	*Baby Animals Learn* by Pamela Chanko and Samantha Berger *Guess Who Hides* by Sharon Gordon *Salamanders* by Robin Nelson *Clocks and Time* by Tracey Steffora *Leaves* by Charlotte Guillain *African Elephants* by Shannon Knudson *Holiday! Celebration Days Around the World* by Deborah Chancellor *Forest Fires* by Janet Piehl	*Counting Seeds* (C) By Margie Burton *Masks* (F) By Pam Holden *The Speedy Cheetah* (G) By Rachel Elliott *Hair* (I) By Valorie Lee Schaefer *Antarctica* (J) By Jill McDougall *Slinky, Scaly Snakes!* (K) By Jennifer Dussling *From Wax to Crayon* (L) By Robin Nelson *Fast Food* (M) By Alex Kelly	*When Rain Falls* by Melissa Stewart *Hurricanes* by Gail Gibbons *What's Out There? A Book About Space* by Lynn Wilson *Sisters and Brothers* by Steve Jenkins and Robin Page *All About Lizards* by Jim Arnosky *Biggest, Strongest, Fastest* by Steve Jenkins
INTERMEDIATE			
Toad or Frog, Swamp or Bog? A Big Book of Nature's Confusables by Linda Graham-Barber	*Crocodiles on the Hunt* by Lori Polydoros *The Bald Eagle* by Elaine Landau *Your Muscles* by Anne Ylvisaker	*The Chocolate Trail* (N) By Julie Haydon *Meercats* (O) By Robin Weever *Earthquakes* (P) By Andrew Whitmore *Skateboarding* (Q) By Eric Preszler *Everything Dog: What Kids Really Want to Know About Dogs* (R) By Marty Crisp	*All About Turkeys* by Jim Arnosky (Grades 2–3) *Bats* by Gail Gibbons (Grades 4–5)

Figure 16.4 Immersing students in expository texts

IMMERSING STUDENTS IN EXPOSITORY TEXTS			
INTERMEDIATE, *(cont.)*			
Interactive Read-Aloud	**Independent Reading (Book Talks)**	**Guided Reading**	**Book Clubs**
Inside Volcanoes by Melissa Stewart (Grades 3–6) *Life in the Boreal Forest* By Benda Guiberson (Grades 4–5) *Muscles: Our Muscular System* by Seymour Simon (Grades 4–8) *A Drop of Water: A Book of Science and Wonder* by Walter Wick (Grades 4–8) *Caves* by Stephen Kramer (Grades 6–8)	*Mighty Mammals* by Sharon Dalgleish *How Do Plants Grow?* by Melissa Stewart *Alligators and Crocodiles* by Karen Dudley *Crocodilians* by Joan Short and Bettina Bird *Arctic and Antarctica* by Barbara Taylor *Forensic Science* by Ron Fridell *Robotics* by Helena Domain	*Midnight Journeys: Travels in the Mysterious World of Sleep* (S) By Maureen Mecozzi *Human Barriers: The Walls of the World* (T) By Nelson Eggleton *Castles: Towers Dungeons, Moats and More* (U) By Matt White *Time Travelers: Adventures in Archaeology* (W) By Sue Bursztynski *Investigating Electromagnetism* (Y) By Elizabeth R.C. Cregan	*Caves and Caverns* by Gail Gibbons (Grades 4–5) *Life in the Boreal Forest* by Brenda Guiberson (Grades 4–5) *A Place for Butterflies* by Melissa Stewart *The Underground Railroad* by Raymond Bial (Grades 5–8) *Life in a Bucket of Soil* by Alvin Silverstein and Virginia Silverstein (Grades 5–8)

Figure 16.4 Immersing students in expository texts *(cont.)*

listing characteristics, students will have focused their thinking, realizing that some apply to *every* expository text and others apply often or only once in awhile. As more texts are read, revisit the list and highlight the characteristics that are critical in forming the working definition.

Define

With your students, construct a concise definition of expository texts, paying attention to the wording. The definition shouldn't simply repeat the characteristics or be too wordy; rather, it should summarize the essential features (see the example in Figure 16.3). Create a chart for reference and have students write the definition in their reader's notebooks.

Teach

Plan and teach minilessons on the specific characteristics of expository texts, using some examples from the mentor texts. Each minilesson principle is stated clearly and displayed in writing so that students can revisit it as they read and apply the principle in their independent reading. Some characteristics of an effective minilesson principle are shown in Figure 16.5. Key ideas to keep in mind when you are writing the minilesson principle include:

1. Use the characteristics generated during the inquiry process but reshape them in terms of what readers do. With the youngest students (e.g., grades K–2) start the principle with "Think about . . ." for example, "Think about

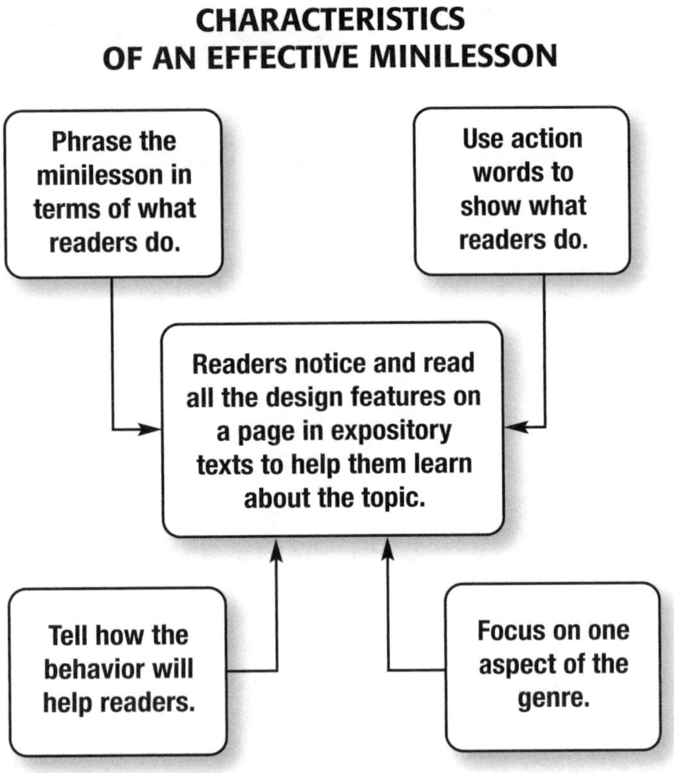

Figure 16-5 Characteristics of an effective minilesson

the information writers show in photographs to help you learn about the topic." (You can always deepen the analysis through further inquiry focused on deeper thinking. For example, once you have helped students see that writers of expository texts frequently use patterns, you can take one pattern like cause and effect, look for it, and discuss how it is used in several mentor texts. Then you can move on to other specific patterns.)

2. Use action words that describe what readers do and that students need to think about as they read.
3. Limit the minilesson to one specific idea so that readers can focus their attention during independent reading and group share.
4. Include the rationale in the statement. Tell how the behaviors will help students as readers—*why* they need to think about the principle. Most of the time, the reason may be broad (*understand, think about, learn*, for example), but it is important.

Older students who are using a reader's notebook can write the minilesson principle in it, make notes, and record some of the mentor text examples (see *Reader's Notebook: Advanced*). Alternatively, students can glue the principle on the page and make notes.

The minilesson principle resurfaces during group share, when students have a chance to talk more (with one or two partners or as a whole group) about their own application of the minilesson principle. For example, in response to the minilesson principle in Figure 16.2, readers might share by saying: "My nonfiction book is ____. I noticed that _____." "In my book, the writer _____." "On this page in my book, _____." For younger students new to readers' workshop, you may want to model sharing behavior using a book you are currently reading and then have students practice the behavior in pairs.

Read and Revisit

Even after beginning to teach minilessons on the genre, continue to read more mentor texts. With your students, you may notice new characteristics, refine a characteristic they've already noticed, or reword the definition.

Minilessons to Learn About Expository Nonfiction Texts

You might begin a study of expository texts by noticing the broad strokes of how texts are written. Here are some possible minilesson principles:

- Readers notice how texts are written so they can identify (name) the type of writing or the genre.
- Readers notice and think about the features the writer or illustrator includes in a text to help them understand it better.

Then, as you read examples of expository texts to students, ask them what they notice. Almost anything will be useful. The idea is for students to become more consciously aware of the characteristics of texts. An example of the process of moving from interactive read-aloud to readers' workshop minilessons in the study of expository texts is laid out in Figure 16.6.

The figure lists quite a few characteristics, but the possibilities are even more extensive. Throughout the

<table>
<tr><th colspan="4">FROM INTERACTIVE READ-ALOUD TO READERS' WORKSHOP: EXPOSITORY NONFICTION TEXTS</th></tr>
<tr><th>Inquiry</th><th colspan="2">Definition</th><th>Minilesson</th></tr>
<tr><td rowspan="7">What we notice about expository nonfiction:
• Provides factual information about a topic
• Information is presented with a clear (non-narrative) organizational structure
• Has a major topic and supporting information

Often:
• Conveys a larger message
• Has information organized by categories or subcategories
• Includes organizational tools (table of contents, headings, index, glossary, pronunciation guide, appendices)
• Includes graphic features that support or enhance the text (photographs, illustrations, captions, insets, charts, diagrams, tables and graphs, timelines)</td><td colspan="2">An expository nonfiction text gives factual information in an organized way with a major topic and supporting information.</td><td>Readers notice and think about the writing and the design features on the page in a nonfiction text to understand all the information.</td></tr>
<tr><th colspan="3">Minilessons to Extend Learning About Expository Nonfiction</th></tr>
<tr><td>Information in the Text</td><td colspan="2">• Readers notice the topic of a text and think about information related to the topic to learn about it.
• Readers think about whether the information in a text is true. They use background information and other sources to be confident about the accuracy.
• Readers notice new information to learn more about a topic.
• Readers notice the way the writer has provided support for the facts in a text to help them understand the topic.
• Readers notice the qualifications of the writer to help them think about the accuracy of the information.</td></tr>
<tr><td>Text Structure</td><td colspan="2">• Readers notice and use the writer's organization to read the text with understanding.
• Readers notice when a writer tells about the topic through information in categories to learn about the topic.
• Readers notice when a writer uses description and detail to give information about a topic.
• Readers notice when a writer uses comparison/contrast to provide information about a topic.
• Readers notice when a writer tells about causes and effects to provide information about a topic.
• Readers notice when a writer identifies problems and tells the solutions to learn about the topic.
• Readers notice when a writer presents events in a time sequence to understand the information.</td></tr>
<tr><td>Big Ideas</td><td colspan="2">• Readers think about the most important messages the writer is telling about the topic to understand it.
• Readers think about the meaning or relevance of the text to people and the world (the "so what?") to appreciate the information.</td></tr>
<tr><td>Tone, Voice, and Attitude</td><td colspan="2">• Readers notice the strong and powerful verbs writers use to help them understand the information.</td></tr>
</table>

Figure 16.6 From interactive read-aloud to readers' workshop: expository nonfiction texts

continues

FROM INTERACTIVE READ-ALOUD TO READERS' WORKSHOP: EXPOSITORY NONFICTION TEXTS		
Inquiry	**Minilessons to Extend Learning About Expository Nonfiction**	
Once students understand the concept of text features and know to read everything on the page, teach individual minilessons on how to use each: • Index • Dedication • Glossary • Author's notes • List of Websites • Headings • Subheadings • Bullets • Chapter titles • Bold print, colored print • Sidebars • Labels • Bullets • Captions • Insets • Diagrams • Charts • Timelines • Cross-sections • Cutaways	**Tone, Voice, and Attitude** *(cont.)*	• Readers notice the specific nouns nonfiction writers use to help them understand the information. • Readers notice and think about new vocabulary words to help them understand the topic. • Readers think about how the writer feels about the topic of an expository text to understand the writer's point of view. • Readers notice when a writer tells both sides of a problem or gives two perspectives on a topic in order to judge the accuracy or authenticity of a text.
	Design Features	• Readers notice and read all the information that is outside the body of the text so they can learn more information and get to information easily. • Readers notice the nonfiction graphic features and the way they are put on the page so they can use them to learn about a topic. • Readers notice and use the organizational tools on a page so they can learn about the topic. • Readers notice how each print feature in a nonfiction book helps them understand the topic. • Readers notice how a table of contents is different from an index to understand when these features are helpful while reading. • Readers think about how a glossary is different from a dictionary to understand how to use it when reading a nonfiction book.

Figure 16.6 From interactive read-aloud to readers' workshop: expository nonfiction texts *(cont.)*

year, each time you read nonfiction expository texts aloud, you can add to the list. The umbrella minilesson prompts readers to notice and think about the writing and the art on the page in a nonfiction text. Following this minilesson, readers can notice and share any aspect they have noticed in the texts they are reading independently. Subsequent minilessons can delve into more details (smaller categories) relative to the characteristics of expository texts. The excerpts in Figures 16.7, 16.8, and 16.9 are from minilessons on the features of nonfiction texts.

The minilesson in Figure 16.7 helps students distinguish the main part, or *body*, of the text so that many of the features that characterize nonfiction texts can be identified and discussed. The minilesson in Figure 16.8 focuses on graphic features such as diagrams, sidebars, and charts. The teacher asks readers to find one graphic feature to share with classmates. As a result (over two or three days), students generate a chart on graphic features and how they help readers.

You can also cluster a series of minilessons to teach a particular group of concepts related to the craft of

EXCERPT FROM A MINILESSON ON THE BODY OF A NONFICTION TEXT	
Statement of principle:	
Readers notice the *body* or main part of a nonfiction text so that they can tell the difference between the body and other information on the page.	
TEACHER:	You have been noticing a lot about nonfiction texts. Let's look at a couple of examples of books you know to help you think about the different kinds of information on a page. The main part of the book—what the writer is telling you—is called the *body*. [Reads the minilesson principle. Shows the body text of *Wild Dogs: Past and Present* and reads a little from pages 16–17.] But you can see on these pages that the writer has included more information in other ways. What do you notice?
CHARLOTTE:	There are pictures and maps, and a diagram that shows subspecies.
JAMES:	There's a section title.
JOSHUA:	There's some writing in a box that is shaded yellow.
TEACHER:	That box tells about a DNA discovery related to the Eastern wolf. The information in these boxes, called *sidebars*, gives you information about wolves but it is very focused—a special kind of information that doesn't quite belong in the body, the main part of the book. It is *set off*, usually in a box. Take a look at page 31. What do you notice here?
FRED:	There's a map and then pictures of the different kinds of wild dogs, like the red fox that we have here. There is a label under the picture.
TEACHER:	Yes, and this information is also set off from the main text—it looks different. You can also notice the chapter title and another sidebar on page 30 with a picture and some information about secrets to wolves' survival. As you read nonfiction today, notice the difference between the body, which is the main information the author is telling, and the extra information that is presented in different ways. When we come back together, share some things that you noticed.

Figure 16.7 Excerpt from a minilesson on the body of a nonfiction text

writing nonfiction texts. One of the greatest benefits of using such minilessons in readers' workshop is that you also build understandings that contribute to students' writing. Students can consider word choice, interesting language, text organization, and the use of underlying text structures as they craft their own expository writing. Some areas of understanding, along with the related minilesson principle, that you can help your students notice in the texts they are reading independently are listed in Figure 16.10 (p. 301). These areas are also important when considering other genres, but they are especially so in learning about nonfiction texts. Each area becomes increasingly more sophisticated as readers process more complex kinds of texts.

Accuracy/authenticity. It is especially important for readers of nonfiction texts to think critically about the accuracy of the writing. The facts and examples should be trustworthy and reliable. Discerning readers notice the writer's qualifications as well as whether the writer documents sources or describes the research on which the content of the book is based. You can also measure the text against your own background knowledge and

EXCERPT FROM A MINILESSON ON GRAPHIC FEATURES

Statement of principle:

Readers notice the graphic features and the way they are put on the page so they can use them to learn about nonfiction topics.

TEACHER: You have been noticing a great deal about nonfiction texts. Today, let's look back at a few of the books we have read to notice some features that help readers. [Reads the minilesson principle.] Do you remember this book, *Do Animals Have Feelings Too?* What graphic features do you notice on this page?

NICOLAS: There are pictures of the animals that the book is talking about.

SOPHIE: There's a box with questions at the bottom.

TEACHER: Look at this page. What do you notice?

MONA: It's the same things as on the other pages and this one has bullets.

TEACHER: In just a few minutes, you have identified some important graphic features that will be helpful in learning about a topic. Let's look quickly at another book we have read, *Wild Dogs: Past and Present.* What do you notice on this page, Ellen? [Show page 29.]

ELLEN: It's got a heading and a box with some information.

TEACHER: That box is called a *sidebar*. We'll be learning more about sidebars later. Anything on page 28?

MARK: There's a chart, Family of Foxes, and then all the kinds of foxes in a line down from it.

TEACHER: These pages have got a great deal of information on them, and a lot of it comes from the graphic features. It's not in what we call the body of the text, which is here [indicates]. It's in boxes and charts and pictures and captions. That's why readers read everything on the page. Today when you read your nonfiction book, notice one graphic feature—not in the body of the text—that gives more information. Think about how it helps you as a reader. Bring your book back to show a partner during share time. We'll make a quick list of what you found and how it helps.

CHART CREATED DURING GROUP SHARE

Readers notice the graphic features and the way they are put on the page so they can use them to learn about nonfiction topics.

GRAPHIC FEATURE	HOW IT HELPS READERS
Sidebar	Gives extra information that is very specific or that summarizes what is in the body
Caption	Tells exactly what is in the picture and sometimes tells how it relates to the body
Label	Helps readers know parts of the picture
Diagram (Sketch or Drawing)	Shows the parts of something or how something works
Chart	Shows important facts and how they are related to each other and to the information in the body of the text
Timeline	Shows the order in which something happened

Figure 16.8 Excerpt from a minilesson on graphic features

EXCERPT FROM A MINILESSON ON NOTICING AND USING THE ORGANIZATIONAL FEATURES OF NONFICTION TEXTS

Statement of principle:

Readers notice and use the organizational features of nonfiction texts so they can learn more information and get to information easily.

TEACHER:	Today we are going to think together about the organizational features of the book. You have noticed information in fiction books that is included in addition to the story. Do you remember examples?
CARA:	Information on the author.
NICOLAS:	Or something that the author writes about himself or that tells who he wrote the book for.
TEACHER:	[Reads minilesson principle.] Let's look at *Wild Dogs: Past and Present.* You really enjoyed this book, and I noticed that several of you went back and read sections of it. When we read this book, we noticed lots of information. I want to show you some features of the book that can help you to find information more easily. [Shows the table of contents.] What do you call this?
SOPHIE:	The table of contents. It tells what is in the book.
TEACHER:	The table of contents helps readers know the topics that the writer is telling about. Also, you can look at the table of contents and quickly get to the section that you are interested in. [Shows the index.] This is the index. It is very helpful. Have some of you used the index?
ANDREW:	You look for the word that you want to find and it tells you the page number.
TEACHER:	That makes it really easy. The table of contents tells you a whole category of information that the author wrote a lot about. But if you are looking for something very specific, the index is a great help. For example, if I know that I want to read about the arctic fox, I can go to pages 13 and 28. [Shows the bibliography.] This is the bibliography. How does it help you?
MARK	It tells where the author got her information.
TEACHER:	The bibliography often helps you investigate the topic more and sometimes the author will also include a list of additional resources. What kinds of things did we find on this page? [Shows pages 62–63.]
ELLEN:	You can go to websites to get more information.
TEACHER:	This page does list websites and also more books you can find as well as interviews. You can look at the bibliography to see all the sources of information that the writer read in order to get accurate information to put in the book. When there is a bibliography, there is a better chance that the information is accurate. Here is a piece of extra information that I always like to read. It's the dedication. This dedication is by the author, Kelly Milner. She says: "To Charles, a Great Dane with regal distinction who taught me how to really love a dog. To Yogi, a domesticated giant with the heart and spirit of these wonderful wild dogs. His memory survives. To Cricket, a faithful, crippled mutt who healed my heart before she said goodbye. And to little Gizmo, a tired, old eight-pounder, not long for this world, who will doubtless run with Charles, Yogi, and Cricket when he gets to the other side. Thanks for bettering my world. KMH." What do you think of that?
ANGIE:	That tells you why she wrote the book!

Figure 16.9 Excerpt from a minilesson on noticing and using organizational features of nonfiction texts

continues

EXCERPT FROM A MINILESSON ON NOTICING AND USING THE ORGANIZATIONAL FEATURES OF NONFICTION TEXTS

NICOLAS: What do you mean?

ANGIE: Well, she loved her dogs and all of them are dead except for the last one. So she wanted to write about dogs.

NICOLAS: But why didn't she write about them instead of the wild dogs?

ANGIE: I don't know, but she loved them.

TEACHER: What do some of the rest of you think?

CHARLES: Maybe she just got real interested in dogs because she liked hers so much.

SOPHIE: You can tell a lot about dogs because all of them are related even to the wild dogs. Remember, they are something like 99 percent alike.

TEACHER: It could be. The author tells us something about herself in the dedication, doesn't she? It gives us some ideas about why she went to all that trouble to write the book. As you read today, notice some of the organizational features of the book and think how they help you as a reader. We'll share some of them later.

CHART CREATED DURING GROUP SHARE

ORGANIZATIONAL FEATURES OF THE BOOK	HOW IT HELPS READERS
Table of Contents	Helps readers know everything that is in the book. Helps them find the kind of information they are interested in.
Index	Helps readers find exactly what they are interested in by looking for the word and finding the page number.
Glossary	Gives definitions of words that are important and that readers might not know.
Author's Notes	Tells why the author wrote the book or what the author thinks about the topic.
List of Additional Resources and Websites	Tells where to go for more information.
Bibliography	Tells where the author got the information to write the book.
Dedication	Tells something personal about the author and may help readers know why the author wrote the book.

Figure 16.9 ***Figure 16.9*** Excerpt from a minilesson on noticing and using organizational features of nonfiction texts *(cont.)*

MINILESSONS TO HELP READERS UNDERSTAND NONFICTION TEXT	
Area to Notice	**Minilesson Principles**
Accuracy/ Authenticity	• Readers use information about the writer and topic to find out if the facts and information are accurate. • Readers notice and think about whether the writer is giving a fair view of the topic to be sure they are gaining accurate information.
Point of View	• Readers notice how a writer shows feelings about a topic to help understand the author's point of view. • Readers notice when the writer uses "I" to tell about the information so that they can understand what the writer is thinking about the topic.
Purpose	• Readers think about the nonfiction writer's purpose in writing a book to help them understand the information.
Voice	• Readers notice what the nonfiction writer does to make a topic interesting to readers. • Readers notice how nonfiction texts inform, instruct, and interest readers to help them understand a topic. • Readers notice how the nonfiction writer tells about a topic in an interesting way. • Readers notice how the vivid language in nonfiction writing helps them understand a topic.
Word Choice	• Readers notice and think about new vocabulary words to help them understand a topic. • Readers notice the specific nouns nonfiction writers use to help them understand the information. • Readers notice the strong verbs nonfiction writers use to help them understand the information. • Readers notice the signal words nonfiction writers use to help them understand the patterns for thinking about the ideas (e.g., sequence–*first, next*).
Text Structure	• Readers notice and think about the patterns a nonfiction writer uses to help them understand the information. • Readers notice when the nonfiction writer is providing information in a list to help them understand the topic. • Readers notice when the nonfiction writer is using description to help them understand the topic. • Readers notice when the nonfiction writer is comparing two or more things to help them understand the topic. • Readers notice when the nonfiction writer is telling about a problem and a solution to help them understand the topic.

Figure 16.10 Minilessons to help readers understand nonfiction text

continues

MINILESSONS TO HELP READERS UNDERSTAND NONFICTION TEXT	
Area to Notice	**Minilesson Principles**
Text Structure *(cont.)*	• Readers notice when the nonfiction writer is telling about the cause of something to help them understand the topic. • Readers notice when the writer is asking the reader a question and giving a factual answer to help them understand the topic.
Text Features	• Readers look at everything on the page to understand the topic. • Readers notice and think about the writing and all the art on the page to understand the information. • Readers can read a nonfiction book from beginning to end to learn all about the topic. • Readers can use the table of contents or index (to dip in and out of a book) in nonfiction books to find specific information. • Readers notice (use) how each text feature in a nonfiction book (heading, chart, timeline, italics) helps them understand the topic. • Readers use each feature in a nonfiction book to help them learn more about the topic. • Readers notice the features in a table of contents to help them think about and find information. • Readers notice how a table of contents is different from an index to understand when these features are helpful while reading nonfiction. • Readers think about how a glossary is different from a dictionary to understand how to use it when reading a nonfiction book.

Figure 16.10 Minilessons to help readers understand nonfiction text *(cont.)*

check other sources of information. Once a writer has established credibility, she becomes a trusted source. Readers of all ages need to gradually acquire a group of authors that they recognize and trust.

Point of view. Every writer is biased; each has a point of view toward the topic that shapes the writing in subtle ways. Readers need to notice how a writer shows feelings about a topic. Sometimes a text (or a portion of it) is written in first person, and that makes it easier for readers to detect the writer's attitudes. But usually readers are expected to infer attitudes and feelings from the writer's language. Point of view is closely related to accuracy and authenticity because the stance taken by the writer affects whether the topic has been fairly and objectively treated. Writers of nonfiction try very hard to be objective by telling both sides of an issue, but in the end the writer's attitudes usually emerge.

Purpose. As mentioned earlier, the characteristics of genres are related to the writer's purpose, so it is important for readers to think (or hypothesize) about the underlying intent of a book. The writer's purpose is also closely related to the larger messages of the text, so awareness of purpose is important for deeper comprehension. Deriving the writer's purpose usually requires delving through layers of meaning. An author may have several purposes in mind, and there may be obvious purposes and underlying purposes. For example, a nonfiction book about an endangered species may have the hidden purpose of persuading people to protect that particular species. Sometimes the author's purpose is clearly revealed. It's important for readers to think about purpose even if their hypotheses are not always accurate. It's the thinking that matters. Readers need to look below the surface of expository texts and think critically.

Voice. Just as writers of fiction work to engage readers, so do writers of nonfiction. In some ways there are more constraints on the writer of nonfiction because of the obligation to be accurate; the writer cannot embellish the facts but can use vivid language and interesting words to make the topic interesting. To do so, the writer must communicate *what is important* about the topic and persuade readers to share that view. Readers should learn to notice aspects of the writer's craft—how the writer uses language in ways that help readers understand the topic and raise awareness and interest.

Word choice. Writers of nonfiction select their words carefully—partly because they must be accurate but also to engage interest and increase readers' understanding. Readers should notice specific nouns and strong verbs as well as key vocabulary words that need to be understood in order to learn about the topic. Signal words help readers detect underlying structures that the writer is using to provide information. For example:

- Sequence is signaled by words and phrases like *after*, *before*, *first*, *second*, *finally*, *not long after*, *then*, and *next*.
- Comparison/contrast is signaled by words and phrases like *although*, *but*, *same as*, *similar to*, *yet*, *on the other hand*, *like*, *unlike*, *in contrast to*, and *compared to*.
- Problem/solution and cause/effect are signaled by words and phrases like *if . . . then*, *so that*, *due to*, *because*, *because of*, *as a result*, *since*, *therefore*, *for this reason*, *so that*, and *that's why*.
- Question/answer is signaled by words and phrases like *who*, *what*, *when*, *where*, *why*, *how*, or *how many*.

Text structure. Nonfiction writers use patterns, or *structures*, to present information to readers. A text will have an *overall* structure that readers must understand to know how the text "works." In addition, readers need to notice the underlying structures that nonfiction writers use to communicate information (comparison/contrast, for example). Untangling these structures helps readers understand how information is *related* within the text and leads to more powerful comprehension than remembering a string of seemingly unrelated facts.

Text features. It is especially important for readers of nonfiction to notice and use text features. You need to read everything on the page in order to understand how the information is related to and extends the information in the body of the text. You need to follow the logical presentation of information within sections in the body of the text but at the same time you scan the page, picking up information from text features such as charts, maps, graphs, pictures with legends, labeled drawings, and other features. You need to notice words or phrases presented in italics or bold print, because they are especially important to the meaning. In addition, you need to learn to use numerous tools such as the table of contents, headings, subheadings, the glossary, and the index, so that you can find information quickly and also understand how the text is organized (larger categories and subcategories of information, for example).

Learning About Narrative Nonfiction

Narrative nonfiction is a unique and increasingly popular kind of nonfiction text. The narrative structure is engaging, and by using it writers of nonfiction can create texts of high literary quality. Some types of nonfiction, such as biography, use narrative structure because they are recounting events in time; however, narrative nonfiction takes a different form. Writers of narrative nonfiction still have the goal of imparting information, but they often break the rules in order to create a highly engaging and literary text.

It is interesting for students to encounter these types of texts, but they first need to know something about the craft and the purposes of the writer. The minilesson in Figure 16.11 helps students understand narrative nonfiction. Readers need to understand how a writer can have the purpose of communicating information yet use structures and sometimes writing techniques that do not fit neatly within nonfiction text characteristics. The flexibility with which students approach nonfiction texts helps them deepen their comprehension.

MINILESSON FOR LEARNING ABOUT NARRATIVE NONFICTION TEXTS	
TEACHER:	Sometimes a writer of a nonfiction text wants to give you information but also wants to create a beautiful, interesting book. To do this, the writer tells a story. Here's a book that we have shared before. [Shows *Wings of Light: The Migration of the Yellow Butterfly.*] Do you remember this one?
CAROLE:	It shows the way they migrate across the world.
TEACHER:	What else would you say about this book?
MARK:	It has beautiful illustrations. They're paintings.
KARA:	There's a map that shows the migration.
LARA:	It's kind of like a cycle.
HAVEH:	It has a good description.
TEACHER:	When we read this book, you really liked the way the writer used language to describe the flight of the butterflies. Also, this writer has given some information and has maps like many nonfiction books but has used the information to tell a story. This is story has a beginning, middle, and an ending, like many fiction stories. Today we are going to read another narrative nonfiction book, *Wolfsnail: A Backyard Predator.* It's about an unusual type of snail. Have you ever heard of a snail that is a predator?
HAVEH:	No, snails usually just eat plants.
TEACHER:	This writer has decided to write about a type of snail that doesn't behave like other snails you may have heard or read about. This type of snail is fast and fierce and it hunts for other smaller, slower snails. It's really interesting. As I read the first part, think about what you are learning about wolfsnails but also about how the writer shares the information and tells a story.

Figure 16.11 Minilesson for learning about narrative nonfiction texts

Using Minilessons and Group Share to Learn About Biography

A suggested plan for using biographical texts during interactive read-aloud is presented in Figure 16.12. An important part of this plan is helping students gain the key understandings listed in column 3. These understandings are not set in stone. Students may express other understandings that are important.

After experiencing and discussing several clear examples of biography over time, students work together with you to create a list of noticings about biography, and a working definition. The definition can be modified as students learn more about the genre. Using the definition as a base, you can plan and teach an umbrella minilesson that builds on what students already know (see Figure 16.13, page 308).

Differentiating the Types of Nonfiction Texts

Nonfiction texts are complex, and it takes many years of study for students to differentiate the various types. Throughout their school years, student readers face an amazing increase in nonfiction text difficulty. For example:

- Overall text structures become increasingly complex.
- Texts switch structures for different purposes.

PLAN FOR USING BIOGRAPHICAL TEXTS DURING INTERACTIVE READ-ALOUD		
Text	**Opening Remarks**	**Places to Invite Conversation**
A Voice from the Wilderness: The Story of Anna Howard Shaw by Don Brown	"We have a new biography today. The information in this book came from Anna Howard Shaw's own autobiography, a book Anna wrote about her own life. Some of the actual words she wrote are included. [Read title, author, and illustrator.] This biography starts in an interesting way: 'By most measures, Anna Howard Shaw's life was hard and filled with struggle. But Anna used her own scale and kept her own measurements, and that made all the difference.' [p. 1] Turn and talk about what you think that could mean.	p. 8—"Turn and talk to a partner about why the writer compared becoming a pioneer to learning to eat a banana." p. 14—"Here is what Anna wrote later about her mother: 'But her face never lost the deep lines those first hours of pioneer life cut upon it.' Turn and talk about what you are thinking. p. 22—"The writer said Anna felt rudderless just like the ship they were on that almost sank. What do you think the writer was trying to tell us?" p. 28—"What did you notice about the ending? [Students will notice that the book ends as it began.] What do you think the author's message was?" Share some information from the author's note. *Key understandings:* **1.** *Anna faced many hardships but she worked hard to overcome them.* **2.** *She loved learning and educated herself.* **3.** *She developed the ability to speak to people by practicing.* **4.** *She decided to enroll in college and worked very hard for education.* **5.** *Anna fought for the rights of women to vote.* **6.** *She was a pioneer as a child and also a pioneer as a woman.*
The Secret World of Walter Anderson by Hester Bass	"Today we are going to read another biography. It's called *The Secret World of Walter Anderson.* Have you ever heard of Walter Anderson? [It would be surprising if students knew about this artist.] I don't think I had heard of him either, but it's not surprising. Walter Anderson was a great artist, but he had a 'secret world.' He Shared much of his art, but he kept his most famous paintings and drawings for himself and no one saw them until after he died. We are going to hear that he loved nature.	p. 12—"Turn and talk about what you are thinking." p. 24—"Turn and talk about why you think Walter was so happy on Horn Island all by himself." p. 28—"How do you think Mrs. Anderson felt when she saw the secret room and all the paintings?" Bring in information from the author's note. Invite students to look at the book independently during readers' workshop.

Figure 16.12 Plan for using biographical texts during interactive read-aloud *continues*

PLAN FOR USING BIOGRAPHICAL TEXTS DURING INTERACTIVE READ-ALOUD		
Text	**Opening Remarks**	**Places to Invite Conversation**
	As I read, be thinking about how this writer is helping us understand Walter's love of art."	Key understandings: 1. *Walter painted to bring himself and nature together in art.* 2. *He painted for the joy of art and nature rather than to sell paintings. (Often he painted his murals for nothing.)*
The Boy who Invented TV: The Story of Philo Farnsworth by Kathleen Krull	"[Show end papers.] Look at the drawings on the endpapers of this biography! What are you thinking? [Students may not at first realize that these are all television sets.] TV was invented many years ago, and it looked like this one with a little round window. It was invented in the 1920s by a 22-year-old man named Philo Farnsworth, and this biography is the story of his life. As I read, be thinking about what kind of boy Philo was and how that may have led him to invent TV."	p. 9—"Turn and talk to a partner about what you noticed about Philo as a boy." p. 15—"Turn and talk about the idea of 'pictures that fly through the air.'" p. 29—He was a real inventor, like his heroes—someone who connected people, a shaper of the world to come. Thanks to him, the future would include TV. "Turn and talk about what you are thinking." [Students may ask why Phil did not become famous.] Bring in information from the author's note. *Key understandings:* 1. *Philo was very curious when he was a boy.* 2. *He dreamed of "capturing light in a bottle" through electricity.* 3. *He invented TV but did not get the credit for it in his lifetime.*
Gregor Mendel: The Friar Who Grew Peas by Cheryl Bardoe	"We have been reading some biographies this week. Some of the people, you have never heard of before. What are some of the things you've learned from these biographies? [Students may cite some specific facts or say they learned more about an invention or a person.] Today I'm going to read a book about Gregor Mendel. You may not have heard of him but you have heard of genes. [Give students a chance to talk about what they know.] Gregor Mendel is the person who discovered how we inherit	p. 6—"Notice that the writer includes some words that Gregor wrote himself: '[I needed to] be spared perpetual anxiety about a means of livelihood.' So he is at a decision point, isn't he? Turn and talk about what you are thinking." p. 12—He focused his attention on one of the hottest scientific questions of his time: How do mothers and fathers—whether they are apple trees, sheep, or humans—pass down traits to their children? "Turn and talk about why you think he was so interested in that question." p. 26—Gregor's hunger for knowledge had led to a great discovery. It was time to tell the world. "Turn and talk about the way Gregor worked to make this discovery."

Figure 16.12 Plan for using biographical texts during interactive read-aloud *(cont.)*

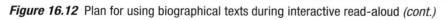

PLAN FOR USING BIOGRAPHICAL TEXTS DURING INTERACTIVE READ-ALOUD		
Text	**Opening Remarks**	**Places to Invite Conversation**
	things like hair color and eye color from grandparents and parents. People don't always look like someone in the family, but has anyone ever said that you look like someone in your family? [Invite talk.] Gregor Mendel discovered the rules of inheritance by growing peas. As I read, be thinking about the way that he worked to make his discoveries. He worked hard for a long time and in a particular way."	p. 30–So even though Gregor did not receive any recognition in his lifetime, today he is known as the first geneticist. "What are you thinking?" Share something from the author's note. *Key understandings:* 1. *Gregor had to overcome obstacles to reach his goal.* 2. *He worked carefully and patiently for years.* 3. *He used the scientific method.* 4. *He reached his dream even though he was not recognized for it while he lived.*
Animals Marco Polo Saw: An Adventure on the Silk Road by Sandra Markle	"Our new biography is about the very exciting adventures of Marco Polo. It happened many years ago–in 1271–800 years ago. Have you heard of Marco Polo? [Students may have heard the name but probably don't realize exactly what Marco did.] In the time of Marco Polo, most people didn't travel and didn't even know what the rest of the world was like, but Marco Polo went to China, Japan, and other countries in East Asia. And he wrote about his travels so that other people wanted to go exploring. As I read, think about how Marco's travels changed things. The writer also tells us about the animals Marco saw on his journeys. They were very important. The title is *Animals Marco Polo Saw: An Adventure on the Silk Road.*	p. 9–"But why did he go in the first place? And what did he discover along the way? You may be surprised to learn about the animals he encountered, some of which played a key part in the journey. Turn and talk with your partner about what it was like in Marco Polo's time." Point out the note in each section that describes the animals. p. 25–"So Marco and his father took a caravan instead of a boat. Turn and talk with your partner about what you have found interesting." p. 41–Suddenly, people wanted to know more about the world. Many European countries sent people out to explore. New interactions between the West and the East had begun. For better and for worse, they would change the world forever. "Let's talk about some of those changes that Marco Polo inspired." Key understandings: 1. *Traveling was an adventure and very dangerous in those days.* 2. *Animals were very important in Marco's journey. They helped him and he learned from them.* 3. *Marco's influence was greater because he wrote about his adventures.* 4. *Travel helps people learn more about their world.*

Figure 16.12 Plan for using biographical texts during interactive read-aloud *(cont.)*

UMBRELLA MINILESSON ON BIOGRAPHY

TEACHER:	We have read quite a few picture biographies, and you have noticed a lot about what they are like. Rachel, would you read the definition we wrote for biography based on what we know now?
RACHEL:	[Reading] A biography is a factual story about all or part of a real person's life. It tells what the person accomplished or overcame.
TEACHER:	What do you think is the most important part of this definition?
RICHARD:	It tells about what the person accomplished or overcame.
TEACHER:	Does everyone agree with that?
STUDENTS:	Yes.
TEACHER:	Usually biographies are about one person, although there are often other people in biographies who are important to the subject. Often the subject of the biography is famous because of what he or she did, though some are not famous or even very well known.
DORISA:	But just because we never heard of them doesn't mean they weren't famous when they lived.
TEACHER:	That's true. You are all noticing something readers think about when they read biographies. Readers think about why a writer might have chosen to write about the subject of a biography. The *subject* is a term we use to describe the person the biography is about. I will write that term here so we can start using it as we talk about our biographies. Let's think for a few minutes about some of the books we have read and why the authors might have chosen to write about the subject. *[The teacher reveals a chart with two columns. One column lists the titles of a few of the books the class has read together during interactive read-aloud. The other column has the heading:* ***Why the author might have chosen this subject****. As they discuss, the teacher records their thinking in this column.]* For example: Why do you think the author chose to write about Anna Howard Shaw in *A Voice from the Wilderness: The Story of Anna Howard Shaw*? Turn and talk to a partner for a moment. *[The teacher gives the students a minute to talk to their partner and then brings everyone back together to share their thinking.]* What were some of the things you and your partner were discussing?
DORISA:	We think the author chose to write about Anna because she helped women get the right to vote.
SARAH:	We also think the author wrote about her to teach us something.
TEACHER:	Can you say more about that?

Figure 16.13 Umbrella minilesson on biography

UMBRELLA MINILESSON ON BIOGRAPHY	
SARAH:	We think the author is trying to say that if you work hard, you can overcome your struggles and make a difference in other people's lives.
TEACHER:	So, are you saying that sometimes authors of biographies choose their subjects because they have something to teach us about our own lives?
SARAH:	Yes.
TEACHER:	Okay, let's look at one more example and then try to sum up what we have been talking about. *[The teacher offers one more example from the books they have read and the students discuss why the author might have chosen the subject of the biography to write about. She again writes the students' ideas on the chart paper.]* So, let's see if we can write a minilesson principle to sum up our thinking. Readers . . . anyone want to offer a suggestion? Larry?
LARRY:	Readers think about why an author has chosen the subject of a biography.
TEACHER:	What does everyone think about that as a start?
STUDENTS:	Good.
TEACHER:	I think that is a good start too. I am going to add a second part to our statement that we will be working on over the course of the week. *[The teacher writes the principle on chart paper.]* Does anyone want to read the principle for us?
CHRISTINA:	Readers think about why the author has chosen the subject of a biography and pay attention to how the writer reveals the reason to better understand and evaluate the information.
TEACHER:	We will be working together this week to think about these ideas in more detail. Today, during your independent reading think about why the author of the biography you are reading chose his subject. Please be prepared to share with the group at the end of readers' workshop. *[The teacher plans to follow up this umbrella minilesson with related minilessons. For example:* *Readers notice the events a writer chooses to include from a subject's life to better understand the subject's significance.* *Readers think about how an author's use of figurative language, imagery, and word choice helps reveal the significance of the subject's life to better understand the information.* *Readers think about why the author chose his subject in order to evaluate the information for accuracy and bias.*

Figure 16.13 Umbrella minilesson on biography *(cont.)*

- Information is embedded within more detailed categories (headings, subheadings, sub-subheadings).
- There are many different embedded text structures.
- Vocabulary becomes highly technical.
- Many kinds of graphics are introduced.
- Information presented in insets can be distracting.
- There is more technical information that is not part of readers' general knowledge.

All nonfiction texts provide information, but they do it in different ways and for different purposes. The minilesson principles in Figure 16.14, used as part of an inquiry into mentor texts, help students understand the different types.

Constructing the Curriculum

Since genre study continues during all the years of schooling, accomplishing the goals of genre study requires collaboration with your colleagues as you map a curriculum. Potential units of study include:

- *Genre*: It is obvious that genre is not the *only* focus for learning about reading. There are all of the systems of strategic actions that readers are required to use to process and understand texts. Aspects of the writer's craft are important beyond genre as well. But it is also true that by studying genre, students learn many more aspects of reading. Genre study of nonfiction texts is essential for promoting deep understanding of the special aspects of this kind of text.

<table>
<tr><th colspan="4">MINILESSON PRINCIPLES THAT HELP STUDENTS UNDERSTAND DIFFERENT KINDS OF NONFICTION TEXTS</th></tr>
<tr><td colspan="4">Umbrella Minilesson Principles:
■ Readers notice the writer's purpose so that they can tell whether a text is meant to tell a story, give facts about a topic, tell how to do something, or persuade.
■ Readers notice how the nonfiction writer organized the information in a nonfiction book—a story, an explanation of facts, steps in a procedure, or points in an argument—so that they can understand the information.</td></tr>
<tr><td>Biographical and Narrative Nonfiction</td><td>Expository Nonfiction</td><td>Procedural Texts</td><td>Persuasive Texts</td></tr>
<tr><td>Minilesson Principle:
Readers notice when the writer of a nonfiction text is using a narrative style so that they can learn about a topic and its importance.</td><td>Minilesson Principle:
Readers notice when the writer of a nonfiction text is telling different kinds of facts so that they can learn about the topic and its importance.</td><td>Minilesson Principle:
Readers notice when the writer of a nonfiction text is explaining procedures (or steps in how to do something) so that they can learn about the sequence and its importance.</td><td>Minilesson Principle:
Readers notice when the writer of a nonfiction text is trying to get them to agree or persuade them so that they can understand the arguments and the evidence.</td></tr>
</table>

Figure 16.14 Minilesson principles that help students understand different kinds of nonfiction texts

- *Craft*: Work to help students understand the writer's craft by examining mentor texts. At the same time, craft is closely related to genre, so it may be possible to study both simultaneously. Craft is just as important in nonfiction as in fiction texts.
- *Conventions*: Conventions are important in the writing of fiction and nonfiction texts and are an aspect of the writer's craft.
- *A specific author/illustrator*: Studying the body of work of an author or an illustrator helps readers notice the details of craft and become more insightful about the deeper meanings of texts. Often, writers specialize in a particular genre, so genre study and author study merge. When writers produce several genres, students notice how they change the style and forms of their writing.
- *Using a reader's notebook and forms for writing about reading:* As student readers study genres, they can extend their thinking through writing. As you teach minilessons, you want students to respond in writing. They may note minilesson principles and jot down examples of texts they know that illustrate them. They may make notes of characteristics of the texts they are reading or respond to some of the language in the text.

- *Minilessons on oneself as a reader*: As they grow in knowledge of genre, students also need to understand more about themselves as readers and build their reading life. Studying genre is not simply an academic exercise. Lifelong readers have favorite genres and within that, favorite authors, time periods, and subject matter. They have preferences they can talk about with others.

There is no one pathway to helping students learn the critical understandings related to each genre. Your students will also bring their noticings and wondering together with your expertise to make genre study filled with new insights and enjoyment of books.

Suggestions for Professional Development

Explicit minilessons are key to developing an in-depth understanding of genres.

1. Form grade-level groups.
2. Collect one type of informational text: biography, narrative nonfiction, expository nonfiction, procedural texts, or persuasive texts.
3 Discuss the characteristics you notice and make a list of large categories or "umbrellas" for your minilessons.
4. Select one umbrella category and list specific minilessons that will develop the idea.
5. For each minilesson, write a statement of the principle. Be sure to tell what readers need to think about and why.

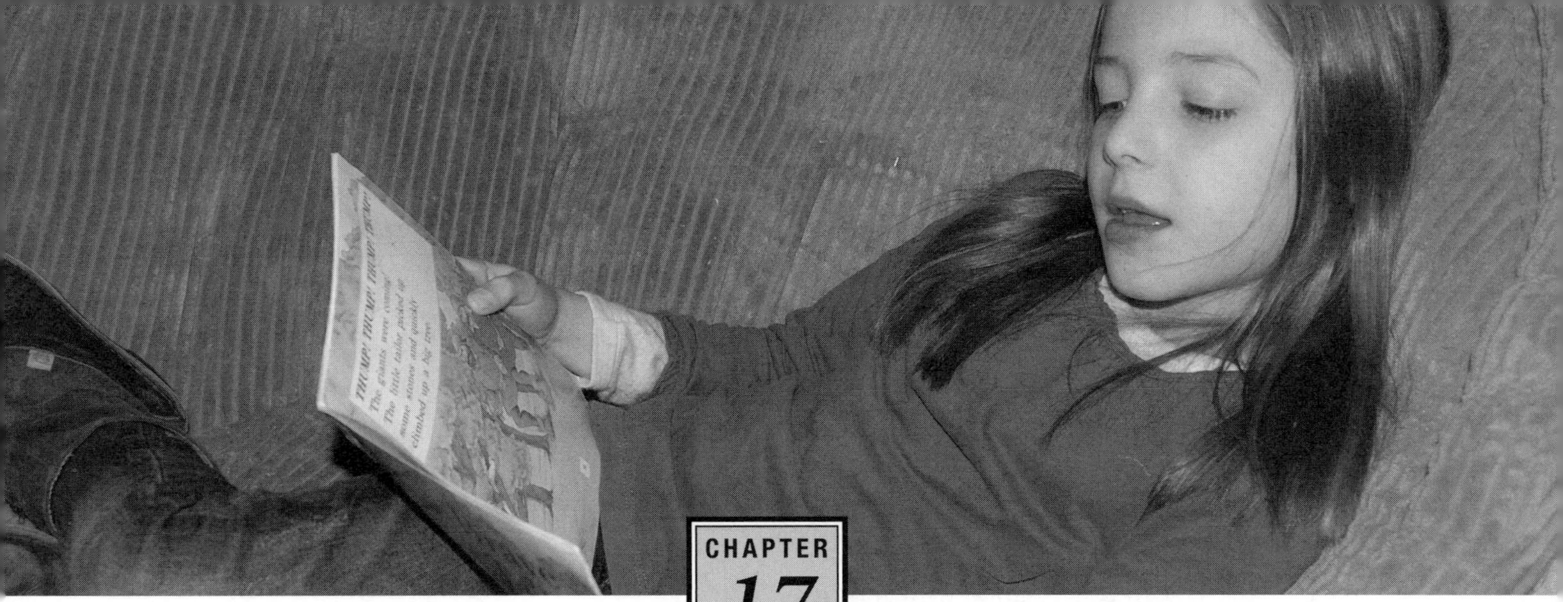

CHAPTER 17

Developing Understandings About Genre Through Reading Conferences and Independent Reading

No single literacy activity has a more positive effect on students' comprehension, vocabulary knowledge, spelling, writing ability, and overall academic achievement than free voluntary reading.

—Stephen Krashen

During a crowded day in the classroom it is difficult to find time for one-to-one interactions, yet students learn as individuals and that is how you need to think of them. The structure of readers' workshop makes a place for individual conferences; it is a way to make the one-to-one time you spend with students especially powerful. The basic structure of readers' workshop includes a book talk and minilesson at the beginning, followed by students' independent reading and teacher-student conferences (often involving writing about reading), and a time for sharing at the end of the period. Once students have learned the routines for independent reading, teachers have forty or forty-five minutes to work with small groups in guided reading or book clubs, and/or meet with individuals in the earliest grades (K–1) students may work at literacy centers. At the beginning of the year, spend the bulk of the time meeting with individuals in reading conferences so you can learn as much as possible about them.

Several big ideas have important implications for planning reading conferences:

- Individual interactions during readers' workshop *help students become lifelong readers.* Talking with others about books increases interest and enjoyment. Also, individual attention makes students feel special and powerful.

- The goal of the conference is to *teach the reader, not the text*. The purpose is not testing or simply helping the student read a particular book. The conference gives the teacher an opportunity to support thinking that the reader can apply to many texts.
- The conference is a *reader-to-reader conversation*. Students learn a great deal about how to talk about books, extending their own thinking through expressing it. Rather than answering a string of questions, students experience the give and take of conversation with another reader. This kind of dialogue works very well even if the teacher has not read the particular book because questions can fall out naturally, just as they would when two literate people recommend books to each other.
- The conference has a definite *structure that supports new learning*. It is not idle conversation. The teacher has the opportunity to gain information about the reader; the student plays a role in guiding the direction of the conference. Both student and teacher talk; the teacher is interested in the reader and the reader's thinking. The teaching is "intentional" and the conference results in learning.
- Lastly, and very importantly, the teacher gets to know the student as a unique person and builds the relationship.

Independent Reading

Independent reading is life's work, not just school work. It is the classroom reading activity that most closely reflects what literate people do voluntarily. Of course, almost everyone reads as part of his job, but the true mark of a literate life is the enjoyment of fiction and nonfiction as a choice. Independent reading within the readers' workshop is framed by strong instruction (minilesson and sharing) and supported by conversations in which teachers use facilitative talk. But strong elements of classroom independent reading are *choice, personal responsibility*, and *sustained time to read*:

- *Choice* has been shown to increase motivation for reading (Guthrie 2006). Sometimes, students have had so few choices (or so little guidance in learning how to choose) that they find it quite difficult to select appropriate texts. Part of the instructional work of readers' workshop is to teach students how to choose books that will engage them. In so doing, you are putting power in their hands. Choosing books is a way to develop the tastes, habits, and attitudes of a reader. According to Daniels and Bizar (2005) student choice is one of the important characteristics of best-practice classrooms.
- *Autonomy*—personal responsibility—is closely related to choice and to the genuine motivation that leads to greater conceptual understanding (Pinker 2009). Students are supported by teaching, but each day they also experience the personal responsibility of processing a text and doing their own thinking about it. They are empowered and in control of their own learning.
- The *volume* of reading is also important. Students read independently for about forty minutes each day and almost the same amount of time each evening for homework. They have opportunities to talk with others about their reading; in the process they clarify their own thinking and benefit from others' ideas. In a classroom with a literate culture, students are always choosing books and recommending them to others. They look for chances to talk with others who have read the same book. They see reading not as an assignment or a test but as part of what they do and enjoy every day.

A frequent practice in schools is to have all the students in a class read the same novel, working with a shared text. And as a teacher you may have your favorite novels that you love. But you can easily build a set of shared texts through interactive read-aloud and book clubs. In addition, allocate substantial time to choice reading.

> Whole-class novels, often chosen with the best of intentions, do not take reading and interest levels into account. There is no one book that will speak to the needs of every student in my class and the large block of time usually devoted to these books does not mimic the type of reading real readers do. The time I have with my students is too valuable to waste on practices that don't push them to grow. (Allison 2009, 4)

It is well worth taking the time to establish the routines of readers' workshop. In doing so, you create the kind of space your students need to read more books and deepen their engagement with those books.

An Environment for Reading

The first step is to create a physical context that supports daily reading. Assemble a good collection of books, as well as readers' tools to support the work of readers' workshop. The school library is an important support, but for a dynamic readers' workshop in which all students participate actively, the texts and tools should be available in the classroom. In some schools, the librarian and classroom teachers together create sets of books that rotate in and out of classroom libraries.

Books and Other Texts

A classroom needs a collection of six hundred to a thousand-plus books (at least thirty books per student). When starting with very few books, you can supplement the collection with books from the school library or public libraries. You can also build the collection by instigating book clubs and asking students to loan some of their own books for the year. *Leveled Books, K–8: Matching Texts to Readers for Effective Teaching* (Fountas and Pinnell 2005) describes in detail how to build and organize a classroom library over time.

The classroom library books should not be labeled with a "level" or organized by level. Students need to learn how to choose books using the criteria readers use (difficulty, interest, genre, or writing style, for example). Also, within any classroom there is a range of reading competencies; the collection needs to reflect the levels of difficulty that students can read. You can of course guide particular students who can't easily choose for themselves, but learning how to choose appropriate books is a life skill. Students need to be taught how.

A great way to connect students with the right books is to make them easy to find. There are many—perhaps hundreds—of ways to organize the classroom library. The least interesting way is on shelves, spine out, in alphabetical order by author. Bookstores are organized by sections so that readers can quickly find the genres they like. Many books are placed face out on tables at the front of the store or in the middle of a section, labeled *bestsellers*, *popular authors*, *summer reading*, *staff recommendations*, and similar designations.

To make the classroom a place that "sells" books, you can organize them in tubs or baskets with the covers facing out so that students can flip through them. You can group books in any way that will interest your students. For example:

- Mischievous or silly characters
- Series books
- Sequels
- New versions of old stories
- Genres:
  - Biographies
  - Cultural tales
  - Humorous books
  - Nonfiction authors
  - Mysteries
- Popular authors (authors you have shared or that many have read).
- Popular illustrators
- Other worlds and times
- Topics
- Graphic texts
- Themes
- Nonfiction magazines
- Maps, brochures, field guides
- Books you have read aloud

Just about any category will work as long as it is of interest to the students, and as you acquire more books and learn about your students' preferences, the categories will grow.

If possible there should be books of a range of difficulty levels within each tub or basket so that all students interested in the topic can find something they can read independently. And you needn't worry if all the books in a category aren't neatly parallel: almost any text fits into two or more categories. It's better to have some variation to match the variety of students exploring the categories. Books that have been read aloud should be easily available in a special basket. Classroom libraries should also include magazines, maps, brochures, field guides, and other everyday literacy materials students need to read and understand.

Examples of how sections of classroom libraries can be organized are shown in Figures 17.1 through 17.4. Each has implications for genre study. The collection of books in Figure 17.1 focuses on genre. Within each basket is a variety of authors and types of texts, as well as books of a range of difficulty appropriate to the group. The organization of sections in Figure 17.2 is by popular author (particular authors will vary by grade level). Many popular authors specialize in a specific genre, but make a point to include those who write in several. Organization can also focus on one genre (nonfiction is the focus of the section in Figure 17.3 and within it a variety of nonfiction genres) or on series books (see Figure 17.4).

Figure 17.1 Section of classroom library with genre baskets

Figure 17.2 Section of classroom library with author baskets

Figure 17.3 Section of classroom library with a focus on nonfiction

Figure 17.4 Section of classroom library with series books

Series books are a great way to help students increase their reading volume. If you read the first book in a series aloud, introduce it in a book talk, or use it with a guided reading group, students who get hooked may read a sequel or several more books in the series. Reading books that have sequels also allows students to meet characters they love and then follow them over time as they change. Students love series and sequels; their confidence increases as they read more and more, because they bring significant background knowledge to the experience. Like all texts, series books fit into genre categories, and sometimes readers can learn a great deal about a genre by reading a whole series. (See the extensive list of books in a series or with sequels on the F&P Resources Site.)

Classroom libraries also need multiple copies of books for genre book clubs: fantasies, mysteries, historical fiction, nonfiction. Meeting with the librarian and grade-level colleagues is a good way to create multiple copy sets that can be passed around to different classrooms. (After a book has been read by a book club, one copy should remain in the classroom library; other students are sure to want to read it.)

Tools

It is important that simple tools to support readers' workshop be readily available to students. (Some may be used in electronic or digital versions.)

Reader's Notebook

The reader's notebook is a vessel for thinking about reading. In this notebook, usually kept in a box or basket labeled with the student's name, readers keep lists of the books they read and their written responses to their reading. The reader's notebook (described in detail in Chapter 18) is also an important source of assessment information; it gives an immediate update on the number and types of books a student has read, how difficult they were, and what they thought about them.

Stick-On Notes

Stick-on notes are a valuable tool (Figure 17.5 shows one in use); they are helpful in many ways:

- Students can mark places they want to talk about during reading conferences or in book clubs.
- They can make a brief notes about places in the text they want to remember when they write a response in the reader's notebook, give a book talk, or write a book review.
- They can mark examples related to a minilesson that they want to share at the end of the workshop.

Genre Thinkmarks

A Genre Thinkmark (see Figure 17.6) is a tool that guides readers to note certain elements in their reading (see *Guiding Readers and Writers* (Fountas and Pinnell 2000) for a general Thinkmark). Readers can quickly note the page numbers of parts of a text where they see evidence of specific genre characteristics, and share them with others. A variety of genre-specific Thinkmarks are included with the additional resources on the F&P Resources Site. They can be used when students are applying their new understandings to their study of genre.

Wall Charts

When you present a minilesson, create a chart with the minilesson principle and some examples—a definition, a list of characteristics, and so on in the process. These charts are a valuable resource for student readers. They help them remember the minilesson principle and decide what to share at the end of readers' workshop or in conferences. Often, teachers have students copy these charts or give a photocopy into their reader's notebooks so they can refer to them there as well. A wall chart defining genres that students in one classroom have studied is shown in Figure 17.7.

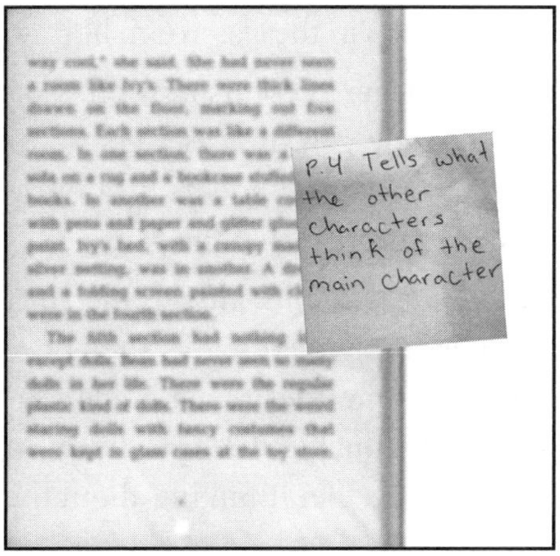

Figure 17.5
A stick-on note marking a page in a book

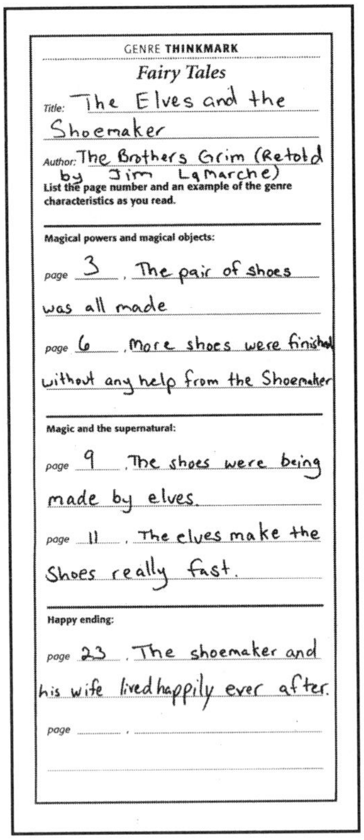

GENRE THINKMARK

Fairy Tales

Title: The Elves and the Shoemaker

Author: The Brothers Grim (Retold by Jim LaMarche)

List the page number and an example of the genre characteristics as you read.

Magical powers and magical objects:

page 3, The pair of shoes was all made

page 6, More shoes were finished without any help from the Shoemaker

Magic and the supernatural:

page 9, The shoes were being made by elves.

page 11, The elves make the Shoes really fast.

Happy ending:

page 23, The shoemaker and his wife lived happily ever after.

page ______, ______

Figure 17.6 A Genre Thinkmark

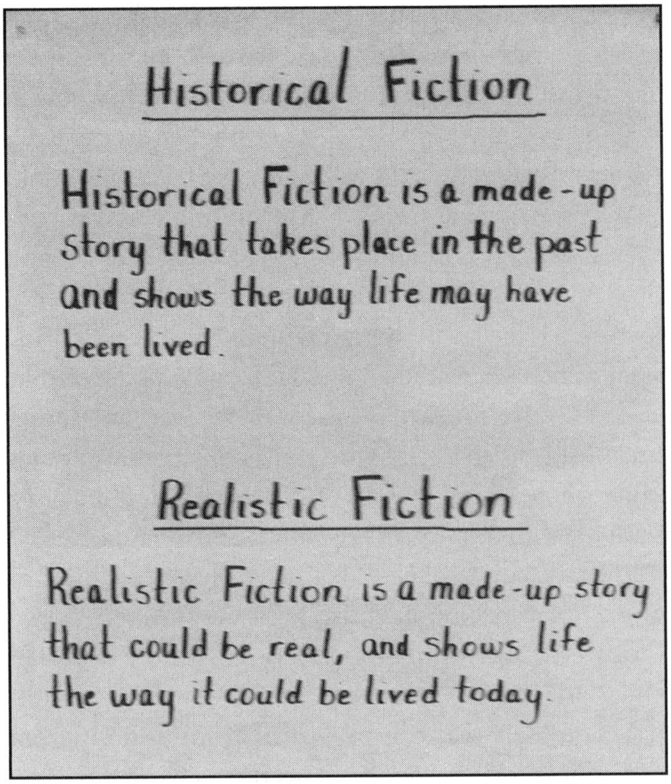
Historical Fiction
Historical Fiction is a made-up story that takes place in the past and shows the way life may have been lived.
Realistic Fiction
Realistic Fiction is a made-up story that could be real, and shows life the way it could be lived today.

Figure 17.7 Chart showing the genres the class has studied so far

Readers' Workshop as a Setting for Individual Conferring

A readers' workshop includes the following components within a recommended sixty-minute period:

1. *Book talk.* The teacher has the option of making one or more book talks, brief descriptions designed to get students to read specific books as part of a genre study. In anywhere from one to three minutes, students get to know particular authors, series, or titles in the classroom library.
2. *Minilesson.* The teacher presents a minilesson on any aspect of reading in this case, a particular genre. Minilessons raise students' awareness of the specific characteristics of the genre.
3. *Independent reading and individual conferring.* Students independently read books they have chosen. During this time, the teacher holds conferences with individuals. Students have an opportunity to express their thinking about the book and the genre.
4. *Group share.* The whole class meets briefly at the end of the workshop. The teacher revisits the minilesson principle. Students report what they have noticed while reading relative to the principle. During a genre study, students may be asked to read at least one book in that genre and notice and share their thinking about characteristics.

Book Talks for Independent Reading

Once you have collected some wonderful examples of texts in the selected genre, take one more step to get readers interested and excited. Select some of the books you think will most interest your students and introduce them in short book talks. The point is to sell the book, telling just enough about it to whet readers' appetites. For example:

> "We have been talking about realistic fiction, and you are choosing some books in that genre. One book I really enjoyed is *The Chalk Box Kid,* by Clyde Robert Bulla. It's about a boy, Gregory, whose father has lost his job. The family has to

move to a new neighborhood, and Gregory has to share a room with his uncle Max, who isn't very nice to him. Some of you remember what it's like to move to a new school. Sometimes making all new friends is hard. Gregory likes to draw, and he tries to find a place that belongs to him. You may want to read this book and find out whether he does that. It's realistic fiction—a story that could happen today."

"I have a new book for our historical fiction collection. The title is *The Witch of Blackbird Pond,* and it's by Elizabeth George Speare. This is one of my favorites. In fact, I read it when I was about your age. It's historical fiction, but the writer has some messages that are important for us to think about today. The story takes place in 1687, in Connecticut. The main character is a girl named Kit, who is sixteen. Kit grew up on Barbados, a tropical island, but after her grandfather died, she had to go to live with her aunt and uncle in Connecticut. At that time, people in Connecticut were very strict Puritans. They wouldn't allow bright colors or other things they thought were fancy. And they believed in witches. It was really dangerous to be accused of being a witch. If you read this book, you can find how Kit tried to adjust to this really different place and to the people. I'll read a bit to let you know how she is feeling at the beginning: "Almost choking with helpless rage she stumbled after Judith, who had moved ahead too absorbed to even notice. Oh, why had she ever come to this hateful place?"

"Several of you have read books by Katherine Paterson, a really good writer. She writes in several genres. I've read some of her historical fiction. Some of you read *The Great Gilly Hopkins,* which is realistic fiction. This book, *Bridge to Terabithia*, is realistic fiction. A couple of you have read it, but I wanted to talk about it quickly, because this is a special book. It's about a friendship between Jess, a boy, and Leslie, a girl. Together they create an imaginary place called Terabithia, and then a terrible tragedy occurs. You'll find out what happens when you read it."

By providing these one- or two-minute talks, you help your students get to know authors, genres, and titles in the classroom library and find books that appeal to them. If the book sounds interesting, students can record the title on the Books to Read list in the reader's notebook, making it quicker and easier to select a new book. (The reader's notebook is described in detail in Chapter 18.) Book talks also create excitement for new books. Most authors have websites that provide interesting information about their books (and often, their lives). Many book reviews can also be found online.

In a book talk, you can:

- Give a brief summary of exciting parts (without giving the climax away).
- Describe interesting characters in the story.
- Identify the type of reader who might enjoy the book.
- Identify the genre and say something about it.
- Describe the setting.
- Read quotes from the back of the book or book jacket.
- Talk about the theme of the book.
- Read aloud an exciting or humorous sentence or short passage to illustrate author's craft.
- Make connections to other books.
- Talk about the author or show a few books by the same author.
- Talk about the conflict in the story.
- Link the book to students' lives.
- Tell students what you liked about the book.
- Tell why the book won an award.
- Link it to another book you have read aloud to the class.
- Tell students what you think they will like about the book.

Students can also learn how to make these brief book talks to sell a book they have enjoyed. Books that their friends like are attractive to students; they enjoy delivering a book talk orally or writing a review on a blog classmates can access. In addition, lots of websites have podcasts of book talks. As an adult reader, you might note the titles of books that are mentioned briefly by your friends; book talks are a great way not only to get students reading good books but also to develop the habit of recommending books to and getting suggestions from others.

Minilesson

After one or two book talks, provide a focused minilesson on any aspect of reading. If you are studying a genre, focus the minilesson on one of the genre characteristics identified through inquiry (see Chapters 15 and 16). The minilesson principle has implications for the shape of the individual reading conferences. The principle and an excerpt from a minilesson on the setting in a biography are presented in Figure 17.8).

In this classroom, students had been advised to select a biography from the classroom collection to read independently when their present books were finished. Within a week, all students were reading biographies. In this minilesson, the teacher explores the idea that the setting is critical to understanding the subject's story in a biography. It is important for readers to understand the context in which the subject lived in order to understand the culture and attitudes at the time. The teacher ends the minilesson with these instructions:

> "As you read your biography today, be sure to notice the setting—what times and people were like when the subject of your biography lived. In past times, people sometimes faced challenges or difficulties that they would not today. You need to understand what life was like when and where the person lived to appreciate what he or she achieved. If we have a conference today, we'll talk about the setting for your biography, and then during group share, you can share a little bit about it with your friends."

The teacher raised students' awareness of an important element of biography and set the scene for powerful future conferences. In them, she'll first talk generally about the work or the thinking that the student is doing as a reader. But there will be a teaching point that supports the reader in learning something new. If appropriate, the teaching point can reflect the minilesson principle. And during group share, students will return to the principle and share their thinking with one another.

The Shape of a Reading Conference

Reading conferences do not take a long time, but any individual interaction with students has a powerful impact. Figure 17.9 is an example of an individual reading conference conducted within the context of a study of biography.

In this conference the teacher revisits the minilesson principle by asking Valerie to talk about the setting for the biography of Laura Ingalls Wilder. These questions and interactions will not always be the same and do not have to follow the minilesson principle. Make decisions appropriate for the individual student. This teacher wants to give Valerie more support and help her prepare for sharing, and at the same time nudge her to think deeply about biography. She begins by listening to Valerie read orally and determines that the text is too easy for her: Valerie needs to try something more challenging. At the same time, Valerie is relatively inexperienced reading biography, so reading the book is productive, and she goes through it quickly.

After checking on how Valerie is doing as a reader, the teacher makes a teaching point that arises from the student's expressed confusion. With Laura Ingalls Wilder, it's difficult to trace the fine line between historical fiction and autobiography. Talking about this text helps Valerie begin to understand the differences among genres. Following the teaching, Valerie is encouraged to read a little more text silently and to think about Laura's experiences. At the end of the conference, the teacher summarizes their conversation and encourages her to begin another biography right away.

A conference takes place at the student's desk or table; pull up next to the student and work eye to eye with her. The conference gives you the opportunity to differentiate instruction and help the reader become more independent in reading choices. Through the conference you can also help your students reflect on and think about their own reading. Meet the learner at the point of need and do a few minutes of powerful individual teaching.

While conferences are tailored to the individual, it is helpful to remember a basic series of steps that support your effectiveness (see Figure 17.10).

EXCERPT FROM A MINILESSON ON SETTING IN A BIOGRAPHY

A biography tells the story of all or a part of a real person's life. It tells about what they accomplished or overcame.

MINILESSON STATEMENT:

Setting—Readers think about the setting in a biography and its influence on the life of the subject to understand the subject's challenges and decisions.

TEACHER:	You have been reading and learning about biographies. Stan, can you read the definition?
STAN:	[Reads the definition.] "A biography tells the story of all or a part of a real person's life. It tells about what they accomplished or overcame." It's usually a person who has done something important or who is famous.
TEACHER:	That's right. There is usually something to be learned from reading about the life of a person who has done something important. Look at our list of things we noticed about biography. Today I'd like you to think more about this one [points]. The setting is critical to understanding the person's story. Remember the setting? It can be where the person lived and what life was like. Why do you think the setting is important in a biography?
JANET:	Because sometimes the person has a lot of problems or things to overcome that might be connected to the time or place they lived in. Like Wilma Rudolph grew up during the Great Depression and her family was poor.
KRISTI:	She grew up in the South too, and there was still segregation back then.
TEACHER:	So, when you think about the setting, think about what the person's life was like–the time and the place. Remember the biography of Philo Farnsworth–the boy who invented television? [Holds it up.] Think about Philo's life in the early 1900s on a farm in the west. What was it like?
HEATHER:	He didn't even have electricity or a telephone.
AARON:	It was just really out in the country. He worked on the farm.
TEACHER:	Right, he didn't have things like a telephone or electricity because many of those things were just being invented. What else do you remember?
PAUL:	He liked inventions and he wanted to invent something, too.
KRISTI:	He was bullied but he kept going and learned to play the violin and then to invent things.
PAUL:	TV's such a big invention but nobody really heard about him.
TEACHER:	It's interesting to read about the childhood of people like Wilma and Philo. Wilma was sickly and couldn't get the medical care she needed because she was African American, but she became the fastest woman in the world. Philo lived on a farm, but he was fascinated by new inventions. Remember Jacques Cousteau? We read a biography about him called *Manfish*. He grew up near the sea and loved it. How did the setting make a difference for him?
HEATHER:	He loved it so much he wanted to explore it and protect it from pollution.
TEACHER:	All of you are reading a biography and you will be able to think about the setting, especially the part about the subject's childhood, and why it is important.

Figure 17.8 Excerpt from a minilesson on setting in a biography

READING CONFERENCE FOCUSING ON CHARACTERISTICS OF BIOGRAPHY		
TEACHER:	I see you are reading *Laura Ingalls Wilder: An Author's Story*. Read a little aloud to me.	**Status**
VALERIE:	[Reads] "Life in South Dakota was very hard. Summers were hot and the winters were freezing cold. One winter, a blizzard hit the town. Store owners had only kept a little food for sale in the stores. Soon that ran out." I read about that time in *The Long Winter.* It's like it really happened.	
TEACHER:	This whole biography is about Laura's real life. Are you enjoying it?	
VALERIE:	I like it because I read some of the Little House books.	
TEACHER:	Did you recognize anything else?	
VALERIE:	The little house in the woods and her sisters, too. Her books are just like her life, but they were fiction—historical fiction I think. It's kind of confusing.	
TEACHER:	Most writers draw from their lives when they tell their stories. But often they just use some of the feelings and the events that happened, and they make up other things, so the work is fiction. It's not wholly factual, but the writer uses what she knows to make a good story. It sounds like Laura's stories are very close to what she experienced in her life. Is that right?	**Teaching Point**
VALERIE:	Yes, she even used the same names and the same places. But maybe she changed just enough that it couldn't be nonfiction. But she isn't a writer yet in this book.	
TEACHER:	Laura didn't start to write until her children were grown up. And then she wrote about what she remembered, so her books are almost autobiographies. But probably she had to make up things like what people said and maybe some characters to make it more interesting. Is this the first biography you read?	
VALERIE:	I read one about Allen Say, who wrote *Grandfather's Journey.*	
TEACHER:	Yes, and *Tree of Cranes*. Was the setting important in Allen's biography?	
VALERIE:	Yes, he was born in Japan and lots of his books are about Japan or about coming from Japan.	
TEACHER:	Read on a little more silently, and then talk about what you are thinking about Laura and the setting in which she lived.	**Have a Go**
VALERIE:	[Reads the rest of page 14 through part of 16.] This is Almanzo. Laura was a teacher and she married him. She met him in the big snow when he got the food to them. But I only read about her as a teenager. Her life is going on after that. Maybe I'll read another of her books. It seems like she had a lot of hardships, but she was happy and she had them to write about.	
TEACHER:	That makes sense to me. So today we talked about the subject of a biography and how experiences in childhood—the setting—is very powerful in the life of the person. We also talked about how writers can use their experiences to create stories. You might want to share your thinking about Laura Ingalls Wilder during group share. It looks like you will finish this biography today. What are you thinking of next?	**Summary and Goals**
VALERIE:	I don't know, but I'd like a little bit longer one.	
TEACHER:	I think you could try a biography that is a little more challenging. Take a look at the biographies of Amelia Earhart and of Rosa Parks. And there is another really fascinating one called *Secret Soldier: The Story of Deborah Sampson.* It's a true story about a girl who pretended to be a boy and became a solder in the Revolutionary War.	**Connection to Independent Reading**

Figure 17.9 Reading conference focusing on characteristics of biography

THE SHAPE OF THE READING CONFERENCE		
Structure	**Description**	**Goals**
Status	The teacher begins by asking the student to talk about what he is reading, sampling some oral reading, looking at the reader's notebook, or looking at some writing about reading.	• Check in with the student. • Gather information about what the student is doing as a reader. • Assess oral reading fluency and problem-solving strengths/needs. • Listen to the reader. • Learn what the student thinks as a reader. • Learn how the reader manages his reading life—what he reads and why. • Determine whether the student is making good choices for independent reading. • Assess the student's comprehension and ability to apply the minilesson principle. • Find out what the student needs help with. • View the reader's history (reading list, genres). • Meet the reader at the point of need. Provide "just-in-time" teaching.
Teaching Point	Based on the conversation and ongoing observational records, the teacher teaches the student something specific. The teaching point is made through conversation that supports the reader in learning something new about reading. The teacher may demonstrate by talking about reading and/or may guide the student to use the reader's notebook.	• Match the individual's needs. • Help the reader become more independent. • Reinforce the minilesson principle if applicable. • Deepen the reader's understandings. • Help the reader think in new ways. • Deal with confusions; clarify concepts. • Help the reader process texts more effectively. • Expand the reader's thinking and ideas. • Confirm and expand understandings. • Talk about the frequency, volume and kinds of reading the student is doing. • Make recommendations to the reader. • Refer to mentor text examples. • Learn about the kinds of books, genres, authors, and series the reader is interested in.
Have a Go	The reader applies the new learning immediately through reading or writing about reading.	• Give the student the opportunity to solidify new learning. • Assess the effectiveness of the teaching point. • Help the reader prepare to talk about his thinking during group share.
Summary and Goals	The teacher summarizes the conference—what was learned.	• Support the reader's memory of new learning. • Bring new learning to conscious awareness so the student can use it while reading or writing about reading. • Set goals—student goals and teacher goals.

Figure 17.10 The shape of the reading conference

Status

Begin with some quick assessment to check the status of the reader. (If you just conferred with the student the day before, this may not be necessary.) Begin by simply asking the student, "Talk about what you are thinking about your reading" or "How can I help you with your reading?" or "What would you like to talk about?" You can also sample some oral reading if you want to check the ease and fluency with which the student is reading the chosen book. If you are focusing on genre study, this is a good time to ask the student to identify the genre of the text and talk about specific characteristics related to the genre. You may also look with the student at her reading list in the reader's notebook. This list gives you an opportunity to check on her life as a reader—the kinds of reading, the frequency, and the volume. You can discuss the reader's genre history. Some options for checking a reader's status are:

- Ask an open-ended question such as, "Talk about what you are thinking as you read this book." (Other openings are provided in Figure 17.11).
- Look at and discuss the student's reading list in her reader's notebook. (Students keep a record of all books read for independent reading; the list includes the title, author, and genre.) Ask a question such as, "What do you notice about the kinds of books you have been reading?" (Figure 17.12 presents additional possibilities.)
- Look at the student's writing—either her letters about her reading or any other kind of writing about reading that she has produced. Have the student read a bit of the writing and then talk about the thinking behind it.

(See *Prompting Guide, Part 2*—Prompts for Reading Conferences (Fountas and Pinnell 2012) for specific language to support individual conferences.)

WAYS TO OPEN A READING CONFERENCE

- What would you like to talk about?
- What are you reading? Talk about your thinking.
- What are you thinking about this book?
- Talk about your thinking right now.
- Where are you in your reading of this book?
- Are you enjoying this book? What do you like about it?
- You said in our last conference that you were going to try to ______. How are you doing with that?
- Since last time, you chose a new book. How is it going?
- How is this book choice working for you?
- Is there a part you'd like help thinking about?
- Point to where you are. Start reading aloud.
- Choose a paragraph to read aloud.
- Show a part you loved. Read it aloud.
- You are still reading [book]. How is it going?

Figure 17.11 Ways to open a reading conference

Teaching Point

After checking on the reader's status, make a specific teaching point designed to help the reader become more independent. Sometimes the teaching point will come from the student. Aways consider the student's agenda. The student may ask for specific support with her reading or writing about reading. Your goal is to lift the reader's understanding in some way by getting him to think in new ways or process texts more effectively. The teaching point is based not only on your brief status conversation but also on your ongoing assessment and knowledge of the student's accomplishments and needs. You can deal with confusions he encountered while reading the selected text and clarify concepts he doesn't understand, but your primary goal is to help him learn something that will improve his ability to read all texts.

This goal might be more efficient processing, which might involve learning how to take words apart, search for and use information, monitor reading, read with fluency and phrasing, or adjust reading for different genres. You can demonstrate or prompt students to act in ways that make their reading more proficient.

QUESTIONS TO ASK ABOUT THE READING LIST

- What do you notice about the kinds of books you have been reading?
- How do you feel about the number of books you have read?
- What genres seem to be your favorites?
- Do you see any favorite topics in the record of your reading?
- Do you see any favorite authors in the record of your reading?
- What kind of books do you think you should choose during the next month?
- What kinds of books are missing from your record of reading?

Figure 17.12 Questions to ask about the reading list

OPENINGS FOR A CONFERENCE ABOUT GENRE

- What is the genre of your book?
- What helped you realize that your book is [genre]?
- What have you noticed about this book that is like the list of characteristics we made for [genre]?
- Is the setting important in your book? Why?
- Talk about the subject of your biography. Why is the subject important?
- What did the writer do to help you understand the fantasy setting?
- Does this story seem like it could really happen? Show a place where the writer made the story (characters, setting) seem real and talk about it.
- How did the writer help you understand what times were like at that time? Show me a place.
- What lesson did this story teach you?

Figure 17.13 Openings for a conference about genre

Prompting Guide, Part 1 (Fountas and Pinnell 2008) will be helpful in this teaching.

You could also help the student think in new ways about his reading. You might discuss characters—how they feel and what motivates them—or have a conversation about the author's message or new information the student has gained from reading the text. The goal is that by thinking deeply about this text, the reader will learn how to approach and understand other texts.

If the focus is genre study, an individual conference is an ideal time to clarify understanding and clear up confusions. You might ask the student to talk about the book he has chosen in relation to genre. Some suggested questions are provided in Figure 7.13. *Genre Prompting Guide for Fiction* (Fountas & Pinnell 2012); *Genre Prompting Guide for Nonfiction, Poetry, and Test Taking* (Fountas & Pinnell 2012); and *Prompting Guide, Part 2* (Fountas and Pinnell 2012), described in Chapter 19, will also be helpful tools for selecting language that will open up the conversation about genre and expand students' thinking.

You may also decide to help the student use the reader's notebook to reflect on his reading. The reader's notebook captures the student's work for the year. In it, the reader catalogues accomplishments and documents the thinking he has been doing. It is not so much counting the number of texts and it is certainly not about the level. In fact, students do not select the book by level or record the level in the notebook. It is compiling a body of work that represents not only the volume of reading but tastes, preferences, and thoughts.

In the notebook, the student keeps a reading list of titles with author and genre and the date completed; he also keeps a list of topics, genres/types of books, authors, and some specific titles that are interesting. In addition, he writes once a week to his teacher about any reading he has done. He explains his thinking about reading, and the teacher responds. In addition, in other sections, the student writes notes from minilessons as well as examples of genre and genre characteristics. The following are examples of interactions in a conference using the reader's notebook:

- Look at the list of texts the student has read, as well as the Reading Interests lists to help him reflect on the body of his reading. Potential questions are shown in Figure 17.14.
- Select one of the student's letters about reading. Ask: "I noticed that you wrote [read the writing] about [book]. Can you talk more about that?" Or, "You read your first book this year in this genre. Can you talk more about what you notice about this genre?"
- Revisit a minilesson principle that the student has recorded in his reader's notebook. Ask, "How does your book fit the characteristics of the genre? Talk about your book and the lesson that we had then [today]."

Always, the goal of the teaching point is to help the student better understand some aspect of the reading process, including genre. Some suggestions for an effective teaching point are:

- Give clear, precise feedback to the student.
- Cue the student that you are teaching by saying something like this: "There's something I want to teach you how to do today [show you today], something readers do."
- Give an explanation of what you are teaching—what it is, and why it's important to learn.
- Explain how readers do what you want the student to learn how to do—describe how to do it, and/or give examples from your own reading.

REFLECTING ON THE STUDENT'S READING LIST IN THE READER'S NOTEBOOK

- Look at all of the books you have read. What do you notice about your reading list?
- You've read [number] books so far. That's [number] books a week. What do you think about that?
- Looking at this list, what would you say are the kinds of books that you like?
- You really like [genre]. What do you like about it? Why do you think you like it?
- From this list, what were some of your favorite books? Why?
- Are there any genres that you see missing from this list? Why is that?
- I notice that you haven't read any [many] books in [genre]. Why is that?
- Can I suggest some books for you in [genre]?
- I notice that you read [book] in [genre]. There's another book that I think you would like–[title].
- On your Reading Interests list, I noticed [topic]. I'd suggest [book].
- You have listed a lot of genres on the list of types of books that interest you. But you don't have many books of [genre] on your reading list. Can I suggest some?
- After listening to book talks and reading book reviews, you have listed some titles that you would like to read, and you have already read some of them. I think you would really like [book].
- You have listed [author] on your list of authors that interest you. Did you know that this author also wrote [title] in [another genre]?
- I see that you are reading almost all fiction [nonfiction] books. Let's look at some nonfiction [fiction] books that fit with the interests you have listed.
- How do you think you are doing with reading all the genres we are studying?
- You are reading a lot of books that are easy for you. Do you think you should try some that are more challenging?
- I noticed that you have abandoned several books. Do these books have things in common that don't appeal to you?
- What genre are you going to try next?

Figure 17.14 Reflecting on the student's reading list in the reader's notebook

- Name what you are teaching the student how to do—for example, how to think in a new way, how to notice character change, think about the facts in historical fiction.

Have a Go

Have the student try what you've just taught her, usually by having her talk about how she will do it, or by reading and then reflecting on it. Then ask the student to have a go by applying the new learning immediately to her reading or to book selection or to writing about reading. The application might involve asking the student to read for a specific purpose while you observe, or it might mean asking the student to take action after the conference and report to you in the next conference.

Summary and Goals

At the end of the conference, summarize the conversation and remind the student to use what you have taught him to do. A concise statement that repeats the teaching point or summarizes the learning as well as agreed upon goals will help the student remember the specific action that he needs to take. Record this summary in your notes so you can go back to it and/or build on it during your next conference with the student. These notes also help you summarize group learning during share time.

Group Share

At the end of readers' workshop, bring the whole class together for a brief sharing period. During this time, reinforce the minilesson principle, and have students share examples from their own reading that are relevant. When you work on genre characteristics, have students choose a book in that genre for independent reading. That way, they will have many examples to bring up during the discussion. If you are focusing on the setting for biography, for example, students can share with a partner or in triads the setting for the subjects in their own books and why it is important. Anticipating the group share brings a layer of raised consciousness to students' independent reading choices and creates accountability for thinking. Sharing gives them a chance to make the principle their own, providing examples.

Intentional Teaching in the Reading Conference

An individual conference with a reader offers many opportunities for teaching. The conversation is purposeful and intentional; you help students monitor their understandings and expand their thinking about what they are reading. The example of a reading conference in Figure 17.15 demonstrates how genre knowledge can be explored. In the conference, the teacher refers to the student's Reading List (see Figure 17.16, page 329) and Books to Read list (see Figure 17.17, page 330), both kept in the reader's notebook

In this conversation with Tenisha, the teacher's goal was to raise Tenisha's awareness of her favorite genre, realistic fiction, but also to help her broaden the range of texts she was reading. The teacher noticed that Tenisha tends to gravitate to series books, reading several of them quickly. She was building mileage and stamina as a reader but not experiencing the variety of genres she needed.

READING CONFERENCE FOCUSING ON GENRE	
TEACHER:	What book you are reading?
TENISHA:	*Frindle*, by Andrew Clements.
TEACHER:	And you just chose that today?
TENISHA:	I've had it two days.
TEACHER:	Have you read any other books by that author?
TENISHA:	I read *The Report Card* and I liked it so I chose this one.
TEACHER:	What do you like about Andrew Clements?
TENISHA:	Well, he writes about stuff that could really happen and kind of does really happen, like kids being afraid of their report card grades.
TEACHER:	His books do seem real, don't they? What's the genre?
TENISHA:	Realistic fiction.
TEACHER:	I wonder if his books seem real because of the problems he chooses or because of his characters and the way they act.
TENISHA:	It's both really.
TEACHER:	Can you think of an example from the book you are reading?
TENISHA:	Well, I just started this one, but there's a girl who is kind of quiet and nobody notices much, but she's smart. And she is in this really funny classroom; he really describes it. I never saw a classroom like it, but it could happen, and it's kind of exciting to think about it.
TEACHER:	So Andrew Clements makes you feel almost like you are there?
TENISHA:	Yes, like that girl is like me kind of.
TEACHER:	I sometimes feel like that when I read. Let's look at your reading list. Take a look at all the reading you have done and talk about what you notice about it.
TENISHA:	I read some easy books at the beginning of the year but they were really fun. I also like series books.
TEACHER:	I see that once you read a book in a series, you often read two or three more books in that series. What do you notice about the genres you've been choosing?
TENISHA:	I read one biography the week everyone was reading them. It was about Clara Barton. And I started to read *The Greek Gods*, but it was hard to understand so I abandoned it. I guess it's mostly realistic fiction.
TEACHER:	I see that. You must really like those kinds of books. You read one book, *The Bracelet*, that was historical fiction. That was one I presented in book talks. Did you like it?
TENISHA:	Yes, it was kind of sad but good.
TEACHER:	And you started *Misty of Chincoteague*. I remember that you abandoned it because it seemed hard, and that was a good decision. You can keep reading realistic fiction, but find some books in other genres that you like just as much. Let's look at your Books to Read list. [Looking at list.] You said here that you were interested in reading some fantasy.
TENISHA:	Yes, but I just never thought of one.

Figure 17.15 Reading conference focusing on genre

READING CONFERENCE FOCUSING ON GENRE

TEACHER:	What I enjoy about reading fantasy is that surprising things happen—really unexpected. And they are things that couldn't be real, but in a good fantasy, they seem real while I am reading. And also in a good fantasy, the characters can seem just as real as in realistic fiction. And the writer uses these imaginary events to give you a really strong message as a reader.
TENISHA:	I liked *James and the Giant Peach* when my mom read it to me.
TEACHER:	Roald Dahl does write good books of fantasy, so you could check out more of those. There's another really interesting one that you might like called *The Castle in the Attic*. It begins with a boy living in the real world but then he finds a castle and a knight who comes to life. Lots of kids really like it. Maybe *Princess for a Week* would be fun for you too. Ask Carrie about it. Also, you like series books. There is a series about a hamster named Humphrey that is really funny. I think you'd like it. Why don't you take a look at the fantasy basket and also the series books that are fantasy. Then you would have one in mind after finishing *Frindle*.
TENISHA:	Okay.
TEACHER:	When I talk with you next, maybe we can list two or three fantasy books, and we can also look for some biographies that you might put on your list of titles.

Figure 17.15 Reading conference focusing on genre *(cont.)*

Reading List

Select a book to read. Enter the title and author on your reading list. When you have completed it, write the genre and the date. If you have abandoned it, write an **A** and the date you abandoned it in the date column. Write an **E** if the book was easy for you to read, a **JR** if it was just right for you, and a **D** if it was difficult for you to read and understand. Place an asterisk (*) next to the code in the genre column if your book is a graphic text.

#	Title	Author	Genre Code	Date Completed	E, JR, D
1	Russell Sprouts	Joanna Horwitz	RF	9/10	E
2	Russell and Elysa	Joanna Horwitz	RF	9/15	E
3	The Boxcar Children	Gertrude Warner	RF	9/16	JR
4	Amanda Joins the Circus	Avi	RF	9/18	E
5	The Report Card	Andrew Clements	RF	9/20	JR
6	Marvin Redpost Class President	Louis Sacher	RF	9/25	E
7	The Boxcar children: the Hurricane Mystery	Gertrude Warner	RF	9/27	E
8	The Boxcar Children: the chocolate Sundae Mystery	Gertrude Warner	RF	10/1	JR
9	the Boxcar children return	Gertrude Warner	RF	10/3	JR
10	Misty of Chincoteague	Marguerite Henry	RF	10/7	E
11	Beezus and Ramona	Betsy Byers	NF	4	[illegible]
12	the Pinballs	Betsy Byers	RF	10/12	E
13	Clara Barton: Founder of American Red Cross	Augusta Stevenson	RF	10/21	JR

Figure 17.16 Tenisha's reading list

Tenisha would benefit from inquiry into nonfiction and fantasy. After the conference, the teacher made a note to monitor Tenisha's book selections and support her in finding both fantasy and nonfiction books. The planned inquiry into biography would be helpful.

Mark's reading list (see Figure 17.18) reveals a different pattern. Like many students who are taken with fantasy, Mark is adding steadily to the volume of fantasy texts but spending less time on nonfiction genres, although he has read several biographies and is beginning to sample other informational texts. After a reading conference (see Figure 17.19), his teacher made a note to continue to encourage Mark to vary his reading, especially during the upcoming genre study of nonfiction books.

Students are expected to develop tastes and preferences as readers: that's characteristic of all readers. Most adults have genres they choose more often than others. Students need to have the opportunity to get to know a range of genres so that they see their value, understand them, and even make new favorites. Inquiry into different genres can develop these understandings as well as some new experiences as readers.

Books to Read

Title	Author	Check When Completed
The Boxcar children Return	Gertrude Warner	✓
The Night Swimmers	Betsy Byars	✓
Otis Spofford	Beverly Cleary	✓
The Music of Dolphins	Karen Hesse	✓
Something upstairs	Avi	
George's Marvelous Medicine	Roald Dahl	
Frindle	Andrew Clements	✓
The Cat's Meow	Gary Soto	
Everything Dog	Marty Crisp	
The Castle in the Attic	Elizabeth Winthrop	
Princess for a Week	Betty Ren Wright	
Humphrey the Hamster Series	Betty G. Birney	

Figure 17.17 Tenisha's Books to Read list

Reading List

Select a book to read. Enter the title and author on your reading list. When you have completed it, write the genre and the date. If you have abandoned it, write an **A** and the date you abandoned it in the date column. Write an **E** if the book was easy for you to read, a **JR** if it was just right for you, and a **D** if it was difficult for you to read and understand. Place an asterisk (*) next to the code in the genre column if your book is a graphic text.

#	Title	Author	Genre Code	Date Completed	E, JR, D
1.	Commander Toad and the Voyage Home	Jane Yolen	F	9/5	E
2.	The Littles Go Exploring	John Peterson	F	9/7	E
3.	Pinky and Rex and the School Play	James Howe	F	9/10	E
4.	The Magic Finger	Roald Dahl	F	9/16	E
5.	The Twits	Roald Dahl	F	9/21	D
6.	Luke's Bully	Elizabeth Winthrop	RF	9/27	JR
7.	The Chocolate Touch	Patrick Catling	RF	10/1	JR
8.	Postcards from Australia	Helen Arnold	I	10/3	JR
9.	George's Marvelous Medicine	Roald Dahl	F	10/7	JR
10.	The Aliens are Coming	Colin McNaughton	F	10/10	E
11.	Pee-Wee's Tale	Johanna Hurwitz	F	10/16	E
12.	Pee Wee and Plush	Johanna Hurwitz	F	10/22	E
13.	I'm Too Fond of My Fur	Geronimo Stilton	F	10/25	E

Figure 17.18 Mark's reading list

Principles for increasing the power of the reading conference include:

- Listen carefully to the student; make eye contact and show with nonverbal gestures that you are listening and interested in what he is saying.
- Find out what the reader wants help with and is feeling good about.
- Prompt for more talk about thinking.
- Work for ways to make the reader independent rather than dependent on you. Help the reader use the resources in the classroom.
- Make notes on each conference so that you can find patterns over time and note progress.
- After the conference, use the recorded information to follow up in the next conference.
- Use the information from the conference to support the reader in guided reading lessons and inform your selection of minilessons.

Vary the reading conference by pulling together two or three students who are reading a particular genre (e.g., realistic fiction), to talk about and compare the characters and their problems. You might also have pairs of students confer with each other. Generally, students do not have ability to provide the lift that you do, but they can have productive conversations that increase their commitment to reading and their ability to use language to share their thinking.

The Role of Facilitative Talk in Helping Students Learn About Genre

Once you have set up the routines of readers' workshop and are using the structure of the reading conference, use conversation to expand students' thinking. This is called *facilitative talk* because it supports learners in deepening their understanding of texts. When your goal is helping them learn more about text genres, your knowledge of the particular genre helps you be very specific.

We have created a number of comprehensive tools designed to support teachers in using facilitative talk across many instructional contexts (see *Prompting Guide, Part 1*, *Prompting Guide, Part 2*, and *Genre Prompting Guide for Fiction* and *Nonfiction*). Figure 17.20 includes some examples of the kinds of prompts that facilitate and expand student thinking that can be found in these tools.

The conversations you have with students in individual reading conferences have huge potential for supporting their learning. The same kind of facilitative talk will also be important in all other settings—interactive read-aloud, guided reading, book clubs, and writers' workshop. Students are being asked to think in new ways across these contexts, and they benefit from hearing the same messages over and over. The goal is a thinking curriculum.

READING CONFERENCE FOCUSING ON GENRE	
TEACHER:	Hi Mark! How are you enjoying the informational book you're reading?
MARK:	It's okay. I really liked *Bats* and I've just finished this one on bugs. It's pretty cool.
TEACHER:	I'm glad to see you are reading some nonfiction. I know you really like fantasy.
MARK:	Fantasy is my favorite and that's mostly what I read, but I did some biography too.
TEACHER:	Yes, I see that you did. Can you talk about what feels different when you read fantasy than when you read nonfiction like biography or informational books?
MARK:	In fantasy, you just kind of become part of the story. And it can be funny or exciting and the characters are really interesting. You know it isn't true, but it still feels real when you're reading it. I'm going to read Harry Potter at home.
TEACHER:	And when you read nonfiction?
MARK:	Well, it feels more serious and you know it's real. I don't think it's as much fun to read, but you learn some interesting things. And afterward, you know more.
TEACHER:	I feel that way too when I read a good nonfiction book. I especially notice information that is new to me and then I come away knowing more and it's interesting. What else have you noticed about the nonfiction books you've read?
MARK:	Well, they have photographs of real animals like bats and there are sections that show different kinds of information. [Shows several sections.] You can find what you are interested in. I read all of this, but I could have just gone to the section that I was studying.
TEACHER:	That's right. And sometimes you do that when you are doing research. You don't always read the whole book. The author has organized it so that one kind of information is in the same section. Are you going to try some more nonfiction books?
MARK:	Yes, I'm looking for one about sled dogs.
TEACHER:	I think there might be one in the basket with the dog books. I'm going to be reading some nonfiction books aloud to all of you next week, so keep in mind some of the important things you are noticing about nonfiction and you can share them.

Figure 17.19 Reading conference focusing on genre

EXAMPLES OF FACILITATIVE TALK	
Getting the Reader to Talk About Thinking	• What are you thinking? • What is your best thinking about that? • What is most important in this chapter [section]? • What is the writer saying to you? • Show a part that confused you. Read it aloud. What was confusing? • What are your questions as you read this book? • What does the writer make you think more about? • Can you say more? • Talk about why you think that.
Helping the Reader Reflect	• You have been reading this book for awhile. When are you planning to finish it? • You have been reading a lot of [genre] books. When you finish you might want to consider [other genre]. • You seem to be very interested in [author, topic, series, genre]. You might like to read [book]. • You are still reading [book]. How is it going for you? • How is this book choice working for you?
Helping the Reader Think About Genre	• What is the genre? How do you know? • Why do you think the writer chose this genre? • What did you notice about this book that helped you know the genre? • How does this book fit in that genre? • How is this mystery like the last mystery you read? • Is your book a fiction or a nonfiction text? How do you know? • Does you nonfiction book tell a story or does it give you information in sections? • How is the genre helping you think about what to expect in this book? • Talk about the quest in the fantasy book you are reading.
Helping the Reader Think About Literary Elements	• Why do you think the writer chose this setting for the story? • Talk about the main character [protagonist] in your book. • What do the main character's actions tell you about her?

Figure 17.20 Examples of facilitative talk

Suggestions for Professional Development

With a group of colleagues, establish the routines needed so that each of you can hold some individual conferences with students during the study of a particular genre.

OPTION I:

- Have a meeting to discuss conferences and set some goals. Take a look at the facilitative talk and select some language that you think would be helpful to you in working with students around genre.
- Video- or audio-record a conference to share with colleagues.
- Meet again to listen to the conference. If you are working on your own, watch your video and think about the following questions:
  - What is the evidence of student understanding?
  - What confusions did you notice?
  - How did facilitative talk help the student reveal/expand thinking?
  - What specific understandings about genre were built during the conference?
  - What does the student need to learn in the next conference?

OPTION 2:

- Select two students to follow as case studies as you look closer at supporting genre study through your reading conferences. Try to pick students who are reading at different levels.
- Take three weeks to concentrate on conferring with these two students while you are in the inquiry stages of the genre study and during the follow-up minilessons. Make notes of each interaction and think about how they gained as readers from each conference.
  - What evidence of their learning do you see from one conference to another?
  - What specific understandings about genre were built during the conferences? What is your evidence?
  - What do these students need to learn next as readers? What will you help them to understand next in terms of genre?
- Meet with colleagues to talk about your findings. You may want to discuss the following:
  - What language did you find particularly useful during these conferences?
  - What did you learn about your teaching from these two students that you can apply to conferring with the rest of the readers in your class?
  - What insight did you gain into the inquiry process of genre study and your minilessons from your conferences with these two students?

CHAPTER 18

Writing About Reading in a Reader's Notebook

Learning to respond powerfully to books is one of the great truths [students] will learn in school. It reflects their thinking and their learning lives.

—Janet Angelillo

Readers extend their understandings through language interactions with others, either orally or in writing. In either form they are communicating their thinking. Writing about reading can vary greatly in volume and form. The particular forms students use to write about reading depend on their grade level and their current abilities. The writing can take a variety of forms. You can vary the writing task from "short writes" of just a few minutes (half a page to a page) to polished essays that may fill three or more pages. Writing about reading can be entirely open-ended, in which students write expressively about their thinking, or you can establish some requirements while still allowing open response. At some point, older students should also learn how to write a totally structured response, although the observations and ideas must be their own.

Elsewhere (Fountas and Pinnell 2000, 2006) we have discussed writing as a powerful way to increase readers' engagement with texts, help them become more involved in their reading both intellectually and emotionally, and support more organized and analytical ways of thinking about texts. We recommend using a reader's notebook in which students keep records of their reading and write letters to and participate in other forms of dialogue with their teacher, as well as introducing other kinds of writing about reading as part of small-group instruction (guided reading and literature discussion, for example).

We recently revised the original *Reader's Notebook* to focus specifically on students in grades 2–4. A new *Reader's Notebook: Advanced* (2011), for grades 4–8, focuses more on genre (we discuss *Reader's Notebook: Advanced* in more detail later). Both notebooks offer valuable experiences and resources that increase students' ability to articulate their understandings about texts in a variety of written forms.

Reader's Notebook includes an introduction especially helpful for students who have not used one before. Teachers in grade 4 who have students who have already used a *Reader's Notebook* for two years may want to use *Reader's Notebook: Advanced.* It's aimed at students who understand all the routines of readers' workshop and are ready for formal genre study. Students' experience and foundational understanding guide decisions about using the notebook.

Using *Reader's Notebook*

The newly revised *Reader's Notebook* (Heinemann 2012) includes four sections: Reading List, Choosing Books, Minilessons, and Writing About Reading. (In kindergarten and grade 1 children may draw and write in blank notebooks.)

In the Reading List section students record the total number of books they read during the year. There is space for specifying reading requirements and a Genres at a Glance chart that defines each genre and assigns it a corresponding code. The Reading List form includes space for recording book titles, authors, genre codes, dates completed, and a code for whether the book was easy, just right, or difficult. Students can also indicate whether they abandoned the book and why. (Graphic texts are given an asterisk.)

The Choosing Books section provides tips for choosing books and giving a book talk. A form on which students can record books they want to read in the future is also included, the assumption being that students will hear about interesting books from their peers or the teacher's book talks.

The Minilessons section offers tips for how to use their notebooks during minilessons. It includes simple diagrams illustrating how fiction and nonfiction texts are organized. For each minilesson presented, students use blank, lined Record of Minilessons pages to copy or glue on information, make notes about what they want to remember, and list books that are good examples.

A chart in the Writing About Reading section lists different formats students can use to write about reading, from brief notes to longer essays. The goal for the student is to interpret the meaning of the text and respond to it. Letters to the teacher give students an authentic audience for sharing their voice. There is a simple letter form to use as a starting point, as well as guidelines students can use to check their writing.

The inside front cover of the revised *Reader's Notebook* states guidelines for readers' workshop; the inside back cover lists ways to have a good book discussion.

Using *Reader's Notebook: Advanced*

In this chapter we describe in detail the organization of *Reader's Notebook: Advanced* and the way it functions within readers' workshop. We discuss, with examples, a number of ways students can explore genre through writing about reading. Students bring their notebooks to readers' workshop and may use them during any and every part of this instructional period:

- *Book talks and minilesson.* During book talks, students can note titles they are interested in reading. During genre study minilessons, they write down the things they notice, the genre definition, and examples of mentor texts in the Genre Studies section. During other minilessons, they write down the principle, any notes, and mentor texts in the Minilessons section.
- *Independent reading and conferring.* At first, students might write one thoughtful letter a week to the teacher (who responds). This helps students learn how to share their genuine thinking with a real audience. Following minilessons on different forms of writing about reading, students can choose their form of response. The notebook also contains sections for keeping a record of reading, particularly types of genres.
- *Guided reading* and *literature discussion (book clubs).* During the workshop, teachers sometimes bring together small groups of students for guided reading or book clubs. Guided reading (see Chapter 19) provides intensive instruction for a small group of students who are reading at about the same level of text. In book clubs (see Chapter 14), students either read or listen to a shared text and then discuss

it following literature discussion routines. Students can use their notebook in either situation to note points they want to discuss, jot down things they notice, refer to previous minilessons, remember examples, or analyze texts using graphic organizers.

- *Group share.* At the end of readers' workshop, students bring their notebooks to the sharing session. It helps them remember what they want to share with a partner, a small group, or the whole group.

Parts and Tools in *Reader's Notebook: Advanced*

The notebook includes a collection of helpful tools, as well as specific sections that help students organize their writing. It's designed to be used efficiently. It is amazing how much time can be wasted searching through a notebook to find a specific section or item. The published version (the cover is shown in Figure 18.1) includes tabbed sections that make teaching more efficient and lessons move more quickly:

- The Reading List section supports readers' workshop routines. It includes Guidelines for Readers' Workshop, Reading Requirements, Books to Read, and the Reading List (books read) form.
- The Genre Studies section supports inquiry. It includes a chart to help students understand fiction and nonfiction genres and their relationships, as well as forms on which to record a particular genre's characteristics, definition, and examples.
- The Minilessons section supports the direct lessons taught at the beginning of the workshop (and is referred to during share time). It includes a record of minilessons, along with reference charts describing basic fiction and nonfiction.
- The Writing About Reading section supports a variety of student writing about reading. It includes a chart with definitions of different forms for writing about reading, some guidelines students can use to check their writing, a letter explaining how to use the notebook, a list of suggestions for writing about reading, and blank pages for student work.
- The Glossary lists useful terms and their definitions, so students can find definitions quickly.

Figure 18.1 Cover and tabbed sections from *Reader's Notebook: Advanced*

Inside Front Cover

Inside the front cover is Guidelines for Readers' Workshop, a set of simple guidelines for the community of readers and writers (see Figure 18.2).

Section 1: Reading List

During the workshop, students read a book of their own choosing and share their thinking about the book with others. The time spent reading is silent. Students

Guidelines for Readers' Workshop

1. Read a book or write down your thoughts about your reading.
2. Work silently so that you and your peers can do your best thinking.
3. Use a soft voice when conferring with your teacher.
4. Choose books that you think you'll enjoy and abandon books that aren't working for you after you've given them a good chance.
5. List the book information when you begin reading and record the date and a one-word response when you finish the book.
6. Think about the genre of the book you are reading and what you notice.
7. Always do your best work.

For more information on using *Reader's Notebook: Advanced* see *Guiding Readers and Writers*, and *Teaching for Comprehending and Fluency* by I. C. Fountas and G. S. Pinnell. Published by Heinemann, Portsmouth, NH.

Figure 18.2 Guidelines for Readers' Workshop from *Reader's Notebook: Advanced*

Reading List

Reading Requirements

Total Books: 45

Requirement	Genre	Tally
3	(RF) Realistic Fiction	||
2	(HF) Historical Fiction	|
2	(TL) Traditional Literature (Folktales, Fables, Myths, Legends)	|
2	(F) Fantasy	||
2	(SF) Science Fiction	
3	(B) Biography/Autobiography	|
2	(M) Memoir	
10	(I) Informational	||||
2	(P) Poetry	|
2	(H) Hybrid	
15	Genre Free Choice	||

Figure 18.3 Reading Requirements from *Reader's Notebook: Advanced*

do not talk with others unless they are conferring individually with the teacher or engaged in small-group instruction (guided reading or book clubs). Everyone uses soft voices when conferring or working in small groups. There are expectations about how books are chosen, and students have the opportunity to choose books they think they will enjoy.

Books should be accessible—that is, within the student's current reading ability—but students should not choose books by text level (see Chapter 19). If students have difficulty selecting appropriate books, you can assist them in individual conferences. If minilessons on selecting books haven't been successful for particular students, you need to reteach them how to choose well—have them read a little of the book and think about whether they can read it independently and whether they understand it. Sometimes you need to help a student get started, especially in a new genre, by setting genre and quantity requirements for student reading (see Figure 18.3). Students use the Reading Requirements chart to tally the number of texts read in each category and thus are able to monitor their own reading progress.

If readers' workshop is conducted four or five days a week and students are also reading at home, they can finish approximately one book a week (often more titles of challenging but shorter fiction and nonfiction). Some texts may take longer than a week but others will take less. Whatever the text difficulty, students select texts they can read independently—with accuracy, understanding, and good momentum.

One Reading Requirement category is Genre Free Choice. Having students do a great deal of reading of their own choosing is strongly supported by research (see Chapter 16). But you also want to ensure that over the years students learn to understand many genres. Therefore, at the same time you engage students in genre inquiry and present genre minilessons, have them choose their own examples of the genre to read independently.

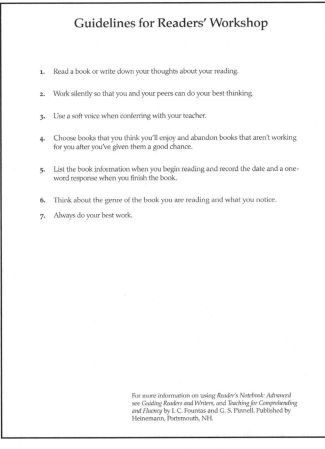

Reading List

Books to Read

Title	Author	Genre	Check When Completed
The Boxcar Children Return	Gertrude Warner		✓
The Night Swimmers	Betsy Byars		✓
Otis Spofford	Beverly Cleary		✓
The Music of Dolphins	Karen Hesse		✓
Something Upstairs	Avi		
George's Marvelous Medicine	Roald Dahl		
Frindle	Andrew Clements		✓
The Cat's Meow	Gary Soto		
Everything Dog	Marty Crisp		
The Castle in the Attic	Elizabeth Wintrop		
Princess for a Week	Betty Ren Wright		
Humphrey the Hamster Series	Betty G. Birney		

Figure 18.4 Books to Read from *Reader's Notebook: Advanced*

Reading List

Select a book to read. Enter the title and author on your reading list. When you have completed the book, write the genre and the date. If you abandoned the book, write an **(A)** and the date you abandoned it in the date column. Write a one-word response that shows your reaction to the book. Place an asterisk **(*)** next to the code in the genre column if your book is a graphic text

#	Title	Author	Genre Code	Date Completed	One-Word Response
1	Commander Toad and the Voyage Home	Jane Yolen	F	9/5	E
2	The Littles Go Exploring	John Peterson	F	9/7	E
3	Pinky and Rex and the School Play	James Howe	F	9/10	E
4	The Magic Finger	Roald Dahl	F	9/16	E
5	The Twits	Roald Dahl	F	9/21	D
6	Luke's Bully	Elizabeth Winthrop	RF	9/27	JR
7	The Chocolate Touch	Patrick Catling	RF	10/1	JR
8	Postcards from Australia	Helen Arnold	I	10/3	JR
9	George's Marvelous Medicine	Roald Dahl	F	10/7	JR
10	The Aliens are Coming	Colin McNaughton	F	10/10	E
11	Pee-Wee's Tale	Johanna Hurwitz	F	10/16	E
12	Pee Wee and Plush	Johanna Hurwitz	F	10/16	E
13	I'm Too Fond of My Fur	Geronimo Stilton	F	10/25	E

Figure 18.5 Reading List from *Reader's Notebook: Advanced*

It is a good idea for grade-level colleagues to determine genre requirements together. Working across grade levels is also a good idea. You want to know your students' previous experiences in genre study, for example. Working together also helps you and your colleagues take a longer-term perspective. When making these decisions, consider:

- Requirements of district or state curriculum guides and standards.
- National Curriculum standards (for example, Common Core Standards).
- The emphases codified in *The Continuum of Literacy Learning.*
- The strands of genre study you plan to implement across the year.

The Books to Read form (see Figure 18.4) helps students select books. As they hear book talks or get recommendations from friends, they write interesting titles on the form. If they have heard about the book in a book talk or read a peer book review of it, they know the genre. If not, they leave the genre notation column blank until they have a chance to read the book.

This list becomes a resource for selecting a new book. When you have a list of interesting books in mind, it's easy to pick a new one. Also, if students need to read in a particular genre, they can quickly identify examples of books they intend to read in that genre. Using this form helps students become readers who always have potential "reads" in mind.

Students use the Reading List form (see Figure 18.5) to keep records on their own reading throughout the year (several pages are provided). They list each title they have read, along with the author, genre, date completed, and a one-word response. Looking at this list together during individual conferences, you and your students can see reading patterns and set goals. The list represents a large and connected body of work on the

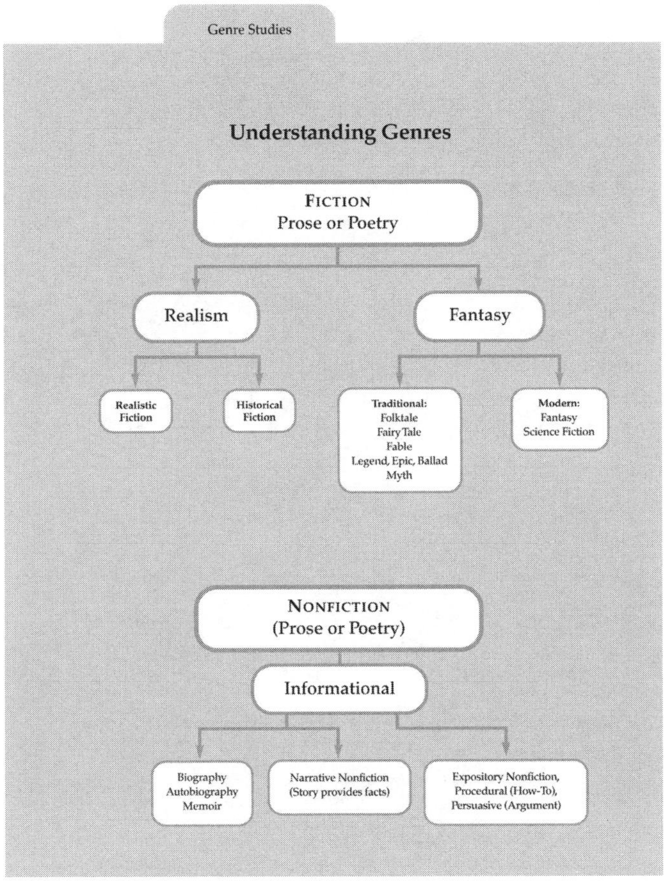

Figure 18.6 Understanding Genres chart

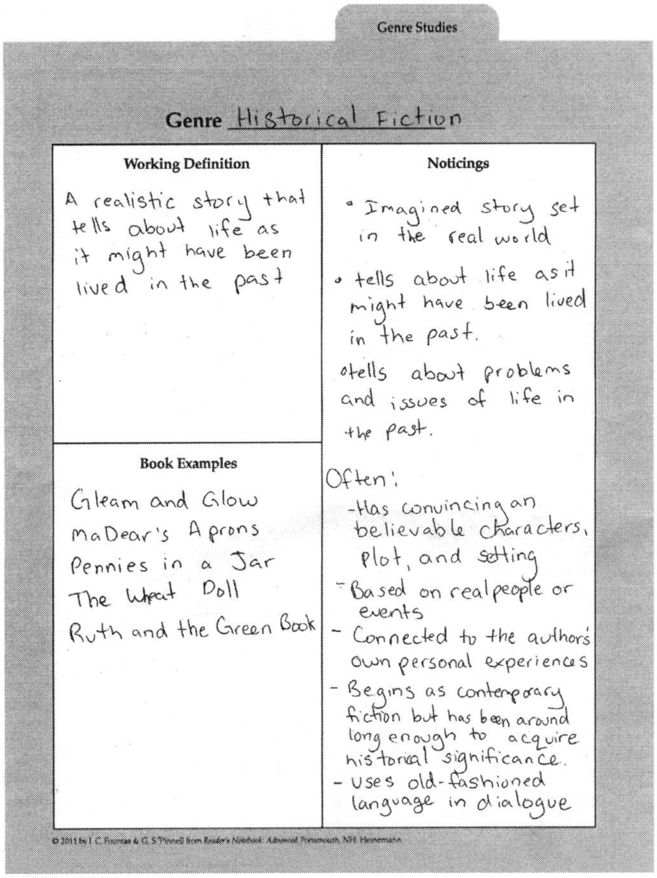
Genre Studies

Genre Historical Fiction

Working Definition	Noticings
A realistic story that tells about life as it might have been lived in the past	• Imagined story set in the real world • tells about life as it might have been lived in the past. • tells about problems and issues of life in the past.
Book Examples	
Gleam and Glow MaDear's Aprons Pennies in a Jar The Wheat Doll Ruth and the Green Book	Often: -Has convincing an believable characters, plot, and setting - Based on real people or events - Connected to the author's own personal experiences - Begins as contemporary fiction but has been around long enough to acquire historical significance. - Uses old-fashioned language in dialogue

© 2011 by I. C. Fountas & G. S. Pinnell from Reader's Notebook: Advanced. Portsmouth, NH: Heinemann.

Figure 18.7 A page from Genre Studies section

part of the student. Your students can use it to get back to their thinking about particular texts and realize their own growth across the year.

Section 2: Genre Studies

The Genre Studies section of the notebook supports students as they learn about the various genres of written texts. It begins with a quick-reference chart that breaks out fiction and nonfiction genres and shows their relationships (see Figure 18.6). Students can refer to it during interactive read-aloud, minilessons, guided reading, and individual conferences.

Following the chart are several pages students can use to record their participation in genre inquiry. During interactive read-aloud you chart your students' shared thinking about what they notice about a genre, and together you and your students use these characteristics to create a working definition. Students record this shared thinking on the Genre Studies form (see Figure 18.7), because the characteristics and working definition become the basis for minilessons. Once students are very familiar with genre inquiry, they can also list some of the things they notice independently, for later sharing. Students also list here some examples of texts in each genre, from interactive read-aloud, literature discussion, and independent reading. Remembering mentor texts supports concrete understandings of the genre.

Section 3: Minilessons

As you move from inquiry to minilessons, help your students learn how to make their own record of minilesson principles so that they can look back on what they have learned and think about the minilesson and how it helps them as readers and writers. They can also list titles of books in the genre, give examples from a book, or make notes of what they want to remember. Instructions are provided at the beginning of the section.

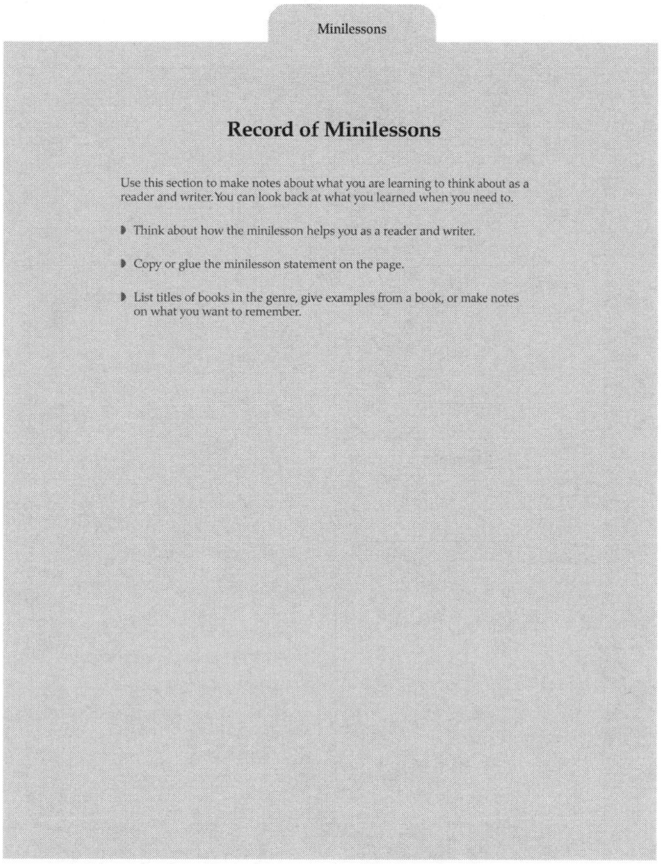

Figure 18.8 Record of Minilessons page from *Reader's Notebook: Advanced*

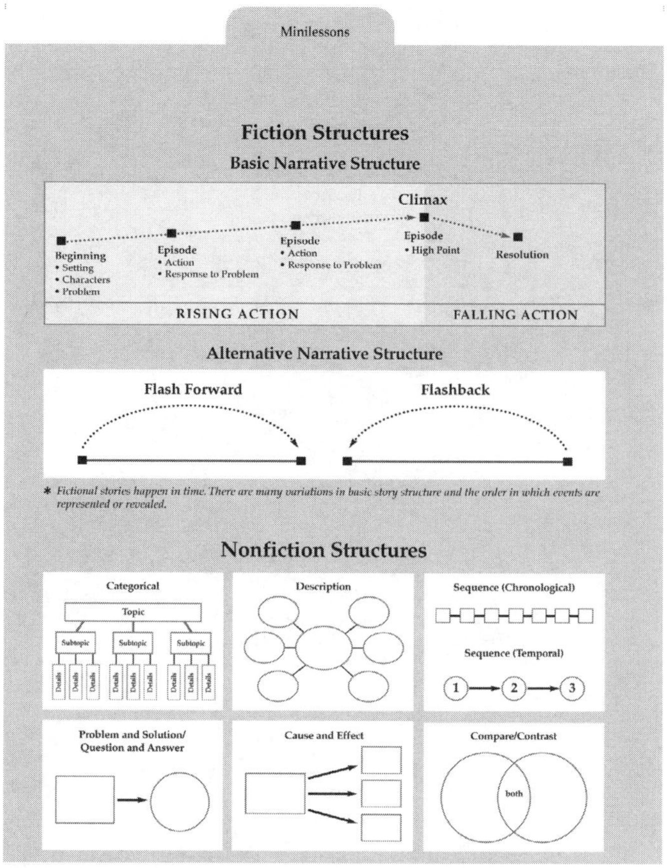

Figure 18.9 Text Structures page from *Reader's Notebook: Advanced*

The Record of Minilessons page (see Figure 18.8) is followed by several diagrams depicting fiction and nonfiction text structures that students need to be familiar with: basic narrative structure, an alternative narrative structure for fiction, and the most important nonfiction text structures (see Figure 18.9). Students can refer to these diagrams while reading independently and during small-group reading instruction and interactive read-alouds. Following the diagrams are a number of blank pages on which students can take notes on the minilessons: the minilesson principle, text examples, any other notes that will be helpful.

Section 4: Writing About Reading

Here students collect the letters they write about books as well as other kinds of writing about reading they have completed. The section begins with a list of forms of writing about reading and related definitions (see Figure 18.10). Each of these types of writing (introduced through minilessons and demonstrations) is discussed in detail later in this chapter.

Following this page is a list of guidelines students can use to check their writing (see Figure 18.11). First on the list, students need to reread their writing to be sure it makes sense. They also need to include standard parts of a letter (the date and a greeting and closing, for example) and respond to what the teacher (or peer) has written to them. They need to include the title of the book that is the subject of the letter or dialogue journal. They learn some conventions such as underlining the title of a book and putting direct quotes in quotation marks, followed by the page number. They also need to proofread to be sure that the writing is neat and that spelling, capitalization, and punctuation are correct. These criteria apply to all writing about reading that students do.

Next, a letter explains the procedures of the notebook and readers' workshop to the students (see Figure 18.12).

Writing About Reading

Forms for Writing About Reading

Tally	Kind of Writing	Definition
III	**Letter to your teacher (or another reader)**	a letter to share your thinking about your reading with another reader who writes back to you
I	**Letter — Essay**	a structured analysis of a whole book, written as a letter
II	**Short Write**	an open-ended response or focused response to a specific prompt or a question
I	**Notes**	words, phrases, or quick drawing to help you remember the book
	List	words, phrases, or sentences written one under the other
	Sketch	a quick drawing or series of drawings to show your thinking
	Double Column Entry (T-chart)	a phrase, sentence, or quote on the left and your thinking on the right
II	**Graphic Organizer (for example, a web, T-chart, story map, grid, or timeline)**	a chart that helps you see the way information is organized
	Plot Summary	a few sentences that tell the problem or conflict
	Summary	a few sentences that tell the most important information
I	**Book Recommendation**	writing that gives another reader some information and advice on a book
	Book Review	an opinion and analysis that includes comments on the quality of a book and gives another reader advice
	Poem	a poetic piece that responds to a book (characters, setting, story events)
	Blog	a blend of the term "web log," a blog has entries of comments, descriptions of events, or other information

Figure 18.10 Forms for Writing about Reading page from *Reader's Notebook: Advanced*

Writing About Reading

Guidelines for Checking Your Writing

1. Reread what you have written to be sure it makes sense.
2. If you are writing a letter:
   - write the date.
   - include the greeting and closing.
   - be sure you have responded to what the teacher or a peer wrote to you.
3. Be sure to include the title of the book and underline it.
4. Put quotation marks (" ") around sentences that are direct quotes from the book. Document the page where you found the quote, and explain the context and/or significance.
5. Check that your writing is neat and easy to read.
6. Check your spelling, capitalization, and punctuation.

Figure 18.11 Guidelines for Checking Your Writing from *Reader's Notebook: Advanced*

It covers book talks, how to use the reading list tally chart, how to use the section for writing about reading, and the reason for minilessons. The letter is addressed to students, but parents also find it valuable. You can modify the letter and ask students to glue your letter over this one, or you can add your comments at the bottom.

The next page (see Figure 18.13) provides suggestions for writing about reading, which are especially helpful when students write their letters about their reading. Sometimes students write very superficial letters or comment only about one aspect of the text. They can use this list as a resource for making their letters more interesting. The list is also a resource for your writing-about-reading instruction: each suggestion can be used as the basis for one or more minilessons. You can demonstrate with your own letters or the letters of students in the class. Following the suggestions are lined, blank pages on which students can write letters and other kinds of writing about reading.

Section 5: Glossary

At the end of the notebook is a quick-reference glossary of academic terms that students need to understand in order to talk and write about texts and their genres (for example, *argument, major characters, minor characters, conflict, narrator, persuasive, setting, theme*). Terms that are new to students are introduced in minilessons. Over time, these terms become part of students' known vocabulary, used automatically in conversation, but that takes time and repeated opportunities to use them.

Inside Back Cover

The inside back cover of the notebook (see Figure 18.14) contains suggestions for supporting students in literature discussion. The Talking About Reading suggestions help students prepare for book clubs or individual conferences with you (or write about reading)

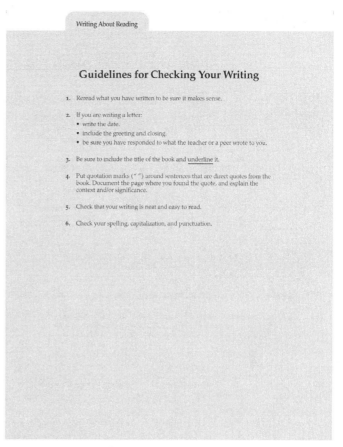

Date

Dear ______________________________,

This year we will spend time thinking, talking, and writing about books. We will talk about books as a group, with partners, or you and I will have a conversation with each other in a reading conference. In class you will learn about different fiction and nonfiction genres and how to recognize some of the common characteristics of each. I hope you will learn about many new books, authors, topics, and genres, and have a year filled with interesting reading.

You can use the tally chart in the Reading List section of this notebook to keep a record of the reading you do at school and at home. You will have a good amount of time to read at school and are also expected to read for _____ minutes at home each evening.

Use this section of your notebook to share your thinking about the books you read. Your writing is a record of your thinking and this notebook will serve as the place to collect your thoughts and share them with others. Some of our book conversations will be in the form of letters to each other, and some will be letters to your peers. Be sure to write in letter form, with a date, greeting, and closing. Include the title and author of your book in your response, using capital letters and underlining the title.

During minilessons, I will teach you how to write about your reading using a variety of forms. Use the chart at the front of the Writing About Reading section to keep a record of the different forms of writing you use to respond to your reading.

I look forward to sharing books with you and learning more about your thinking.

Sincerely,

Figure 18.12 Example of letter from *Reader's Notebook: Advanced*

Suggestions for Writing About Reading

Share your thinking about:

- The genre and its characteristics
- Why you chose to read a book in this genre
- Whether you would choose this genre again and why
- How the book is like other books by the same author, or on the same topic
- What clues about the genre the title and illustrations provide
- What made it easy or difficult to identify the genre
- What makes this a good example of the genre
- Something that surprised you or that you found interesting about the genre
- What you learned from the genre and how this fits with what you already know
- How the genre helped you to think about what to expect in the story
- How the setting and characters support the genre
- How the characters are shaped by the setting and/or time period
- How the character's choices or actions helped to reveal who he or she is
- Whether the main character is also the narrator and how this affects the story
- Whether the characters are believable
- Whether you can relate to the characters and/or the challenges they faced
- How the setting shapes the events in the story
- What words helped you to picture the setting
- What sounds, smells, sights, or feelings helped the setting seem real
- What you learned about the time period
- The author's use of time in history
- Whether the setting could be a real place that exists now

Figure 18.13 Suggestions for Writing about Reading from *Reader's Notebook: Advanced*

by marking places they want to comment on, ask questions about, or write about. Students are always expected to share their thinking about texts. The Ways to Have a Good Book Discussion list reminds students of the routines of literature discussion or book clubs. Students don't necessarily come to the discussion knowing social conventions like looking at the person who is talking, asking questions, waiting for the speaker to finish, being sure everyone gets a turn, and keeping the discussion on a topic before changing the subject. However, after these discussion skills become automatic, they last a lifetime.

The tools in *Reader's Notebook: Advanced* support a literate life in the classroom. You may want to post materials and have students send their letters and other work via email. If electronic notebooks are used, it is still important to have easy access, by date and topic, to the student's entire body of work during the school day and from home. Loose pages, emails, or electronic files can disappear. A great part of students' motivation is the concrete evidence of their progress.

Studying Genre Through Writing About Reading

Writing about reading always takes place when students are working independently in readers' workshop and is also often integrated into interactive read-aloud, the minilesson, and group share; used as preparation for or response to book clubs; and completed as homework. More complex writing about reading may be developed during writers' workshop.

Writing about reading can be separated into four broad categories (see *Teaching for Comprehending and Fluency*):

Talking About Reading

Reading is thinking. You will have many opportunities to talk about your thinking.

- Mark places you want to talk or write about with a stick-on note, or make a list with page numbers.
- Talk about your thinking in conferences with your teacher, or in group-share.
- Share your thinking during book club meetings.

Ways to Have a Good Book Discussion

1. Be prepared.
2. Sit so everyone can see each other.
3. Get started right away.
4. Share your best thinking.
5. Look at the person who is talking.
6. Listen to understand each other's thinking.
7. Ask questions to understand better.
8. Speak clearly but not too loudly.
9. Wait for the speaker to finish.
10. Use language that invites others to share their ideas.
11. Be sure everyone gets a turn.
12. Build on one another's thinking.
13. Respect the thinking of your peers.
14. Be sure everyone has shared their thinking on a topic before moving on to another topic.
15. Provide evidence from your experience or from the text to support your thinking.

Figure 18.14 Talking about Reading and Ways to Have a Good Book Discussion from *Reader's Notebook: Advanced*

1. *Functional* writing about reading supports memory and expands understanding. It is undertaken for communication or to help students understand big ideas, text structures, or other aspects of texts. Functional writing includes the letters students write about texts and the notes they take to help them remember what they notice while reading. Functional writing also includes graphic organizers, diagrams, and outlines. This kind of writing about reading supports analytical thinking.
2. *Narrative* writing about reading tells a story. Students use narrative text structure to represent their understandings or thinking. They might retell some or all of a plot, relate the text to stories from their own life, or summarize a fiction or nonfiction text.
3. *Informational* writing about reading communicates facts in an organized and logical way. Students organize data into categories, often the same ones used in the fiction or nonfiction text they are responding to. Informational writing about reading includes reports, news articles, interviews, and literary essays.
4. *Poetic* writing about reading responds to texts in a poetic way. Students select and arrange words to convey meaning in ways that evoke feelings and/or sensory images.

This book discusses the possibilities of these types of writing about reading for extending students' understandings of genre.

Functional Writing About Reading

Much of students' writing about reading in-school is functional (see Figure 18.15). The main purpose of this kind of writing, which includes weekly letters students write about the texts they read, is to help students extend their understandings of written texts and share that thinking with others. Writing is an excellent way to help students internalize the characteristics of genres.

Notes and Sketches

Notes are essential tools for readers who want or need to share thinking with others. Many of us jot down notes or record quotes we like even if we have no immediate plans for talking with others about a book. Note-taking supports memory and enables us to get back quickly to our thinking about important parts of the book. When students use writing or sketching as a tool, they come prepared for discussion with a small group or the whole class. Students can also take notes during interactive read-aloud and reading minilessons and use these notes as a guide when they read and write. Stick-on notes are a very handy way for students to make notes on anything; as part of genre study they are a quick way for students

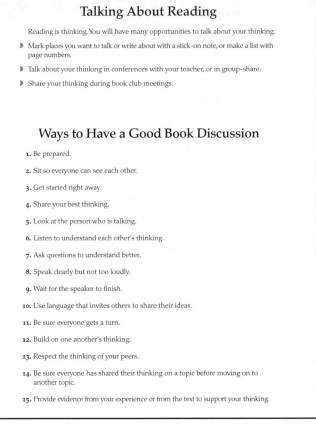

FUNCTIONAL WRITING ABOUT READING	
Description and General Examples	**Connection to Genre Study**
Notes and sketches—words, phrases, or sketches on stick-on notes or Thinkmarks in the reader's notebook: • Connections • Predictions • Wonderings • Noticings • Confusions • New or memorable language • New learning	Used to note: • Examples of genre characteristics • Places the text is like other texts in the genre • Examples of writer's craft related to the genre • Confusions about the genre or a particular aspect of it • New learning about the genre
Short writes—a few sentences or paragraphs produced quickly in the notebook or on a large sticky note: • Response to a quote. • Reaction to a writer's style • Thoughts about craft, message, or characters • Comments on point of view • New understandings or insights • Predictions or connections	Used to: • Reflect on why the writer selected the genre • Reflect on how the writer exemplified the genre • Reflect on the writer's unique way of using the genre • Note and describe elements of genre, with examples • Describe how a quote showed characteristics of the genre • Reflect on how understanding the genre supported our reading
Graphic organizers—words, phrases, sketches, or sentences in charts that show the way a text is organized—on paper or in the notebook: • Story maps • Webs that connect information • Time sequences • Comparison/contrast chart • Cause and effect chart • Problem/solution chart • Informal outlines • Double-column entries	Used to: • Show the internal structure of informational texts • Show the internal structure of narrative texts • Show how categories of information are related in nonfiction texts • Show how story elements (characters, setting, and problem) are related in fiction texts • Show underlying text structures in informational texts • Show the plot structure in fiction texts

Figure 18.15 Functional writing about reading

FUNCTIONAL WRITING ABOUT READING	
Description and General Examples	**Connection to Genre Study**
Letters about reading—letters written to the teacher or to other students about reading as well as letters to authors or illustrators: • Thoughts about reading—connections, new insights, opinions • Comments on character, plot, theme, or structure • Evidence for thinking	Used to: • Identify the genre • Talk about what students like (or don't like) about the genre • Identify characteristics of the genre evident in the text (structure, story elements, setting, organization)
Longer responses—longer written responses elaborating on thinking about one or several texts: • Double-column entry—two-column responses with material from the text, a category, or questions on the left and response or comments on the right • Expansion of thinking from the notes, sketches, short writes, or graphic organizers	Used to: • Analyze the text as an example of the genre • Draw out key characteristics of the text • Elaborate on genre characteristics
Book review—structured piece, journalistic in style and geared to an audience, that evaluates and does or does not recommend a particular text	Used to: • Evaluate the text as an example of the genre • Comment on the writer's ability to use the genre

Figure 18.15 Functional writing about reading *(cont.)*

to record what they notice. (See the examples in Figures 18.16 and 18.17.) Important stick-on notes can later be placed in the reader's notebook.

Another helpful note-taking tool is the Genre Thinkmark. Leslie's notes (see Figure 18.18), noting important places in the text, help her remember or refer quickly to important thinking about the characteristics of the genre. The Thinkmark is a good resource for discussion and more formal writing about reading.

Short Writes

Because students are always reading independently, listening to books read aloud, and discussing books with others, they have plenty of source material for "short writes," quick responses to a specific prompt. These short pieces help students become accustomed to thinking and writing quickly and easily. Students can do short writes just about any time—after or during a read-aloud, as an extension of guided reading, or during independent reading. (Examples are provided in Figures 18.19, 18.20, and 18.21).

Readers of biography need to understand that the writer in this genre selects the important events and decisions from a subject's life. A biography is not just a chronicle of a series of events. It is a *selected series* that provides important insights into the subject's decisions and builds a case for his or her impact on others. The short write in Figure 18.19 shows that this reader has

Acid rain kills trees with poison that goes into the ground and they soak it up. Birds can die too.

Has real photographs and drawings.

Figure 18.16 Observations captured on a stick-on note

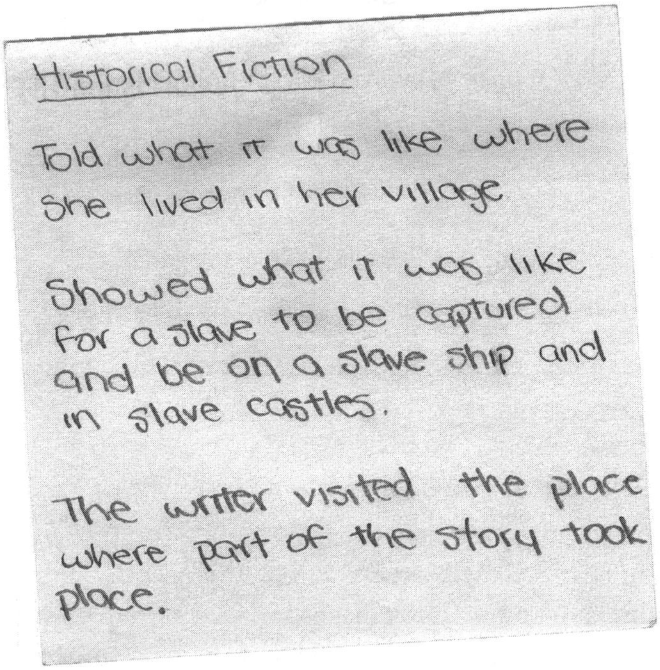
Historical Fiction

Told what it was like where She lived in her village

Showed what it was like for a slave to be captured and be on a slave ship and in slave castles.

The writer visited the place where part of the story took place.

Figure 18.17 Observations about the setting in a historical fiction book

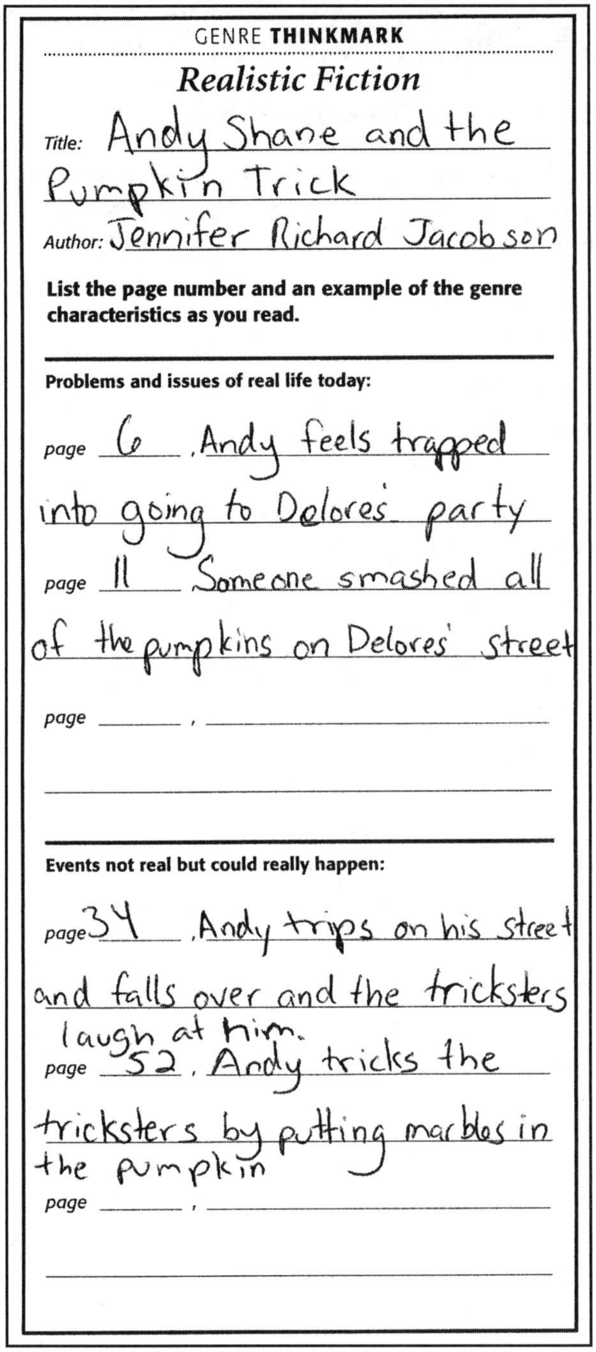
GENRE **THINKMARK**

Realistic Fiction

Title: Andy Shane and the Pumpkin Trick

Author: Jennifer Richard Jacobson

List the page number and an example of the genre characteristics as you read.

Problems and issues of real life today:

page 6, Andy feels trapped into going to Delores' party

page 11 Someone smashed all of the pumpkins on Delores' street

page ______, ______________

Events not real but could really happen:

page 34, Andy trips on his street and falls over and the tricksters laugh at him.

page 52, Andy tricks the tricksters by putting marbles in the pumpkin

page ______, ______________

Figure 18.18 Genre Thinkmark

taken important ideas from the reading and discussion of a biography during a guided reading lesson. The teacher's instructions after the discussion were: "That was a good discussion of the biography of Laura Ingalls Wilder. Take your reader's notebook and write for ten minutes about how the writer showed why Laura became a writer."

Figure 18.20 is a short write based on a read-aloud/discussion of *The Librarian of Basra* (Winter 2004), a partial biography of Alia Muhammad Baker, the librarian of Basra, Iraq. When war came, Alia was very worried about the books and took measures to remove them in secrecy. Because of her efforts, the books were saved when the library burned. This

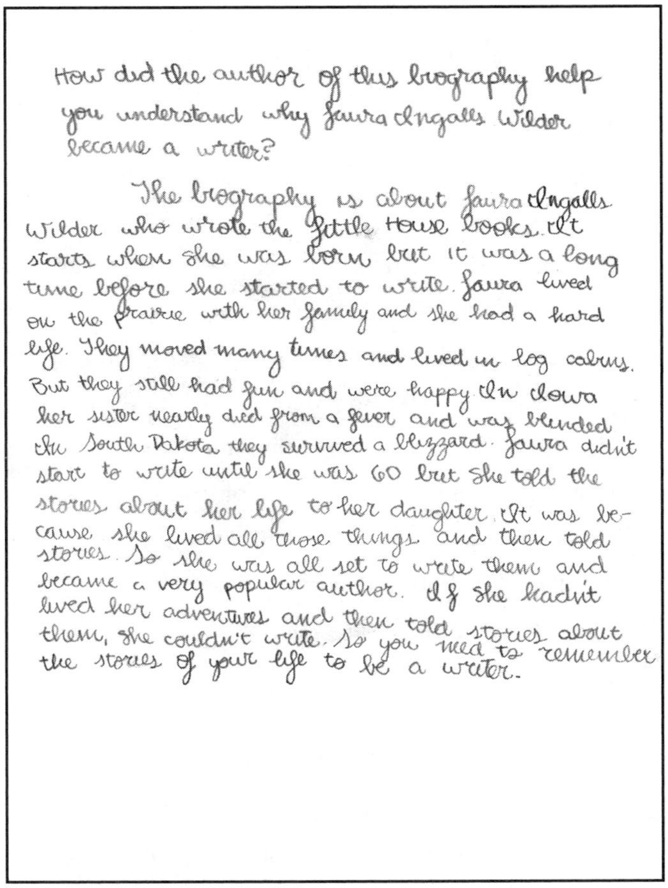

How did the author of this biography help you understand why Laura Ingalls Wilder became a writer?

The biography is about Laura Ingalls Wilder who wrote the Little House books. It starts when she was born but it was a long time before she started to write. Laura lived on the prairie with her family and she had a hard life. They moved many times and lived in log cabins. But they still had fun and were happy. In Iowa her sister nearly died from a fever and was blended. In South Dakota they survived a blizzard. Laura didn't start to write until she was 60 but she told the stories about her life to her daughter. It was because she lived all those things and then told stories. So she was all set to write them and became a very popular author. If she hadn't lived her adventures and then told stories about them, she couldn't write. So you need to remember the stories of your life to be a writer.

Figure 18.19 Short write from guided reading lesson

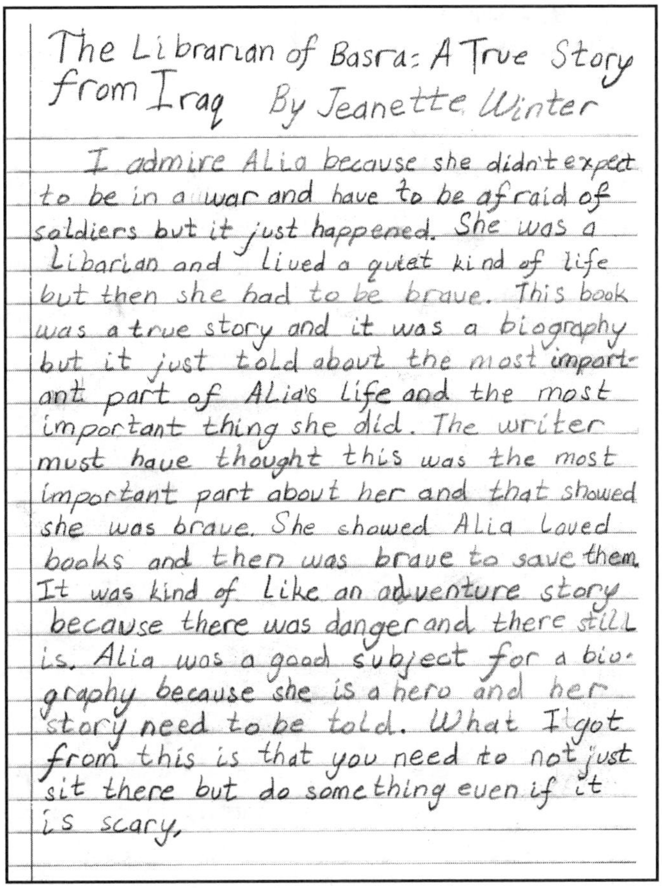

The Librarian of Basra: A True Story from Iraq By Jeanette Winter

I admire Alia because she didn't expect to be in a war and have to be afraid of soldiers but it just happened. She was a Libarian and lived a quiet kind of life but then she had to be brave. This book was a true story and it was a biography but it just told about the most important part of Alia's life and the most important thing she did. The writer must have thought this was the most important part about her and that showed she was brave. She showed Alia loved books and then was brave to save them. It was kind of like an adventure story because there was danger and there still is. Alia was a good subject for a biography because she is a hero and her story need to be told. What I got from this is that you need to not just sit there but do something even if it is scary.

Figure 18.20 Short write in reader's notebook after interactive read-aloud

ordinary librarian acted heroically and continued to guard the books while hoping for a new library. In the discussion students said they admired Alia, and there was also some talk about how the writer showed the subject's courage in just a few pages. The teacher's instructions after the discussion were: "Now open your reader's notebook and write for a short time about why you think the writer wanted to tell the story of Alia."

Since students are always reading a book of their own choosing independently, they can use that book as the basis for a short write on any topic. In the example in Figure 18.21, a student writes about *The Giver* in response to these instructions: "You know that we have been thinking about how writers of fiction create a mood with the words and language they choose. Most of you are reading fantasy because we are studying this genre, and some of you are just finishing up your realistic fiction books. Take out your reader's notebook and write for a short time about the mood in the book you are reading. Try to provide some examples of how the writer created the mood of the story." This student was able to identify a change of mood in the text and to provide examples that showed the writer's craft.

These short writes take only five or ten minutes for students to produce and also take very little time for teachers to read. They are excellent evidence of the student's ability to write in an articulate way about reading. Also, they help students prepare for the kinds of responses expected on tests.

Graphic Organizers

Graphic organizers are widely used to help students understand overall organizational structures as well as underlying structures in every genre. *Guiding Readers and Writers* and *Teaching for Comprehending and Fluency* discuss graphic organizers in detail and provide

Figure 18.21 Short write response to a general prompt

Tell what you noticed about the mood of the fantasy you are reading.

The Giver is the fantasy I am reading. The mood was interesting to me because it changes from normal and comfortable to tense and closed in as the story goes on. As Jonas learns things from the Giver the way he feels about the Community changes and so does the mood. In the earlier part of the book Jonas feels very comfortable in his community, which connects to the theme. At this point he doesn't have any reason to question his life. I could say he is content. This is an example of how the writing changed over the course of the book. Both quotes I've chosen are from the dinner discussions. The first (p. 4–5): "It was one of the rituals, the evening telling of feelings. Sometimes Jonas and his sister, Lily, argued over turns, over who would go first. Their parents, of course were part of the ritual; they, too, told their feelings each evening. But like all parents—all adults—they didn't fight and wheedle for their turn." This quote reminds me of the happy innocence of childhood and the mood is feeling simple and relaxed. The second quote (p. 164): "The family unit was eating together as always: Lily chattering away, Mother and Father making their customary comments (and lies, Jonas knew) about the day. . . ." The mood here is completely different than it was before. Instead of juvenile and innocent now it seems knowing and wary of the lies underneath what is really happening. Jonas is suspicious of what is happening and instead of feeling comfortable in his home, he now feels suspicious and angry.

hundreds of examples. However, there are some attendant cautions. They should not be overused or treated as worksheets (for students to fill out as seatwork or homework without talking about them with others, for example). They are most productive when they are:

- Simple and quick to complete.
- Completed with a partner.
- Introduced and demonstrated in a group lesson.
- Completed as shared writing
- Directly related to the characteristics of texts students are studying.
- Discussed in small groups or pairs.
- Kept in the reader's notebook and referred to in the future.

The last two points are especially important. If a graphic organizer is well chosen and students put in the effort needed to complete it, they deserve to discuss it with others and they should be able to use it in other situations.

Figure 18.22 is a simple three-box graphic organizer in which the student summarizes the story. She notes the beginning of the text (with setting and problem), the turning point, and the satisfying ending that allows readers to predict how the main character will put what she learned to good use in helping others.

The example in Figure 18.23 shows how a group of students identified the underlying cause-and-effect structure used by the writer of the nonfiction book *Acid Rain*. Often, a graphic organizer can bring rigor to a discussion.

Figure 18.22 Graphic organizer summarizing *The Dot* (Reynolds 2003)

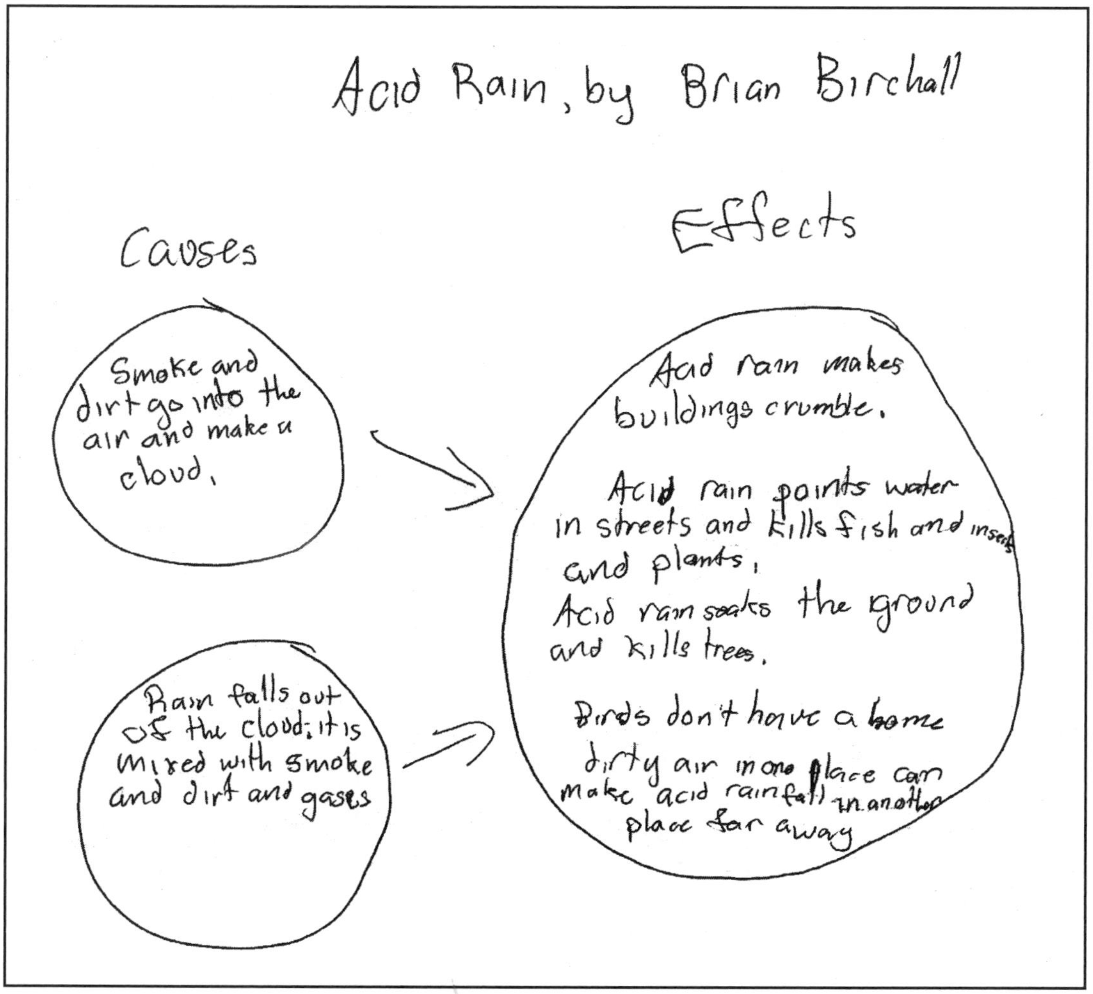

Figure 18.23 Graphic organizer plotting the organization of *Acid Rain*

In *The Boy Who Invented TV* (Krull 2009), the biographer reveals important character traits related to Philo Farnsworth achievements. The web in Figure 18.24 represents these qualities graphically.

Letters About Reading

In readers' workshop students write about their reading in a weekly (or bimonthly) letter to the teacher, who then responds. This written dialogue is a great opportunity to learn what students have noticed about genre and to nudge their thinking. In the example in Figure 18.25, Ethan is developing insights into realistic fiction and fantasy (which he calls "epics"). That's understandable since he is journeying through *The Fellowship of the Ring* (Tolkien 2005). He has grasped the general idea of the "other world" created by the writer.

The interchange of letters between teacher and students is an ideal way to work genre into the ongoing conversation. The concept of genre should be part of the language students use all the time as they talk and write about books. In the exchange between Royi and her teacher in Figure 18.26, it is clear that Royi is vary familiar with fiction and has noticed differences among the genres. She is working to sort out the different labels.

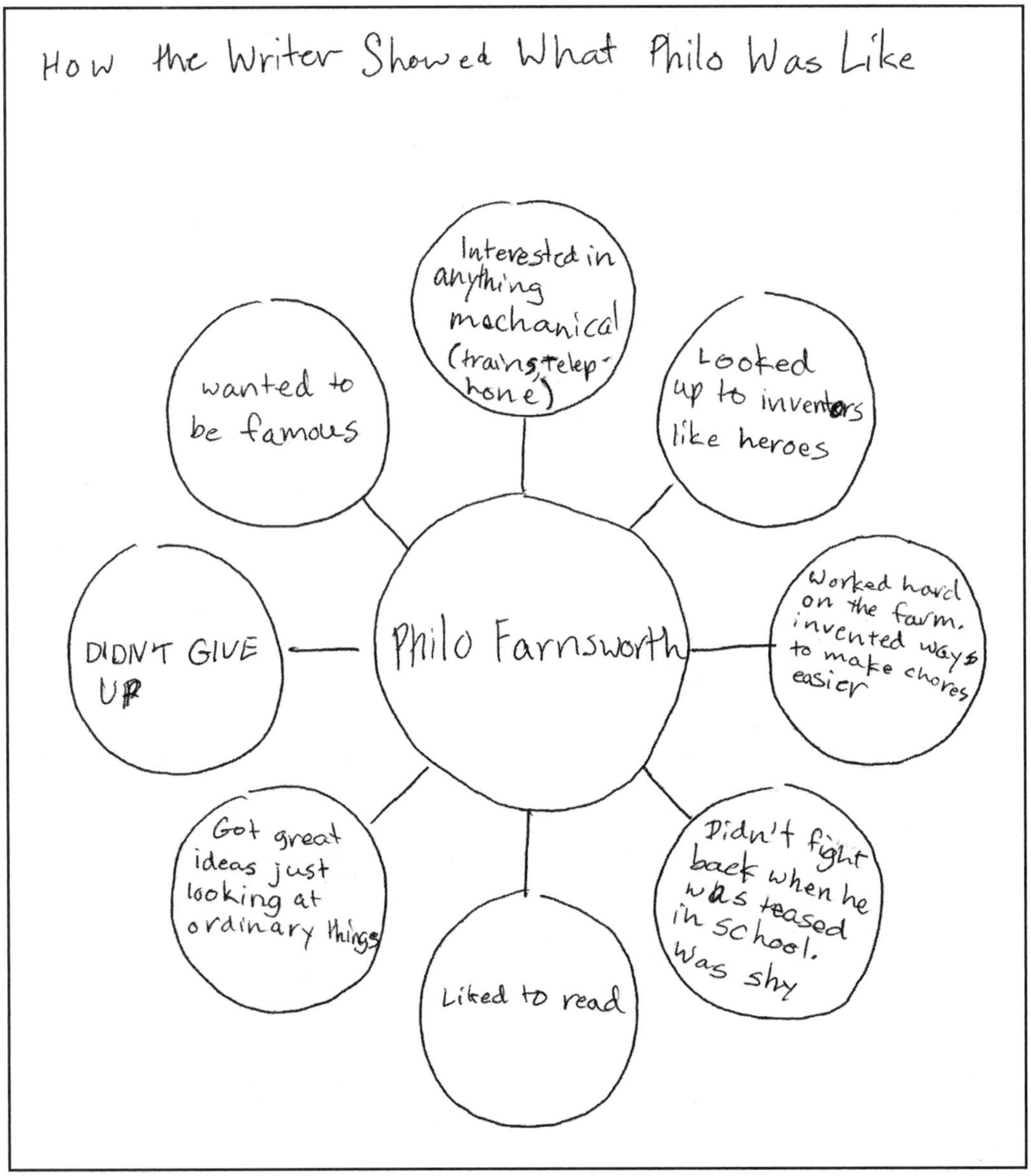

Figure 18.24 Graphic organizer highlighting Philo Farnsworth's character traits

Another exchange between Ms. Won and a student is shown in Figure 18.27. Reading these letters, you can infer their previous dialogue. Ms. Won has expressed interest in a book because she had not yet read it. (You probably can't read every one of the books your students choose for independent reading, although over the years you will come close! However, you can still have conversations about what students are thinking.) Per is so careful not to "ruin" the story that he provides little detail! Ms. Won then probes about Per's preference for fantasy and is no doubt surprised when he says he needs more science books. His lack of awareness of the depth of the book collection alerts her to weaknesses in his ability to select books, and she can make a plan to help him.

You can also use reader's notebooks to gather information about what your students know about the elements of literature and include some individual teaching in your responses. Ms. Won's letter exchange with another student (see Figure 18.28) focuses on story elements, particularly characters. Misha is finding her voice—a way to talk about books.

Your students (grade 1) can begin to draw or write short letters to you. As they grow more sophisticated and learn more about genre, they can begin to formalize their writing and move toward longer responses. The continuum in Figure 18.29 shows how a simple letter develops into a letter-essay over time. (Examples of the first three categories of responses are shown in Figure 18.30. An example of a letter-essay is provided in Figure 18.31.) Where you position your curriculum along this continuum depends on our students' experience and level of sophistication; your instruction should be customized to meet their needs and current skills.

Dear Mrs. D.,

I think it is half true that all stories need happy endings. Sometimes, books like <u>Snowbound</u> just end. Epics tend to have a good ending, although it feels there is always something else to be told. And realistic fictions seem to end super-happy. Personally, I prefer the "epic" ending (that I described). And what I said about "extreme" fantastical elements is that there are things like Ringwraith pursuit, and dangers of orcas, etc.

Well, for a brief update of the book. The Fellowship has "met up" with Haldar and his two brothers, with the same quote, "you breathe so loud we could have shot you in the dark" (pretty much the same quote, but under different circumstances). A thing I've noticed is that in each realm of the book (i.e., elves, hobbits, men, and dwarves) the species in the realm which they "belong to", the person(s) that is of that race, temporarily takes leadership] of the group. I think that J.R.R. Tolkein makes each place seem new, and mysterious, too. And here's a question, if you were a species of Middle-Earth, which one would you like to be? I'd choose to be an elf or man.

Sincerely, Ethan

Figure 18.25 Ethan's letter about *The Fellowship of the Rings*

LETTERS BETWEEN ROYI AND MS. WON	
Dear Ms. Won, I think realistic fiction and just fiction books have a difference. The difference is that realistic fiction could really happen. But still I don't mind reading realistic fiction. I'm reading a book called *Walk Two Moons*. I really like it because it is an adventure book (I like adventure books too). I also like it because it has a lot of suspense in it. I can't wait until I get to the end of the book. I want to find out what happens to Sal's grandma after she gets bitten by the poisonous snake. From, Royi	Dear Royi, If realistic fiction "could really happen," then why is it called *fiction*? How can the words *realistic* and *fiction* go together when they seem to be opposite? Then how would you describe fiction that is not realistic fiction? Isn't it interesting that there are different genres of fiction? I think you might be noticing that some fiction couldn't be real. We called that kind of fiction *fantasy*. The book you are reading now could have happened, so it is called *realistic fiction*. How would you explain what in the book *Walk Two Moons* is suspenseful? What are you thinking as you read it? Love, Ms. Won

Figure 18.26 Letters between Royi and Ms. Won

LETTERS BETWEEN PER AND MS. WON	
Dear Per, Thanks for filling me in. Don't worry about telling me what happens in the story. Are you concerned about ruining it for me? Actually I want to hear all of your thoughts about the books you read. I want to know about what happens in the stories but more than that, what do you think about it all? I've noticed that you really enjoy fantasy. What is it that draws you to this genre? What do you like about it? Well, I know you are reading *Miss Bianca* now. Tell me what you think about it so far. What are the characters like? Love, Ms. Won	Dear Ms. Won, I am drawn not only to fantasy, but to science books also. You have not noticed this because there aren't enough science books in our library! I have none to bring to school from home. I also like zoology. (Same case as with science.) I like fantasy because it is unreal. It is exciting and likely to consist of magical things. Now about *Miss Bianca*. It is a good book. It shows women in leadership. I think it is a good book. I like Miss Bianca's poems. From, Per

Figure 18.27 Letters between Per and Ms. Won

LETTERS BETWEEN MISHA AND MS. WON

Dear Misha,

I can see that you have started reading *Trespassers*. It sounds as though you like mysteries. This one is realistic fiction, and in this genre, the characters are very important. From what you described, it seems to have many interesting characters who give you a lot to think about. Aside from all of the mysterious and suspenseful events in the story, it's great to be able to think about the characters, too. They can be complicated and make us think about our own lives and our own personalities. I really like how books can offer so much for us to think about.

Characters are so important to stories. They're the ones who make decisions and make the books come alive. If Grub had a different personality, he might do different things and the events in the story might change.

How do you feel about the importance of characters in a book?

Love,
Ms. Won

P.S. Don't forget to sign your letters!

Dear Ms. Won,

I'm still reading *Trespassers*. In the mystery Grub is an interesting character. Grub is sort of like me because sometimes nothing can cheer him up. It's like me. Sometimes nothing can cheer me up but then I see something interesting. For example, when my mom did not let me have a play date, I was sad. But when I was sad I saw a woodpecker in my tree and that made me happy again. Same with him. So that is how I relate to the character in the story.

I feel that the characters are a very important part of the book. If the characters would be boring, then the book would be boring, unless the book is talking about what happened and not what the characters did. If I read the back of a book that said that the characters were boring people, I'd not read the book. It's like a chain: Setting, characters, the focus, and the plot. If one of them breaks or gets boring the story falls apart. It's like a building. If one of the columns breaks, the building falls in. The characters are as important as anything in the story—they're even. And that is what I think of the characters.

Sincerely,
Misha

Dear Misha,

I found what you wrote about characters really interesting. I like how you compared a story to a building. That is called an *analogy*. It is when you describe something by comparing it to something else, just like how to describe a story by comparing it to a building.

You make a good point about how all of the parts of a story are very important parts of the book and how they are all so closely connected with each other. It's like each part is good and can even seem better if the other parts are good too. It would be hard to have really fascinating characters but a totally boring plot, or a beautiful and captivating setting but drab characters.

Do you find that there is one that you as a reader tend to focus more on as you read a story? From your last letter, it seems you're saying that each part is equally important. What book are you reading now? As you are reading it, are you thinking about all o f the "parts" (characters, setting, plot, etc.) equally? Does one stand out in any way?

Love,
Ms. Won

Figure 18.28 Letters between Misha and Ms. Won

WRITING ABOUT READING: A CONTINUUM FOR TEACHER DECISION MAKING			
Beginning → *Highly Proficient*			
Letter	**Letter**	**Letter**	**Letter-Essay**
• Open-ended response	• Open-ended response with requirement—one paragraph focused on minilesson principle applied to student's book choice	• One paragraph open response with three or more paragraphs of focused responses	• Structured multi-paragraph personal response featuring an in-depth analysis of one book
• Half page to start, then to full page	• Minimum one page	• Minimum one page	• Minimum two pages
• Weekly or every other week	• Weekly or every other week	• Weekly or every other week	• Once per month

Figure 18.29 Writing about reading: a continuum for teacher decision making

Weekly open-ended responses (column one) simply encourage the student to express thinking; when you respond to their letters, you can ask questions that require an answer. Students start with half a page and increase writing to about a page. After students are accustomed to producing open responses and do so easily, you can begin requiring, as part of the open response, one paragraph that responds directly to the day's minilesson principle (column two). As students become more experienced, you increase the required paragraphs so that they write about structural elements as a matter of habit (column three). Finally, at highly sophisticated levels, have your students produce a letter-essay (column four).

Longer Responses

Sometimes you want students to write a longer, more extended and detailed response to their independent reading (or a read-aloud book). While short writes represent thinking that students record quickly and expressively, longer responses require looking back through the book, using notes, outlining or listing major points, drafting, and revising. The writing may be accomplished in either readers' workshop or writers' workshop. The longer response may also be an extended version of the graphic organizer. For example, a student may use a double column with character, problem, or quote on the left and an extended personal response on the right. An example of a longer response is shown in Figure 18.31.

Book Review

Reviewing books is an authentic reason for writing about reading. Anyone can publish a review now via the Internet, and many people do. A book review is a structured piece of writing, (journalistic in style and geared to an audience), that evaluates and does or does not recommend a particular text. The recommendation may be explicit or implicit.

To help students learn how to write book reviews, plan for a series of writers' minilessons (see Chapter 20). Writers of book reviews usually start with an opening that catches readers' attention. Notice Molly's attention-grabbing opening in her review in Figure 18.32. She

EXAMPLES OF THREE CATEGORIES OF WRITING-ABOUT-READING LETTERS		
Letter (Open-Ended Response)	**Letter (Open + One Structured Paragraph)**	**Letter (Open + Structured Paragraphs)**
Dear Mr. Wall, The book I am reading is *Understanding September 11th.* My favorite part of the book was when the planes were flying in the air in New York City cause they were still flying in the air. I felt really bad for the people who died because of the plane crash because a country killed the pilot and made the crash. It happened. This makes me think that this book teaches me about not doing bad things that can hurt our country. Sincerely, Laura P.S. Please read three times!	Dear Ms. Won, I am reading *Yang the Youngest and His Terrible Ear* by Lensey Namioka. In this book it is about a young boy (the youngest in his family) and about how he struggles playing the violin. His whole entire family thinks he plays horrible and so does he. Yang is having trouble getting friends. He also is not looking forward to a recital where Yang plays a second violin. Soon Yang meets Matthew and becomes friends. What does Yang want Matthew to get lessons for the violin from his family so much? You want me to talk about what the author of the book is trying to say. I think the message of this book is going to be that you always want to please your family but you also have to get to know yourself and what you can do. I think it will also be that friends are important in helping you. Love, Jessica	Dear Mrs. Gordon, I am reading *Bridge to Terabithia.* Jess and Lesley are interesting characters. I learned in the book that Jess is really sneaky. I like Lesley because she is smart and creative. Her and Jess created Terabithia their own world. I think that Jess and Leslie are best friends and Terabithia will get better. [characters] The writer made this book seem real because there are a lot of details. I know that this book has its own world. Terabithia seems like a real place even though it is not. I really wish there was a real Terabithia and I could be friends with Leslie and Jess. [author's craft] I predict that Jess will think of more ideas and Leslie will get really better at running. I know Leslie will help Jess a lot. [prediction] I think that the author wrote this book to show friendship and kindness. I haven't finished the book but it seems that Jess and Leslie need to be friends. [author's message] *Bridge to Terabithia* is a very good book and it is interesting because it shows that a boy and girl can be best friends even if they are not very much alike. I have lots of friends that are girls and some that are boys too. But I don't think I have any friends like Leslie. Love, Katie

Figure 18.30 Examples of three categories of writing-about-reading letters

Response to *They Cage the Animals at Night,* by Jennings Michael Burch

Prompt: Write about any connections you see between the book you are reading and your own life or the world today.

As I read *They Cage the Animals at Night* by Jennings Michael Burch, I continuously marveled at the terrible things that some people are capable of doing to a young child. The book is about an 8-year-old boy named Jennings whose mother is sick, and having a hard time caring for him. Because his mother is sick, Jennings has to live at many different orphanages and foster houses when she cannot take care of him. Some of the places he stays at are good, most are not though. *They Cage the Animals at Night* is a book that makes me think about how lucky I am to have a good home, enough food, and a caring family. It also reminds me of my mom's work. So many sad things happen to Jennings that sometimes I can barely believe that it is a true story. It is an autobiography or a memoir.

Often when I read *They Cage the Animals at Night*, I compared what is going on with Jennings to my own life. I also thought about how lucky I am. When I started the book, I imagined how I would feel if my mom dropped me off at an orphanage. On page 6, Jennings' mother left him at the orphanage and I felt sorry for him. Jennings was afraid. He cried and begged for his mother because he had no idea what was happening. If that happened to me, I would probably react the same way. I also compared Jennings life with my own when Jennings found out his father was alive. Jennings learned that his father was not dead but that he was an alcoholic and he felt surprised and then mad because his father did not help his mother to take care of their family at all. Jennings' father never wanted to see him or take care of him. If I were Jennings, I would feel similarly, and I would also feel like my father doesn't care about me. Jennings' experience with foster care also made me think about my mom's work.

When I started reading *They Cage the Animals at Night*, I thought about my mom's job. My mom is a children's psychologist and many of the kids she works with have had some type of violence in their family, just like Jennings had at the orphanages and at one of his foster homes, with the Carpenters. Some of the kids my mom works with live in foster families because their parents did not take care of them well. Since I know about my mom's work, I know that this kind of situation actually happens to children besides Jennings. When the nun pulled Jennings across the hard wood floor giving him splinters all over his body not even caring about his pain I was shocked and horrified. I could barely believe this had really happened. Many of the things Jennings experienced sounded too terrible to be true but the stories my mom has told me about the children she works with helped me to know that these things really happened to Jennings, and still do today.

This book is amazing, sad, and inspiring. I enjoyed it very much and hope to read the sequel when it comes out.

Figure 18.31 Letter-essay response to *They Cage the Animals at Night*

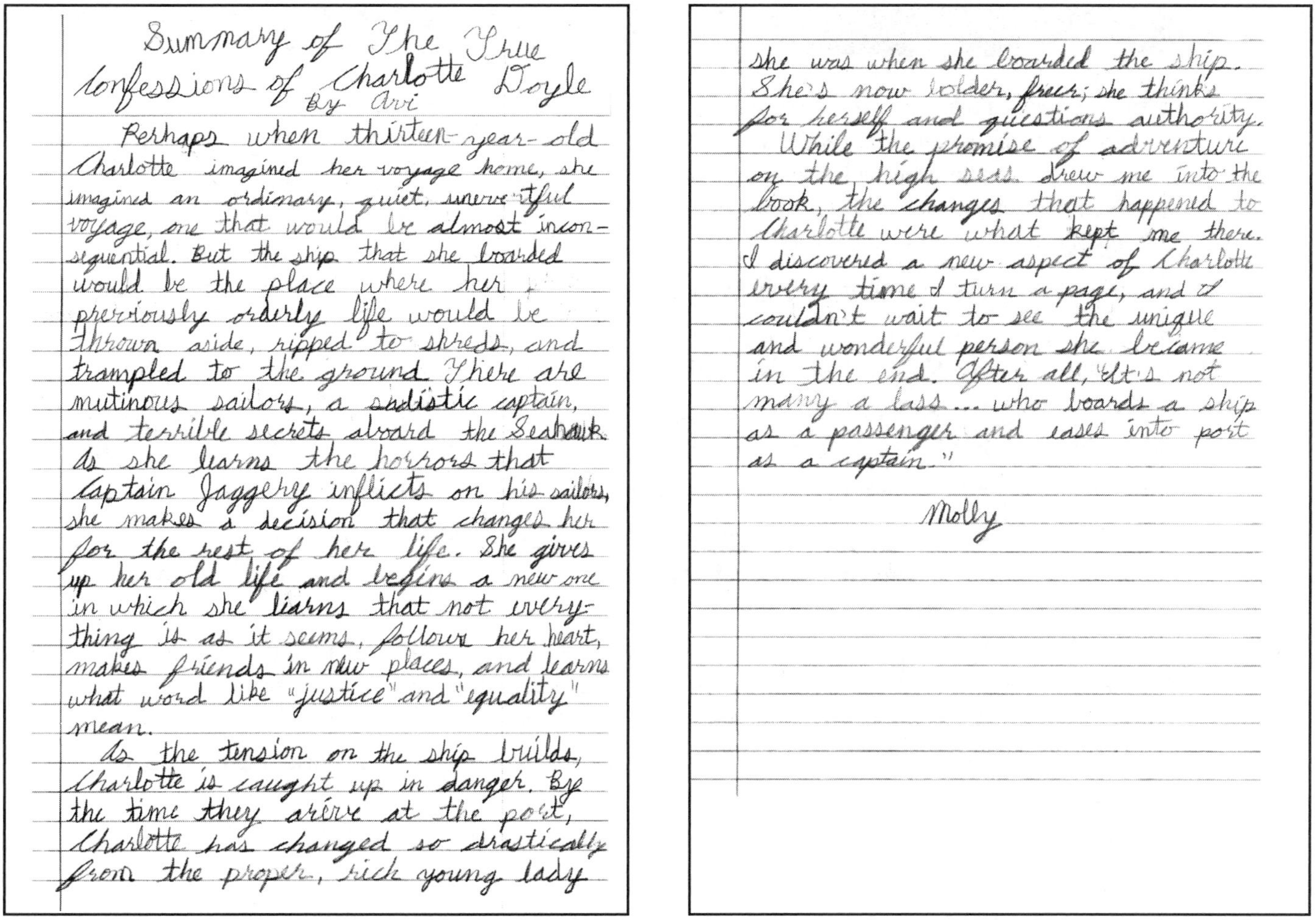
Summary of The True
Confessions of Charlotte Doyle
By Avi

Perhaps when thirteen-year-old Charlotte imagined her voyage home, she imagined an ordinary, quiet, uneventful voyage, one that would be almost inconsequential. But the ship that she boarded would be the place where her previously orderly life would be thrown aside, ripped to shreds, and trampled to the ground. There are mutinous sailors, a sadistic captain, and terrible secrets aboard the Seahawk. As she learns the horrors that Captain Jaggery inflicts on his sailors, she makes a decision that changes her for the rest of her life. She gives up her old life and begins a new one in which she learns that not everything is as it seems, follow her heart, makes friends in new places, and learns what word like "justice" and "equality" mean.

As the tension on the ship builds, Charlotte is caught up in danger. By the time they arrive at the port, Charlotte has changed so drastically from the proper, rich young lady she was when she boarded the ship. She's now older, freer; she thinks for herself and questions authority.

While the promise of adventure on the high seas drew me into the book, the changes that happened to Charlotte were what kept me there. I discovered a new aspect of Charlotte every time I turn a page, and I couldn't wait to see the unique and wonderful person she became in the end. After all, "It's not many a lass... who boards a ship as a passenger and eases into port as a captain."

Molly

Figure 18.32 Molly's review of *The True Confessions of Charlotte Doyle*

also summarizes the important parts of the book so that her readers will understand what it is about, and she foreshadows the outcome without giving away the exciting parts. She ends with a concluding statement that leaves readers thinking about the book.

Letter-Essays

Ms. Quest-Neubert used a letter-essay checklist with her students that they inserted into their reader's notebooks and used as they moved from open-ended response letters to letter-essays (Figure 18.33). It takes into account responding to the teacher's latest letter and can be modified or simplified according to students' current understandings.

Graphic Planner

A structured tool to help writers organize information in logical ways and avoid redundancy is a graphic planner like the one shown in Figure 18.34. Carlos has found three kinds of evidence (taken from three points in the story), but a writer might use only two boxes or might add boxes. A simple chart like this helps students begin with the main idea or argument (thesis), then provides evidence that supports the main argument. The summary and conclusions refer back to the main argument, which by now has been supported by the details. Carlos' final essay (see Figure 18.35) is based on his graphic planner. He makes an important thesis statement and supports it by revealing the plot sequence and emphasizing character development.

LETTER-ESSAY CHECKLIST

Your reader's notebook is a place for you to consider books, reading, authors, and writing. Since you've now written a number of informal responses in your reader's notebook and your home reading records, we're ready to raise the level of our written conversations about books. You'll write about your books in informal essays directed to me, and I'll write back to you about your ideas and observations. These letter-essays and responses will become a record of the reading, thinking, learning, and teaching we accomplished together.

As you write your letter-essays, as well as after you've finished, look at this checklist to make sure you have met all the requirements.

- ☐ Is your letter-essay **at least 2 full pages long**, and about just one book?
- ☐ Does it have a **proper greeting** (Dear Ms. ______)?
- ☐ Did you include the **date**?
- ☐ Is it broken into **at least** 6 paragraphs by the idea or subject?
    - ☐ **Response paragraph** responding to teacher comments and questions from the previous letter-essay.
    - ☐ **2 paragraphs** about different **literary elements** in the book—what you notice and think about how the author used these different elements.
    - ☐ **1 paragraph** about a quote that stood out to you—why the quote stood out to you and what it shows about the book (or part of the book) or why it's important in the book. Remember that the quote needs to include quotation marks and page numbers.
    - ☐ **Conclusion paragraph** summarizing your overall thoughts about the book, including reasons and recommendations.
- ☐ Is it **mostly your opinion**: what you like and dislike about the book?
- ☐ Do you *explain* your opinion: why you think what you think? Do you give examples?
- ☐ Does it have a **proper signature** *(Sincerely, From, Your Friend)?*

If the answer to any of these questions is no, go back to your letter-essay and revise it to include the missing pieces.

LITERARY ELEMENTS IN FICTION

Characters/Character Development	**Plot**	**Setting**
• Who characters are • How characters change	• Action (what happens) • Tension/conflict	• Where the book takes place • When the book takes place
Theme	**Perspective**	**Structure**
• Message/so what? • What the author is trying to tell the reader	• Point of view of the narrator(s)	• How the text is set up • How it "works"

Style and Language

- How the author uses language to convey (express) meaning
- Figurative language
- Imagery and symbolism
- Mood
- How realistic the writing is or how the author makes characters and events seem real (realistic or historical fiction)

Figure 18.33 Letter-essay checklist developed by Ms. Quest-Neubert

CARLOS'S GRAPHIC PLANNER		
Main Idea (argument), Introductory or Thesis Paragraph In this novel *Lord of the Flies,* by William Golding, people are forced to change because of a new environment (to survive). They react in different ways. Jack is the main character (antagonist) and he changed in a very negative way.		
Support/Proof Details • Jack hunts for his own food. • Kills the pig and starts to sing "Kill the beast! Cut his throat! Spill his blood!" • After he found out about the beast they cut off pig's head for the beast. • He started to release his savage nature.	**Support/Proof Details** • Jack has his own camp and becomes a leader. • Uses war paint. • They killed Simon because they thought he was the beast, so they beat him to death. • After Jack became a leader they attacked Ralph's group and stole Piggy's glasses. • Feels invincible.	**Support/Proof Details** • Jack was the almighty chief. • He lost his humanity because he became obsessed and gives permission to kill people. • All but one became part of his crew and he wanted to kill that one. • The island has changed him to kill everyone in his way.
Summary/Conclusion All boys adapted to the new environment in different ways, some leaders and some followers. Jack is a dynamic character who is always changing. He is the kind of person who hides his fear by showing off and making fun of people to make him feel better and to make others laugh to draw attention to himself. Jack adapted to the environment in a negative way and became so savage that he killed others.		

Figure 18.34 Carlos's graphic planner for *Lord of the Flies*

Grading is a school reality, especially at the upper levels. Expect your students to work hard at writing letters or letter-essays and to take them seriously. We provide a form for grading letters in *Teaching for Comprehending and Fluency.* Ms. Quest-Neubert developed her own grading system for her students letter-essays (see Figure 18.36) Teachers who want to use this form only as a reflection instrument can take off the columns related to grading. The form can be modified to make requirements more open.

Narrative Writing About Reading

Narrative writing about reading is similar to all response writing, but it is presented as a story. Narrative writing includes a plot summary or general summary, a readers' theater script, or a cartoon/storyboard (a visual summary). Figure 18.37 lists four different forms of narrative writing, all of which help students learn to think in deeper ways about their reading. Each form can be used to focus students' attention on genre.

Figure 18.35 Carlos's Essay About *Lord of the Flies*

Essay: *Lord of the Flies*

Lord of the Flies by William Golding is a dramatic story of children trying to survive only by using their wits. The antagonist, Jack, had to adjust to a new island environment. A plane crashed and only a group of young boys survived. At first Jack became a simple hunter to search and provide food for the group. Soon enough after killing a pig he starts becoming a savage and all he wants to do is kill. Those urges to kill grow even stronger to the point where he actually kills someone. Jack wanted to be the leader of the group but never had the chance to, but he makes his own crew and almost everyone joins out of fear. The Jack that was once part of the choirboys is now a full-fledged savage.

The first thing Jack did was become a hunter and help out with small things like tending to fire. It was supposed to be a simple job of providing food for the group. He was ashamed at first because he couldn't catch the pig. When he finally got a successful technique down, they caught the pig. They started to sing "Kill the beast! Cut his throat! Spill his blood!" With success comes greed. Jack starts to think he's high and mighty because he brought everyone food. That all starts to go to his head and he'd rather hunt than help out the group. The savage nature with Jack is being released.

As the savage in Jack is awakening the others are scared of him. He becomes wild and doesn't show respect to anyone. He starts to use war paint to show he's a true hunter. Jack and his hunters have a feast and invite everyone to show off. While the feast is going on one of the boys who wandered off comes back with a spear in his back. He died. The next day they murder yet another boy. At the moment Jack feels invincible.

Jack did not become all that powerful on his own. By fear, he got to conjure up his own crew to help him hunt. At first he had his choir boys help him but by the end he had everyone except one. He disliked the last boy very much. He thought of him as a rebel and wanted to kill him. The war paint they used to hunt was also a group symbol. Jack was the almighty chief of this group but he lost his humanity.

In the book *Lord of the Flies*, all the boys adapted to the environment in many different ways. Some were leaders, others were followers. Jack was the antagonist of the story. He was obsessed with hunting. He always wanted to be chief. Jack even became so savage he killed other boys because he could. Jack adapted to his environment in a negative way. It was like there was a demon inside him. The story shows that when people are put into a new environment where they have to survive and some try to get power over others, some can turn into savages and do terrible things. Jack went from choir boy to savage killer. The fear for survival made his inner evil come out.

LETTER-ESSAY GRADING CRITERIA		
Student ______________ **Letter-Essay #** ______________		
Requirement	**Points Possible**	**Points Received**
Includes a **proper greeting** (including the date!)	1	
At least **2 pages** long	2	
Includes an **introductory paragraph**, including the **title** of the book (underlined), and its **author**, as well as a quick **summary**	2	
Includes at least **one paragraph** responding to teacher comments and questions from the previous letter-essay	2	
Includes at least **2 paragraphs** about different **literary elements** in the book–what you notice and think about how the author used these different elements	4	
Includes **1 paragraph** about a **quote** that stood out to you and what it shows about the book, or why it's important in the book	2	
Includes a **conclusion paragrap**h summarizing your **overall thoughts** about the book,including **reasons** and **recommendations**	2	
The letter is **mostly opinion**: what you like and dislike about the book	2	
Your opinions are backed up with **explanations** (why you think what you think) and includes **examples**	2	
Includes a **proper signature**	1	
TOTAL	**20**	

Figure 18.36 Ms. Quest-Neubert's grading criteria for letter-essays

NARRATIVE WRITING ABOUT READING	
Description and General Benefits	**Connection to Genre Study**
Plot summary—a brief statement of the text's plot: • Supports readers' memory • Helps readers determine what is most important information in the text • Provides a basis for sharing thinking • Provides a good record to help readers get back to the meaning even much later	• Helps readers notice the characteristics of fiction texts • Helps readers differentiate types of plots in various forms of fiction (mystery, adventure, etc.) • Helps readers remember what they noticed about the characteristics of genre
Summary—a few sentences that tell the most important information in a text: • Enables readers to evaluate information in a text • Requires that readers select the information that is most important • Helps readers remember the important information in order to inform further reading or discussion • Helps readers record important information so they can connect to other texts while reading	• Helps readers keep in mind the whole text while talking about characteristics of genre • Helps readers remember and use the characteristics of genre to support further reading or discussion • Can be used as a resource when writing about genre
Scene for readers' theater—a script with a narrator and parts designed to enable readers to become the voices of characters; may be prepared by teacher as a model or prepared by experienced students: • Expands readers' understanding of the narrator in a text • Requires practice in identifying dialogue • Requires thoughtful attention to the important and interesting parts of a text • Involves thinking about the characters' feelings, motivations, and ways of expressing themselves • Provides much practice in fluent, expressive reading	• Helps readers notice aspects of the writer's craft related to the characteristics of genre • Enables readers to change the genre of a text (for example, a fictionalized script based on biography or informational texts) • Helps readers notice key characteristics of the genre
Cartoon/storyboard—a succession of graphics or stick figures used to present a story or information: • Enables readers to communicate ideas in images that tell a story or give a sequence • Helps readers learn to select important information • Helps readers learn to summarize • Can be used as a basis for writing	• Enables readers to communicate the characteristics of the genre visually • Can help students identify the key characteristics of a genre

Figure 18.37 Narrative writing about reading

Plot Summary or General Summary

Narrative writing might take the form of a plot summary. Even younger readers can learn to summarize by selecting the important parts of the plot. A very simple summary of the fable "The City Mouse and the Country Mouse" is shown in Figure 18.38.

Scene for Readers' Theater or Writing for Other Dramatic Purpose

Selecting sections of text suitable for dramatic reading requires careful thought about the writer's craft. It helps readers notice the details of texts as well as aspects of genre.

A readers' theater script can be a simple scene with assigned parts. Your students can select a scene and write the parts. It is a valuable task for understanding the nuances of a text and developing fluency. Readers who are writing dramatic narratives can change the genre of a text or its form. In Figure 18.39, Amy has created two monologues for separate characters in the book *Homecoming*, by Cynthia Voigt.

Cartoon/Storyboard

Creating cartoons or making storyboards is an enjoyable activity for students and has instructional value. Students quickly draw pictures or sketches representing significant events or information in a text. These sketches are arranged to match the structure of the text and can be used as a basis for writing. To create a storyboard readers have to select important events or literary elements. The storyboard may reveal the structure or organization of a text or present an analysis.

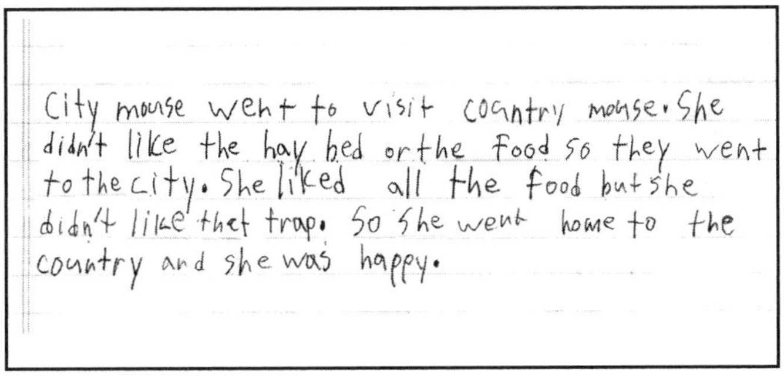
City mouse went to visit country mouse. She didn't like the hay bed or the food so they went to the city. She liked all the food but she didn't like thet trap. So she went home to the country and she was happy.

Figure 18.38 Summary of "The City Mouse and the Country Mouse"

Nonfiction Writing About Reading

Nonfiction or informational writing organizes facts into a coherent whole. Drawing from their knowledge of the different genres and forms of written language, student readers can produce a wide range of informational writing, as shown in Figure 18.40.

Outline

Outlining can be overdone, but it can help readers understand the organization of a text, and it is particularly helpful when working with nonfiction genres. Outlining can be used even if a text does not include readers' tools such as headings and subheadings. An outline for the informational text *Acid Rain* is shown in Figure 18.41.

Outlining can reveal the internal structure of a text, which is closely related to the genre, and it can support readers in noticing the characteristics of genre. Noel's outline for *Acid Rain* is spare but shows his ability to see the organization of the text even when headings are not provided. An outline like this can be useful in looking across texts to make connections or draw out big ideas and information.

Author Study

An author study is the result of much reading and research. When engaging in a class study of an author students learn the process for an in-depth noticing of an author's works. Students read a body of work by an author and sometimes do research on the writer's life. The study may involve comparison, analysis, and/or critique. Students note and discuss the genres the writer uses. They hypothesize why the writer chose certain genres. Sometimes, studying a body of work by an author gives students an opportunity to notice how the writer's style and language change when writing in different genres.

Illustrator Study

An illustrator study is similar to an author study. Looking across a body of work, students may notice consistent aspects of an illustrator's style and may also

AMY'S MONOLOGUES FOR DRAMATIC READING FROM *HOMECOMING*	
Maybeth Thinks About What's Taking Place (pages 144–64)	**Sammy Expresses Her Point of View** (Chapters 1–3)
Oh God, what do I do now? When we arrived at this house I felt comfortable, like this was our final stop. I guess I was wrong. I'm lying in bed pretending to be asleep. The police car that had come before pulled up to the house a while ago. Downstairs I can hear my sister and the grownups talking. I think they are talking about mama but I can't make out the words. Nobody thinks I know this but I heard Cousin Eunice talking about me with Dicey. They (the father and the nuns) think I'm retarded. I don't quite know what it means but I know it's not good. All I can do to keep calm is sing. The time I sang the first night mama was gone is running through my mind. "I gave my love a cherry that had no stone . . ." What is retarded: does it mean they think I'm stupid? . . . "I gave my love a chicken that had no bone . . . I gave my love a . . . " maybe not stupid, but slow ". . . ring that had no end . . . " I admit that I am slow but once its explained I catch on easily ". . . I gave my love a baby with no crying . . ." I hope we leave this place. I'm thankful to Eunice but I'm not comfortable here. "A cherry when it's blooming it has no stone, a chicken when it's piping it has no bone, a ring when it's rolling it has no end, a baby when it's sleeping has no crying." Oh here comes Dicey. She looks worried. I think she wants to tell me something. **NOTE:** I knew the song Maybeth sang in the beginning and thought it would be neat to tie it into the entry.	Yesterday my mother left me in a car all alone. Even though she left me with my sisters and one brother I still feel alone. Nobody has ever looked after or even cared about me except for my mother. I want to believe my mother will come find me but I know she won't. Why does she hate me? I remember how kids made fun of my family. I never told mama because I didn't want her to worry. My sister doesn't know about the kids either. She would hate me even more than she already does. I wish she could see my side like Maybeth does. Maybeth is my other sister. She is the only one who can comfort me. Everyone thinks she's so sweet but I think she also knows mother won't come back. I miss mama so much but I'm also mad at her. I don't know what to think. Tonight we're staying in an abandoned campsite. I'm tired and my feet hurt. As the fire burns out so does my strength. Tomorrow I hope will be a better day.

Figure 18.39 Amy's monologues for dramatic reading from *Homecoming*

INFORMATIONAL WRITING ABOUT READING	
Description and General Benefits	**Connection to Genre Study**
Outline—a list of headings and phrases that identify main points and sub-points in an organized way to show their relationship visually: • Helps readers identify and understand the major ideas and supporting ideas in a text • Helps readers show evidence for conclusions • Provides a quick way for readers to look back over the whole text and how it is organized	• Reveals the internal structure of a text, which is related to genre • Helps readers quickly find examples of genre characteristics • Provides a foundation for writing analytically about the text
Author study—writing that provides information about an author and his/her craft as exemplified in several specified works; may involve comparison, analysis, critique: • Engages readers in analytical and critical thinking about the writer's craft • Prompts noticing a writer's style and how it may change in response to a subject • Provides opportunities to express analytical or critical thinking in writing • Requires using evidence from the text to support thinking	• Helps readers notice how an author's work demonstrates the characteristics of the genre • Helps readers think about why the author selected the genre • Provides readers the opportunity to notice how a writer's work may change for different genres • Helps readers think about why a writer might prefer certain genres
Illustrator study—writing that provides information on an illustrator and his/her craft as exemplified in several specified works; may involve artistic analysis, response to mood, analysis of integration of ideas and visual images, observation of technique: • Provides opportunity to think of the text as an artistic whole • Provides opportunities for artistic appreciation • Requires thinking about the meaning of the text in comparison to the visual images • Requires drawing evidence from visual images and describing them	• Helps readers notice whether and how the illustrations fit the genre (photographs or drawings for expository texts, for example) • Sometimes provides readers the opportunity to notice how the illustrations can change the genre by adding information or a second story line
Literary essay—a formal essay that presents ideas about a text or texts and may include a short summary: • Requires planning and organizing • Involves drafting, revising, and editing to be sure the argument is clear to readers • Involves developing a new understanding from a well-presented argument • Requires analytical and critical thinking • Requires using evidence from the text to support thinking • Requires reaching the quality of publication	• Requires readers to identify the genre • Requires readers to use their knowledge of the genre to analyze the text • Requires readers to evaluate whether a text is an example of a genre • Requires readers to use evidence from the text to identify and discuss the genre

Figure 18.40 Informational writing about reading

continues

INFORMATIONAL WRITING ABOUT READING	
Description and General Benefits	**Connection to Genre Study**
Interview (author or expert)–a series of questions and responses that provide information about an author or expert on a topic: • Requires deeper thinking about a topic or author's work • Provides an opportunity to use interaction to create a written text • Provides experiences in using firsthand sources • Provides experience in using question-and-answer format • Requires readers to know enough about a topic to determine points of inquiry	• Provides the opportunity for readers to question the author about the use of genre • Sometimes requires readers to think about a body of work in a genre or across genres • Requires readers to understand the underlying structure–question and answer
How-to article–article that explains to readers how something is made or done and gives specialized knowledge: • Requires readers to be "experts" on the topic through reading about it • Requires careful attention to sequence • Requires readers to think about the audience's understanding	• Requires readers to understand how procedural texts are organized and written • Requires readers to think about how the audience would need to read a procedural text
Photo essay, picture essay, PowerPoint or multimedia presentation–a series of photographs, drawings, or digital photography sometimes with sound or video, that explains a topic or event: • Provides opportunity to use visual imagines to communicate thoughts and ideas • Provides opportunity to connect illustrations and brief pieces of text as an integral whole • Requires the organization of visual, written, and digital information	• Provides readers the possibility of presenting information from one text in another form or genre • Requires readers to understand how information is presented in a variety of genres
Report–factual information presented in an organized way: • Requires gathering, organizing, and selecting information from different sources • Requires the use of a variety of text features • Provides experience in organizing information in a logical way • Requires attention to what the audience understands • Requires selection of terms and concepts that must be defined in the text • Requires documentation of informational sources • Requires citing of evidence to support exposition or argument	• Requires readers to use their knowledge of nonfiction genres to engage in research • Provides readers the opportunity to use underlying text structures in nonfiction genres • Requires readers to know how nonfiction genres are organized

Figure 18.40 Informational writing about reading *(cont.)*

INFORMATIONAL WRITING ABOUT READING	
Description and General Benefits	**Connection to Genre Study**
News or feature article—factual information written to inform readers about and share interest in a topic: • Requires readers to select a compelling topic • Requires readers to evaluate, select, and organize important information • Requires readers to organize and present information in a form that will make it accessible and interesting to the audience (e.g., prose, brochure)	• Requires readers to understand a particular form of a nonfiction genre • Requires readers to develop skill in writing in the form
Editorial/op-ed pieces—ideas organized and presented in writing to communicate information or a specific opinion on a topic or issue: • Requires organizing information to support an argument • Requires use of structures and signal words and phrases that are characteristic of argument (*because of, as a result, the evidence is, we must conclude*) • Requires citing of evidence to support argument or opinion • Requires documentation of the truth of evidence to support argument or opinion	• Requires readers to understand persuasive texts • Provides readers opportunities to notice the language writers of persuasive texts use • Promotes critical thinking about persuasive texts
Biographical sketch—a short article that provides information about a person's life or achievements; written to show appreciation for a person's accomplishments: • Requires selection of the most important information about a subject • Allows the reader to express appreciation for individuals and to say why	• Extends readers' understanding of biography • Extends readers' understanding of the way writers of biography make decisions.
Review or recommendation—an article written to give readers advice on a book, topic, product, or place • Requires thinking about how to produce a text that will persuade or influence an audience • Requires careful consideration of all aspects of the topic, product, book, or place • Requires selection of what is important information • Requires selection of the kind of information that will be important to an audience	• Extends readers' understanding of the way writers of reviews work • Extends readers' understanding of the kinds of style and language used in persuasive texts

Figure 18.40 Informational writing about reading *(cont.)*

continues

INFORMATIONAL WRITING ABOUT READING	
Description and General Benefits	**Connection to Genre Study**
Project–a creative body of work that presents ideas and opinions about texts or topics in an organized way: • Provides the opportunity for an extended and creative piece of work • Incorporates many different kinds of information gathering • Requires organization and representation of different kinds of visual and print information. • Produces a public piece of work	• Requires readers to use information about many different genres in the production of the project • Extends readers' understanding of how information can be gained and communicated across different genres and forms of text

Figure 18.40 Informational writing about reading *(cont.)*

***Acid Rain* by Brian Birchall**
Illustrated by Bob Kerr

Outline

1. The City
   a. The city is busy.
   b. The city has planes and cars
   c. The city has factories with smoke
2. Smoke in the Air
   a. Smoke mixes with air.
   b. There is a cloud of smoke over the city.
3. Rain
   a. Raindrops fall.
   b. Raindrops have smoke and dirt and gas in them.
4. Acid Rain
   a. Rain with dirt is dangerous.
   b. Acid rain destroys things
   c. Acid rain makes the water poison.
   d. Acid rain kills trees
5. Garbage
   a. Acid rain can blow away
   b. It's like throwing garbage on other people.
6. People Working Together
   a. We need to know how to keep air clean.
   b. People need to work on this.

Note: This book didn't have any headings so I made up some and told what would be under each.

Noel

Figure 18.41 Noel's outline for *Acid Rain*

see how style changes subtly to respond to different topics or genres. In some texts, aspects of genre are determined by the illustrations; for example, fanciful illustrations may contrast a serious text. Studying an illustrator's work requires thinking about the meaning and mood of texts and the role of the illustrator in communicating both.

Literary Essay

The literary essay is a formal piece of writing that presents ideas about a text and may include a short summary. The purpose is not to prove, "book report" style, that a book has been read but to present analytical and critical thinking. Sometimes an essay discusses several related texts. Producing a literary essay requires students to identify the genre and to think about the work as an example of the genre. It requires planning and organizing, drafting, revising, and editing. The example in Figure 18.42 combines the literary essay with a book recommendation. Amy includes specific citations from the text as evidence. She also addresses character traits, setting, and the theme of the story.

Interview

It may seem that an interview is easy to write because you are simply quoting a person's answers, but this form can be quite challenging. Students must know the work of the person being interviewed and/or the topic well enough to compose a series of well-planned

Figure 18.42 Amy's literary essay on *Homecoming*

Homecoming

Literary Essay

by Amy

Homecoming by Cynthia Voigt is an adventure; and yet, it was such a realistic story. I was amazed at how the writer could take a realistic fiction story and make it seem true to life. The characters in this book faced an immense predicament and turned it into a not-so-complicated bad one. The author added funny effects, and good effects, so that the story was not only about a ruined and bad family. It was engaging, descriptive, informative, and well written.

I especially loved Cynthia Voigt's style of writing. I really liked how she made up a lot of different characters and described so well their different personalities. She really zooms in on the characters. As you read you experience the pride, anger, and forlornness that Dicey (the main character) encounters throughout her journeys. The author also showed every single little detail about the person. It was like you were looking at the person this instant. Here is an example: "She slung her purse over her shoulder and walked away, her stride made uneven by broken sandal thongs, thin elbows showing through holes in the oversized sweater, her jeans faded and baggy." I wonder if Cynthia Voigt is like one of these characters because she described them like they were her own children.

Cynthia Voigt's writing is so descriptive. This passage from page 299 is so well done that you can almost reach out and touch the surroundings: "At the first signs of dawn, the first pink glimmers, the first watery bird songs, Dicey opened her eyes. She lay on her back with James on one side and Maybeth curled against the other and Sammy on his belly beside James. Her eyes looked up through the delicate leaves of trees into a depthless sky. She smiled and her eyes closed." I thought this was a great example of a description of scenes.

My favorite part of the book was when the Tillermans stayed with Will's circus. This was because the children finally got to act like real kids; they got treated like them too. They also got good food, shelter, and new clothes, plus the fact that they got to stay with a circus. What more could a kid want? Each child got to do something different and exhilarating. For instance, Sammy was in an act with Claire; Maybeth was going to make a costume for him; and James was busy with the machinery that ran the carousel.

For me, one of the most entertaining parts of the book was when the Tillermans met their grandmother. The quarrels between Dicey and Gram were sometimes very funny. Even though that was a good part, I still believe an even more entertaining part has to be on page 167 when they are about to leave Cousin Eunice's in search of their grandmother:

"Where are we going," Maybeth asked.

"We're going to see the place Momma lived in when she was a little girl," Dicey answered.

continues

Figure 18.42 Amy's literary essay on *Homecoming (cont.)*

> "All of us together?"
>
> "All of us together," Dicey said. "That's the only way the Tillermans travel."
>
> I thought that brought out the overall feeling that Dicey had about how everything would end up. It is a very powerful passage because it is simple, to the point, but also very decided. Dicey knew that no matter what, she would keep her family together.
>
> Homecoming is the beautiful story about a family of children sticking together to overcome a terrible predicament. I found myself laughing, gasping, and tearing all throughout the story. I would definitely recommend this book to anyone who likes writing with a lot of description. It is a complex but easy read. It was humorous and adventurous. If you like a book that once you pick it up, you can't put it down, Homecoming will be perfect. I was caught up in the story and wanted more. I guess I will have to read the sequel to quench this insatiable thirst with which Cynthia Voigt has left me.

questions and probes to help the subject elaborate on points. Constructing an interview requires deeper thinking about a body of work, which may include thinking about the writer's choice of genre or the genres used as resources to learn about a topic. Transcribing the interview requires understanding how to organize the information so that it flows naturally and how to use the questions and answers so that the interview will be comprehensible.

How-To Article

A how-to article can be about any process or procedure; it requires students to act as "experts" on the topic, which often requires reading and drawing out information across texts. This kind of article also requires and extends students' understanding of how procedural texts are organized and written. They need to see the procedural texts from the audience's point of view in order to produce a clearly sequenced set of directions.

Photo Essay, Picture Essay, or PowerPoint Presentation

Using even very simple technology, students have endless possibilities when it comes to communicating information. They can combine visual images that they find or take themselves, video, diagrams, and abstract designs to create overall messages and/or to explain a topic or phenomenon. This kind of presentation requires students to organize visual, written, and digital information as well as write in a variety of genres.

Report

Writing a report involves gathering, organizing, and selecting information from different sources, some of which may involve reading in several genres. It requires using nonfiction genres for research and helps students extend their understanding of the many underlying text structures in nonfiction (see Chapter 10). To prepare a report students need to organize and present information in a logical way, often using nonfiction text features such as headings, subheadings, illustrations, and graphics. They may need to define content words. The example in Figure 18.43 is an excerpt from a report on Ecuador. The writer has incorporated both print information from several sources. She has placed like information in categories, reflecting the usual organization of an expository text.

News or Feature Article

A news or feature article is written in a journalistic style. Students read a variety of nonfiction material, then evaluate, select, and organize important information as well

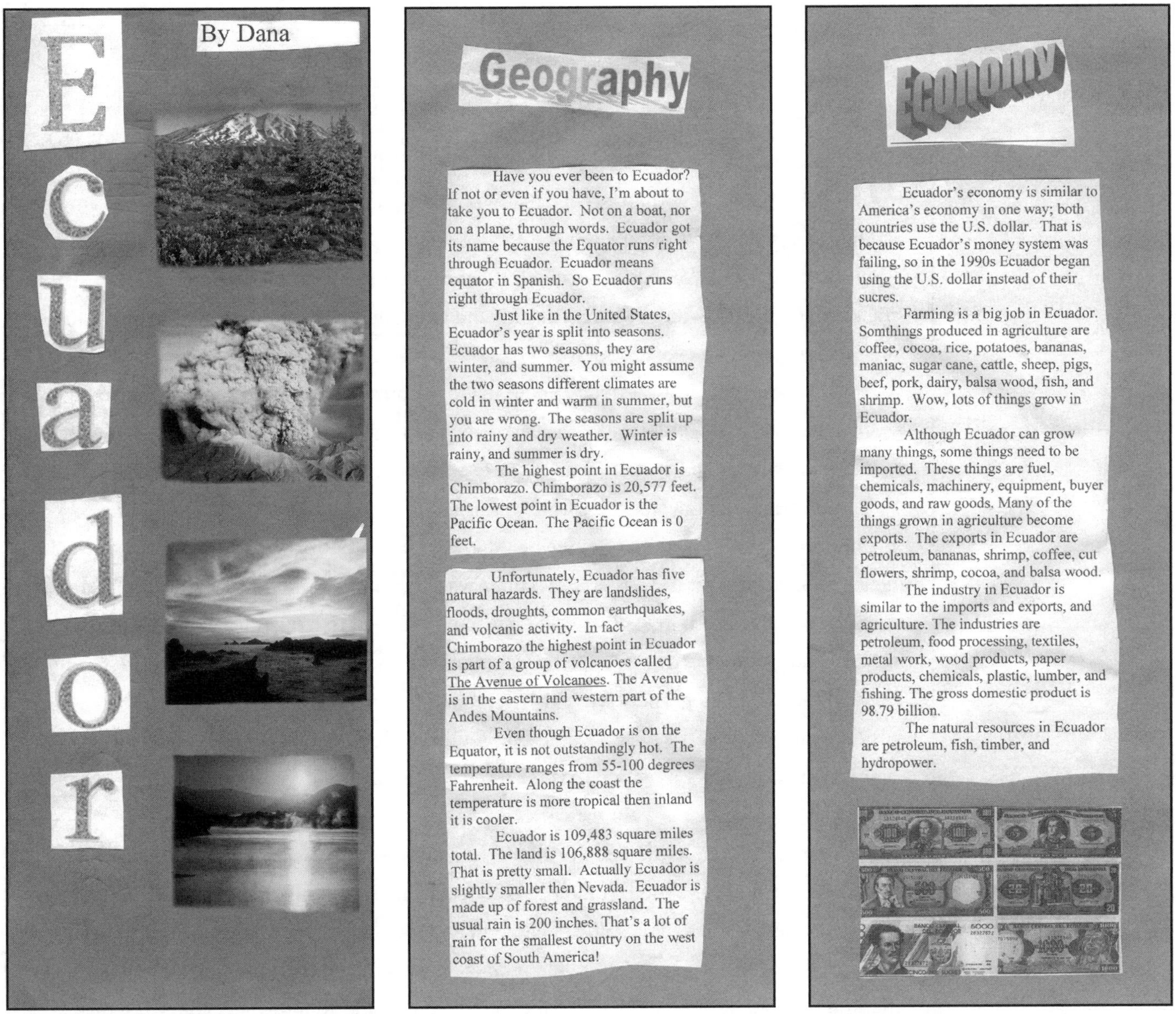
Ecuador

By Dana

Geography

Have you ever been to Ecuador? If not or even if you have, I'm about to take you to Ecuador. Not on a boat, nor on a plane, through words. Ecuador got its name because the Equator runs right through Ecuador. Ecuador means equator in Spanish. So Ecuador runs right through Ecuador.

Just like in the United States, Ecuador's year is split into seasons. Ecuador has two seasons, they are winter, and summer. You might assume the two seasons different climates are cold in winter and warm in summer, but you are wrong. The seasons are split up into rainy and dry weather. Winter is rainy, and summer is dry.

The highest point in Ecuador is Chimborazo. Chimborazo is 20,577 feet. The lowest point in Ecuador is the Pacific Ocean. The Pacific Ocean is 0 feet.

Unfortunately, Ecuador has five natural hazards. They are landslides, floods, droughts, common earthquakes, and volcanic activity. In fact Chimborazo the highest point in Ecuador is part of a group of volcanoes called The Avenue of Volcanoes. The Avenue is in the eastern and western part of the Andes Mountains.

Even though Ecuador is on the Equator, it is not outstandingly hot. The temperature ranges from 55-100 degrees Fahrenheit. Along the coast the temperature is more tropical then inland it is cooler.

Ecuador is 109,483 square miles total. The land is 106,888 square miles. That is pretty small. Actually Ecuador is slightly smaller then Nevada. Ecuador is made up of forest and grassland. The usual rain is 200 inches. That's a lot of rain for the smallest country on the west coast of South America!

Economy

Ecuador's economy is similar to America's economy in one way; both countries use the U.S. dollar. That is because Ecuador's money system was failing, so in the 1990s Ecuador began using the U.S. dollar instead of their sucres.

Farming is a big job in Ecuador. Somthings produced in agriculture are coffee, cocoa, rice, potatoes, bananas, maniac, sugar cane, cattle, sheep, pigs, beef, pork, dairy, balsa wood, fish, and shrimp. Wow, lots of things grow in Ecuador.

Although Ecuador can grow many things, some things need to be imported. These things are fuel, chemicals, machinery, equipment, buyer goods, and raw goods. Many of the things grown in agriculture become exports. The exports in Ecuador are petroleum, bananas, shrimp, coffee, cut flowers, shrimp, cocoa, and balsa wood.

The industry in Ecuador is similar to the imports and exports, and agriculture. The industries are petroleum, food processing, textiles, metal work, wood products, paper products, chemicals, plastic, lumber, and fishing. The gross domestic product is 98.79 billion.

The natural resources in Ecuador are petroleum, fish, timber, and hydropower.

Figure 18.43 Excerpt from a student report on Ecuador

as make the topic or idea attractive and interesting to the audience. An article may be expository or persuasive or a combination of both of these nonfiction genres.

Editorials/Op-Ed Pieces

Similar to a news article, an editorial or op-ed piece must be written in spare, journalistic style. However, this form is usually persuasive: students convey an opinion with compelling evidence to back it up. They use structures and signal phrases that are characteristic of argument: *because of, due to, that is why, as a result, the evidence is, we must conclude, the outcome must be, for these reasons.* Writing an editorial extends students' understanding of persuasive texts.

Biographical Sketch

A biographical sketch is a short article written to show appreciation for accomplishments. The sketch provides information about a subject. Students need to carefully select and organize information that communicates a larger message drawn from the life of a subject. An example of a biographical sketch is shown in Figure 18.44.

Figure 18.44
Amelia's biographical sketch of Anne Frank

Anne Frank

by Amelia

It all started in 1949 when World War II began with Hitler as the leader of Germany. He was trying to kill all Jews and anyone that would object. Annellese Marie Frank was Jewish and this affected her life completely.

On June 12, 1939, Anne was born into a Jewish family, the Franks. She lived in Frankfurt, Germany, with her parents Edith and Otto and her sister Margot. She also had a Grandma who she was very close to.

Ann celebrated her 13th birthday and got a lot of presents but the most important one was a diary. She called it Kitty. It was very special to her because, since her life had to be so secretive, writing in her diary was the only way she could express herself. She wrote in it every day (including when she was in hiding).

Anne was still living in Germany when the war started but instead of Frankfurt she had moved to an apartment in Amsterdam. Hitler was becoming more powerful and her parents were getting worried so in 1942 she and her family moved to a hideout. They called it the Secret Annex. They lived there with the Van Pels family too. There was Mr. and Mrs. Van Pels and their son Peter. There were also helpers. Their names were Miep Gies, Bep Vosievijl and Fritz Pfeffer. They would buy food and clothing and bring them to the families but they didn't live in the Secret Annex with the Franks and Van Pels. The helpers put their lives in danger to help their friends.

Both families lived in the Secret Annex for about two years. But then, a couple of months before the war ended, Anne heard footsteps and shouting coming up the hidden stairs. She hid her diary. The soldiers came in and took everyone to a concentration camp. Anne died there from a sickness called typhus. Her dad, Otto, was the only one who lived after the war ended. He went back to the Secret Annex and found Anne's diary. He had always known she kept a diary but he never knew how wonderful her writing was. He brought it to an office and made it into a book. It always was her dream to be a writer and her dream finally came true.

Despite all the sadness in Anne's life she was always a joyful and kind spirit. When she was little she had lived a very normal life but when the war began things started to change. But she was never affected by any of this. She stayed the same throughout her whole life. That is the biggest reason we will always remember Anne Frank.

Quotes from Anne Frank's diary:

"Despite everything, I believe that people are really good at heart."

"I live in a crazy time."

"I don't think of all the misery but of all the beauty that still remains."

Anne Frank was amazing in many ways.

Review or Recommendation

A review or recommendation is similar to an article except that it is written to give readers advice on a book, topic, product or place. Amy's essay on *Homecoming* (Figure 18.42) includes some aspects of a recommendation. Writing a review extends students' understanding of the way reviews work. They select information and think about how to construct the text so that it persuades or influences the audience. Of all the forms of nonfiction writing about reading, articles, editorials, and reviews require the most intensive thinking about audience.

Project

A *project* is a creative body of work that presents ideas and opinions about texts or topics in an organized way. The project may incorporate many kinds of nonfiction writing about reading as well as multiple media. Putting together a variety of textual resources to communicate an overarching message is a highly sophisticated act, but one that young students are becoming increasingly able to accomplish. They experience such presentations almost every day via the Internet.

Poetic Writing About Reading

A poetic text may be written in response to any genre—fiction or nonfiction. It may focus on any aspect of text—character, plot, setting, an individual's achievement (biography). Such a text may be written for one or more voices and stretches thinking by enabling the student to express thoughts in another genre. Turning nonfiction or fiction into poetry sharpens students' awareness of the characteristics of genre and provokes deeper thinking about some aspect of a text. Poems written in response to texts are presented in Figures 18.45 and 18.46.

The language of good books suggests poetry to readers. Feel free to borrow language and imagery from writers and to feel the emotion carried in good literature. By translating one genre into another, you can get inside the structure and put words together in new ways.

Teacher Reflection on Writing About Reading

Writing about reading is evidence of your students' reading comprehension as well as their ability to put together coherent pieces of writing. As you examine each piece of writing, you may want to ask such questions as:

1. Does the writer include enough information about the book that the reader can understand the review or essay?
2. Does the writer tell briefly what the book is about?
3. Does the writer demonstrate comprehension of the book or story?

The Librarian

Alia loved the books.
And the talk of world and spirit.
Alia feared for the books.
For the talk of bombs and war.
Alia hid the books.
From the consuming fire.
Alia keeps the books.
For the future of her country.
Alia loved the books.

Figure 18.45 Nara's poem in response to *The Librarian of Basra*

Philo Farnsworth

The farm boy
Having nothing
Worked the fields
Watched the plowed rows.
The inventor
Having a dream
Danced light in a bottle
The world watched . . . TV.

Figure 18.46 Saul's poem in response to *The Boy Who Invented TV*

4. Does the writer demonstrate analytic thinking?
5. Does the writer make clear statements and support them with evidence?
6. Is there a clear beginning, middle, and end?
7. Is there evidence that the writer can identify the author's messages or themes—the big ideas?
8. Does the writer use specific parts of the text as evidence?
9. Does the writer express judgments and opinions about the text and tell why? (Is the book worth reading?)
10. Does the piece show evidence of careful reading and understanding?
11. Does the writer discuss main characters, their actions, and their development?
12. Does the writer use appropriate punctuation for sentences, paragraphs, and quotes?
13. Does the writer use a variety of sentences to make the piece engaging?
14. Does the writer express his own feelings?
15. Does the writer avoid repetition and extraneous detail?

If the answer to any one of the questions is partially or very little, plan a minilesson or series of lessons or writing about reading to help students expand their capabilities. These and other characteristics are incorporated into the form in Figure 18.49.

Self as Reader and Writer

One of the added benefits of writing about reading is that students can become much more self-aware of their literate lives. These written records help students reflect on their reading habits and realize how they have grown over time. Many teachers ask students—once or twice a year—to look back through their reader's notebook, reflect on their development as readers, and write a reflective paper. An excerpt from one student's reflective paper is shown in Figure 18.47)

A middle school student's reflection at the end of the year is provided in Figure 18.48. It is obvious that Meg has progressed beyond children's literature and is reading at an adult level. That's the goal we want all our students to achieve.

The journey to this level of self-awareness is a long one. We expect students to write and draw about their reading from the time they enter school. Even the youngest children can represent their thoughts and responses to literature. Doing a variety of writing about reading, from short and quick to highly complex, supports and extends students' thinking over time. The ways to write about reading explored in this chapter are not "assignments" to keep students busy or to make them read. Rather, they are tools student readers can use to find their own voices and learn more about themselves. For each student, the reader's notebook becomes a repository of a rich history of reading.

I think I mostly read realistic fiction books because those are the kind of books I can relate to. I also like to read fantasy and science fiction books that have teens in them. I really like series because you get to know the characters so well when there are multiple books about the same characters and situations. If the book is really good and you don't want it to end, reading a series is perfect for me because it is like a part of the whole picture. The only bad thing about a series is that you sometimes have to wait a whole year for the next one to come out and in that time you might forget what was happening. You usually have to reread the books, but sometimes you don't when the author gives you a hint of what happened in previous books to help you. Also if I like a certain author I will want to read all their books even if it is about different characters because I like the writing style or subjects, for example Karen Hesse or Gary Paulsen.

Figure 18.47 Excerpt from a reflective essay

Dear Ms. Q-N,

First, let me just step back and say thank you. You taught me that the Language Arts class can be fun, informative, and useful. You taught me about what makes a good book, and about evaluating books, and a whole lot about writing. I thank you for all your help during the year, for your book suggestions, for helping me write things that I'm proud of. I thank you for your carefully planned assignments, your minimal homework, your collection of books. But most of all, you gave me the tools to evaluate and learn on my own, for many years into the future. For that I thank you.

As a writer, I think I have grown into more of a person who can analyze writing and provide constructive feedback on it. I now notice certain errors with organization, phrasing, grammar, and inconsistency that I would not have noticed or cared about before. I also notice more of the differences between different authors' writing styles. The letter essays and discussions helped me learn how to see these things, as they made me look for them, think about them, and provide my opinion and views on them. If fact, noticing writing styles seems to have become one of my strengths. My only other strength is my love for reading. It's one of the most important aspects of my personality. My weakness stems from this, as I tend to throw myself into too many things at once, too many books, too many projects, all at once and all with an insufficient amount of time to even complete one, let alone the vast sea of work I drown myself in.

I definitely read a lot this year, but I'm a fairly avid reader in general. I read a lot, all the time, for personal enjoyment, without being told to. Because I read for pleasure, I found myself reading mostly fictional stories, mostly fantasy and science fiction. In fact, my favorite book this year was a piece of science fiction. *1984* was by far the most amazing book I've read this year. George Orwell, the author, created such a beautifully twisted world. He sent his protagonist through an amazing, dangerous rebellion against an oppressive government, made it absolutely clear that the protagonist was doing the right thing, and then made his protagonist lose. He lost his mind, his free will, his love, his trust in himself. It was an amazing reminder about the dangers of doing the right thing, and made so many important points about human psychology. It was not only a great story; it was also an iconic read for me. It was the first time I've actually succeeded reading a book that complicated, while actually understanding a lot of it. I still have things left to decipher, and I will probably have to re-read it in a few years. It prompted a lot of discussions with my family about human nature and governments today.

My goals for the future are fairly simple. I wish to become good enough to write. Writers are the ultimate form of readers, and show mastery of the works that come before them; they set paths for others to follow, and give other people peeks into their minds, to the fantastic worlds that like within. You must read to write, and you must read often and consistently. You must read to learn, to enjoy, to expand your own worlds. When I have achieved this, I believe that I will be happy.

Thank you,
Meg

Figure 18.48
Meg's reflective essay

ANALYZING WRITING ABOUT READING		
	Does the writer . . .	**Notes**
Evidence of Comprehension	• Identify the author's message (big ideas) or theme? • Tell what the book is about? (synopsis or summary statement) • Use evidence from the text to support statements? • Interpret the text? • Show careful reading? • Quote directly from the text? • Justify comments with references to the text or other texts? • Make connections between the text and problems of the real world?	
Evidence of Analytical Thinking	• Express own thinking? • Express own feelings? • Comment on the writer's craft? • Notice and comment on literary elements (character, setting, plot, problem and problem resolution)? • Discuss characters and character development? • Make connections between the text and others? • Comment on the author's style?	
Evidence of Critical Reading	• Evaluate the quality or authenticity of the text? • Back up opinions with evidence? • Comment on the quality of the writing?	
Organization	• Have a clear beginning, middle, and end? • Include a summary early in the piece? • Show awareness of audience? • Present information and ideas in a logical way? • Have a clear conclusion? • Use descriptive details to support points? • Use a variety of sentences to make meaning clear?	
Conventions	• Provide the date and sign the piece? • Give the title, author, and illustrator of the book? • Use appropriate capitalization and underlining (book titles)? • Use appropriate sentence structure and punctuation (the best the student knows at this time)? • Show evidence of proofreading?	
Overall Goal	• Demonstrate deep thinking about a text? • Present ideas in an articulate and organized way?	

Figure 18.49 Analyzing writing about reading

Suggestions for Professional Development

1. Meet with grade-level colleagues or across two or three grade levels.
2. Discuss various kinds of writing about reading.
3. Plan to implement one kind of writing about reading. (Individual teachers may want to make different choices so that there is variety to discuss at the next meeting, or every teacher can implement the same kind.) Talk about how the kind of writing about reading you choose will help your students in understanding more about genre. Use Figures 18.13, 18.37, and 18.40. Discuss:
   - What will my students need to understand about a genre before they accomplish this type of writing?
   - What do I hope my students learn about a genre through this writing about reading?

The plan should include:

- A series of minilessons to introduce students to the type of writing about reading.
- Good examples to help students internalize the characteristics of the writing.
- Time for students to perform the writing at school.
- Individual conferences to support students.
- Times when students can share their work with each other.

4. After about a month, schedule another meeting to share samples of the writing. Discuss what your students have learned about genre through their writing about reading.
5. Work in small groups to share samples and analyze them using the form in Figure 18.49.
6. Discuss the next steps in instruction.

CHAPTER 19

Using Guided Reading to Develop Understandings About Genre

Guided reading is dependent on the teacher being aware of the students' competencies, interests, and experiences, being able to determine the supports and challenges offered by a book; and accepting the role of supporting learning rather than directing teaching.

—Margaret Mooney

Guided reading is powerful small-group instruction that lifts and expands students' ability to read increasingly challenging texts. The lessons can include very specific teaching about genre and its characteristics to support effective processing of the text.

Small-group reading instruction is appropriate from kindergarten through upper elementary grades and, if necessary, beyond. Guided reading is needed not only to develop beginning literacy skills. The strategic actions readers need to comprehend deeply and understand the nuances of genre take many years to develop, and doing so requires explicit instruction, demonstration, and teacher support. We have written extensively about guided reading in *Guided Reading*, *Guiding Readers and Writers*, and *Teaching for Comprehending and Fluency*; this chapter addresses aspects of guided reading in relation to genre.

Understanding genre helps you adjust your reading in subtle but important ways so that you gain the maximum benefit. For example, you read a news article to get information on a topic that has caught your eye as you perused the newspaper or magazine. You know that the most important information will be presented up front; you read on for elaboration and explanation or skip the additional information and move on to another article. When you begin a realistic novel, you've likely already done some thinking about the book when you selected it. You expect characters, a plot or story line, a building toward resolution of the problem(s), and you hope for a satisfying ending. You may have automatically asked, "Can I identify with these characters? Will I like them? Will I find the story interesting? Will this help me understand more about [content]?" If you pick up a work of fantasy, you expect to read closely to understand elements of the unreal world—the "rules" of the fantasy setting. You know that to enjoy the story you will need to suspend your disbelief for the time you spend with the book.

What we've just described is typical of sophisticated readers. The strategic actions you use go far beyond simple proficiency in decoding words, although that is certainly necessary; effective reading entails a great deal more than accuracy. The goal of guided reading is to help students develop a full range of strategic actions.

A Text Gradient to Support Effective Teaching

Over a period of many years we have created a text gradient that helps students gradually improve their reading abilities and helps teachers provide supportive instruction that accelerates student progress. The gradient is a "ladder of progress" that readers climb, rung by rung, not just toward higher reading levels but also to develop deeper understanding and greater ability to think analytically about texts— skills required by national and state tests and state standards.

We describe this gradient in *The Continuum of Literacy Learning* and provide detailed descriptions of behaviors and understandings to notice, teach, and support for every level. These behaviors include understanding and using genre knowledge to process texts well.

Begin with Assessment

Guided reading provides teaching at the reader's instructional level. Select a text that is just a little more difficult than the reader can process independently. Your teaching support makes it possible for the reader to read with accuracy and excellent comprehension. Therefore, the first step in implementing guided reading is to find what your students know and can do as readers so you know where to begin.

Using Instructional Level Texts

The ideal level to place students for effective teaching is the *instructional level*—the highest level on the text gradient at which the student is able to process a text with 90%–94% accuracy (levels A–K) or 94%–97% accuracy (levels L–Z) with satisfactory or excellent comprehension. A student's independent level is the highest level read at 95%–100% accuracy (levels A–K) or 98%–100% accuracy (levels L–Z) with satisfactory to excellent comprehension. A child's fluency score is helpful in guiding teaching but is not reliable enough to be the basis for determining instructional or independent reading levels.

An instructional level text is within the student's control but offers opportunities to learn and expand systems of strategic actions. Working at a student's instructional level allows you to provide strong teaching that helps the reader process challenging material proficiently. Students can read independent level text without your support, and identifying this level helps you guide their independent reading. However, they should not use text levels to select their own books for independent reading. Instead, teach them how to sample a book and decide whether it will be interesting and easy enough to read without help. Typically, students will read according to their interests in a range of levels.

Determining Reading Level

We recommend using a systematic benchmark system like the *Fountas & Pinnell Benchmark Assessment System* (*BAS*) (2011) to determine accurate reading levels. The *BAS* includes one fiction text and one nonfiction text specially written for each level. These texts have been field-tested for reliability and are used in the context of standardized, technologically supported procedures that include introductions, key understandings, and probes/questions. The *BAS* can be administered at the beginning of the year, midyear, or toward the end of the year to determine student reading levels. Between administrations, ongoing reading records and observations provide systematic evidence of students' reading to make decisions in moving groups up a level or regrouping students.

Using Guided Reading to Support Genre Study

The organizational structure of guided reading makes it an ideal support for learning more about genre. The way each guiding reading lesson component supports genre awareness is laid out in Figure 19.1. A description and an example follow.

Selecting the Text

Although the text should be at an appropriate level for students to be able to process, genre is an important secondary consideration.

The classroom library for independent reading should have texts at every level in each genre being studied. It makes sense to introduce a genre in a guided reading lesson at the same time you are reading that genre aloud. Provide baskets of books, labeled by genre and including texts at a variety of levels, from which students can choose their independent reading.

For guided reading, select texts from a leveled book collection (separate from the classroom library). As you select the text and plan the introduction, consider the text features your student readers will need to notice and understand:

1. *Genre and forms.* Students need to use their current understandings of the genre to help them make predictions and understand the text. Knowledge of the form is also helpful—realistic fiction might take the form of a mystery or a survival story, for example. The text may also help students learn *more* about the genre or form.
2. *Structure.* Fiction and nonfiction genres are organized and presented in various ways. Students need to recognize if texts are narratives (fiction, narrative nonfiction, and biography) or if they are organized categorically or topically, with underlying structures like comparison/contrast.
3. *Content.* Content refers to the subject matter of the text—the concepts that are important to understand. In fiction, content may be related to the setting or the kinds of problems characters have. In factual texts, content is the topic. Student readers' level of understanding is related to the degree their prior knowledge matches the new content.
4. *Themes and ideas.* These are the big ideas communicated by the writer. Ideas may be concrete and accessible or complex and abstract. Fiction genres usually communicate a message about human relationships or life. Nonfiction writers also have overarching messages; they may be highly persuasive or guide readers to draw conclusions, form opinions, or develop attitudes from the facts they present.
5. *Language and literary features.* All written language is qualitatively different from spoken language. Fiction writers use dialogue, figurative language, and other literary features such as plot, character development, and setting. Nonfiction writers use description and sometimes technical language. Many writers of nonfiction use literary language to make a topic more accessible or engaging.
6. *Sentence complexity.* In any fiction or nonfiction text, the writer maps meaning onto syntax (grammar). Texts with simpler, more natural sentences are easier to process. Sentences with embedded and conjoined clauses make a text more difficult. In fiction texts, dialogue increases complexity. The topics of nonfiction text may be so complex or technical that they cannot be explained in simple syntax but require more complex structures.
7. *Vocabulary.* The more known vocabulary in a text, the easier it will be. Students' *reading and writing vocabularies* are words they understand and can also read or write. Nonfiction texts often include highly technical words,

sometimes but not always defined within the context. Often readers rely on background knowledge or a glossary.

8. *Words.* In general, the more multisyllable words a text contains, the more challenging it is for students to decode. In fiction texts, interesting and highly descriptive language often means more challenging words. In nonfiction, the topic often requires technical words.

9. *Illustrations.* Drawings, paintings, or photographs may accompany the text and add meaning and enjoyment. Often, readers are

STRUCTURE OF GUIDED READING AND IMPLICATIONS FOR DEVELOPING GENRE KNOWLEDGE AND GENRE STUDY		
Component	**Description**	**Significance for Genre Study**
Selecting the Text	Select a text at the students' instructional level.	Select some texts that represent the genre being studied.
Introducing the Text	Introduce the text in a way that supports students' understanding.	Set the scene by naming (or asking students to name) the genre and talk about specific aspects of this text that they expect will fit what they know about the genre.
Reading the Text	Each student reads the text individually and silently. Ask individual students to raise their voices to an audible level while they listen to a short piece of oral reading (a couple of sentences or a paragraph) and also interact briefly to prompt for strategic actions.	As you interact with students, point out characteristics of the genre and/or invite them to notice them (see *Prompting Guide, Part 1* and *Part 2*).
Discussing the Text	Students talk about their thinking.	Guide the discussion to help students notice characteristics of the genre, use language to talk about the genre, and use their understandings to understand the genre (see *Prompting Guide, Part 2*).
Teaching for Strategic Actions	Make an explicit teaching point to demonstrate and help students use strategic actions.	If appropriate, point out aspects of the genre and help students connect them to other texts they have read or heard read.
Working with Words	Lead students in two or three minutes of active word work to support decoding using word parts and developing vocabulary.	Build vocabulary and word knowledge needed to effectively process future texts while thinking about the genre.
Extending Understanding	(Optional) Students write or draw to reflect on their understandings of the text.	Ask students to include the genre and what they noticed about the text in their writing about their reading. You may give specific writing assignments that will help them express their thinking about the genre (see Chapter 18).

Figure 19.1 Structure of guided reading and implications for developing genre knowledge and genre study

expected to notice how illustrations contribute to the mood of the text. In factual texts, illustrations also include graphics that provide a great deal of information that readers must integrate with the text.

10. *Book and print features.* Book and print features are the physical aspects of the text—length, size, and layout. Book and print features also include readers' tools such as table of contents, glossary, pronunciation guides, indexes, and sidebars. Graphic texts include unique features that signal readers how to process and interpret the text.

These ten factors help you think analytically about the texts you use, and genre characteristics are central to that analysis.

Let's look an example. Ann has chosen *How Do Plants Grow?* (Stewart 2007), a level S nonfiction text, to use with a reading group. As she reads through the text, she does a quick analysis of the ten text factors (see Figure 19.2) so that she can begin to plan the introduction.

Introducing the Text

The introduction grows from Ann's knowledge of her students and her analysis of the text. These students have become accustomed to guided reading routines and know that participating in the introduction will help them read better. At this level readers have already had a great deal of experience reading informational texts that present information in categories. They can use readers' tools like a table of contents, headings, and glossary, and they understand what it means when words are in bold type.

As part of the genre study that Ann is implementing, she wants her students to become more aware of the craft of writing nonfiction. This ability to notice genre features will not only help them read with deeper understanding but will also give them a broader repertoire of skills to use in their own writing. Ann has in mind some possible points to make during the introduction:

- Point out the concept that there is a great variety of plants on earth but they all need to grow and make seeds to survive (section 1, pages 5 through 7).
- Point out the word *species* on page 5 and help students notice how the word is defined in the sentence (set off by commas).

ANN'S ANALYSIS OF *HOW DO PLANTS GROW?*

As I read *How Do Plants Grow?* I noticed that:

- The information is organized into categories that correspond with the sections of the book listed in the table of contents.
- In the body of the text, the writer speaks directly to readers using clear, friendly language.
- The text is illustrated with photographs that have captions.
- There are some technical words in each section (*organelles*, for example).
- Key words are in bold type and usually defined in context; many are in the glossary.
- At the end of each section, there is a sidebar posing a question that prompts readers to reflect on the content.
- There are two diagrams, one showing the temporal sequence of a plant growing from a seed.
- The content shows the interdependence of animals and plants (birds carrying seeds, for example).
- At the end of the book is an activity to help readers perform an experiment.
- There is a glossary, references for finding more information, and an index.
- The text builds from a general introduction to a great deal of detail about complex processes. The information becomes more technical, but concepts build well on one another.
- A big idea is that plants are complex living things that require food, light, and water to grow. They use complex processes to process food and they, in turn, produce food for people and animals.

Figure 19.2 Ann's analysis of *How Do Plants Grow?*

- Ask students to think about why the writer sometimes talks directly to us as readers (at the beginning of the section on page 9, for example).
- Remind students to think about the questions in the sidebar at the end of each section.
- Point out the diagram on page 23 and ask students what information is being shown (temporal sequence of growth of a plant from a seed).
- Point out the suggested activity on pages 26 and 27 and ask students why the writer might have included it.
- Ask students, as they read, to think about the writer's purpose and the big ideas she wants to convey to the reader.

Figure 19.3 is an excerpt from Ann's introduction to *How Do Plants Grow?* This conversation before reading not only alerts students to some of the words, language, and concepts they will meet in the text but also prompts them to think in certain ways about it. Ann shares some ideas about purpose and content that the group can return to in their later discussion.

Reading the Text

As students read the text individually and silently, Ann listens to some oral reading, signaling each student, in turn, to read a little aloud, softly. She interacts quickly with students (see Figures 19.4 and 19.5) to prompt for strategic actions (see Chapter 14). These quick interactions help students attend to important information that they can use to understand the text. They also learn more about the characteristics of expository nonfiction and how writers of expository (or nonfiction) texts present information.

To support Dara's comprehension, Ann draws her attention to the writer's use of a photograph to illustrate concepts; she also previews the next section. In this text, it is important for readers to accumulate information and keep the big picture in mind, because the text first presents the parts of plants and then goes into details about the smaller components and their functions.

Ann supports Robert's understanding of photosynthesis, a complex process explained only briefly in the text. Readers don't have to remember every detail and all the technical words but should come away with the general understanding that all plants have parts, made up of very small cells, that create food that enables the plant to grow and survive.

INTRODUCTION TO *HOW DO PLANTS GROW?*	
TEACHER:	Today you are going to read another expository (nonfiction) book called *How Do Plants Grow?* The writer, Melissa Stewart, has written about some things that all kinds of plants need in order to grow. Take a look at the title page.
DARA:	It looks like different pictures of a bean growing.
TEACHER:	That's what it is. You see five pictures of how a seed looks as it grows into a plant. There are thousands of kinds of plants and almost all of them grow from seeds like that. You'll see that drawing again later in the book and will read about what happens. Turn to page 5. Look at the two species, or kinds, of plants on this page layout. Read the captions and talk about your thinking.
ROBERT:	I didn't think about grass like a plant.
LINDA:	It's a green plant and a kind of dead one in the desert. There's only sand.
TEACHER:	In this first section you will learn that there are very many different kinds of plants. Listen while I read the first paragraph and tell what you notice. [Reads.]

Figure 19.3 Ann's introduction to *How Do Plants Grow?*

continues

INTRODUCTION TO *HOW DO PLANTS GROW?*	
NORAH:	It says grass is a plant.
ROBERT:	A plant can be a tree or a grass. They are both plants.
DARA:	It's kind of talking to you.
TEACHER:	It sounds friendly, doesn't it? Do you see how the writer has used you as if she is talking right to us? Sometimes writers of nonfiction do that. It may be to get us interested in the topic. What do you think?
JORDAN:	She is telling us to go outside and look so it is kind of like talking.
TEACHER:	Now listen while I read the next sentence, because this is an important idea. [Reads.] Say *species*. Put your finger under it. It's in bold type. Can someone talk about what that word means?
JORDAN:	It means kinds, 260,000 kinds of plants.
TEACHER:	So this writer has identified a key word in bold and put the meaning of the word right there after it. What else do you notice?
ROBERT:	It has commas.
TEACHER:	Yes, whenever you see a word, then a comma, and then *or*, look carefully because it might help you know what the word means. As you read today, be looking for the definitions of some of the important words. Okay. There are so many different kinds of plants, but they all have to survive. Look at page 9 and read the heading and the first sentence. [Students read silently.] What is the writer telling you here?
LINDA:	To think about what people need to survive.
TEACHER:	She is trying to get you to think about what you know about yourselves and apply that to plants. Let's look at a couple of words. On page 11, find the word *absorb*. Read the whole sentence and think about what the word means.
STUDENTS:	To take in.
ROBERT:	To sort of suck in the water and the minerals.
DARA:	It might be the way they drink.
TEACHER:	That is an interesting way to think about it. You can see a close-up photograph of the tiny tubes that carry the water, minerals, and food to all parts of the plan after it is absorbed by the roots.
Ann goes on to have students locate the word organelles*, say it, and notice how to derive the definition from the sentence by using the word* called*. She then examines a couple more headings to be sure the students understand the organization of the text.*	
TEACHER:	This writer is giving a great deal of information about what plants need to grow and how they make food. As you read, be thinking about why the writer might have written all these ideas about plants. Why do you need to know this information?

Figure 19.3 Ann's introduction to *How Do Plants Grow? (cont.)*

Discussing the Text

After everyone has read the book, Ann invites the students to talk about what they learned from and noticed about the text. Based on this discussion, she will then focus students' attention on strategic actions, in this case, particularly the characteristics of informational texts. An excerpt from the beginning of the discussion is provided in Figure 19.6.

The discussion here is fairly brief but can be extended if time permits. You want to hear from as many students as possible and can learn a great deal from these first open responses. For example:

- What students noticed and remembered about the content and the way the writer presented it.
- What was new information for the readers.
- The degree to which they can support their statements with evidence.
- What may have surprised or confused them.
- Their understanding of the larger ideas and the purposes of texts.
- Their understanding of why the writer selected the topic.
- Their understanding of the relevance of the text to themselves and the world.

In a discussion after a fiction text, look for evidence that students understand the plot and setting. They can discuss the author's messages and the theme, notice character development, and discuss aspects of the writer's craft (see *Prompting Guide, Part 2* for a variety of discussion prompts).

Teaching for Strategic Actions

In the excerpt in Figure 19.7, the discussion moves seamlessly into a teaching point Ann has selected to move students forward in the development of strategic actions.

Working with Words

Students spend few minutes after the lesson learning some important principles about how words work. To effectively read texts at level S, for example, students must be able to work flexibly with base words, making new words by changing prefixes and suffixes. Prefixes and suffixes change the meaning and function of the

BRIEF INTERACTION WITH DARA WHILE STUDENTS ARE READING *HOW DO PLANTS GROW?*

After Dara reads page 11:

TEACHER:	Were you able to answer the question, Dara?
DARA:	Yes, the parts are roots, leaves, and the stem, and that was right because I checked it upside down.
TEACHER:	Take a look at the next page and you'll see those parts clearly in the tree.
DARA:	The trunk of the tree is like the stem of it.
TEACHER:	What do you expect to learn in this next section?
DARA:	It's going to tell what the inside of a plant is like.
TEACHER:	Take a look at the photograph and read the caption. [Dara reads.] How does this photograph help you understand more about plants?
DARA:	It's really close up and shows the little cells that are the leaf.
TEACHER:	So in this section you will read about those cells and what they are and how they work. Remember we talked about the tiny parts called organelles that have their own jobs to do.

Figure 19.4 Ann's brief interaction with Dara

word in a sentence. Recognizing and using them helps readers take words apart smoothly and derive their meaning more easily, so they can think about the meaning of the text.

Ann works with words that change meaning and function by adding *-ly* or *-y*. She uses examples like *juice, juicy*; *week, weekly*; *day, daily*; *sweet, sweetly*; and *fair, fairly*. She points out examples in the text (*juicy, sugary*), not to "teach" the words, but so her students will learn word-solving principles they can use to read many words. She wants her student readers to notice the connections between words, not learn them as isolated units.

Extending Understanding

This optional lesson component helps students further their understanding of the text through writing, drawing, or more talk. Students can engage in these activities very quickly as they finish reading, or they can write or draw independently after the lesson. Chapter 18 suggests a range of possibilities for writing about reading. Ann asks her students to do a short write about what they think the writer's message is.

The Goal of Guided Reading Lessons

A guided reading lesson places a strong instructional frame around readers' processing of a new text that offers just enough challenge. With each reading, your goal is to help students do more than read the book accurately: your teaching offers specific scaffolds, important background, and demonstrations that allow readers to learn something more about how to read many books at the level. The goal is to establish the range of strategic actions described for each level of the gradient (see *The Continuum of Literacy Learning*). Over time, the texts will become easy enough for readers to process independently, and the guided reading lesson then shifts to a higher level text. In guided reading, students are always working at the far edge of their current abilities, with your expert teaching.

BRIEF INTERACTION WITH ROBERT WHILE STUDENTS ARE READING *HOW DO PLANTS GROW?*	
After Robert reads page 19:	
TEACHER:	What did you learn from this page?
ROBERT:	This is a cell and those parts do the photosynthesis. That's when light comes in. The water comes from the roots and the carbon dioxide comes in through little holes in the leaf. They mix and they make a food. That how the plant gets food, but I'm not sure how it eats it.
TEACHER:	Could be that it is just absorbed in the cells–sinks into it–and that's how the plant grows. It's a complicated process, isn't it? Why do you think the writer tried to explain it?
ROBERT:	It's so you would know more about how the plant works than just watering it and give it light. It's a lot of details.
TEACHER:	The section headed "Inside a Plant" did go into a lot of detail. I'm thinking that this writer wants readers to understand some really important information. Did you notice that the book started in a general way and got more and more detailed?
ROBERT:	Yes, it made it kind of. You started by thinking just what is needed to survive, and then it began to tell about the inside and how plants do it.
TEACHER:	I guess the writer wanted to show exactly how plants made food so that we could understand how important the process is to plant survival. Read on to find out how animals help.

Figure 19.5 Ann's brief interaction with Robert

EXCERPT FROM DISCUSSION AFTER READING *HOW DO PLANTS GROW?*	
TEACHER:	What did you learn about plants?
LINDA:	They are all plants, even trees and grass. There are so many kinds.
DARA:	They all grow from seeds but different kinds. They have the same things like stems but on a tree the stem is like a trunk.
ROBERT:	The roots of the tree are almost as big as the top of the tree but the leaves make it look bigger.
TEACHER:	This writer told about how plants grow. Talk about that a little.
ROBERT:	The seed is underground and the plant sprouts from it and grows to above the ground.
NORAH:	The leaves make the food when the water comes up and the light hits them.
JORDAN:	It's photo-something.
TEACHER:	Take us to the page where you learned that.
JORDAN:	Page 19. The picture shows a cell when you look at it in a microscope. They make the food like sugar because the light and water come in. Photosynthesis.
ROBERT:	Then the plant can grow.
TEACHER:	We couldn't see these cells with our eyes, but the photograph through a microscope not only shows the cell but all of the parts that work to create food for the plant to grow. What else did you find interesting?
LINDA:	I liked how the animals help the plants.
TEACHER:	Show where you learned that and talk more about it.
LINDA:	Page 21. The insects fly around and get pollen stuck to them. Then they fly to other plants and the pollen helps them.
JORDAN:	The butterfly is drinking the sugar like bees do, too.
ROBERT:	The animals eat the seeds sometimes and then they spit them out somewhere else so a new plant grows.
DARA:	No, they go through their bodies and then they poop them out.
TEACHER:	What were you thinking about why the author might have written this book?
JORDAN:	She wanted to show how plants make their food so they can grow.
LINDA:	It was maybe that plants are really important and they have special ways of making their own food.
DARA:	I think it could be that it's interesting to find out the little parts of plants and how they work together. And there's the directions in the back to make a plant grow so you can see it sprout, so it's just about how surprising it is.
TEACHER:	It seems like the writer wanted us to appreciate the way plants work. We all depend on plants for food and shelter, so it's important to understand what they need.

Figure 19.6 Excerpt from discussion after reading *How Do Plants Grow?*

TEACHING FOR STRATEGIC ACTIONS AFTER STUDENTS HAVE READ *HOW DO PLANTS GROW?*	
TEACHER:	We've been studying the kind of nonfiction texts that are expository—they explain or give information about something. Do you think this book is a good example of an expository (nonfiction text)? And if you do, why?
LINDA:	It's good because there are pictures that really help you understand the things that are hard. Some of it I knew but there was a lot that I didn't know.
DARA:	I think parts of it were hard to understand. It got boring when there were just too many details.
TEACHER:	There were some complicated ideas that probably need more study, but did you get some good understandings?
ROBERT:	Yes, I think the pictures really helped and it wasn't too hard to read. There were some big words.
NORAH:	The headings really helped. In a way, the plant growing is just kind of like people growing from babies or dogs growing from puppies.
TEACHER:	Let's talk about some of the comparisons the writer used to help you understand. Look at page 9 and read the first two sentences. What is the writer trying to help you understand?
JORDAN:	She's making us think about what everyone needs to live. It's food, water, and a place to live where you can be warm.
ROBERT:	You're supposed to think about that everyone—people and animals and plants all need things to survive.
TEACHER:	That's one of the big ideas, I agree. Also, the writer may have wanted to show that living things like plants and animals depend on each other. Was there evidence of that in the book?
LINDA:	The animals eat the fruit from the plant and then scatter the seeds so that there can be more plants growing.
TEACHER:	Nonfiction writers do present facts, but they usually have some bigger ideas that they want to communicate to readers too. The writer has a purpose that is more than just listing facts. So always be thinking about what the writer is really trying to say, and as you are writing your own nonfiction pieces, think about one or more big ideas that you want your readers to understand about the topic.

Figure 19.7 Teaching for strategic actions after students have read *How Do Plants Grow?*

Connecting Guided Reading to Genre Study

A collection of leveled texts that includes a variety of genres allows you to connect guided reading with the genre you are studying and help students apply to their own reading the concepts they have developed by participating in interactive read-aloud. Thinking across the variety of texts strengthens comprehension and awareness of genre characteristics.

Elizabeth's students have been studying nonfiction texts, and over several days produced a chart of things they noticed and a working definition. Charts like these let student readers quickly access the characteristics of the genre. They have a raised awareness of the characteristics and can apply the concepts immediately.

The introduction from a guided reading lesson in which Elizabeth helps students connect the genre with its features using the expository nonfiction text *Bird Fact File* (Haydon 2005) is shown in Figure 19.8.

INTRODUCTION TO *BIRD FACT FILE*	
TEACHER:	[Hands out books.] Your book today is *Bird Fact File*. Take a look at it. Can you identify the genre?
RAPHAEL:	It's nonfiction.
TEACHER:	Take a look at the chart we have been making. Does anything about this book stand out for you?
JANE:	It has headings for sections. They tell you what you are going to be reading about.
STEPHANIE:	Each subheading tells a fact about a bird, and it shows examples.
RICHARD:	It has pictures that look like pages from a notebook.
TEACHER:	The facts in this book tell how all birds are similar. But then when you read the examples, what do you learn?
JANE:	That there are a lot of different birds. They all have something like a beak, but the beaks are different.
RICHARD:	They do different things with their beaks or they have different nests. Not all birds build nests, but lots of them do.
DI:	They have to have different things like beaks because they live in different kinds of climates and they have to eat what they find there.
STEPHANIE:	Some birds don't even fly, like an ostrich.
TEACHER:	So it sounds as if one big important idea is that all or most birds have something in common that makes them birds, but there is a lot of variety, too. What's another thing you think this writer is trying to say?
STEPHANIE:	Maybe that birds are different because of their environments.
TEACHER:	I agree. Their bodies are made to help them survive where they live. Nonfiction writers have some important ideas to communicate in addition to just the facts. They want readers to think about why the information is important. Take a look at our chart on nonfiction texts. We said that writers want readers to get the message but we could add big ideas to the chart. Is there anything else on the chart that you noticed?
DI:	This writer tells how things are alike and how they are different but also tells why.
TEACHER:	So as you are reading nonfiction, notice when the writer is doing that and you might do something similar in your own writing if you think it would help readers understand the topic.

Figure 19.8 Introduction to *Bird Fact File*

The students preview several sections and talk about the organization of the book and the headings and subheadings. The students note that the writer has presented information on the torn-out pages of a notebook with writing and pictures of birds glued in. Students comment that it looks a bit like a science notebook and that now people often use electronic folders on the computer to store such information. Elizabeth then returns to aspects of genre in her teaching point.

Don't select a book for guided reading *only* because of the genre. The appropriate level is the first priority. Consider a wide range of student needs and interests and the quality of the text. But using an appropriate book in the genre during guided reading lessons intensifies the learning. These "echoes" across instructional contexts help students think more analytically about texts and notice and use aspects of genre.

Using Specific Language to Support Strategic Actions

You can use very specific language throughout a guided reading lesson to support students' thinking. In the introduction, demonstrate how readers think as you preview parts of the text, and prompt students to take a strategic action while reading. Reading a text for the *purpose* of using a strategy is heavy handed and interferes with comprehension. But a simple suggestion such as, "As you read, be thinking about ____ and we'll talk about it afterward," can lightly scaffold readers' thinking. As you interact with individual students while they are reading, prompt their thinking with specific language that helps them learn how to problem solve their way through the text. (See *Prompting Guide, Part 1.*) These interactions need to be *very* brief so they don't interfere with the reader's understanding of the story.

After students have finished reading, you can use specific prompts to guide the discussion and also to make specific teaching points. *Prompting Guide, Part 2* and *Genre Prompting Guide*s suggest some language that will expand students' thinking in the discussion following the reading. *Prompting Guide, Part 2* includes a large selection of highly specific prompts that help students think within, beyond, and about texts. These prompts are organized by systems of strategic actions, as well as by genre and literary elements and structure.

Selecting and using language is a complex process. It is based on your knowledge of students, texts, and the continua of progress students make toward proficiency as readers. As readers, they learn in individual ways, but guided reading provides the context in which each student can respond to and process increasingly complex texts and take on new learning. Teacher language scaffolds the process.

Suggestions for Professional Development

OPTION I: Create resources for connecting guided reading with genre study.

- With grade-level colleagues, identify an area for genre study. Then spend some time looking for appropriate leveled books that are also good examples of the genre. Match the range of levels needed.
- Organize the books as a set so that all teachers can easily find and use them. (Remember that you can refer back to genre charts weeks or even months later).
- Discuss as many of the books as you can, thinking together about the genre characteristics and how you might use the charts in the introduction or discussion of a text. (You can put stick-on notes on each book to record some of your thinking.)
- As you think about how you might introduce the text and integrate the noticings charts, talk about the different needs of the students in your guided reading groups. Remember there will not be a one-size-fits-all introduction. Discuss how introductions to the same book might be different depending on the needs of the group, their experiences with different genres, and their understanding of the genre of the book you are introducing. Have teachers share the leveled books for a period of time and then meet again to discuss results in terms of student progress in both reading and genre understanding. Try to be as specific as possible about the way you supported the students' thinking around genre during your guided reading lessons. Share how you chose to introduce different texts and talk about why you made the decisions you did based on your students' understandings and needs.

OPTION 2: Work on the language of instruction.

- With a partner at your grade level (or a lower or higher level), examine the strategic actions called for by the statements or prompts in *Prompting Guide, Part 2* or *Genre Prompting Guides*.
- Look over assessment information for students in one guided reading group and share some specific needs of individuals and some that are common to the group.
- Put some sample prompts from the prompting guides on your clipboard or on stick-on notes.
- Select two books for the guided reading group and go through them looking for possible learning outcomes. Plan the introduction and think of possible teaching points.
- Teach the guided reading group for two days; use appropriate prompts.

Meet with your partner and talk about the prompts you used and their impact on students.

CHAPTER 20

The Reading–Writing Connection

> *"I read a lot, which helps me to know how to write as well as what to write about. My best advice for anyone who would like to be a writer is: Read!!!"*
>
> —Mem Fox

Every interesting and memorable experience students have with texts nourishes them as writers. As they listen to a text read aloud and participate in whole-group discussions, they explore the text's message and notice aspects of the writer's craft. In small-group settings like guided reading and book clubs, they notice how the writer reveals plot and characters, organizes information, and expresses a point of view. All of these experiences help students notice more as they read independently; in addition, you can draw their attention to aspects of writing during individual conferences. All the texts students encounter are potential mentors for them as growing writers, examples of how to write a variety of fiction and nonfiction pieces.

One of your most important goals as a teacher is to enable students to *read like writers* so that they constantly add to their writing repertoire as they do a massive amount of reading:

> When children have a chance to become writers themselves, they begin to notice how other authors work. While literature suggests the many forms which stories, information, or poetry may take, it is only as children experiment with the model that they begin to develop a sensitivity to the conventions of the form. This awareness in turn allows them to bring a wider frame of reference to the reading and writing that follow. (Kiefer, Hepler, and Hickman 2010, 794–95)

This process eventually becomes unconscious, but it is built through careful teaching that raises students' awareness. The many kinds of texts students know and remember are a treasure chest into which they can reach in search of inspiration and examples for their own writing. The experience is even better if many of the texts have been discussed by the whole class, in a small group, or with a partner.

A strong connection between reading and writing supports students' writing in many genres. All other contexts—reading aloud, literature discussion, guided reading, minilessons, conferences, and group share all support your work in writers' workshop. The writing section of *The Continuum of Literacy Learning* is a helpful tool in creating links across the language arts curriculum so that the work you do in one area contributes to learning in others. School becomes a *coherent* relevant experience for students; it all makes sense to the learner. Most importantly, the students work toward the same goals.

A Seamless Approach to Reading and Writing Genres

This chapter discusses genres that students are likely to write as part of curricular requirements, generally the same genres as those they are reading. However, students are not likely to write long novels or extensive nonfiction texts like scholarly histories and in-depth biographies. They can nevertheless use the knowledge they are gaining from reading long, complex genres to begin producing shorter pieces in those genres. Then they can apply what they learned how to do as a reader or writer in the short piece to longer pieces.

Figure 20.1 is a conceptual diagram representing a comprehensive approach to supporting writing in specific genres. The degree to which to use this very thorough approach depends on the genre's appropriateness for student writing, other demands of the curriculum, and the amount of time you can give to the process. But the period of time does not need to be lengthy. Also, everything needn't be done at once. You can (even weeks or months later) refer back to the characteristics charts and definitions created during genre study.

The steps below can be done in sequence or reordered, and they can be spaced out over time; but teachers often work intensively on a genre for a chunk of time to maximize and accelerate learning.

1. *Collect.* Select the genre of interest and gather a collection of texts:
   a. Text sets for reading aloud (immersion). Find interesting texts appropriate for the students' age level.
   b. Books in the genre that can be placed in the classroom library for independent reading. Although books will not be labeled by level, ensure a good variety so that students can find books they like and can read independently. Place the books in a basket or two labeled with the genre. Subdivide by topic or setting if appropriate.
   c. Three or four sets of books that will be the basis of book club discussions. Students can indicate their first and second choices.
   d. Leveled books in the genre from which to select for guided reading groups.
2. *Immerse.* Begin the immersion process using interactive read-aloud.
3. *Study.* Help students explore the genre through examples and the connections between them. Write a working definition of the genre.
4. *Read and revise.*
   a. Make books in the genre available for independent reading; introduce them with book talks; ask students to talk about what they noticed during group share.
   b. Provide readers' workshop minilessons on the specific characteristics of the genre.
   c. Have students discuss examples of the genre in book clubs.
5. *Teach.* Introduce books in the genre to students in small-group guided reading and guide them to talk about what they noticed after reading, citing examples from the text. Teach writing workshop minilessons using mentor texts in the genre.

The process is not as linear as it might seem. Some steps will be taken on the same day. You can move experiences with the genre in and out of instructional contexts, always using the basic investigation work as a foundation and touchstone.

Figure 20.1 A comprehensive approach to supporting writing in specific genres

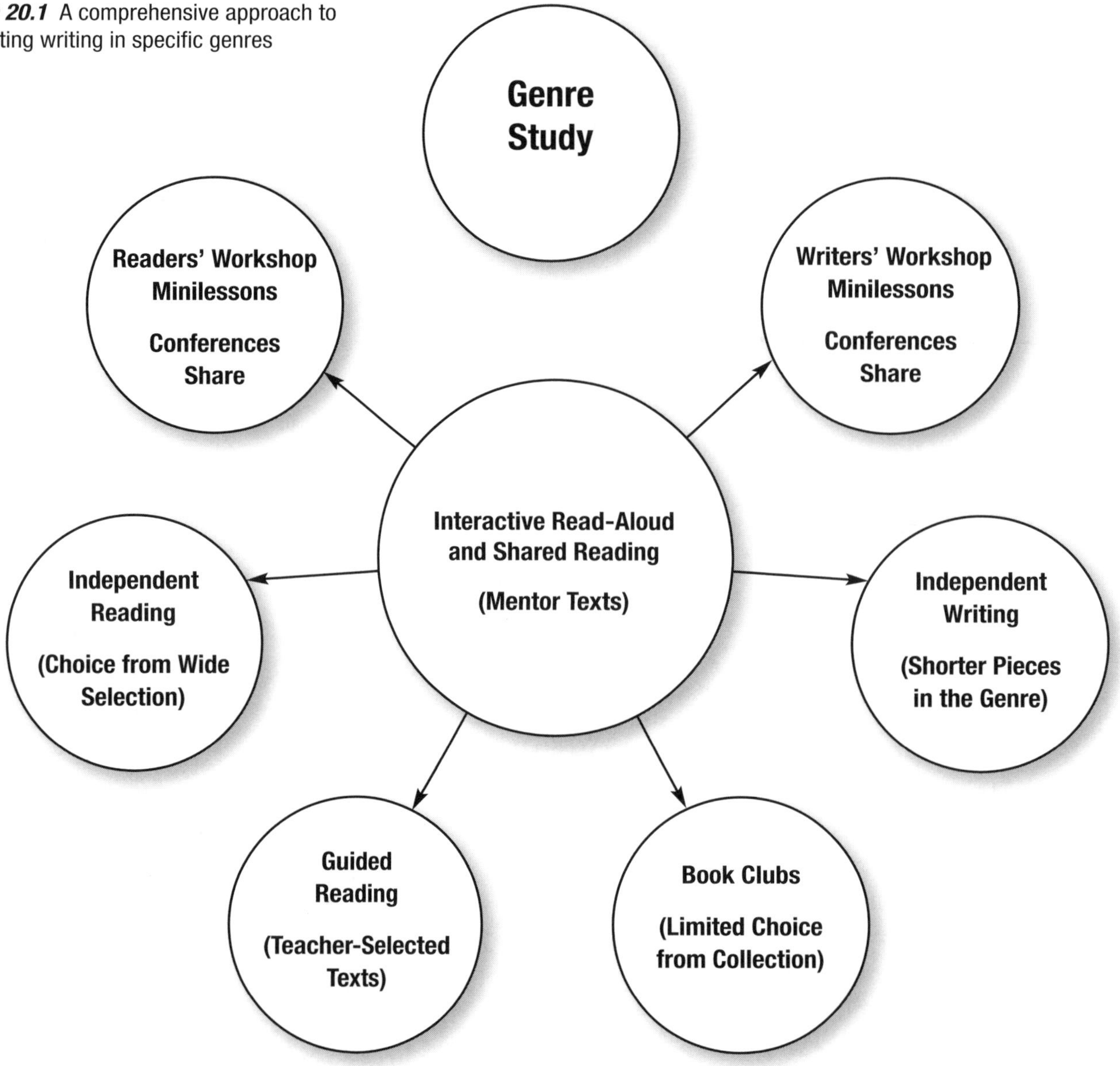

The Writing Process

In writers' workshop students are immersed in the processes writers use to bring documents from ideas to final drafts and occasionally publication. The writing process (see Figure 20.2) involves proceeding through a series of actions through which the writer gradually drafts and refines the piece. These steps are not rigid; they are recursive. At any time a writer might back up to an earlier phase in order to change direction or reshape an idea. When working on a draft or publishing a piece, a writer who has an experience or gets some ideas might jot down those ideas in a notebook to be used in later pieces. The writer's notebook is a rich resource—it is where the writer stores ideas, language, images, drafts and notes, feelings, and descriptions to be revisited later.

The circular path reinforces that students in the writers' workshop are always working at some phase of the process. When they complete a final draft or publish, they move back to rehearsing and planning for another piece of writing. Writers may set aside a piece at the draft stage and begin another, returning to the first piece later. Also, almost all writers do a bit of editing and proofreading even while they are producing a first draft. Or they may stop and draft or review material even while finishing a final publication.

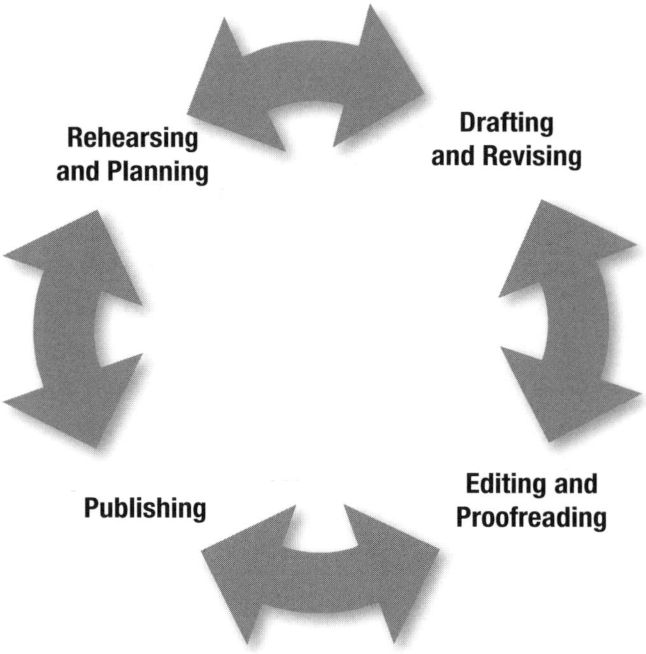

Figure 20.2 The writing process

Ray (2006) also argues against thinking of the writing process as a sequence of steps. Students need to engage in the process and talk about it with others many times, always realizing that moving from ideas to a finished piece takes many twists and turns. The more they do it, the better they will be able to describe what they do as writers and learn from others. You can help them look closely at what writers really do—not just the process sequence but issues like these:

- What they do when they are "stuck."
- How they get their ideas and then elaborate them.
- How they know when a piece is finished.
- How they know when to put something aside because it isn't working.
- When to seek help or feedback from others.
- When to read for inspiration.
- How to revise the beginning or middle when the end isn't working.
- How to cut out information that doesn't fit or distracts the reader.
- How to redirect the writing when it goes in a wrong direction.

Rehearsing and Planning

Rehearsing and planning involve gathering information, trying out ideas, and considering critical aspects of the text (see *The Continuum of Literacy Learning*):

- Writers have a clear *purpose* for writing the text. This purpose influences the genre they choose as well as the way they organize and present information.
- Writers think of the *audience* for the text. For students, the audience may be their classmates, others in the school, or their families. Occasionally, students publish for a wider, unknown audience. Students need to think of the audience as all readers of the text—not just the teacher.
- Writers find it easier to produce notes and drafts if they have opportunity to *talk with others* about their ideas.
- The writer's notebook is an important tool. In it, writers can "gather seeds"—collect ideas and quotes, make sketches and diagrams, write quick pieces on any topic. The notebook can be revisited as a resource for ideas.
- Writers carefully select the *content* and the *topics* so that they can achieve their purposes. They have a clear idea of the *message* or *theme* so that everything in the text supports the ideas they want to communicate.
- With audience, content, purpose, and message in mind, writers select the *genre* and *form* for the piece.

Drafting and Revising

Writers use basic processes to produce an initial draft and then revise it so that it communicates the message more effectively. Genre knowledge is important because it guides the writer in crafting the piece to reflect genre characteristics. Procedures include:

- Writers *produce an initial draft* by getting ideas down quickly. This is sometimes called a "discovery draft" because, often, the writer discovers more ideas and messages while drafting. During this process, writers do not worry much about editing and revising, although most will catch minor mistakes and cross out words to rewrite a sentence or substitute a better word even while drafting.

- Writers *reread* to remember what has been written so that they can improve the piece's clarity and appeal.
- Writers *add information*—details, adjectives, phrases that clarify, dialogue, for example—to make the piece more interesting or clearer.
- Writers *delete information* that gets in the way of the message by providing confusing and irrelevant details. Writers also delete redundant information and extraneous details. Every piece of information in the text should be necessary and work toward the message.
- Writers *reorganize information*, moving sentences and paragraphs around to create a logical sequence.
- Writers *change the text*. They work on transitions, change words to make the text more interesting or clear, and make vague parts more specific.
- Writers use a repertoire of *tools and techniques* for drafting and revising texts; for example, editing tools like carets (^), "spider legs" (a piece of inserted text taped to a page), standard symbols for revising and editing, cut-and-paste. (Writers working on the computer use word-processing tools.)
- Writers *understand the writing process*. As they work on drafting and revising, they may consult other writers as mentors and peer reviewers.

Editing and Proofreading

Once a satisfactory draft has been produced, the piece can be polished to the point of a final draft or publication. Now, writers focus on the form of the composition. While students do their own editing and proofreading, professional writers have editors, copy editors, and proofreaders who help them.

- Writers *edit for conventions*. They use everything they know about the conventions of spelling, punctuation, grammar and sentence structure, and text organization to edit the document.
- Writers often *use tools* to help them edit and proofread. They may use a printed or electronic dictionary or thesaurus. They may use a spelling or grammar check on the computer (these tools require knowledge and understanding, and cannot be blindly depended on).
- Writers *understand the editing and proofreading processes*; they use computer tools effectively and know when, how, and why to get editing help.

Publishing

Students produce a final draft that may be shared with others in the classroom and placed in the writing folder. This final draft is the best piece of writing the student can do at this time. You may assist on some final proofreading, but students need to learn the skills of editing and proofreading. As they increase proficiency, they can use editors' tools. A piece being published is teacher-edited before being formally printed.

It isn't necessary for students to bring every piece of writing to publication—that takes a great deal of time. It is better for students to produce many final drafts so that they become highly productive as writers and have many writing experiences. Producing many pieces is particularly important if you want them to experiment with writing in different genres. They need to try their hand at producing several pieces in the genre so that they internalize some of the important characteristics. But it is important to take the final step to publication several times a year so that students have the entire writing experience.

The Structure of Writers' Workshop

You contribute to your students' writing throughout your language arts teaching, but writers' workshop is a time (about an hour) in which you develop writers by teaching and applying principles related to the conventions, craft, or process of writing. The overarching purpose of writers' workshop is to help students become excellent writers by:

- Setting aside a daily time, with structured routines, dedicated to writing (see Figure 20.3).
- Providing strong instruction on the craft, process, and conventions of writing, including those related to specific genres.
- Introducing excellent and clear examples of writing in many genres (mentor texts).
- Teaching how to use writer's tools such as the writer's notebook.
- Teaching the *process* of writing, from getting ideas to publication.
- Providing whole-class, small-group, and individual instruction as students engage in the writing process.
- Creating a learning community around the development of writers.
- Teaching how to talk with others about their writing.
- Teaching how to read like writers.
- Teaching how to write with their readers in mind.

The workshop begins with whole-class instruction. As an option, you may first provide one or two "writer talks." These brief descriptions (one or two minutes) let students into the lives and processes of writers that they know. You wouldn't always use a quotation, but it is sometimes great to hear the writer's voice. The writer talks are more meaningful if students have listened to or read books by the author. (Numerous examples of writer talks are included in Chapter 28 of *Teaching for Comprehending and Fluency*.)

Following the brief writer talks (if provided), you present a minilesson on any aspect of the writing process. Typically, at the beginning of the year the minilessons help students learn the routines of writers' workshop and begin to use a writer's notebook. Through further minilessons, they learn the steps of the writing process, which they will use again and again on different pieces. As students become deeply involved in genre study, you begin to provide minilessons directly related to genre and to writing in a specific genre. An excerpt from a minilesson on writing memoir is provided in Figure 20.4.

Before ending the minilesson, it is important to have students try, immediately and actively, to apply the principle you have been teaching. In Figure 20.4, students quickly write one or two feelings and some notes on how they might show them. Students could also:

- Note language or a genre characteristic they want to incorporate into the piece they are writing or planning to write.
- Begin to write about the topic and then share with a partner.
- Reread a piece they have been working on to find genre characteristics and share with the group or a partner.
- Look at "seeds" (thoughts put down quickly in their writer's notebook) to find a topic and decide whether it might fit the genre.
- Look at examples of titles in the genre and select a text or two they want to use as resources for writing.
- Do some quick writing about a genre element in a piece in their writer's notebook.
- Try writing about the topic in one genre and then write about it in a different genre.
- Try writing several "leads" or endings for a piece.

Following the whole-class minilesson, students work on their writing individually; the room is silent except for conferences with individuals or discussion in small group work that can help students incorporate the characteristics of a genre into their own writing. A conversation with J.G. during a writing conference is provided in Figure 20.5. In a guided writing lesson each student is wrestling with the same kinds of problems but is working on her or his own example; you provide additional teaching that will help them along in their writing.

As the writers' workshop ends, students gather for a brief sharing period during which they talk about what they have accomplished or learned and you reinforce the minilesson principle. Sometimes students turn

STRUCTURE OF WRITERS' WORKSHOP		
Minilesson	**Writer Talks (optional)**	• The teacher provides one or two short pieces of information about a writer. • Talks may provide interesting information about the writer or describe how the writer gets ideas or processes texts. • Talks may highlight the genre(s) the writer uses and tell or discuss why. (Some writers stay with one genre, some work in a variety of genres.) • Students look at several examples of writing to derive an important principle. • Examples come from mentor texts that demonstrate characteristics of the genre in which they are writing.
	Statement of the Principle	• The teacher helps shape the principle in clear, explicit, and concise language (see the writing section of *The Continuum of Literacy Learning* for ideas). • The principle explains what writers do and why. • The principle is related to the characteristics chart that students have produced or to anything else the teacher wants them to learn about a genre.
	Examples	• The teacher invites students to offer more examples. • Students see how the examples help them think as writers and can refer to them while writing.
	Have a Try (when applicable)	• Students may try a short piece of writing in the genre in their notebooks. • Students may write the principle and a few examples or notes in their notebooks. • Focuses students' attention, helps them actively process the information, and gets them started.
Apply	**Independent Writing** **Conferring with the Teacher** **Guided Writing**	• Students apply what they have learned about writing in a genre as they write in their writer's notebooks or produce their own pieces of writing. • The teacher holds brief individual conferences to support students' writing in the genre. • The teacher may reinforce the minilesson principle and help the students use the information. • The teacher may bring a small group of students together to help them learn more about writing in the genre.
Share	**Group Share**	• Students share new learning with the whole group. • Students may share new insights into the genre. • Students may share examples from their own writing. • The group evaluates how today's writing workshop went.

Figure 20.3 Structure of writers' workshop

AN EXCERPT FROM A MINILESSON ON WRITING MEMOIR

NOTICINGS ABOUT MEMOIR

- Tells the story (memory) of a significant time or event in a subject's life
- Told by the subject
- Uses a narrative structure
- Provides factual information about the subject's life
- Tells why the time or event is important enough to be written about
- Has a limited perspective (subjective)

Often:

- Includes direct quotes
- Has photographs
- Tells the story at a significant point in subject's life
- Tells the setting and the culture the person lived in and what influenced the subject
- Adds factual statements as additional information
- Conveys a larger message

Writers of memoir show their strong feelings to help readers understand why the memory is important to them.

Grandma's Records—the writer told how the music made him and Grandma feel, and that it reminded her of home.

In Coal Country—the writer told that it was hard growing up in coal country but she loved her family and they were proud.

The Upside Down Boy—the writer told what it felt like to adjust to a new school and find his voice.

A memoir tells the story of or describes a significant time or event in the author's life.

TEACHER: Let's look at some of the memoirs we have read together so you can think about what you have learned as writers. Do you remember *Grandma's Records*, by Eric Velasquez? What were some of the feelings Velasquez showed?

RICHARD: He remembered his grandma always played records and loved music.

MARJA: He was very happy when he played the music and when they went to the concert. His grandma liked the music, too, because it reminded her of her home.

JORGE: And he wrote the story because he loved his grandma.

TEACHER: He helped you understand that he had strong feelings about his grandmother and about music. He even got a job playing music on the radio. Strong feeling is one of the things you noticed about the memoirs we read.

The teacher writes and then reads the minilesson principle. Then she writes a summary of the students' comments on *Grandma's Records*, *In Coal Country*, and *The Upside Down Boy*.

TEACHER: Each of these writers showed what they were feeling. They didn't just say they felt happy or proud. By what they showed, they helped you know. You could understand the feelings. Do you remember any examples?

GARETH: The author of *Grandma's Records* showed them dancing to music and also grandma putting a hand to her heart.

TEACHER: That's a good example. We have been working on showing, not just telling. Open your writer's notebooks and list one or two of the feelings you want your readers to understand in your memoir, and make some notes on how you will show them.

Students write for a few minutes and then talk with a partner. Before they begin writing independently, the teacher reminds them to think about the feelings they want to communicate and how they can show them.

Figure 20.4 An excerpt from a minilesson on writing memoir

EXAMPLE OF A CONVERSATION DURING A WRITING CONFERENCE	
TEACHER:	I see you are still working on your bow-and-arrow memoir. Read what you have so far.
J.G.:	[Reads]: "I chose a sleek black one with a green grip and paid the man at the cashier. It was twenty dollars. I hoped I had enough money. I did. I started to take the box apart in the car. Mom said no. Then we got home."
TEACHER:	How were you feeling about that bow? I know it must have been special for you to tell about it.
J. G.:	I was really excited. I couldn't wait to get it out and shoot it with Ian.
TEACHER:	So you were excited when you went into the store and when you finally found the one you liked. I can tell you really liked it by some of the words you used to describe it. Talk about what it was like getting the bow home and using it.
J. G.:	I was ripping the box open in the car and then Mom said I had to read the instructions first. But when we got home I ran in and called Ian and then finally we got to go out to use it.
TEACHER:	Ripping open the box sounds exciting. If you write what you just explained, your readers will know how excited and impatient you were. Your story moves fast there. Then it sounds like your Mom slowed you down but only for a while. Why don't you think of going fast, then slowing down, and then going fast again. Did you run to Ian's? How could you show that?
J. G.:	I ran, like, about thirty miles an hour!
TEACHER:	Think about how you can show your excitement by describing that.

Figure 20.5 Example of a conversation during a writing conference

and talk with a partner. At other times, several students share with the entire group. An excerpt from a group share is provided in Figure 20.6.

The structure of writers' workshop is a strong framework within which you can teach students to write in different genres. The instruction is effective because it rests on the work you have previously done—and simultaneously are doing—in genre study during interactive read-aloud and readers' workshop.

Purpose and Genre

Writers select a genre according to their purpose. For example, Anna Quindlin has written many best-selling works of realistic fiction like *One True Thing* (2006) and *Every Last One* (2010). But she has also produced personal memoirs like *Being Perfect* (2005) and *How Reading Changed My Life* (1998), and her newspaper column expresses opinions and sometimes includes narratives. She selects the genre according to her purpose and audience, but only writers who understand various genres are able to make those decisions.

Your students may not have a broad repertoire of genres, and they likely are not skilled writers in many of them, so you need to encourage (and often require) them to write in a variety of genres so they expand their writing abilities. You accompany this requirement with demonstration and teaching that will give student writers confidence and get them interested in trying out the genre—minilessons, individual conferences, small-group instruction, and group share. Students will also be bolstered by the many examples of the genre they have encountered during interactive read-aloud and readers' workshop.

The Continuum of Literacy Learning categorizes writing genres under four purposes: narrative, informational,

AN EXCERPT FROM A WRITERS' WORKSHOP GROUP SHARE	
TEACHER:	As you wrote today, you were thinking about how to show your strong feelings in your memoirs. You all have your pieces. Take a look and find a place where you tried to show feelings in your memoir. [Students take a moment to look.] Now turn to a partner and share what you wrote. [Students talk to a partner for a short time.] J.G. would you share the part you added to your memoir?
J. G.:	I wanted to show how excited I was to get my new bow and how I wanted to just rip into it. But my mom slowed me down to read instructions and then I couldn't get out and use it for a while. [Reads:] "I shot like a bullet out the front door of the store and madly began ripping the box open but my mom said you have to read the instructions first. Okay, I sighed. When I finished reading them we were already at home. I ran to the door and blasted through it. I sprinted to the phone and called Ian my friend. Then I waited a couple of hours then finally got to go. I ran at least 30 miles an hour all the way to Ian's house. 'Come on!!' I yelled."
TEACHER:	So J.G.'s memoir was about a very exciting time–when he got his new bow and arrow. What showed you he was excited?
GRETCHEN:	He was yelling.
ADRIANA:	He ran thirty miles an hour. I don't think he really did, but he made it sound like he did.
SARAH:	He said he shot like a bullet. I guess he couldn't have done that either, but it kind of helped you know how fast he went.
TEACHER	J.G. used some exaggeration in his memoir "shot like a bullet" is figurative language. He was comparing himself to a bullet to show how excited he was and that helps us know what he was feeling. Also, it helped you know why the memory was important to him. It's okay to do something like that because readers know what the writer is doing. What you have been working on today is an important characteristic of memoir–writers show their strong feelings to help readers understand why the memory is important to them. Tomorrow we'll continue working on memoirs.

Figure 20.6 Excerpt from a writers' workshop group share

poetic, and functional. These genres correspond to those we have discussed for literature. We have also added a fifth category—hybrids—because once students are familiar with and have tried the fiction and nonfiction categories and have studied hybrid texts, they may want to try putting genres together in interesting ways. The continuum lists key understandings particular to each genre (what students *need to know*) and includes statements that describe the way students demonstrate understanding by taking on the various kinds of writing within the genre (what students *can do* with the genre). It also includes examples of important forms in the writing curriculum.

Generally, young children love to write stories about their own lives—expressive writing that is descriptive or tells a simple tale, such as first-grader Jesse's account of turtle hunting, which is really a memoir (see Figure 20.7).

As students grow as writers from prekindergarten through grade 8, they understand new genres but also write increasingly complex and sophisticated examples within each genre category: narrative, expository, poetic, and functional. All the categories can be connected to the genres students study in readers' workshop (see Figure 20.8).

Turtel hunting
Jesse
Today im going tutrle hunting It is a nice day. 1
I went to get a Life Jacit so did my cosins and 2
and Then I went to the doke. My grandPa was un- 3
dad
aunt rebcea
doing the bote. When he was done we all got in. 4
My dad startdd rowing. we moved throw the 5
cove. When we were by the big log. We sowe a 6
turtul!!!!!!!!!!!! We all took a net and- 7

Figure 20.7 Jesse's account of turtle hunting

workd together to cach
it and we COT IT, "Woho"
8
I said, thats so cool,
I no!!!! evreione else
9
said. Lets bring it back
to the lodge I said.
10
Good idesaid my
Aunt. We slowly moved
11
back thow the cove back
to the lodge and put the
12
turtal in the turtal cage.
We showd nanaleb and
13
Grandpa Steve. then we let
it go. "Bye turtel we all"
14
said. It slipd back into the
water. The end
15

Figure 20.7 Jesse's account of turtle hunting *(cont.)*

GENRES FOR WRITERS' WORKSHOP: RELATIONSHIP TO GENRE STUDY IN READERS' WORKSHOP		
Genres Studies for Writers' Workshop		**Genres for Study in Readers' Workshop**
Narrative Genres	Short Fiction	Realistic Fiction
		Historical Fiction
		Traditional Literature
		Modern Fantasy (including science fiction)
	Memoir	Memoir
		Autobiography
	Biography	Biography
	Narrative Nonfiction	Narrative Nonfiction
Informational Genres (non-narrative)	Expository Nonfiction	Expository/Persuasive
	Essay and Letter-Essay	Persuasive
	Editorial	Persuasive
	Book Review	Expository/Persuasive
Poetic Genres	Poetry (various forms)	Poetry (various forms)
Functional Genres	Friendly and Formal Letters	Expository/Narrative
	Lists and Procedures	Procedural Texts
	Test Writing	Procedural/Expository/Persuasive/ Narrative
	Writing About Reading	Variety of Fiction/Nonfiction Genres
Hybrids	Hybrids	Variety of Hybrids

Figure 20.8 Genres for writers' workshop: relationship to genre study in readers' workshop

Narrative Genres

Through genre study, students learn to recognize the structure of narrative—from very simple to highly complex. They encounter narrative structure in realistic and historical fiction as well as all forms of fantasy. They also encounter narrative structure in memoir, biography, autobiography, and narrative nonfiction. Narratives may also be evident in hybrid texts.

Short Fiction

When they study works of realistic fiction, historical fiction, or fantasy, students may like to produce short pieces of their own. When they first participate in writing workshop, students benefit from mining significant topics from their own lives, including stories that have narrative structure. They learn about many of the features of fiction through these personal narratives. If they attempt fiction too soon, they may produce long strings of dialogue with little narrative and no point, episode after episode with no real structure, and "far out" science fiction with no real narrative. You want to push them to a deeper awareness of the features of the genre as they write.

Stories have the classic structure described in Chapter 6. Characters, setting, and the story problem are introduced and then developed over a few or many episodes. Rising action builds to a climax or high point when the problem is resolved, and falling action moves quickly to the end. As they encounter works of fiction, students start to craft short stories that reflect elements of the genre.

Sean has just started to craft fiction. In his (to be continued) short story "Robert and the Protector: The Secret Meeting," he uses a first person narrative, which he is familiar with from writing memoir, to craft a fantasy/mystery. The cover has some of the characteristics of graphic texts (see Figure 20.9).

On the first page, Sean sets the scene (see Figure 20.10). He has an action-oriented, engaging beginning that lets the reader know that the narrator's parents have left and that he has two siblings, Bob and Mary. The fantasy element also emerges. As the story goes on, Robert enters Might Manor and encounters mysterious signs that he and his brother and sister follow by car, which crashes. (See the vivid description in Figure 20.11.) Robert's parents are finally discovered being held captive in a secret chamber. An example of the author's character description is shown in Figure 20.12. He ends the story by having Robert rescue his parents but then leaves a cliffhanger (see Figure 20.13), page 407.

Figure 20.9 Cover of "Robert and the Protector: The Secret Meeting"

Figure 20.10 Setting the scene for "Robert and the Protector"

I sat down regretting I didn't do it earlier. "Bob, you will be done with your homework when your father and I get back! You will never wait until last minute again!" With that, my mom left. I picked up my pencil and forced myself to do the first question. With a struggle, I did the second one, then the third. Minutes passed and then finally, I finished the last question with a sigh of relief. I fell down on the couch and clicked on the T.V. Cartoons and shows and movies passed, until finally I looked up and jumped.

"9:30!" I yelled.

"What's wrong now, Bob?" my sister, Mary, said, bored.

I yelled back upstairs, "It's been 9 hours since mom left!"

"No, it hasn'- Wow! What do you think happened to her?"

"I don't know. Ask Ben, he's the oldest," I said.

"He never knows what to do!" Mary screeched. She had a point, though. My older brother never acts his age, much less knows what to do in these situations.

"I'm going to go and investigate the neighborhood. I'll be right back," I said.

"Fine, but we're not coming with you," Mary said.

I walked out the door and hopped down the steps. My feet clicked against the pavement. The crisp night air blew in my face. Then, as I was walking along, something caught the corner of my eye. A giant black mansion loomed above me to my left. But the strange thing is, it's never been there before until tonight.

So many thoughts were whizzing through my head, I thought my brain would explode. A tiny part of me wanted to go inside, but the sane part of me told me to keep walking. Almost in a trance, I walked over slowly and cautiously. I heard a rustle and jumped out of my body. Then I realized that it was just a squirrel playing in the bushes. The plaque on the door read in fancy letters: Might Manor.

Sean's story reflects his reading of fiction. It is very action oriented and probably will not involve much character development. If he is to develop further as a fiction writer, he will need to think about more than action. Characters' feelings and perspectives matter, and they change in response to experiences. But Sean has good facility with language and is ready to consider these other elements.

Jesse, a younger student, has written a short fantasy story in which he talks directly to his audience (see Figure 20.14). Jesse obviously has much to learn in terms of conventions, but he does use punctuation (although he overuses exclamation points) and his spelling indicates his awareness of more complex spelling (*muninits*); he is not afraid to use sophisticated vocabulary even if he is unsure of the spelling. He seems to have borrowed freely from his own hearing and reading of stories. He has a beginning, a series of events, and a satisfying ending. He has grasped some of the characteristics of traditional tales (the story of how a place got its name) as well as science fiction.

Some questions you can ask about our students' short fiction are provided in Figure 20.15, page 411.

We slammed into the giant boulder jutting out of the ground. We flew into the air, and left my stomach behind. Our car went impossibly far before slamming into the ground, upside down. Huge cracks stretched over the roof of the car as it bounced, ripping me out of my seatbelt. I tumbled around the car until finally I grabbed onto the door. Then I realized that it was the handle.

The car shook and it threw me across it. Even with that much force on the handle, it wouldn't budge. It was jammed. Then I felt my back slam into the arm rest. I was facing the door. I was in perfect position…BAM! I used all of my strength and force in my feet and legs that my they went numb. As soon as my feet connected with the door, it broke clean off. Ben, Mary, and I all tumbled out of the door on top of each other. We hit the rocks and rolled away fast, avoiding the tumbling upside down car by just an inch. I fell off a ledge and my eyesight went as black as the rocks.

Figure 20.11 Description from "Robert and the Protector"

A crazy man burst into the room and immediately interrupted the men's conversation. I couldn't tell how old he was because of how he looked. He had a brown, oversized lab coat that seemed to have been white, black pants flecked with small holes, and suspicious purple smoke flowing off of his cracked glasses. Just to top it off, his spiked up, white hair matched his shoes and ghostly pale skin. He looked deeply into the man on the left's eyes with his electric blue ones. His wrinkled skin twitched as he talked nervously in a loud enough voice for me to barely hear him.

Figure 20.12 Character description from "Robert and the Protector"

As the world ended, I saw my brother and sister in the broken and smashed car, half tumbling, half driving, at about 200miles per hour. It whipped past, and I dove after it, my parents holding on and dangling behind me like a chain. I managed to grab the top of the car, my parents' weight pulling me down, my fingers slipping…my sister quickly slid the smashed car door open and I swung down into it, my parents right behind me. We got into our seats and managed to close the door. We didn't bother putting our seat belts on.

"What happened, guys?" I said, gasping for air.

My mom replied, "Someone got us in the neighborhood as we were leaving. I saw his nametag, I think his last name was Might, but it was so long ago..." I was thinking of Might. My mind brought me back to the mansion… "I hope you finished your homework," my mom said as we drove out of the exploding, crumbling cliffs, screaming and booming behind us.

To be Continued...

Figure 20.13 The ending of "Robert and the Protector"

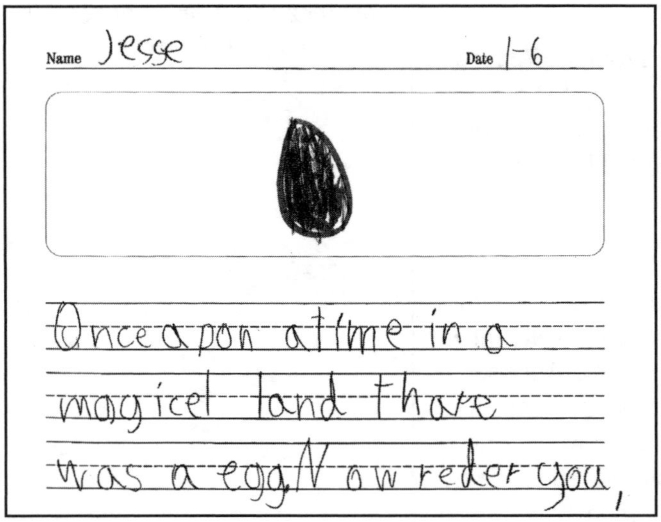
Name Jesse Date 1-6

Once apon atime in a magicel land thare was a egg. Now reder you, 1

Figure 20.14 Jesse's short fantasy story, **p. 1**

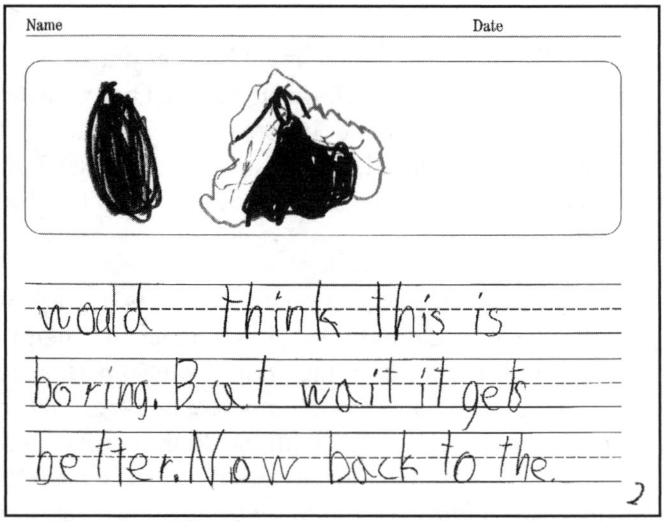
Name Date

would think this is boring. But wait it gets better. Now back to the 2

p. 2

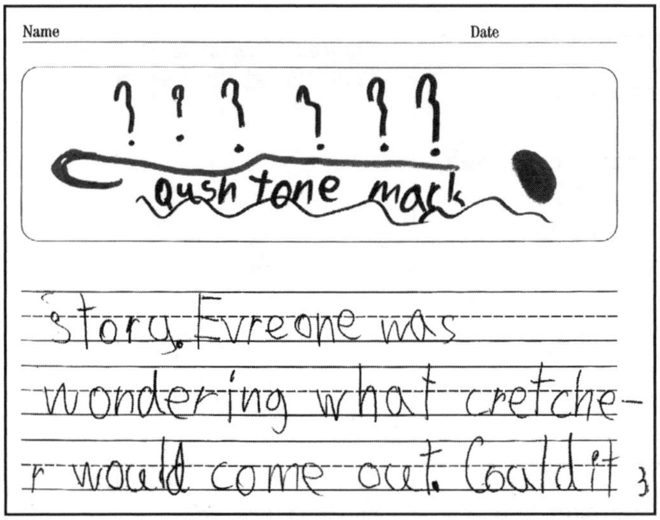
Name Date

story. Evreone was wondering what cretche-r would come out. Could it 3

p. 3

Name Date

be a griffin could it be a banshee? All they new that they ave never seen 4

p. 4

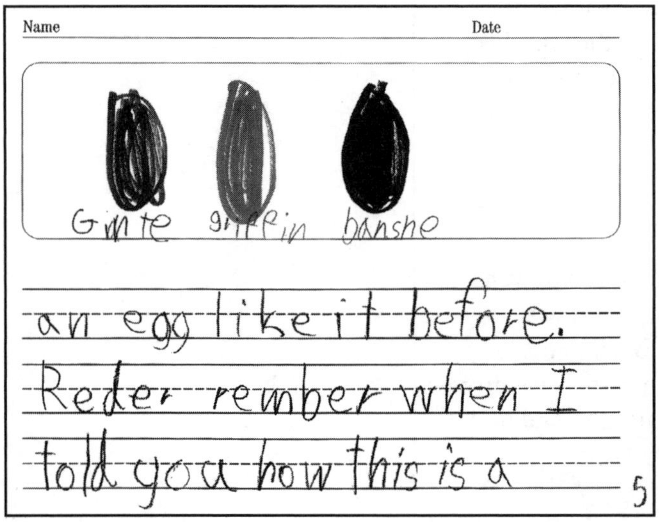
Name Date

an egg like it before. Reder rember when I told you how this is a 5

p. 5

Name Date

magicil land. Well this magcil land was on a Planit fare out in space and 6

p. 6

Name Date

at the time I was telling you about the egg. on erith a big spaceship was taking off to 7

p. 7

Name Date

go to this planet. Wait they weren't exactly going to this planit they were serching 8

p. 8

Name Date

for life. So the astonots who are going in space do not no where they are going. 9

p. 9

Name Date

USA

Now I will tell you about earth a littebit on earth at NASA they were 10

p. 10

Name Date

five four three two one blast off

blasting off now! FIVE Four Three two one blast off!!!! 11

p. 11

Name Date

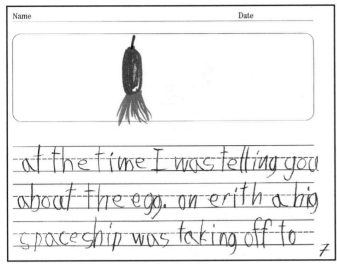

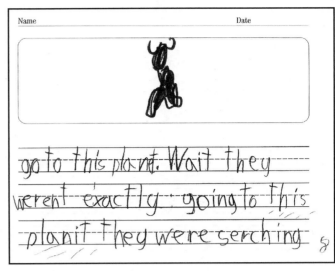

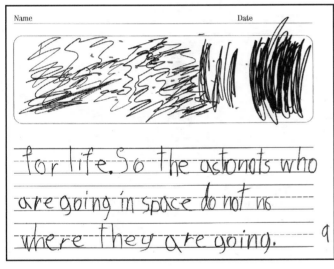

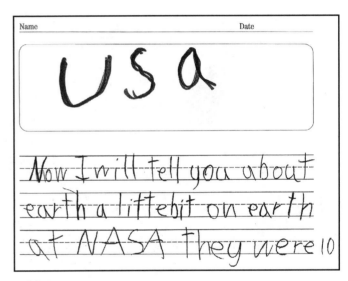

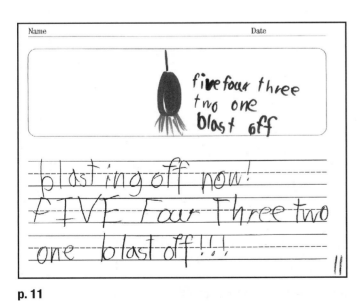

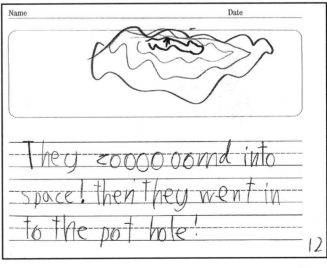

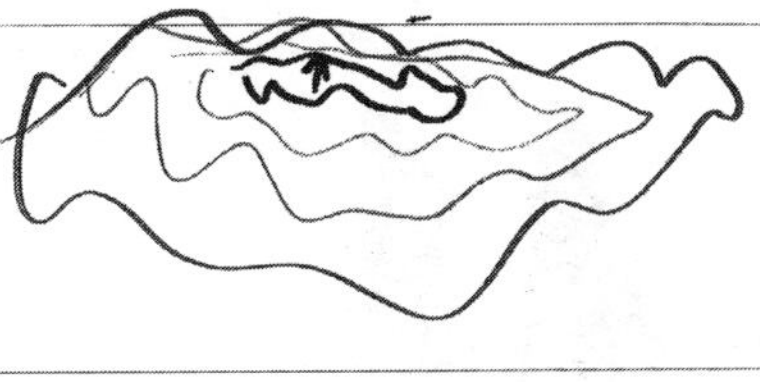

They zooooomd into space! then they went in to the pot hole! 12

p. 12

continues

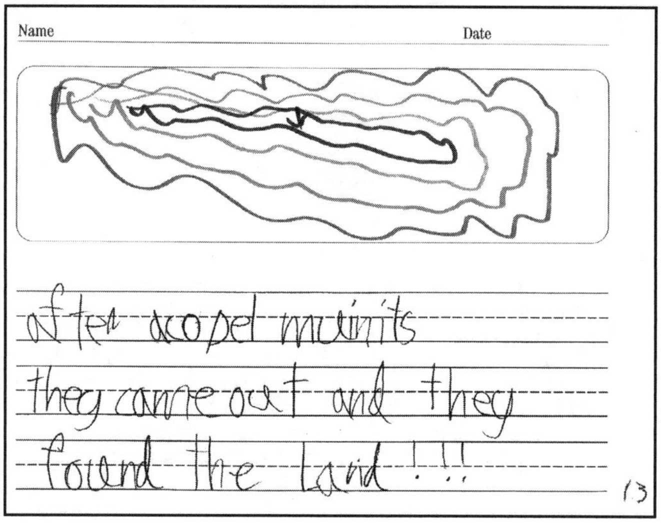

p. 13

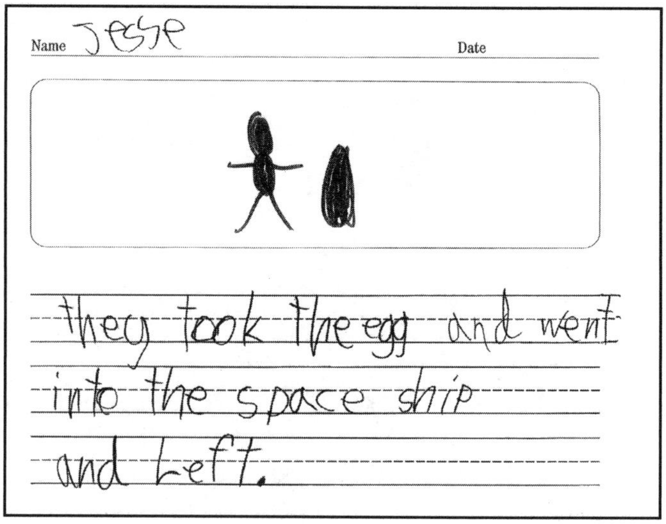

Name Jesse
Date
after acopel muinits
they came out and they
found the land !!!
back to earth and
wacht it. after a month...
It was a dragen!
They put it in blace
land and now the
name of thozs mountens
is? Dragens of Blue land'
they took the egg and went
into the space ship
and Left.

p. 14

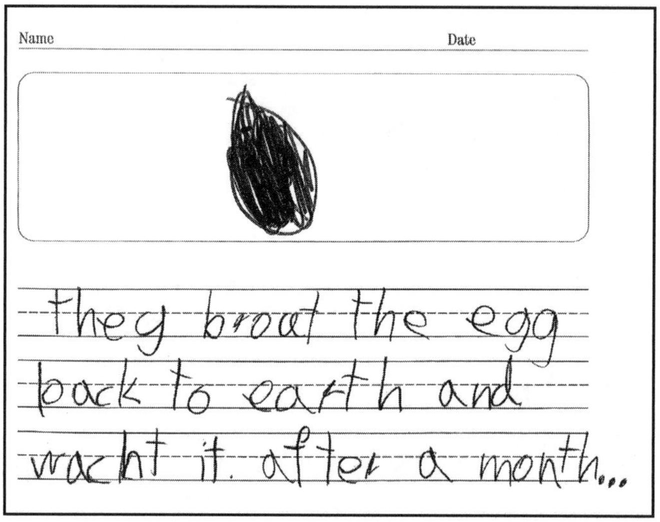

p. 15

p. 16

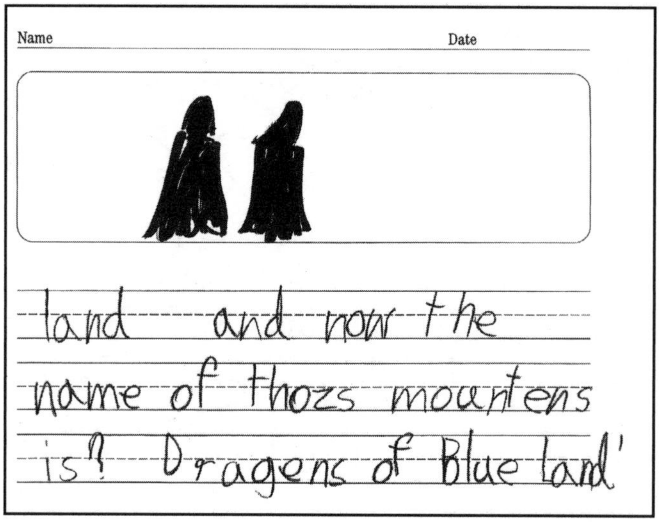

p. 17

Figure 20.14 Jesse's short fantasy story *(cont.)*

QUESTIONS TO ASK ABOUT STUDENTS' SHORT FICTION

- Have they considered the audience while writing?
- Have they written realistic fiction, historical fiction, fantasy, science fiction, or stories that resemble traditional literature?
- Do they understand that the short story should communicate a larger message?
- Do they understand and use the elements of fiction, including setting, problem characters, plot, and problem resolution?
- Do they understand the structure of narrative and ways it can be varied (flashback, circular plot, multiple narrators)?
- Have they taken the point of view of one character (or switch points of view) in a way that works?
- Do they show (rather than tell) character traits by what they do, what they say and think, and what others say about them?
- Have they written in an interesting way (engaging plot, compelling lead, satisfying ending)?
- Do they use dialogue skillfully (without overusing)?
- Do they use literary features such as figurative and/or descriptive language, imagery, or personification?

Figure 20.15 Questions to ask about students' short fiction

Memoir

Many memoir writers are unpublished but find pleasure reflecting in writing about their own lives. Young writers often begin with memoir to develop their voice. Writing about important events in their lives, they describe characters, setting, a series of events, and their own sensory experiences and feelings, all of which are important aspects of writing fiction. Figure 20.16 is J.G.'s finished memoir about his new bow and arrow. He uses many of the techniques of fiction writers to make his memoir exciting.

The first paragraph establishes the setting. The action moves quickly as they enter the store but slows down as he looks through the bows, lovingly describes his choice, goes home, and waits for his friend. It speeds up again when the two boys go to try out the bow. J.G. even describes an exciting point when the arrow almost hits his friend. It is also obvious that J.G. is trying to spice up his writing with strong verbs; he has overdone it a bit, but some of the action words he uses work very well. He has an engaging beginning and a satisfying ending. He uses words like *finally* to show the passing of time and uses literary language different from everyday conversation. J.G.'s memoir reflects some of the important characteristics of memoir. He tells about a moment in time and even includes an explicit moral lesson.

Figure 20.17 lists some characteristics to look for in students' memoir pieces. They need to understand that a memoir is a personal narrative that reflects a memorable experience. Mentor texts mentioned during minilessons are good examples for them. A memoir describes a time, event, person, or setting that had an impact on the writer—something unforgettable. It may be one event or something that happened with regularity, as in *Nana Upstairs and Nana Downstairs* (de Paola 2000). Students who see themselves as writers will find it useful to carry a notebook and jot down notes to help them remember meaningful topics that can be turned into memoirs.

My Bow and Arrow J.G

We were at Dick's, the sports store.
I barreled twoards the hunting section. I stared
in awe at all the hunting knives and rifles. there
were some bows that wer more than $400!
I finally chase a sleek black one with a green
grip and paid the man at the cashier. It wa
twenty dollars I hoped I had enough money. I did
I shot like a bulled out the front door of the
store and madly began ripping the box open but
my mom said you have to read the instructio
-s first. Okay I sighed. When I finished reading
them we were all ready at home, I ran to the
door and blasted through them. I sprinted to
the phone and called Ian my friend.
Then I waited a couple of hours then finall
got to go. I ran at least 30 miles
an hour all the way to Ian's house
"Come on!!" I yelled. Then we zoomed even faste
towards the other side of the street. I ra
to the top of the biggest hill not even
stopping to think how tired I should be, took th
bow off my back, pulled an arrow from my
quiver, nached the arrow. It shot from
my bow like a bullet it flew through
the air. Just then my friend came over
the hill, the arrow was headed straigh
for him! "Duck!!!!!" I yelled, hee threw himsel
at the ground. It worked the arrow missed.

We took turns shooting the bow for the rest
of the afternoon with only a couple of close
calls so in the end it was a pretty nice
day.

(moral): Never shoot a bow at a
person!)

Figure 20.16 J.G.'s "My Bow and Arrow"

THINGS STUDENTS SHOULD KEEP IN MIND WHEN WRITING MEMOIR

As writers of memoir, students need to:

- Think of how they want readers to feel while reading the memoir.
- Select memorable experiences that have been significant in their lives.
- Reveal something about themselves through their writing.
- Use different forms, such as story, poem, vivid description, "slice of life" vignettes.
- Sometimes use dialogue to show feelings and attributes of self and others.
- Use only the important details, eliminating extraneous and unnecessary information that gets in the way of the message.
- Communicate the larger meaning of the memoir (usually at the end).
- Use literary language, for example, strong verbs, imagery, descriptive language, metaphor and simile.

Figure 20.17 Things students should keep in mind when writing memoir

Biography

In Chapter 9, we discuss the study of biography. As students go deeper into learning the key characteristics of biography, they enjoy writing their own. The availability of a great deal of information on the Internet, including pictures, makes it interesting and easy to do the background research. But you don't want students simply to compile a dull list of (largely copied) facts (as they used to do years ago from the encyclopedia and now may cut and paste from the Internet). A biography, even a biographical sketch, is *crafted.*

Kaylee's biography of Albert Einstein is shown in Figure 20.18. Kaylee is just learning to write short biographies. It took her some time to place information in paragraphs and to order the paragraphs so that events were unfolding in a logical way. The characteristics of biography she was able to incorporate in her own writing include chronology, quotations, and challenges faced by the subject.

Student writers need to understand a biography as the true story of someone's life (or a part of it). They need to convey the importance and/or influence of their subject and the significance of events and personal decisions made by the subject. Biographers reveal their own stance toward the subject by their selection of facts and events and how they describe them. They describe the important decisions and turning points and try to engage their readers by writing in an interesting way. Biographers have choices in the information they report and how they report it. They can provide information in chronological order or use techniques such as flashbacks; they can focus on an individual's childhood or describe a short period of time in the context of background information. Figure 20.19 lists some things students need to be aware of when writing biography.

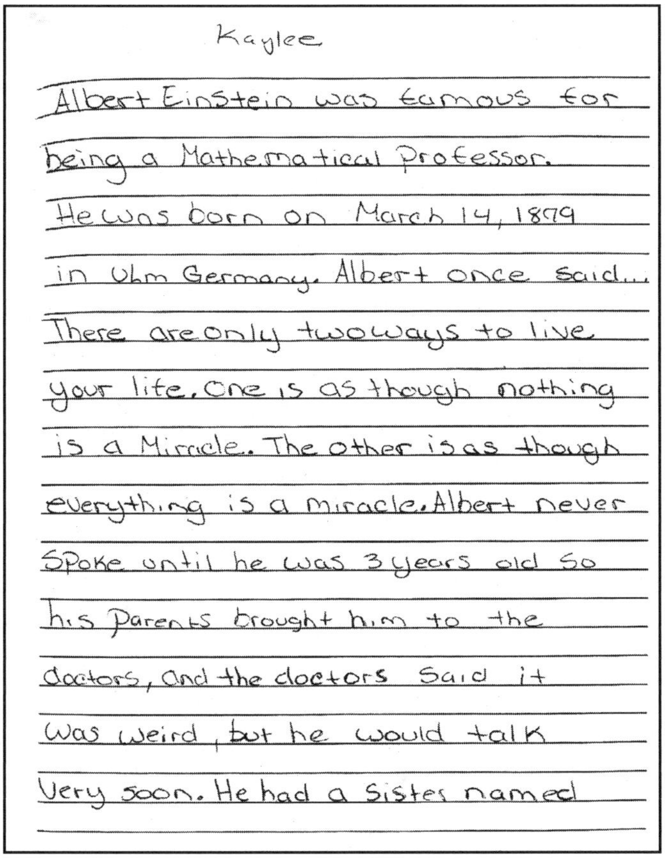
Kaylee
Albert Einstein was famous for
being a Mathematical Professor.
He was born on March 14, 1879
in Ulm Germany. Albert once said...
There are only two ways to live
your life. One is as though nothing
is a Mircale. The other is as though
everything is a miracle. Albert never
Spoke until he was 3 years old So
his Parents brought him to the
doctors, and the doctors Said it
Was weird, but he would talk
Very soon. He had a Sistes named

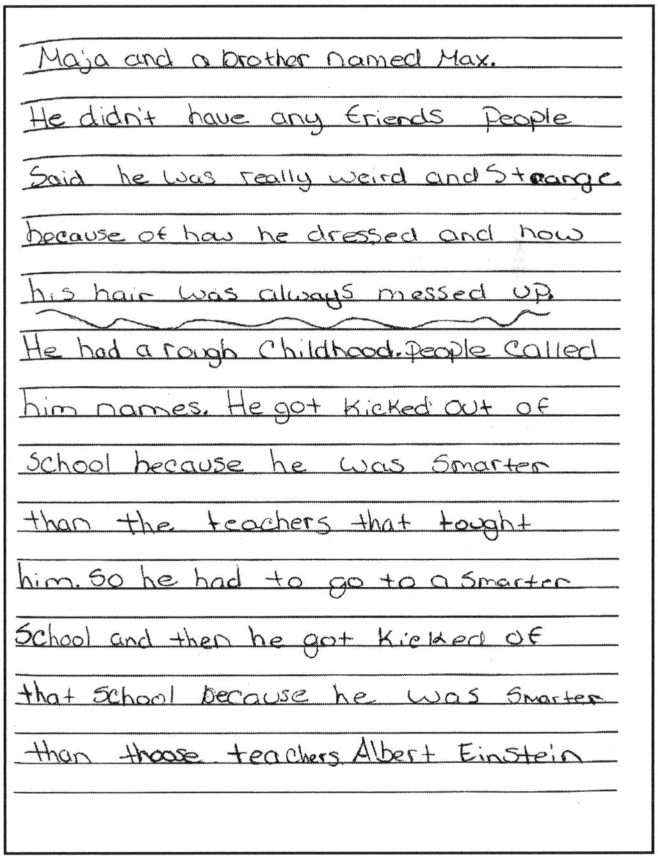
Maja and a brother named Max.
He didn't have any friends People
Said he was really weird and Strange
because of how he dressed and how
his hair was always messed up.
He had a rough Childhood. People called
him names. He got kicked out of
School because he was Smarter
than the teachers that tought
him. So he had to go to a Smarter
School and then he got kicked of
that School because he was Smarter
than thoose teachers. Albert Einstein

Figure 20.18 Kaylee's biography of Albert Einstein

p. 2

continues

did poorly in school he didn't want to read and memorize that wasn't his style.

When Albert Einstein got older he ended up being a mathemacial professor at a collage. Everyone loved him and took him serious. He made up new things like the formula $E = Mc^2$. E stands for enery and M is for mass and the third thing C is for the speed of light. Albert also made a bomb it wasn't to hurt anybody he just made it because

p. 3

because he knew how to make it. Albert Einstein hated war because it was so vilent and he was a peaceful person.

After years and years Albert meet somebody her name was mileva they were friends for a while and they were dating and got married and had 2 sons. Albert took long walks with mileva and his sons. Some people told him to go to this place so that he could be the greatest scientist

p. 4

and mathemacian, he said yes and left his sons and wife mileva and didn't come back. mileva died in 1948.

After that were Albert was staying he meet this girl and her name was Elsa. They got married and moved to princeton New jersey. Three years later Elsa died In 1936.

Albert Einstein published a paper about relativity in 1905.

After Elsa died Albert was upset

p. 5

when Elsa died. He didn't do any of the stuff he used to do it slowed him down because Elsa died. Albert died on April 8, 1955. When Albert died he ask to donate his brain to science.

Alberts last quote was.......

Everything is determined the begining as well as the end, by forces over which we have no control. It is determined for the insect as well as for

p. 6

Figure 20.18 Kaylee's biography of Albert Einstein, *(cont.)*

the Star Human beings,
Vegetables or Cosmic dust.
We all dance to a mysterious
tune intoned in the distance
by an invisble Player.

p. 7

THINGS STUDENTS SHOULD KEEP IN MIND WHEN WRITING BIOGRAPHY

As writers of biography, students need to:

- Use mentor texts to learn about craft.
- Keep the reader in mind while planning and writing.
- Select the subject for a reason and help readers understand it.
- Understand that the text should have a larger message or lesson for readers.
- Select important information to report.
- Leave out unimportant details or information that does not contribute to the overall message.
- Understand the need for accuracy and objectivity in reporting.
- Do background research and base their writing on verifiable sources.
- Describe the subject's important decisions and turning points, and show how those decisions influenced his or her life or the lives of others.
- Create interest in the subject.
- Reveal the subject's feelings through what he does, what he has said or written, and what others say about him.
- Tell events in chronological order or some other clear organization (categories, flashbacks, sidebars).
- Reveal own point of view through the information selected and reported.

Figure 20.19 Things students should keep in mind when writing biography

Narrative Nonfiction

Writers of nonfiction select genres as carefully as do writers of fiction. One way to convey factual information is through a narrative. Both narratives and expository texts can be literary—that is, incorporate descriptive language, figurative language, imagery, or illustrations/graphics; but narrative nonfiction follows a story-like arc. *The Continuum of Literacy Learning* provides information on both narrative and expository nonfiction texts in the writing continuum under "Nonfiction." Biographers of course use narrative structure, but writers of other kinds of informational texts can also select this way of organizing texts.

Why would a nonfiction writer choose narrative structure? Some overarching reasons are to find an effective way to communicate information and to produce a high-quality work of literature. Other reasons include:

- Narratives seem more familiar to readers and may be easier to follow.
- Some topics, such as historical accounts, lend themselves to narrative.
- Problem/solution and cause/effect structures sometimes take the form of a story (for example, reporting a problem and describing the actions of scientists who explore causes and attempt solutions).
- Narrative helps readers see what life is like for other living things (for example, a day/year in the life of . . . or the story of . . .).

Figure 20.20 lists some things students' need to be aware of when writing narrative nonfiction pieces.

Teaching Narrative Genres

You need to help students use narrative structure effectively, according to purpose. Short fiction entertains by weaving a story with believable characters and tension. Memoir communicates the writer's feelings and experiences. Biography engages readers' interest in and evokes feelings about the subject while at the same time communicating true information. Narrative nonfiction can take a wide variety of forms and can be applied to almost any topic. Adding narrative to exposition can make a text more engaging to readers. Ideally, students should move away from assembling dry "reports" meant only for their teacher to creating texts with a broader group of readers in mind. A deep knowledge of narrative structure and how to use it effectively helps writers of both fiction and nonfiction.

THINGS STUDENTS SHOULD KEEP IN MIND WHEN WRITING NARRATIVE NONFICTION

As writers of narrative nonfiction, students need to:

- Use narrative structure in an appropriate and interesting way.
- Understand that the writer of narrative nonfiction tries to interest readers in the topic.
- May use literary language, including figurative language, to make the topic interesting.
- Present details and information within the narrative structure.
- Write with the audience's interests and background knowledge in mind.
- Include text features (graphics, maps, sidebars, etc.) as appropriate.
- Bring the narrative to a satisfying and interesting conclusion.
- Avoid fictionalizing the topic (unless writing a hybrid text).

Figure 20.20 Things students should keep in mind when writing narrative nonfiction

Katie Gribben, a middle school teacher, approaches the teaching of nonfiction narrative systematically, and her students keep records of minilessons and examples. Figure 20.21 is a page from the notebook of a student reader who is learning to notice the writer's craft by thinking about how meaning and significance affect a writer's decisions to write biography, autobiography, or memoir.

Non-Narrative Genres

Writers must also know how to craft interesting, engaging non-narrative nonfiction texts that inform, explain, persuade, and argue.

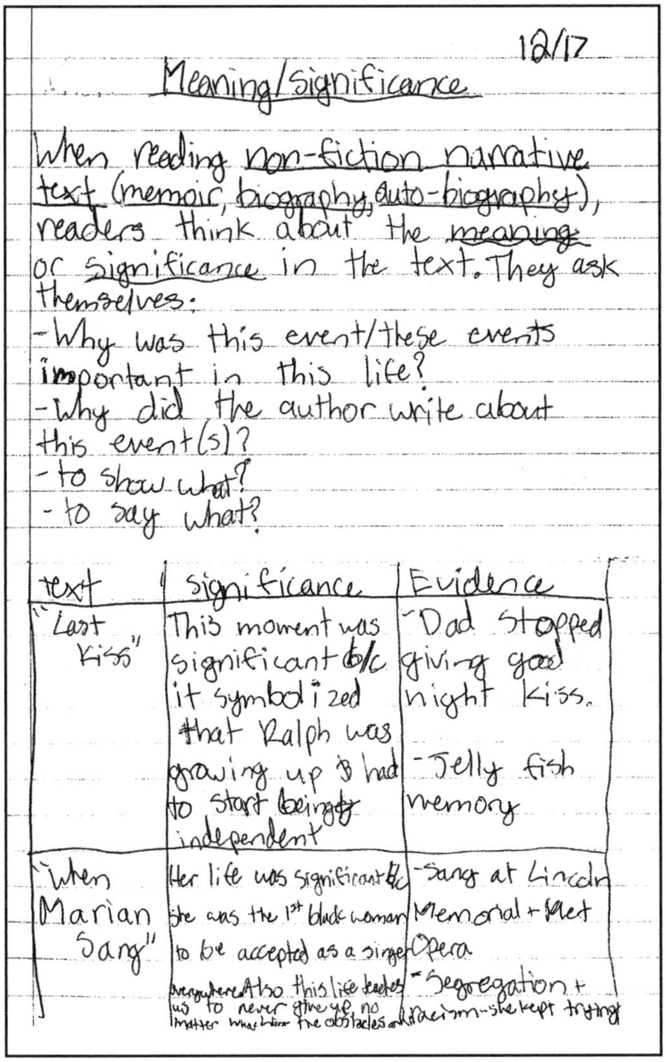

12/17

Meaning/significance

When reading non-fiction narrative text (memoir, biography, auto-biography), readers think about the meaning or significance in the text. They ask themselves:
- Why was this event/these events important in this life?
- Why did the author write about this event(s)?
- to show what?
- to say what?

text	significance	Evidence
"Last Kiss"	This moment was significant b/c it symbolized that Ralph was growing up & had to start being independent	-Dad stopped giving good night kiss. -Jelly fish memory
"When Marian Sang"	Her life was significant b/c she was the 1st black woman to be accepted as a singer everywhere. Also this life teaches us to never give up no matter what the obstacles are	-Sang at Lincoln Memorial + Met Opera -Segregation + racism-she kept trying

Figure 20.21 Meaning and significance of narrative nonfiction texts

Expository Nonfiction

Writing expository nonfiction such as a report or feature article requires research and the ability to order and present information logically. A report brings together a body of information and may include several aspects or categories of information related in some way. Often, reports, feature articles, and editorials involve persuasive writing. Excellent expository writing, particularly persuasive writing, requires students to see themselves as thoughtful people who are able to express their own opinions well. According to Caine (2008), it can be complicated to separate objective reporting from persuasion—so often a piece becomes a combination of the two. The difference may be one of degree: "Some writing is noticeably persuasive; other writing is persuasive in a more subtle way" (Caine xiii).

A feature article usually focuses on one aspect of a topic and includes a lead paragraph, more detailed information in subsequent paragraphs, and a conclusion. Even younger children can begin to find and organize information into a report that reads well. The cover of second-grader Jade's report "Freaky Awesome Sharks!" is shown in Figure 20.22. She has a table of contents (Figure 20.23). She has included an organizing device (web) to help her remember important subtopics that she wants to include (Figure 20.24). She even has a chart showing all four kinds of sharks (Figure 20.25) She has devoted a page with at least two sentences and an illustration to each subtopic (Figure 20.26).

Older students prepare a few longer, more elaborate reports. These reports take a great deal of time and increasingly involve a variety of media. Students need to understand that a report has an introductory section, followed by more information in categories or sections. Figure 20.27 lists some of the requirements of excellent report writing. Students will be moving toward these goals.

Students also learn a great deal by writing feature articles. Feature articles require writers to perform all the actions listed in Figure 20.27 but more concisely. A feature article can focus on any topic and includes many of the features of expository text. By writing many feature articles, students experience again and

Figure 20.22 The cover of Jade's report "Freaky Awesome Sharks!"

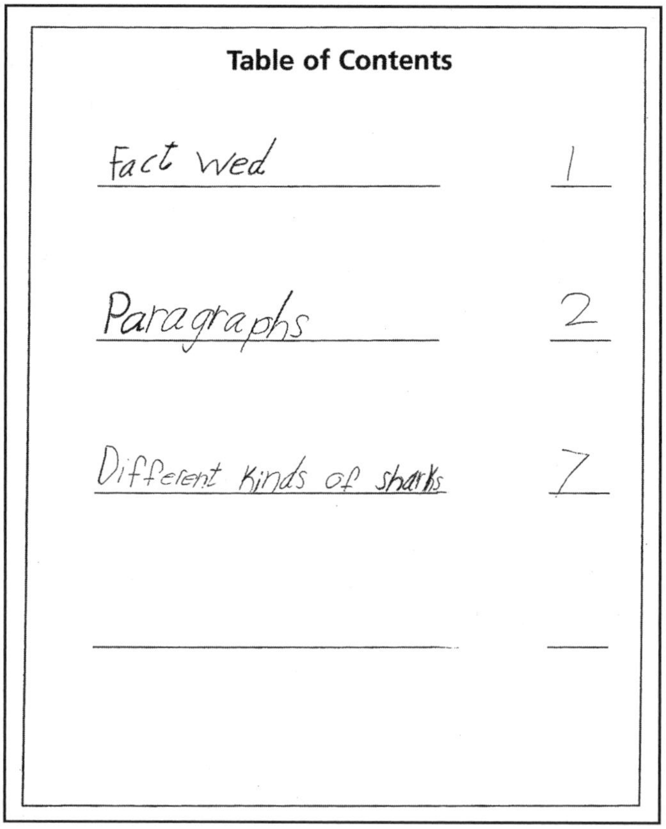

Figure 20.23 Table of Contents from "Freaky Awesome Sharks!"

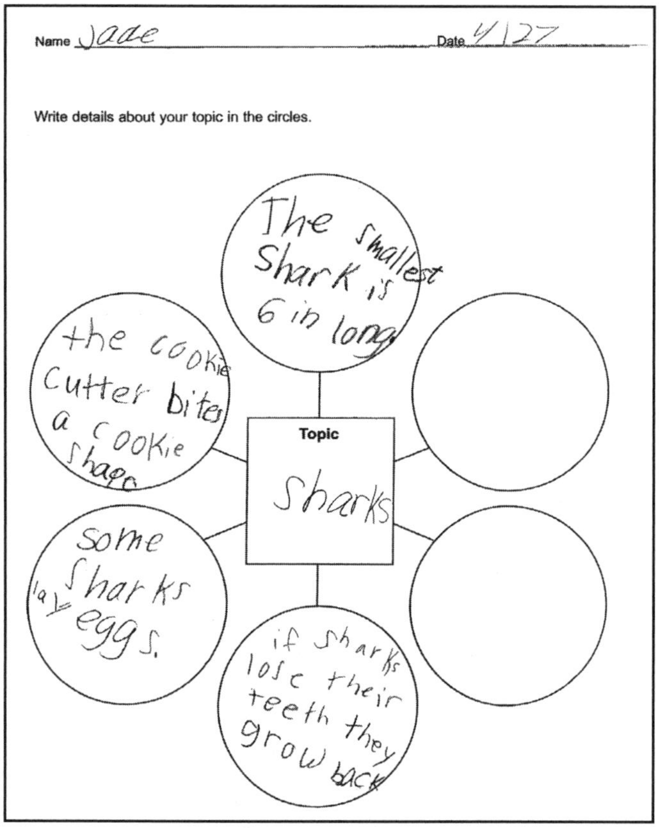

Figure 20.24 Jade's organizing web

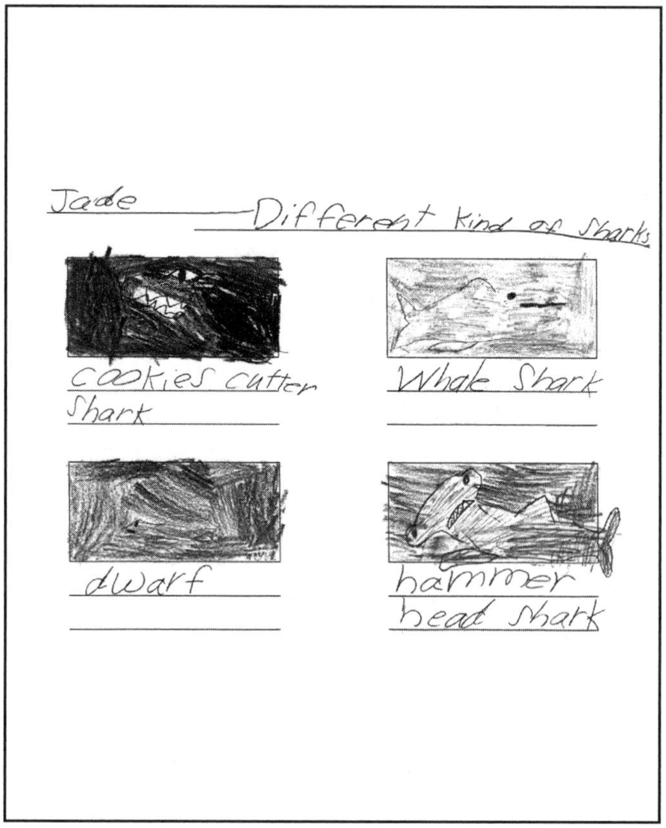

Figure 20.25 Chart from "Freaky Awesome Sharks!"

Sharks

The cookie cutter shark bites a cookie shape. The bite goes though the 2 part of the skin.

Figure 20.26 Page 1 of "Freaky Awesome Sharks!"

If a shark loses its teeth they will grow back. The teeth grow back on the out side of the mouth.

p. 2

The smallest shark is 6 in long. It can fit in your hand. It is not much biger than a gold fish.

p. 3

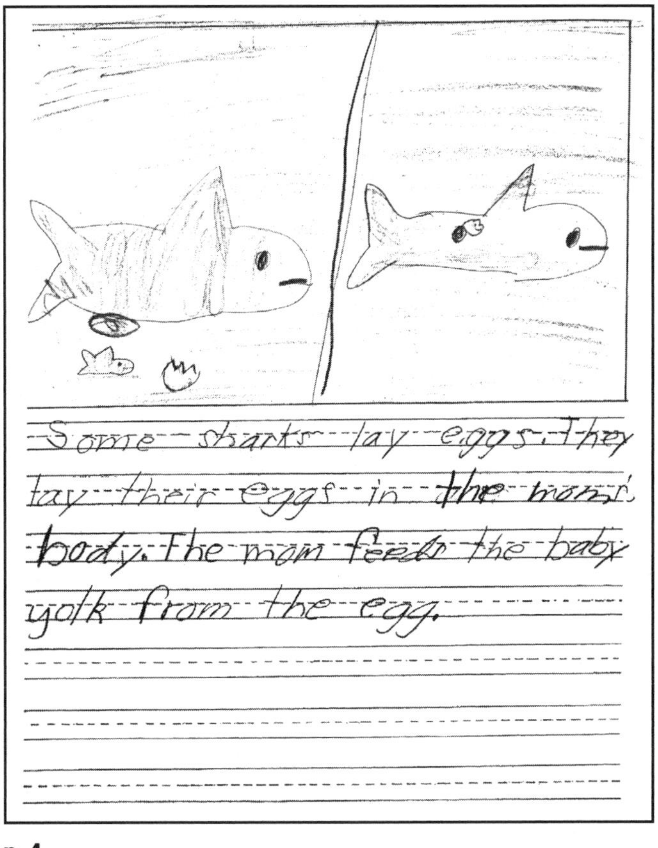
Some sharks lay eggs. They lay their eggs in the moms' body. The mom feeds the baby yolk from the egg.

p. 4

REQUIREMENTS OF REPORT WRITING

As writers of reports, students need to:

- Analyze and use mentor texts.
- Include several aspects of the same topic.
- Engage in research and organization.
- Include an introductory section, followed by more information in categories or sections.
- Present related information in categories and organize categories logically throughout the report.
- Include facts, statistics, examples, and anecdotes.
- Document statements with references (footnotes and citations).
- Use vocabulary that is specific to the topic.
- Use quotes from experts or other knowledgeable people when appropriate.
- Write with the audience in mind.
- Use headings and subheadings when appropriate.
- Use features of nonfiction texts such as sidebars if appropriate.
- Include a bibliography of sources.
- Include graphics when needed to illustrate the topic.
- Write legends and label graphics when needed.

Figure 20.27 Requirements of report writing

again the composition and publication of an expository text, each time internalizing deeper awareness of the genre and developing voice as a nonfiction writer.

Maggie's feature article about Ray Allen is shown in Figure 20.28. She is aware of journalistic style, using catchy headlines and presenting the big news at the very top followed by three sections of explanatory details. She quotes several fans as well as the subject; she mentions websites. She has headings and subheadings and a nice graphic showing the subject's three-pointers across his career. There is a nice contrast between Ray's breaking "The Big 3" and the Celtics' eighteenth championship.

Anne's feature article "Who Is Watson?" (about a computer that competed on Jeopardy) is shown in Figure 20.29. Anne has worked hard to engage readers in this short piece. She includes a labeled photograph and leads with a question for readers to consider. She has two short sections and a sidebar.

Reports and feature articles can be persuasive as well, as in Sean's feature article "Bad Foods and Restaurants" (see Figure 20.30). Sean begins by presenting his readers with some surprising facts that should engage them and make them think about their own diets. Then he attempts to persuade readers to improve their dietary habits. He has a table of contents ("Inside This Issue"), and he cites sources.

Figure 20.31 is Lila's feature article persuading readers to avoid drinking diet soda. Lila begins with a generic quote designed to help readers connect their own habits to the article. She then raises questions about the value of diet soda. In the next section, she presents statistics comparing the risks of regular and diet soda. She reveals the ingredients in diet soda and connects them to problems with teeth and high blood pressure (cause and effect). She includes a photograph with more information in a legend, and she cites her sources.

In "A Misunderstood Hobby" (see Figure 20.32), Tim's purpose is to clarify the purposes and benefits of Civil War reenactments. He has several main arguments:

- Civil War reenactments educate participants about the details of the Civil War.
- Reenactments help us learn how people in that time period lived, acted, and talked.
- We can learn more from reenactments than from textbooks because we are living the details and talking about things that happened at the time.

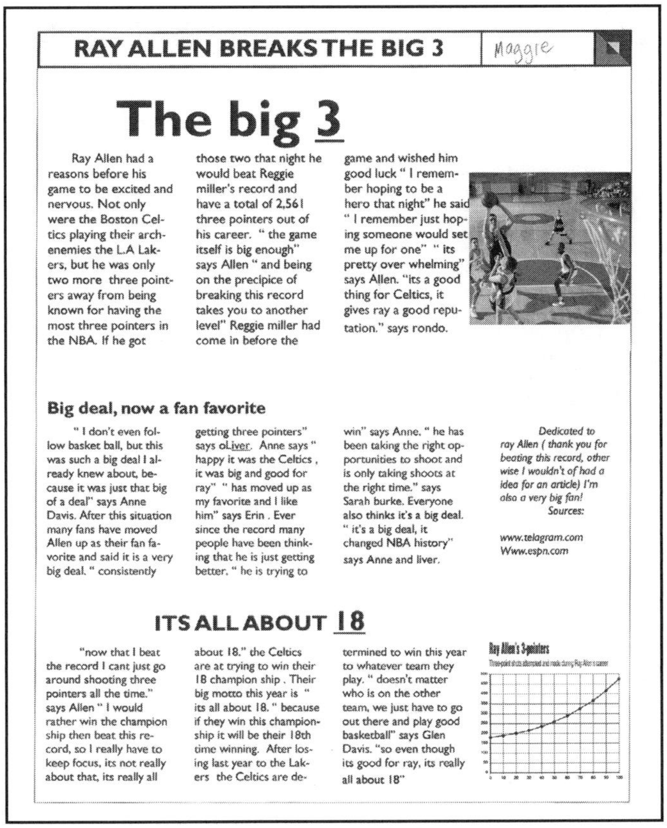

RAY ALLEN BREAKS THE BIG 3 | Maggie

The big 3

Ray Allen had a reasons before his game to be excited and nervous. Not only were the Boston Celtics playing their arch-enemies the L.A Lakers, but he was only two more three pointers away from being known for having the most three pointers in the NBA. If he got those two that night he would beat Reggie miller's record and have a total of 2,561 three pointers out of his career. " the game itself is big enough" says Allen " and being on the precipice of breaking this record takes you to another level" Reggie miller had come in before the game and wished him good luck " I remember hoping to be a hero that night" he said " I remember just hoping someone would set me up for one" " its pretty over whelming" says Allen. "its a good thing for Celtics, it gives ray a good reputation." says rondo.

Big deal, now a fan favorite

" I don't even follow basket ball, but this was such a big deal I already knew about, because it was just that big of a deal" says Anne Davis. After this situation many fans have moved Allen up as their fan favorite and said it is a very big deal. " consistently getting three pointers" says oLiver. Anne says " happy it was the Celtics , it was big and good for ray" " has moved up as my favorite and I like him" says Erin . Ever since the record many people have been thinking that he is just getting better. " he is trying to win" says Anne. " he has been taking the right opportunities to shoot and is only taking shoots at the right time." says Sarah burke. Everyone also thinks it's a big deal. " it's a big deal, it changed NBA history" says Anne and liver.

Dedicated to ray Allen (thank you for beating this record, other wise I wouldn't of had a idea for an article) I'm also a very big fan!

Sources:

www.telagram.com
Www.espn.com

ITS ALL ABOUT 18

"now that I beat the record I cant just go around shooting three pointers all the time." says Allen " I would rather win the champion ship then beat this record, so I really have to keep focus, its not really about that, its really all about 18." the Celtics are at trying to win their 18 champion ship . Their big motto this year is " its all about 18. " because if they win this championship it will be their 18th time winning. After losing last year to the Lakers the Celtics are determined to win this year to whatever team they play. " doesn't matter who is on the other team, we just have to go out there and play good basketball" says Glen Davis. "so even though its good for ray, its really all about 18"

Ray Allen's 3-pointers

Figure 20.28 Maggie's feature article about "The Big 3"

Who is Watson?

Anne

March

Perfect?

A couple of years a go did you think it would be possible for a computer to compete on "Jeopardy!"? Let alone win it, while facing Ken Jennings, famous for winning 74 games of "Jeopardy!", and Brad Rutter another champion. Watson proved to have a strategy of calling in before he knew the answer then found the answer before time ran out. Watson is not perfect, he answered Toronto when the category was "U.S Cities" the question was "What city's largest airport is named after a World War 2 hero, it's second biggest a World War 2 battle. The answer was Chicago.

The Challenge

After Watson won, I.B.M donated the million dollar prize to charity. Ken Jennings said "I've studied artificial intelligence all my life and I can say that this is a impressive and unprecended moment." I.B.M. is getting closer to the of talking, smart, computers.

Sources

Jeopardy. com

New York Times .com

In The End

Watson came in first with 77,147 dollars, next came Ken Jennings with 24,100 dollars and with a close third Brad Rutter with $21,600.

Figure 20.29 Anne's feature article "Who Is Watson?"

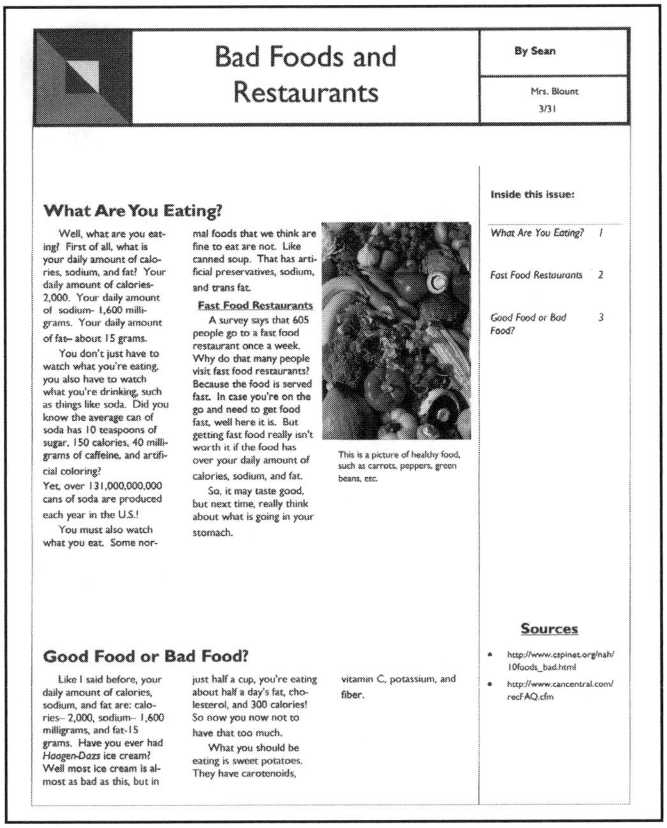

Bad Foods and Restaurants

By Sean

Mrs. Blount
3/31

What Are You Eating?

Well, what are you eating? First of all, what is your daily amount of calories, sodium, and fat? Your daily amount of calories- 2,000. Your daily amount of sodium- 1,600 milligrams. Your daily amount of fat– about 15 grams.

You don't just have to watch what you're eating, you also have to watch what you're drinking, such as things like soda. Did you know the average can of soda has 10 teaspoons of sugar, 150 calories, 40 milligrams of caffeine, and artificial coloring?
Yet, over 131,000,000,000 cans of soda are produced each year in the U.S.!

You must also watch what you eat. Some normal foods that we think are fine to eat are not. Like canned soup. That has artificial preservatives, sodium, and trans fat.

Fast Food Restaurants

A survey says that 605 people go to a fast food restaurant once a week. Why do that many people visit fast food restaurants? Because the food is served fast. In case you're on the go and need to get food fast, well here it is. But getting fast food really isn't worth it if the food has over your daily amount of calories, sodium, and fat.

So, it may taste good, but next time, really think about what is going in your stomach.

This is a picture of healthy food, such as carrots, peppers, green beans, etc.

Inside this issue:

What Are You Eating?	*1*
Fast Food Restaurants	*2*
Good Food or Bad Food?	*3*

Good Food or Bad Food?

Like I said before, your daily amount of calories, sodium, and fat are: calories– 2,000, sodium– 1,600 milligrams, and fat-15 grams. Have you ever had *Haagen-Dazs* ice cream? Well most ice cream is almost as bad as this, but in just half a cup, you're eating about half a day's fat, cholesterol, and 300 calories! So now you now not to have that too much.

What you should be eating is sweet potatoes. They have carotenoids, vitamin C, potassium, and fiber.

Sources

- http://www.cspinet.org/nah/10foods_bad.html
- http://www.cancentral.com/recFAQ.cfm

Figure 20.30 Sean's feature article "Bad Foods and Restaurants"

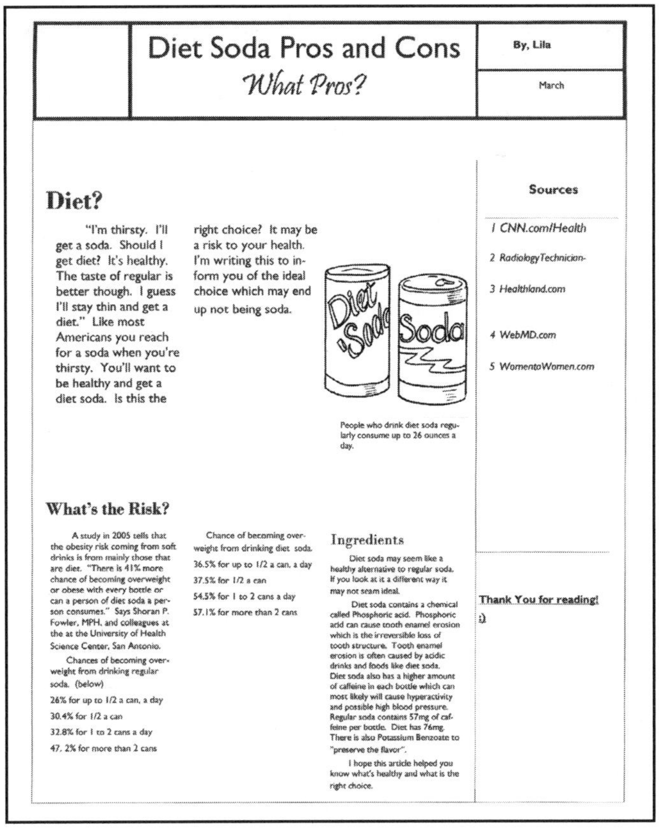

Diet Soda Pros and Cons

What Pros?

By, Lila

March

Diet?

"I'm thirsty. I'll get a soda. Should I get diet? It's healthy. The taste of regular is better though. I guess I'll stay thin and get a diet." Like most Americans you reach for a soda when you're thirsty. You'll want to be healthy and get a diet soda. Is this the right choice? It may be a risk to your health. I'm writing this to inform you of the ideal choice which may end up not being soda.

People who drink diet soda regularly consume up to 26 ounces a day.

What's the Risk?

A study in 2005 tells that the obesity risk coming from soft drinks is from mainly those that are diet. "There is 41% more chance of becoming overweight or obese with every bottle or can a person of diet soda a person consumes." Says Shoran P. Fowler, MPH, and colleagues at the at the University of Health Science Center, San Antonio.

Chances of becoming overweight from drinking regular soda. (below)

26% for up to 1/2 a can, a day

30.4% for 1/2 a can

32.8% for 1 to 2 cans a day

47. 2% for more than 2 cans

Chance of becoming overweight from drinking diet soda.

36.5% for up to 1/2 a can, a day

37.5% for 1/2 a can

54.5% for 1 to 2 cans a day

57.1% for more than 2 cans

Ingredients

Diet soda may seem like a healthy alternative to regular soda. If you look at it a different way it may not seam ideal.

Diet soda contains a chemical called Phosphoric acid. Phosphoric acid can cause tooth enamel erosion which is the irreversible loss of tooth structure. Tooth enamel erosion is often caused by acidic drinks and foods like diet soda. Diet soda also has a higher amount of caffeine in each bottle which can most likely will cause hyperactivity and possible high blood pressure. Regular soda contains 57mg of caffeine per bottle. Diet has 76mg. There is also Potassium Benzoate to "preserve the flavor".

I hope this article helped you know what's healthy and what is the right choice.

Sources

1 CNN.com/Health

2 RadiologyTechnician-

3 Healthland.com

4 WebMD.com

5 WomentoWomen.com

Thank You for reading!

:)

Figure 20.31 Lila's feature article "Diet Soda Pros and Cons"

A Misunderstood Hobby

The first time I played Bugle over a civil war battlefield was September of 2009.

In the beginning of September 2009 I started doing civil war reenactments which is just like any other hobby it is fun and expensive. You can learn many things from Civil War reenactments. Text books don't give enough details about the Civil War. When you go to Civil War reenactments you can learn the details about the Civil War, because we wear the same type of clothes, use the same kind of guns, use the same kind of instruments, sleep in the same kind of tents, and we speak about things that would have happened back then.

Some people think that Civil War reenacting is stupid or geeky, but the truth is it is a good learning experience. When people call reenactments stupid they don't understand what the reenactment represents. Also most people don't know why they should go to or even join reenactments.

I and many other people have joined Civil War reenacting to preserve history and to have a little fun doing it to. If you don't preserve history then you won't know what happened in that time period and the same mistakes that happened in the past which is actually pretty stupid. If you preserve history then you aren't as likely to make the same mistakes that were made in the past. To preserve history is to show people what it was like to live in that time period. To do that Civil War reenacters wear the same clothes, shoot the same guns, sleep in the same tents, and play the same instruments and every thing else that people would use or do in that time period.

Most of the time people want to know what battle we are doing. Well the truth is most of the time we do the small skirmishes or small battles that weren't written about and that aren't all that popular. These reenactments aren't just about \hooting guns or playing instruments. It's about the learning experience. Like I said it is a better experience then in text books. What you learn at a Civil War reenactment is how people of that people would live, act, and talk.

So go out there with this information and either join a reenactment group or go watch a reenactment to help this misunderstood hobby preserve history. If you don't preserve history stupid things can happen to start another Civil War or any other war. So go out there and do your part in preserving history. I know I have.

By Tim

Figure 20.32 Tim's feature article "A Misunderstood Hobby"

- If we preserve history, we will not be as likely (as citizens) to make the same mistakes.

Tim does not present facts or research, but he speaks from his own experiences. The piece was written as a feature article but it could also qualify as an essay.

Editorials

An editorial is an opinion piece. The writer presents an opinion and then backs it up with evidence in the form of facts or people's experiences. Often, an editorial argues against other opinions, acts, or circumstances. Sometimes an editorial presents both sides of an argument fairly, but usually the writer takes a stance.

Let's look at the process of writing an editorial using the writer's notebook of another of Katie's students. Katie has read several editorials aloud for her students to analyze, using inquiry to develop their understandings as readers and writers. Lanah has pulled out the writer's main thesis as well as the major arguments and evidence offered (see Figure 20.33).

Working on these examples allows Katie's students to see the "bones" of an editorial. The next day they look again at the editorials, plus one more, to learn to think critically about these opinion pieces (see Figure 20.34).

Later, Katie has students brainstorm topics so they can select something interesting; another page from Lanah's notebook is shown in Figure 20.35. The principle at the top is the focus of the minilesson, in which Katie helps students learn how to choose topics they care about enough to include in an editorial. Lanah has circled three potential topics.

It is important for students to consider a topic carefully; the more the writer cares about the topic, the easier it will be to compose the essay. The next day, Katie's students develop their editorial topic. Lanah notes possible aspects of the topics she is considering (see Figure 20.36), then selects greyhound racing.

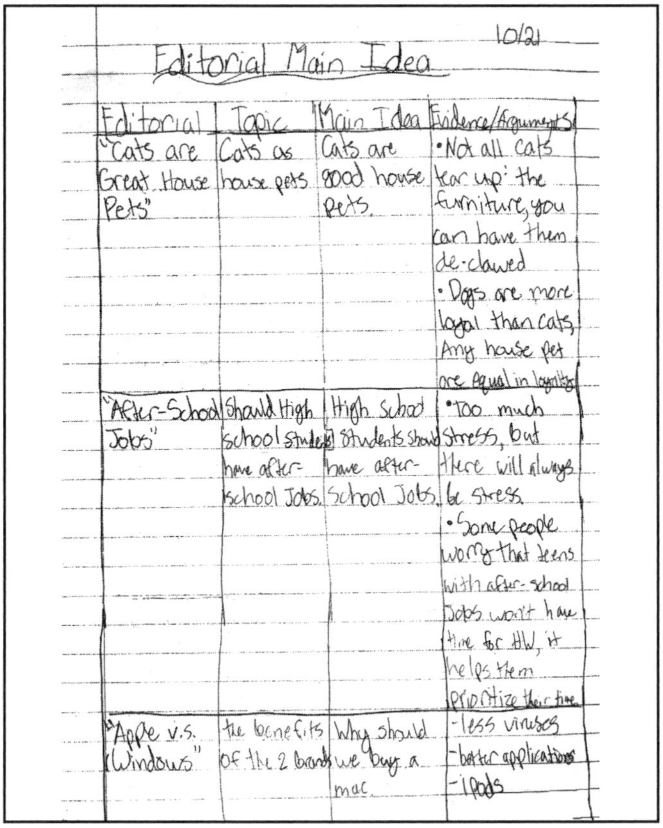

10/21

Editorial Main Idea

Editorial	Topic	Main Idea	Evidence/Arguments
"Cats are Great House Pets"	Cats as house pets	Cats are good house pets.	• Not all cats tear up the furniture, you can have them de-clawed • Dogs are more loyal than cats, Any house pet are equal in loyalty
"After-School Jobs"	Should High school students have after-school Jobs.	High school students should have after-school Jobs.	• Too much stress, but there will always be stress. • Some people worry that teens with after-school Jobs won't have time for HW, it helps them prioritize their time.
"Apple v.s. Windows"	the benefits of the 2 brands	Why should we buy a mac	- less viruses - better applications - ipods

Figure 20.33 Lanah's notes on editorial main idea

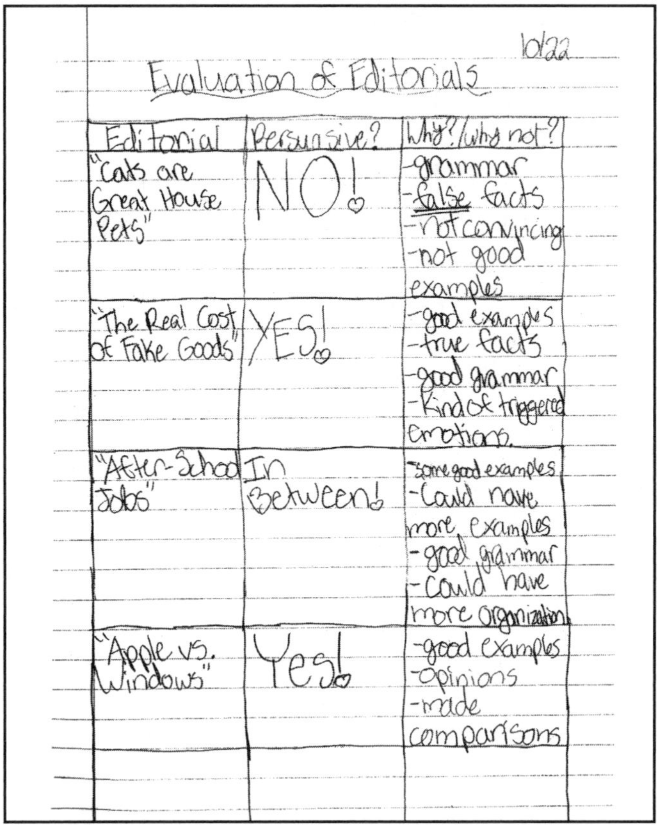

10/22

Evaluation of Editorials

Editorial	Persuasive?	Why?/why not?
"Cats are Great House Pets"	NO!	-grammar -false facts -not convincing -not good examples
"The Real Cost of Fake Goods"	YES!	-good examples -true facts -good grammar -Kind of triggered emotions.
"After-School Jobs"	In Between!	-some good examples -Could have more examples -good grammar -could have more organization
"Apple vs. Windows"	Yes!	-good examples -opinions -made comparisons

Figure 20.34 Lanah's evaluation of editorials

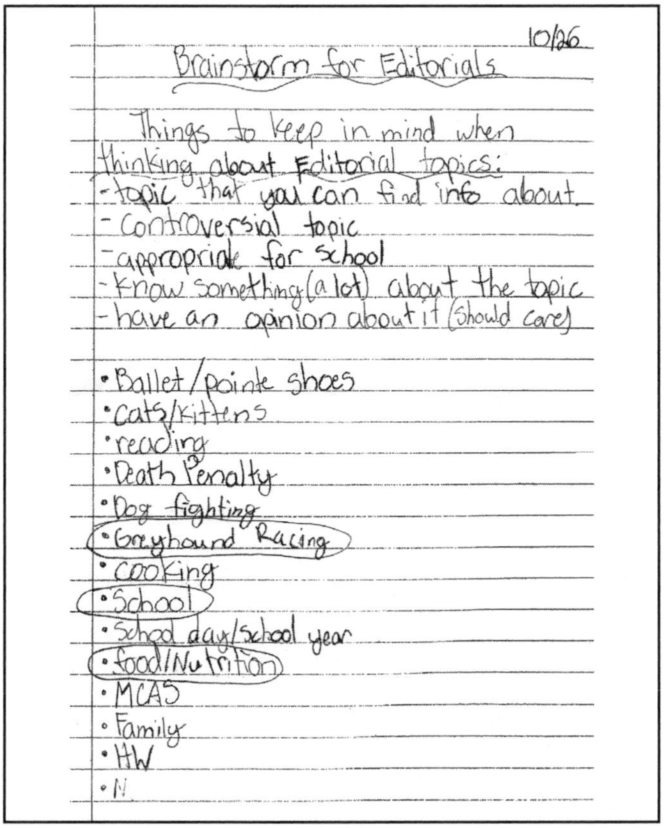

10/26

Brainstorm for Editorials

Things to keep in mind when thinking about Editorial topics:
- topic that you can find info about.
- Controversial topic
- appropriate for school
- know something (a lot) about the topic
- have an opinion about it (should care)

• Ballet/pointe shoes
• cats/kittens
• reading
• Death Penalty
• Dog fighting
• Greyhound Racing
• cooking
• School
• School day/School year
• food/Nutrition
• MCAS
• Family
• HW
• N

Figure 20.35 Lanah's editorial topic brainstorm

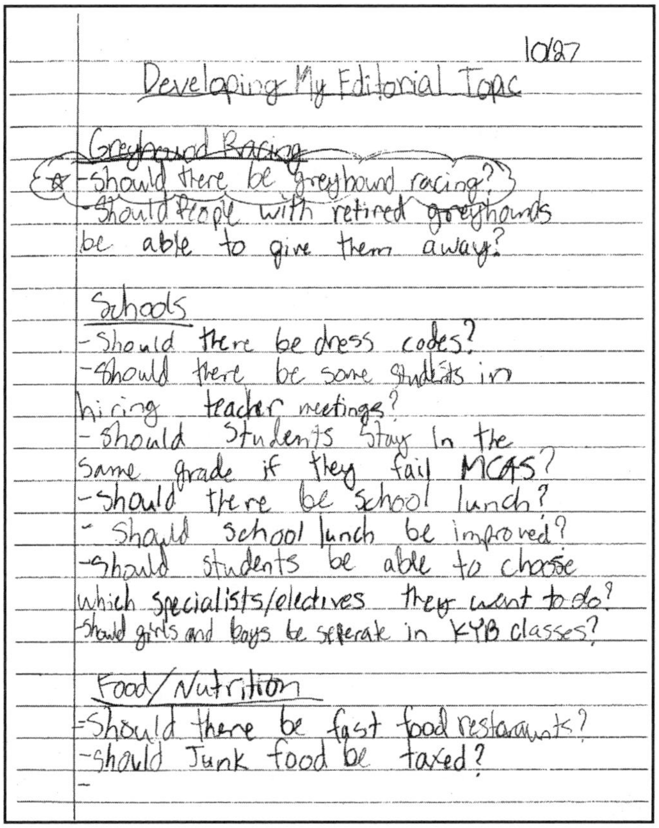

10/27

Developing My Editorial Topic

Greyhound Racing
☆ -Should there be greyhound racing?
-Should People with retired greyhounds be able to give them away?

Schools
-Should there be dress codes?
-Should there be some students in hiring teacher meetings?
-Should Students stay in the same grade if they fail MCAS?
-Should there be school lunch?
-Should school lunch be improved?
-Should students be able to choose which specialists/electives they want to do?
Should girls and boys be seperate in KYB classes?

Food/Nutrition
-Should there be fast food restaurants?
-Should Junk food be taxed?
-

Figure 20.36 Lanah develops her editorial topic

Next, Katie's students pose a question and collect information showing both sides of an argument. At this point, Lanah has begun to do research on her topic (see Figure 20.37). Learning from Katie's demonstration, she places information gained from reading into *pro* and *con* (yes and no) categories. When making an argument, students need to identify the counterarguments so that they can effectively argue against them.

Katie's next minilesson focuses on expanding information and forming a statement of point of view. Students gather information and began to draft material for their editorials. Lanah's work expanding information is shown in Figure 20.38.

Later Katie demonstrates the construction of an introductory paragraph and suggests students try a couple of options. Lanah's options are shown in Figure 20.39.

Next, Katie works with the students on organizing their editorials in a logical way. Lanah tries out some topic sentences and copies a diagram that will help her organize her editorial (see Figure 20.40). Finally, Lanah records her understandings of how to write counterarguments, along with some helpful vocabulary (see Figure 20.41).

Writing editorials has benefit beyond the task itself. In both reports and editorials, students learn to argue persuasively, which can be part of any informational writing. It is a good idea for younger students to write short pieces arguing a point so that they get used to clear, persuasive writing. They can practice writing letters to individuals and to newspapers on any issue important to them. The kind of precise instruction provided by Katie helps students write more organized, polished pieces. Heller (1991) recommends studying advertising to help students both read critically and learn the techniques of persuasion.

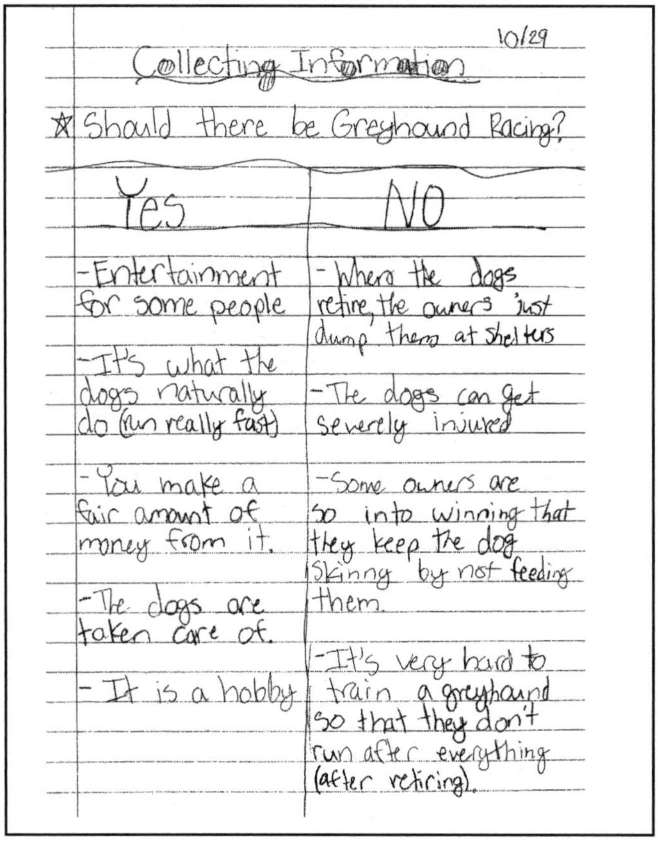
10/29

Collecting Information

☆ Should there be Greyhound Racing?

Yes	NO
- Entertainment for some people	- When the dogs retire, the owners just dump them at shelters
- It's what the dogs naturally do (run really fast)	- The dogs can get severely injured
- You make a fair amount of money from it.	- Some owners are so into winning that they keep the dog skinny by not feeding them.
- The dogs are taken care of.	- It's very hard to train a greyhound so that they don't run after everything (after retiring).
- It is a hobby	

Figure 20.37 Lanah collects information

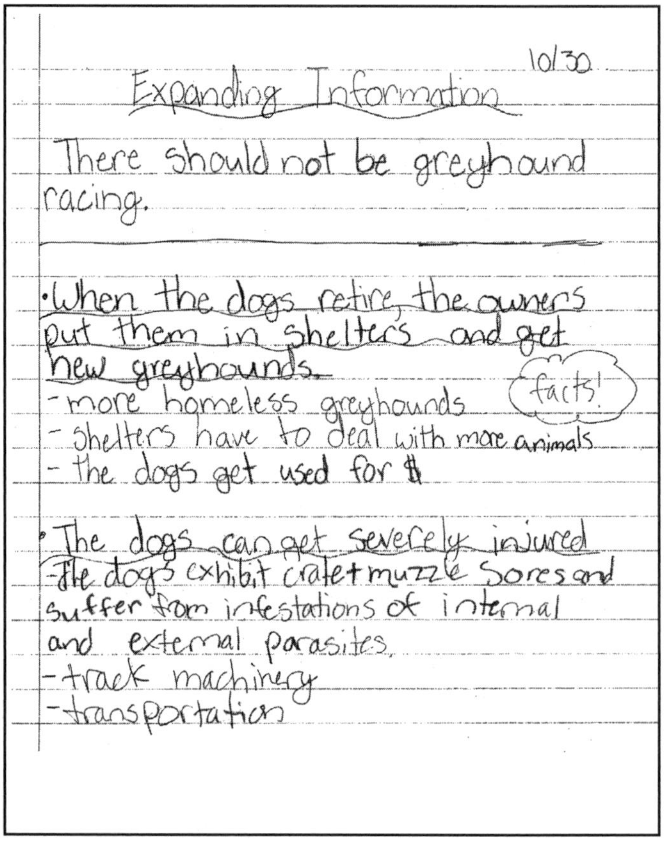
10/30

Expanding Information

There should not be greyhound racing.

• When the dogs retire, the owners put them in shelters and get new greyhounds.
- more homeless greyhounds (facts!)
- shelters have to deal with more animals
- the dogs get used for $

• The dogs can get severely injured
- The dogs exhibit crate + muzzle sores and suffer from infestations of internal and external parasites.
- track machinery
- transportation

Figure 20.38 Lanah expands her information

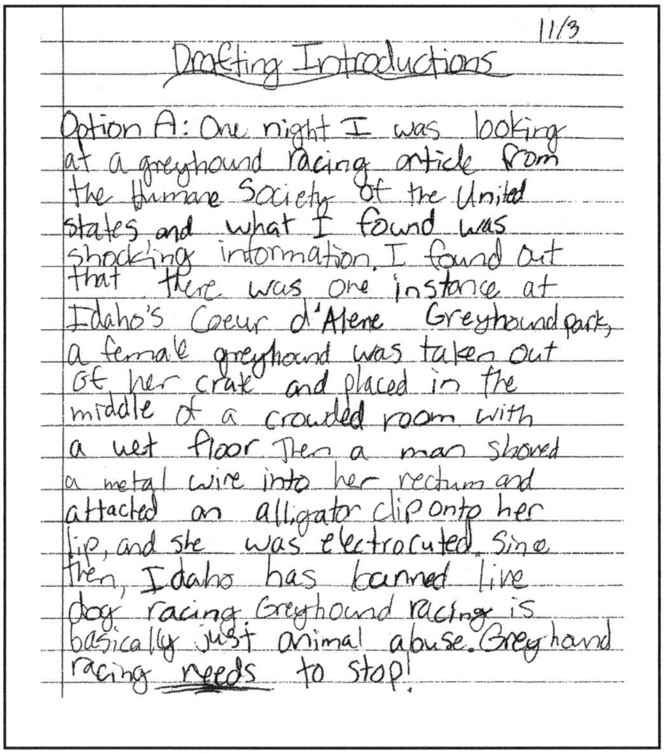
11/3

Drafting Introductions

Option A: One night I was looking at a greyhound racing article from the Humane Society of the United States and what I found was shocking information. I found out that there was one instance at Idaho's Coeur d'Alene Greyhound park, a female greyhound was taken out of her crate and placed in the middle of a crowded room with a wet floor. Then a man shoved a metal wire into her rectum and attached an alligator clip onto her lip, and she was electrocuted. Since then, Idaho has banned live dog racing. Greyhound racing is basically just animal abuse. Greyhound racing needs to stop!

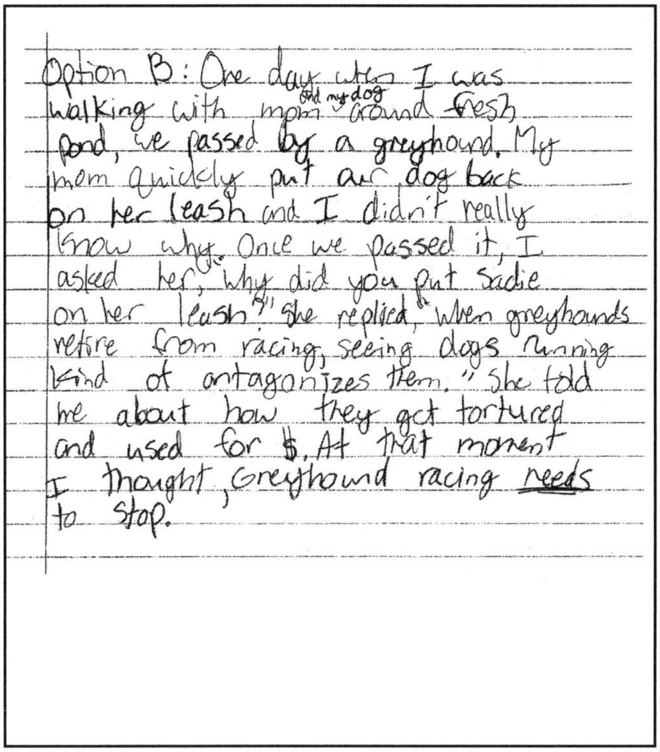
Option B: One day when I was walking with mom and my dog around Fresh pond, we passed by a greyhound. My mom quickly put our dog back on her leash and I didn't really know why. Once we passed it, I asked her, "why did you put Sadie on her leash?" She replied, "when greyhounds retire from racing, seeing dogs running kind of antagonizes them." She told me about how they get tortured and used for $. At that moment I thought, Greyhound racing needs to stop.

Figure 20.39 Lanah's options for introductory paragraphs

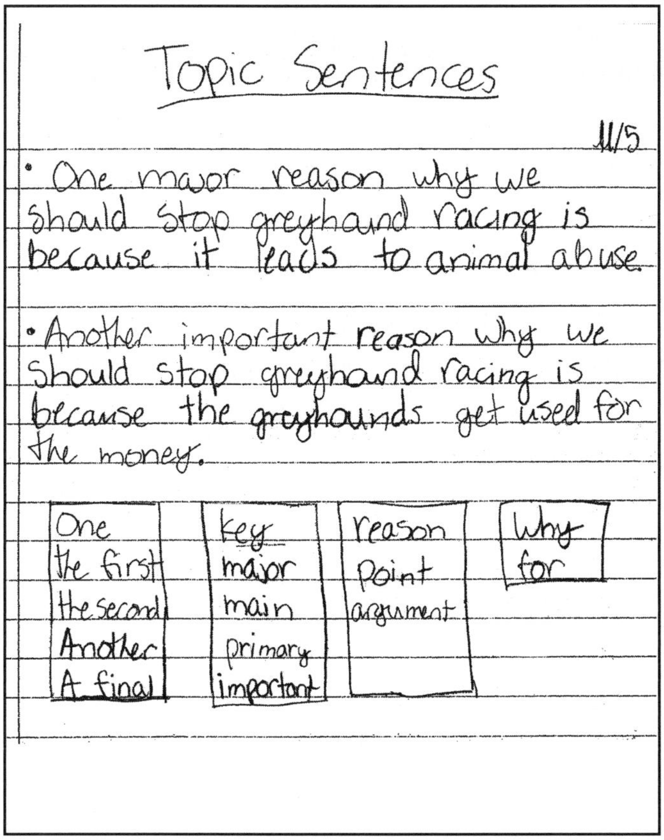
Topic Sentences

11/5

• One major reason why we should stop greyhound racing is because it leads to animal abuse.

• Another important reason why we should stop greyhound racing is because the greyhounds get used for the money.

One	key	reason	Why
the first	major	point	for
the second	main	argument	
Another	primary		
A final	important		

Figure 20.40 Lanah's topic sentences and diagram

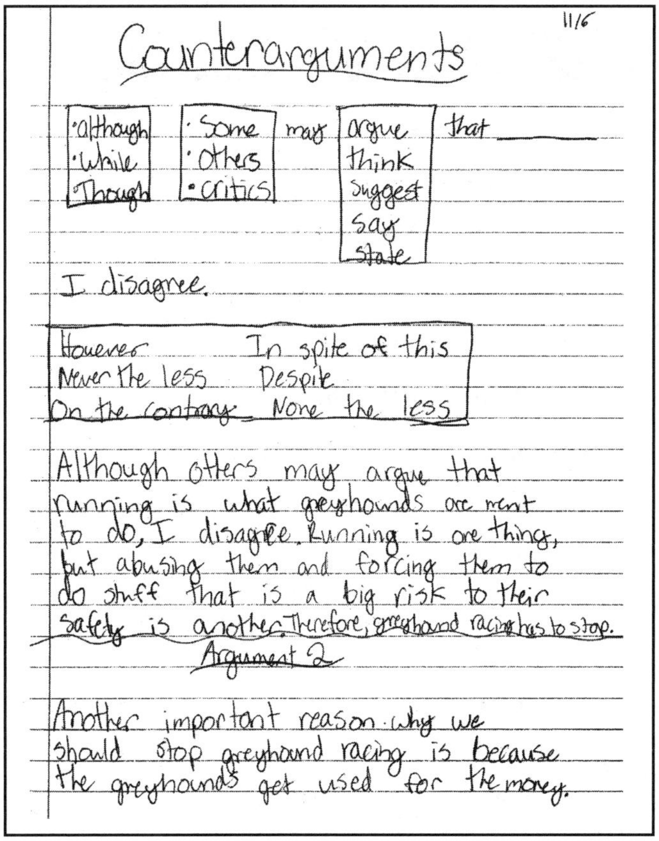
11/6

Counterarguments

although	Some	may	argue	that ______
While	Others		think	
Though	critics		suggest	
			say	
			state	

I disagree.

However	In spite of this
Never the less	Despite
On the contrary	None the less

Although others may argue that running is what greyhounds are ment to do, I disagree. Running is one thing, but abusing them and forcing them to do stuff that is a big risk to their safety is another. Therefore, greyhound racing has to stop.

Argument 2

Another important reason why we should stop greyhound racing is because the greyhounds get used for the money.

Figure 20.41 Lanah's counterarguments

Book Reviews

A book review is another kind of persuasive writing about reading. Writers must think analytically and write concisely. A book review also requires critical thinking. A book review can be approached through genre study as a type of expository writing.

After reading several book reviews, Carol's class generates a list of things they notice (see Figure 20.42).

Then Carol teaches a series of minilessons in readers' and writers' workshop to help students notice more and write their own book reviews. She draws principles from the important characteristics they have noticed:

- *Readers' workshop*: Readers notice and think about the information the writer includes in a book review to help them judge the quality of the book.
- *Writers' workshop*: Writers use what they notice about book reviews (a genre or type of writing) to help them write well in that genre.
- *Readers' workshop*: Readers notice the writer's point of view and opinions when they read a book review and they look for examples to support the opinion.
- *Writers' workshop*: In writing a review, writers give their opinions about the book and back them up with examples.
- *Readers' workshop*: Readers notice that the writer of a book review gives a short summary but does not reveal the ending or solution to the problem, so that they can think about whether they want to read the book.
- *Writers' workshop*: Writers of book reviews give a short summary of the story but do not show how the story ended; they write just enough to interest their readers.
- *Readers' workshop*: Readers notice how the writer of a book review reveals the main themes or big ideas of the book so that they can decide whether to read it.

CHARACTERISTICS OF BOOK REVIEWS

Reviewers of Books:

- Explain the genre
- Give a short summary (main events)
- Reveal the main themes
- Give basic information about characters in stories
- Tell who might enjoy the book
- Give opinion and back up with examples
- Tell the writer's point of view if important
- Tell the writer's style
- Tell information about the author or other books by the author
- Use quotes to make a point or share impact on the reader
- Tell about the conflict (fiction)
- Build interest or wonderings
- Drive home opinion at end in conclusion statement
- Leave readers thinking about the book
- Show something about self as reader
- Recommend books to certain readers (or no readers)
- May begin with a quote or question to capture the reader's attention
- Indicate any awards
- Recommend an audience by interest and/or age
- Ask cliffhanger questions
- Provide personal reactions and opinions
- Mention other books by the author
- Make comparisons with other books
- Use strong, convincing words

Figure 20.42 Characteristics of book reviews

- *Writers' workshop*: Writers of reviews think about the theme or message in the book and decide how to write about it.
- *Readers' workshop*: Readers notice how a writer of a book review builds interest in the book and invites others to read it.
- *Writers' workshop*: Writers of a book review recommend (or don't recommend) the book to the readers and they may tell readers why they would like the book (language, quotes, awards).

Figure 20.43 is an example of a book review.

Essay and Letter-Essay

Another opinion piece is the essay. Students need to understand that an essay is a literary composition that clearly states the author's point of view. Students can begin writing essays using their own experiences. For example, Emily's essay "Heroes" (see Figure 20.44) focuses on her family and friends.

Emily has crafted a beginning paragraph that states her thesis clearly (that a true hero is an ordinary person who is a friend rather than a super power). In the next two paragraphs, she offers two examples that elaborate the thesis, and in the final paragraph she implies the same comparison, stating the thesis again in a different way and elaborating on her definition of heroes. She also reveals some things about herself. (She illustrates her essay with photographs of family and friends.) As a writer of essays, Emily has made a very good beginning.

A more sophisticated example is shown in Figure 20.45. Patrick begins by introducing the topic and setting the scene for his treatment of it. In his second paragraph, He uses examples from the book and the film to show the many similarities between the book *Fahrenheit 451* and the film by the same name. He has selected significant details and correctly documents quotes by page number. He is able to write about the theme, characters, symbolism, references to Greek mythology, the larger conflict, dramatic effects, and plot. In the last paragraph, Patrick takes a position with a rationale.

Chapter 18 describes how students use a reader's notebook to write about their reading. Student writers become more and more sophisticated over time as they think analytically about texts and record their thoughts. Many teachers of middle school students use

Book Review for *The Emperor's Code*
by Gordon Korman

This book is about two orphan siblings named Amy and Dan. In this book, number 8 of the 39 Clues series, Amy and Dan Cahill travel to China on a hunch that the next clue is there. Then when they found out that their parents were Madrigals, a notorious part of their family who is known for violent behavior. In China, Amy says some bad things about their parents, and Dan runs off, then he is kidnapped, and Amy and their au pair, Nellie, don't even know who took him. Then Amy has to either get the next clue, or find Dan.

I really enjoyed this book because it was so full of suspense and it was fun to try to figure out what would happen next. I liked the main character, Amy, because like her, I am very interested in foreign places, and their geography. I also enjoyed learning about China because they have such a different writing system. This is a very interesting book, and it really kept me on my toes.

Figure 20.43 Kerry's book review

a letter-essay to prepare students for the literary essays that are required in middle and high school, as well as take them to a new level of analytic thinking.

Let's follow Liam as he plans and creates his letter-essay on *Papa's Parrot*, a short story by Cynthia Rylant. Some of his notes are shown in Figure 20.46. Figure 20.47 is a kind of map Liam makes of the story. The top row of boxes summarizes events in the story, and the line tracks the rising and falling action. On the pages shown in Figure 20.48, Liam begins to organize evidence of Harry's change in feelings. He lays out more thoughts in Figure 20.49, after a minilesson on how readers can respond in writing. Finally, Liam uses all this thinking and planning material in his notebook to produce a draft, which he then revises and edits. Figure 20.50 is his published letter-essay.

Heroes
by Emily

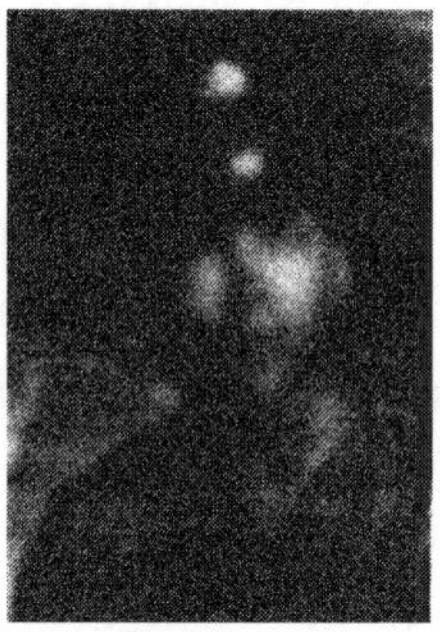

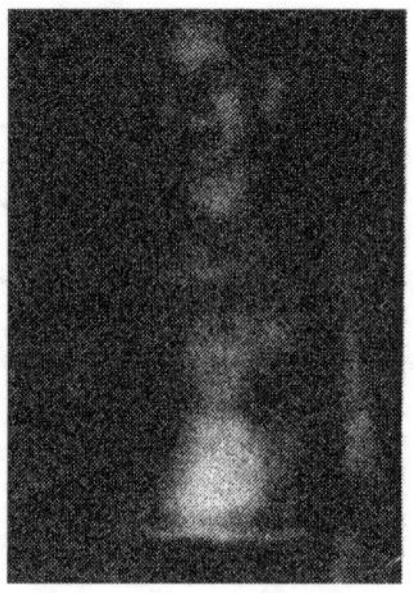

A hero to me is a person that people look up to. They help you when you are stuck in a problem and need someone to talk to. Heroes should be smart, brave, and strong with lots of courage. They should be trustworthy and true with everything they do. Heroes don't have to be super people with super powers to have people look up to them; they have just be themselves and nothing more.

My hero is my gramps. He fought cancer for about 2 years and lost in the end. When he was alive, I could talk to him about everything and anything. I trusted him with the secrets I told him and nobody else. I looked up to my gramps because he was there when others weren't. My gramps and I would always go fishing on a sunny day, hunting on a winter morning, and swimming when all the work needed to be done was done. My gramps was my hero for many reasons; he was also my best friend. Although my gramps is not here, to this day nobody can change the way I feel about him. In my heart, I can still talk to him when I need him. Whenever I go hunting, fishing or ride horses I still imagine him right next to me telling me stories about his amazing life, just like he used to.

I am a hero to my friend, Rachel. Whenever I am at her house or she's at mine, she tells me things that nobody else knows. Rachel trusts me in every way because I am a true friend to her. Sometimes when I am with my friends, she will ask to come hang out with us. When we walk places she follows me like a loyal pig follows their rightful owner. Rachel talks to me because I can understand what she is going through since I am older. Knowing that a little girl looks up to me because I am myself makes me feel very great, but it also scares me when I mess up because I don't want her to follow what I did wrong. Rachel looks up to me in every way possible and I enjoy being her hero.

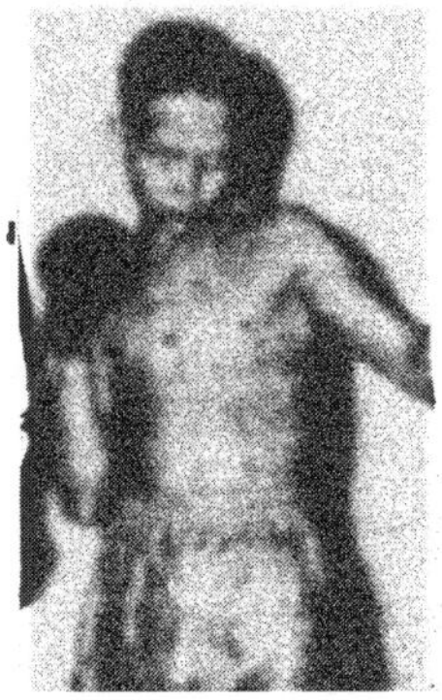

People need heroes not just to save their lives, but someone to talk to. We need heroes to look up to and be friends with in the most horrid times in our lives. People need heroes to help them feel safe and secure. Many people need heroes to understand them when they're having trouble or problems. I think heroes shape our lives because whoever our hero was or still is we try to be like them.

Figure 20.44 Emily's essay "Heroes"

Patrick

Literature versus Video; the Benefits of Both

Ray Bradbury's science fiction novel Fahrenheit 451 is a story about Guy Montag, and average fireman, taking on a journey to change society's view on books. After viewing the movie and reading the book, there are many similarities in the plot, characterization, themes, famous quotes and symbolism. Yet there are several noted differences in character portrayal, critical characters, dramatic effects, burning scenes, and emotional elements.

The book and movie share similar aspects. The plot includes Montag meeting Clarisse, who opens his eyes to the world and the details in it, convincing Montag to begin a journey to bring back literature to his world. Characterization of Guy Montag, his wife Mildred, and Beatty are depicted similarly. Guy questions himself and his happiness in both versions, Montag's wife is still self-absorbed and glued to the parlor walls, Beatty is the captain of the fire station and is still cynical. Bradbury emphasizes the theme of censorship by taking away the light in his world of darkness by burning books and leaving the population clueless. There were recognizable quotes in both versions ~~in both versions~~ of the story. When Beatty says, "Light the first page, light the second page. Each becomes a black butterfly." (pg.76) Beatty believes that the burning of books is beautiful and rare, like the sight of a black butterfly. Another quote was when the intellectuals posing as hobos quote, "Don't judge a book by its cover." (pg.155) This talks about what the condition of the intellectuals is. The men and women dress and live as hobos, but have memorized countless amounts of books between themselves, with which they plan to spread. Symbolism is present in the forms of the number 451 and the image of a salamander. The number 451 is the temperature at which paper burns, which is the lifestyle that Montag lives. The salamander is a reference to Greek mythology, in which the salamander spews flames yet is immune to the effect of fire. In both versions this is exactly what the fireman are; destructive forces not affected by the tools used to create the destruction. These similarities helped Bradbury emphasize the theme of censorship in both versions.

There are similar qualities; however, there were many differences. One example is that in the book the main character Clarisse is much younger than that of the Clarisse in the movie. Clarisse is also believed to have been killed by a car in the novel, yet she simply runs away from the police. Other critical characters in the story such as Faber, Montag's mentor, and the Mechanical Hound, are not present in the film. Major events that created dramatic effects such as the war and the bombing of the town are no longer present in the plot. The war setting helped to create tension and suspense, while the bombing of the war cleared the path for the intellectuals to spread literature once again. Without these effects available, the viewer is left wondering just how the intellectuals are going to accomplish their plan to bring books back into common life. Other notable things like the burning scenes depicted by Bradbury are changed from version to version. Bradbury makes the burning of houses a spectacle, or a circus like event, while the director has the books burnt alone in the day. Montag's home also differs in each story. On paper the reader learns that he is truly empty and alone, and not connected at all to his wife. The screen gives the story an adult appeal, filling in his emptiness with passion and romance. These differences show the details missed in the conversion, and help the reader and viewer compare the two stories.

The most similar aspect of the two stories is the basic plot, a man who strives to change his life and the life of the others around him. A major difference between the two tales is the loss of two major characters; Faber who guided Montag and the hound which made him need to change his culture. The void of these two characters is filled by Clarisse, which in turn altered her part to fit the storyline. I believe the book gives the reader a stronger storyline, and sets up a real plan on how to accomplish the revival of books. I feel the movie leaves you to wonder how this is to achieved. All in all, Bradbury made a magnificent piece of literature out of Fahrenheit 451.

Figure 20.45 Patrick's essay "Literature versus Video: the Benefits of Both"

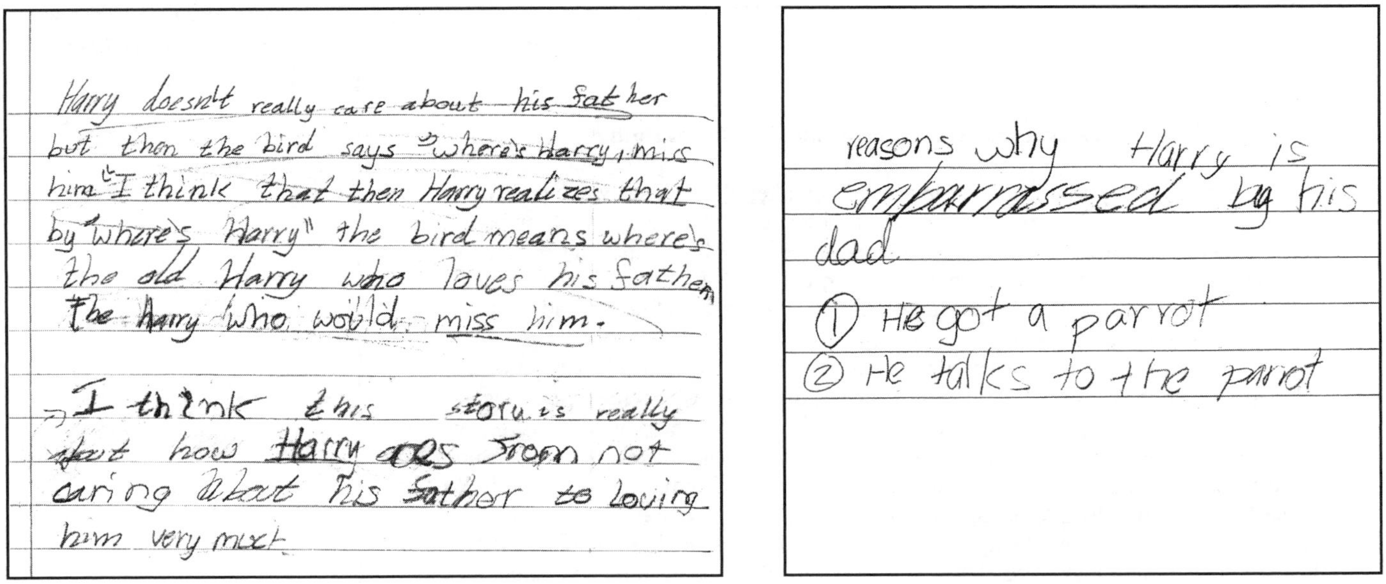

Harry doesn't really care about his father but then the bird says "where's Harry, miss him" I think that then Harry realizes that by "where's Harry" the bird means where's the old Harry who loves his father The harry who would miss him.

I think this story is really about how Harry goes from not caring about his Sather to loving him very much

reasons why Harry is embarrassed by his dad

① He got a parrot

② He talks to the parrot

Figure 20.46 Liam's notes for a letter-essay

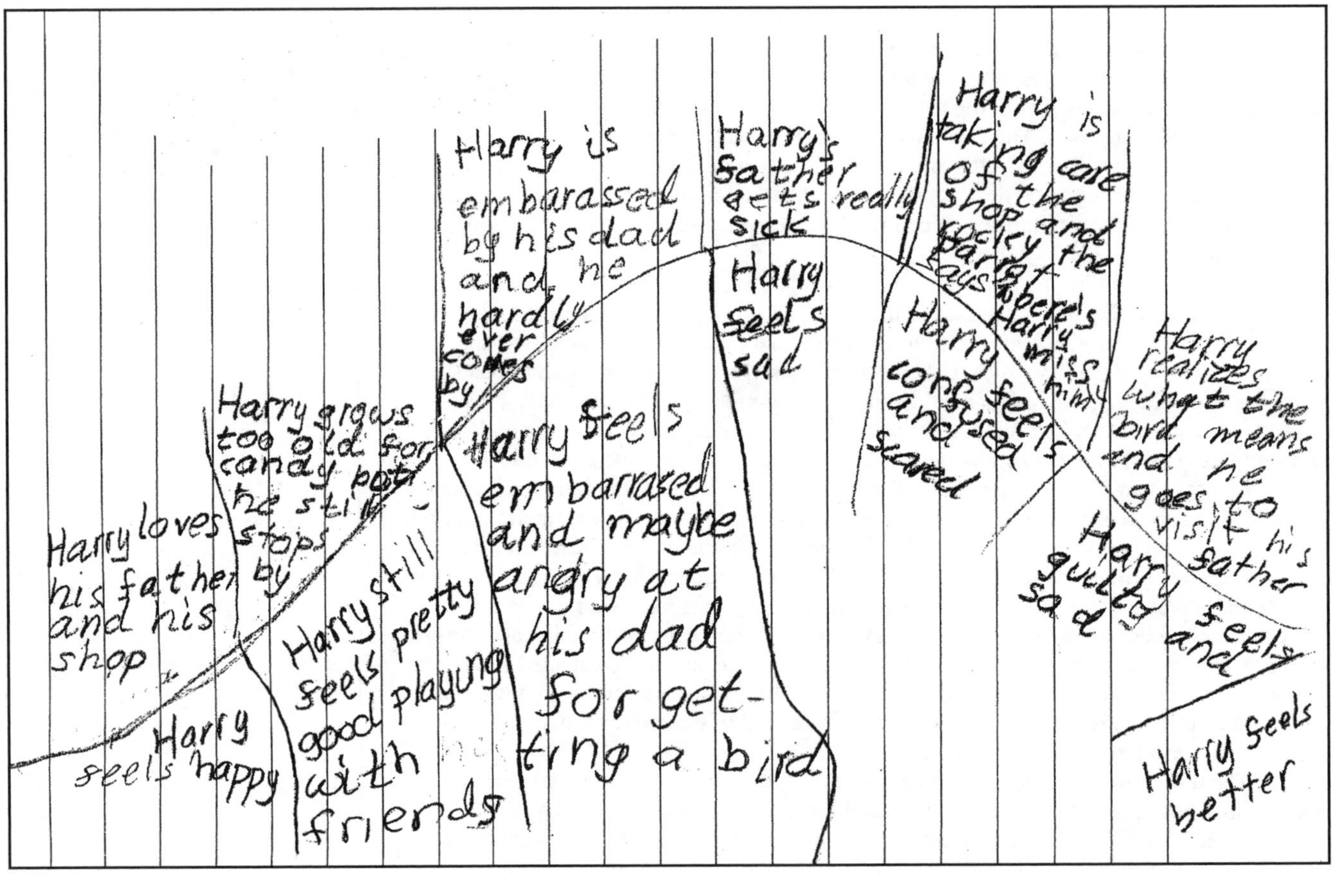

Figure 20.47 Liam's story map

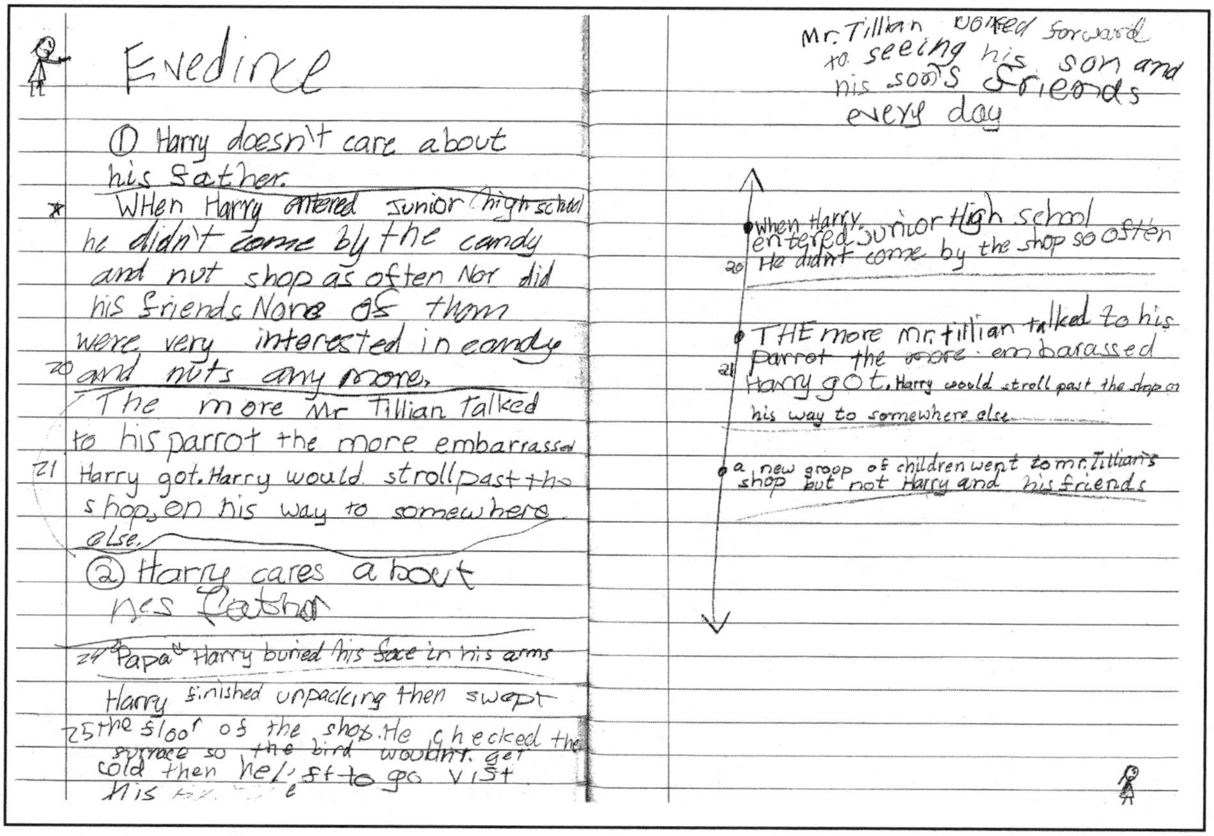

Evedince

① Harry doesn't care about his father.

WHen Harry entered Junior high school he didn't come by the candy and nut shop as often Nor did his friends None of them were very interested in candy 20 and nuts any more.

The more Mr Tillian talked to his parrot the more embarrassed 21 Harry got. Harry would stroll past the shop, on his way to somewhere else.

② Harry cares about his father

24 "Papa" Harry buried his face in his arms

Harry finished unpacking then swept 25 the floor of the shop. He checked the furnace so the bird wouldn't get cold then he left to go visit his

Mr. Tillian looked forward to seeing his son and his son's friends every day

- When Harry entered Junior High school 20 He didn't come by the shop so often
- THE more mr. tillian talked to his parrot the more embarassed 21 Harry got. Harry would stroll past the shop on his way to somewhere else.
- a new group of children went to mr. Tillian's shop but not Harry and his friends

Figure 20.48 Liam organizes his evidence

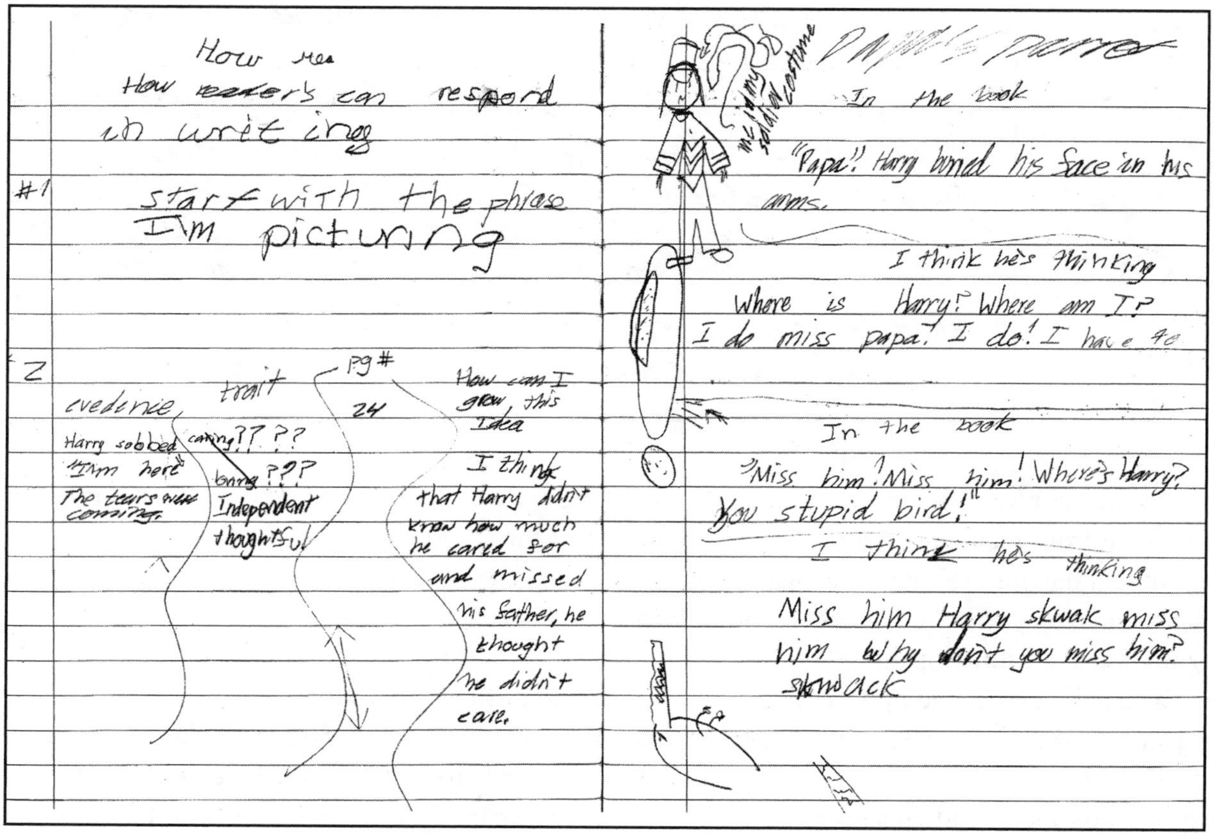

How rea
How reader's can respond in writing

#1 start with the phrase I'm picturing

2 evedence, trait, pg #, How can I grow, this Idea

Harry sobbed "I'm here" The tears were coming. — caring??? ??? boring ??? Independent thoughtful — 24 — I think that Harry didn't know how much he cared for and missed his father, he thought he didn't care.

Mr. Tillian's parrot

In the book

"Papa"! Harry buried his face in his arms.

I think he's thinking

Where is Harry? Where am I? I do miss papa! I do! I have to

In the book

"Miss him! Miss him! Where's Harry? You stupid bird!"

I think he's thinking

Miss him Harry skwak miss him why don't you miss him? skwack

Figure 20.49 Liam's notes on responding in writing

Figure 20.50 Liam's published letter-essay

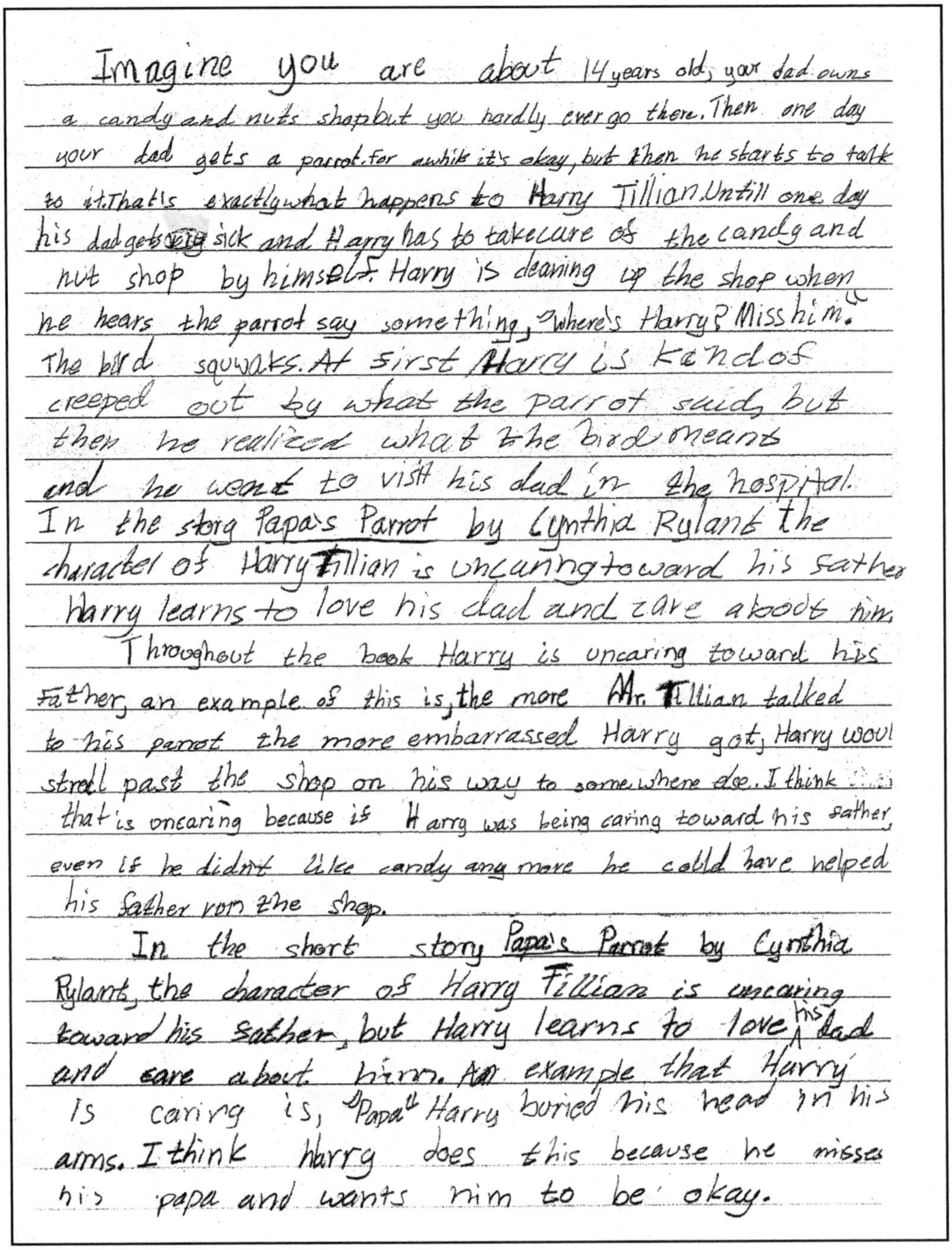

Imagine you are about 14 years old, your dad owns a candy and nuts shop but you hardly ever go there. Then one day your dad gets a parrot. For awhile it's okay, but then he starts to talk to it. That's exactly what happens to Harry Tillian. Untill one day his dad gets sick and Harry has to take care of the candy and nut shop by himself. Harry is cleaning up the shop when he hears the parrot say something, "Where's Harry? Miss him." The bird squawks. At first Harry is kind of creeped out by what the parrot said, but then he realized what the bird means and he went to visit his dad in the hospital. In the story Papa's Parrot by Cynthia Rylant the character of Harry Tillian is uncaring toward his sather Harry learns to love his dad and care about him.

Throughout the book Harry is uncaring toward his father, an example of this is, the more Mr. Tillian talked to his parrot the more embarrassed Harry got, Harry woul stroll past the shop on his way to somewhere else. I think that is uncaring because if Harry was being caring toward his sather, even if he didnt like candy any more he colld have helped his sather run the shop.

In the short story Papa's Parrot by Cynthia Rylant, the character of Harry Tillian is uncaring toward his sather, but Harry learns to love his dad and care about him. An example that Harry is caring is, "Papa" Harry buried his head in his arms. I think harry does this because he misses his papa and wants him to be okay.

Liam's notebook entries reveal the kind of thinking that goes into moving from dialogue essays to letter essays. He has examined the story closely, noticing evidence of character change in terms of dialogue and behavior. The kind of analytic thinking this young student is doing will help him in both reading and writing. Some questions you can ask about your students' essays are listed in Figure 20.51.

Nonfiction genres vary widely, and students will benefit from reading many examples and writing their own short pieces in a range of forms. All nonfiction genres can be approached as genre inquiry, in which students first notice characteristics of the texts and use those characteristics to formulate and internalize definitions of the various genres and forms. Minilessons presented in both readers' and writers' workshops help them write the best pieces they can at the time. It is more helpful to students to make many attempts, gradually learning more and improving, than to work for a very long time on one piece of nonfiction writing. A guiding principle for you

QUESTIONS TO ASK ABOUT STUDENT ESSAYS

As writers of essays, do students:

- Begin with an opening that tells the reader what is being argued or explained?
- State the thesis clearly?
- Provide a series of arguments to support the thesis?
- Provide examples from the text to support points (literary essay)?
- State arguments clearly?
- Provide details to make examples clear?
- Include illustrations, charts, or diagrams to inform or persuade readers?
- Cite the opinions or research findings of experts?
- Support opinions by facts?
- Craft sentences that clearly express the writer's beliefs?
- Write a logical, thoughtful ending?

Figure 20.51 Questions to ask about student essays

as a teacher is to help students select topics they care about. Assigning nonfiction writing is an inevitable part of school, but allowing students to choose the topic will engage them and they will learn more.

Poetic Genres

Young writers have traditionally found writing poetry one of their most onerous assignments, but in recent years teachers from elementary to high school have been introducing poetry through personal poetry anthologies. Students read or listen to a wide variety of poems several times, select those that mean something to them, copy or glue them into their notebook, and illustrate them, thus creating a personal collection that is very meaningful. Students who have been immersed in poetry they have selected for themselves find it much easier to write poems themselves.

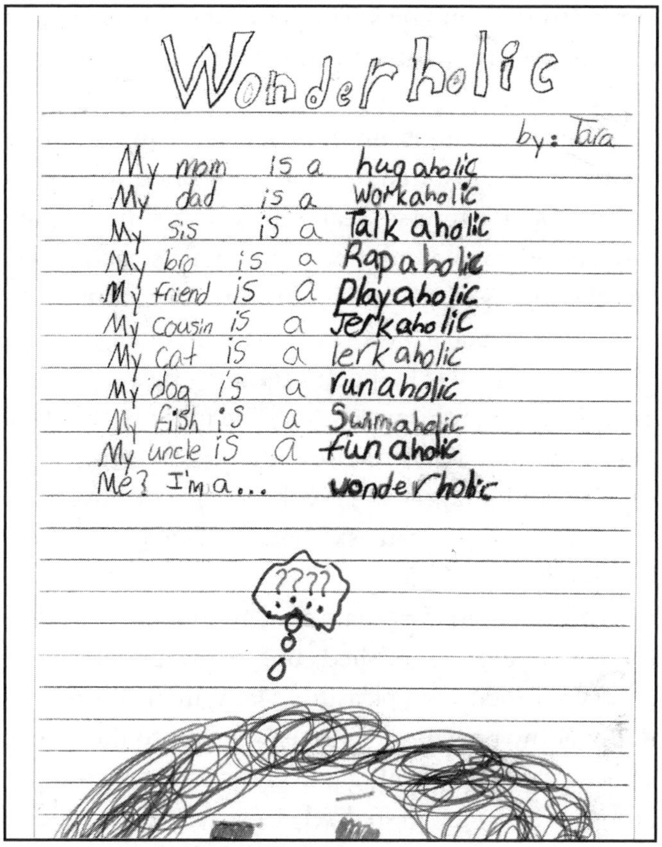

Figure 20.52 Tara's poem "Wonderholic"

Poetry, like prose, is a form of writing, and as discussed in Chapter 13, it can appear in many different genres—realistic fiction, historical fiction, nonfiction, and others. Poetry also has a wide variety of structural forms, and students can experience all of them through inquiry as well as by trying to write them.

Young poets need to understand that studying mentor texts will help them write their own poems. They can understand poetry as a unique way of communicating feelings and ideas, and as they explore the different forms they can compare how they communicate moods. Poems are all about symbolism and sensory images, communicated through language that is different from ordinary language. You want your students to be able to recognize the forms of poetry. Trying to write poems will help students "get inside" the forms and learn how they work.

Writing poetry does not have to be hard. The most important thing is for students to enjoy the process and their creations. In "Wonderholic" (see Figure 20.52), Tara plays with words to produce a poem about her family, friends, and pets. The patterns in this poem are pleasing, as are the descriptive words and sentiments of the poem.

A more serious example is Deon's poem "You" (see Figure 20.53), inspired by his reading about homeless people. Deon expresses real feelings in a simple, spare way. His poem does not rhyme, but it has structure. He has chosen his words and his line breaks carefully.

Poems can take the form of memoir; often students find it easiest to write poetry recalling pleasant times and using sensory imagery. In "The Little Beach" (see Figure 20.54), Rebecca uses alliteration, repetition, rhythm, and imagery to describe a place she loves.

Questions you can ask about students' poetry are listed in Figure 20.55.

Few poets are fortunate enough to become widely known or even published, but many people write poetry for their own pleasure. Many, many more find that reading poetry adds real enjoyment to their lives. The more your students get to know poetry by reading and writing it, the more likely they are to continue to read and write poetry throughout their lives.

You

You have a house,
Good clothes,
But look at me.
Do I?
I don't look as good as you,
No roof over my head,
Only sky, rain, darkness,
And most of all,
Lonely forever.

By Deon

Figure 20.53 Deon's poem "You"

The Little Beach
By Rebecca

Salty sand
soft as a cloud
slowly shifting
to and fro
to and fro

Ocean rocking
bobbing rowboats
pulling sand
in and out
in and out

Seagulls crying
screaming loudly
swirling, twisting
getting ready to steal...
someone's lunch!

Figure 20.54 Rebecca's poem "The Little Beach"

QUESTIONS TO ASK ABOUT STUDENTS' POETRY

As poets, do students:

- Select subjects that have strong meaning for the writer?
- Collect language and images that can be used as a resource for poetry?
- Use words to evoke imagery and feelings?
- Select the form appropriate to the meaning and purpose of the poem?
- Write poetic texts in response to other poems and fiction and nonfiction texts?
- Remove extra words to clarify the meaning and make the writing more powerful?
- Use repetition, refrain, rhythm, and other poetic techniques?
- Use figurative language such as alliteration, personification, onomatopoeia, or metaphor?
- Help readers see the world in a new way?

Figure 20.55 Questions to ask about students' poetry

Functional Genres

Writing in functional genres includes much of the writing we do as part of our everyday lives. Functional genres include formal letters (including letters to the editor), test writing (extended responses, essays, and short answers), and writing about reading, which is discussed in detail in Chapter 18.

Formal Letters

Students begin by writing friendly letters, and as they learn the purposes and general form of letters, they move on to formal letters. The letters students write in their reader's notebook as a response to reading are very helpful. They are friendly letters, but students write one each week, so they get lots of authentic practice (see Chapter 18).

Eventually, students should learn to write a well-crafted, clear, and concise formal letter for a number of purposes, including:

- Expressing opinions in a letter to the editor of a newspaper, magazine, or website.
- Writing letters to authors, artists, and other people with whom they are not personally acquainted.
- Writing letters of application for jobs.
- Writing business letters of all kinds.
- Writing letters in support of causes or people.

These days, people tend to write fewer traditional letters because much written communication takes place electronically. Email varies from quick, informal notes to something that resembles traditional letters. All that means is it is more important than ever to communicate clearly in writing. Except in very informal, friendly exchanges between friends, even electronic forms of communication like email, websites, and blogs require good writing. In business, professional, or more formal social exchanges, an individual does not make a good impression or get points across through hastily written, disorganized communications with poor spelling or grammar. Students, and all of us, need to remember that words in electronic media last forever.

Lists and Procedures

We read and write lists and procedures every day—directions, recipes, how-to texts, and operating manuals. Increasingly, these procedural texts are in electronic forms, but the craft is the same. Procedural texts need to be clear, sequential, descriptive, and easy to follow. Some people make a career out of procedural writing, but all of us need to know how to write directions. Even younger students will enjoy writing directions for something that they know well, as in Carli's "How to Tie Your Shoes" (see Figure 20.56).

Some students' how-to texts can be expanded and published, especially if they focus on procedures that other students find interesting. There are a number of great how-to books you can use as mentor texts (see the list at the end of Chapter 10).

Studying procedural texts, students notice aspects of the genre like these:

- Tell readers what the procedure is.
- Usually number or list steps.
- Describe the steps in order.
- Explain what happens in each step.
- Use lots of bullets, diagrams, and other illustrations.
- Explain everything readers need to know (don't make them guess at steps).
- Write in a very clear way.
- Show readers what will happen at the end if its done right.

The ability to write clear directions is valuable in real life in all kinds of ways. It is part of being a competent communicator in the social and business world and well worth exploring in the classroom.

Test Writing

In *Guiding Readers and Writers* (2001) we discuss understanding the "testing genre" in order to prepare students for high-quality test-taking performances. To perform well on tests, students first must be competent readers and writers, and that is the goal of literacy education. But student readers and writers must also be able to display knowledge and skills that will be

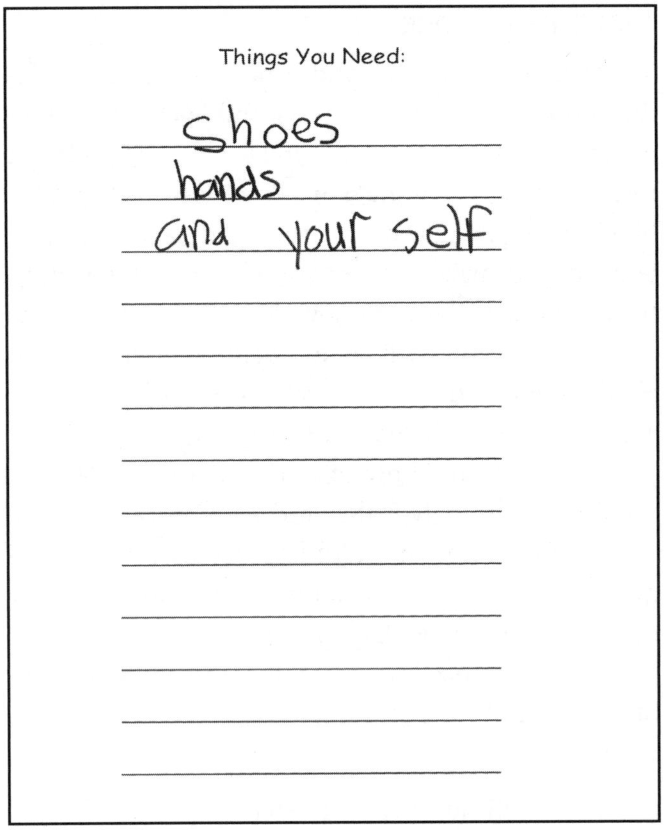
Things You Need:
Shoes
hands
and your self

Figure 20.56 “How to Tie Your Shoes” by Carli, **p. 1**

1. get your Shoes and hold both ends.
2. Make a X With the lases and put one lases under and pull.
3. Make 1 one Bunny ear.

p. 2

4. you take the one 1 with no Bunny ear and rap it arownd.
5. you pull it Not to tight.
How to Dooble Knot take both bunny ears Make a X.

p. 3

pull and you did it
You tide your Shoe all done!!!
It will not come out.

p. 4

expected of them in test performance, and that means understanding the language and requirements of tests.

A test is a genre—"a type of discourse that is distinguishable by characteristics of form, style, and content" (Fountas and Pinnell 2001, 463). Tests vary, of course, but students can learn to notice or detect some common patterns and act accordingly. For example, if they have a chance to read several sample tests, students might notice:

- Some words are used in very specific ways (*selection, summary, answer, which, why*).
- There will be questions that must be answered.
- Sometimes the question will be in a statement form.
- Sometimes you are asked to give your opinion.
- Unless there are graphics, the print is all you have from which to answer the questions.
- You may be asked to write what you have learned from looking at a map, diagram, chart, or graph.
- Selections usually have no pictures.
- Selections are usually short and not related to one another.
- On some tests, you may have to read two or more related selections and write your answers with both (all) selections in mind.
- There are several kinds of questions: (1) multiple choice—more than one may seem right but choose the best answer; (2) short response—write a very concise answer that goes right to the question; and (3) long response—think and organize before you write.
- You have to stick to the topic you are asked to write.
- You have to write in the genre you are asked to write.
- Sometimes you are asked to support your answers with excerpts from the selection.

Kelley and Clausen-Grace (2010) found that students who had spent time consciously examining features of nonfiction texts were able to write better predictions and learn more from reading the text. So

it's a good idea to have students stop and quickly write predictions about what they are going to learn or to make a quick list of what they learned from a text.

Heller (1991) claims that "the process of summary writing may be the ultimate example of making connections between reading and writing" (p. 158.) Summaries require writers first to read and fully comprehend the prose and then to reduce the text to its *gist,* or main ideas. Taking three to five minutes to write a summary and then comparing and analyzing it with a partner can give students facility with this kind of writing, which may be required on its own or as part of a longer response.

Just as you do with other genres, you can teach minilessons on test genres, work with test questions during guided reading, and have students practice all kinds of responses in their reader's or writer's notebook. For example, in guided reading, you could use a few quick questions like these from *Prompting Guide, Part 2*:

- Find the sentence that tells you ______.
- Say (or quickly write) what this section is mostly about (summarize).

- Who is telling the story?
- The story is being told form the perspective of ______.
- _____ says "______." What do you think that means?
- What does the writer want you to think about the topic?
- Write a quick summary of the text.
- Summarize the main ideas of the text in your notebook.
- What do these two books have in common? How are they different?
- What does this section tell you about ______? How do you know?

Learning the test reading/writing genres need not take a great deal of time away from the mainstream literacy curriculum. In general, tests of writing require the same processes that all writers use, so we can embed test writing into classroom instruction. However, in test writing, students rarely can choose their own topics but must instead write on an assigned topic within a defined period of time. During interactive read-aloud or the workshop minilesson, we can have students practice writing quickly in their reader's or writer's notebook in response to questions about characters, plot, craft, text organization, key understandings, summaries, comparisons, problems/solutions, issues raised, significance of topic, and so on. An example of test writing is provided in Figure 20.57. Figure 20.58 lists some questions you can ask about your students' test writing.

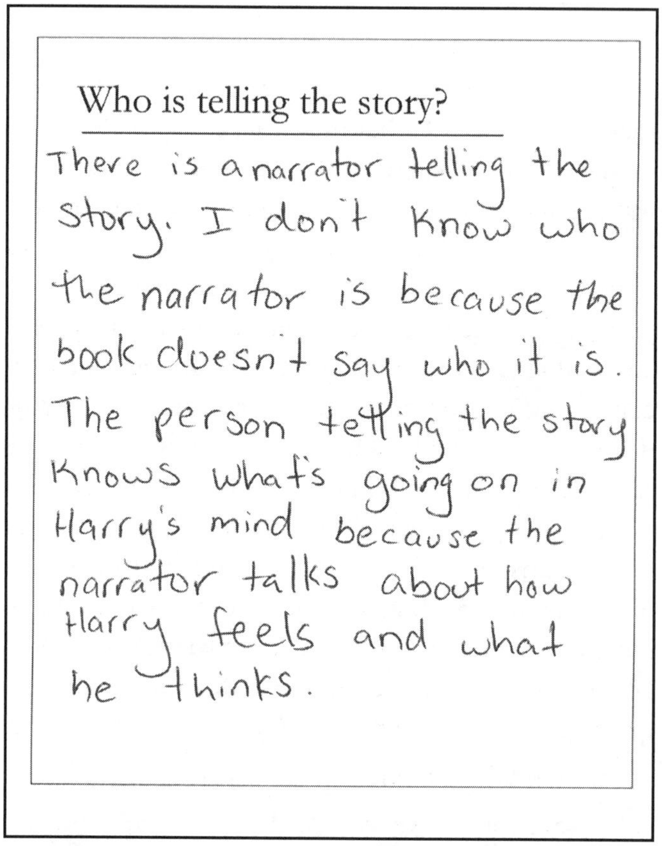
Who is telling the story?

There is a narrator telling the story. I don't know who the narrator is because the book doesn't say who it is. The person telling the story knows what's going on in Harry's mind because the narrator talks about how Harry feels and what he thinks.

Figure 20.57 Sample of test writing

QUESTIONS TO ASK ABOUT STUDENTS' TEST WRITING

As test writers, are students able to:

- Analyze prompts or questions to determine what is being asked?
- Write concisely and to the direction of the question or prompt?
- Write a clear, focused response with no extraneous information?
- Write a response that evaluators will be able to understand?
- Articulate the qualities of a written response that will get a good evaluation?
- Elaborate on points or support them with evidence when appropriate?
- State a point of view and support it with evidence?
- Restate a claim and support it with further evidence?
- Compose a strong lead and concluding sentences?
- Avoid repeating the same points over and over?
- State alternate points of view and the evidence for each?
- Critically examine alternate points of view and take a stance, with evidence?

Figure 20.58 Questions to ask about students' test writing

Writing and Its Connection to Reading

There is a definite connection between reading and writing; the processes are similar. But at the same time, they are different. They are distinct cognitive processes. Readers and writers call on the same sources of knowledge, but understanding a text and creating one are different processes.

As readers, you are always noticing characteristics of the texts you read, and this works to your advantage as writers. Ray says, "I read like a teacher of writing even when I'm reading the morning paper, and I see rich text possibilities all around me" (2006, 64). Ray advises you to be on the lookout for all kinds of texts that can be used as interesting examples for young writers—catalog copy, articles, pamphlets, short stories, books, magazines, excerpts, Internet sites. She advises that when planning a study, the stack of texts that students experience will "form the vision toward which students will draft, and that stack will help students know where their writing 'fits' into the larger world of writing" (65).

The ultimate goal of connecting reading and writing through genre study is to help students understand that mentor texts of all kinds can help—and impel—them to take on the task in an independent way. Ray (2006) describes students who have learned to collect their own examples. After a great deal of demonstration and group work, students can:

- Decide on a topic that is compelling to them.
- Select the appropriate genre or genres.
- Search for mentor texts in the classroom library, school library, or Internet.
- Evaluate the texts as to their quality and usefulness.
- Examine the mentor texts and make a list (mentally or on paper) of the characteristics they want their own writing to demonstrate in the genre.
- Plan and start to write the piece.
- Use mentor texts as resources (not to copy but to remember what writers do).
- Compare their finished piece to the mentor texts (what they did as a writer and what they chose not to do).

It will take many experiences for student to become independent in this process. They need to know how to use examples rather than cutting and pasting from the Internet or simply copying. Thoughtful connections between reading and writing can help them find their voice and at the same time strengthen their ability to read like writers.

Suggestions for Professional Development

1. With a group of grade-level colleagues, select a genre and plan writing minilessons. You may want to look at your grade-level standards and/or the writing genres that will be tested.
2. Collect a group of mentor texts in the genre.
3. Read the texts together and generate a list of the criteria for students' writing. (This would be same as noticing characteristics except that you are going to intentionally teach for them and then assess student writing using them. You'll need to decide which features you can expect students at the grade level to demonstrate.)
4. Make a list of questions such as the ones in this chapter.
5. Develop a list of principles that can be the focus of a series of minilessons.
6. Plan a genre inquiry using the mentor texts over a series of days. The same set of mentor texts can be used in each minilesson focused on a different aspect of the genre (lead, dialogue, organization, word choice, conclusion, nonfiction text features, etc.).
7. Have each of your colleagues implement the plan by doing the genre study and then using the mentor texts in writers' workshop.
8. Ask colleagues to bring students' work in process or finished pieces to a follow-up meeting to share progress. Possible points to discuss:
   - How did the inquiry process prepare your students to write in the genre?
   - How did their noticings in reading impact their writing in the genre?
   - How were your writing minilessons effective? What would you change in the future?
   - What did your students learn from writing within the genre that they will take back to their reading of that genre?

Appendix

Access to Additional Resources on the F&P Resources Site, including:

- Lists of series and sequels books
- Links to sites listing various award-winning books
- Printable Genre Thinkmarks

How to Access the *Genre Study* F&P Resources Site

STEP 1. Go to www.fountasandpinnell.com/resources

STEP 2. Follow the directions on the site to login and register for access to to your e-product

STEP 3. When prompted use fpgenreappendix12 as the "Product Code"

Mentor Texts, Grades K–1

POTENTIAL GENRE STUDIES FOR GRADES K–1 In Chapter 15, we discuss the genres that students at each grade level might study through inquiry, as well as other genres they might be exposed to through read-aloud, book clubs, or independent reading. (see Figure 15.3, p. 242). Within these genres, students might be reading many different forms of texts (e.g., picture books, plays, and series books) as well as different types of fiction (e.g., mysteries, adventure stories, and humorous stories). The mentor texts lists for grades K-1 reflect these genre study suggestions, but use your own judgment regarding what your individual students are ready for, and utilize the mentor text lists for other grades and genres as you see fit.

AUTHOR	TITLE
Realistic Fiction	
Bang, Molly	*When Sophie Gets Angry – Really, Really Angry...*
Chodos-Irvine, Margaret	*Ella Sarah Gets Dressed*
Daly, Niki	*Jamela's Dress*
Frazee, Marla	*Roller Coaster*
Graham, Bob	*A Bus Called Heaven*
Graham, Bob	*How to Heal a Broken Wing*
Harper, Dan	*Sit, Truman!*
Harper, Isabelle	*My Cats Nick and Nora*
Harper, Isabelle	*My Dog Rosie*
Harper, Isabelle	*Our New Puppy*
Henkes, Kevin	*A Good Day*
Keats, Ezra Jack	*The Snowy Day*
Manning, Maurie J.	*Kitchen Dance*
Messner, Kate	*Over and Under the Snow*
Mora, Pat	*Gracias/Thanks*
Myron, Vicki and Witter, Bret	*Dewey: There's a Cat in the Library!*
Newberry, Clare Turlay	*Marshmallow*
Newman, Leslea	*Miss Tutu's Star*
Raschka, Chris	*A Ball for Daisy*
Rylant, Cynthia	*Night in the Country*
Shannon, David	*No, David!*
Takabayashi, Mari	*I Live in Tokyo*
Tarpley, Natasha Anastasia	*I Love My Hair*
Williams, Vera	*A Chair for My Mother*
Folktales	
Aylesworth, Jim	*The Gingerbread Man*
Brett, Jan	*Gingerbread Baby*
Brett, Jan	*The Mitten*
Bruchac, Joseph	*How Chipmunk Got His Stripes*
Bruchac, Joseph	*Raccoon's Last Race*

**Common Core State Standards Exemplar Text*

AUTHOR	TITLE
Dwyer, Mindy	*Coyote in Love*
Galdone, Paul	*Henny Penny*
Galdone, Paul	*The Little Red Hen*
Hagrogian, Noni	*One Fine Day*
MacDonald, Margaret Read	*Tunjur! Tunjur! Tunjur! A Palestinian Folktale*
Morgan, Pierr (illustrated by)	*The Turnip: An Old Russian Folktale*
Moroney, Lynn	*Baby Rattlesnake*
Pinkney, Jerry	*Little Red Riding Hood*
Shulevitz, Uri	*The Treasure**
Spirin, Gennady	*Goldilocks and the Three Bears*
Stevens, Janet	*Tops and Bottoms**

Fairy Tales

Alderson, Brian	*Thumbelina*
dePaola, Tomie	*Strega Nona*
Galdone, Paul	*The Magic Porridge Pot*
Isadora, Rachel	*Hansel and Gretel*
Isadora, Rachel	*The Princess and the Pea*
Isadora, Rachel	*Rapunzel*
Isadora, Rachel	*The Twelve Dancing Princesses*
Isadora, Rachel	*The Fisherman and His Wife*
Littledale, Freya	*The Magic Fish*
Karlin, Barbara	*Cinderella*
Kellogg, Steven	*Jack and the Beanstalk*
Knight, Hillary	*Cinderella*
LaMarche, Jim	*The Elves and the Shoemaker*
MacDonald, Margaret Read	*The Great, Smelly, Slobbery, Small-Tooth Dog*
Meade, Holly	*The Rabbit's Bride*
Philip, Neil	*The Golden Bird*

Animal Fantasy

Brown, Ken	*The Scarecrow's Hat*
Burningham, John	*Mr. Gumpy's Outing*
Cannon, Janell	*Stellaluna*
Dewdney, Anna	*Llama Llama Misses Mama*
Eastman, P.D.	*Are You My Mother?**
Falconer, Ian	*Olivia*
Henkes, Kevin	*Lily's Big Day*
Henkes, Kevin	*Lily's Purple Plastic Purse*
Henkes, Kevin	*Owen*
Hest, Amy	*Little Chick*

**Common Core State Standards Exemplar Text*

AUTHOR	TITLE
Animal Fantasy, *cont.*	
Hoban, Russell	*Bread and Jam for Frances*
Hobbie, Holly	*Toot and Puddle*
Hobbie, Holly	*Toot and Puddle: A Present for Toot*
Hobbie, Holly	*Toot and Puddle: Top of the World*
Hobbie, Holly	*Toot and Puddle: The One and Only*
Hobbie, Holly	*Toot and Puddle: You Are My Sunshine*
Kasza, Keiko	*The Dog Who Cried Wolf*
Kasza, Keiko	*The Wolf's Chicken Stew*
Keller, Holly	*Farfallina and Marcel*
Kirk, Daniel	*Library Mouse*
Kirk, Daniel	*Library Mouse: A Friend's Tale*
Kirk, Daniel	*Library Mouse: A World to Explore*
Lobel, Arnold	*Frog and Toad are Friends**
McPhail, David	*Waddles*
Minarik, Else Holmelund	*Little Bear**
Numeroff, Laura	*Otis and Sydney and the Best Birthday Ever*
Puttock, Simon	*Little Lost Cowboy*
Rohmann, Eric	*My Friend Rabbit*
Saunders, Karen	*Baby Badger's Wonderful Night*
Springman, I.C.	*More*
Steig, William	*Amos and Boris**
Tillman, Nancy	*Tumford the Terrible*
Waddell, Martin	*Owl Babies*
Wells, Rosemary	*Yoko*
Narrative Nonfiction	
Bauer, Marion Dane	*If You Were Born a Kitten*
Blackford, Harriet	*Elephant's Story*
Gibbons, Gail	*Fire! Fire!**
Halfmann, Janet	*Star of the Sea: A Day in the Life of a Starfish*
Harvey, Tom and Allie	*Tiger Pups*
Kerby, Johanna	*Little Pink Pup*
Marzollo, Jean	*Pierre the Penguin*
Ray, Mary Lyn	*Mud*
Ryder, Joanne	*Panda Kindergarten*
Schaefer, Lola	*An Island Grows*
Springett, Martin	*Kate and Pippin: An Unlikely Love Story*

**Common Core State Standards Exemplar Text*

AUTHOR	TITLE
Expository Nonfiction	
Aliki	*My Five Senses**
Bulla, Clyde Robert	*A Tree is a Plant**
Hartman, Gail	*As the Crow Flies: A First Book of Maps*
Hoban, Tana	*I Read Signs**
Hurd, Edith Thacher	*Starfish**
Kerley, Barbara	*A Cool Drink of Water*
Most, Bernard	*How Big Were the Dinosaurs?*
Ray, Mary Lyn	*Stars*
Rose, Deborah Lee	*Ocean Babies*
Sill, Cathryn	*About Crustaceans: A Guide for Children*
Sill, Cathryn	*About Fish: A Guide for Children*
Sill, Cathryn	*About Insects: A Guide for Children*
Stockdale, Susan	*Fabulous Fishes*
Swinburne, Stephen	*Lots and Lots of Zebra Stripes: Patterns in Nature*
Zuckerman, Andrew	*Creature*
Procedural Texts	
Ehlert, Lois	*Growing Vegetable Soup*
Hill, Mary	*Let's Make Pizza*
Potter, Beatrix and Bray-Moffatt, Naia	*The Peter Rabbit and Friends Cookbook*
Snyder, Inez	*Milk to Ice Cream*
Snyder, Inez	*Wax to Crayons*
Tuckfield, Liyala	*How to Make a Bird Feeder*
Whitford, Rebecca	*Little Yoga*
Poetry	
Beaumont, Karen	*I Ain't Gonna Paint No More!*
Ehlert, Lois	*Lot's of Spots*
Greenfield, Eloise	*In the Land of Words: New and Selected Poems**
Lear, Edward	*The Owl and the Pussycat*
Merriam, Eve	*You be Good and I'll be Night**
Moss, Lloyd	*Zin! Zin! Zin! A Violin**
Muldrow, Diane	*We Planted a Tree*
George, Kristine O'Connell	*Little Dog Poems*
Prelutsky, Jack	*Real Aloud Rhymes for the Very Young*
Roemer, Heidi	*Come to My Party and Other Shape Poems*
Scanlon, Liz Garton	*All the World*
Sidman, Joyce	*Red Sings From Treetops: A Year in Colors*
Stockdale, Susan	*Bring on the Birds*
Yolen, Jane (compiled by)	*Here's a Little Poem: A Very First Book of Poetry*

Common Core State Standards Exemplar Text

Mentor Texts, Grades 2–3

POTENTIAL GENRE STUDIES FOR GRADES 2–3 In Chapter 15, we discuss the genres that students at each grade level might study through inquiry, as well as other genres they might be exposed to through read-aloud, book clubs, or independent reading. (see Figure 15.3, p. 242). Within these genres, students might be reading many different forms of texts (e.g., picture books, plays, and series books) as well as different types of fiction (e.g., mysteries, adventure stories, and humorous stories). The mentor texts lists for grades 2–3 reflect these genre study suggestions, but use your own judgment regarding what your individual students are ready for, and utilize the mentor text lists for other grades and genres as you see fit.

AUTHOR	TITLE
Realistic Fiction	
Brandenberg, Aliki	*Marianthe's Story: Painted Words*
Brandenberg, Aliki	*Marianthe's Story: Spoken Memories*
Brinckloe, Julie	*Fireflies!*
Buchanan, Jane	*Seed Magic*
Bunting, Eve	*A Day's Work*
Bunting, Eve	*Butterfly House*
Cisneros, Sandra	*Hairs = Pelitos*
Choi, Yangsook	*The Name Jar*
Coffelt, Nancy	*Fred Stays with Me!*
Compestine, Ying Chang	*Crouching Tiger*
Harrington, Janice N.	*The Chicken-Chasing Queen of Lamar County*
Harrison, Troon	*Courage to Fly*
Hest, Amy	*The Dog Who Belonged to No One*
Hoffman, Mary	*Amazing Grace*
Howard, Elizabeth Fitzgerald	*Aunt Flossie's Hats (and Crab Cakes Later)*
Hundal, Nancy	*Camping*
Hutchins, Hazel	*Mattland*
Javaherbin, Mina	*Goal!*
Juster, Norton	*Neville*
LaMarche, Jim	*The Raft**
Laminack, Lester L.	*The Sunsets of Miss Olivia Wiggins*
Mackintosh, David	*Marshall Armstrong is New to Our School*
Medina, Meg	*Tia Isa Wants a Car*
Mora, Pat	*Tomas and the Library Lady**
Morris, Carla	*The Boy Who Was Raised by Librarians*
Munson, Derek	*Enemy Pie*
Paulsen, Gary	*Canoe Days*
Pinkney, Andrea Davis	*Fishing Day*
Polacco, Patricia	*My Rotten Redheaded Older Brother*

**Common Core State Standards Exemplar Text*

AUTHOR	TITLE
Rattigan, Jama Kim	*Dumpling Soup*
Recorvits, Helen	*My Name is Yoon*
Rocco, John	*Blackout*
Rylant, Cynthia	*Henry and Mudge: The First Book of Their Adventures**
Rylant, Cynthia	*In November*
Rylant, Cynthia	*The Relatives Came*
Schubert, Leda	*The Princess of Borscht*
Sheth, Kashmira	*Monsoon Afternoon*
Simont, Marc	*The Stray Dog*
Viorst, Judith	*Super Completely and Totally the Messiest*
Viorst, Judith	*The Tenth Good Thing About Barney*
Winthrop, Elizabeth	*Squashed in the Middle*
Wood, Douglas	*A Quiet Place*
Woodson, Jacqueline	*Sweet Sweet Memory*
Woodson, Jacqueline	*We Had a Picnic This Sunday Past*
Wyeth, Sharon Dennis	*Something Beautiful*
Yolen, Jane	*Owl Moon*

Historical Fiction

Aston, Diana Hutts	*The Moon Over Star*
Bedard, Michael	*Emily*
Bunting, Eve	*Dandelions*
Buzzeo, Toni	*The Sea Chest*
Cooney, Barbara	*Hattie and the Wild Waves*
Cooney, Barbara	*Island Boy*
Hall, Donald	*Ox-Cart Man*
Hopkinson, Deborah	*Apples to Oregon*
Hopkinson, Deborah	*Stagecoach Sal*
Lasky, Kathryn	*She's Wearing a Dead Bird on Her Head!*
McCully, Emily Arnold	*Mirette on the Highwire*
McCully, Emily Arnold	*Starring Mirette and Bellini*
McKissack, Patricia C.	*Goin' Someplace Special*
Michelson, Richard	*Across the Alley*
Miller, William	*The Piano*
Moser, Lisa	*Kisses on the Wind*
Randall, Alison L.	*The Wheat Doll*
Ransom, Candice F.	*The Promise Quilt*
Woodson, Jacqueline	*The Other Side*

**Common Core State Standards Exemplar Text*

AUTHOR	TITLE
Folktales	
Aardema, Verna	*Borreguita and the Coyote*
Ada, Alma Flor	*With Love, Little Red Hen*
Bryan, Ashley	*Beautiful Blackbird*
Dabcovich, Lydia	*The Polar Bear Son: An Inuit Tale*
Diakite, Baba Wague	*The Hatseller and the Monkeys: A West African Folktale*
Diakite, Baba Wague	*The Hunterman and the Crocodile*
Deedy, Carmen	*Martina the Beautiful Cockroach: A Cuban Folktale*
Haley, Gail E.	*A Story, A Story**
Kimmel, Eric	*Joha Makes a Wish: A Middle Eastern Tale*
McDermott, Gerald	*Anansi the Spider: A Tale from the Ashanti*
McDermott, Gerald	*Arrow to the Sun: A Pueblo Indian Tale*
McDermott, Gerald	*Pig-Boy: A Trickster Tale from Hawai'i*
McDermott, Gerald	*Raven: A Trickster Tale from the Pacific Northwest*
McDermott, Gerald	*Monkey: A Trickster Tale from India*
McDermott, Gerald	*Coyote: A Trickster Tale from the American Southwest*
Mikolaycak, Charles	*Babushka*
Mosel, Arlene	*Tikki Tikki Tembo*
San Souci, Robert	*The Talking Eggs*
Steptoe, John	*Mufaro's Beautiful Daughters*
Steptoe, John	*The Story of Jumping Mouse*
Tchana, Katrin	*Sense Pass King: A Story from Cameroon*
Tolhurst, Marilyn	*Somebody and the Three Blairs*
Yussof Day, Noreha	*Kancil and the Crocodiles: A Tale from Malaysia*
Fairy Tales	
Anderson, Brian	*The Prince's New Pet*
Bazilian, Barbara	*The Red Shoes*
Climo, Shirley	*The Egyptian Cinderella*
Craft, Mahlon	*Sleeping Beauty*
Dalton, Annie	*The Starlight Princess and Other Princess Stories*
Daly, Jude	*Fair, Brown and Trembling: An Irish Cinderella Story*
Duntze, Dorothee (illustrated by)	*The Six Swans*
Fleischman, Paul	*Glass Slipper, Gold Sandal: A Worldwide Cinderella*
Geringer, Laura	*The Seven Ravens*
Kimmel, Eric	*The Castle of Cats*
Mayer, Marianna	*Beauty and the Beast*
Ogburn, Jacqueline K.	*The Magic Nesting Doll*
San Souci, Robert	*Cendrillon: A Caribbean Cinderella*

**Common Core State Standards Exemplar Text*

AUTHOR	TITLE
Scieszka, Jon	*The Frog Prince Continued*
Seidler, Tor	*The Steadfast Tin Soldier*
Sierra, Judy	*The Gift of the Crocodile*
Wilson, Tony	*The Princess and the Packet of Frozen Peas*

Fables

Brett, Jan	*Town Mouse, Country Mouse*
Climo, Shirley	*Tuko and the Birds: A Tale from the Philippines*
Forest, Heather	*The Contest Between the Sun and the Wind: An Aesop's Fable*
Guarnaccia, Steven	*Goldilocks and the Three Bears: A Tale Moderne*
Hartman, Bob	*The Wolf Who Cried Boy*
Hennessy, B.G.	*The Boy Who Cried Wolf*
Lobel, Arnold	*Fables*
Kimmel, Eric A.	*The Frog Princess: A Tlingit Legend from Alaska*
Naidoo, Beverley	*Aesop's Fables*
Osborne, Will, and Mary Osborne	*Sleeping Bobby*
Poole, Amy Lowry	*The Ant and the Grasshopper*
Rosales, Melodye Benson	*Leola and the Honeybears: An African-American Retelling of Goldilocks and the Three Bears*
Scieszka, Jon	*The True Story of the 3 Little Pigs!*
Sogabe, Aki	*Aesop's Fox*
Uribe, Veronica	*Little Book of Fables*
Wague Diakite, Baba	*The Magic Gourd*
Wormell, Christopher	*Mice, Morals, and Monkey Business*
Young, Ed	*Seven Blind Mice*

Myths

Day, Nancy Raines	*Piecing Earth and Sky Together*
Kahanu, Noelle	*Raven and the Sun*
Karas, G. Brian	*Young Zeus*
Lewis, Paul Owen	*Storm Boy*
Wells, Rosemary	*Max and Ruby's First Greek Myth: Pandora's Box*
Wells, Rosemary	*Max and Ruby's Midas: Another Greek Myth*
Young, Ed	*Moon Mother*

Modern Fantasy

Andreae, Giles	*Captain Flinn and the Pirate Dinosaurs*
Atwater, Richard	*Mr. Popper's Penguins**
Cronin, Doreen	*Click, Clack, Moo: Cows that Type*
Cronin, Doreen	*Diary of a Spider*
Foreman, Michael	*Fortunately, Unfortunately*

**Common Core State Standards Exemplar Text*

AUTHOR	TITLE
Modern Fantasy, *cont.*	
Gall, Chris	*Dear Fish*
Gall, Chris	*There's Nothing to Do on Mars*
Graham, Bob	*April and Esme: Tooth Fairies*
Jeffers, Oliver	*The Incredible Book Eating Boy*
Joyce, William	*George Shrinks*
Lehman, Barbara	*Museum Trip*
Lehman, Barbara	*The Red Book*
Lehman, Barbara	*The Secret Box*
McPhail, David	*Edward and the Pirates*
McPhail, David	*Edward in the Jungle*
Novak, Matt	*The Everything Machine*
Rathman, Peggy	*10 Minutes Till Bedtime*
Rathman, Peggy	*Officer Buckle and Gloria*
Rylant, Cynthia	*Poppleton in Winter**
Stead, Philip	*A Sick Day for Amos McGee*
Steig, William	*Doctor De Soto*
Teague, Mark	*The Secret Shortcut*
Yorinks, Mark	*Hey, Al*
Biography	
Aliki	*A Weed is a Flower: The Life of George Washington Carver**
Bass, Hester	*The Secret World of Walter Anderson*
Brown, Don	*Teedie: The Story of Young Teddy Roosevelt*
Brown, Don	*Uncommon Traveler: Mary Kingsley in Africa*
Brown, Monica	*My Name is Celia: The Life of Celia Cruz*
Brown, Monica	*Pablo Neruda: Poet of the People*
Coles, Robert	*The Story of Ruby Bridges**
Greenstein, Elaine	*The Goose Man: The Story of Konrad Lorenz*
McDonnell, Patrick	*Me . . . Jane*
Novesky, Amy	*Me, Frida*
Rappaport, Doreen	*Martin's Big Words: The LIfe of Dr. Martin Luther King, Jr.*
Schanzer, Rosalyn	*How Ben Franklin Stole the Lightning*
Stone, Tanya Lee	*Elizabeth Leads the Way: Elizabeth Cady Stanton and the Right to Vote*
Sweet, Melissa	*Balloons Over Broadway: The True Story of the Puppeteer of Macy's Parade*
Tonatiuh, Duncan	*Diego Rivera: His World and Ours*
Warren, Sarah	*Dolores Huerta: A Hero to Migrant Workers*
Winter, Jonah	*Frida*

**Common Core State Standards Exemplar Text*

AUTHOR	TITLE
Memoir	
Crews, Donald	*Bigmama's*
Crews, Donald	*Shortcut*
dePaola, Tomie	*26 Fairmount Avenue*
dePaola, Tomie	*Nana Upstairs and Nana Downstairs*
dePaola, Tomie	*What a Year!*
Hendershot, Judith	*In Coal Country*
Herrera, Juan Felipe	*Calling the Doves*
Herrera, Juan Felipe	*The Upside Down Boy*
Laminack, Lester L.	*Saturdays and Teacakes*
Rylant, Cynthia	*When I Was Young in the Mountains*
Velasquez, Eric	*Grandma's Records*
Yaccarino, Dan	*All the Way to America*
Narrative Nonfiction	
Aliki	*A Medieval Feast**
Blackford, Harriet	*Elephant's Story*
Campbell, Sarah C.	*Wolfsnail: a Backyard Predator*
Cowley, Joy	*Red-Eyed Tree Frog*
Crandell, Rachel	*Hands of the Maya: Villagers at Work and Play*
Davies, Nicola	*One Tiny Turtle*
Franco, Betsy	*Birdsongs*
Frost, Helen and Gore, Leonid	*Monarch and Milkweed*
Hutts Aston, Dianna	*An Egg is Quiet*
Hutts Aston, Dianna	*A Seed is Sleepy*
Katz, John	*Meet the Dog's of Bedlam Farm*
McMillan, Bruce	*Salmon Summer*
Paulsen, Gary	*The Tortilla Factory*
Pfeffer, Wendy	*A Log's Life*
Provensen, Alice and Martin	*The Year at Maple Hill Farm**
Reed-Jones, Carol	*Salmon Stream*
Stewart, Melissa	*Under the Snow*
Swinburne, Stephen	*Wings of Light: The Migration of the Yellow Butterfly*
Thomson, Sarah L.	*Where Do Polar Bears Live?**
Wadsworth, Ginger	*Up, Up, and Away!*
Winters, Kay	*Wolf Watch*

Common Core State Standards Exemplar Text

AUTHOR	TITLE
Expository Nonfiction	
Arnosky, Jim	*All About Owls*
Arnosky, Jim	*All About Turkeys*
Arnosky, Jim	*Wild Tracks! A Guide to Nature's Footprints**
Bateman, Robert	*Safari*
Batten, Mary	*Who Has a Belly Button?*
Beeler, Selby	*Throw Your Tooth on the Roof: Tooth Traditions Around the World**
Berger, Melvin and Gilda	*Does It Always Rain in the Rain Forest? Questions and Answers About Tropical Rain Forests*
Berger, Melvin and Gilda	*How Do Bats See in the Dark? Questions and Answers About Night Creatures*
Brocket, Jane	*Jane Brocket's Clever Concepts: Spotty, Stripy, Swirly*
Crossingham, John and Kalman, Bobbie	*The Life Cycle of a Snake*
Davies, Nicola	*Big Blue Whale*
Davies, Nicola	*Outside Your Window: A First Book of Nature*
Davies, Nicola	*Surprising Sharks*
Esbaum, Jill	*Apples for Everyone*
Franco, Betsy and Jenkins, Steve	*Bees, Snails, & Peacock Tails: Patterns & Shapes . . . Naturally*
Gans, Roma	*How Do Birds Find Their Way?*
Gibbons, Gail	*Horses!*
Gibbons, Gail	*Tell Me, Tree: All About Trees for Kids*
Gibbons, Gail	*Bats*
Gibbons, Gail	*The Pumpkin Book*
Gibbons, Gail	*Snakes*
Hodge, Deborah	*Whales: Killer Whales, Blue Whales, and More*
Jenkins, Steve	*Actual Size*
Jenkins, Steve	*Dogs and Cats*
Jenkins, Steve	*What Do You Do With a Tail Like This?*
Judge, Lita	*Bird Talk: What Birds Are Saying and Why*
Komiya, Teruyuki	*Life-Size Aquarium*
Komiya, Teruyuki	*Life-Size Zoo*
Komiya, Teruyuki	*More Life-Size Zoo*
Koontz, Robin	*What's the Difference Between a Butterfly and a Moth?*
Kudlinski, Kathleen	*Boy, Were We Wrong About Dinosaurs**
Llewellyn, Claire	*Earthworms**
Loewer, Peter and Jean	*The Moonflower*
Munro, Roxie	*Hatch!*
Pringle, Laurence	*Bats! Strange and Wonderful*
Pringle, Laurence	*Crows! Strange and Wonderful*
Pringle, Laurence	*Dinosaurs! Strange and Wonderful*

**Common Core State Standards Exemplar Text*

AUTHOR	TITLE
Rauzon, Mark and Bix, Cynthia Overbeck	*Water, Water Everywhere**
Simon, Seymour	*Animals Nobody Loves*
Simon, Seymour	*Our Solar System*
Sidman, Joyce	*Swirl by Swirl*
Silver, Donald M.	*One Small Square: Backyard*
Silver, Donald M.	*One Small Square: Pond*
Silver, Donald M.	*One Small Square: Woods*
St. George, Judith	*So You Want to be President?**

Procedural Texts

Barton, Byron	*Building a House*
Charles, Oz	*How Is a Crayon Made?*
Egan, Robert	*From Wheat to Pasta*
Emberley, Ed	*Ed Emberley's Drawing Book: Make a World*
Gibbons, Gail	*How a House is Built*
Gibbons, Gail	*Ice Cream: The Full Scoop*
Irvine, Joan	*How to Make Pop Ups*
Krasny Brown, Laurie	*How to be a Friend: A Guide to Making Friends and Keeping Them*
Luby, Thia	*The Children's Book of Yoga*
Marshall, Pam	*From Idea to Book*
Priceman, Marjorie	*How to Make an Apple Pie and See the World*
Walker, Barbara	*The Little House Cookbook*

Persuasive Texts

Asch, Frank	*The Earth and I*
Parr, Todd	*The Earth Book*
Pasquali, Elena	*It's My World Too: Discover Endangered Animals and Their Habitats*
Arnosky, Jim	*All About Frogs*
Berger, Melvin	*Oil Spill!*
Carrick, Carol	*The Polar Bears Are Hungry*
Drummond, Allan	*Energy Island: How One Community Harnessed the Wind and Changed Their World*
Gibbons, Gail	*Recycle: A Handbook for Kids*
Gibbons, Gail	*The Vegetables We Eat*
Guiberson, Brenda	*Moon Bear*
Jenkins, Steve	*Almost Gone: The World's Rarest Animals*
Rockwell, Anne	*What's So Bad About Gasoline? Fossil Fuels and What They Do*
Rockwell, Lizzy	*The Busy Body Book: A Kid's Guide to Fitness*
Rotner, Shelley	*The Buzz on Bees: Why Are They Disappearing?*
Yezerski, Thomas F.	*Meadowlands: A Wetlands Survival Story*

**Common Core State Standards Exemplar Text*

AUTHOR	TITLE
Poetry	
Davies, Nicola	*Outside Your Window: A First Book of Nature*
Dean Myers, Walter	*Looking Like Me*
De Regniers, Beatrice Schenk (editor)	*Sing a Song of Popcorn*
Elliott, David	*In the Wild*
Florian, Douglas	*Beast Feast*
Florian, Douglas	*Bow Wow Meow Meow: It's Rhyming Cats and Dogs*
Florian, Douglas	*Insectlopedia*
Frost, Helen	*Step Gently Out*
Gerstein, Mordicai	*Dear Hot Dog*
Gottfried, Maya	*Our Farm*
Graham, Joan Bransfield	*Flicker Flash*
Graham, Joan Bransfield	*Splish Splash*
Gray, Rita	*One Big Rain: Poems for Rainy Days*
Havill, Juanita	*I Heard It From Alice Zucchini: Poems About the Garden*
Lewis, J. Patrick	*Doodle Dandies: Poems that Take Shape*
Lewis, J. Patrick and Yolen, Jane	*Take Two! A Celebration of Twins*
O'Connell George, Kristine	*The Great Frog Race*
O'Connell George, Kristine	*Old Elm Speaks: Tree Poems*
O'Connell George, Kristine	*Toasting Marshmallows: Camping Poems*
Prelutsky, Jack	*Behold the Bold Umbrellaphant: and Other Poems*
Prelutsky, Jack	*It's Raining Pigs and Noodles*
Prelutsky, Jack	*Scranimals*
Prelutsky, Jack (compiled by)	*The Random House Book of Poetry for Children*
Salas, Laura Purdie	*A Leaf Can Be...*
Sidman, Joyce	*Swirl by Swirl: Spirals in Nature*
Worth, Valerie	*All the Small Poems and Fourteen More*

**Common Core State Standards Exemplar Text*

Mentor Texts, Grades 4–5

POTENTIAL GENRE STUDIES FOR GRADES 2–3 In Chapter 15, we discuss the genres that students at each grade level might study through inquiry, as well as other genres they might be exposed to through read-aloud or independent reading. (see Figure 15.3, p. 242). Within these genres, students might be reading many different forms of texts (e.g., picture books, plays, and series books) as well as different types of fiction (e.g., mysteries, adventure stories, and humorous stories). The mentor texts lists for grades 2–3 reflect these genre study suggestions, but use your own judgment regarding what your individual students are ready for, and utilize the mentor text lists for other grades and genres as you see fit.

AUTHOR	TITLE
Realistic Fiction	
Bunting, Eve	*One Green Apple*
Castaneda, Omar	*Abuela's Weave*
Fletcher, Ralph	*Hello, Harvest Moon*
Fletcher, Ralph	*Twilight Comes Twice*
Graber, Janet	*Muktar and the Camels*
Hesse, Karen	*Come On, Rain!*
High, Linda Oatman	*Beekeepers*
Hundal, Nancy	*Camping*
Laínez, René Colato	*My Shoes and I*
Markle, Sandra	*Butterfly Tree*
McCloskey, Robert	*Time of Wonder*
McKay, Lawrence	*Journey Home*
Ringgold, Faith	*Dinner at Aunt Connie's House*
Schotter, Roni	*Nothing Ever Happens on 90th Street*
Stock, Catherine	*Gugu's House*
Thomas, Patricia	*Firefly Mountain*
Whelan, Gloria	*Waiting for the Owl's Call*
Woodson, Jacqueline	*Our Gracie Aunt*
Historical Fiction	
Anderson, M. T.	*The Serpent Came To Gloucester*
Bartone, Elisa	*Peppe the Lamplighter*
Bruchac, Joseph	*Crazy Horse's Vision*
Bunting, Eve	*Cheyenne Again*
Bunting, Eve	*Gleam and Glow*
Bunting, Eve	*So Far from the Sea*
Chaconas, Dori	*Pennies in a Jar*

**Common Core State Standards Exemplar Text*

AUTHOR	TITLE
Historical Fiction, *cont.*	
Crowe, Chris	*Just As Good*
Fuchs, Bernie	*Ride Like the Wind: A Tale of the Pony Express*
Harrington, Janice N.	*Going North*
Hest, Amy	*When Jessie Came Across the Sea*
Hopkinson, Deborah	*A Band of Angels: A Story Inspired by the Jubilee Singers*
Hopkinson, Deborah	*Sky Boys: How They Built the Empire State Building*
Kimmelman, Leslie	*Mind Your Manners, Alice Roosevelt!*
King Mitchell, Margaree	*Uncle Jed's Barbershop*
Kirkpatrick, Katherine	*Redcoats and Petticoats*
Lowry, Lois	*Crow Call*
McKissack, Patricia C.	*Ma Dear's Aprons*
Miller, Debbie S.	*The Great Serum Race: Blazing the Iditarod Trail*
Moss, Marissa	*True Heart*
Nelson, Vaunda Micheaux	*Almost to Freedom*
Park, Linda Su	*The Third Gift*
Polacco, Patricia	*Pink and Say*
Rappaport, Doreen	*Freedom Ship*
Slate, Joseph	*I Want to be Free*
Soentpiet, Chris	*Coolies*
Stroud, Bettye	*The Patchwork Path: A Quilt Map to Freedom*
Theis Raven, Margot	*Night Boat to Freedom*
Theis Raven, Margot	*Circle Unbroken*
Turner, Ann	*Katie's Trunk*
Weatherford, Carole Boston	*Freedom on the Menu: The Greensboro Sit-ins*
Wells, Rosemary	*Streets of Gold*
Wiles, Deborah	*Freedom Summer*
Woodson, Jacqueline	*Coming on Home Soon*
Yang, Belle	*Hannah is My Name*
Yee, Paul	*Ghost Train*
Yolen, Jane	*The Ballad of the Pirate Queens*
Chapter Books	
Burnett, Frances Hodgson	*The Secret Garden**
Curtis, Christopher Paul	*Bud, Not Buddy**
MacLachlan, Patricia	*Sarah, Plain and Tall**
Folktales	
Aardema, Verna	*Why Mosquitos Buzz in People's Ears*
Bouchard, David	*The Dragon New Year: A Chinese Legend*
Burns, Batt	*The King with Horse's Ears: And Other Irish Folktales*

**Common Core State Standards Exemplar Text*

AUTHOR	TITLE
Crunk, Tony	*Railroad John and the Red Rock Run*
Day, Nancy Raines	*The Lion's Whiskers: An Ethiopian Folktale*
Hamilton, Virginia	*The People Could Fly: American Black Folktales*
Kurtz, Jane	*Fire on the Mountain*
Mayer, Marianna	*Baba Yaga and Vasilisa the Brave*
Medearis, Angela Shelf	*The Singing Man: Adapted from a West African Folktale*
Merrill, Jean	*The Girl Who Loved Caterpillars*
Paterson, Katherine	*The Tale of the Mandarin Ducks**
Phillip, Neal	*Stockings of Buttermilk: American Folktales*
Robinson, Sandra Chisholm	*The Rainstick, A Fable*
Tingle, Tim	*Crossing Bok Chitto: A Choctaw Tale of Friendship & Freedom*
Wolkstein, Diane	*The Magic Orange Tree and Other Haitian Folktales*
Yee, Paul	*Tales from Gold Mountain*
Young, Ed	*Night Visitors*

Fairy Tales

Bedard, Michael	*The Night-In-Gale*
Bateman, Teresa	*The Eyes of the Unicorn*
Bazilian, Barbara	*The Red Shoes*
Craft, Kinuko Y. (illustrated by)	*Cinderella*
Craft, Kinuko Y. (illustrated by)	*Sleeping Beauty*
de la Mare, Walter	*The Turnip*
Eilenberg, Max	*Beauty and the Beast*
Hale, Shannon	*Princess Academy (chapter book)*
Levine, Gail Carson	*Ella Enchanted (chapter book)*
Louie, Ai-Ling	*Yeh-Shen: A Cinderella Story from China*
Martin, Rafe	*The Rough-Face Girl*
Mayer, Marianna	*The Twelve Dancing Princesses*
Mitchell, Stephen	*Iron Hans*
Philip, Neil	*The Golden Bird*
Pinkney, Jerry	*The Nightingale*
Schlitz, Laura Amy	*The Bearskinner: A Tale of the Brothers Grimm*
Scieszka, Jon	*The Stinky Cheese Man and Other Fairly Stupid Tales*
Spirin, Gennady	*The Tale of the Firebird*
Young, Ed	*Lon Po Po**
Zelinsky, Paul	*Rapunzel*
Zelinsky, Paul	*Rumpelstiltskin*

Fables

Bader, Barbara	*Aesop and Company*
Burton, Virginia Lee (illustrated by)	*The Emperor's New Clothes*
Cherry, Lynne	*The Great Kapok Tree: A Tale of the Amazon Rain Forest*

**Common Core State Standards Exemplar Text*

AUTHOR	TITLE
Fables, *cont.*	
Cooney, Barbara	*Chanticleer and the Fox*
Giovanni, Nikki	*The Grasshopper's Song*
Lewis, J. Patrick	*The Frog Princess*
Mora, Pat	*A Tale About a Giant Woman With a Great Big Heart: Doña Flor*
Palatini, Margie	*Lousy, Rotten, Stinkin' Grapes*
Pollock, Penny	*The Turkey Girl: A Zuni Cinderella Story*
Valentino, Jim, and Kristen K. Simon (edited by)	*Fractured Fables*
Zwerger, Lisbeth (selected by)	*Aesop's Fables*
Legends, Epics, Ballads	
Bruchac, Joseph	*Between Earth and Sky: Legends of Native American Sacred Places*
Crunk, Tony	*Railroad John and the Red Rock Run*
Cullen, Lynn	*The Mightiest Heart*
dePaola, Tomie	*The Legend of the Bluebonnet*
dePaola, Tomie	*The Legend of the Indian Paintbrush*
Goble, Paul	*Buffalo Woman*
Goble, Paul	*Storm Maker's Tipi*
Henrichs, Wendy	*I Am Tama, Lucky Cat: A Japanese Legend*
Heyer, Marilee	*The Weaving of a Dream*
Kimmel, Eric A.	*The Hero Beowulf*
Lester, Julius	*John Henry*
San Souci, Robert	*Robin Hood and the Golden Arrow*
San Souci, Robert	*Young Arthur*
Souhami, Jessica	*Rama and the Demon King*
Steptoe, John	*The Story of Jumping Mouse*
Tavares, Matt	*Mudball*
Van Laan, Nancy	*Rainbow Crow*
Wargin, Kathy-jo	*The Legend of the Lady's Slipper*
Wiesner, David	*The Loathsome Dragon*
Yolen, Jane	*Merlin and the Dragons*
Young, Ed	*Monkey King*
Myths	
Burleigh, Robert	*Pandora*
Byrd, Robert	*The Hero and the Minotaur*
Climo, Shirley	*Atalanta's Race*

**Common Core State Standards Exemplar Text*

AUTHOR	TITLE
D'Aulaire, Ingri and Edgar Parin	*D'Aulaires' Book of Greek Myths*
D'Aulaire, Ingri and Edgar Parin	*D'Aulaires' Book of Norse Myths*
Demi	*King Midas: The Golden Touch*
Jaffe, Nina	*The Golden Flower: A Taino Myth from Puerto Rico*
Kessler, Timothy	*When God Made the Dakotas*
McCaughreen, Geraldine	*Greek Gods and Goddesses*
Pomme Clayton, Sally	*Persephone*
Stewig, John	*King Midas*
Wolkstein, Diane	*Sun Mother Wakes the World*
Yolen, Jane	*Pegasus, the Flying Horse*
Yolen, Jane	*Wings*

Modern Fantasy

Because of the nature of modern fantasy at this level, in addition to the picture books listed below you may want to select two or three chapter books and read a section of each across several days. We have included several chapter books for this purpose. You may also choose to use the picture books listed for this genre under other grade levels.

Barrett, Judi	*Cloudy with a Chance of Meatballs*
Barrett, Judi	*Pickles to Pittsburgh*
Bearn, Emily	*The Adventures of Tumtum and Nutmeg* (short stories)
Cannon, Jannell	*Crickwing*
Cannon, Jannell	*Verdi*
Conrad, Pam	*The Tub People*
Fleischman, Paul	*Weslandia*
Joyce, William	*The Leaf Men*
Joyce, William	*The Man in the Moon (Guardians of Childhood)*
Lehman, Barbara	*Rainstorm*
McLerran, Alice	*Roxaboxen*
O'Conner, Jane	*The Snow Globe Family*
O'Malley, Kevin	*Captain Raptor and the Moon Mystery*
Steig, William	*The Amazing Bone*
Steig, William	*Brave Irene*
Steig, William	*Rotten Island*
Steig, William	*Sylvester and the Magic Pebble*
Van Allsburg, Chris	*Jumanji*
Van Allsburg, Chris	*The Polar Express*
Wiesner, David	*Flotsam*
Wiesner, David	*Sector 7*
Wiesner, David	*Tuesday*

**Common Core State Standards Exemplar Text*

AUTHOR	TITLE
Chapter Books	
Appelt, Kathi	*The Underneath*
Baum, L. Frank	*The Wonderful Wizard of Oz**
Cameron, Eleanor	*The Wonderful Flight to the Mushroom Planet*
Carman, Patrick	*Stargazer*
Carroll, Lewis	*Alice's Adventures in Wonderland**
Eager, Edward	*Half Magic*
Gannett, Ruth Stiles	*My Father's Dragon**
Greenburg, Dan	*Thrills, Spills, and Cosmic Chills*
Jansson, Tove	*Finn Family Moomintroll**
King-Smith, Dick	*The Fox Busters*
Law, Ingrid	*Savvy*
L'Engle, Madeleine	*A Wrinkle in Time**
Lewis, C.S.	*The Lion, the Witch, and the Wardrobe*
Nelson, Peter	*Herbert's Wormhole*
O'Rourke Dowell, Francis	*Falling In*
Paton Walsh, Jill	*The Green Book*
Pearce, Philippa	*Tom's Midnight Garden*
Prineas, Sarah	*The Magic Thief*
Riordan, Rick	*Percy Jackson and the Olympians (Books 1-5)*
Rowling, J.K.	*Harry Potter (Books 1-7)*
Sauer, Julia	*Fog Magic*
Winthrop, Elizabeth	*The Castle in the Attic*
Biography	
Barretta, Gene	*Neo Leo: The Ageless Ideas of Leonardo da Vinci*
Bass, Hester	*The Secret World of Walter Anderson*
Berne, Jennifer	*Manfish: A Story of Jacques Cousteau*
Brown, Don	*A Voice from the Wilderness: The Story of Anna Howard Shaw*
Brown, Tami Lewis	*Soar, Elinor!*
Christensen, Bonnie	*Django: World's Greatest Jazz Guitarist*
Coerr, Eleanor	*Sadako*
Cooper, Floyd	*Coming Home: From the Life of Langston Hughes*
Cooper,Floyd	*Mandela, from the life of the South African statesman*
D'Agnese, Joseph	*Blockhead: The Life of Fibonacci*
de la Peña, Matt	*A Nation's Hope: The Story of Boxing Legend Joe Louis*
Fishman, Cathy Goldberg	*When Jackie and Hank Met*
Greenwood, Mark	*The Donkey of Gallipoli: A True Story of Courage in World War I*
Hill, Laban Carrick	*Dave the Potter Artist, Poet, Slave*
Krull, Kathleen	*The Boy Who Invented TV: The Story of Philo Farnsworth*

**Common Core State Standards Exemplar Text*

AUTHOR	TITLE
Krull, Kathleen	*Harvesting Hope: The Story of Cesar Chavez*
Krull, Kathleen	*Houdini: World's Greatest Mystery Man and Escape King*
Lewis Brown, Tami	*Soar, Elinor!*
Love, D. Anne	*Of Numbers and Stars: The Story of Hypatia*
Markle, Sandra	*Animals Marco Polo Saw*
McCully, Emily Arnold	*Wonder Horse: The True Story of the World's Smartest Horse*
McDonough, Yona Leldis	*Louisa: The Life of Louisa May Alcott*
Meltzer, Milton	*Albert Einstein: A Biography*
Micheaux Nelson, Vaunda	*Bad News for Outlaws: The Remarkable Life of Bass Reeves, Deputy U.S. Marshall*
Muñoz Ryan, Pam	*When Marian Sang*
Napoli, Donna Jo	*Mama Miti*
Pinkney, Andrea Davis and Brian	*Ella Fitzgerald: The Tale of a Vocal Virtuosa*
Rappaport, Doreen	*Abe's Honest Words: The Life of Abraham Lincoln*
Rappaport, Doreen	*Eleanor, Quiet No More: The Life of Eleanor Roosevelt*
Rockwell, Anne	*Big George: How a Shy Boy Became President Washington*
Shange, Ntozake	*Coretta Scott*
Spielman, Gloria	*Marcel Marceau: Master of Mime*
Stanley, Fay	*The Last Princess: The Story of Princess Ka'iulani of Hawai'i*
Tavares, Matt	*Henry Aaron's Dream*
Tavares, Matt	*There Goes Ted Williams*
Van Allsburg, Chris	*The Queen of the Falls*
Wallner, Alexandra	*Lucy Maud Montgomery: The Author of Anne of Green Gables*
Wargin, Kathy-Jo	*Alfred Nobel: The Man Behind the Peace Prize*
Weatherford, Carole Boston	*Moses: When Harriet Tubman Led Her People to Freedom*
Wing, Natasha	*An Eye for Color: The Story of Joseph Albers*
Winter, Jeanette	*The Librarian of Basra*
Winter, Jeanette	*Wangari's Trees of Peace*
Yolen, Jane	*All Star! Honus Wagner and the Most Famous Baseball Card Ever*

Autobiography and Memoir

Cole, Joanna / Saul, Wendy	*On the Bus with Joanna Cole*
Cunxin, Li	*Dancing to Freedom: The True Story of Mao's Last Dancer*
Egan, Anna Smucker	*No Star Nights*
Fendler, Donn	*Lost on a Mountain in Maine*
Hoestlandt, Jo	*Star of Fear, Star of Hope*
Hopkinson, Deborah	*Sweet Land of Liberty*
Huynh, Quang Nhuong	*The Land I Lost: Adventures of a Boy in Vietnam*
Lester, Helen	*Author: A True Story*
Moss, Marissa, and John Hendrix	*Nurse, Soldier, Spy*

**Common Core State Standards Exemplar Text*

AUTHOR	TITLE
Autobiography and Memoir, *cont.*	
Park, Frances and Ginger	*My Freedom Trip: A Child's Escape from North Korea*
Parks, Rosa	*I Am Rosa Parks*
Robinson, Sharon and Nelson, Kadir	*Testing the Ice: A True Story About Jackie Robinson*
Uhlberg, Myron	*Dad, Jackie, and Me*
Wells, Rosemary	*Streets of Gold*
Wyk, Chris Van	*Nelson Mandela, Long Walk to Freedom*
Narrative Nonfiction	
Brindell Fradin, Dennis	*Duel! Burr and Hamilton's Deadly War of Words*
Cherry, Lynne	*A River Ran Wild: An Environmental History*
Cowcher, Helen	*Desert Elephants*
Craighead George, Jean	*Look to the North: A Wolf Pup Diary*
Crenson, Victoria	*Horseshoe Crabs and Shorebirds*
Curlee, Lynn	*Ballpark: The Story of America's Baseball Fields*
Dowson, Nick	*North: The Amazing Story of Arctic Migration*
Floca, Brian	*Moonshot: The Flight of Apollo 11*
Giblin, James Cross	*The Mystery of the Mammoth Bones: And How It Was Solved*
Greenberg, Jan	*Ballet for Martha: Making Appalachian Spring*
Guiberson, Brenda	*Life in the Boreal Forest*
Hatkoff, Juliana	*Looking for Miza: The True Story of the Mountain Gorilla Family Who Rescued One of Their Own*
Jenkins, Steve	*Down, Down, Down: A Journey to the Bottom of the Sea*
Kroll, Steven	*The Boston Tea Party*
Schulman, Janet	*Pale Male: Citizen Hawk of New York City*
Swinburne, Stephen	*Turtle Tide: The Ways of Sea Turtles*
Wulffson, Don	*Toys! Amazing Stories Behind Some Great Inventions**
Expository Nonfiction	
Arnosky, Jim	*All About Alligators*
Facklam, Margery	*The Big Bug Book*
Gibbons, Gail	*Nature's Green Umbrella: Tropical Rain Forests*
Gibbons, Gail	*The Reasons for Seasons*
Gibbons, Gail	*The Honey Makers*
Heos, Bridget	*What to Expect When You're Expecting Hatchlings: A Guide for Crocodilian Parents (and Curious Kids)*
Jenkins, Steve	*Just a Second*
Kalman, Bobbie	*Forest Mammals*
Knowlton, Jack	*Geography From A to Z: A Picture Glossary*

**Common Core State Standards Exemplar Text*

AUTHOR	TITLE
Koscielniak, Bruce	*About Time: A First Look at Time and Clocks**
Krull, Kathleen	*Big Wig: A Little History of Hair*
Lauber, Patricia	*Dinosaurs Walked Here and Other Stories Fossils Tell*
Ling, Mary, and Mary Atkinson (written and edited by)	*The Snake Book: A Breathtaking Close-up Look at Splendid, Scaly, Slithery Snakes*
Markle, Sandra	*Outside and Inside Kangaroos*
McMillan, Bruce	*The Baby Zoo*
Quinlan, Susan E.	*Puffins*
Ruurs, Margaret	*My Librarian is a Camel: How Books Are Brought to Children Around the World**
Simon, Seymour	*Bones: Our Skeletal System*
Simon, Seymour	*Crocodiles and Alligators*
Simon, Seymour	*Horses**
Simon, Seymour	*Volcanoes**
Steedman, Scott	*Egyptian Town*
Sturges, Philemon	*Bridges Are to Cross*
Wick, Walter	*A Drop of Water: A Book of Science and Wonder**

Procedural Texts

Craighead George, Jean	*How to Talk to Your Cat*
Craighead George, Jean	*How to Talk to Your Dog*
Irvine, Joan	*How to Make Pop-Ups*
Lagasse, Emeril	*Emeril's There's a Chef in My Soup! Recipes for the Kid in Everyone*
Macauley, David	*The Way We Work*
Scholastic	*The Games Book: How to Play the Games of Yesterday*
Walker, Lester R.	*Housebuilding for Children: Step-by-Step Plans for Houses Children Can Build Themselves*

Persuasive Texts

Bang, Molly	*Common Ground: The Water, Earth, and Air We Share*
Bang, Molly	*Nobody Particular: One Woman's Fight to Save the Bays*
Cherry, Lynne	*A River Ran Wild*
Craighead George, Jean	*The Buffalo Are Back*
Craighead George, Jean	*The Wolves Are Back*
Goodall, Jane	*The Chimpanzees I Love: Saving Their World and Ours*
Jenkins, Martin	*Can We Save the Tiger?*
McLimans, David	*Gone Wild: An Endangered Animal Alphabet*
Miller, Edward	*The Monster Health Book: A Guide to Eating Healthy, Being Active, and Feeling Great*

**Common Core State Standards Exemplar Text*

AUTHOR	TITLE	
Persuasive Texts, *cont.*		
Papastavrou, Vassili	*Seals and Sea Lions*	
Smith, Lane	*It's a Book*	
Stewart, Melissa	*A Place for Bats*	
Stewart, Melissa	*A Place for Birds*	
Stewart, Melissa	*A Place for Butterflies*	
Stewart, Melissa	*A Place for Fish*	
Stewart, Melissa	*A Place for Frogs*	
Swinburne, Stephen R.	*Saving Manatees*	
Hybrid Texts		
Chin, Jason	*Redwoods*	expository nonfiction modern fantasy
Cole, Henry	*Jack's Garden*	expository nonfiction realistic fiction
Cole, Joanna	*The Magic School Bus on the Ocean Floor*	expository nonfiction modern fantasy
Cole, Joanna	*The Magic School Bus inside the Human Body*	expository nonfiction modern fantasy
Davies, Nicola	*Bat Loves the Night*	expository nonfiction realistic fiction
Davies, Nicola	*Just Ducks*	expository nonfiction realistic fiction
Davies, Nicola	*One Tiny Turtle*	expository nonfiction realistic fiction
Davies, Nicola	*White Owl, Barn Owl*	expository nonfiction realistic fiction
French, Vivian	*Yucky Worms*	expository nonfiction realistic fiction
Harper, Charise Mericle	*Henry's Heart: A Boy, His Heart, and a New Best Friend*	expository nonfiction realistic fiction
Lewis, Patrick J., and Jane Yolen	*Take Two! A Celebration of Twins*	expository nonfiction poetry
O'Brien, Patrick	*The Making of a Knight*	expository nonfiction historical fiction
Peacock, Louise	*At Ellis Island: A History in Many Voices*	historical fiction expository nonfiction
Wallace, Karen	*Bears in the Forest*	expository nonfiction realistic fiction
Wright-Frierson, Virginia	*A North American Rain Forest Scrapbook*	memoir expository nonfiction persuasive text

**Common Core State Standards Exemplar Text*

AUTHOR	TITLE	
Heinz, Brian J.	*The Wolves*	realistic fiction expository nonfiction
Schoenherr, John	*Bear*	realistic fiction expository nonfiction
Williams, Marcia	*Archie's War: My Scrapbook of the First World War, 1914–1918*	historical fiction expository nonfiction
Yolen, Jane and Stemple, Heidi	*The Mary Celeste: An Unsolved Mystery from History*	expository nonfiction historical fiction

Poetry

Baylor, Bird	*The Way to Start a Day*
Christian, Peggy	*If You Find a Rock*
Dant, Traci	*Some Kind of Love: A Family Reunion in Poems*
Fletcher, Ralph	*Moving Day*
Fletcher, Ralph	*Ordinary Things*
Fletcher, Ralph	*A Writing Kind of Day: Poems for Young Poets*
Florian, Douglas	*Poetrees*
George, Kristine O'Connell	*Hummingbird Nest*
Greenfield, Eloise	*Honey I Love and Other Poems*
Grimes, Nikki	*Danitra Brown Leaves Town*
Grimes, Nikki	*Thanks a Million*
Guthrie, Woody (words and music by)	*This Land Is Your Land*
Harley, Avis	*African Acrostics: A Word in Edgeways*
Heard, Georgia (edited by)	*Falling Down the Page: A Book of List Poems*
Heard, Georgia	*This Place I Know: Poems of Comfort*
Hopkins, Lee Bennett (selected by)	*Amazing Faces*
Hopkins, Lee Bennett (selected by)	*Sharing the Seasons: A Book of Poems*
Hopkinson, Deborah	*Under the Quilt of Night*
Janeczko, Paul B. and Raschka, Chris	*A Foot in the Mouth: Poems to Speak, Sing, and Shout*
Janeczko, Paul B. and Raschka, Chris	*A Kick in the Head: An Everyday Guide to Poetic Forms*
Janeczko, Paul B. and Raschka, Chris	*A Poke in the I: A Collection of Concrete Poems*
Lewis, J. Patrick	*Earth Verses and Water Rhymes*
Raczka, Bob	*Lemonade: and Other Poems Squeezed from a Single Word*
Sidman, Joyce	*Song of the Water Boatman and Other Pond Poems*
Sidman, Joyce	*This Is Just to Say: Poems of Apology and Forgiveness*
Singer, Marilyn	*The Company of Crows: A Book of Poems*
Singer, Marilyn	*Footprints on the Roof: Poems About the Earth*
Singer, Marilyn	*Mirror, Mirror*
Young, Ed	*Beyond the Great Mountains: A Visual Poem About China*
Various authors	*Poetry for Young People* (series)

**Common Core State Standards Exemplar Text*

Mentor Texts, Grades 6–8

POTENTIAL GENRE STUDIES FOR GRADES 6–8 In Chapter 15, we discuss the genres that students at each grade level might study through inquiry, as well as other genres they might be exposed to through read-aloud, book clubs, or independent reading. (see Figure 15.3, p. 242). Within these genres, students might be reading many different forms of text (e.g., plays, series, chapter books, graphic texts, picture books) as well as different types of fiction (e.g., mysteries, adventure stories, horror, humorous stories), and nonfiction (e.g., reports, literary essays, feature articles, interviews) The mentor texts lists for grades 6–8 reflect these genre study suggestions, but use your own judgment regarding what your individual students are ready for, and utilize the mentor text lists for other grades and genres as you see fit.

Realistic Fiction

Because of the nature of this genre at this level, in addition to the picture books listed below you may want to select two or three longer texts and read a section of each across several days. We have included several chapter books for this purpose. You may also choose to use the picture books listed for this genre under other grade levels.

AUTHOR	TITLE
Belton, Sandra	*From Miss Ida's Porch*
Bromley, Anne C.	*The Lunch Thief*
Bunting, Eve	*Smoky Night*
Bunting, Eve	*How Many Days to America?*
Bunting, Eve	*The Wall*
Deitz-Shea, Pegi	*The Carpet Boy's Gift*
Garland, Sherry	*I Never Knew Your Name*
Heinz, Brian	*Nanuk Lord of the Ice*
Kittinger, Jo S.	*The House on Dirty-third Street*
Kooser, Ted	*House Held Up By Trees*
Paulsen, Gary	*Dogteam*
Rumford, James	*Silent Music: A Story of Baghdad*
Rylant, Cynthia	*An Angel for Solomon Singer*
Rylant,Cynthia	*The Old Woman Who Named Thing*
Uhlberg, Myron	*A Storm Called Katrina*
Williams, Karen Lynn	*Four Feet, Two Sandals*

Chapter Books

AUTHOR	TITLE
Buchanan Smith, Doris	*A Taste of Blackberries*
Canales, Viola	*The Tequila Worm*
Gantos, Jack	*Joey Pigza Loses Control*
Giff, Patricia Reilly	*Pictures of Hollis Woods*
Henkes, Kevin	*Olive's Ocean*
Hiaasen, Carl	*Hoot*
Lord, Cynthia	*Rules*
Lowry, Lois	*Anastasia Krupnik*
Paterson, Katherine	*Bridge to Terabithia*
Paulsen, Gary	*Hatchet*
Perkins, Lynne Ray	*Criss Cross*
Voigt, Cynthia	*Homecoming* (trilogy)

**Common Core State Standards Exemplar Text*

AUTHOR	TITLE

Historical Fiction

Because of the nature of this genre at this level, in addition to the picture books listed below you may want to select two or three longer texts and read a section of each across several days. We have included several chapter books for this purpose. You may also choose to use the picture books listed for this genre under other grade levels.

AUTHOR	TITLE
Albright, Flossie	*My War Diary*
Crow, Chris	*Just As Good*
Garland, Sherry	*The Lotus Seed*
Hoestlandt, Jo	*Star of Fear, Star of Hope*
Innocenti, Roberto	*Rose Blanche*
Johnston, Tony	*The Harmonica*
Lee, Milly	*Nim and the War Effort*
Littlesugar, Amy	*Willy & Max: A Holocaust Story*
Mochizuki, Ken	*Baseball Saved Us*
Patt, Beverly	*Best Friends Forever: A World War II Scrapbook*
Peacock, Louise	*At Ellis Island: A History in Many Voices*
Ramsey, Calvin	*Ruth and the Green Book*
Soentpiet, Chris	*Coolies*

Chapter Books

AUTHOR	TITLE
Anderson, Laurie Halse	*Chains*
Avi	*The Fighting Ground*
Holm, Jennifer	*Penny from Heaven*
Chaikin, Miriam	*I Should Worry, I Should Care*
Choi, Sook Nyul	*The Year of Impossible Goodbyes*
Choldenko, Gennifer	*Al Capone Does My Shirts*
Choldenko, Gennifer	*Al Capone Shines My Shoes*
Cushman, Karen	*Catherine, Called Birdy*
Cushman, Karen	*The Midwife's Apprentice*
Erdrich, Louise	*The Birchbark House**
Hesse, Karen	*A Time of Angels*
Hesse, Karen	*Out of the Dust*
Kadohata, Cynthia	*Kira-Kira*
Paulsen, Gary	*Sarny: A Life Remembered*
Schmidt, Gary	*The Wednesday Wars*
Taylor, Mildred D.	*Roll of Thunder, Hear My Cry**
Twain, Mark	*The Adventures of Tom Sawyer**

Legends, Epics, Ballads

AUTHOR	TITLE
Bower, Tamara	*How the Amazon Queen Fought the Prince of Egypt*
Bruchac, Joseph	*Between Earth and Sky: Legends of Native American Sacred Places*
Cooper, Susan	*The Selkie Girl*

**Common Core State Standards Exemplar Text*

AUTHOR	TITLE

Legends, Epics, Ballads, *cont.*

Cullen, Lynn	*The Mightiest Heart*
Early, Margaret (illustrated by)	*William Tell*
Hodges, Margaret	*The Kitchen Knight: A Tale of King Arthur*
Hodges, Margaret	*Merlin and the Making of the King*
Hodges, Margaret	*Saint George and the Dragon*
McCaughrean, Geraldine	*Gilgamesh the Hero*
Osborne, Mary Pope	*The One-Eyed Giant**
Rogasky, Barbara	*Dybbuk*
Rumford, James	*Beowulf: A Hero's Tale Retold*
Shannon, Mark	*Gawain and the Green Knight*
Shephard, Aaron	*The Sea King's Daughter: A Russian Legend*
Sutcliff, Rosemary	*Black Ships Before Troy: The Story of 'The Iliad'**
Talbott, Hudson	*Excalibur*
Talbott, Hudson	*King Arthur and the Round Table*
Talbott, Hudson	*Lancelot*
Verma, Jatinder	*The Story of Divaali*
Zeman, Ludmila	*Gilgamesh the King*
Zeman, Ludmila	*The Revenge of Ishtar*

Myths

Craft, M. Charlotte	*Cupid and Psyche*
Climo, Shirley	*Atalanta's Race*
Craft, Charlotte	*King Midas and the Golden Touch*
Gavin, Jamila	*Tales From India: Stories of Creation and the Cosmos*
Hamilton, Virginia	*In the Beginning: Creation Stories from Around the World*
Low, Alice	*The Simon and Schuster Book of Greek Gods and Heroes*
Mayer, Marianna	*Pegasus*
McDermott, Gerald	*Musicians of the Sun*
Osborne, Mary Pope	*Favorite Norse Myths*
Riordan, James	*Jason and the Golden Fleece*
Williams, Marcia	*Ancient Egypt: Tales of Gods and Pharaohs*

Modern Fantasy

Because of the nature of modern fantasy at this level, in addition to the picture books listed below you may want to select two or three longer texts and read a section of each across several days. We have included several chapter books and short story collections for this purpose. You may also choose to use the picture books listed for this genre under other grade levels.

Avi	*Strange Happening: Five Tales of Transformation* (short stories)
Rowling, J.K.	*The Tales of Beedle the Bard*
Steig, William	*Shrek*
Turner, Megan Whelan	*Instead of Three Wishes* (short stories)
Willis, Jennifer Schwamm	*Wizards: Stories of Magic, Mischief, and Mayhem* (story collection)
Van Allsburg, Chris (and various authors)	*The Chronicles of Harris Burdick*

**Common Core State Standards Exemplar Text*

AUTHOR	TITLE
Van Allsburg, Chris	*The Garden of Abdul Gasazi*
Van Allsburg, Chris	*The Mysteries of Harris Burdick*
Van Allsburg, Chris	*The Wreck of the Zephyr*
Van Allsburg, Chris	*Two Bad Ants*
Van Allsburg, Chris	*Zathura*

Chapter Books

Almond, David	*Skellig*
Babbitt, Natalie	*The Search for Delicious**
Babbitt, Natalie	*Tuck Everlasting**
Billingsley, Frannie	*The Folk Keeper*
Browne, Anthony	*Voices in the Dark*
Cooper, Susan	*Over Sea, Under Stone*
Cooper, Susan	*The Dark is Rising**
Hardinge, Frances	*Fly Trap*
Kendall, Carol	*The Gammage Cup*
Le Guin, Ursula K.	*A Wizard of Earthsea*
Oppel, Kenneth	*Silverwing* (trilogy)
Pullman, Philip	*The Golden Compass*
Rowling, J.K.	*Harry Potter* (Books 1–7)
Spudvilas, Wild	*Woolvs in the Sitee*
Stewart, Trenton Lee	*The Mysterious Benedict Society*
Stewart, Trenton Lee	*The Mysterious Benedict Society and the Perilous Journey*
Stewart, Trenton Lee	*The Mysterious Benedict Society and the Prisoner's Dilemma*
Yep, Lawrence	*The Tiger's Apprentice*
Yolen, Jane	*The Devil's Arithmetic*
Yolen, Jane	*Foiled*

Science Fiction

Because of the nature of science fiction at this level, you may want to select two or three longer texts and read a section of each across several days. We have included several chapter books for this purpose.

Chapter Books

Duprau, Jean	*The City of Ember*
Dunkle, Clare	*The Sky Inside*
Engdahl, Sylvia	*Enchantress from The Stars*
Falkner, Brian	*The Tomorrow Code*
Fox, Helen	*Eager*
Haddix, Margaret	*Among the Hidden*
Hobbs, Will	*Go Big or Go Home*
Klause, Annette	*Alien Secrets*
L'Engle, Madeleine	*A Swiftly Tilting Planet*
Lowry, Lois	*The Giver*
Lowry, Lois	*Gathering Blue*

**Common Core State Standards Exemplar Text*

AUTHOR	TITLE
Science Fiction, *cont.*	
Oppel, Kenneth	*Airborn*
Park, Linda Sue	*Archer's Quest*
Paulsen, Gary	*The Time Hackers*
Pearson, Mary	*The Adoration of Jenna Fox*
Peck, Richard	*Lost in Cyberspace*
Peck, Richard	*The Great Interactive Dream Machine*
Walsh, Jill Paton	*The Green Book*
Biography	
Bardoe, Cheryl	*Gregor Mendel: The Friar Who Grew Peas*
Bernier-Grand, Carmen	*Frida*
Bolden, Tonya	*Maritcha: A Nineteenth-Century American Girl*
Bryant, Jen	*A River of Words: The Story of William Carlos Williams*
De La Peña, Matt	*A Nation's Hope: the Story of Boxing Legend Joe Louis*
Freedman, Russell	*Lincoln: A Photobiography**
Giovanni, Nikki	*Rosa*
Greenberg, Jan	*Vincent Van Gogh: Portrait of An Artist**
Hendrix, John	*John Brown: His Fight for Freedom*
Kerley, Barbara	*The Dinosaurs of Waterhouse Hawkins*
Lasky, Kathryn	*John Muir: America's First Environmentalist*
McGinty, Alice B.	*Darwin: With Glimpses into His Private Journal & Letters*
Mochizuki, Ken	*Passage to Freedom: The Sugihara Story*
Petry, Ann	*Harriet Tubman: Conductor on the Underground Railroad**
Poole, Josephine	*Anne Frank*
Rubin, Susan Goldman	*Jean Laffite: The Pirate Who Saved America*
Sís, Peter	*Starry Messenger: Galileo Galilei*
Stanley, Diane, and Peter Vennema	*Bard of Avon: The Story of William Shakespeare*
Usher, M. D.	*Wise Guy: the Life and Philosophy of Socrates*
Weatherford, Carole Boston	*Jesse Owens: Fastest Man Alive*
Winter, Jonah	*You Never Heard of Sandy Koufax?*
Weaver, Janice	*Harry Houdini: The Legend of the World's Greatest Escape Artist*
Yoo, Paula	*Sixteen Years in Sixteen Seconds: The Sammy Lee Story*
Autobiography and Memoir	
Bierman, Carol	*Journey to Ellis Island: How My Father Came to America*
Bridges, Ruby	*Through My Eyes*
Bryan, Ashley	*Ashley Bryan: Words to My Life's Song*
Capaldi, Gina (adapted by)	*Red Bird Sings: The Story of Zitkala-Sa*
Close, Chuck	*Face Book*
Darrow, Sharon	*Through the Tempests Dark and Wild: A Story of Mary Shelley*
Douglass, Frederick	*Narrative of the Life of Frederick Douglass an American Slave, Written by Himself**
Gibbons, Alan	*Charles Darwin*

**Common Core State Standards Exemplar Text*

AUTHOR	TITLE
Hong, Chen Jiang	*Mao and Me*
Hoose, Philip	*Claudette Colvin: Twice Toward Justice*
O'Brien, Tony, and Mike Sullivan	*Afghan Dreams: Young Voices of Afghanistan*
Park, Frances and Ginger Park	*My Freedom Trip: A Child's Escape from North Korea*
Paulsen, Gary	*Guts*
Paulsen, Gary	*My Life in Dog Years*
Robinson, Anthony, and Annemarie Young	*Gervelie's Journey: A Refugee Diary*
Sís, Peter	*The Wall: Growing Up Behind the Iron Curtain*
Steinbeck, John	*Travels with Charley: In Search of America*

Narrative Nonfiction

Blumberg, Rhoda	*Commodore Perry in the Land of the Shogun*
Burleigh, Robert	*Black Whiteness, Admiral Byrd Alone in the Antarctic*
Deedy, Carmen Agra	*14 Cows for America**
Freedman, Russell	*The Adventures of Marco Polo*
Freedman, Russell	*Freedom Walkers: The Story of the Montgomery Bus Boycott**
Griffin Burns, Loree	*The Hive Detectives: Chronicle of a Honey Bee Catastrophe*
Montgomery, Sy	*Quest for the Tree Kangaroo: An Expedition to the Cloud Forest of New Guinea**
Montgomery, Sy	*Saving the Ghost of the Mountain: An Expedition Among Snow Leopards in Mongolia*
Montgomery, Sy	*The Man-Eating Tigers of Sundarbans*
Murphy, Jim	*An American Plague: The True and Terrifying Story of the Yellow Fever Epidemic of 1793*
Murphy, Jim	*The Great Fire**
Murphy, Jim	*Truce: The Day the Soldiers Stopped Fighting*
Nelson, Kadir	*We Are the Ship: The Story of Negro League Baseball*
Rappaport, Doreen	*Lady Liberty, A Biography*
Ruelle, Karen Gray and Durland DeSaix, Deborah	*The Grand Mosque of Paris: A Story of How Muslims Rescued Jews During the Holocaust*
Sobol, Richard	*The Mysteries of Angkor Wat: Exploring Cambodia's ancient Temple*
Tilley Turner, Glennette	*Fort Mose*
Walker, Sally M.	*Secrets of a Civil War Submarine: Solving the Mysteries of the H. L. Hunley*

Expository Nonfiction

Bishop, Nic	*Marsupials*
Carrick Hill, Laban	*Harlem Stomp!*
Christensen, Bonnie	*Pompeii: Lost & Found*
Compoint, Stephane	*Buried Treasures: Uncovering Secrets of the Past*
D'Aluisio, Faith	*What the World Eats**
DK Publishing	*Eyewitness Expert: Shark*
Freedman, Russell	*Cowboys of the Wild West*
Giblin, James Cross	*Secrets of the Sphinx*
Halls, Kelly Milner	*Wild Dogs: Past & Present*

**Common Core State Standards Exemplar Text*

AUTHOR	TITLE	
Expository Nonfiction, *cont.*		
Jackson, Donna M.	*The Bone Detectives: How Forensic Anthropologists Solve Crimes and Uncover Mysteries of the Dead*	
Jackson, Ellen	*The Mysterious Universe: Supernovae, Dark Energy, and Black Holes*	
Kerley, Barbara	*A Cool Drink of Water*	
Markle, Sandra	*Vultures: Animal Scavengers*	
Milner Halls, Kelly	*Tales of the Cryptids: Mysterious Creatures that May or May Not Exist*	
Montgomery, Sy	*The Snake Scientist*	
Short, Joan and Bird, Bettina	*Crocodilians*	
Simon, Seymour	*Destination: Mars*	
Skerry, Brian	*Face to Face with Manatees*	
Snedden, Robert	*Yuck! A Big Book of Little Horrors*	
Vogel, Carole Garbuny, and Yossi Leshem	*The Man Who Flies With Birds*	
Procedural Texts		
Anderson, Maxine	*Amazing Leonardo da Vinci Inventions You Can Build Yourself*	
Bucholz, Dinah	*The Unofficial Harry Potter Cookbook*	
Gurstelle, William	*The Art of the Catapult: Build Greek Ballistae, Roman Onagers, English Trebuchets, and More Ancient Artillery*	
Macaulay, David	*Built to Last*	
Macaulay, David	*The New Way Things Work*	
Slavin, Bill	*Transformed: How Everyday Things Are Made*	
Stephens, Sarah Hines	*Show Off: How to do Absolutely Everything. One Step at a Time*	
Whitehead, Sarah	*How to Speak Dog*	
Woodford, Chris	*Cool Stuff And How It Works*	
Woodford, Chris	*Cool Stuff 2.0: And How It Works*	
Persuasive Texts		
Collard, Sneed B.	*Science Warriors: The Battle Against Invasive Species*	
Griffin Burns, Loree	*Tracking Trash: Flotsam, Jetsam, and the Science of Ocean Motion*	
Guiberson, Brenda	*Life in the Boreal Forest*	
Kurlansky, Mark	*World Without Fish*	
Markle, Sandra	*The Case of the Vanishing Golden Frogs*	
Silhol, Sandrine and Guerive, Gaelle	*Extraordinary Endangered Animals*	
Simon, Seymour	*Global Warming*	
Swinburne, Stephen R.	*Once a Wolf: How Wildlife Biologists Fought to Bring Back the Gray Wolf*	
Strauss, Rochelle	*One Well: The Story of Water on Earth*	
Turner, Pamela	*A Life in the Wild: George Schaller's Struggle to Save the Last Great Beasts*	
Hybrid Texts		
Abdul-Jabbar, Kareem	*What Color is My World? The Lost History of African-American Inventors*	biography realistic fiction
Albright, Archie	*Archie's War: My Scrapbook of the First World War (1914-1918)*	historical fiction expository nonfiction
Darrow, Sharon	*Through the Tempests Dark and Wild*	biographical text historical fiction

**Common Core State Standards Exemplar Text*

AUTHOR	TITLE	
Denenberg, Barry	*Titanic Sinks!*	narrative nonfiction historical fiction
Macaulay, David	*City: A Story of Roman Planning and Construction*	expository nonfiction historical fiction
Sidman, Joyce	*Dark Emperor & Other Poems of the Night*	expository nonfiction poetry (fiction)
Sidman, Joyce	*Ubiquitous: Celebrating Nature's Survivors*	expository nonfiction poetry (fiction)
Smith Jr., Charles R.	*Twelve Rounds to Glory: The Story of Muhammad Ali*	biography/poetry

Poetry

Atkins, Jeannine	*Borrowed Names*
Bernier-Grand, Carmen T.	*Frida*
Browning, Robert	*Robert Browning's The Pied Piper of Hamelin**
Carlson, Lori Marie	*Red Hot Salsa: Bilingual Poems About Being Young and Latino in the United States*
Fletcher, Ralph	*Buried Alive: The Elements of Love*
Holbrook, Sara	*Am I Naturally this Crazy?*
Holbrook, Sara	*I Never Said I Wasn't Difficult*
Holbrook, Sara	*Some Families*
Holbrook, Sara	*The Dog Ate My Homework*
Holbrook, Sara	*Walking on the Boundaries of Change*
Hughes, Langston	*The Dream Keepr and Other Poems*
Janeczko, Paul B.	*Requiem: Poems of the Terezín Ghetto*
Lear, Edward	*Edward Lear: Poetry for Young People*
Lewis, J. Patrick	*Skywriting: Poems to Fly*
McLaughlin, Timothy P. (edited by)	*Walking on Earth & Touching the Sky*
Myers, Walter Dean	*Harlem*
Myers, Walter Dean	*Jazz*
Myers, Walter Dean	*Looking Like Me*
Myers, Walter Dean	*A Blues Journey*
Nelson, Marilyn	*Carver: A Life in Poems*
Nelson, Marilyn	*A Wreath for Emmett Till*
Nye, Naomi Shihab	*19 Varieties of Gazelle: Poems of the Middle East*
Peters, Lisa Westberg	*Volcano Wakes Up!*
Rylant, Cynthia	*Waiting to Waltz: A Childhood*
Sidman, Joyce	*Dark Emperor and Other Poems of the Night*
Singer, Marilyn	*All We Needed to Say: Poems About School from Tanya and Sophie*
Singer, Marilyn	*Central Heating: Poems About Fire and Warmth*
Smith, Phillip (edited by)	*100 Best-Loved Poems*
Soto, Gary	*Canto Familiar**
Soto, Gary	*Neighborhood Odes**
Thayer, Ernest	*Casey at the Bat: A Ballad of the Republic Sung in the Year 1888*
Willard, Nancy	*A Visit to William Blake's Inn*
Young, Ed	*Beyond the Great Mountains: A Visual Poem About China*

**Common Core State Standards Exemplar Text*

Glossary

ADVENTURE / ADVENTURE STORY A contemporary realistic or historical fiction or fantasy text that presents a series of exciting or suspenseful events, often involving a main character taking a journey and overcoming danger and risk.

ALLITERATION The repetition of identical or similar initial consonant sounds in consecutive or nearby words or syllables.

ANIMAL FANTASY A modern fantasy text geared to a very young audience in which animals act like people and encounter human problems.

ANIMAL STORY A contemporary realistic or historical fiction or fantasy text that involves animals and that often focuses on the relationships between humans and animals.

ARGUMENT A persuasive nonfiction text that presents a series of logically organized reasons for a belief, attitude, or proposed action. The term *argument* can also be used to mean "main idea" in a persuasive nonfiction text. See also *discussion* and *persuasive essay*.

ARGUMENTATIVE An underlying structural pattern used especially in nonfiction texts to present a series of persuasive statements or opinions with reasons attached.

ASSONANCE The repetition of identical or similar vowel sounds in stressed syllables in words that usually end with different consonant sounds. Compare with *rhyme*.

AUDIENCE The readers of a text. Often a writer crafts a text with a particular audience (with specific characteristics such as age or level of understanding) in mind. Readers can sharpen their appreciation and understanding of a text by identifying the writer's intended audience.

AUTHENTIC BIOGRAPHY A biography that is thoroughly grounded in research, that recounts only documented events, that includes no imagined details or dialogue, that does not attribute feelings to characters, and that is written by someone who has searched for actual comments by the subject or comments from those who have written or talked about the subject. Compare with *fictionalized biography* and *biographical fiction*.

AUTOBIOGRAPHY A biographical text in which the story of a person's life is written and narrated by that person. Autobiography is usually told in chronological sequence but may be in another order.

BALLAD A traditional poem or tale, often recited or sung, and usually telling a story important to a particular region or culture. First handed down orally and later in writing, ballads usually feature a hero whose deeds and attributes have grown and become exaggerated over time.

BEAST TALE A folktale featuring animals that talk.

BIOGRAPHICAL FICTION A fiction text in which a real person may be identified and used as a starting point, but in which the writer imagines many events, actions, and characters, as well as dialogue. Compare with *authentic biography*.

BIOGRAPHICAL TEXT A nonfiction text that is focused on the story (or part of the story) of a real person's life. Biographical texts include biography, autobiography, and memoir.

BIOGRAPHY A biographical text in which the story (or part of the story) of a real person's life is written and narrated by another person. Biography is usually told in chronological sequence but may be in another order.

CATEGORICAL TEXT An expository nonfiction text that presents information in logical categories (and subcategories) of related material. All such categories are clearly related to a major topic, and there may be diagrams to show how categories of information are related. Another term for categorical text is *enumeration*.

CAUSE AND EFFECT An underlying structural pattern used especially in nonfiction texts, often to propose the reasons or explanations for how and why something occurs.

CHAPTER BOOK A text that is divided into chapters, each of which narrates an episode in the whole (usually called so by younger readers).

CHARACTER An individual, usually a person or animal, in a text.

CHRONOLOGICAL SEQUENCE An underlying structural pattern used especially in nonfiction texts to describe a series of events in the order they happened in time. See also *recount*.

CINQUAIN A Japanese-inspired poem of five lines composed usually with two, four, six, eight, and two syllables.

CLASSIC/CLASSIC BOOK A book that over time is considered to epitomize the characteristics of high-quality literature. Classics exist in all genres and include themes that have been important in many different eras.

COLLECTION An expository text that presents a body of material as a list. Items are organized, sometimes with descriptors, into a database that may be printed, accessed via Internet, or on a computer disk. A collection may be included as a reference tool in a factual text.

COMBINATION An underlying structural pattern used in nonfiction texts, in which two or more structural patterns are present within a single text. Many nonfiction texts use a combination of structural patterns including argumentative, cause and effect, chronological sequence, compare and contrast, descriptive, problem and solution, question and answer, and temporal sequence.

COMEDY Formerly, a fiction text that ends happily and that is intended to amuse through humor and wit. Like tragedy, satire, and epic, comedy once was a widely produced genre but now appears in different forms or embedded within other genres.

COMIC BOOK A volume presenting strips of comics that tell a longer story about the same characters.

COMIC STRIP Panels of graphics and print that tell a continuing story about the same characters. Comic strips often appear in magazines and newspapers.

COMPARE AND CONTRAST An underlying structural pattern used especially in nonfiction texts to compare two ideas, events, or phenomena by showing how they are alike and how they are different.

CONCRETE POETRY Poems with words (and sometimes punctuation) arranged to present a concrete picture of the idea the poem is conveying. See also *shape poem*.

CONFLICT In fiction texts, a central problem within the plot that is resolved near the end of the story. In literature, characters are usually in conflict with nature, with other people, with society as a whole, or with themselves.

CONSONANCE The repetition of the final consonant sounds in words with different vowels. Compare with *assonance*.

CRIME/CRIME STORY A contemporary realistic or historical fiction or fantasy text focused on how a criminal commits a crime and is (usually) brought to justice.

CUMULATIVE TALE A folktale in which story events are repeated with each new episode, giving them a rhythmic quality.

DESCRIPTIVE An underlying structural pattern used especially in nonfiction texts to provide sensory and emotional details so that readers can determine how something looks, moves, tastes, smells, or feels.

DESIGN FEATURES The characteristics of a text's appearance on the page. Design features of nonfiction texts include text divisions, organizational tools and sources of information, graphic features, print features, and layout. Readers can analyze design features to help them evaluate nonfiction texts.

DIALOGUE Spoken words, usually set off with quotation marks in text. Dialogue is an element of a writer's style.

DIARY A record of events and observations written in the first person and kept regularly in sequential, dated entries.

DIRECTIONS (HOW-TO) A procedural nonfiction text that shows the steps involved in performing a task. A set of directions may include diagrams or drawings with labels.

DISCUSSION A persuasive nonfiction text that presents the pros and cons of a situation, event, or phenomenon. Discussion generally seeks full disclosure of information in an objective way and presents specific information. See also *argument* and *persuasive essay*.

EDITORIAL A persuasive nonfiction text in which the purpose is to state and defend an opinion, usually by an editor of a magazine, newspaper, or TV news show. Editorials are usually written in spare, journalistic style.

ELEMENTS OF BIOGRAPHY Important elements of biography include characters, sequence of events, theme, setting, and perspective, as well as graphic features and print features.

ELEMENTS OF FICTION Important elements of fiction include narrator, characters, plot, setting, theme, and style.

ELEMENTS OF POETRY Important elements of poetry include figurative language, imagery, personification, rhythm, rhyme, repetition, alliteration, assonance, consonance, onomatopoeia, and aspects of layout.

ENUMERATION See *categorical text.*

EPIC A traditional tale or long narrative poem, first handed down orally and later in writing. Usually an epic involves a journey and a set of tasks or tests in which the hero triumphs. Generally the nature of the deeds and attributes of the hero have grown and become exaggerated over time. Like comedy, tragedy, and satire, epic was once was a widely produced genre but now appears in different forms or embedded within other genres.

ESSAY An analytic or interpretive piece of expository writing with a focused point of view, or a persuasive text that provided a body of information related to a social or scientific issue.

EXPOSITORY TEXT A nonfiction text that gives the reader information about a topic. Expository texts use a variety of text structures, such as compare and contrast, cause and effect, chronological sequence, problem and solution, and temporal sequence. Seven forms of expository text are categorical text, recount, collection, interview, report, feature article, and literary essay.

FABLE A folktale that demonstrates a useful truth and teaches a lesson. Usually including personified animals or natural elements such as the sun, fables appear to be simple but often convey abstract ideas.

FAIRY TALE A folktale about real problems but also involving magic and magical creatures. Also called "wonder tales," fairy tales have been handed down through oral language over the years.

FANTASY A category of fiction that includes the following genres—traditional literature, folktale, fairy tale, fable, legend, epic, ballad, myth, modern fantasy, animal fantasy, low fantasy, high fantasy, and science fiction.

FEATURE ARTICLE An expository text that presents information organized around a central theme or idea, or one particular aspect of a topic. A feature article may use one or more structural patterns to weave a cohesive sequence of ideas. Feature articles usually are published in newspapers and magazines.

FICTION Invented, imaginative prose or poetry that tells a story. Fiction texts can be organized into the categories realism and fantasy. Along with nonfiction, fiction is one of two basic genres of literature.

FICTIONALIZED BIOGRAPHY A biography based on research in which the main events of the story and characters are authentic, but in which the author imagines some details, guesses at a subject's thoughts and motivations, or invents dialogue. Compare with *authentic biography* and *biographical fiction.*

FIGURATIVE LANGUAGE Language that compares two objects or ideas to allow the reader to see something more clearly or understand something in a new way. An element of a writer's style, figurative language changes or goes beyond literal meaning. Two common types of figurative language are metaphor (a direct comparison) and simile (a comparison that uses *like* or *as*).

FLASH-FORWARD A literary device in which the action moves suddenly into the future to relate events that have relevance for understanding the present.

FLASHBACK A literary device in which the action moves suddenly into the past to relate events that have relevance for understanding the present.

FOLKTALE A traditional fiction text about a people or "folk," originally handed down orally from generation to generation. Folktales are usually simple tales and often involve talking animals. Fables, fairy tales, beast tales, trickster tales, tall tales, realistic tales, cumulative tales, noodlehead tales, and pourquoi tales are some types of folktales.

FORM A kind of text that is characterized by particular elements. Mystery, for example, is a form of writing within the realistic fiction genre. Another term for form is *subgenre*.

FORMAL LETTER A functional nonfiction text usually addressed to a stranger, in which the form (for example, a business letter) follows specific conventions.

FOUND POEM A piece of writing declared to be a poem because of some poetic even quality though the writing was not intended to be a poem.

FREE VERSE A form of poetry with irregular meter. Free verse may include rhyme, alliteration, and other poetic sound devices.

FRIENDLY LETTER A functional nonfiction text usually addressed to friends and family that may take the form of notes, letters, invitations, or email.

FUNCTIONAL TEXT A nonfiction text intended to accomplish a practical task. Letters, lists, test writing, and writing about reading are examples of functional text.

GENRE A kind of category of text or artistic work or a class of artistic endeavor that has a characteristic form or technique, including music, drama, and studio arts.

GRAPHIC FEATURE In fiction texts, graphic features are usually illustrations. In nonfiction texts, graphic features include photographs, paintings and drawings, captions, charts, diagrams, tables and graphs, maps, and timelines.

GRAPHIC NONFICTION TEXT A book-length nonfiction text with comic strips on every page and factual information presented in categories or sequence.

GRAPHIC NOVEL A book-length fiction text with comic strips or other illustrations on every page and a story line that continues across the text. Illustrations, which depict moment-to-moment actions and characters' emotions, are usually accompanied by dialogue in speech balloons and occasional narrative description of actions.

GRAPHICA Fiction or nonfiction texts that integrate pictures and words and arrange them cumulatively to tell a story or convey information.

HAIKU An ancient Japanese form of non-rhyming poetry that creates a mental picture and makes a concise emotional statement.

HIGH FANTASY A long, complex modern fantasy text characterized by the motifs of traditional literature—the quest, struggle between good and evil, the hero. High fantasy involves stories that take place in an alternative world alongside the real world, or where our world does not exist. Compare with *low fantasy*.

HISTORICAL FICTION A fiction text that takes place in a realistically (and often factually) portrayed setting of a past era. Historical fiction focuses on the problems and issues of life in a particular historic time period. Compare with *realistic fiction*.

HORROR / HORROR STORY A fiction text in which events evoke a feeling of dread in both the characters and the reader. Horror stories often involve elements of fantasy, but they may also fit into the category of realism.

HOW-TO See *directions (how-to)*.

HUMOR / HUMOR STORY A realistic fiction text that is full of fun and meant to entertain.

HYBRID / HYBRID TEXT A text that includes at least one nonfiction genre and at least one fiction genre blended in a coherent whole. In some hybrid texts, genres are smoothly blended. Sometimes a text of a certain genre is embedded within a text of another genre. Other times, the primary text is one genre with different sections of text (of another genre) set apart.

ILLUSTRATION Graphic representation of important content (for example, art, photos, maps, graphs, charts) in a fiction or nonfiction text.

IMAGERY The use of language—descriptions, comparisons, and figures of speech—that helps the mind form sensory impressions. Imagery is an element of a writer's style.

INFORMATIONAL TEXT A nonfiction text including the following genres—biography, autobiography, memoir, and narrative nonfiction, as well as expository texts, procedural texts, and persuasive texts.

INTERVIEW An expository text that organizes information in a series of questions with responses. Interviews may be based on a verbal or written interview, or on frequently arising or logical questions about a topic. See also *question and answer.*

IRONY The use of words to express the opposite of the literal meaning. Irony is an important device in many genres of fiction and nonfiction texts, and it is crucial to works of satire.

LAYOUT The way print and illustration are arranged on a page. For example, poets sometimes use line breaks after particular words to support the central meaning of a poem or to add additional meaning to it. In nonfiction texts, aspects of layout include the use of columns, shading, bullets, and white space. See also *design features.*

LEGEND A traditional tale, first handed down orally and later in writing, that tells about a noteworthy person or event. Legends are believed to have some root in history, but the accuracy of the events and people they describe is not always verifiable. Some legends developed in relation to modern phenomena, such as technological inventions or unexplained events.

LIMERICK A form of rhyming verse, usually surprising and humorous and frequently nonsensical.

LIST POEM A rhymed or unrhymed poem of any length that is an itemization of things or events. Another term for list poem is *catalog poem.*

LITERARY ESSAY An expository text that presents ideas about a work (or works) of literature in a formal, analytic way.

LITERARY NONFICTION Nonfiction texts that employ literary techniques, such as figurative language, to present information in engaging ways.

LOW FANTASY A modern fantasy text that takes place in the real world but which also includes characters, places, and events that do not and could not exist in the real world. Low fantasy may be contemporary or historical. Though low fantasy does not come from an oral tradition, it sometimes reflects characteristics of traditional literature. In general, low fantasy requires less suspension of disbelief than high fantasy because the author provides a bridge between the real world and a world of fantasy. Compare with *high fantasy.*

LYRIC A songlike poem that has rhythm and sometimes rhyme and is memorable for sensory images and description.

MANGA A form of graphic storytelling that uses stylized Japanese illustrations to represent characters. Manga is sometimes intended for middle-school or young adult readers, and it is often separated into *shojo* for females and *shonen* for males.

MEMOIR A biographical text in which a writer takes a reflective stance in looking back on a particular time or person. Usually written in the first person, memoirs are often briefer and more intense accounts of a memory or set of memories than the accounts found in biographies and autobiographies.

MENTOR TEXT A book or other text that serves as an example of excellent writing. Mentor texts provide models of specific genres for literature discussion and student writing.

METAPHOR A type of figurative language that describes one thing by comparing it to something else without using the words *like* or *as*. Compare with *simile*.

METER The rhythmical pattern in verse. See also *rhythm*.

MODERN FANTASY Fantasy texts that have contemporary content. Unlike traditional literature, modern fantasy does not come from an oral tradition. Modern fantasy texts can be divided into four more specific genres: animal fantasy, low fantasy, high fantasy, and science fiction.

MOOD The emotional atmosphere communicated by an author in his or her work, or how a text makes readers feel. An element of a writer's style, mood is established by details, imagery, figurative language, and setting. See also *tone*.

MOTIF A characteristic feature of a text, such as a recurring theme, idea, or subject. For example, six basic motifs in modern fantasy and traditional literature are the struggle between good and evil, magic, secondary or alternative worlds, the hero's quest, special character types, and fantastic or magical objects.

MYSTERY / MYSTERY STORY A contemporary realistic or historical fiction or fantasy text that deals with the solution of a crime or the unraveling of secrets. A mystery has a plot that hinges on a puzzling situation or event that is resolved by the end.

MYTH A traditional narrative text, often based in part on historical events, that explains human behavior and natural events or phenomena such as seasons and the sky.

NARRATIVE NONFICTION Nonfiction texts that tell a story using a narrative structure and literary language to make a topic interesting and appealing to readers.

NARRATIVE POEM A story poem with rhyme and rhythm that relates an event or episode.

NARRATIVE STRUCTURE A method of organizing a text. A simple narrative structure follows a traditional sequence that includes a beginning, a problem, a series of events, a resolution of the problem, and an ending. Alternative narrative structures may include devices, such as flashback or flash-forward, to change the sequence of events or have multiple narrators.

NARRATOR The teller of the story of a text. The terms *perspective* and *point of view* also indicate the angle from which the story is told, usually the first person (the narrator is a character in the story) or the third person (the unnamed narrator is not a character in the story).

NON-NARRATIVE STRUCTURE A method of organizing a text. Non-narrative structures are used especially in three genres of nonfiction—expository texts, procedural texts, and persuasive texts. In non-narrative nonfiction texts, structural patterns include argumentative, categorical, descriptive, chronological, temporal, compare and contrast, cause and effect, problem and solution, and question and answer.

NONFICTION Prose or poetry that provides factual information. Along with fiction, nonfiction is one of the two basic genres of literature. According to their structures, nonfiction texts can be organized into the categories of narrative and non-narrative.

NOODLEHEAD STORY A humorous folktale featuring one or more foolish characters who often behave in surprising ways, often making mistake after mistake but coming out on top in the end.

NOVEL A work of prose fiction that is usually long and complex and focused on human experience as it is revealed in a series of interrelated events.

ONOMATOPOEIA The representation of sound with words.

ORAL TRADITION The handing down of literary material—such as songs, poems, and stories—from person to person over many generations through memory and word of mouth.

ORGANIZATION The arrangement of ideas in a text according to a logical structure, either narrative or non-narrative. Another term for organization is *text structure*.

ORGANIZATIONAL TOOLS AND SOURCES OF INFORMATION A design feature of nonfiction texts. Organizational tools and sources of information help a reader process and understand nonfiction texts. Examples include table of contents, headings, index, glossary, appendices, about the author, and references.

PERSONIFICATION A figure of speech in which an animal is spoken of or portrayed as if it were a person, or in which a lifeless thing or idea is spoken of or portrayed as a living thing. Personification is one type of figurative language.

PERSPECTIVE The angle from which the story is told, usually the first person (the narrator is a character in the story) or the third person (the unnamed narrator is not a character in the story). Another term for perspective is *point of view*. See also *narrator*.

PERSUASIVE ESSAY A persuasive nonfiction text that provides a body of information related to social or scientific issues. Persuasive essays encourage the reader to develop generalizations and principles on which to make decisions. See also *argument* and *discussion*.

PERSUASIVE TEXT A nonfiction text intended to convince the reader of the validity of a set of ideas—usually a particular point of view. Three forms of persuasive text are argument, discussion, and persuasive essay.

PICTURE BOOK An illustrated fiction or nonfiction text in which pictures work with the text to tell a story or provide information.

PLOT The events and actions, the conflict, and the order in which this information is presented in a fiction text. A simple plot progresses chronologically from start to end, whereas more complex plots may shift back and forth in time.

POETRY Compact, metrical writing characterized by imagination and artistry and imbued with intense meaning. Along with prose, poetry is one of the two broad categories into which all literature can be divided.

POINT OF VIEW The angle from which the story is told, usually the first person (the narrator is a character in the story) or the third person (the unnamed narrator is not a character in the story). Another term for point of view is *perspective*. See also *narrator*.

POURQUOI TALE A folktale intended to explain why things are the way they are, usually having to do with natural phenomena.

PRINT FEATURE In nonfiction texts, print features include the color, size, style, and font of type, as well as various aspects of layout.

PROBLEM AND SOLUTION An underlying structural pattern used especially in nonfiction texts, often in persuasive and expository texts. This structural pattern allows a writer to define a problem and clearly propose a solution.

PROCEDURAL TEXT A nonfiction text that explains how to do something. Procedural texts are almost always organized in temporal sequence and take the form of directions (or "how-to" texts) or descriptions of a process.

PROSE The ordinary form of spoken or written language in sentences and paragraphs and without the metrical structure of poetry. Along with poetry, prose is one of the two broad categories into which all literature can be divided. Prose includes two basic genres, fiction and nonfiction.

PURPOSE A writer's overall intention in creating a text, or a reader's overall intention in reading a text. To tell a story is one example of a writer's purpose, and to be entertained is one example of a reader's purpose.

QUATRAIN In poetry, a four-line stanza with a rhyming pattern.

QUESTION AND ANSWER An underlying structural pattern used especially in nonfiction texts to organize information in a series of questions with responses. Question-and-answer texts may be based on a verbal or written interview, or on frequently arising or logical questions about a topic. See also *interview*.

REALISM A category of fiction that includes two genres—contemporary realistic fiction and historical fiction. Realism presents events that take place in the real world, either past or present.

REALISTIC FICTION A fiction text that takes place in contemporary or modern times about believable characters involved in events that could happen. Contemporary realistic fiction usually presents modern problems that are typical for the characters, and it may highlight social issues. Compare with *historical fiction.*

REALISTIC TALE A folktale that does not involve talking animals but has been passed down orally over time. Realistic tales are often humorous, portraying the customs and foibles of rural people.

RECOUNT An expository text that presents events in chronological sequence. Sometimes a recounting may start in the present and move backwards in time. A recount may include timelines and diagrams that show time periods clearly. See also *chronological sequence.*

REPETITION Repeated words or phrases that help to create rhythm and emphasis in poetry or prose.

REPORT An expository text that synthesizes information from several sources in order to inform the reader about some general principles.

RHYME The repetition of vowel and consonant sounds in the stressed syllables of words in verse, especially at the ends of lines.

RHYTHM The regular or ordered repetition of stressed and unstressed syllables in speech or writing, especially poetry. See also *meter.*

ROMANCE A contemporary realistic or historical fiction text focused on the development of romantic (and sometimes sexual) attraction between characters.

SAGA A long, sophisticated traditional tale or narrative poem. See also *epic.*

SATIRE Formerly, a fiction text that uses sarcasm and irony to portray and ridicule human failures. Like comedy, tragedy, and epic, satire once was a widely produced genre but now appears in different forms or embedded within other genres.

SCIENCE FICTION Modern fantasy texts that involve technology, futuristic scenarios, and real or imagined scientific phenomena. Science fiction texts usually fall into one of four categories: blend of fantasy and science, technology and science, outer space and alien worlds, or futuristic stories.

SEQUEL A literary work, typically a fiction text, that continues a story begun in a previous book. The central character usually remains the same, and new secondary characters may be introduced. Books with sequels are generally meant to be read in order. A sequel is a type of series book.

SEQUENCE See *chronological sequence* and *temporal sequence.*

SERIES A set of books that are connected by the same character(s) or setting. Each book in a series stands alone, and often books may be read in any order.

SETTING The place and time in which a fiction text or biographical text takes place.

SHAPE POEM Poetry with words (and sometimes punctuation) arranged in interesting ways that may be tied to the poem's meaning. See also *concrete poetry.*

SHORT STORY A work of prose fiction that is focused on human experience as it is revealed in a series of interrelated events. Shorter and less complex structurally than novels, short stories use most of the same literary elements that are found in novels.

SIMILE A type of figurative language that makes a comparison of two different things using the words *like* or *as*. Compare with *metaphor*.

SONNET A form of poetry consisting of fourteen lines, usually with three four-line stanzas—each with its own rhyme pattern—and ending with a couplet. Sonnets are written in regular meter (ten beats per line).

SPORTS STORY A contemporary realistic or historical fiction text focused on athletes and sports.

STORY A series of events in narrative form, either fiction or nonfiction.

STORY ABOUT FAMILY, FRIENDS, AND SCHOOL A contemporary realistic or historical fiction text that focuses on the everyday experiences of children of a variety of ages, including relationships with family and friends and experiences at school.

STORY WITHIN A STORY A structural device occasionally used in fiction texts to present a shorter, self-contained narrative within the context of the longer primary narrative.

STYLE The way a writer chooses and arranges words to create a meaningful text. Aspects of style include sentence length, word choice, and the use of figurative language and symbolism.

SUBGENRE A kind of text that is characterized by particular elements. See also *form.*

SURVIVAL STORY A contemporary realistic or historical fiction text in which a character or characters must struggle against nature or other people in order to stay alive.

SYMBOLISM A literary device in which a writer uses an object, person, or situation to represent a larger idea that goes beyond a literal meaning. For example, a writer might use an object such as a tree symbolically to represent nature, or a writer might use a particular character to represent an idea such as loyalty or treachery. Symbolism is an element of a writer's style.

TALL TALE A folktale that revolves around a central legendary character with extraordinary physical features or abilities. Tall tales are characterized by a great deal of exaggeration.

TEMPORAL SEQUENCE An underlying structural pattern used especially in nonfiction texts to describe the sequence in which something always or usually occurs, such as the steps in a process. See also *procedural text,* and *directions (how-to).*

TEXT DIVISION A design feature of nonfiction and fiction texts. Text divisions including chapters, sections, subsections, and paragraphs signal to readers the way a text "works"—that is, the way a writer has structured or organized it.

TEXT STRUCTURE The overall architecture or organization of a piece of writing. Another term for text structure is *organization.* See also *narrative structure* and *non-narrative structure.*

THEME The central underlying idea, concept, or message that the author conveys in a text.

TONE An expression of the author's attitude or feelings toward a subject reflected in the style of writing. For instance, a reader might characterize an author's tone as ironic or earnest. Sometimes the term *tone* is used to identify the mood of a scene or a work of literature. For example, a text might be said to have a somber or carefree tone. See also *mood.*

TRADITIONAL LITERATURE Stories passed down in oral or written form through history. An integral part of world culture, traditional literature includes the following genres—folktales, fairy tales, fables, legends, epics, sagas, ballads, and myths. See also *oral tradition.*

TRAGEDY Formerly, a fiction text that ends unhappily and that is intended to evoke strong emotions in the audience. Tragedy often involves a noble or otherwise dignified hero who struggles against eventual defeat. Like comedy, satire, and epic, tragedy once was a widely produced genre but now appears in different forms or embedded within other genres.

TRICKSTER TALE A folktale featuring a clever, usually physically weaker or smaller animal who outsmarts larger or more powerful animals.

VOICE The unique way that a writer uses language to convey ideas.

WESTERN / WESTERN STORY A fiction text set in the rural parts of the American West, primarily in the latter half of the nineteenth century, though some are set in more contemporary times. Westerns often involve cattle herding and strong, tough characters who must pit themselves against the harsh elements and customs of the landscape and time period.

ANALYZING TEXT FACTORS FOR FICTION

Analysis of ______________________________ **Level** __________

Text Factor	**Analysis**
Genre	
Text Structure	
Content	
Themes and Ideas	
Language and Literary Features	
Sentence Complexity	
Vocabulary	
Words	
Illustrations	
Book and Print Features	

ANALYZING TEXT FACTORS FOR NONFICTION		
MEANING		
Ideas and Themes	Important ideas:	Emerging theme:
ORGANIZATION/STRUCTURE		
Overall Organizational Structure	Present in the text:	Description:
Underlying Structural Patterns	Present in the text:	Description:

ANALYZING TEXT FACTORS FOR NONFICTION

DESIGN

Structural Features	Important ideas:	Emerging theme:
Organizational Features	Important ideas:	Emerging theme:
Graphic Features	Important ideas:	Emerging theme:
Print Features	Important ideas:	Emerging theme:
Layout Features	Important ideas:	Emerging theme:

List of Children's Books That Appear in *Genre Study*

AUTHOR	TITLE
Aardema	*Why Mosquitoes Buzz in People's Ears*
Abells, Chana Byers	*The Children We Remember*
Ada, Alma Flor	*Me llamo María Isabel*
Adams, Richard	*Watership Down*
Aesop	*The Tortoise and the Hare*
Aesop	*The Wind and the Sun*
Aesop (adapted by Jerry Pinkney)	*The Lion and the Mouse*
Alcott, Louisa May	*Little Women*
Alexander, Lloyd	*The Book of Three* (The Chronicles of Prydain)
Alexander, Lloyd	*The Black Cauldron* (The Chronicles of Prydain)
Alexander, Lloyd	*The Castle of Llry* (The Chronicles of Prydain)
Alexander, Lloyd	*Taran Wanderer* (The Chronicles of Prydain)
Alexander, Lloyd	*The High King* (The Chronicles of Prydain)
Alexander, Lloyd	*Westmark* (The Westmark Trilogy)
Alexander, Lloyd	*The Kestrel* (The Westmark Trilogy)
Alexander, Lloyd	*The Beggar Queen* (The Westmark Trilogy)
Aliki	*Those Summers*
America's Test Kitchen	*Cook's Illustrated Cookbook*
Anderson, Laurie Halse	*Independent Dames: What You Never Knew About the Women and Girls of the American Revolution*
Applegate, K. A.	Animorphs series
Arnold, Helen	*Postcards from Australia*
Arnosky, Jim	*All About Frogs*
Arnosky, Jim	*All About Lizards*
Arnosky, Jim	*All About Turkeys*
Arnosky, Jim	*Slow Down for Manatees*
Avi	*Amanda Joins the Circus*
Avi	*The Fighting Ground*
Avi	*Something Upstairs*
Avi	*The True Confessions of Charlotte Doyle*
Babbitt, Natalie	*The Search for Delicious*
Babbitt, Natalie	*Tuck Everlasting*
Bacon, Ron	*Amazing Journeys*
Bacon, Ron	*The Sun*
Bardoe, Cheryl	*Gregor Mendel: The Friar Who Grew Peas*
Barrows, Annie	Ivy + Bean series
Bass, Hester	*The Secret World of Walter Anderson*

AUTHOR	TITLE
Bateman, Robert	*Safari*
Baum, L. Frank	*The Wonderful Wizard of Oz*
Berenstain, Stan, and Jan Berenstain	Berenstain Bears series
Berne, Jennifer	*Manfish: A Story of Jacques Cousteau*
Bial, Raymond	*The Underground Railroad*
Birchall, Brian	*Acid Rain*
Birney, Betty G.	Humphrey the Hamster series
Blackford, Harriet and Manja Stojic	*Elephant's Story*
Blume, Judy	*Are You There God? It's Me, Margaret*
Blume, Judy	*Tales of a Fourth Grade Nothing*
Blume, Judy	*Then Again, Maybe I Won't*
Boyd, Candy Dawson	*Circle of Gold*
Bradbury, Ray	*Fahrenheit 451*
Brown, Don	*A Voice from the Wilderness: The Story of Anna Howard Shaw*
Brown, Marc	Arthur series
Brown, Marcia	*Once a Mouse*
Brown, Margaret Wise	*Goodnight Moon*
Bulla, Clyde Robert	*The Chalk Box Kid*
Bunting, Eve	*Butterfly House*
Bunting, Eve	*Coffin on a Case*
Bunting, Eve	*Dandelions*
Bunting, Eve	*Jumping the Nail*
Bunting, Eve	*One Green Apple*
Burch, Jennings Michael	*They Cage the Animals at Night*
Burnford, Sheila	*The Incredible Journey*
Burns, Batt	*The King with Horse's Ears and Other Irish Folktales*
Burrowes, Adjoa J.	*Grandma's Purple Flowers*
Byars, Betsy	*The Night Swimmers*
Byars, Betsy	*The Pinballs*
Cameron, Eleanor	*The Wonderful Flight to the Mushroom Planet*
Campbell, Sarah C.	*Wolfsnail: A Backyard Predator*
Capstone Press	Graphic Science and Graphic History series
Card, Orson Scott	*Ender's Game*
Carroll, Lewis	*Alice's Adventures in Wonderland*
Cassino, Mark with Jon Nelson, Ph.D.	*The Story of Snow: The Science of Winter's Wonder*
Catling, Patrick	*The Chocolate Touch*
Chaconas, Dori	*Pennies in a Jar*
Chanko, Pamela and Samantha Berger	*Baby Animals Learn*
Chen, Jiang Hong	*Mao and Me: The Little Red Guard*

AUTHOR	TITLE
Cherry, Lynne	*The Great Kapok Tree: A Tale of the Amazon Rain Forest*
Cherry, Lynne	*A River Ran Wild: An Environmental History*
Children's Press	Rookie Biography series
Choi, Sook Nyul	*Year of Impossible Goodbyes*
Christelow, Eileen	Five Little Monkeys books
Christensen, Bonnie	*Django: World's Greatest Jazz Guitarist*
Christopher, Matt	Peach Street Mudders series
Cleary, Beverly	Beezus and Ramona series
Cleary, Beverly	*Dear Mr. Henshaw*
Cleary, Beverly	*Otis Spofford*
Clements, Andrew	*Frindle*
Clements, Andrew	*Lost and Found*
Clements, Andrew	*The Report Card*
Clinton, Catherine	*When Harriet Met Sojourner*
Cobb, Vicki	*I Face the Wind*
Coerr, Eleanor	*Mieko and the Fifth Treasure*
Coffelt, Nancy	*Fred Stays with Me!*
Cohen, Barbara	*Thank You, Jackie Robinson*
Cole, Henry	*A Nest for Celeste: A Story About Art, Inspiration, and the Meaning of Home*
Cole, Joanna	The Magic School Bus series
Cole, Joanna and Bruce Degen	*The Magic School Bus on the Ocean Floor*
Collier, James Lincoln	*Jump Ship to Freedom*
Collins, Suzanne	*The Hunger Games*
Collins, Suzanne	*Catching Fire*
Collins, Suzanne	*Mockingjay*
Collodi, Carlo	*Pinocchio*
Cooper, Floyd	*Mandela: From the Life of the South African Statesman*
Cooper, Susan	*The Dark Is Rising*
Cooper, Susan	*The Grey King*
Cooper, Susan	*Greenwitch*
Cooper, Susan	*Over Sea, Under Stone*
Cooper, Susan	*Silver on the Tree*
Couper, Heather and Nigel Henbest	*Black Holes: A Journey to the Heart of a Black Hole–and into One of the Greatest Mysteries of the Universe*
Craft, Charlotte	*King Midas and the Golden Touch*
Cray, Jordan	danger.com series
Creech, Sharon	*Walk Two Moons*
Crews, Donald	*Bigmama's*
Crisp, Marty	*Everything Dog*

AUTHOR	TITLE
Curtis, Christopher Paul	*Elijah of Buxton*
Curtis, Christopher Paul	*The Watsons Go to Birmingham—1963*
Cushman, Karen	*Catherine, Called Birdy*
D'Aulaire, Ingri and Edgar Parin	*Abraham Lincoln*
D'Aulaire, Ingri and Edgar Parin	*D'Aulaires' Book of Greek Myths*
D'Aulaire, Ingri and Edgar Parin	*D'Aulaires' Book of Norse Myths*
Dahl, Roald	*Charlie and the Chocolate Factory*
Dahl, Roald	*George's Marvelous Medicine*
Dahl, Roald	*James and the Giant Peach*
Dahl, Roald	*The Magic Finger*
Dahl, Roald	*The Twits*
De la Peña, Matt	*A Nation's Hope: The Story of Boxing Legend Joe Louis*
Deedy, Carmen Agra	*Martina the Beautiful Cockroach: A Cuban Folktale*
Defoe, Daniel	*Robinson Crusoe*
DePaola, Tomie	*Nana Upstairs and Nana Downstairs*
DiCamillo, Kate	*Because of Winn-Dixie*
Dickinson, Peter	*Eva*
Dixon, Franklin W.	Hardy Boys series
DK Children	DK Eyewitness set
DK Publishing	*Holiday! Celebration Days Around the World*
Doeden, Matt	*The Sinking of the Titanic*
Dogar, Sharon	*Annexed*
Domain, Helena	*Robotics*
Douglass, Frederick	*Escape from Slavery: The Boyhood of Frederick Douglass in His Own Words*
Doyle, Arthur Conan	Sherlock Holmes mysteries
Editors at America's Test Kitchen	*The Cook's Illustrated Cookbook*
Ehlert, Lois	*Growing Vegetable Soup*
Engdahl, Sylvia Louise	*The Enchantress from the Stars*
Erickson, Paul	*Daily Life in a Covered Wagon*
Estes, Eleanor	*The Hundred Dresses*
Exploring the Earth	*Mighty Mammals*
Falconer, Ian	*Olivia*
Fandel, Jennifer	*Alexander Graham Bell and the Telephone*
Fandel, Jennifer	*George Eastman and the Kodak Camera*
Farmer, Nancy	*The Ear, the Eye, and the Arm*
Farmer, Nancy	*A Girl Named Disaster*
Fergus, Mary Pat	*I'm a Chef*
Field, Rachel	*Hitty: Her First Hundred Years*
Finley, Martha	*Elsie Dinsmore*
Fleischman, Paul	*Glass Slipper, Gold Sandal: A Worldwide Cinderella*

AUTHOR	TITLE
Fleischman, Paul	*Seedfolks*
Fleschmein, Paul	*Weslandia*
Fletcher, Ralph	*Fig Pudding*
Florian, Douglas	*Beast Feast: Poems and Paintings*
Florian, Douglas	*POETREES*
Fountas & Pinnell LLI Blue System	*All About Astronauts*
Fountas & Pinnell LLI Blue System	*All About Bats*
Fountas & Pinnell LLI Blue System	*All About Dinosaurs*
Fountas & Pinnell LLI Blue System	*All About Redwood Trees*
Fountas & Pinnell LLI Blue System	*All About the Sonoran Desert*
Fountas & Pinnell LLI Blue System	*All About Spiders*
Fountas & Pinnell LLI Blue System	*All About Volcanoes*
Fountas & Pinnell LLI Blue System	*Eugenie Clark, Shark Lady*
Fountas & Pinnell LLI Blue System	*From Milk to Ice Cream*
Fountas & Pinnell LLI Blue System	*Mother Sea Turtle*
Fountas & Pinnell LLI Red System	*You Can't Stop Trudy*
Fox, Mem	*Wilfrid Gordon McDonald Partridge*
Fradin, Judy	*Witness to Disaster: Tsunamis*
Frank, Anne	*The Diary Of A Young Girl*
Frank, Mitch	*Understanding September 11th: Answering Questions About the Attacks on America*
Fridell, Ron	*Forensic Science* (Cool Science)
Fritz, Jean	*And Then What Happened, Paul Revere?*
Fritz, Jean	*Will You Sign Here, John Hancock?*
George, Jean Craighead	*My Side of the Mountain*
George, Jean Craighead	*The Wolves Are Back*
George, Kristine O'Connell	*The Great Frog Race and Other Poems*
George, Kristine O'Connell	*Toasting Marshmallows: Camping Poems*
Gibbons, Gail	*Bats*
Gibbons, Gail	*Caves and Caverns*
Gibbons, Gail	*Deserts*
Gibbons, Gail	*How a House Is Built*
Gibbons, Gail	*Hurricanes!*
Gibbons, Gail	*Nature's Green Umbrella: Tropical Rain Forests*
Gibbons, Gail	*Trains*
Giovanni, Nikki	*Spin a Soft Black Song: Poems for Children*
Glasscock, Sarah	*Laura Ingalls Wilder: An Author's Story*
Golding, William	*Lord of the Flies*
Goldschmidt, Judy	*The Secret Blog of Raisin Rodriguez*
Goodman, Susan E.	*Stones, Bones, and Petroglyphs: Digging into Southwest Archaeology*
Gordon Sharon	*Guess Who Hides*

AUTHOR	TITLE
Graber, Janet	*Muktar and the Camels*
Graham-Barber, Linda	*Todd or Frog, Swamp or Bog? A Big Book of Nature's Confusables*
Greenfield, Eloise	*Honey, I Love and Other Love Poems*
Gregory, Kristiana	Cabin Creek Mysteries series
Grimes, Nikki	*Danitra Brown Leaves Town*
Grimm, The Brothers	*Snow White and the Seven Dwarfs*
Guiberson, Brenda Z.	*Life in the Boreal Forest*
Guiberson, Brenda Z.	*Moon Bear*
Guillain, Charlotte	*Leaves*
Hahn, Mary Downing	*Wait Till Helen Comes: A Ghost Story*
Hale, Bruce	Chet Gecko Mystery series
Hale, Shannon and Dean Hale	*Rapunzel's Revenge*
Halls, Kelly Milner	*Mysteries of the Mummy Kids*
Halls, Kelly Milner	*Wild Dogs: Past & Present*
Hamilton, Martha and Mitch Weiss	*Noodlehead Stories*
Hamilton, Virginia	*Cousins*
Hamilton, Virginia	*The House Of Dies Drear*
Hamilton, Virginia	*In the Beginning: Creation Stories from Around the World*
Hart-Lovelace, Maud	Betsy/Tacy series
Haydon, Julie	*Bird Fact File*
Hayes, Geoffrey	Benny and Penny series
Hearne, Betsy	*Seven Brave Women*
Heller, Ruth	World of Language series
Hendershot, Judith	*In Coal Country*
Henry, Marguerite	*Misty of Chincoteague*
Hesse, Karen	*Lester's Dog*
Hesse, Karen	*The Music of Dolphins*
Hesse, Karen	*Sable*
Hesse, Karen	*A Time of Angels*
Hiaasen, Carl	*Flush*
Hiaasen, Carl	*Hoot*
Hinds, Gareth	*Beowulf*
Hinds, Gareth	*King Lear*
Hinds, Gareth	*The Merchant of Venice*
Hinds, Gareth	*The Odyssey*
Hoena, Blake A. (retold by) and Ricardo Tercio	*Jack and the Beanstalk: The Graphic Novel*
Holling, Holling Clancy	*Paddle-to-the-Sea*
Holm, Jennifer L. and Matthew Holm	Babymouse series
Homer	*The Iliad*
Homer	*The Odyssey*

AUTHOR	TITLE
Hopkinson, Deborah and James E. Ransome	*Sky Boys: How They Built the Empire State Building*
Howard, Elizabeth Fitzgerald	*Aunt Flossie's Hats (and Crab Cakes Later)*
Howe, James	*Pinky and Rex and the School Play*
Hudson, Wade	*Five Brave Explorers*
Hunter, Mollie	*A Stranger Came Ashore*
Hurwitz, Johanna	*Pee Wee & Plush*
Hurwitz, Johanna	*Pee-Wee's Tale*
Hurwitz, Johanna	*Russell and Elysa*
Hurwitz, Johanna	*Russell Sprouts*
InfoTrek Plus	*Earthquakes*
Jacques, Brian	The Redwall Adventures series
Jenkins, Steve	*Biggest, Strongest, Fastest*
Jenkins, Steve and Robin Page	*How to Clean a Hippopotamus: A Look at Unusual Animal Partnerships*
Jenkins, Steve and Robin Page	*Sisters and Brothers: Sibling Relationships in the Animal World*
Johnston, Tony	*The Harmonica*
Juster, Norton	*Neville*
Keene, Carolyn	Nancy Drew Mystery Stories series
Kellogg, Stephen	*The Three Sillies*
Kendall, Carol	*The Gammage Cup: A Novel of the Minnipins*
Killer Animals	*Crocodiles on the Hunt*
Kim, Susan, Laurence Klavan, and Faith Erin Hicks	*Brain Camp*
Kimmel, Elizabeth Cody	*The Frog Princess: A Tlingit Legend from Alaska*
Kinney, Jeff	*Diary of a Wimpy Kid: Greg Heffley's Journal*
Kinney, Jeff	Diary of a Wimpy Kid series
Kirk, Bill	*All About Volcanoes*
Knight, Amelia Stewart	*The Way West: Journal of a Pioneer Woman*
Knopf	Eyewitness Juniors set
Konigsburg, E. L.	*The View from Saturday*
Kooser, Ted	*Bag in the Wind*
Korman, Gordon	*The Emperor's Code*
Kramer, Stephen	*Caves*
Kroll, Steven	*Lewis and Clark: Explorers of the American West*
Krull, Kathleen	*The Boy Who Invented TV: The Story of Philo Farnsworth*
Krull, Kathleen	*Wilma Unlimited: How Wilma Rudolph Became the World's Fastest Woman*
Lagasse, Emeril	*Emeril's There's a Chef in My Soup! Recipes for the Kid in Everyone*
Laminack, Lester L.	*Saturdays and Teacakes*
Landau, Elaine	*The Bald Eagle*
Larrick, Nancy (editor)	*Piping Down the Valleys Wild: A Merry Mix of Verse for All Ages*
Lasky, Kathryn	*Sugaring Time*

AUTHOR	TITLE
Le Guin, Ursula K.	*A Wizard of Earthsea* (Earthsea series)
Le Guin, Ursula K.	*The Tombs of Atuan* (Earthsea series)
Le Guin, Ursula K.	*The Farthest Shore* (Earthsea series)
Le Guin, Ursula K.	*Tehanu* (Earthsea series)
Le Guin, Ursula K.	*Tales from Earthsea* (Earthsea series)
Le Guin, Ursula K.	*The Other Wind* (Earthsea series)
Lester, Helen	*Author: A True Story*
Lester, Julius	*John Henry*
Lester, Julius	*When Dad Killed Mom*
Levine, Gail Carson	*Ella Enchanted*
Lewis, C. S.	*The Lion, the Witch, and the Wardrobe* (The Chronicles of Narnia series)
Lewis, C. S.	*Prince Caspian: The Return to Narnia* (The Chronicles of Narnia series)
Lewis, C. S.	*The Voyage of the Dawn Treader* (The Chronicles of Narnia series)
Lewis, C. S.	*The Silver Chair* (The Chronicles of Narnia series)
Lewis, C. S.	*The Horse and His Boy* (The Chronicles of Narnia series)
Lewis, C. S.	*The Magician's Nephew* (The Chronicles of Narnia series)
Lewis, C. S.	*The Last Battle* (The Chronicles of Narnia series)
Lewis, Rose A. and Grace Zong	*Orange Peel's Pocket*
Li, Cunxin	*Dancing to Freedom: The True Story of Mao's Last Dancer*
Lies, Brian	*Bats at the Library*
Lindgren, Astrid	*Pippi Longstocking*
Littlesugar, Amy	*Willy & Max: A Holocaust Story*
Llewellyn, Claire	*Killer Creatures*
Lofting, Hugh	*Dr. Doolittle*
Lord, Cynthia	*Rules*
Louie, Ai-Ling	*Yeh-Shen: A Cinderella Story from China*
Lovelace, Maud Hart	Betsy-Tacy series
Lowry, Lois	*Autumn Street*
Lowry, Lois	*Gathering Blue*
Lowry, Lois	*The Giver*
Lunn, Janet	*The Root Cellar*
Macaulay, David	*Building Big*
Macaulay, David	*Built to Last*
Macaulay, David	*Castle*
Macaulay, David	*Cathedral*
Macauley, David	*The New Way Things Work*
Macauley, David	*Pyramid*
Macauley, David	*The Way We Work*
Macintosh, David	*Marshall Armstrong Is New to Our School*

AUTHOR	**TITLE**
Malory, Sir Thomas	*Le Morte d'Arthur*
Markle, Sandra	*Animals Marco Polo Saw: An Adventure on the Silk Road*
Markle, Sandra	*Outside and Inside Bats*
Markle, Sandra	*Vultures: Animal Scavengers*
Martin, Ann	*The Doll People*
Martin, Ann	*The Meanest Doll in the World*
Martin, Ann	*The Runaway Dolls*
Martin, Jacqueline Briggs	*Snowflake Bentley*
Martin, Rafe	*The Rough-Face Girl*
Matas, Carol	*After the War*
Mazer, Norma Fox	*Good Night, Maman*
McCloskey, Robert	*Make Way for Ducklings*
McDermott, Gerald	*Coyote: A Trickster Tale*
McDermott, Gerald	*Jabuti the Tortoise*
McDermott, Gerald	*Monkey: A Trickster Tale*
McDermott, Gerald	*Raven: A Trickster Tale*
McDermott, Gerald	*Zomo the Rabbit*
McDonnell, Patrick	*Me . . . Jane*
McGovern, Ann	*The Secret Soldier: The Story of Deborah Sampson*
McKissack, Patricia C.	*Ma Dear's Aprons*
McMillan, Bruce	*Salmon Summer*
McNaughton, Colin	*The Aliens Are Coming!*
McNish, Cliff	*Breathe*
Meltzer, Milton	*Albert Einstein: A Biography*
Merrill, Jean	*The Pushcart War*
Meyer, Kai	*The Glass Word*
Meyer, Kai	*The Stone Light*
Meyer, Kai	*The Water Mirror*
Miles, Miska	*Annie and the Old One*
Mitchell, Margaree King	*Uncle Jed's Barbershop*
Mora, Pat	*Doña Flor*
Moss, Marissa	*True Heart*
Most, Bernard	*How Big Were the Dinosaurs?*
Munson, Derek	*Enemy Pie*
Muth, Jon (retold by)	*Stone Soup*
Myers, Walter Dean	*Monster*
Namioka, Lensey	*Yang the Youngest and His Terrible Ear*
Napoli, Donna Jo	*Mama Miti: Wangari Mathaai and the Trees of Kenya*
Nelson, Robin	*Salamanders*
Nixon, Joan Lowery	*The Other Side of Dark*

AUTHOR	TITLE
Nolen, Jerdine	*Thunder Rose*
Norton, Mary	*The Borrowers*
Noyes, Deborah	*Red Butterfly: How a Princess Smuggled the Secret of Silk Out of China*
O'Brien, Robert C.	*Mrs. Frisby and the Rats of NIMH*
O'Hara, Mary	*My Friend Flicka*
Ondaatje, Michael	*The Collected Works of Billy the Kid*
Onyefulu, Ifeoma	*A Is for Africa*
Orwell, George	*1984*
Osborne, Mary Pope	Magic Tree House series
Parker, Vic	*What Living Things Need: Water*
Parks, Rosa with Jim Haskins	*I Am Rosa Parks*
Pascal, Francine	Sweet Valley High series
Paterson, Katherine	*Bridge to Terabithia*
Paterson, Katherine	*The Day of the Pelican*
Paterson, Katherine	*The Great Gilly Hopkins*
Paterson, Katherine	*Lyddie*
Patron, Susan	*The Higher Power of Lucky*
Paulson, Gary	*Guts: The True Stories Behind* Hatchet *and the Brian Books*
Paulson, Gary	*Hatchet*
Paulson, Gary	*My Life in Dog Years*
Paulson, Gary	*Sarny: A Life Remembered*
Paulson, Gary	*Winterdance: The Fine Madness of Running the Iditarod*
Pavlova, Anna	*I Dreamed I Was a Ballerina*
Pearce, Philippa	*Tom's Midnight Garden*
Pearce, Philippa	*The Way to Sattin Shore*
Peterson, John	*The Littles Go Exploring*
Pinkney, Andrea Davis	*Alvin Ailey*
Pinkney, Andrea Davis	*Bill Pickett: Rodeo-Ridin' Cowboy*
Pinkney, Andrea Davis	*Ella Fitzgerald: The Tale of a Vocal Virtuosa*
Polacco, Patricia	*Pink and Say*
Potter, Beatrix	*The Tale of Peter Rabbit*
Potts, Steve	*The Grizzly Bear*
Pringle, Laurence	*Fire in the Forest: A Cycle of Growth and Renewal*
Pull Ahead Books	*African Elephants*
Pull Ahead Books	*Forest Fires*
Pullman, Philip	*The Golden Compass*
Quindlin, Anna	*Being Perfect*
Quindlin, Anna	*Every Last One*
Quindlin, Anna	*How Reading Changed My Life*
Quindlin, Anna	*One True Thing*

AUTHOR	TITLE
Raczka, Bob	*Name That Style: All About Isms in Art*
Raczka, Bob	*The Vermeer Interviews*
Ramsey, Calvin Alexander	*Ruth and the Green Book*
Randall, Alison L.	*The Wheat Doll*
Rappaport, Doreen	*Eleanor, Quiet No More: The Life of Eleanor Roosevelt*
Rappaport, Doreen	*Lady Liberty: A Biography*
Raskin, Ellen	*The Westing Game*
Raven, Margot Theis	*America's White Table*
Raven, Margot Theis	*Night Boat to Freedom*
Recorvits, Helen	*My Name Is Yoon*
Reeder, Carolyn	*Foster's War*
Renier, Aaron	*The Unsinkable Walker Bean*
Rey, H. A.	Curious George books
Reynolds, Peter H.	*The Dot*
Rice, David L.	*Do Animals Have Feelings Too?*
Rice, David L.	*Lifetimes*
Rigby Focus	*The Chocolate Trail*
Rigby Sails	*Burrows, Tunnels, and Chambers*
Ringgold, Faith	*Dinner at Aunt Connie's House*
Riordan, James	*Jason and the Golden Fleece*
Riordan, Rick	39 Clues series
Riordan, Rick	Percy Jackson series
Robinson, Anthony	*Hamzat's Journey: A Refugee Diary*
Robinson, Sharon	*Testing the Ice: A True Story About Jackie Robinson*
Rockwell, Thomas	*How to Eat Fried Worms*
Rollins, Prentis	*The Making of a Graphic Novel / The Resonator*
Rowling, J. K.	*Harry Potter and the Sorcerer's Stone*
Rowling, J. K.	*Harry Potter and the Chamber of Secrets*
Rowling, J. K.	*Harry Potter and the Prisoner of Azkaban*
Rowling, J. K.	*Harry Potter and the Goblet of Fire*
Rowling, J. K.	*Harry Potter and the Order of the Phoenix*
Rowling, J. K.	*Harry Potter and the Half-Blood Prince*
Rowling, J. K.	*Harry Potter and the Deathly Hallows*
Ryan, Pam Muñoz	*Amelia and Eleanor Go for a Ride*
Ryan, Pam Muñoz	*Becoming Naomi: León*
Ryan, Pam Muñoz	*When Marian Sang: The True Recital of Marian Anderson*
Rylant, Cynthia	*An Angel for Solomon Singer*
Rylant, Cynthia	*But I'll Be Back Again*
Rylant, Cynthia	Henry and Mudge series
Rylant, Cynthia	*Missing May*

AUTHOR	TITLE
Rylant, Cynthia	*Night in the Country*
Rylant, Cynthia	*The Relatives Came*
Rylant, Cynthia	*When I Was Young in the Mountains*
Sachar, Louis	*Marvin Redpost: Class President*
San Souci, Robert D.	*Cendrillon: A Caribbean Cinderella*
Say, Allen	*Grandfather's Journey*
Say, Allen	*Tree of Cranes*
Scarce, Carolyn	*Journey of a Butterfly*
Schachner, Judy	Skippyjon Jones series
Scholastic	If You . . . series
Scholastic	Geronimo Stilton series
Sciezka, Jon	The Time Warp Trio series
Seidler, Tor	*The Wainscott Weasel*
Selznick, Brian	*The Invention of Hugo Cabret*
Sendak, Maurice	*Where the Wild Things Are*
Seuss, Dr.	*The Butter Battle Book*
Shannon, David	*No, David!*
Sharmat, Marjorie Weinman	Nate the Great series
Sharp, Margery	*Miss Bianca: A Fantasy*
Short, Joan and Bettina Bird	*Crocodilians*
Silverstein, Alvin and Virginia Silverstein	*Life in a Bucket of Soil*
Simon, Seymour	*Muscles: Our Muscular System*
Simply Science	*Fossils*
Singer, Marilyn	*Footprints on the Roof: Poems About the Earth*
Sís, Peter	*The Wall: Growing Up Behind the Iron Curtain*
Smith, Doris Buchanan	*A Taste of Blackberries*
Smith, Jeff	Bone series
Smith, Jeff	*Little Mouse Gets Ready*
Smucker, Anna Egan	*No Star Nights*
Snyder, Zilpha Keatley	*The Trespassers*
Sobol, Donald J.	Encyclopedia Brown series
Soto, Gary	*The Afterlife*
Soto, Gary	*The Cat's Meow*
Souhami, Jessica	*Rama and the Demon King*
Speare, Elizabeth George	*The Witch of Blackbird Pond*
Spiegelman, Art	*Maus I: A Survivor's Tale: My Father Bleeds History*
Spinelli, Jerry	*Maniac Magee*
Squires, Janet	*The Gingerbread Cowboy*
Stanley, Diane	*Elena*
Stead, Philip	*A Sick Day for Amos McGee*

AUTHOR	TITLE
Steffora, Tracy	*Clocks and Time*
Steig, William	*Abel's Island*
Steig, William	*The Amazing Bone*
Steig, William	*Amos and Boris*
Steig, William	*Sylvester and the Magic Pebble*
Steinbeck, John	*The Red Pony*
Steptoe, John (retold by)	*Mufaro's Beautiful Daughters*
Stevenson, Augusta	*Clara Barton: Founder of the American Red Cross*
Stewart, Melissa	*How Do Plants Grow?*
Stewart, Melissa	*Inside Volcanoes*
Stewart, Melissa	*A Place for Butterflies*
Stewart, Melissa	*When Rain Falls*
Stilton, Geronimo	*I'm Too Fond of My Fur*
Sturm, James, Andrew Arnold, and Alexis Frederick-Frost	*Adventures in Cartooning*
Sturm, James and Rich Tommaso	*Satchel Paige: Striking Out Jim Crow*
Sussman, Susan and Robert James	*Lies (People Believe) About Animals*
Sutcliff, Rosemary	*The Sword and the Circle*
Swift, Jonathan	*Gulliver's Travels*
Swift, Jonathan	"A Modest Proposal"
Swinburne, Stephen	*Lots and Lots of Zebra Stripes: Patterns in Nature*
Swinburne, Stephen	*Once a Wolf*
Swinburne, Stephen	*Wings of Light: The Migration of the Yellow Butterfly*
Tan, Shaun	*The Arrival*
Taylor, Barbara	*Arctic and Antarctica* (Eyewitness Books)
Taylor, Mildred D.	*Roll of Thunder, Hear My Cry*
Tinkham, Kelly A.	*Hair for Mama*
Tolkien, J. R. R.	*The Fellowship of the Ring (The Lord of the Rings* trilogy*)*
Tolkien, J. R. R.	*The Two Towers (The Lord of the Rings* trilogy*)*
Tolkien, J. R. R.	*The Return of the King (The Lord of the Rings* trilogy*)*
Travers, P. L.	*Mary Poppins*
Troll Books	First Start Biographies series
Tunnell, Michael	*Mailing May*
Twain, Mark	*The Adventures of Tom Sawyer*
Tyler, Michael	*Frogs*
Uchida, Yoshiko	*The Bracelet*
Uhlberg, Myron	*Dad, Jackie, and Me*
Untamed World, The	*Alligators and Crocodiles*
Van Allsburg, Chris	*Queen of the Falls*
Velasquez, Eric	*Grandma's Records*
Verne, Jules	*Journey to the Center of the Earth*

AUTHOR	TITLE
Voigt, Cynthia	*Dicey's Song* (Tillerman series)
Voigt, Cynthia	*Homecoming* (Tillerman series)
Voigt, Cynthia	*A Solitary Blue* (Tillerman series)
Walsh, Jill Paton	*The Green Book*
Warner, Gertrude	The Boxcar Children series
Weatherford, Carole Boston	*Moses: When Harriet Tubman Led Her People to Freedom*
Webb, Sophie	*Far from Shore: Chronicles of an Open Ocean Voyage*
Weever, Robin	*Meercats*
Wells, Rosemary	*Max and Ruby's First Greek Myth: Pandora's Box*
Wells, Rosemary	*Max and Ruby's Midas: Another Greek Myth*
White, E. B.	*Charlotte's Web*
White, T. H.	*The Once and Future King*
Wick, Walter	*A Drop of Water: A Book of Science and Wonder*
Wilder, Laura Ingalls	Little House series
Wilder, Laura Ingalls	*The Long Winter*
Wiles, Deborah	*Freedom Summer*
Willems, Mo	Knufle Bunny books
Willems, Mo	Elephant and Piggie series
Williams, Margery	*The Veleteen Rabbit*
Wilson, Lynn	*What's Out There? A Book About Space*
Winter, Jeanette	*The Librarian of Basra: A True Story from Iraq*
Winter, Jeanette	*Nasreen's Secret School: A True Story from Afghanistan*
Winter, Jeanette	*Wangari's Trees of Peace*
Winter, Jonah	*You Never Heard of Sandy Koufax?!*
Winthrop, Elizabeth	*The Castle in the Attic*
Winthrop, Elizabeth	*Luke's Bully*
Worth, Valerie	*All the Small Poems and Fourteen More*
Wright, Betty Ren	*Princess for a Week*
X-Sports	*Skateboarding*
Yang, Belle	*Hannah Is My Name*
Yang, Gene Luen	*American Born Chinese*
Yolen, Jane	*Commander Toad and the Voyage Home*
Yolen, Jane	*The Devil's Arithmetic*
Yolen, Jane	*Foiled*
Young, Ed	*The Night Visitors*
Your Body	*Your Muscles*
Zee, Ruth Vander	*Erika's Story*
Zeman, Ludmila	*Gilgamesh the King*

Professional References

Ada, A. F. 1993. *Me Llamo Maria Isabel.* New York: Simon & Schuster/Aladdin.

Allison, N. 2009. *Middle School Readers.* Portsmouth, NH: Heinemann.

Allyn, P. 2009. *What to Read When.* New York: Penguin.

Anderson, C. 2005. *Assessing Writers.* Portsmouth, NH: Heinemann.

Arnosky, J. 1998. *All About Turkeys.* New York: Scholastic.

Babbitt, N. 1975. *Tuck Everlasting.* New York: Farrar, Straus and Giroux/Square Fish.

Bateman, R. 1998. *Safari.* Boston, MA: Little, Brown and Company.

Barrows, A. 2006. *Ivy and Bean.* San Francisco, CA: Chronicle Books.

Bennett-Armistead, V. S., and N. Duke. 2007. *Beyond Bedtime Stories: A Parent's Guide to Promoting Reading, Writing, and Other Literacy Skills.* New York: Scholastic.

Bomer, R. 1995. *Time for Meaning: Crafting Literate Lives in Middle & High School.* Portsmouth, NH: Heinemann.

Bradbury, R. 1951, 1953, 1967, 1979, 1981, 1995. *Fahrenheit 451.* New York: Simon & Schuster

Buckner, A. 2005. *Notebook Know-How: Strategies for the Writer's Notebook.* Portland, ME: Stenhouse.

Burroway, J. 2000. *Writing Fiction: A Guide to Narrative Craft.* New York: Addison Wesley Longman.

Buss, K., and L. Karnowski. 2000. *Reading and Writing Literary Genres.* Newark, DE: International Reading Association.

Caine, K. 2008. *Writing to Persuade: Minilessons to Help Students Plan, Draft, and Revise, Grades 3–8.* Portsmouth, NH: Heinemann.

Campbell, J.R., K. E. Voelkl, and P. L. Donahue. 1996. *NAEP 1996 Trends in Academic Progress.* Washington, D.C.: Department of Education.

Coerr, E. 1993. *Mieko and the Fifth Treasure.* New York: Puffin.

Collins, S. 2008. *The Hunger Games.* New York: Scholastic

Cornog, M., and T. Perper. 2009. *Graphic Novels Beyond the Basics.* Santa Barbara, CA: Libraries Unlimited.

Craighead-George, J. 1959, 1988. *My Side of the Mountain.* New York: Puffin.

Daniels, H., M. Bizar, and S. Zemelman. 2000. *Rethinking High School: Best Practice in Teaching, Learning, and Leadership.* Portsmouth, NH: Heinemann.

Darrigan, D., M. Tunnell, and J. Jacobs. 2002. *Children's Literature: Engaging Teachers and Children in Good Books.* New York: Prentice Hall.

Dowdy, J., T. Duncko, and A. Hartz. 2011. "From Visual Arts to the Big Screen: Comic Strips Enhance Literacy; A Workshop Approach." *Ohio Reading Teacher.*

Duke, N., and V. S. Bennett-Armistead. 2003. *Reading and Writing Informational Texts in the Primary Grades.* New York: Scholastic.

Dymock, S. 2007. "Comprehension Strategy Instruction: Teaching Narrative Text Structure Awareness." *The Reading Teacher,* 61 (2).

Fletcher, R., and J. Portalupi. 2001. *Writing Workshop.* Portsmouth, NH: Heinemann.

Fletcher, R. 1997. *Ordinary Things: Poems from a Walk in Early Spring.* New York: Atheneum/Simon and Schuster.

Fountas, I., and G. S. Pinnell. 1996. *Guided Reading: Good First Teaching for All Children.* Portsmouth, NH: Heinemann.

Fountas, I., and G. S. Pinnell. 2000. *Guiding Readers and Writers: Teaching Comprehension, Genre, and Content Literacy.* Portsmouth, NH: Heinemann.

Fountas, I., and G. S. Pinnell. 2005. *Leveled Books, K–8: Matching Texts to Readers for Effective Teaching.* Portmouth, NH: Heinemann.

Fountas, I., and G. S. Pinnell. 2006. *Teaching for Comprehending and Fluency: Thinking, Talking, and Writing About Reading, K-8.* Portsmouth, NH: Heinemann.

Fountas, I., and G. S. Pinnell. 2008. *Prompting Guide, Part 1: A Tool for Literacy Teachers.* Portsmouth, NH: Heinemann.

Fountas, I., and G. S. Pinnell. 2011. *Fountas & Pinnell Benchmark Assessment System*. Portsmouth, NH: Heinemann.

Fountas, I., and G. S. Pinnell. 2012. *Prompting Guide, Part 2, for Comprehension: Thinking, Talking, and Writing*. Portsmouth, NH: Heinemann.

Fountas, I., and G. S. Pinnell. 2012. *Genre Prompting Guide for Fiction*. Portsmouth, NH: Heinemann.

Fountas, I., and G. S. Pinnell. 2012. *Genre Prompting Guide for Nonfiction, Poetry, and Test Taking*. Portsmouth, NH: Heinemann.

Fountas, I., and G. S. Pinnell. 2012. *Genre Quick Guide*. Portsmouth, NH: Heinemann.

Frank, Anne. 1991, 2001. *The Diary of a Young Girl*. New York: Random House/Doubleday.

Gamble, N. S., and S. Yates. 2008. *Exploring Children's Literature*. Thousand Oaks, CA: Sage Publications.

Gibbons, P. 2009. *English Learners, Academic Literacy, and Thinking: Learning in the Challenge Zone*. Portsmouth, NH: Heinemann.

Gill, S. R. 2009. "What Teachers Need to Know About the 'New' Nonfiction." *The Reading Teacher, 63* (4), 260–67.

Golding, W. 1954. *Lord of the Flies*. New York: Penguin/The Berkley Publishing Group.

Goodman, S. 2000. *Stones, Bones, and Petroglyphs*. New York: Simon and Schuster/Aladdin.

Guthrie, J. T., L. W. Hoa, and A. Wigfield. 2006. "From Spark to Fire: Can Situational Reading Interest Lead to Long-Term Reading Motivation?" *Reading Research and Instruction, 45*(2), 91–117.

Harvey, S., & Daniels, H. 2009. *Comprehension Collaboration: Inquiry Circles in Action*. Portsmouth, NH: Heinemann.

Heard, G. 1998. *Awakening the Heart: Exploring Poetry in Elementary and Middle School*. Portsmouth, NH: Heinemann.

Heller, M.F. 1991. *Reading-Writing Connections: From Theory to Practice*. New York: Longman.

Hicks, T. 2009. *The Digital Writing Workshop*. Portsmouth, NH: Heinemann.

Hopkinson, D. 2012. *Sky Boys: How They Built the Empire State Building*. New York: Random House/Dragonfly Books.

Johnson, D. 2009. *School Libraries Head for the Edge*. Santa Barbara, CA: Linworth Publishing.

Johnston, P. 2004. *Choice Words: How Our Language Affects Children's Learning*. Portland, ME: Stenhouse.

Johnston, T. 2008. *The Harmonica*. Watertown, MA: Charlesbridge.

Kelley, M., and N. Clausen-Grace. 2010. "Guiding Students Through Expository Texts with Text Feature Walks." *The Reading Teacher*. *64* (3), 191–95.

Kiefer, B., with S. Hepler, and J. Hickman. 2010. *Charlotte Huck's Children's Literature*. Edition 9. Boston: McGraw-Hill.

Lattimer, H. 2003. *Thinking Through Genre: Units of Study in Reading and Writing Workshops, 4–12*. Portland, ME: Stenhouse.

Levine, G. 1997. *Ella Enchanted*. New York: HarperCollins.

Lies, B. 2008. *Bats at the Library*. New York: Houghton Mifflin.

Lowry, L. 1980. *Autumn Street*. New York: Random House.

Lindfors, J. W. 1999. *Children's Inquiry: Using Language to Make Sense of the World (Language and Literacy Series, Teachers College Press)*. New York: Teachers College Press.

Markle, S. 1997. *Outside and Inside Bats*. New York: Walker & Company.

McKenna and Robinson. 1993. *Teaching Through Text: A Content Literacy Approach to Content Area Reading*. New York: Longman.

Neufeld, P. 2005/2006. "Comprehension Instruction in Content Area Classes." *The Reading Teacher*. 59 (4).

Nia, I. T. 1999. "Units of Study in the Writing Workshop." *Primary Voices, K–6. (8)* 1: pp. 3–12.

O'Conner, B. 2010. "Keeping It Real: How Realistic Does Realistic Fiction for Children Need to Be?" *Language Arts*, 87. No. 6.: pp. 465–71.

Oliver, M. 1994. *A Poetry Handbook*. Boston, MA: Mariner Books/Houghton Mifflin Harcourt.

Paulsen, G. 1994. *Winterdance: The Fine Madness of Running the Iditarod*. Orlando, FL: Harcourt, Inc.

Pavlova, A. 2001. *I Dreamed I Was a Ballerina*. New York: Simon & Schuster/Atheneum.

Peterson, R., and M. Eeds. 1990. *Grand Conversations: Literature Groups in Action*. New York: Scholastic Teaching Resources.

Pinker, S. 2009. *How the Mind Works*. New York: W.W. Norton and Co.

Pinnell, G. S., and Fountas, I. 2008, 2011. *The Continuum of Literacy Learning*. Portsmouth, NH: Heinemann.

Pinnell, G. S., and I. Fountas. 2011. *Reader's Notebook: Advanced*. Portsmouth, NH: Heinemann.

Pinnell, G. S., and I. Fountas. 2011. *Reader's Notebook*. Portsmouth, NH: Heinemann.

Quindlen, A. 1998. *How Reading Changed My Life*. New York: Ballantine Books.

Ray, K. W. 1999. *Wondrous Words: Writers and Writing in the Elementary Classroom*. Urbana, IL: National Council of Teachers of English.

Ray, K. W. 2002. *What You Know by Heart: How to Develop Curriculum for Your Writing Workshop*. Portsmouth, NH: Heinemann.

Ray, K. W. 2006. "Exploring Inquiry as a Teaching Stance in the Writing Workshop." *Language Arts, 83:3*. 238–47.

Ray, K. W. 2006. *Study Driven: A Framework for Planning Units of Study in the Writing Workshop*. Portsmouth, NH: Heinemann.

Ray, K. W. 2007. *About the Authors*. Portsmouth, NH: Heinemann.

Rollins, P. 2006. *The Making of a Graphic Novel: The Resonator*. New York: Crown Publishing/Random House.

Romano, T. 2000. *Blending Genre, Altering Style: Writing Multigenre Papers*. Portsmouth, NH: Heinemann.

Rosenblatt, L. 1994. "The Transactional Theory of Reading and Writing." In *Theoretical Models and Processes of Reading*, R. B. Ruddell, M. R. Ruddell, and H. Singer, Eds. Fourth Edition. Newark, DE: International Reading Association.

Rycik, M. T., and B. Rosler. 2009. "The Return of Historical Fiction." *The Reading Teacher, 63*(2), 163–66.

Rylant, C. 1995. *But I'll Be Back Again*. New York: HarperCollins.

Sankovitch, N. 2011. *Tolstoy and the Purple Chair: My Year of Magical Reading*. New York: HarperCollins.

Schwartz, G. 2006. "Expanding Literacies Through Graphic Novels." *The English Journal*. Stony Brook, NY: National Council of Teachers of English.

Sharmat, M. 2002. *Nate the Great*. New York: Random House/Delacorte.

Short, K., J. Harste, and C. Burke. 1995. *Creating Classrooms for Authors and Inquirers*. Second Edition. Portsmouth, NH: Heinemann.

Steig, W. 1971. *Amos and Boris*. New York: Farrar, Straus and Giroux.

Swinburne, S. 1999. *Once a Wolf: How Wildlife Biologists Fought to Bring Back the Gray Wolf*. New York: Houghton Mifflin.

Thompson, T. 2008. *Adventures in Graphica*. Portland, ME: Stenhouse.

Tolan, K., and L. Calkins. 2010. *Units of Study for Teaching Reading*. Portsmouth, NH: Heinemann.

Tunnell, M., and J. Jacobs. 2000. *Children's Literature, Briefly*. Boston, MA: Allyn and Bacon.

Voigt, C. 1981. *Homecoming*. New York: Simon & Schuster/Aladdin

White, E.B. 1952, 1980. *Charlotte's Web*. New York: HarperCollins.

Wilson, L. 2002 *Reading to Live: How to Teach Reading for Today's World*. Portsmouth, NH: Heinemann.

Wolf, M. and Barzillai, M. 2009. "The Importance of Deep Reading." *Educational Leadership*. Vol. 66, No. 6.

Wood, J. 2008. *How Fiction Works*. New York: Farrar, Straus and Giroux.

Zarnowski, M. 2003. *History Makers: A Questioning Approach to Reading and Writing Biographies*. Portsmouth, NH: Heinemann.

Zemelman, S., H. Daniels, and A. Hyde. 2005. *Best Practice, Third Edition*. Portsmouth, NH: Heinemann.

Index